The Student's Guide to Cognitive Neuroscience

Second edition

Jamie Ward

Psychology Press
Taylor & Francis Group

HOVE AND NEW YORK

First edition published 2006
Second edition published 2010
by Psychology Press
27 Church Road, Hove, East Sussex BN3 2FA

Simultaneously published in the USA and Canada
by Psychology Press
711 Third Avenue, New York, NY 10017

*Psychology Press is an imprint of the Taylor & Francis Group,
an informa business*

© 2010 Psychology Press

British Library Cataloguing in Publication Data
A catalogue record for this book is available from the British Library

Library of Congress Cataloging in Publication Data
Ward, Jamie.
   The student's guide to cognitive neuroscience / Jamie Ward.—2nd ed.
      p. cm.
Includes bibliographical references and index.
ISBN 978–1–84872–002–2 (hardcover) – ISBN 978–1–84872–003–9 (pbk.)
   1. Cognitive neuroscience. I. Title.
   QP360.5.W37 2010
   612.8′233—dc22   2009011169

ISBN: 978–1–84872–003–9 (pbk)
ISBN: 978–1–84872–002–2 (hbk)

Typeset in by Newgen Imaging Systems (P) Ltd, Chennai, India
Cover design by Aubergine Design
Printed and bound in India by Replika Press Pvt. Ltd.

For Mum and Dad

The Student's Guide to Cognitive Neuroscience

Contents

About the author

Dr. Jamie Ward is a Reader (Associate Professor) at the University of Sussex, UK. He completed degrees at the University of Cambridge (1991–1994) and the University of Birmingham (1994–1997). He subsequently worked as a Research Fellow at the University of Sussex (1997–1999) and as Lecturer and Senior Lecturer at University College London (1999–2007). His principal research interest lies in the cognitive neuroscience of synesthesia, although he has published on many other topics, including frontal lobe function, memory and disorders of reading and spelling. His research uses a number of methods in cognitive neuroscience, including human neuropsychology, functional imaging, EEG and TMS. His other books include *The Frog who Croaked Blue: Synesthesia and the Mixing of the Senses* published by Routledge.

Preface to the first edition

The motivation for writing this book came out of my experiences of teaching cognitive neuroscience. When asked by students which book they should buy, I felt that none of the existing books would satisfactorily meet their needs. Other books in the market were variously too encyclopedic, too advanced, not up-to-date or gave short shrift to explaining the methods of the field. My brief for writing this textbook was to provide a text that presents key ideas and findings but is not too long, that is up-to-date, and that considers both method and theory. I hope that it will be useful to both lecturers and students.

In writing a book on cognitive neuroscience I had to make a decision as to how much would be "cognitive" and how much would be "neuroscience". In my opinion, the theoretical underpinnings of cognitive neuroscience lie within the cognitive psychology tradition. Some of the most elegant studies using methods such as fMRI and TMS have been motivated by previous research in cognitive psychology and neuropsychology. The ultimate aim of cognitive neuroscience is to provide a brain-based account of cognition, and so the methods of cognitive neuroscience must necessarily speak to some aspect of brain function. However, I believe that cognitive neuroscience has much to learn from cognitive psychology in terms of which theoretically interesting questions to ask.

In Chapter 1, I discuss the current status of cognitive neuroscience as I see it. Some of the topics raised in this chapter are directly aimed at other researchers in the field who are sceptical about the merits of the newer methodologies. I suspect that students who are new to the field will approach the topic with open-mindedness rather than scepticism, but I hope that they will nevertheless be able to gain something from this debate.

Chapter 2 is intended primarily as a reference source that can be referred back to. It is deliberately pitched at a need-to-know level. Chapters 3 to 5 describe in detail the methods of cognitive neuroscience. The aim of an undergraduate course in cognitive neuroscience is presumably to enable students to critically evaluate the field and, in my opinion, this can only be achieved if the students fully understand the limitations of the methods on which the field is based. I also hope that these chapters will be of use to researchers who are starting out in the field.

Chapters 6 to 14 outline the main theories and findings in the field. I hope that they convey something of the excitement and optimism that currently exists. Some of the chapters deal with up-and-coming areas that are not necessarily covered by other textbooks – numerical cognition (Chapter 12) and social cognitive neuroscience (Chapter 14) being the two obvious examples.

I have found writing this book to be a significant personal and academic challenge. There have been frustrating moments but, overall, I regard the experience to have been stimulating and rewarding. In these days of greater and greater specialization, it is very satisfying to be able to have an overview of most of the major topics and theories in the field.

There are a number of people whom I wish to thank. Katie Brett has been a constant and loving companion throughout and I'd like to thank her for her patience and support while I have been locked away writing. Ruben Hale at Psychology Press provided much-needed help and guidance in putting together the manuscript. A substantial proportion of the manuscript was written in the Borre Basse, France, in summer 2004 and I am grateful to Teddy and Amelia for making their home available. The following people provided constructive comments on earlier drafts of chapters: Alan Baddeley, Marlene Behrmann, James Blair, Daniel Bor, Brian Butterworth, Jamie Campbell, Alfonso Caramazza, Bhismadev Chakrabarti, Chris Frith, Uta Frith, Karl Friston, Elaine Funnell, Rick Hanley, Rik Henson, Glyn Humphreys, John Marshall, Andrew Mayes, David Milner, Morris Moscovitch, Alvaro Pascual-Leone, Cathy Price, Lynn Robertson, Noam Sagiv, Robert Savoy and Anna Woollams. I am also grateful for the critical but constructive comments provided by a number of anonymous referees.

Jamie Ward
jamie.ward@ucl.ac.uk
London, July 2005

Preface to the second edition

The first thing that you will probably notice about the second edition is a superficial change. The book is now in full color. The second stylistic change is that North American spellings have been adopted throughout. I have also tried to ensure that the examples chosen are not too culturally biased or, at least, drawn from different countries.

There have also been more substantive changes to the text. All chapters have been updated with new references to new research, and there are two new chapters. The first edition lacked a dedicated chapter on hearing, although basic auditory processing was covered in the context of speech perception. A new chapter, "The Hearing Brain", covers in more detail early auditory processes, and provides an opportunity to cover topics such as music and voice perception, as well as incorporating some of the material on speech perception. The second new chapter, "The Developing Brain", provides an introduction to the exciting field of developmental cognitive neuroscience. Rather than presenting an overview of development in each area of cognition (vision, memory, language, etc.), the approach that I've taken is to highlight some general brain-behavior principles in development that offer a contemporary take on the nature–nurture debate – a topic that still continues to draw students to psychology degrees.

I'd like to draw your attention to the new resources, accessible from http://psychology-textbooks.com, which contain material for lecturers including PowerPoint slides and suggested course structures. There are quizzes that can be used either by lecturers (for assessment, i.e. the students do not access them) or by students (so that they can test their own progress). There are also links to many of the research papers cited in the book.

The following people provided helpful comments at various stages in the writing of the second edition: Michelle de Haan, Fatima Felisberti, Alison Lee, Jennifer Mangels, Sandhi Patchay, Lauren Stewart and Robert Zatorre.

Jamie Ward
December 2008

CHAPTER 1

CONTENTS

Introducing cognitive neuroscience

Between 1928 and 1947, Wilder Penfield and colleagues carried out a series of remarkable experiments on over 400 living human brains (e.g. Penfield & Rasmussen, 1950). The patients in question were undergoing brain surgery for epilepsy. To identify and spare regions of the brain involved in movement and sensation, Penfield electrically stimulated regions of the cortex while the patient was still conscious. The procedure was not painful (the surface of the brain does not contain pain receptors) but the patients did report some fascinating experiences. When stimulating the occipital lobe one patient reported, "a star came down towards my nose". Upon stimulating a region near the central sulcus, another patient commented, "those fingers and my thumb gave a jump". After temporal lobe stimulation, another patient claimed, "I heard the music again; it is like the radio." She was later able to recall the tune she heard and was absolutely convinced that there must have been a radio in the operating theatre. Of course, the patients had no idea when the electrical stimulation was being applied – they couldn't physically feel it or see it. As far as they were concerned, an electrical stimulation applied to the brain felt pretty much like a mental/cognitive event.

This book tells the emerging story of how mental processes such as thoughts, memories and perceptions are organized and implemented by the brain. It is also

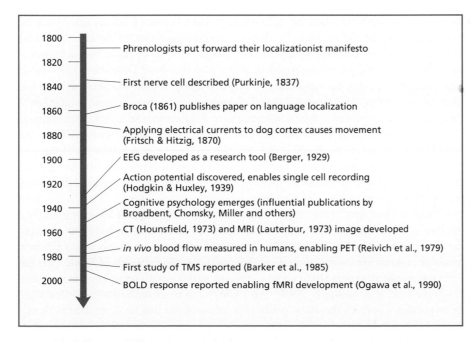

A timeline for the development of methods and findings relevant to cognitive neuroscience, from phrenology to present day.

concerned with how it is possible to study the mind and brain, and how we know what we know. The term **cognition** collectively refers to a variety of higher mental processes such as thinking, perceiving, imagining, speaking, acting and planning. **Cognitive neuroscience** is a bridging discipline between cognitive science and cognitive psychology, on the one hand, and biology and neuroscience, on the other. It has emerged as a distinct enterprise only recently and has been driven by methodological advances that enable the study of the human brain safely in the laboratory. It is perhaps not too surprising that earlier methods, such as direct electrical stimulation of the brain, failed to enter into the mainstream of research.

This chapter begins by placing a number of philosophical and scientific approaches to the mind and brain in an historical perspective. The coverage is selective rather than exhaustive, and students with a particular interest in these issues might want to read more deeply elsewhere (e.g. Finger, 2000). The chapter then provides a basic overview of the current methods used in cognitive neuroscience. A more detailed analysis and comparison of the different methods is provided in Chapters 3 to 5. Finally, the chapter attempts to address some of the criticisms of the cognitive neuroscience approach that have recently been articulated.

COGNITIVE NEUROSCIENCE IN HISTORICAL PERSPECTIVE

Philosophical approaches to mind and brain

Philosophers as well as scientists have long been interested in how the brain can create our mental world. How is it that a physical substance can give rise to our feelings, thoughts and emotions? This has been termed the **mind–body problem**, although it should more properly be called the mind–brain problem because it is now agreed that the brain is the key part of the body for cognition. One position is that the mind and brain are made up of different kinds of substance, even though they may interact. This is known as **dualism**, and the most famous proponent of this idea was René Descartes (1596–1650). Descartes believed that the mind was non-physical and immortal whereas the body was physical and mortal. He suggested that they interact in the pineal gland, which lies at the center of the brain and is now considered part of the endocrine system. According to Descartes, stimulation of the sense organs would cause vibrations in the body/brain that would be picked up in the pineal gland, and this would create a non-physical sense of awareness. There is little hope for cognitive neuroscience if dualism is true because the methods of physical and biological sciences cannot tap into the non-physical domain (if such a thing were to exist).

Even in Descartes' time, there were critics of his position. One can identify a number of broad approaches to the mind–body problem that still have a contemporary resonance. Spinoza (1632–1677) argued that mind and brain were two different levels of explanation for the same thing, but not two different kinds of thing. This has been termed **dual-aspect theory** and it remains popular with some current researchers in the field (e.g. Velmans, 2000). An analogy can be drawn to wave–particle duality in physics, in which the same entity (e.g. an electron) can be described both as a wave and as a particle.

An alternative approach to the mind–body problem that is endorsed by many contemporary thinkers is **reductionism** (e.g. Churchland, 1995; Crick, 1994). This position states that, although cognitive, mind-based concepts (e.g. emotions, memories, attention) are currently useful for scientific exploration, they will eventually be replaced by purely biological constructs (e.g. patterns of neuronal firings, neurotransmitter release). As such, psychology will eventually reduce to biology as we learn more and more about the brain. Advocates of this approach note that there are many historical precedents in which scientific constructs are abandoned when a better explanation is found. In the seventeenth century, scientists believed that flammable materials contained a substance, called *phlogiston*, which was released when burned. This is similar to classical notions that fire was a basic element along with water, air and earth. Eventually, this construct was replaced by an understanding of how chemicals combine with oxygen. The process of burning became just one example (along with rusting) of this particular chemical reaction. Reductionists believe that mind-based concepts, and conscious experiences in particular, will have the same status as phlogiston in a future theory of the brain. Those who favor dual-aspect theory over reductionism point out that an emotion will still *feel* like an emotion even if we were to fully understand its neural basis and, as such, the usefulness of cognitive, mind-based concepts will never be fully replaced.

Scientific approaches to mind and brain

Our understanding of the brain emerged historically late, largely in the nineteenth century, although some important insights were gained during classical times. Aristotle (384–322 BC) noted that the ratio of brain size to body size was greatest in more intellectually advanced species, such as humans. Unfortunately, he made the error of claiming that cognition was a product of the heart rather than the brain. He believed that the brain acted as a coolant system: the higher the intellect, the larger the cooling system needed. In the Roman age, Galen (circa AD 129–199) observed brain injury in gladiators and noted that nerves project to and from the brain. Nonetheless, he believed that mental experiences themselves resided in the ventricles of the brain. This idea went essentially unchallenged for well over 1500 years. For example, when Vesalius (1514–1564), the father of modern anatomy, published his plates of dissected brains, the ventricles were drawn in exacting detail whereas the cortex was drawn crudely and schematically. Others followed in this tradition, often drawing the surface of the brain like the intestines. This situation probably reflected a lack of interest in the cortex rather than a lack of penmanship. It is not until one looks at the drawings of Gall and Spurzheim (1810) that the features of the brain become recognizable to modern eyes.

Gall (1758–1828) and Spurzheim (1776–1832) received a bad press, historically speaking, because of their invention and advocacy of **phrenology**. Phrenology had two key assumptions; first, that different regions of the brain perform different functions and are associated with different behaviors; and second, that the size of these regions produces distortions of the skull and correlates with individual differences in cognition and personality. Taking these two ideas in turn, the notion of **functional specialization** within the brain has effectively endured into modern cognitive neuroscience, having seen off a number of challenges over the years (Flourens, 1824; Lashley, 1929). The observations of Penfield and co-workers on the electrically stimulated brain provide some striking examples of this principle. However, the functional specializations of phrenology were not empirically derived and were not constrained by theories of cognition. For example, Fowler's famous phrenologist's head had regions dedicated to "parental love", "destructiveness" and "firmness". Moreover, skull shape has nothing to do with cognitive function.

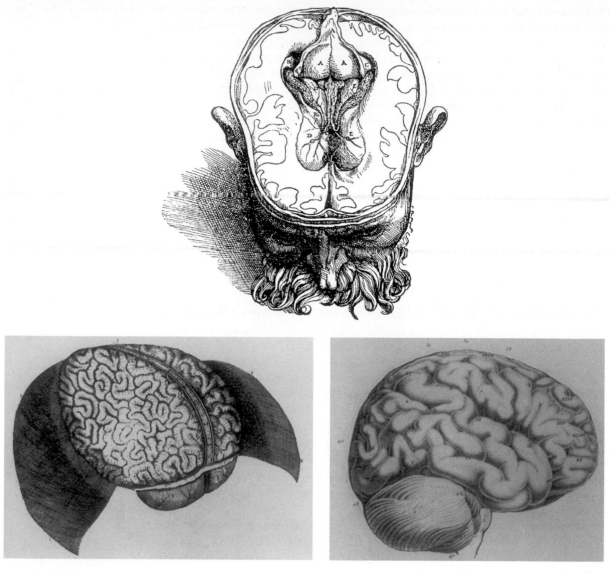

Different drawings of the brain from Vesalius (1543) (top), de Viessens (1685) (bottom left) and Gall and Spurzheim (1810) (bottom right). Note how the earlier two drawings emphasized the ventricles and/or misrepresented the cortical surface.

Although phrenology was fatally flawed, the basic idea of different parts of the brain serving different functions paved the way for future developments in the nineteenth century, the most notable of which are Broca's (1861) reports of two brain-damaged patients. Broca documented two cases in which acquired brain damage had impaired the ability to speak but left other aspects of cognition relatively intact. He concluded that language could be localized to a particular region of the brain. Subsequent studies argued that language itself was not a single entity but could be further subdivided into speech recognition, speech production and conceptual knowledge (Lichtheim, 1885; Wernicke, 1874). This was motivated by the observation that brain damage can lead either to poor speech comprehension and good production, or good speech comprehension and poor production (see Chapter 11 for full details). This suggests that there are at least two speech faculties in the brain and that each can be independently impaired by brain damage. This body of work was a huge step forward in terms of thinking about mind and brain. First, empirical observations were being used to determine what the building blocks of cognition are (is language a single faculty?) rather than listing them from first principles. Second, and related, they were developing models of cognition that did not make direct reference to the brain. That is, one could infer that speech recognition and production were separable without necessarily knowing *where* in the brain they were located, or how the underlying neurons brought these processes about. The approach of using patients with acquired brain damage to inform theories of normal cognition is called **cognitive neuropsychology** and remains influential today (Chapter 5 discusses the logic of this method in detail). Cognitive neuropsychology is now effectively subsumed within the term "cognitive neuroscience", where the latter phrase is seen as being less restrictive in terms of methodology.

Whereas discoveries in the neurosciences continued apace throughout the nineteenth and twentieth centuries, the formation of psychology as a discipline at the end of the nineteenth century took the study of the mind away from its biological underpinnings. This did not reflect a belief in dualism. It was due, in part, to some pragmatic constraints. Early pioneers of psychology, such as William James and Sigmund Freud, were interested in topics like consciousness, attention and personality. Neuroscience has had virtually nothing to say about these issues until quite recently. Another reason for the schism between psychology and biology lies in the notion that one can develop coherent and testable theories of cognition that do not make claims about the brain. The modern foundations of cognitive psychology lie in the computer metaphor of the brain and the **information-processing** approach, popular from the 1950s onwards. For example, Broadbent (1958) argued that much of cognition consists of a sequence of processing stages. In his simple model, perceptual processes occur, followed by attentional processes that transfer information to short-term memory and thence to long-term memory (see also Atkinson & Shiffrin, 1968). These were often drawn as a series of box-and-arrow diagrams. The implication was that one could understand the cognitive system in the same way as one could understand the series of steps performed by a computer program, and without reference to the brain. The idea of the mind as a computer program has advanced over the years along with advances in computational science. For example, many cognitive models contain some element of interactivity and parallel processing. **Interactivity** refers to the fact that stages in processing may not be strictly separate and that later stages can begin before earlier stages are complete. Moreover, later stages can influence

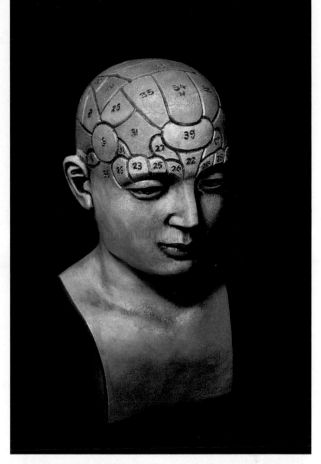

The phrenologist's head was used to represent the hypothetical functions of different regions of the brain.

KEY TERMS

Cognitive neuropsychology
The study of brain-damaged patients to inform theories of normal cognition.

Information processing
An approach in which behavior is described in terms of a sequence of cognitive stages.

Interactivity
Later stages of processing can begin before earlier stages are complete.

Examples of box-and-arrow and connectionist models of cognition. Both represent ways of describing cognitive processes that need not make direct reference to the brain.

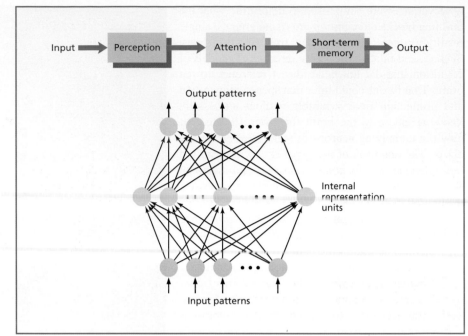

the outcome of early ones (**top-down processing**). **Parallel processing** refers to the fact that lots of different information can be processed simultaneously (serial computers process each piece of information one at a time). Although these computationally explicit models are more sophisticated than earlier box-and-arrow diagrams they, like their predecessors, do not always make contact with the neuroscience literature (Ellis & Humphreys, 1999).

COMPUTATIONAL AND CONNECTIONIST MODELS OF COGNITION

In the 1980s, powerful computers became widely accessible as never before. This enabled cognitive psychologists to develop computationally explicit models of cognition (that literally calculate a set of outputs given a set of inputs) rather than the computationally inspired, but underspecified, box-and-arrow approach. One particular way of implementing computational models has been very influential; namely the **neural network**, connectionist or parallel distributed processing (PDP) approach (McClelland, Rumelhart, & Group, 1986). These models are considered in a number of places throughout this book, notably in the chapters dealing with memory, speaking and literacy.

Connectionist models have a number of architectural features. First, they are composed of arrays of simple information-carrying units called nodes. **Nodes** are information-carrying in the sense that they respond to a particular set of inputs (e.g. certain letters, certain sounds) and produce a restricted set of outputs. The responsiveness of a node depends on how strongly it is connected to other nodes in the network (the "weight" of the connection) and how active the other nodes are. It is possible to calculate, mathematically, what the output of any node would be, given a set of input activations and a set of weights. There are a number of advantages to this type of model. For example, by adjusting the weights over time as a result of experience, the model can develop and learn. The parallel processing enables large amounts of data to be processed simultaneously. A more controversial claim is that they have "neural plausibility". Nodes, activation and weights are in many ways analogous to neurons, firing rates and neural connectivity, respectively. However, these models have been criticized for being too powerful in that they can learn many things that real brains cannot (e.g. Pinker & Prince, 1988). A more moderate view is that connectionist models provide examples of ways in which the brain *might* implement a given cognitive function. Whether or not the brain actually *does* implement cognition in that particular way will ultimately be a question for empirical research in cognitive neuroscience.

KEY TERM

Nodes
The basic units of neural network models that are activated in response to activity in other parts of the network.

The birth of cognitive neuroscience

It was largely advances in imaging technology that provided the driving force for modern-day cognitive neuroscience. Raichle (1998) describes how brain imaging was in a "state of indifference and obscurity in the neuroscience community in the 1970s" and might never have reached prominence if it were not for the involvement of cognitive psychologists in the 1980s. Cognitive psychologists had already established experimental designs and information-processing models that could potentially fit well with these emerging methods. It is important to note that the technological advances in imaging not only led to the development of functional imaging, but also enabled brain lesions to be described precisely in ways that were never possible before (except at post mortem).

Present-day cognitive neuroscience is composed of a broad diversity of methods. These will be discussed in detail in subsequent chapters. At this juncture, it is useful to compare and contrast some of the most prominent methods. The distinction between *recording* methods and *stimulation* methods is crucial in cognitive neuroscience. Electrical stimulation of the brain in humans is now rarely carried out. The modern-day equivalent of these studies uses magnetic, not electric, fields and is called transcranial magnetic stimulation (TMS). This can be applied across the skull rather than directly to the brain. This method will be considered in Chapter 5, alongside the effect of organic brain lesions. Electrophysiological methods (EEG/ERP and single-cell recordings) and magnetophysiological methods (MEG) record the electrical and magnetic properties of neurons themselves. These methods are considered in Chapter 3. In contrast, functional imaging methods (PET and fMRI) record physiological changes associated with blood supply to the brain, which evolve more slowly over time. These are called hemodynamic methods and are considered in Chapter 4.

The methods of cognitive neuroscience can be placed on a number of dimensions:

- The **temporal resolution** refers to the accuracy with which one can measure *when* an event is occurring. The effects of brain damage are permanent and so this has no temporal resolution as such. Methods such as EEG, MEG, TMS and single-cell recording have millisecond resolution. PET and fMRI have temporal resolutions of minutes and seconds, respectively, that reflect the slower hemodynamic response.
- The **spatial resolution** refers to the accuracy with which one can measure *where* an event is occurring. Lesion and functional imaging methods have comparable resolution at the millimeter level, whereas single-cell recordings have spatial resolution at the level of the neuron.
- The *invasiveness* of a method refers to whether or not the equipment is located internally or externally. PET is invasive because it requires an injection of a radio-labeled isotope. Single-cell recordings are performed on the brain itself and are normally only carried out in non-human animals.

THE DIFFERENT METHODS USED IN COGNITIVE NEUROSCIENCE

Method	Method type	Invasiveness	Brain property used
EEG/ERP	Recording	Non-invasive	Electrical
Single-cell (and multi-unit) recordings	Recording	Invasive	Electrical
TMS	Stimulation	Non-invasive	Electromagnetic
MEG	Recording	Non-invasive	Magnetic
PET	Recording	Invasive	Hemodynamic
fMRI	Recording	Non-invasive	Hemodynamic

The methods of cognitive neuroscience can be categorized according to their spatial and temporal resolution. Adapted from Churchland and Sejnowski (1988).

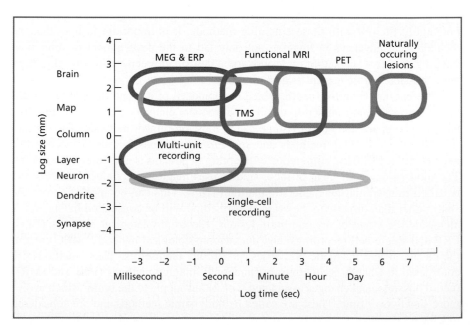

DOES COGNITIVE PSYCHOLOGY NEED THE BRAIN?

As already noted, cognitive psychology developed substantially from the 1950s, using information-processing models that do not make direct reference to the brain. If this way of doing things remains successful, then why change? Of course, there is no reason why it should change. The claim is not that cognitive neuroscience is replacing cognitive psychology (although some might endorse this view), but merely that cognitive psychological theories can inform theories and experiments in the neurosciences and vice versa. However, others have argued that this is not possible by virtue of the fact that information-processing models do not make claims about the brain (Coltheart, 2004b; Harley, 2004).

Coltheart (2004b) poses the question: "Has cognitive neuroscience, or if not might it ever (in principle, or even in practice), successfully used data from cognitive neuro-imaging to make theoretical decisions entirely at the cognitive level (e.g. to adjudicate between competing information-processing models of some cognitive system)?" (p. 21). Henson (2005) argues that it can in principle and that it does in practice. He argues that data from functional imaging (blood flow, blood oxygen) comprise just another dependent variable that one can measure. For example, there are a number of things that one could measure in a standard forced-choice reaction-time task: reaction time, error rates, sweating (skin conductance response), muscle contraction (electromyograph), scalp electrical recordings (EEG) or hemodynamic changes in the brain (PET, fMRI). Each measure will relate to the task in some way and can be used to inform theories about the task.

To illustrate this point, consider one example. One could ask a simple question such as: "Does visual recognition of words and letters involve computing a representation that is independent of case?" For example, does the reading system treat "E" and "e" as equivalent at an early stage in processing or are "E" and "e" treated as different letters until some later stage (e.g. saying them aloud)? A way of investigating this using a reaction-time measure is to present the same word twice in the same or different case (e.g. radio-RADIO, RADIO-RADIO) and compare this with situations in which the word differs (e.g. mouse-RADIO, MOUSE-RADIO). One general finding in reaction-time studies is that it is faster to process a stimulus if the same stimulus has recently been presented. For example, if asked to make a speeded decision about RADIO (e.g. is it animate or inanimate?) then performance will be faster if it has been previously encountered. Dehaene et al. (2001) investigated this mechanism by comparing reaction-time measures with functional imaging (fMRI) measures. In this task, the first word in each pair was presented very briefly and was followed by visual noise. This prevents the participants from consciously perceiving it and, hence, one can be sure that they are not saying the word. The second word is consciously seen and requires a response. Dehaene et al. found that reaction times are faster to the second word when it follows the same word, irrespective of case. Importantly, there is a region in the left fusiform cortex that shows the same effect (although in terms of "activation" rather than response time). In this concrete example, it is meaningless to argue that one

One could take many different measures in a forced-choice response task: behavioral (reaction time [RT], errors) or biological (electromyographic [EMG], lateralized readiness potential [LRP], lateralized BOLD response [LBR]). All measures could potentially be used to inform cognitive theory. Adapted from Henson (2005), by kind permission of the Experimental Psychology Society.

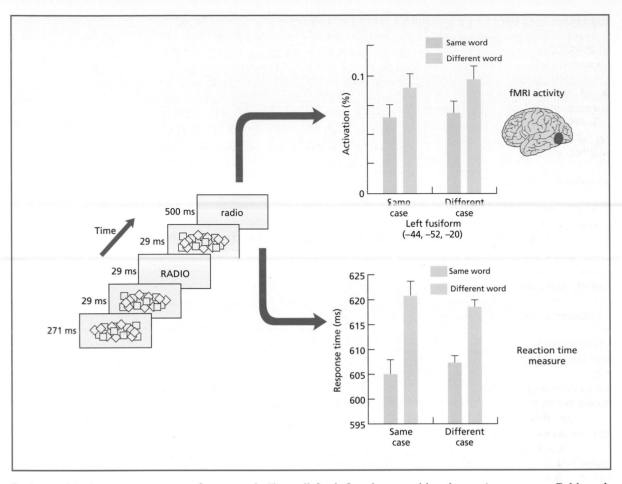

Both reaction times and fMRI activation in the left fusiform region demonstrate more efficient processing of words if they are preceded by subliminal presentation of the same word, irrespective of case. Adapted from Dehaene et al. (2001).

type of measure is "better" for informing cognitive theory (to return to Coltheart's question) given that both are measuring different aspects of the same thing. One could explore the nature of this effect further by, for instance, presenting the same word in different languages (in bilingual speakers), presenting the words in different locations on the screen and so on. This would provide further insights into the nature of this mechanism (e.g. what aspects of vision does it entail, does it depend on word meaning?). However, both reaction-time measures and brain-based measures could be potentially informative. It is not the case that functional imaging is merely telling us *where* cognition is happening and not *how* it is happening.

Another distinction that has been used to contrast cognitive psychology and cognitive neuroscience is that between software and hardware, respectively (Coltheart, 2004b; Harley, 2004). This derives from the familiar computer analogy in which one can, supposedly, learn about information processing (software) without knowing about the brain (hardware). As has been shown, to some extent this is true. But the computer analogy is a little misleading. Computer software is written by computer programmers (who, incidentally, have human brains). However, information processing is not written by some third person and then inscribed into the brain. Rather, the brain provides causal constraints on the nature of information processing. This is not analogous to the computer domain in which the link between software and hardware is arbitrarily determined by a computer programmer. To give a simple example, one model of word recognition suggests that words are recognized by searching words in a mental dictionary one by one until a match is found (Forster, 1976). The weight of evidence from cognitive psychology argues against this serial search, and in favor of words being searched in parallel (i.e. all candidate words are considered at the same time). But *why* does human cognition work like this? Computer programs can be made to recognize words adequately with both serial search and parallel search. The reason why human information processing uses a parallel search and not a serial search probably lies in the relatively slow *neural* response time (acting against serial search). This constraint does not apply to the fast processing of computers. Thus, cognitive psychology may be sufficient to tell us the structure of information processing but it may not answer deeper questions about why information processing should be configured in that particular way.

DOES NEUROSCIENCE NEED COGNITIVE PSYCHOLOGY?

It would be no exaggeration to say that the advent of techniques such as functional imaging have revolutionized the brain sciences. For example, consider some of the newspaper headlines that have appeared in recent years. Of course, it has been well known since the nineteenth century that pain, mood, intelligence and sexual desire are largely products of processes in the brain. The reason why headlines such as these are extraordinary is because now the technology exists to be able to study these processes *in vivo*. Of course, when one looks inside the brain one does not "see" memories, thoughts, perceptions and so on (i.e. the stuff of cognitive psychology). Instead, what one sees is grey matter, white matter, blood vessels and so on (i.e. the stuff of neuroscience). It is the latter, not the former, that one observes when conducting a functional imaging

The media loves to simplify the findings of cognitive neuroscience. Many newspaper stories appear to regard it as counterintuitive that sex, pain and mood would be products of the brain. *Sunday Times*, 21 November 1999; *Metro* 5 January 2001; *The Observer*, 12 March 2000; *The Independent*, 27 May 1999.

experiment. Developing a framework for linking the two will necessarily entail dealing with the mind–body problem either tacitly or explicitly. This is a daunting challenge.

Is functional imaging going to lead to a more sophisticated understanding of the mind and brain than was achieved by the phrenologists? Some of the newspaper reports in the figure suggest it might not. One reason why phrenology failed is because the method had no real scientific grounding; the same cannot be said of functional imaging. Another reason why phrenology failed was that the psychological concepts used were naïve. It is for this reason that functional imaging and other advances in neuroscience do require the insights from cognitive psychology to frame appropriate research questions and avoid becoming a new phrenology (Uttal, 2001).

The question of whether cognitive, mind-based concepts will eventually become redundant (under a reductionist account) or coexist with neural-based accounts (e.g. as in dual-aspect theory) is for the future to decide. But for now, cognitive, mind-based concepts have an essential role to play in cognitive neuroscience.

IS THE BRAIN MODULAR?

The notion that the brain contains different regions of functional specialization has been around in various guises for 200 years. However, one particular variation on this theme has attracted particular attention and controversy – namely, Fodor's (1983, 1998) theory of **modularity**. First, Fodor makes a distinction between two different classes of cognitive process: central systems versus modules. The key difference between them relates to the types of information they can process. Modules are held to demonstrate **domain specificity** in that they process only one particular type of information (e.g. color, shape, words, faces), whereas central systems are held to be domain independent in that the type of information processed is non-specific (candidates would be memory, attention, executive functions). According to Fodor, one advantage of modular systems is that, by processing only a limited type of information, they can operate rapidly, efficiently and in isolation from other cognitive systems. An additional claim is that modules may be innately specified in the genetic code.

Many of these ideas have been criticized on empirical and theoretical grounds. For example, it has been suggested that domain specificity is not innate, although the means of acquiring it could be (Karmiloff-Smith, 1992). Moreover, systems like reading appear modular in some respects but cannot be innate because they are recent in evolution. Others have argued that evidence for interactivity suggests that modules are not isolated from other cognitive processes (Farah, 1994).

On balance, the empirical evidence does not strongly favor this version of modularity. However, the extent to which the brain contains regions of functional specialization and domain specificity is still an active area of debate.

SUMMARY AND KEY POINTS OF THE CHAPTER

- The mind–body problem refers to the question of how physical matter (the brain) can produce mental experiences, and this remains an enduring issue in cognitive neuroscience.
- To some extent, the different regions of the brain are specialized for different functions.
- Functional neuroimaging has provided the driving force for much of the development of cognitive neuroscience, but there is a danger in merely using these methods to localize cognitive functions without understanding how they work.
- Cognitive psychology has developed as a discipline without making explicit references to the brain. However, biological measures can provide an alternative source of evidence to inform cognitive theory and the brain must provide constraining factors on the nature and development of the information-processing models of cognitive science.

EXAMPLE ESSAY QUESTIONS

- What is the "mind–body problem" and what frameworks have been put forward to solve it?
- Is cognitive neuroscience the new phrenology?
- Does cognitive psychology need the brain? Does neuroscience need cognitive psychology?

RECOMMENDED FURTHER READING

- Finger, S. (2000). *Minds behind the brain: A history of the pioneers and their discoveries*. New York: Oxford University Press. A good place to start for the history of neuroscience.
- Henson, R. (2005). What can functional neuroimaging tell the experimental psychologist? *Quarterly Journal of Experimental Psychology, 58A*, 193–233. An excellent summary of the role of functional imaging in psychology and a rebuttal of common criticisms. This debate can also be followed in a series of articles in *Cortex (2006, 42, 387–427).*
- Uttal, W. R. (2001). *The new phrenology: The limits of localizing cognitive processes in the brain*. Cambridge, MA: MIT Press. An interesting overview of the methods and limitations of cognitive neuroscience.
- Velmans, M. (2009). *Understanding consciousness* (second edition). London: Routledge. In-depth coverage of the mind–body problem, drawing on some evidence from cognitive neuroscience.

CHAPTER 2

CONTENTS

Introducing the brain

It is hard to begin a chapter about the brain without waxing lyrical. The brain is the physical organ that makes all our mental life possible. It enables us to read these words, and to consider thoughts that we have never considered before – or even to create thoughts that no human has considered before. This book will scratch the surface of how this is all possible, but the purpose of this chapter is more mundane. It offers a basic guide to the structure of the brain, starting from a description of neurons and working up to a description of how these are organized into different neuroanatomical systems. The emphasis is on the human brain rather than the brain of other species.

TEN INTERESTING FACTS ABOUT THE HUMAN BRAIN

(1) There are 100 billion neurons in the human brain.

(2) Each neuron may connect with around 10,000 other neurons.

(3) If each neuron connected with every single other neuron, our brain would be 12.5 miles in diameter (Nelson & Bower, 1990). This is the length of Manhattan Island. This leads to an important conclusion – namely, that neurons only connect with a small subset of other neurons. Neurons may tend to communicate only with their neighbors and long-range connections are the exception rather than the rule.

(4) Neurons make up only 10% of the cells in our brain. This may have given rise to the common myth that we only ever use 10% of our brain (Beyerstein, 1999). The other cells are called glia and they serve a number of essential support functions. For example, they are involved in tissue repair and in the formation of myelin.

(5) The brain makes up only 2% of body weight.

(6) It is no longer believed that neurons in the brain are incapable of being regenerated. It was once widely believed that we are born with our full complement of neurons and that new neurons are not generated. This idea is now untenable, at least in a region called the dentate gyrus (for a review, see Gross, 2000).

(7) On average, we lose a net amount of one cortical neuron per second. A study has shown that around 10% of our cortical neurons perish between the ages of 20 and 90 years – equivalent to 85,000 neurons per day (Pakkenberg & Gundersen, 1997).

(8) Identical twins do not have anatomically identical brains. A comparison of identical and non-identical twins suggests that the three-dimensional cortical gyral pattern is determined primarily by non-genetic factors, although brain size is strongly heritable (Bartley, Jones, & Weinberger, 1997).

(9) Autistic people have larger brains (Abell et al., 1999). They also have larger heads to accommodate them. There is unlikely to be a simple relationship between brain size and intellect (most autistic people have low IQ) and brain efficiency may be unrelated to size.

(10) Men have larger brains than women, but women have more folded brains. The total number of cortical neurons is related to gender but not overall height or weight (Pakkenberg & Gundersen, 1997). The female brain is more folded, implying an increase in surface area that may offset any size difference (Luders et al., 2004).

STRUCTURE AND FUNCTION OF THE NEURON

All **neurons** have basically the same structure. They consist of three components: a **cell body** (or soma), **dendrites** and an **axon**. Although neurons have the same basic structure and function, it is important to note that there are some significant differences between different types of neurons in terms of the spatial arrangements of the dendrites and axon.

The cell body contains the nucleus and other organelles. The nucleus contains the genetic code, and this is involved in protein synthesis (e.g. of certain neurotransmitters). Neurons receive information from other neurons and they make a "decision" about this information (by changing their own activity) that can then be passed on to other neurons. From the cell body, a number of branching structures called dendrites enable communication with other neurons. Dendrites receive information from other neurons in close proximity. The number and structure of the dendritic branches can vary significantly depending on the type of neuron (i.e. where it is to be found in the brain). The axon, by contrast, sends information to other neurons. Each neuron consists of many dendrites but only a single axon (although the axon may be divided into several branches called collaterals).

Neurons consist of three basic features: a cell body, dendrites that receive information and axons that send information. In this diagram the axon is myelinated (see p. 20) to speed the conduction time.

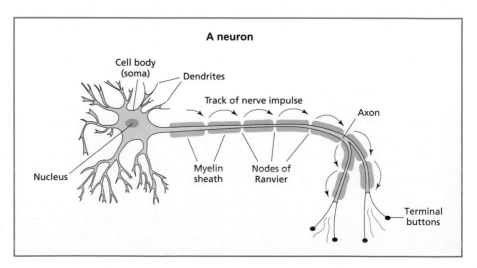

A neuron

Cell body (soma)
Dendrites
Track of nerve impulse
Axon
Nucleus
Myelin sheath
Nodes of Ranvier
Terminal buttons

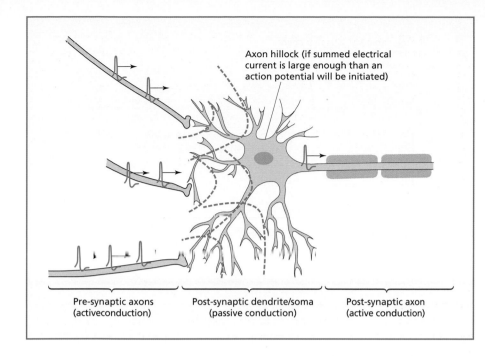

Axon hillock (if summed electrical current is large enough than an action potential will be initiated)

Pre-synaptic axons (activeconduction)

Post-synaptic dendrite/soma (passive conduction)

Post-synaptic axon (active conduction)

Electrical currents are actively transmitted through axons by an action potential. Electrical currents flow passively through dendrites and soma of neurons but will initiate an action potential if their summed potential is strong enough at the start of the axon (called the hillock).

The terminal of an axon flattens out into a disc-shaped structure. It is here that chemical signals enable communication between neurons via a small gap termed a **synapse**. The two neurons forming the synapse are referred to as presynaptic (before the synapse) and postsynaptic (after the synapse), reflecting the direction of information flow (from axon to dendrite). When a presynaptic neuron is active, an electrical current (termed an **action potential**) is propagated down the length of the axon. When the action potential reaches the axon terminal, chemicals are released into the synaptic cleft. These chemicals are termed **neurotransmitters**. (Note that a small proportion of synapses, such as retinal gap junctions, signal electrically and not chemically). Neurotransmitters bind to receptors on the dendrites or cell body of the postsynaptic neuron and create a synaptic potential. The synaptic potential is conducted passively (i.e. without creating an action potential) through the dendrites and soma of the postsynaptic neuron. If these passive currents are sufficiently strong when they reach the beginning of the axon in the postsynaptic neuron, then an action potential (an *active* electrical current) will be triggered in this neuron. It is important to note that each postsynaptic neuron sums together many synaptic potentials, which are generated at many different and distant dendritic sites (as opposed to a simple chain reaction between one neuron and the next). Passive conduction tends to be short range because the electrical signal is impeded by the resistance of the surrounding matter. Active conduction enables long-range signalling between neurons by the propagation of action potentials.

Electrical signalling and the action potential

Each neuron is surrounded by a cell membrane that acts as a barrier to the passage of certain chemicals. Within the membrane, certain protein molecules act as gatekeepers and allow particular chemicals in and out under certain conditions. These chemicals consist, amongst others, of charged sodium (Na^+) and potassium (K^+) ions.

KEY TERMS

Synapse
The small gap between neurons in which neurotransmitters are released, permitting signalling between neurons.

Action potential
A sudden change (depolarization and repolarization) in the electrical properties of the neuron membrane in an axon.

Neurotransmitters
Chemical signals that are released by one neuron and affect the properties of other neurons.

The action potential consists of a number of phases.

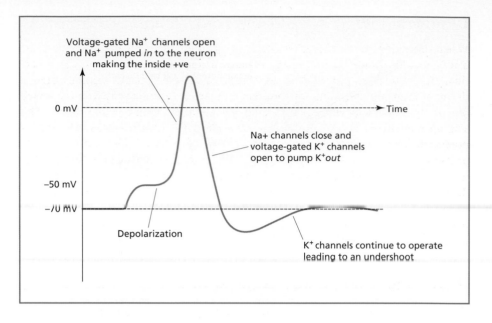

Voltage-gated Na⁺ channels open and Na⁺ pumped *in* to the neuron making the inside +ve

0 mV

Time

Na+ channels close and voltage-gated K⁺ channels open to pump K⁺*out*

−50 mV

−70 mV

Depolarization

K⁺ channels continue to operate leading to an undershoot

The balance between these ions on the inside and outside of the membrane is such that there is normally a resting potential of –70 mV across the membrane (the inside being negative relative to the outside).

Voltage-gated ion channels are of particular importance in the generation of an action potential. They are found only in axons, which is why only the axon is capable of producing action potentials. The sequence of events is as follows:

1. If a passive current of sufficient strength flows across the axon membrane, this begins to open the voltage-gated Na⁺ channels.
2. When the channel is opened, then Na⁺ may enter the cell and the negative potential normally found on the inside is reduced (the cell is said to *depolarize*). At about –50 mV, the cell membrane becomes completely permeable and the charge on the inside of the cell momentarily reverses. This sudden depolarization and subsequent repolarization in electrical charge across the membrane is the action potential.
3. The negative potential of the cell is restored via the *outward* flow of K⁺ through voltage-gated K⁺ channels and closing of the voltage-gated Na⁺ channels.
4. There is a brief period in which hyperpolarization occurs (the inside is more negative than at rest). This makes it more difficult for the axon to depolarize straight away and prevents the action potential from travelling backwards.

An action potential in one part of the axon opens adjacent voltage-sensitive Na⁺ channels, and so the action potential moves progressively down the length of the axon, starting from the cell body and ending at the axon terminal. The conduction of the action potential along the axon may be speeded up if the axon is myelinated. **Myelin** is a fatty substance that is deposited around the axon of some cells (especially those that carry motor signals). It blocks the normal Na⁺/K⁺ transfer and so the action potential jumps, via passive conduction, down the length of the axon at the points at which the myelin is absent (called *nodes of Ranvier*). Destruction of myelin is found in a number of pathologies, notably *multiple sclerosis*.

Chemical signalling and the postsynaptic neuron

When the action potential reaches the axon terminal, the electrical signal initiates a sequence of events leading to the release of neurotransmitters into the synaptic cleft. Protein *receptors* in the membrane of the postsynaptic neurons bind to the neurotransmitters. Many of the receptors are transmitter-gated ion channels (not to be confused with voltage-gated ion channels found in the axon). This sets up a localized flow of Na^+, K^+ or chloride (Cl^-), which creates the synaptic potential. Some neurotransmitters (e.g. GABA) have an inhibitory effect on the postsynaptic neuron (i.e. by making it less likely to fire). This can be achieved by making the inside of the neuron more negative than normal and hence harder to depolarize (e.g. by opening transmitter-gated Cl^- channels). Other neurotransmitters (e.g. acetylcholine) have excitatory effects on the post-synaptic neuron (i.e. by making it more likely to fire). These synaptic potentials are then passively conducted as already described.

How do neurons code information?

The amplitude of an action potential does not vary, but the number of action potentials propagated per second varies along a continuum. This rate of responding (also called the "spiking rate") relates to the informational "code" carried by that neuron. For example, some neurons may have a high spiking rate in some situations (e.g. during speech) but not others (e.g. during vision), whereas other neurons would have a complementary profile. Neurons responding to similar types of information tend to be grouped together. This gives rise to the functional specialization of brain regions that was introduced in Chapter 1.

If information is carried in the response rate of a neuron, what determines the *type* of information that the neuron responds to? The type of information that a neuron carries is related to the input it receives and the output it sends to other neurons. For example, the reason why neurons in the primary auditory cortex can be considered to carry information about sound is because they receive input from a pathway originating in the cochlea and they send information to other neurons involved in more advanced stages of auditory processing (e.g. speech perception). However, imagine that one were to re-wire the brain such that the primary auditory cortex was to receive inputs from the retinal pathway rather than the auditory pathway (e.g. Sur & Leamey, 2001). In this case, the function of the primary "auditory" cortex would have changed (as would the type of information it carries) even though the region itself was not directly modified (only the inputs to it were modified). This general point is worth bearing in mind when one considers what the function of a given region is. The function of a region is determined by its inputs and outputs. As such, the extent to which a function can be strictly localized is a moot point.

THE GROSS ORGANIZATION OF THE BRAIN

Gray matter, white matter and cerebrospinal fluid

Neurons are organized within the brain to form white matter and gray matter. **Gray matter** consists of neuronal cell bodies. **White matter** consists of axons and support

There are three different kinds of white matter tract, depending on the nature of the regions that are connected. Adapted from Diamond et al. (1986). © 1986 by Coloring Concepts, Inc. Reprinted by permission of HarperCollins Publishers.

cells (**glia**). The brain consists of a highly convoluted folded sheet of gray matter (the cerebral cortex), beneath which lies the white matter. In the center of the brain, beneath the bulk of the white matter fibers, lies another collection of gray matter structures (the subcortex), which includes the basal ganglia, the limbic system and the diencephalon.

White matter tracts may project between different cortical regions within the same hemisphere (called *association tracts*), may project between different cortical regions in different hemispheres (called *commisures*; the most important commisure being the **corpus callosum**) or may project between cortical and subcortical structures (called *projection tracts*).

The brain also contains a number of hollow chambers termed **ventricles**. These were incorrectly revered for 1500 years as being the seat of mental life. The ventricles are filled with *cerebrospinal fluid* (CSF), which does serve some useful functions, albeit non-cognitive. The CSF carries waste metabolites, transfers some messenger signals and provides a protective cushion for the brain.

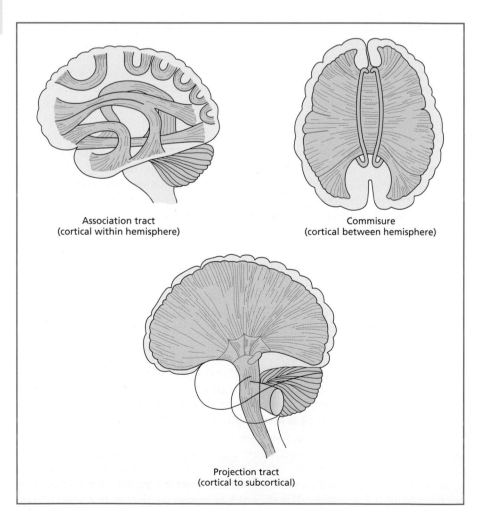

Association tract
(cortical within hemisphere)

Commisure
(cortical between hemisphere)

Projection tract
(cortical to subcortical)

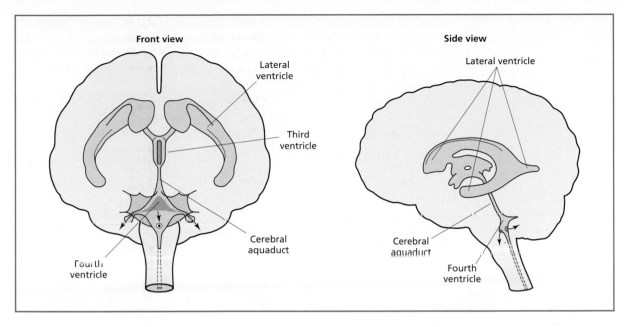

The brain consists of four ventricles filled with cerebrospinal fluid (CSF): the lateral ventricles are found in each hemisphere, the third ventricle lies centrally around the subcortical structures, and the fourth ventricle lies in the brainstem (hindbrain).

A hierarchical view of the central nervous system

Brain evolution can be thought of as adding additional structures onto older ones, rather than replacing older structures with newer ones. For example, the main visual pathway in humans travels from the retina to the occipital lobe, but a number of older visual pathways also exist and contribute to vision (see Chapter 6). These older pathways constitute the dominant form of seeing for other species such as birds and reptiles.

Terms of reference and section

There are conventional directions for navigating around the brain, just as there is a north, south, east and west for navigating around maps. **Anterior** and **posterior** refer to directions towards the front and the back of the brain, respectively. These are also called *rostral* and *caudal*, respectively, particularly in other species that have a tail (caudal refers to the tail end). Directions towards the top and the bottom are referred to as **superior** and **inferior**, respectively; they are also known as **dorsal** and **ventral**, respectively. The terms anterior, posterior, superior and inferior (or rostral, caudal, dorsal and ventral) enable navigation in two dimensions: front–back and top–bottom. Needless to say, the brain is three-dimensional and so a further dimension is required. The terms **lateral** and *medial* are used to refer to directions towards the outer surface and the center of the brain, respectively; the term "medial" is ambiguous because it is also used in another context. Although it is used to refer to the center of the brain, it is also used to refer to the middle of structures more generally. For example, the

KEY TERMS

Anterior
Towards the front.

Posterior
Towards the back.

Superior
Towards the top.

Inferior
Towards the bottom.

Dorsal
Towards the top.

Ventral
Towards the bottom.

Lateral
The outer part (cf. medial).

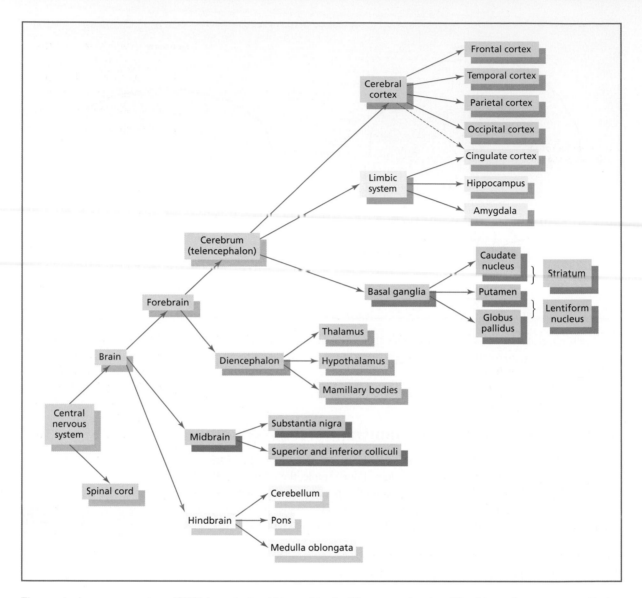

The central nervous system (CNS) is organized hierarchically. The upper levels of the hierarchy, corresponding to the upper branches of this diagram, are the newest structures from an evolutionary perspective.

medial temporal gyrus lies on the lateral surface of the brain (not the medial). It is called "medial" because it lies midway between the superior and inferior temporal gyri.

The brain can be sectioned into two-dimensional slices in a number of ways. A *coronal* cross-section refers to a slice in the vertical plane through both hemispheres (the brain appears roundish in this section). A *sagittal* section refers to a slice in the vertical plane going through one of the hemispheres. When the sagittal section lies between the hemispheres it is called a *midline* or medial section. An *axial* (or horizontal) section is taken in the horizontal plane.

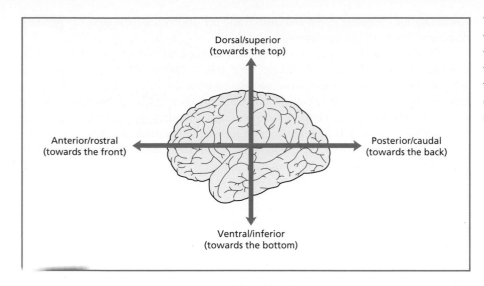

Terms of reference in the brain. Note also the terms *lateral* (referring to the outer surface of the brain) and *medial* (referring to the central regions).

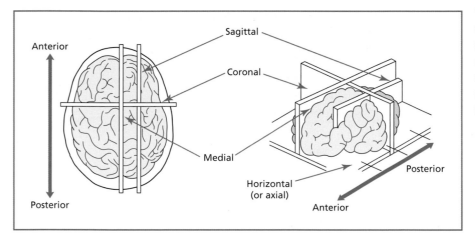

Terms of sections of the brain. Adapted from Diamond et al. (1986). © 1986 by Coloring Concepts Inc. Reprinted by permission of HarperCollins Publishers.

THE CEREBRAL CORTEX

The cerebral cortex consists of two folded sheets of gray matter organized into two hemispheres (left and right). The surface of the cortex has become increasingly more convoluted with evolutionary development. Having a folded structure permits a high surface area to volume ratio and thereby permits efficient packaging. The raised surfaces of the cortex are termed **gyri** (or gyrus in the singular). The dips or folds are called **sulci** (or sulcus in the singular).

The cortex is only around 3 mm thick and is organized into different layers that can be seen when viewed in cross-section. The different layers reflect the grouping of different cell types. Different parts of the cortex have different densities in each of the layers. Most of the cortex contains six main cortical layers and this is termed the *neocortex* (meaning "new cortex"). Other cortical regions are the mesocortex

KEY TERMS

Gyri (gyrus = singular)
The raised folds of the cortex.

Sulci (sulcus = singular)
The buried grooves of the cortex.

(including the cingulate gyrus and insula) and the allocortex (including the primary olfactory cortex and hippocampus).

The lateral surface of the cortex of each hemisphere is divided into four lobes: the frontal, parietal, temporal and occipital lobes. The dividing line between the lobes is sometimes prominent, as is the case between the frontal and temporal lobes (divided by the lateral or *sylvian fissure*), but in other cases the boundary cannot readily be observed (e.g. between temporal and occipital lobes). Other regions of the cortex are observable only in a medial section, for example the cingulate cortex. Finally, an island of cortex lies buried underneath the temporal lobe; this is called the *insula* (which literally means "island" in Latin).

The main gyri of the lateral (top) and medial (bottom) surface of the brain. The cortical sulci tend to be labeled according to terms of reference. For example, the superior temporal sulcus lies between the superior and medial temporal gyri.

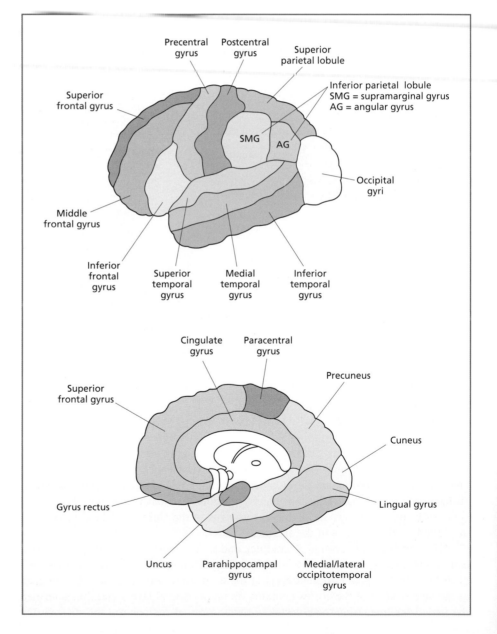

There are three different ways in which regions of cerebral cortex may be divided and, hence, labeled:

1. *Regions divided by the pattern of gyri and sulci.* The same pattern of gyri and sulci is found in everyone (although the precise shape and size varies greatly). As such, it is possible to label different regions of the brain accordingly.
2. *Regions divided by cytoarchitecture.* One of the most influential ways of dividing up the cerebral cortex is in terms of **Brodmann's areas**. Brodmann divided the cortex up into approximately 52 areas (labeled from BA1 to BA52), based on the relative distribution of cell types across cortical layers. Areas are labeled in a circular spiral starting from the middle, like the numbering system of Parisian suburbs. Over the years, the map has been modified.
3. *Regions divided by function.* This method tends only to be used for primary sensory and motor areas. For example, Brodmann areas 17 and 6 are also termed the primary visual cortex and the primary motor cortex, respectively. Higher cortical regions are harder (if not impossible) to ascribe unique functions to.

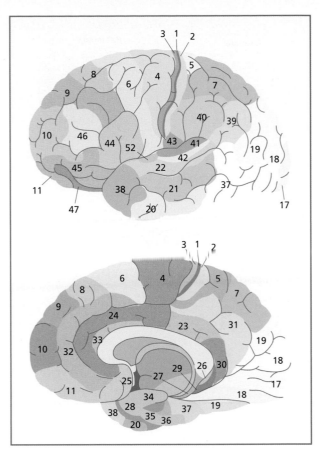

The Brodmann areas of the brain on the lateral (top) and medial (bottom) surface.

THE SUBCORTEX

Beneath the cortical surface and the intervening white matter lies another collection of gray matter nuclei termed the subcortex. The subcortex is typically divided into a number of different systems with different evolutionary and functional histories.

The basal ganglia

The **basal ganglia** are large rounded masses that lie in each hemisphere. They surround and overhang the thalamus in the center of the brain. They are involved in regulating motor activity and the programming and termination of action (see Chapter 8). Disorders of the basal ganglia can be characterized as hypokinetic (poverty of movement)

KEY TERMS

Brodmann's areas
Regions of cortex defined by the relative distribution of cell types across cortical layers (cytoarchitecture).

Basal ganglia
Regions of subcortical gray matter involved in aspects of motor control and skill learning; they consist of structures such as the caudate nucleus, putamen and globus pallidus.

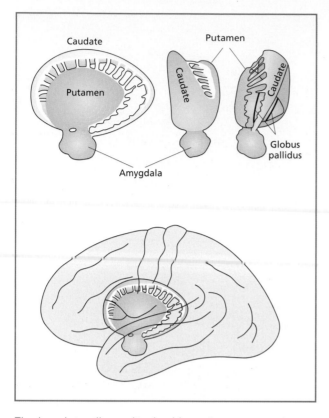

The basal ganglia are involved in motor programming and skill learning.

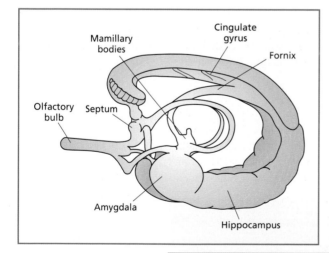

The limbic system.

or hyperkinetic (excess of movement). Examples of these include Parkinson's and Huntington's disease, respectively (see Chapter 8). The basal ganglia are also implicated in the learning of skills and habits (see Chapter 9). The main structures comprising the basal ganglia are: the *caudate nucleus* (an elongated tail-like structure), the *putamen* (lying more laterally) and the *globus pallidus* (lying more medially). The caudate and putamen funnel cortical inputs into the globus pallidus, from which fibers reach into the thalamus. Different circuits passing through these regions either increase or decrease the probability and amplitude of movement.

The limbic system

The **limbic system** is important for relating the organism to its environment based on current needs and the present situation, and based on previous experience. It is involved in the detection and expression of emotional responses. For example, the *amygdala* has been implicated in the detection of fearful or threatening stimuli (see Chapter 15) and parts of the *cingulate gyrus* have been implicated in the detection of emotional and cognitive conflicts (see Chapter 14). The *hippocampus* is particularly important for learning and memory (see Chapter 9) and has also been hypothesized to act as a novelty detector (e.g. Knight, 1996). Both the amygdala and hippocampus lie buried in the temporal lobes of each hemisphere. Other limbic structures are clearly visible on the underside (ventral surface) of the brain. The *mamillary bodies* are two small round protrusions that have traditionally been implicated in memory (e.g. Dusoir, Kapur, Byrnes, McKinstry, & Hoare, 1990). The *olfactory bulbs* lie on the under surface of the frontal lobes. Their connections to the limbic system underscore the importance of smell for detecting environmentally salient stimuli (e.g. food, other animals) and its influence on mood and memory.

The diencephalon

The two main structures that make up the diencephalon are the thalamus and the hypothalamus.

The **thalamus** consists of two interconnected egg-shaped masses that lie in the center of the brain and appear prominent in a medial section. The thalamus is the main sensory relay for all senses (except smell) between the sense organs (eyes, ears, etc.) and the cortex. It also contains projections to almost all parts of the cortex and the basal ganglia. At the posterior end of the thalamus lie the *lateral geniculate nucleus* and the *medial geniculate nucleus*. These are the main sensory relays to the primary visual and primary auditory cortices, respectively.

The **hypothalamus** lies beneath the thalamus and consists of a variety of nuclei that are specialized

The ventral surface of the brain shows the limbic structures of the olfactory bulbs and mamillary bodies. Other visible structures include the hypothalamus, optic nerves, pons and medulla.

KEY TERMS

Thalamus
A major subcortical relay center; for instance, it is a processing station between all sensory organs (except smell) and the cortex.

Hypothalamus
Consists of a variety of nuclei that are specialized for different functions that are primarily concerned with the body and its regulation.

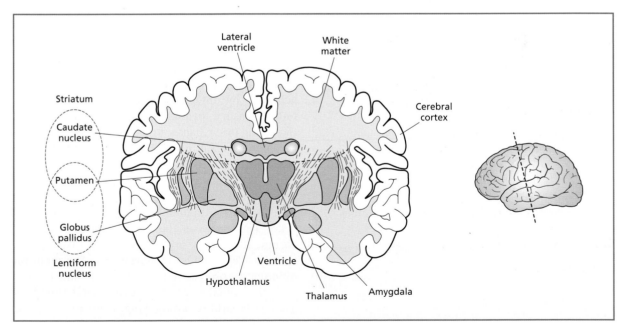

A coronal section through the amygdala and basal ganglia shows the thalamus and hypothalamus as prominent in the midline.

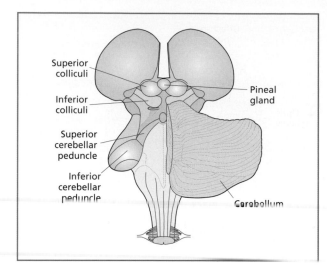

A posterior view of the midbrain and hindbrain. Visible structures include the thalamus, pineal gland, superior colliculi, inferior colliculi, cerebellum, cerebellar peduncle and medulla oblongata (the pons is not visible but lies on the other side of the cerebellum).

for different functions primarily concerned with the body. These include body temperature, hunger and thirst, sexual activity and regulation of endocrine functions (e.g. regulating body growth). Tumors in this region can lead to eating and drinking disorders, precocious puberty, dwarfism and gigantism.

THE MIDBRAIN AND HINDBRAIN

The midbrain region consists of a number of structures, only a few of which will be considered here. The **superior colliculi** and **inferior colliculi** (or colliculus in singular) are gray-matter nuclei. The superior colliculi integrate information from several senses (vision, hearing and touch), whereas the inferior colliculi are specialized for auditory processing. These pathways are different from the main cortical sensory pathways and are evolutionarily older. They may provide a fast route that enables rapid orienting to stimuli (flashes or bangs) before the stimulus is consciously seen or heard (e.g. Sparks, 1999). The midbrain also contains a region called the *substantia nigra*, which is connected to the basal ganglia. Cell loss in this region is associated with the symptoms of Parkinson's disease.

The **cerebellum** (literally "little brain") is attached to the posterior of the hindbrain via the cerebellar peduncles. It consists of highly convoluted folds of gray matter. It is organized into two interconnected lobes. The cerebellum is important for dexterity and smooth execution of movement. This function may be achieved by integrating motor commands with online sensory feedback about the current state of the action (see Chapter 8). Unilateral lesions to the cerebellum result in poor coordination on the same side of the body as the lesion (i.e. ipsilesional side). Bilateral lesions result in a wide and staggering gait, slurred speech (dysarthria) and eyes moving in a to-and-fro motion (nystagmus). The **pons** is a key link between the cerebellum and the cerebrum. It receives information from visual areas to control eye and body movements. The **medulla oblongata** protrudes from the pons and merges with the spinal cord. It regulates vital functions such as breathing, swallowing, heart rate and the wake–sleep cycle.

KEY TERMS

Superior colliculi
A midbrain nucleus that forms part of a subcortical sensory pathway involved in programming fast eye movements.

Inferior colliculi
A midbrain nucleus that forms part of a subcortical auditory pathway.

Cerebellum
Structure attached to the hindbrain; important for dexterity and smooth execution of movement.

Pons
Part of the hindbrain; a key link between the cerebellum and the cerebrum.

Medulla oblongata
Part of the hindbrain; it regulates vital functions such as breathing, swallowing, heart rate and the wake–sleep cycle.

SUMMARY AND KEY POINTS OF THE CHAPTER

- The neuron is the basic cell type that supports cognition. Neurons form a densely interconnected network of connections. Axons send signals to other cells and dendrites receive signals.
- Neurons code information in terms of a response rate. They only respond in certain situations (determined by the input they receive from elsewhere).
- Neurons are grouped together to form gray matter (cell bodies) and white matter (axons and other cells). The cortical surface consists of a folded sheet of gray matter organized into two hemispheres.
- There is another set of gray matter in the subcortex that includes the basal ganglia (important in regulating movement), the limbic system (important for emotion and memory functions) and the diencephalon (the thalamus is a sensory relay center and the hypothalamus is concerned with hemostatic functions).

EXAMPLE ESSAY QUESTIONS

- How do neurons communicate with each other?
- Describe how electrical and chemical signals are generated by neurons.
- Compare and contrast the different functions of the forebrain, midbrain and hindbrain.

RECOMMENDED FURTHER READING

- Bear, M. F., Connors, B. W., & Paradiso, M. A. (2006). *Neuroscience: Exploring the brain* (third edition). Baltimore, MA: Lippincott Williams & Wilkins. A detailed book that covers all aspects of neuroscience. It is recommended for students whose degree contains significant neuroscience components. The book may be beyond the need of many psychology students.

- Crossman, A. R. & Neary, D. (2000). *Neuroanatomy: An illustrated colour text* (second edition). Edinburgh: Harcourt Publishers. A good and clear guide that is not too detailed.

- Gupta, K. (2001). *Human brain coloring workbook*. The Princeton Review. Don't be fooled by the title – this is a serious book. It takes neuroanatomy to an advanced level and is a good way to learn.

CHAPTER 3

CONTENTS

The electrophysiological brain

3

How is it possible that the world "out there" comes to be perceived, comprehended and acted upon by a set of neurons operating "in here"? Chapter 2 introduced some of the basic properties of the neuron, including the fact that the rate of responding of a neuron (in terms of the number of action potentials or "spikes") is a continuous variable that reflects the informational content of that neuron. Some neurons may respond, say, when looking at an object but not when listening to a sound. Other neurons may respond when listening to a sound but not looking at an object and still others may respond when both a sound and an object are present. As such, there is a sense in which the world "out there" is reflected by properties of the system "in here". Cognitive and neural systems are sometimes said to create **representations** of the world. Representations need not only concern physical properties of the world (e.g. sounds, colors) but may also relate to more abstract forms of knowledge (e.g. knowledge of the beliefs of other people, factual knowledge).

Cognitive psychologists may refer to a *mental representation* of, say, your grandmother, being accessed in an information-processing model of face processing. However, it is important to distinguish this from its *neural representation*. There is unlikely to be a one-to-one relationship between a hypothetical mental representation and the response properties of single neurons. The outside world is not copied inside the head, neither literally nor metaphorically; rather, the response properties of neurons (and brain regions) correlate with certain real-world features. As such, the relationship between a mental representation and a neural one is unlikely to be straightforward. The electrophysiological method of **single-cell recordings** has been used to investigate questions related to neural representations and this method will be considered first in this chapter.

The other electrophysiological method that will be considered in this chapter is the event-related potential (or ERP). This is based on measurements of electrical signals generated by the brain through electrodes placed on different points on the scalp (EEG or electroencephalography). Changes in electrical signal associated with cognitive processing are conducted instantaneously to the scalp and this method is therefore particularly useful for measuring the relative *timing* of cognitive events. ERP measurements have much in common with the main method of cognitive psychology, namely, the **reaction time** measure. It is important to note that the absolute time to perform a task is not normally the thing of interest. It is of little theoretical interest to know that one reads the word "HOUSE" within 500 ms (ms = milliseconds). However, relative differences in timing can be used to make inferences about the cognitive system. For example, knowing that people are slower at

KEY TERMS

Representations
Properties of the world that are manifested in cognitive systems (mental representation) and neural systems (neural representation).

Single-cell recordings (or single-unit recordings)
Measure the responsiveness of a neuron to a given stimulus (in terms of action potentials per second).

Reaction time
The time taken between the onset of a stimulus/event and the production of a behavioral response (e.g. a button press).

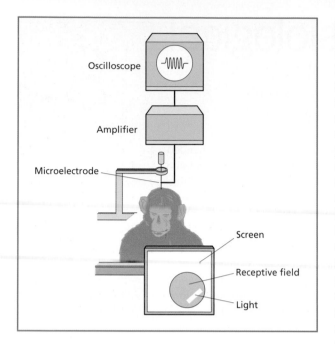

Oscilloscope

Amplifier

Microelectrode

Screen

Receptive field

Light

An illustration of a typical experimental set-up for single-cell recording.

reading "HoUsE" when printed in mIxEd CaSe could be used to infer that, perhaps, our mental representations of visual words are case-specific (e.g. Mayall, Humphreys, & Olson, 1997). The extra processing time for "HoUsE" relative to "HOUSE" may reflect the need to transform this representation into a more standard one. Other methods in cognitive neuroscience are sensitive to measures other than timing. For example, functional imaging methods (PET and fMRI) have a better spatial resolution than temporal resolution (see Chapter 4). Lesion methods tend to rely on measuring error rates rather than reaction times (see Chapter 5). Methods such as transcranial magnetic stimulation (TMS) have both good spatial and temporal resolution (see Chapter 5). It is important to stress that all these methods converge on the question of "how" cognitive processes are carried out by the brain. Just because one method is sensitive to timing differences and another is sensitive to spatial differences does not mean that the methods just tell us "when" and "where". The "when" and "where" constitute the data and the "how" is the theory that accounts for them.

IN SEARCH OF NEURAL REPRESENTATIONS: SINGLE-CELL RECORDINGS

How are single-cell recordings obtained?

By measuring changes in the responsiveness of a neuron to changes in a stimulus or changes in a task, it is possible to make inferences about the building blocks of cognitive processing. The action potential is directly measured in the method of single-cell (and multi-unit) recordings. Single-cell recordings can be obtained by implanting a very small electrode either into the axon itself (intracellular recording) or outside the membrane (extracellular recording) and counting the number of times that an action potential is produced (spikes per second) in response to a given stimulus (e.g. a face). This is an *invasive* method. As such, the procedure is normally conducted on experimental animals only. It is occasionally conducted on humans undergoing brain surgery (see Engel, Moll, Fried, & Ojemann, 2005). It is impossible to measure action potentials from a single neuron non-invasively (i.e. from the scalp) because the signal is too weak and the noise from other neurons is too high. Technology has now advanced such that it is possible to simultaneously record from 100 neurons in multi-electrode arrays. This is termed **multi-cell recordings**.

Distributed versus sparse coding

Hubel and Wiesel (1959) conducted pioneering studies of the early visual cortical areas (see Chapter 6 for detailed discussion). They argued that visual perception is hierarchical in that it starts from the most basic visual elements (e.g. small patches of light and dark) that combine into more complex elements (e.g. lines and edges), that combine into

KEY TERMS

Multi-cell recordings (or multi-unit recordings)

The electrical activity (in terms of action potentials per second) of many individually recorded neurons.

Grandmother cell

A hypothetical neuron that just responds to one particular stimulus (e.g. the sight of one's grandmother).

yet more complex elements (e.g. shapes). But what is the highest level of the hierarchy? Is there a neuron that responds to one particular stimulus? A hypothetical neuron such as this has been termed a **grandmother cell** because it may respond, for example, just to one's own grandmother (for a historical review, see Gross, 2002). The term was originally conceived to be multi-modal, in that the neuron may respond to her voice, and the thought of her, as well as the sight of her. It is now commonly referred to as a cell that responds to the sight of her (although from any viewpoint).

Rolls and Deco (2002) distinguish between three different types of representation that may be found at the neural level:

Could there be a single neuron in our brain that responds to only one stimulus, such as our grandmother? These hypothetical cells are called "grandmother cells".

1. *Fine of representation*. All the information about a stimulus/event is carried in one of the neurons (as in a grandmother cell).
2. *Fully distributed representation*. All the information about a stimulus/event is carried in all the neurons of a given population.
3. *Sparse distributed representation*. A distributed representation in which a small proportion of the neurons carry information about a stimulus/event.

Several studies have attempted to distinguish between these accounts. Bayliss, Rolls, and Leonard (1985) found that neurons in the temporal cortex of monkeys

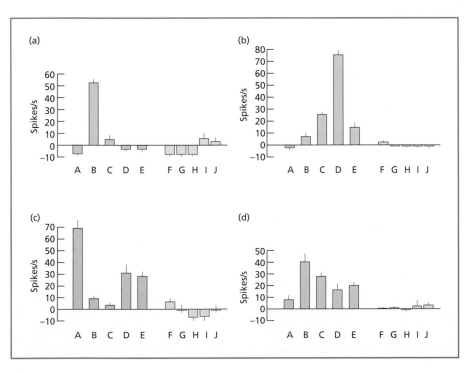

These four neurons respond to different faces (A–E) but not different objects (F–J). They typically respond to several faces, albeit in a graded fashion. Reprinted from Bayliss et al. (1985), Copyright (1985), with permission from Elsevier.

KEY TERM

Grandmother cell

A hypothetical neuron that just responds to one particular stimulus (e.g. the sight of one's grandmother).

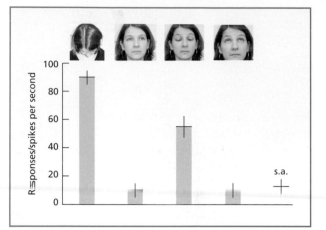

This neuron responds when gaze is oriented downwards. The activity of the neuron (spikes per second) is shown when presented with four faces and during spontaneous activity (s.a.). Adapted from Perrett et al. (1992).

responded to several different faces (from a set of five), albeit to different degrees. Similar results have been found with much larger sets of faces in both monkeys (Rolls & Tovee, 1995) and more recently in humans undergoing surgery for epilepsy (Quiroga, Reddy, Kreiman, Koch, & Fried, 2005). The neurons typically respond to several different stimuli from within the same category (e.g. responding to several faces but no objects). This is inconsistent with a strict definition of a grandmother cell. However, they also showed a surprising degree of specificity. In the study on humans, Quiroga et al. (2005) recorded from neurons in parts of the brain traditionally implicated in memory rather than perception (i.e. medial temporal lobes). They found some neurons that responded maximally to celebrities such as Jennifer Aniston or Halle Berry, irrespective of the particular image used, clothes worn, etc. The "Halle Berry neuron" even responded to the sight of her name and to her dressed up as Cat Woman, but not to other actresses dressed up as Cat Woman. However, it is impossible to conclude that the neuron *only* responds to Halle Berry without probing an infinite number of stimuli. These studies support the notion of "sparse" coding at the top of the visual hierarchy, although the coding is likely to be distributed amongst a group of neurons rather than invested in single neurons.

Some neurons code for other aspects of a stimulus than facial identity. For example, consider the pattern of responding of a particular neuron taken from the superior temporal sulcus (STS) of an alert macaque monkey (Perrett, Hietanen, Oram, & Benson, 1992). The activity of the neuron when shown four different views of faces is compared with spontaneous activity in which no face is shown. The neuron responds strongly to a downward gaze, both with the eyes and the whole head, but not an upward or straight-ahead gaze. In this instance, the two stimuli that elicit the strongest response (head down and head forward with eyes down) do not resemble each other physically, although they are related conceptually. Coding of gaze direction may be important for cognitive processes involved in interpreting social cues (eye contact is perceived as a threat by many species), or for orienting attention and action systems. Perhaps there is something interesting down there that would warrant our attention.

The studies described above can all be classified as **rate coding** of information by neurons in that a given stimulus/event is associated with an increase in the rate of neural firing. An alternative way for neurons to represent information about stimuli/events is in terms of **temporal coding**, in that a given stimulus/event is associated with greater synchronization of firing across different neurons. Engel, Konig and Singer (1991) obtained multi-cell recordings from neurons in the primary visual cortex. This region contains a spatial map of the retinal image (see Chapter 6). If two regions were stimulated with a single bar of light, the two regions synchronized their neural firing. But, if the two regions were stimulated by two different bars of light, there was no synchronization even though both regions showed a response in terms of increased rate of firing. Temporal coding may be one mechanism for integrating information across spatially separated populations of neurons.

KEY TERMS

Rate coding
The informational content of a neuron may be related to the number of action potentials per second.

Temporal coding
The synchrony of firing may be used by a population of neurons to code the same stimulus or event.

Evaluation

Information is represented in neurons by the response rates to a given stimulus or event and, in some circumstances, by the synchronization of their firing. This can be experimentally measured by the methods of single-cell and multi-cell recordings. Both ways of representing information may depend on sparse distributed coding such that activity in several neurons is required to represent a stimulus (e.g. a particular face). The sparseness of coding may enable the brain to have a high memory capacity, and conserves energy. Distributed representation may protect against information loss if synapses or neurons are lost. It may also allow the cognitive system to generalize and categorize (e.g. a novel stimulus that resembles a stored representation would partially activate this representation).

ELECTROENCEPHALOGRAPHY AND EVENT RELATED POTENTIALS

This section considers the basic principles behind the electrophysiological method known as electroencephalography (EEG). The following sections go on to consider some concrete examples of how EEG is used in contemporary cognitive neuroscience and contrast it with other methods used in cognitive psychology and cognitive neuroscience (principally the reaction-time measure).

How does EEG work?

The physiological basis of the EEG signal originates in the postsynaptic dendritic currents rather than the axonal currents associated with the action potential (Nunez, 1981). These were described as passive and active currents, respectively, in Chapter 2. Electroencephalography (EEG) records electrical signals generated

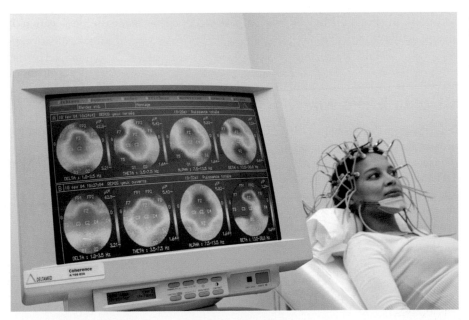

A participant in an EEG experiment. AJ Photo / HOP AMERICAIN / Science Photo Library.

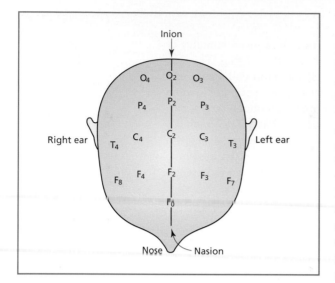

The 10–20 system of electrodes used in a typical EEG/ERP experiment.

by the brain through electrodes placed on different points on the scalp. As the procedure is non-invasive and involves recording (not stimulation), it is completely harmless as a method. For an electrical signal to be detectable at the scalp a number of basic requirements need to be met in terms of underlying neural firing. First, a whole population of neurons must be active in synchrony to generate a large enough electrical field. Second, this population of neurons must be aligned in a parallel orientation so that they summate rather than cancel out. Fortunately, neurons are arranged in this way in the cerebral cortex. However, the same cannot necessarily be said about all regions of the brain. For example, the orientation of neurons in the thalamus may render its activity invisible to this recording method.

To gain an EEG measure one needs to compare the voltage between two or more different sites. A reference site is often chosen that is likely to be relatively uninfluenced by the variable under investigation. One common reference point is the mastoid bone behind the ears or a nasal reference; another alternative is to reference to the average of all electrodes. The experimental electrodes themselves are often arranged at various locations on the scalp, and often described with reference to the so-called *10–20 system* of Jasper (1958). The electrodes are labeled according to their location (F = frontal, P = parietal, O = occipital, T = temporal, C = central) and the hemisphere involved (odd numbers for left, even numbers for right, and "z" for the midline). For example, the O_2 electrode is located over the right occipital lobe and the F_z electrode is located over the midline of the frontal lobes. It is important to stress that the activity recorded at each location cannot necessarily be attributed to neural activity near to that region. Electrical activity in one location can be detected at distant locations. In general, EEG/ERP is not best equipped for detecting the location of neural activity.

How do ERPs work?

The modern-day usage of EEG in cognitive neuroscience is in the context of electrophysiological changes elicited by particular stimuli and cognitive tasks. These are referred to as *event-related potentials* (ERPs). The EEG waveform reflects neural activity from all parts of the brain. Some of this activity may specifically relate to the current task (e.g. reading, listening, calculating) but most of it will relate to spontaneous activity of other neurons that don't directly contribute to the task. As such, the *signal-to-noise ratio* in a single trial of EEG is very low (the signal being the electrical response to the event and the noise being the background level of electrical activity). The ratio can be increased by averaging the EEG signal over many presentations of the stimulus (e.g. 50–100 trials), relative to the onset of a stimulus. The results are represented graphically by plotting time (milliseconds) on the *x*-axis and electrode potential (microvolts) on the *y*-axis. The graph consists of a series of positive and negative peaks, with an asymptote at 0 μV. This is done for each electrode, and each will have a slightly different profile. The positive and negative peaks are labeled with "P" or "N" and their corresponding number. Thus, P1, P2 and P3 refer to the first, second and third positive peaks, respectively. Alternatively, they can be labeled with "P" or "N" and the approximate timing of the peak. Thus, P300 and N400 refer to a positive peak at 300 ms and a negative peak at 400 ms (*not* the 300th positive and 400th negative peak!). It is to be noted that the polarity of the peaks (i.e. whether positive or negative) is of no real significance either cognitively or neurophysiologically (e.g. Otten & Rugg, 2005). It depends, for instance, on the baseline electrical activity and position of the reference electrode. What is of interest in ERP data is the timing and the amplitude of the peaks. This will be considered with some specific examples in the next section.

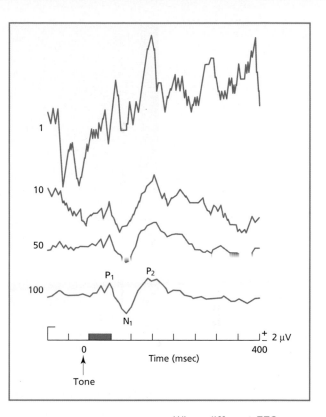

When different EEG waves are averaged relative to presentation of a stimulus (e.g. a tone) then the signal-to-noise ratio is enhanced and an event-related potential is observed. The figure shows average EEG signal to 1, 10, 50, and 100 trials. From Kolb and Whishaw (2002) © 2002 by Worth Publishers. Used with permission.

SOME PRACTICAL ISSUES TO CONSIDER WHEN CONDUCTING EEG/ERP RESEARCH

Where can a set of guidelines for conducting and reporting ERP experiments be found?

A detailed set of guidelines is provided by Picton et al. (2000) and is based on a consensus agreed by 11 leading laboratories in the field. This is recommended reading for all new researchers in the field.

What behavioral measures should be obtained?

In almost all ERP experiments, participants are required to perform a task in which an overt behavioral response is required (e.g. a button press) and this can be analyzed independently (e.g. in terms of reaction times and/or error rates). One exception to this is ERP responses to unattended stimuli (e.g. ignored stimuli, stimuli presented subliminally). It is not possible to record vocal responses (e.g. picture naming) because jaw movements disrupt the EEG signal.

It is important that the initial hypothesis places constraints on the ERP component of interest (e.g. "the experimental manipulation will affect the latency of P300 component") rather than predicting non-specific

ERP changes (e.g. "the experimental manipulation will affect the ERP in some way"). This is because the dataset generated from a typical ERP experiment is large and the chance of finding a "significant" result that is not justified by theory or reliable on replication is high.

How can interference from eye movement be avoided?

Not all of the electrical activity measured at the scalp reflects neural processes. One major source of interference comes from movement of the eyes and eyelids. These movements occur at the same frequencies as important components in the EEG signal. There are a number of ways of reducing or eliminating these effects. One can instruct the participant not to blink or to blink only at specified times in the experiment (e.g. after making their response). The problem with this method is that it imposes a secondary task on the participant (the task of not moving their eyes) that may affect the main task of interest. It is also possible to discard or filter out the effect of eye movements in trials in which they have occurred.

MENTAL CHRONOMETRY IN ELECTROPHYSIOLOGY AND COGNITIVE PSYCHOLOGY

Mental chronometry can be defined as the study of the time-course of information processing in the human nervous system (Posner, 1978). The basic idea is that changes in the nature or efficiency of information processing will manifest themselves in the time it takes to complete a task. For example, participants are faster at verifying that 4 + 2 = 6 than they are to verify that 4 + 3 = 7, and this is faster than verifying that 4 + 4 = 8 (Parkman & Groen, 1971). What can be concluded from this? First of all, it suggests that mathematical sums such as these are not just stored as a set of facts. If this were so, then all the reaction times would be expected to be the same because all statements are equally true. It suggests, instead, that the task involves a stage in processing that encodes numerical size together with the further assumption that larger sums place more limits on the efficiency of information processing (manifested as a slower verification time). This provides one example of how it is possible to make inferences about the nature of cognitive processes from timing measures.

A task such as verification of sums is likely to involve a series of stages, including visual recognition of the digits, computing the sum and producing a response. The reaction time measure is the end product of all these stages. Sternberg (1969) developed a general method for dividing reaction times into different stages termed the **additive factors method**. His experiment involved a working memory task in which participants were given an array of one, two or four digits to hold in mind (e.g. 5, 9, 3, 2). They were then shown a single probe digit (e.g. 9) and asked to press one of two buttons (labeled "yes" and "no") to indicate whether this item had been in

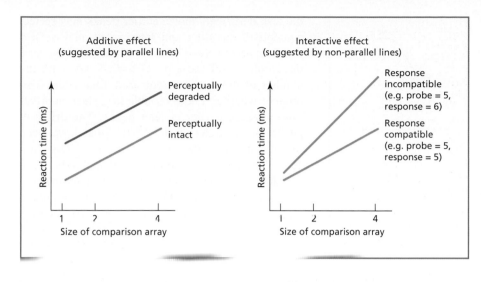

Sternberg's additive factors method assumes that if two variables affect different stages of processing then they should have an additive effect on the overall reaction time (left), but if two variables affect the same stage of processing then the factors should have an interactive effect (right). His task involved comparing a probe digit (e.g. 5) with an array of one, two or four digits held in mind.

the previous array. Sternberg proposed that the task could be divided into a number of separate stages, including:

1. *Encoding* the probe digit.
2. *Comparing* the probe digit with the items held in memory.
3. *Decision* about which response to make.
4. *Responding* by executing the button press.

He further postulated that each of these stages could be independently influenced by different factors affecting the task. For instance, the encoding stage may be affected by the perceptibility of the probe digit (e.g. presenting it on a patterned background). The comparison stage may be affected by the number of items in the array (the more items in the array, the slower the task). He reasoned that, if different factors affect different stages of processing, then the effects should have additive effects on the overall reaction time, whereas if they affect the same processing stage, they should have interactive effects. The strength of this method is that one could then take an unknown factor (e.g. sleep deprivation, Parkinson's disease, reading ability) and determine whether this has an interactive effect on stimulus perceptibility (implying that the new factor affects perceptual encoding) or whether it has an interactive effect with the number of items in the array (implying the new factor affects the comparison stage) or both (implying the new factor has effects at multiple levels).

The additive factors approach has been very influential in cognitive psychology research, although it is to be noted that the assumptions do not always apply. For example, the model assumes that the stages are strictly sequential (i.e. later stages do not occur until earlier ones are complete) but this assumption is not always valid.

At this juncture it is useful to consider how the mental chronometry approach applies to the analysis and interpretation of ERP data. Whereas a reaction time consists of a *single* measure that is assumed to reflect different stages/components, an ERP waveform consists of a series of peaks and troughs that vary continuously over time. These peaks and troughs are likely to have some degree of correspondence with different cognitive stages of processing. For example, in

Graph (a) shows an observed ERP waveform and graphs (b) and (c) show two different sets of hidden components that could have given rise to it. This illustrates the point that there is not a one-to-one mapping between ERP components and the activity of underlying cognitive/neural components. From Luck (2005), © 2004 Massachusetts Institute of Technology by permission of the MIT Press.

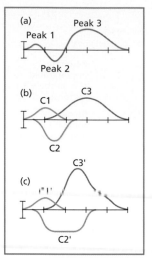

the task described above, earlier peaks may reflect perceptual encoding and later peaks may reflect the comparison stage. One could then observe how the amplitude of those peaks varied, say, with the number of items to be compared. One could also observe whether a new variable (e.g. sleep deprivation) affected earlier or later peaks. The different peaks and troughs of the ERP signal have been referred to as *ERP components* (e.g. Donchin, 1981). There may not be a simple mapping between an ERP component and a cognitive component of a task. For example, a single cognitive component may reflect the action of several spatially separate neural populations (i.e. one cognitive component could affect several ERP components) or several cognitive components may be active at once and sum together, or cancel each other out, in the ERP waveform (i.e. several cognitive components affect a single ERP component). As such, some researchers prefer to use the more neutral term ERP *deflection* rather than ERP *component*.

Investigating face processing with ERPs and reaction times

This chapter has already considered the neural representation of faces as measured by single-cell recordings. ERP studies have also investigated the way that faces are processed. A full model of face processing is discussed in Chapter 6 but a consideration of a few basic stages will suffice for the present needs. An initial stage consists of perceptual coding of the facial image (e.g. location of eyes, mouth), followed by a stage in which the facial identity is computed. This stage is assumed to map the perceptual code onto a store of known faces and represents the face irrespective of viewing conditions (e.g. lighting, viewing angle). (Note that this doesn't assume grandmother cells because facial identity could be computed by a population of neurons.) Finally, there may be a representation of the identity of the person that is not tied to any modality (e.g. responds to faces and names) and may enable retrieval of other types of knowledge (e.g. their occupation).

As with the single-cell results, there is evidence for an ERP component that is relatively selective in relation to the processing of faces compared with other classes of visual objects. This has been termed the N170 (a negative peak at 170 ms) and is strongest over right posterior temporal electrode sites (e.g. Bentin, Allison, Puce, Perez, & McCarthy, 1996). This component is

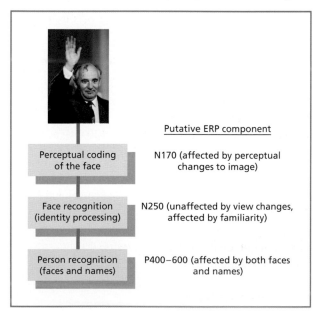

A simple model of several hypothetical stages involved in face processing together with their putative ERP manifestations. Photo © Bernard Bisson and Thierry Orban/Sygma/Corbis.

uninfluenced by whether the face is famous or not (Bentin & Deouell, 2000) and is also found for cartoon "smiley" faces (Sagiv & Bentin, 2001). It is, however, reduced if the face is perceptually degraded (Schweinberger, 1996). The N250, by contrast, is larger for famous and personally familiar faces relative to unfamiliar faces (Herzmann, Schweinberger, Sommer, & Jentzsch, 2004) and responds to presentation of different images of the same person (Schweinberger, Pickering, Jentzsch, Burton, & Kaufmann, 2002b). This suggests that it codes properties of the specific face rather than the specific image. Later, positive-going components (from 300 ms onwards) are also sensitive to the

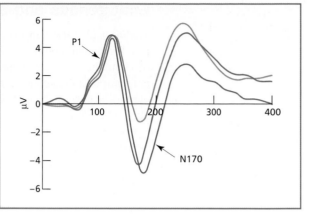

repetition and familiarity of specific person identities but the effects generalize to names as well as faces (Schweinberger, Pickering, Burton, & Kaufmann, 2002a).

The N170 is observed for both human faces (purple) and animal faces (blue) but not other objects (green). Rousselet et al. (2004). With permission of ARVO.

Having sketched out a plausible relationship between different components of the ERP waveform and different cognitive processes, it is possible to use these electrophysiological markers to adjudicate between different theories of face processing. One debate in the cognitive psychology literature concerns the locus of associative priming. **Associative priming** refers to the fact that reaction times are faster to a stimulus if that stimulus is preceded by a stimulus of similar meaning (this is also known as semantic priming). For example, judging that the face of Mikhail Gorbachev (the last President of the Soviet Union) is familiar is performed faster if it immediately follows Boris Yeltsin's face (former President of Russia) or even Yeltsin's name (Young, Hellawell, & De Haan, 1988). The fact that associative priming is found between names and faces might imply that the effect arises at a late stage of processing. However, there is evidence inconsistent with this. Using Sternberg's (1969) method it has been found that

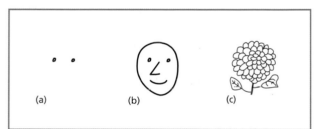

associative priming interacts with stimulus degradation (Bruce & Valentine, 1986) and that associative priming interacts with how perceptually distinctive a face is (Rhodes & Tremewan, 1993). This would imply that associative priming has a perceptual locus such that perceiving Gorbachev's face also activates the perceptual face representation of Yeltsin. Schweinberger (1996) used ERP measures to determine the locus of associative priming of faces and names. He found that associative priming has a late effect (after 300 ms) on the ERP waveform that is more consistent with a postperceptual locus. Effects of stimulus degradation were found under 150 ms. Schweinberger (1996) suggests that, in this instance, the Sternberg method may have led to an invalid conclusion because it assumes discrete stages. ERP was suitable for addressing this question because it enables early and late time points to be measured separately.

Two horizontally spaced symbols (the dots in (a)) do not elicit an N170 unless they have previously been presented in the context of a face (b). The participant's task was merely to count flowers (e.g. (c)), and so both the faces and "eyes" were irrelevant to the task. From Bentin et al. (2002). Reprinted by permission of Blackwell Publishing.

Endogenous and exogenous ERP components

Traditionally, ERP components have been classified as belonging to one of two categories. **Exogenous** components are those that appear to depend on the physical properties of a stimulus (e.g. sensory modality, size, intensity). These have also been called *evoked potentials*. **Endogenous** components, in contrast, appear to depend on properties of the task (e.g. what the participant is required to do with the stimulus). These can even occur in the absence of an external stimulus (e.g. if an expected stimulus does not occur; Sutton, Tueting, Zubin, & John 1967). Exogenous components tend to be earlier than endogenous components.

Although the exogenous–endogenous classification is useful, it should be considered as a dimension rather than a true categorical distinction. To remain with the current example of face processing, consider the nature of the ERP waveform when viewing two repeated symbols that are horizontally spaced (e.g. + +). Typically, such symbols do not evoke the N170 response characteristic of face processing (Bentin, Sagiv, Mecklinger, Friederici, & von Cramon, 2002). However, if the symbols have previously been shown embedded in a face context (as eyes), then the pair of symbols do elicit the N170 response (Bentin et al., 2002). Is this an endogenous or exogenous component? It is impossible to say. Although the N170 is normally taken as indicative of perceptual processing (an exogenous component), in this instance it is entirely dependent on the interpretive bias given.

The spatial resolution of ERPs

The discussion so far has emphasized the importance of ERPs in the timing of cognition. The reason why the spatial resolution of this method is poor is related to the **inverse problem**. If one had, say, three sources of electrical activity in the brain during a given task and the magnitude and location of the activity were known, then it would be possible to calculate the electrical potential that we would expect to observe some distance away at the scalp. However, this is not the situation that is encountered in an ERP study; it is the inverse. In an ERP study, the electrical potential at the scalp is known (because it is measured) but the number, location and magnitude of the electrical sources in the brain are unknown. Mathematically, there are an infinite number of solutions to the problem.

The most common way of attempting to solve the inverse problem involves a procedure called **dipole modeling**. This requires assumptions to be made about how many regions of the brain are critical for generating the observed pattern of scalp potentials. Attempts at dipole modeling with the N250 and N170 evoked by face processing (see above) revealed probable loci in the fusiform gyrus and the posterior occipital region, respectively (Schweinberger et al., 2002b). However, the most common way of obtaining good spatial resolution is to use a different method altogether, such as fMRI or PET (see Chapter 4) or magnetoencephalography (MEG; (see p. 46). (For similar results from fMRI concerning face processing, see Eger, Schyns, & Kleinschmidt, 2004.)

Evaluation

Investigating the time-course of cognitive processes is an important method in cognitive psychology and cognitive neuroscience. Event-related potentials have excellent temporal resolution. This method has a number of benefits over and above reaction-time measurements, such as: it provides a continuous measurement of changes over time (rather than a single timing measure) and it is, at least in theory, easier to link to neural processes in the brain. ERP also enables electrophysiological changes associated with unattended stimuli (that are not responded to) to be measured whereas a reaction-time measure always requires an overt behavioral response.

WHY ARE CARICATURES EASY TO RECOGNIZE?

Caricatures of faces are typically considered humorous and are often used for deliberate mockery or propaganda. As Richard Nixon's unpopularity grew during the Watergate scandal, so did his nose and jowls in published caricatures (see Rhodes, 1996). The paradox of caricatures is that the face is instantly recognizable despite being perceptibly wrong. In fact, people can sometimes be twice as fast at recognizing a caricature of a face as the same face undistorted (Rhodes, Brennan, & Carey, 1987); the caricature appears to be more like the face than the face itself. What does this reveal about the way that faces are processed and represented?

This caricature is instantly recognizable despite significant distortions. We are sometimes faster at recognizing caricatures than actual depictions. Why might this be?

First of all, it is important to clarify how caricatures are created. Caricatures exaggerate the distinctive features of an individual. Computer routines now exist that compare, for example, the size of an individual's nose with the average nose size. If the person has a larger than average nose, then this will be enlarged further in the caricature. If someone has a smaller than average nose, it will be shrunk in the caricature. It is also possible to morph a face to make it look more average (a so-called anti-caricature), and such faces are typically rated as more attractive than the real or caricatured face. One explanation for the effect of caricatures is to assume that our memory representations of faces are caricatured themselves; that is, we store the distinctive properties of a face rather than the face as it is. However, explanations such as these must assume that a "norm" or prototype face exists from which to infer what constitutes a distinctive feature. Another hypothesis is that it is the distinctiveness of caricatures *per se* that aids their recognition because there are fewer similar-looking competitor faces (Valentine, 1991). This account does not need to assume the existence of a face prototype, or that the stored representations themselves are caricatured.

A recent ERP study is consistent with this view. Photographic caricatures of unfamiliar people lead, initially, to an enhancement of the N170 component relative to undistorted images or anti-caricatures (Kaufmann & Schweinberger, 2008). As this component is normally associated with perceptual coding of faces rather than memory of faces, it suggests that the effect is more likely to be due to perceptual distinctiveness than the way faces are coded in memory.

MAGNETOENCEPHALOGRAPHY

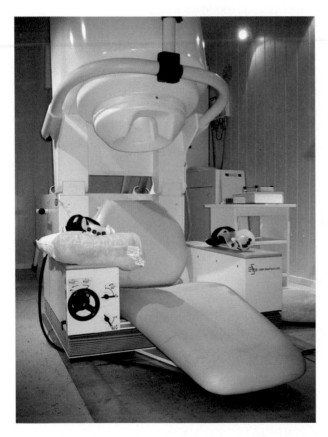

An MEG scanner. This extremely powerful machine measures the magnetic fields produced by electrical activity in the brain.

The recording of magnetic signals, as opposed to electrical ones, generated by the brain has a much shorter history in cognitive neuroscience and still remains in its infancy (for reviews, see Papanicolaou, 1995; Singh, 2006). All electric currents, including those generated by the brain, have an associated magnetic field that is potentially measurable. However, the size of this field is very small relative to the ambient magnetic field of the earth. As such, the development of magneto-encephalography (MEG) had to wait for suitable technological advances to become a viable enterprise. This technological advance came in the form of superconducting devices termed SQUIDs (an acronym of Superconducting Quantum Interference Device). A whole-head MEG contains 200–300 of these devices. The apparatus used requires extreme cooling, using liquid helium, and isolation of the system in a magnetically shielded room. As such, the costs and practicalities associated with MEG are far greater than those needed for EEG. However, the biggest potential advantage of MEG over EEG is that it permits a much better spatial resolution.

MEG	EEG/ERP
• Signal unaffected by skull, meninges, etc.	• Signal affected by skull, meninges, etc.
• Poor at detecting deep dipoles	• Detects deep and shallow dipoles
• More sensitive to activity at sulci	• Sensitive to gyri and sulci activity
• Millisecond temporal resolution	• Millisecond temporal resolution
• Potentially good spatial resolution (2–3 mm)	• Poor spatial resolution
• Expensive and limited availability	• Cheaper and widely available

SUMMARY AND KEY POINTS OF THE CHAPTER

- Neuronal activity generates electrical and magnetic fields that can be measured either invasively (e.g. single-cell recording) or non-invasively (e.g. EEG).
- Studies of single-cell recordings are based on measuring the number of action potentials generated and provide clues about how neurons code information, by measuring the specificity of their responses to external stimuli.
- When populations of neurons are active in synchrony they produce an electric field that can be detected at the scalp (EEG). When many such waves are averaged together and linked to the onset of a stimulus (or response), then an event-related potential (ERP) is obtained.
- An ERP waveform is an electrical signature of all the different cognitive components that contribute to the processing of that stimulus. Systematically varying certain aspects of the stimulus or task may lead to systematic variations in particular aspects of the ERP waveform. This enables inferences to be drawn about the timing and independence of cognitive processes.

EXAMPLE ESSAY QUESTIONS

- How does the brain generate electrical signals, and how are these used in electrophysiological techniques?
- How do neurons code information?
- What is an "event-related potential" (or ERP) and how can it be used to inform theories of cognition?
- What have electrophysiological studies contributed to our understanding of how faces are represented and processed by the brain?

RECOMMENDED FURTHER READING

- Luck, S. J. (2005). *An introduction to the event-related potential technique*. Cambridge, MA: MIT Press. This is the place to start if you are going to conduct research using EEG/ERPs.
- Senior, C., Russell, T., & Gazzaniga, M. S. (2006). *Methods in mind*. Cambridge, MA: MIT Press. Includes chapters on single-cell recording, EEG and MEG.
- Zani, A. & Proverbio, A. M. (2003). *The cognitive electrophysiology of mind and brain*. London: Academic Press. A good summary of the findings of ERP and MEG research in perception, attention, memory, language, and so on.

CHAPTER 4

CONTENTS

The imaged brain

If George Orwell had written *Nineteen eighty-four* during our times, would he have put an MRI scanner in the Ministry of Truth? Could we ever really know the content of someone else's thoughts using functional imaging technology? This chapter will consider how the functional imaging methods of PET (positron emission tomography) and fMRI (functional magnetic resonance imaging) work. This chapter is broadly divided into three parts. The first part considers how functional and structural brain imaging works, with particular reference to underlying neurophysiology. The second part considers methodological factors that are important in ensuring that the results obtained can indeed be meaningfully linked to cognitive theory. The third part considers how functional imaging data are analyzed to find regions of activation and considers some of the pitfalls in their interpretation. Finally, the chapter returns to the question of whether functional imaging could be used as an Orwellian-like mind reader.

STRUCTURAL IMAGING

One key distinction is the difference between **structural imaging** methods and **functional imaging** methods. Structural imaging is based on the fact that different types of tissue (e.g. skull, gray matter, white matter, cerebrospinal fluid) have different physical properties. These different properties can be used to construct detailed *static* maps of the physical structure of the brain. The most common structural imaging methods are computerized tomography (CT) and magnetic resonance imaging (MRI). Functional imaging is based on the assumption that neural activity produces local physiological changes in that region of the brain. This can be used to produce *dynamic* maps of the moment-to-moment activity of the brain when engaged in cognitive tasks.

Computerized tomography

Computerized tomography (CT) scans are constructed according to the amount of X-ray absorption in different types of tissue. The amount of absorption is related to tissue density: bone absorbs the most (and so the skull appears white), cerebrospinal fluid absorbs the least (so the ventricles appear black) and the brain matter is intermediate (and appears gray). Given that CT uses X-rays, the person being scanned is exposed to a small amount of radiation.

CT scans are typically used only in clinical settings, for example to diagnose tumors or to identify hemorrhaging or other gross brain anomalies. CT cannot distinguish between gray matter and white matter in the same way as MRI, and it cannot be adapted for functional imaging purposes.

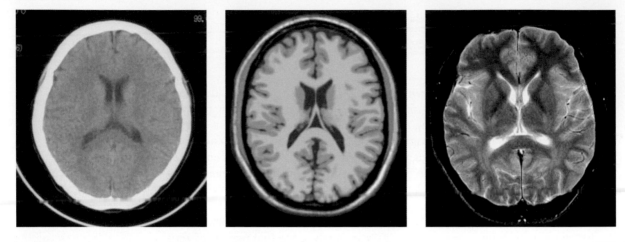

An example of CT (left), T1-weighted MRI (center) and T2-weighted MRI (right) scans of the brain. Note how the MRI scans are able to distinguish between gray matter and white matter. On the T1-weighted scan (normally used for structural images), gray matter appears gray and white matter appears lighter.

Magnetic resonance imaging

Magnetic resonance imaging (MRI) was one of the most important advances in medicine made during the twentieth century. Its importance was recognized by the awarding of the 2003 Nobel Prize to its inventors – Sir Peter Mansfield and Paul Lauterbur. There are a number of advantages of this method over CT scanning, as summarized below:

- It does not use ionizing radiation and so is completely safe (people can be scanned many times).
- It provides a much better spatial resolution, which allows the folds of individual gyri to be discerned.
- It provides better discrimination between white matter and gray matter (see also the box on p. 52).
- It can be adapted for use in detecting the changes in blood oxygenation associated with neural activity, and in this context is called functional MRI (fMRI).

MRI physics for non-physicists

MRI is used to create images of soft tissue of the body, which X-rays pass through largely undistorted. Most human tissue is water-based and the amount of water in each type of tissue varies. Different types of tissue will thus behave in slightly different ways when stimulated, and this can be used to construct a three-dimensional image of the layout of these tissues (for an accessible but more detailed description, see Savoy, 2002).

The sequence of events for acquiring an MRI scan is as follows. First, a strong magnetic field is applied across the part of the body being scanned (e.g. the brain). The single protons that are found in water molecules in the body (the hydrogen nuclei in H_2O) have weak magnetic fields. (Other atoms and nuclei also have magnetic moments but in MRI it is the hydrogen nuclei in water that form the source of the signal.) Initially, these fields will be oriented randomly, but when the strong external field is applied a small fraction of them will align themselves with this. The external field is applied constantly during the scanning process. The strength of the magnetic field is measured in units called tesla (T). Typical scanners have field strengths between 1.5 T and 3 T; the Earth's magnetic field is of the order of 0.0001 T.

When the protons are in the aligned state a brief radio frequency pulse is applied that knocks the orientation of the aligned protons by 90 degrees to their original orientation. As the protons spin (or *precess*) in this new state they produce a detectable change in the magnetic field and this is what forms the basis of the MR signal. The protons will eventually be pulled back into their original alignment with the magnetic field (they "*relax*"). The scanner repeats this process serially by sending the radio wave to excite different slices of the brain in turn. With the advent of acquisition methods such as echo planar imaging, a whole brain can typically be scanned in about two seconds with slices of around 3 mm.

Different types of image can be created from different components of the MR signal. Variations in the rate at which the protons return back to the aligned state following the radio frequency pulse (called the T1 relaxation time) can be used to distinguish between different types of tissue. These T1-weighted images are typically used for structural images of the brain. In a T1-weighted image, gray matter looks gray and white matter looks white. When in the misaligned state, at 90 degrees to the magnetic field, the MR signal also decays because of local interactions with nearby molecules. This is termed the T2 component. Deoxyhemoglobin produces distortions in this component and this forms the basis of the image created in functional MRI experiments (called a T2* image, "tee-two-star").

FUNCTIONAL IMAGING

Whereas structural imaging measures the permanent characteristics of the brain, functional imaging is designed to measure the moment-to-moment variable characteristics of the brain that may be associated with changes in cognitive processing.

Basic physiology underpinning functional imaging

The brain consumes 20% of the body's oxygen uptake; it does not store oxygen and it stores little glucose. Most of the brain's oxygen and energy needs are supplied from the local blood supply. When the metabolic activity of neurons increases, the blood supply to that region increases to meet the demand (but see Attwell and Iadecola, 2002; for a review, see Raichle, 1987). Techniques such as PET measure the change in blood flow to a region directly, whereas fMRI is sensitive to the concentration of oxygen in the blood.

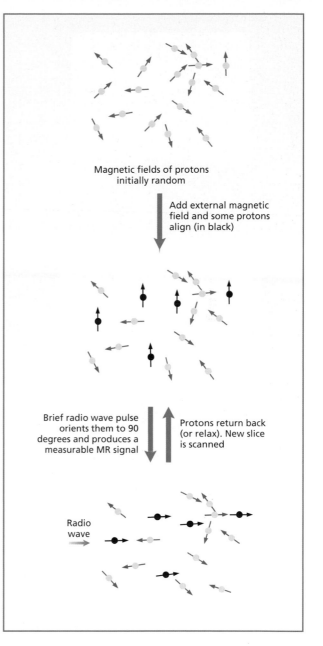

Magnetic fields of protons initially random

Add external magnetic field and some protons align (in black)

Brief radio wave pulse orients them to 90 degrees and produces a measurable MR signal

Protons return back (or relax). New slice is scanned

Radio wave

The sequence of events in the acquisition of an MRI scan.

Visualization of a DTI measurement of a human brain. Depicted are reconstructed fiber tracts that run through the mid-sagittal plane. Image by Thomas Schultz from http://upload.wikimedia.org/wikipedia/commons/8/82/DTI-sagittal-fibers.jpg.

LINKING STRUCTURE TO FUNCTION BY IMAGING WHITE MATTER AND GRAY MATTER

Small scale differences (at the millimeter level) in the organization and concentration of white matter and gray matter can now be analyzed non-invasively using MRI. This is providing important clues about how individual differences in brain structure are linked to individual differences in cognition. Two important methods are **voxel-based morphometry**, or VBM, and **diffusion tensor imaging**, or DTI.

Voxel-based morphometry (VBM) capitalizes on the ability of structural MRI to detect differences between gray matter and white matter (Ashburner & Friston, 2000). VBM divides the brain into tens of thousands of little regions (called voxels) and the concentration of white/gray matter in each voxel is estimated. It is then possible to use this measure to compare across individuals by asking questions such as these: If I learn a new skill, such as a second language, will my gray matter density increase in some regions? Will it decrease in other regions? How does a particular genetic variant affect brain development? Which brain regions are larger, or smaller, in people with good social skills versus those who are less socially competent?

Diffusion tensor imaging (DTI) is different from VBM in that it measures the white matter connectivity between regions (Le Bihan et al., 2001). (Note: VBM measures the *amount* of white matter without any consideration of how it is connected.) It is able to do this because water molecules trapped in axons tend to diffuse in some directions but not others. Specifically, a water molecule is free to travel down the length of the axon but is prevented from traveling out of the axon by the fatty membrane. When many such axons are arranged together it is possible to quantify this effect with MRI (using a measure called "fractional anisotropy"). As an example of a cognitive study using DTI, Bengtsson, Nagy, Skare, Forsman, Forssberg and Ullen (2005) found that learning to play the piano affects the development of certain white matter fibers. However, different fibers were implicated depending on whether they were learned during childhood, adolescence or adulthood.

The brain is always physiologically active. Neurons would die if they were starved of oxygen for more than a few minutes. This has important consequences for using physiological markers as the basis of neural "activity" in functional imaging experiments. It would be meaningless to place someone in a scanner, with a view to understanding cognition, and simply observe which regions were receiving blood and using oxygen because this is a basic requirement of all neurons, all of the time. As such, when functional imaging researchers refer to a region being "active", what they mean is that the physiological response in one task is greater *relative* to some other condition. There is a basic requirement in all functional imaging studies that the physiological response must be compared to one or more baseline responses. Good experimental practice is needed to ensure that the baseline task is appropriately matched to the experimental task otherwise the results will be very hard to interpret.

It is also worth pointing out that PET and fMRI are not measuring the activity of neurons directly too, rather are measuring a downstream consequence of neural activity (i.e. changes in blood flow/oxygen to meet metabolic needs). This is to be contrasted with methods such as EEG (electroencephalography) and MEG (magnetoencephalography) that measure the electrical/magnetic fields generated by the activity of neurons themselves.

Positron emission tomography

Positron emission tomography (PET) uses a radioactive tracer injected into the bloodstream. The greater the blood flow in a region, the greater the signal emitted by the tracer in that region. The most commonly used tracers are oxygen-15, administered in the form of water, and fluorine-18, administered in the form of a glucose sugar. However, it is also possible to use other tracers. For example, it is possible to use radiolabeled neurotransmitters to investigate particular neural pathways and to study the effects of drugs on the brain. Volkow et al. (1997), for instance, were able to study how different aspects of cocaine abuse (e.g. euphoria, craving, restlessness) are implemented by different systems in the brain by administering a radiolabeled tracer with a similar profile to the drug.

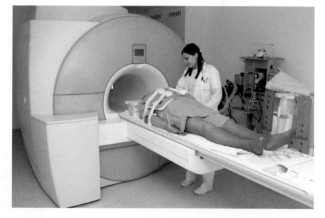

The temporal and spatial resolution of PET is worse than for fMRI. In PET it takes 30 seconds for the tracer to enter the brain and a further 30 seconds for the radiation to peak to its maximum. This is the critical window for obtaining changes in blood flow related to cognitive activity. The temporal resolution of PET is therefore around 30 seconds. The temporal resolution refers to the accuracy with which one can measure *when* a cognitive event is occurring. Given that most cognitive events take place within a second, this is very slow indeed.

Over the last ten years functional magnetic resonance imaging (fMRI) has overtaken PET scans in functional imaging experiments.

When the tracer is in the bloodstream it converts back from the unstable radioactive form into the normal stable form. As it does so, it emits a particle (called a positron) that then collides with an electron, releasing two photons that can be detected by detectors positioned around the head, thus enabling a spatial image to be constructed.

The positron travels 2–3 mm before collision. However, the need to average across participants in PET means that the effective spatial resolution is somewhat worse than this (about 10 mm). The spatial resolution refers to the accuracy with which one can measure *where* a cognitive event (or more accurately, a physiological change) is occurring.

Functional magnetic resonance imaging

Functional magnetic resonance imaging (fMRI) uses standard MRI equipment and, unlike PET, there is no need for ionizing radiation. As such, it means that participants can be re-tested in the scanner many times, if need be. Given that one does not have to wait for the isotope to peak and then decay, the amount of time that each participant spends in the scanner is much less than for PET. Testing of a single participant can normally be completed in under an hour, allowing 30–40 minutes to complete the experiment and 10 minutes for a high-resolution structural MRI scan to be obtained.

The component of the MR signal that is used in fMRI is sensitive to the amount of deoxyhemoglobin in the blood. When neurons consume oxygen they convert oxyhemoglobin to deoxyhemoglobin. Deoxyhemoglobin has strong paramagnetic properties and this introduces distortions in the local magnetic field. This distortion can itself be measured to give an indication of the concentration of deoxyhemoglobin present in the blood. This technique has therefore been termed **BOLD** (for blood oxygen-level-dependent contrast; Ogawa, Lee, Kay, & Tank, 1990). The way that the BOLD signal evolves over time in response to an increase in neural activity is called the **hemodynamic response function** (HRF). The HRF has three phases, as plotted and discussed below (see also Hoge & Pike, 2001):

1. *Initial dip.* As neurons consume oxygen there is a small rise in the amount of deoxyhemoglobin, which results in a reduction of the BOLD signal (this is not always observed in the standard 1.5 T magnets).
2. *Overcompensation.* In response to the increased consumption of oxygen, the blood flow to the region increases. The increase in blood flow is greater than the increased consumption, which means that the BOLD signal increases significantly. This is the component that is normally measured in fMRI.
3. *Undershoot.* Finally, the blood flow and oxygen consumption dip before returning to their original levels. This may reflect a relaxation of the venous system, causing a temporary increase in deoxyhemoglobin again.

The hemodynamic signal changes are small – approximately 1–3% with moderately sized magnets (1.5 T). The hemodynamic response function is relatively stable across sessions with the same participant in the same region, but is more variable across different regions within the same individual and more variable between individuals (Aguirre, Zarahn, & D'Esposito, 1998).

The temporal resolution of fMRI is several seconds and related to the rather sluggish hemodynamic response. Although this is a considerable improvement on PET and allows use of event-related designs (see later), it is still slow compared to the speed at which cognitive processes take place. The spatial resolution is also better than PET, at around 1 mm depending on the size of the voxel.

Which method is best – PET or fMRI?

Over the last ten years, fMRI has largely taken over from the use of PET in functional imaging experiments. The key advantages of fMRI are the better temporal and spatial resolution, the fact that event-related designs are possible, and the fact that it does not use radioactivity. Nevertheless, there are some disadvantages of fMRI that are less of a problem for PET. The MRI scanner is very noisy, which makes it a less attractive candidate for studying auditory processes (although this problem can now be overcome by having periods of silence during the scanning phase in which auditory stimuli can be presented). Another difficulty with fMRI relative to PET is that small movements can distort the signal measured. Producing overt speech is often avoided in fMRI procedures (but not PET) for this reason. Similarly, some brain regions are susceptible to signal distortion because nearby tissue has different magnetic properties (notably air voids – sinuses, oral cavity and ear canals). This makes certain regions such as the orbitofrontal cortex and some temporal lobe regions hard to image in fMRI. Finally, PET can be used to trace the pathways of certain chemicals in vivo by, for example, administering radiolabeled pharmacological agents.

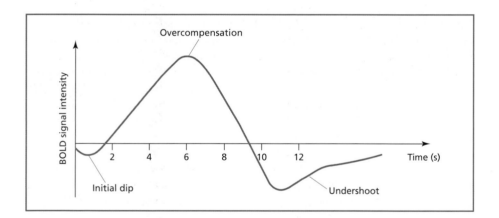

The hemodynamic response function (HRF) has a number of distinct phases.

PET	fMRI
• Based on blood volume	• Based on blood oxygen concentration
• Involves radioactivity (signal depends on radioactive tracer)	• No radioactivity (signal depends on deoxy-hemoglobin levels)
• Participants scanned only once	• Participants scanned many times
• Temporal resolution = 30 seconds	• Temporal resolution = 1–4 seconds
• Effective spatial resolution = 10 mm	• Spatial resolution = 1 mm
• Must use a blocked design	• Can use either blocked or event-related design
• Sensitive to the whole brain	• Some brain regions (e.g. near sinuses) are hard to image
• Can use pharmacological tracers	

FROM IMAGE TO COGNITIVE THEORY: AN EXAMPLE OF COGNITIVE SUBTRACTION METHODOLOGY

One of the groundbreaking studies for establishing the use of PET for imaging cognition was that by Petersen, Fox, Posner, Mintun and Raichle (1988), which was designed to look for brain regions specialized for the processing of written and spoken words. A consideration of this study provides a good introduction to the principle of **cognitive subtraction**. The idea behind cognitive subtraction is that, by comparing the activity of the brain in a task that utilizes a particular cognitive component (e.g. the visual lexicon) to the activity of the brain in a baseline task that does not, it is possible to infer which regions are specialized for this particular cognitive component. As has been noted, the brain is always "active" in the physiological sense and so it is not possible to infer from a single task which regions are dedicated to specific aspects of the task, a comparison between two or more tasks or conditions is always needed.

Let's consider the different processes involved with reading and understanding isolated written words. A simple model of written word recognition is given below, which forms the motivation for the PET study to be described. The Petersen et al. (1988) study was concerned with identifying brain regions involved with: (1) recognizing written words; (2) saying the words; and (3) retrieving the meaning of the words. To do this, the researchers performed a number of cognitive subtractions.

To work out which regions are involved with recognizing written words, Petersen et al. compared brain activity when passively viewing words (e.g. CAKE) versus passively viewing a cross (+), see diagram below. The logic is that both experimental and baseline tasks involve visual processing (and so a subtraction should cancel this out) but only the experimental task involves visual word recognition (so this should remain after subtraction).

To work out which regions are involved with producing spoken words they compared passive viewing of written words (see CAKE) with reading aloud the word (see CAKE, say "cake"). In this instance, both experimental and baseline tasks involve visual processing of the word and word recognition (so subtracting should cancel these out) but only the experimental task involves spoken output (so activity associated with this should remain after subtraction).

To work out which regions are involved with retrieving the meaning of written words they compared a verb-generation task (e.g. see CAKE, say "eat") with reading aloud (e.g. see CAKE, say "cake"). In this instance, both experimental and baseline tasks involve visual processing, word recognition and spoken output (so subtracting should cancel out the activity associated with these processes) but only the experimental task involves generating a semantic associate (so activity associated with this should remain after subtraction).

The results of these subtractions show activity in a number of different sites. Only the principal sites on the left lateral hemisphere are depicted in the diagram.

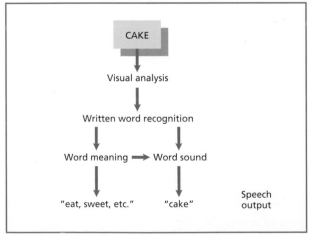

Basic cognitive stages involved in reading written words aloud and producing spoken semantic associates to written words.

Recognizing written words activates bilateral sites in the visual (striate) cortex as well as a site on the left occipito-temporal junction. Producing speech output in the reading aloud condition activates the sensorimotor cortex bilaterally, whereas verb generation activates the left inferior frontal gyrus. This last result has provoked some controversy because of an apparent discrepancy from lesion data; this is discussed later.

Problems with cognitive subtraction

With the benefit of hindsight, there are a number of difficulties with this study, some of which are related to the particular choice of baseline tasks that were employed. However, there are also more general problems with the method of cognitive subtraction itself (e.g. Friston, Price, Fletcher, Moore, Frackowiak, & Dolan, 1996). Consider the subtraction aimed at identifying brain regions associated with written word recognition. The assumption here was that both tasks involve visual processing but that one has the added component of word recognition. That is, one

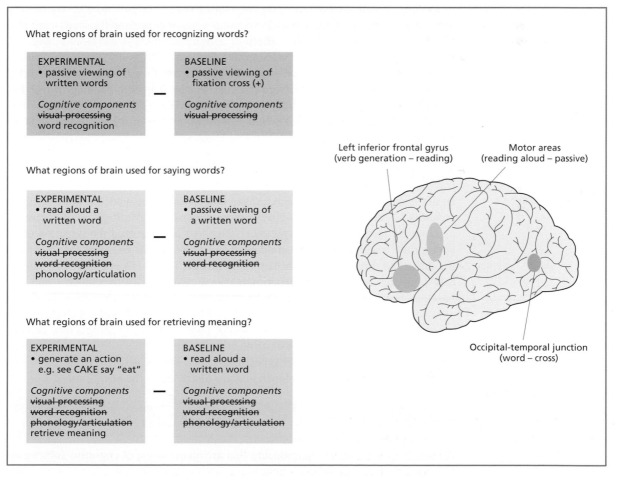

Cognitive subtraction is founded on the assumption that it is possible to find two tasks (an experimental and baseline task) that differ in terms of a small number of cognitive components. The results show several regions of activity but only the main results on the left lateral surface are depicted here.

assumes that adding an extra component does not affect the operation of earlier ones in the sequence. This is referred to as the assumption of **pure insertion** (or pure deletion). It could be that the type or amount of visual processing that deals with written words is not the same as for non-linguistic vision. The fact that the visual information presented in the baseline task (viewing a cross, +) was simpler than in the experimental task makes this a real possibility. However, a more basic problem is common to all functional imaging experiments that employ this methodology. The addition of an extra component in the task has the potential to change the operation of other components in the task. That is, **interactions** are possible that make the imaging data, at best, ambiguous. The next sections consider other types of design that allow one to eliminate or even directly study these interactions.

The choice of baseline is crucial in imaging experiments and can have substantial impacts on the data that is obtained. Ideally, the baseline should be as similar to the experimental task as possible. For example, to find brain regions involved with producing spoken words, the Petersen et al. (1988) study compared reading aloud versus viewing of written words. This is, in fact, likely to involve several stages of processing. It will involve retrieving the word from the brain's store of vocabulary (the mental lexicon), preparing and executing a motor command (to speak) and also listening to what was said. The pattern of activity observed is therefore ambiguous with regards to linking a precise cognitive function with brain structure. Another baseline that could be used is to get the participant to articulate generic verbal responses, such as saying the word "yes" whenever a word comes up (e.g. Price, Moore, Humphreys, Frackowiak, & Friston, 1996). This would enable one to study the lexical retrieval component whilst factoring out the articulation and auditory feedback components.

Evaluation

In summary, functional imaging requires comparisons to be made between different conditions because the brain is always physiologically active. Regions of "activity" can only be meaningfully interpreted relative to a baseline, and the selection of an appropriate baseline requires a good cognitive theory of the elements that comprise the task. The simplest way of achieving this is the method of cognitive subtraction that compares activity in an experimental task with activity in a closely matched baseline task. However, the main problem with cognitive subtraction is that it assumes that a cognitive component can be added on to a task without changing the other components in the task (the problem of pure insertion). Adding a new component to a task may interact with existing components and this interaction may show up as a region of activity. Other types of experimental design that reduce this particular problem have been developed and are discussed in the next section.

BEYOND COGNITIVE SUBTRACTION

A number of experimental approaches that are an extension of cognitive subtraction but that do not rely on the assumption of pure insertion have been described. These methods are strongly favored over cognitive subtraction. Friston (1997) provides a good basic overview. In many respects, these methods are extensions of standard cognitive psychology experimental designs into the functional imaging framework.

Cognitive conjunctions and factorial designs

The method of cognitive conjunction requires that one is able to identify a set of tasks that has a particular component in common. One can then look for regions of activation that are shared across several different subtractions rather than relying on a single subtraction. A baseline task (or tasks) is still required, but the problem of interactions can be reduced. This is because the interaction terms will be different for each pair of subtractions.

Let's consider one concrete example from the literature: why can't we tickle ourselves? Tactile sensations applied to the skin are rated as less ticklish if produced by oneself relative to if they are elicited by another person. The key to explaining this lies in the fact that it is possible to predict the sensory consequences of our own actions. The motor commands that we generate specify where and when the touch will occur and the manner of the touch (e.g. a rough or gentle tickle). This information can then be used to predict what the action will feel like. Thus a representation of the motor command (a so-called "efference copy") is sent to the relevant sensory area, touch in this example, so that the perceptual system knows what to expect. This may help the brain to prioritize incoming sensory information towards the most relevant stimuli in the environment. Being touched by someone or something else is arguably more important to the organism in terms of detecting potential threats than being touched by oneself.

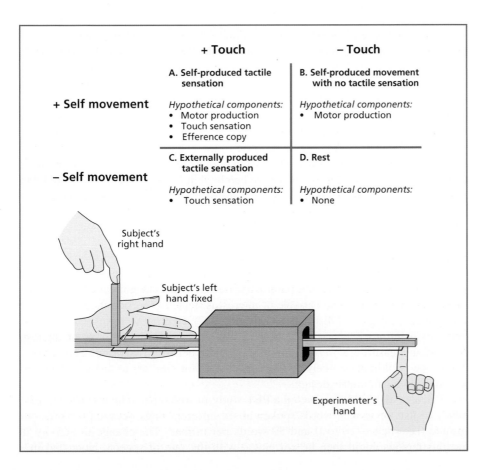

Why can't we tickle ourselves? Self-produced touches (condition A) are less tickly because we can predict their sensory consequences using an "efference copy" of the motor command. Bottom diagram adapted from Blakemore et al. (1998). Copyright © 1998 Elsevier. Reproduced with permission.

To investigate this, Blakemore, Rees and Frith (1998) set up a factorial design with two factors. The first factor was whether or not a tactile stimulus was felt; the second factor was whether or not the participants moved their arm. The experiment involved moving a felt rod that tickled the palm. The rod could be moved either by the experimenter or the participant. It could either make contact with the palm or miss it altogether. In total, this produced four experimental conditions, which have been labeled A to D in the figure.

Before going on to consider the neural basis of the less tickly sensation associated with condition A (hypothetically due to an efference copy), one can perform two cognitive conjunctions to identify regions involved in motor production and the tactile sensation *per se*. Consider the two pairs of subtractions, A – B and C – D. If one asks the question, "What regions do these subtractions have in common [i.e. (A – B) and (C – D)]?" then this can isolate regions involved in tactile sensation. The experiment found activity in the primary and secondary somatosensory cortex in the hemisphere opposite the hand that was stimulated. Consider the two pairs of subtractions, A – C and B – D. If one asks the question, "What regions do these subtractions have in common [i.e. (A – C) and (B – D)]?" then this can isolate regions involved in motor production. In this analysis, the experiment found several active regions, including motor, premotor and prefrontal regions. In terms of methodology, the key point to note is that both of these results are based on conjunctions between two different tasks and baselines and this is sufficient to minimize the problem of pure insertion faced by using a single subtraction alone.

However, these conjunction analyses do not enable one to analyze the neural basis of the "efference copy" or the reduced ticklishness when self-produced. To find this out, one can examine the interaction directly by performing the following analysis: (A – B) – (C – D). This effectively asks the question: is the difference between A and B more (or less) than the difference between C and D (an interaction is simply a difference of differences)? In the present example, it would ask whether the effect of touch is greater in the presence of self-movement than in the presence of other-movement. Blakemore et al. (1998) report that there was decreased activity in the somatosensory cortex. This is likely to be the neural correlate of reduced ticklishness. There were also changes in cerebellum activity that were not found in any other condition and were interpreted as the neural correlate of the efference copy that links self-movement with touch.

Parametric designs

The main difference between a parametric design and a categorical design is that, in a parametric design, the variable of interest is treated as a continuous dimension rather than a categorical distinction (Friston, 1997). In intuitive terms, one is measuring *associations* between brain activity and changes in the variable of interest, rather than measuring *differences* in brain activity between two or more conditions. Thus, one is ultimately likely to use correlations (or similar) to analyze data collected using a parametric design.

Price, et al. (1992) conducted a PET study in which participants listened passively to lists of spoken words spoken at six different rates between 0 words per minute (i.e. silence, or rest) and 90 words per minute. The change in activity in various regions could then be correlated with the rate of speech. Note that in a

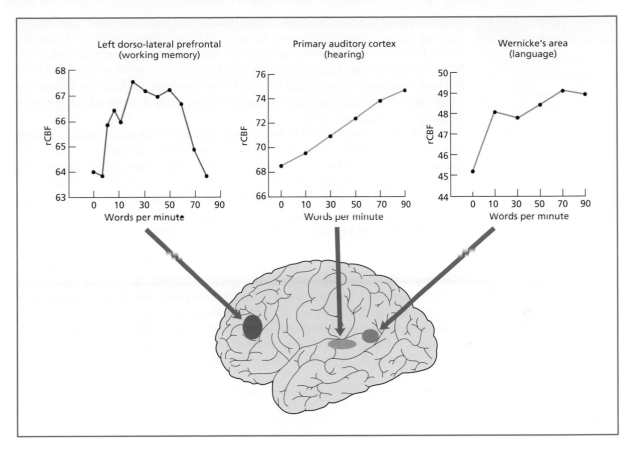

parametric design such as this, a separate baseline condition is not necessary (the effects are evaluated globally across all levels of the factor). In terms of the results, a number of interesting findings were observed. In areas involved in auditory *perception* (e.g. the primary auditory cortex), the faster the speech rate, the greater the activity. However, in regions involved in non-acoustic processing of *language* (e.g. Wernicke's area), the activity was related to the presence of words irrespective of speech rate. In a region often associated with verbal *working memory* (the left dorsolateral prefrontal cortex), a more complex picture was found (Friston, 1997). Activity increased with speech rate but then decreased as the speech rate got faster (an inverted-U function). It suggested that the region has an optimal level at which it functions, beyond which it fails to keep up. This is consistent with the notion of working memory having a limited capacity. One interesting point to note is that, if the experimenters had compared ten words per minute with 90 words per minute in a cognitive subtraction or a factorial design, this region would not have appeared to be implicated in the task.

Different regions of the brain respond to changes in speech rate (words per minute, wpm) in different ways. Note that 0 wpm is equivalent to rest. rCBF = regional cerebral blood flow. Adapted from Price et al. (1992), and Friston (1997).

Functional integration

Most of the functional imaging studies described in this book could be labeled as studies of *functional specialization*. Functional specialization implies that a region responds to a limited range of stimuli/conditions and that this distinguishes it from the responsiveness of other neighboring regions. It is not strictly the same as *localization*, in that it is not necessary to assume that the region is

KEY TERM

Functional integration
The way in which
different regions
communicate with
each other.

solely responsible for performance on a given task or to assume that other regions
may not also respond to the same stimuli/conditions (Phillips, Zeki, & Barlow,
1984). **Functional integration**, on the other hand, refers to the way in which different regions communicate with each other. This is likely to be essential for a
full understanding of how cognition is linked to the brain, and also for dismissing
claims that functional imaging is a new phrenology (e.g. Friston, 2002; Horwitz,
Tagamets, & McIntosh, 1999).

The basic approach of functional integration is to model how activity in different
regions is interdependent. This is used to infer the "*effective connectivity*" or "*functional connectivity*" between regions when performing a task (these methods use
techniques such as structural equation modeling and principal components analysis,
which are beyond the scope of the present discussion). If parametric designs correlate
brain activity with some cognitive/behavioral measure, then designs employing functional integration correlate different regions of brain activity with each other. To give a
concrete example, Friston and Frith (1995) conducted a PET study with a 2 × 2 factorial
design with task instruction as one factor (generate words beginning with "A" versus
repeating letters) and subject group as the other factor (participants either had or had
not been diagnosed as schizophrenic). Although both groups showed a number of similar frontal and temporal lobe activities, there was a strong correlation between activity
in these regions in controls and a striking absence of correlation in the schizophrenics.
Friston and Frith argued that schizophrenia is best characterized in terms of a failure
of communication between distant brain regions (i.e. a functional disconnection).

Setting up a functional
imaging experiment
requires asking oneself
a number of questions,
and making assumptions
about the most
appropriate method. This
flowchart is intended to
be useful rather than
prescriptive.

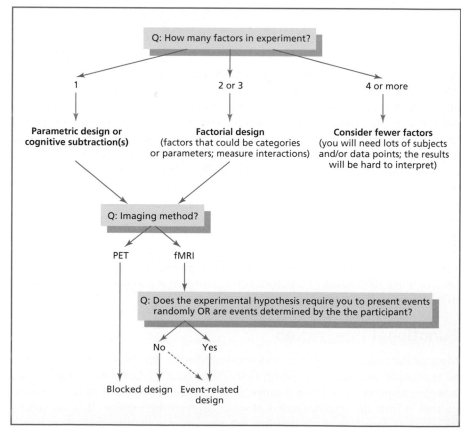

Evaluation

A number of different methods are available for setting up experiments in functional imaging. The main consideration is that the method should be appropriate for the hypothesis being tested (and the level of detail of the hypothesis will vary considerably). Having said this, the diagram on p. 62 offers a number of general points to consider and some suggested outcomes. Note that different labs may have other established methods and that the field itself is developing new methods all the time.

SAFETY AND ETHICAL ISSUES IN FUNCTIONAL IMAGING RESEARCH

It is essential to be aware of the local regulations that apply in your own institution but the following points generally apply.

What are the risks of taking part in functional imaging experiments?

The risks are small (PET) or negligible (fMRI). The risk from PET comes from the fact that it uses a small amount of radioactivity. The amount of radioactivity from a PET scan is equivalent to around 1–3 years of annual background radioactivity. fMRI does not use radiation and the same participants can take part in multiple experiments. Participants wear ear protectors, given that the scanner noise is very loud. Larger magnets (> 3 T) can be associated with dizziness and nausea and participants need to enter the field gradually to prevent this.

Are some people excluded from taking part in functional imaging experiments?

Before entering the scanner, all participants should be given a checklist that asks them about their current and past health. Pregnant women and children cannot take part in PET studies because of the use of radiation. People with metal body parts, cochlear implants, embedded shrapnel or pacemakers will not be allowed to take part in fMRI experiments. In larger magnets, eye make-up should not be worn (it can heat up, causing symptoms similar to sunburn) and women wearing contraceptive coils should not be tested. Before going into the scanner both the researcher and participant should put to one side all metal objects such as keys, jewelry and coins, as well as credit cards, which would be wiped by the magnet. Zips and metal buttons are generally okay, but metal spectacle frames should be avoided. It is important to check that participants don't suffer from claustrophobia as they will be in a confined space for some time. Participants have a rubber ball that can be squeezed to signal an alarm to the experimenter, who can terminate the experiment if necessary.

What happens if a brain abnormality is detected during scanning?

There is always a very small possibility that a brain tumor or some other unsuspected abnormality could be detected during the course of the study. In such instances, the researcher has a duty to double-check this by inviting the participant back for a subsequent scan. Potential abnormalities are followed up by a neurologist (or a clinically qualified member of staff), who would inform the participant and their doctor, if needs be. Wolf et al. (2008) provide a set of ethics concerning the incidental discovery of abnormalities during non-clinical scanning.

How can I find up-to-date details about safety in fMRI experiments?

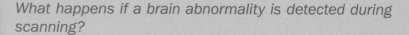

The standard safety reference is by Shellock (2004) and updates can be found at: www.magneticresonancesafetytesting.com.

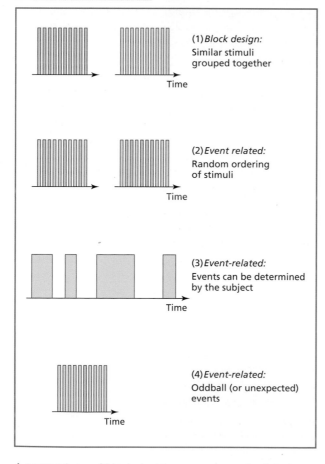

(1) *Block design:* Similar stimuli grouped together

Time

(2) *Event related:* Random ordering of stimuli

Time

(3) *Event-related:* Events can be determined by the subject

Time

(4) *Event-related:* Oddball (or unexpected) events

Time

A comparison of block designs versus event-related designs. The purple and green bars could represent different types of stimuli, conditions or task.

EVENT-RELATED VERSUS BLOCKED DESIGNS

A separate issue as to the choice of experimental design (e.g. categorical versus parametric) is how the different stimuli will be ordered. Broadly speaking, there are two choices. First, stimuli that belong together in one condition could be grouped together. This is termed a **block design**. Second, different stimuli or conditions could be interspersed with each other. This is termed an **event-related design**. In an event-related design the different intermingled conditions are subsequently separated out for the purpose of analysis.

The choice of design is determined by the nature of the task and whether the data comes from PET or fMRI. For PET experiments, the temporal resolution is too poor to enable event-related designs, and so block designs are required. In fMRI one has a choice of event-related designs (also called **efMRI**) or block designs. The advantage of block designs over event-related ones is that the method has more power; that is, it is more able to detect significant but small effects (e.g. Josephs & Henson, 1999). The advantage of event-related designs over blocked ones is that they enable a much wider range of experimental designs and are more closely related to the typical design structure of most cognitive psychology experiments. Certain types of empirical question can be adequately addressed only with event-related designs. In some instances, there is no way of knowing in advance how events should be grouped and so block designs are impossible. For example, one event-related fMRI study investigated participants in a tip-of-the-tongue state (Maril, Wagner, & Schachter, 2001). In this state people are unable to retrieve a name (e.g. the capital of Peru) but have a strong certainty of knowing the answer. In a typical experiment, responses fall into three categories (known, unknown and tip-of-the-tongue). These are defined by each participant and cannot be blocked together at the outset. To give another example of events being defined by a participant, ffytche, Howard, Brammer, David, Woodruff and Williams (1998) studied spontaneously occurring visual hallucinations in patients with progressive blindness. The patients lifted their finger when a hallucination occurred and lowered it when it disappeared. The neural signal in the "on" phase could then be contrasted with the "off" phase. Finally, some events cannot be blocked because the task requires that they are unexpected and occur infrequently.

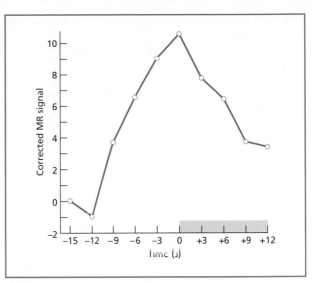

A hemodynamic response function related to the onset of visual hallucinations (at 0 seconds, shown by purple bar). This is derived by averaging together a number of hallucinations involving visual regions of the brain. Note how the brain activity precedes the onset of the conscious experience by as much as 12 seconds. An example of a reported hallucination is as follows: "colored shiny shapes like futuristic cars or objects found in the pyramids. The shapes contained edges within them and did not look like real objects." From ffytch et al. (1998). Reprinted by permission of Macmillan Publishers Ltd, copyright 1998.

ANALYZING DATA FROM FUNCTIONAL IMAGING

The images of brains with superimposed colored blobs are the outcome of several stages of data processing and statistical analysis. In fact, these images are not literal pictures of the workings of the brain at all. What these images depict are the regions of the brain that are computed to be statistically significant given the type of design used. Functional imaging is a statistical science and, as such, is susceptible to error. Although different laboratories use different packages to analyze their data, the challenges faced in analyzing and interpreting functional imaging data are common to them all (for a detailed discussion, see Petersson, Nichols, Poline, & Holmes, 1999a, 1999b).

A central problem faced in the analysis of functional imaging data is how to deal with individual differences. Although the gross brain structure does not differ considerably from one person to the next, there are nevertheless significant individual differences in the size of gyri and the location of folds in the brain. For example, the location of sulci can vary between people by a centimeter or more (Thompson, Schwartz, Lin, Khan, & Toga, 1996).

The most common way of dealing with individual differences is effectively to assume that they don't exist. Or, more properly put, individual differences needn't get in the way of making claims about general brain function. Individual differences are minimized by averaging data over many participants, and one is left with regions of activity that are common to most of us. Before this averaging process can occur, the data from each individual needs to be modified in a number of ways. First, each brain is mapped onto a standard reference brain (called **stereotactic normalization**). This is followed by a process called **smoothing**, which can enhance the signal-to-noise

The main stages of analyzing data in a functional imaging experiment.

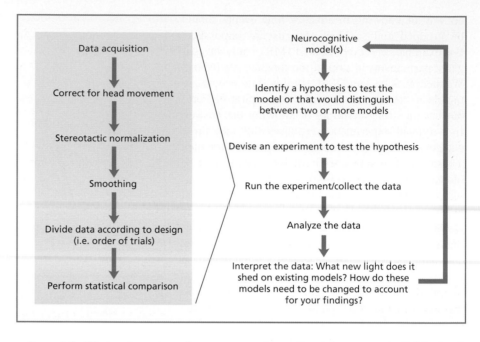

ratio and facilitates detection of common regions of activity across individuals. A flow diagram summarizes the sequence from initial hypothesis to data interpretation that typically occurs in a functional imaging experiment. These main stages will be considered in turn.

Correction for head movement

Perhaps the biggest advantage of the fMRI technique over others is its good spatial resolution. It is able to identify differences in activity over millimeter distances (although this resolution still entails millions of neurons). However, there is a downside to this; namely, that small spatial distortions can produce spurious results. One key problem that has already been noted is that every brain differs spatially in terms of size and shape. The process of stereotactic normalization attempts to correct for this. A different problem is that each person's head might be aligned slightly differently in the scanner over time. If a person wriggles or moves the head in the scanner, then the position of any active region will also move around. This could either result in the region being harder to detect (because the activity is being spread around) or a false-positive result could be obtained (if a region shifts from being active in one condition to being inactive in another condition because the participant has moved his or her head between conditions). It is for this reason that the collected data are corrected for head movement (e.g. Brammer, 2001), which is minimized in the first place by physically restraining the head in position, and instructing participants to keep as still as possible.

Stereotactic normalization

The process of stereotactic normalization involves mapping regions on each individual brain onto a standard brain. Each brain is divided up into thousands of small volumes, called **voxels** (volume elements). Each voxel can be given three-dimensional spatial coordinates (x, y, z). This enables every x, y, z coordinate on a brain to be mapped onto the corresponding x, y, z coordinate on any other brain. Basically, the template of each brain is squashed or stretched (by applying mathematical transformations that entail an optimal solution) to fit into the standard space. The standard space that is used to report functional imaging data across most laboratories in the world is provided by the brain atlas of Talairach and Tournoux (1988). Each point in the brain is assigned a three-dimensional x, y, z coordinate (commonly referred to as the **Talairach coordinates**) with the origin lying at a region called the anterior commisure (small and easily seen in most scans). The x-coordinate refers to left and right (left is negative and right is positive). The y-coordinate refers to front and back (front/anterior is positive and back/posterior is negative) and the z-coordinate refers to top and bottom (top is positive and bottom is negative). This atlas is based on anatomical data from a single post-mortem brain. However, rather than relying on comparisons to this single brain, many contemporary studies use a template based on an average of 305 brains provided by the Montreal Neurological Institute (Collins, Neelin, Peters, & Evans, 1994). This averaged template is then put into Talairach coordinates and used in favor of the single brain originally described in that atlas.

KEY TERM

Talairach coordinates
Locations in the brain defined relative to the atlas of Talairach and Tournoux.

Smoothing

After each brain has been transformed into this standard space, further stages of preprocessing *may* take place before a statistical analysis. The process of "smoothing" sounds like it could waste important information but it is, in fact, an important part of data manipulation. Smoothing spreads some of the raw activation level of a given voxel to neighboring voxels. The closer the neighbor is, the more activation it gets (the mathematically minded might be interested to know that the function used is a Gaussian or normal distribution centered on each voxel). The darker the square, the more active it is. Consider voxel D4. Prior to smoothing, this voxel is inactive, but because it has many active neighbors the voxel gets "switched on" by the smoothing process. In contrast, consider voxel L8. This voxel is initially active but, because it has inactive neighbors, it gets "switched off" by the smoothing process. Smoothing thus enhances the signal-to-noise ratio. In this instance, one assumes that the signal (i.e. the thing of interest) corresponds to the larger cluster of activity and the noise is the isolated voxel. Neighboring voxels that are active mutually reinforce each other and the spatial extent (i.e. size) of the active region is increased. If the brain happened to implement cognition using a mosaic of non-adjacent voxels, then smoothing would work against detecting such a system. It is conceivable that there are some specialized neural populations that are rendered invisible if smoothing is applied.

As well as enhancing the signal-to-noise ratio, smoothing offers an additional advantage for analyzing groups of participants. Smoothing increases the spatial

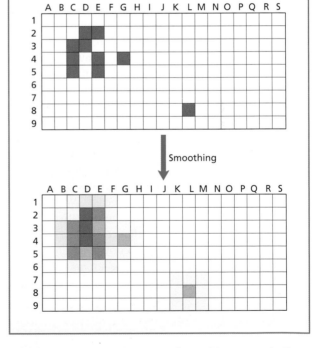

Smoothing spreads the activity across voxels – some voxels (e.g. D4) may be enhanced whereas others (e.g. L8) may be reduced.

extent of active regions. As such, when averaging the activity across individuals there is a greater chance of finding common regions of activity. Of course, if individual differences are the focus of the study, then one may justifiably choose not to smooth the data at all.

Statistical comparison

After the data have been stereotactically normalized, smoothed and corrected for head movement, it is possible to perform a statistical analysis. The standard way to do this is to ask the question: "Is the mean activity at a particular voxel in the experimental condition greater than in the baseline condition?" The same types of statistical test as would be employed in any psychology experiment can be used in functional imaging (e.g. a t-test to compare means). But there are complications. In most psychology experiments one would typically have, at most, only a handful of means to compare. In functional imaging, each brain slice is divided up into tens of thousands of voxels and each one needs to be considered (Cohen, Noll, & Schneider, 1993). If one uses the standard psychology significance level of $P < 0.05$, then there would be thousands of brain voxels active just by chance. (Recall that the significance level represents the probability (P) at which one is willing to say that a result is more than just a chance occurrence. The value of 0.05 represents a 1 in 20 chance level.) How could one prevent lots of brain regions being active by chance? One could have a more conservative criteria (i.e. a lower significance level) but the danger is that this will not detect regions that are important (this is termed a type I error). An analogy here would be trying to count islands by lowering or raising the sea level. If the sea level is too high, there are no islands to observe. If the sea level is too low, there are islands everywhere. One could divide the nominal P value (0.05) by the number of tests (i.e. voxels) – a so-called Bonferroni correction. A difficulty with this is that the activity at each voxel is not independent: neighboring voxels tend to have similar activity, particularly if smoothed. This has led to the development of sophisticated mathematical models of choosing a statistical threshold, based on spatial smoothness (so-called *random field theory*). Other researchers generate thousands of random brain images (e.g. by permuting the data) and select a threshold (e.g. $P < 0.05$) based on random datasets.

When reading papers that have used functional imaging methods, one sometimes observes that they report different significance levels that are "corrected" or "uncorrected". Why is this done and is it acceptable? A corrected level implies that a more conservative criterion has been used to prevent detecting lots of regions just by chance. However, if the interest is in *one* particular voxel, then it is possible to use an uncorrected significance level (e.g. the standard $P < 0.05$) because in this instance there are not multiple comparisons over lots of brain regions. Other procedures are used when investigating effects in a pre-determined region covering several voxels (a so-called *small volume correction*).

INTERPRETING DATA FROM FUNCTIONAL IMAGING

What does it mean to say that a brain region is "active" in a functional imaging experiment? Literally speaking, what this means is that the signal from that region (whether BOLD from fMRI, or level of radiation from PET) is greater in one condition than in other conditions that are being compared (whether in a categorical design, parametric design or whatever). There are several reasons why a region may be active and not all of them are theoretically interesting. Importantly, it need not imply that the particular region is essential for the task. Alternative accounts include: an increase in signal could reflect the strategy that the participants happen to adopt, it could reflect use of some general mechanism (e.g. increased attention) that is not specific to the task, or it could reflect the fact that a region is receiving input but is not responding to the input (i.e. **inhibition**). These competing scenarios can only be ruled out with more rigorous experimentation. Chance occurrences can be ruled out by replicating the results and the necessity of a region for a task can be determined using lesion methods. This is discussed in more detail below.

Inhibition versus excitation

Functional imaging signals are assumed to be correlated with the metabolic activity of neurons, and synapses in particular (see Jueptner & Weiller, 1995). However, neurons can be metabolically active by virtue of both inhibitory interactions (when the presynaptic neuron is active, the postsynaptic neuron is switched off) and excitatory interactions (when the presynaptic neuron is active, the postsynaptic neuron is switched on). Most connections are excitatory in nature. Logothetis, Pauls, Augath, Trinath and Oeltermann (2001) demonstrated that the BOLD signal used in fMRI is more sensitive to the neuronal input into a region rather than the output from the region. Thus, regions that "listen" to other active regions but don't themselves respond to it could appear as areas of activation.

It is unclear whether functional imaging can distinguish between these two types of neural function since both are assumed to be associated with similar physiological changes.

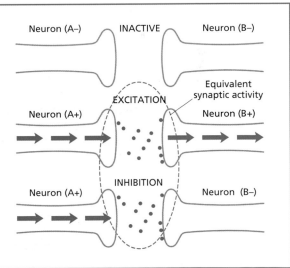

Activation versus deactivation

Activation and deactivation simply refer to the sign (positive or negative) of the difference in signal between two conditions. This is not to be confused with **excitation**/inhibition that refers to the nature of the mechanism by which neurons communicate. If you perform the subtraction (Task A) – (Task B), there could be a set of regions that show a significant positive effect (i.e. "**activation**") because they are used more in Task A than in Task B, and there could also be a set of regions that show a significant negative effect (i.e. "**deactivation**") because they are more active in Task B than in Task A. Of course, if one had done the subtrac-

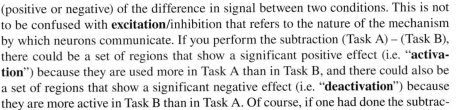

Excitatory and inhibitory synaptic connections both involve metabolic activity and thus an inhibited region could be mistakenly interpreted as a region of activity.

tion (Task B) – (Task A), then the same regions would be identified but the positive and negative signs would merely swap. Thus, the terms activation and deactivation merely refer to whether or not there is a difference in signal between conditions and the direction of that difference. The question of *why* there is a difference is open to theoretical interpretation. If the baseline task is very different from the experimental conditions, the activations and deactivations may be very hard to interpret.

Necessity versus sufficiency

In an intriguingly titled paper "If neuroimaging is the answer, what is the question?", Kosslyn (1999) sets out some of the reasons why functional imaging has its limitations. One particular point that will be picked up on here is the notion that some of the regions that appear "active" may indeed be used during performance of the task but yet might not be critical to the task. For example, a region may appear to be active because of a particular strategy that the participants adopted, even though other strategies might be available. It could also be the case that the tasks being compared differ in some other, more general, way. For example, if one task is harder than the other it could demand more attention, and this demanding of attention would have its own neural correlate. Although paying more attention could certainly help with the performing of the task, it may not in and of itself be crucial for performing the task. As such, it has been claimed that functional imaging gives us a better idea of which regions may be sufficient for performing a particular task but not always which regions are crucial and necessary for performing a task.

The value of functional imaging data is likely to be enhanced when it is used in conjunction with other methods. One early benefit of functional imaging was mooted to be that it could replace lesion-based neuropsychology. However, this is unlikely to happen because the logic of inference is different in these two methods, as illustrated below. In lesion-based neuropsychology, the location of the lesion is manipulated (or selected for in a patient sample) and the resulting behavior is observed. In doing this, a causal connection is assumed between the lesion and the ensuing behavior. In functional imaging the reverse is true. In this instance, the task given to participants in the scanner is manipulated and changes in brain regions are observed. Although some of these changes are likely to be critically related to the performance of the task, other changes may be incidental to it. It is for this reason that functional imaging is unlikely to supplant the traditional lesion-based approach. The next section discusses in more detail how divergent results between imaging and neuropsychology could be reconciled.

Functional brain imaging and lesion-deficit analysis of patients (or TMS, see Chapter 5) are logically different types of methodology. It is unlikely that one will supplant the other.

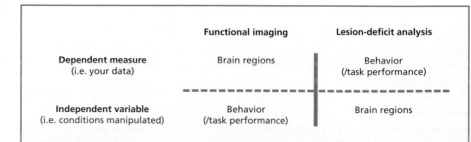

WHY DO FUNCTIONAL IMAGING DATA SOMETIMES DISAGREE WITH LESION DATA?

There are two broad scenarios in which functional imaging data and lesion-deficit data can disagree. These are listed below, together with possible ways of resolving the disagreement, as described in the following box.

Disagreement 1: Imaging data imply that a brain region is used in a given task but lesion data suggest that this region is not essential to the task (imaging +, lesion −)

Possible reasons for disagreement:

- The activated region reflects a particular strategy adopted by the participants that is not essential to performing the task.
- The activated region reflects the recruitment of some general cognitive resource (e.g. due to increased task difficulty, attention or arousal) that is not specific to the task.
- The activated region is being inhibited (i.e. switched off) rather than excited (i.e. switched on).
- The lesion studies have not been powerful enough to detect the importance of the region (e.g. too few patients, lesion not in correct location, tasks used with patients not the same as those used in imaging).

Disagreement 2: Imaging data imply that a brain region is not used in a given task but lesion data suggest that this region is critical to the task (imaging −, lesion +)

Possible reasons for disagreement:

- If the experimental task and baseline task both depend critically on this region, then a comparison between them might produce an artefactual null result.
- It might be intrinsically hard to detect activity in this region of the brain (e.g. it is a very small region, it is in different places in different individuals or genuine activity produces a small signal change).
- The impaired performance after lesion reflects damage to tracts passing through the region rather than the synaptic activity in the gray matter of the region itself.

The above discussion thus highlights the fact that disagreements between results from functional imaging and results from lesion data could lie with imaging results, with the lesion results, or with both. There is no magic solution for resolving the disagreements except through more rigorous experimentation. Each method has some relative merit. As such, disagreements should be viewed as something that is potentially of theoretical interest rather than dismissed as a failure of one or other method (e.g. Henson, 2005). To provide a feel for how this might be achieved, the next section considers a concrete example from the literature.

Having your cake and eating it

A small proportion of unfortunate people in later life start to lose the meanings of words and objects that they previously understood. This deterioration can spare, at least in the early stages, memory for events, calculation abilities and syntax, amongst other things (e.g. Hodges, Patterson, Oxbury, & Funnell, 1992). These patients would probably be given a diagnosis of **semantic dementia**, because their functional lesion is primarily in the **semantic memory** system that stores the meaning of words and objects. Where are the anatomical lesions in these patients? Lesion studies based on voxel-based morphometry (VBM) have shown that the degree of semantic memory impairment is correlated with the amount of atrophy in the left anterior temporal lobe (Mummery, Patterson, Price, Ashburner, Frackowiak, & Hodges, 2000). Given this finding, it would be encouraging if functional imaging studies also activated this particular region when healthy (non-brain-damaged) people are given semantic memory tasks. However, this has not always been the case and a number of studies have reliably shown activation in a different region – the left inferior frontal gyrus (also referred to as the ventrolateral prefrontal cortex). How can these divergent results be explained? It will be argued that a more careful comparison of the tasks used can account for this divergence and reveals, in turn, more about how the brain supports semantic memory.

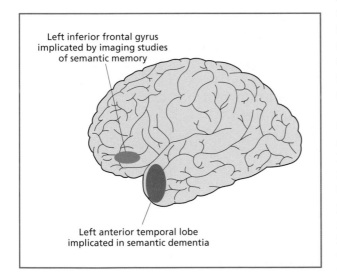

Left inferior frontal gyrus implicated by imaging studies of semantic memory

Left anterior temporal lobe implicated in semantic dementia

Studies of brain-damaged patients with semantic memory and imaging studies of semantic memory have not always highlighted the importance of the same regions.

One of the first ever functional imaging studies of cognition tried to address the question of where semantic memories are stored. As already discussed, Petersen et al. (1988) compared PET brain activation in two tasks: verb generation (e.g. the participant sees CAKE and says "eat") and reading aloud (e.g. the participant sees CAKE and says "cake"). The verb-generation task is assumed to tap semantic memory more than the reading task. However, a comparison of the two tasks shows activity in regions of the left inferior frontal gyrus but not in the same regions that are associated with semantic memory loss. Is the imaging data or the lesion data to be believed? Could it be the case that the left inferior frontal gyrus is really involved in semantic memory (a type 1 disagreement)? To test this hypothesis, instead of taking a group of patients with semantic memory difficulties and asking where the lesion is, one would need to take a group of patients with selective lesions to the left inferior frontal gyrus and give them the same verb-generation task as the healthy people were given when they were scanned. As it turns out, such patients do have subtle but real difficulties with these tasks. Thompson-Schill, Swick, Farah,

D'Esposito, Kan and Knight (1998) asked these patients to generate verbs that had either a low selection demand (e.g. scissors?), in which most people agree upon a verb (i.e. cut), and words with a high selection demand (e.g. cat?), which do not suggest an obvious single answer. The patients are impaired on the latter but not the former. More extensive imaging data on controls shows that the region is responsive to the difficulty of semantic memory retrieval (Thompson-Schill, D'Esposito, Aguirre, & Farah, 1997; Thompson-Schill, D'Esposito, & Kan, 1999). Thus, this disagreement is perhaps more apparent than real. The reason why patients with damage to the left inferior frontal gyrus do not show clinical symptoms of semantic memory impairment is because the region is involved in strategic retrieval operations from semantic memory when no obvious answer comes to mind. By contrast, the temporal regions may be the *store* of semantic information and lesions here can produce more devastating impairments of semantic knowledge. So why didn't these particular imaging studies activate regions that are putatively the store of semantic knowledge? One possibility could be the baseline that was used. Petersen et al. (1988) compared verb generation (their semantic task) with reading (their putatively non-semantic task). However, if word reading does activate the semantic store, and there is in fact good evidence that it might (e.g. Ward, Stott, & Parkin, 2000), then the two things would cancel each other out when subtracted away (a type II disagreement).

In this instance, an initial discrepancy between functional imaging and lesion data has resulted in a more complete understanding of how semantic memory is both stored and retrieved. This is a nice example of how the strengths of different methodologies can be combined in cognitive neuroscience.

IS "BIG BROTHER" ROUND THE CORNER?

This chapter started with the specter of functional imaging being used to reveal one's innermost thoughts to the outside world. It therefore seems appropriate to return to this interesting theme in light of the various points raised so far. It should by now be clear that the process of analyzing and interpreting data produced by functional imaging is not straightforward. It entails a number of stages, each with its own assumptions, rather than a literal reading of the MR signal. Nonetheless, the technology is still relatively new and the amount of progress that has already been made is substantial. Even at this early stage, there are serious studies exploring how functional imaging could be used as a lie detector and studies that try to predict the content of another person's thoughts at some basic level (for a review, see Haynes & Rees, 2006).

COULD FUNCTIONAL IMAGING BE USED AS A LIE DETECTOR?

Lying appears to be a normal component of human social interaction. It is likely to be composed of several cognitive components. For example, it requires an understanding that other people can have states of mind that are different from one's own (so-called theory of mind). Lying also requires an ability to inhibit a truthful response and generate a plausible alternative response. Given this complexity, there will probably be no single "deception module" in the brain dedicated specifically to lying. Nevertheless, there is every reason to believe that studying the brain during deception might lead to more reliable indices of lying than the traditional lie detector (or "polygraph"), given that the brain is the organ that produces the lie in the first place.

The traditional polygraph monitors a number of bodily responses, including sweating, respiration and heart rate, which are considerably downstream from the thought process that creates the lie. As these measures are associated with increased arousal generally (e.g. anxiety), they cannot exclusively detect guilt and their usage is highly questionable. Also, if a liar does not feel guilty there may be no strong arousal response.

A number of studies have used fMRI to measure the neural correlates of deception (e.g. Ganis, Kosslyn, Stose, Thompson, & Yurgelun-Todd, 2003, Langleben et al., 2002). When participants are asked to generate a spontaneous lie to a question (e.g. "Who did you visit during your vacation?", "Was that the card you were shown before?"), a number of regions are activated, including the anterior cingulate cortex. This region is of particular interest in this context, because it has been implicated in monitoring conflicts and errors (Carter, Braver, Barch, Botvinick, Noll, & Cohen, 1998) and also in generating the kinds of bodily response that formed the basis of the traditional polygraph (Critchley et al., 2003). However, not all types of deception may recruit this region. Ganis et al. (2003) found that, if participants memorized a lie in advance of being interviewed in the scanner, then this region was not involved, but regions involved in memory retrieval were involved. Thus, to conclude, although fMRI might have some use in lie detection it is unlikely to offer a simple solution to this complex and important real-world problem (Sip, Roepstorff, McGregor, & Frith, 2007).

Not all lies are as easy to detect.

It is generally believed that different classes of objects (e.g. faces, places, words, tools) activate somewhat different regions of the brain. So is it possible to infer what someone is looking at from brain activity alone? A number of studies have attempted to guess, in a third-person way, what a person is observing (Haxby, Gobbini, Furey, Ishai, Schouten, & Pietrini, 2001) or imagining (O'Craven & Kanwisher, 2000) on a particular trial using only the concomitant neural activity. To achieve this, each person requires pretesting on a whole range of objects to determine the average response to that class of objects relative to some baseline (e.g. all the other objects). Rather than locating the peak area of activity (as in regular fMRI analysis), one can examine the *pattern* of activation over a distributed set of voxels to enable a more fine-grained approach. For example, Haxby et al. (2001) gave participants pictures from eight different types of category, including cats, houses, faces and shoes. The neural activity from an individual trial was then correlated back with the average activity to determine the most probable category that was being viewed. This procedure could predict, given pairwise comparisons, what the person was seeing with 96% accuracy. The same regions of the brain are used, to some extent, when thinking about objects even when they are not physically seen. O'Craven and Kanwisher (2000) obtained comparable results on individual imagery trials.

So, at some basic level, functional imaging can already accurately guess what type of thing someone has in mind. But can it also be used to reveal what we *feel* about the things that we have in mind? One study in the literature has explored the "neural basis of romantic love" (Bartels & Zeki, 2000). This study showed participants a set of photographs of close friends. All the faces were matched for sex, age and length of time that they had been known, but the participant claimed to be deeply in love with only one of them. They did indeed find that there was a neural signature of love as distinct from friendship, although this seems to be distributed amongst several sites in the brain (rather than in a neo-phrenological "love" center).

Can functional imaging distinguish between romantic love and friendship? © Bettmann/ Corbis.

A rather more controversial study has attempted to use fMRI to detect unconscious racial biases in participants who claimed to have no conscious racial prejudices. Phelps et al. (2000) showed white Americans photographs of unfamiliar black or white faces. They measured activity in a region of the brain thought to be involved in processing fear and threat (the amygdala) and they also measured the participants' startle response. Both measures showed a heightened response to these black faces, but not to faces of black positive role models (e.g. Martin Luther King) given in a follow-up study. Are these participants really racist without knowing it? Do they know they are racist but hide their prejudices from the experimenter? Not surprisingly, these strong interpretations soon made it into the popular press. However, a weaker claim (endorsed by the authors) is also possible. Namely, that the results reflect implicit social learning based on one's personal experience (e.g. of growing up in a white neighborhood) and one's own group membership, rather than racism itself (see Eberhardt, 2005, for a review).

Evaluation

In summary, brain imaging can be used to infer the *type* of stimulus that is being processed and how the stimulus is evaluated (e.g. whether it evokes fear or love). However, it is unclear whether fMRI will ever be able to infer the *specific content* of thought. To infer, for example, whether someone in a scanner is thinking about his or her own cat or next-door's cat would require knowledge of how and where an individual stimulus is represented in the brain. We have all been exposed to different cats, houses and so on during the course of our life. Moreover, all our brains differ in subtle ways. This presents a natural boundary on the imaging enterprise that technological developments alone are unlikely to resolve.

SUMMARY AND KEY POINTS OF THE CHAPTER

- Structural imaging reveals the static physical characteristics of the brain (useful in diagnosing disease), whereas functional imaging reveals dynamic changes in brain physiology (that might correlate with cognitive function).
- Neural activity consumes oxygen from the blood. This triggers an increase in blood flow to that region (measured by PET) and a change in the amount of deoxyhemoglobin in that region (measured by fMRI).
- As the brain is always physiologically active, functional imaging needs to measure *relative* changes in physiological activity. The most basic experimental design in functional imaging research is to subtract the activity in each part of the brain whilst doing one task away from the activity in each part of the brain whilst doing a slightly different task. This is called cognitive subtraction.
- Other methods, including parametric and factorial designs, can minimize many of the problems associated with cognitive subtraction.
- There is no foolproof way of mapping a point on one brain onto the putatively same point on another brain because of individual differences in structural and functional anatomy. Current imaging methods cope with this problem by mapping individual data onto a common standard brain (stereotactic normalization) and by diffusing regions of significance (smoothing).
- A region of "activity" refers to a local increase in metabolism in the experimental task compared to the baseline but it does not necessarily mean that the region is essential for performing the task. Lesion studies might provide evidence concerning the necessity of a region for a task.
- Functional imaging can be used to make crude discriminations about what someone is thinking and feeling and could potentially outperform traditional lie detectors. However, it is highly unlikely that they will ever be able to produce detailed accounts of another person's thoughts or memories.

EXAMPLE ESSAY QUESTIONS

- What are the physiological processes that underpin PET and fMRI techniques? What determines the temporal and spatial resolution of these methods?
- What is meant by the method of "cognitive subtraction" in functional imaging research? What problems does this method face?
- Is functional imaging ever likely to completely replace lesion methods for informing theories of cognition?

- If a brain region is shown to be "active" in a given task, does it mean that this region is critical for performing the task? If not, why not?
- Could functional imaging be used in lie detection? Could it be used to read someone else's thoughts and feelings?

RECOMMENDED FURTHER READING

- Friston, K. J. (1997). Imaging cognitive anatomy. *Trends in Cognitive Sciences, 1,* 21–27. A clear and simple account of different experimental designs.

- Jezzard, P., Matthews, P. M., & Smith, S. M. (2001). *Functional MRI: An introduction to methods*. Oxford: Oxford University Press. An advanced text that is only recommended to those who have a very good understanding of the basics, or those who wish to know more about the math and physics of fMRI.

- Savoy, R. L. (2001). History and future directions of human brain mapping and functional neuroimaging. *Acta Psychologica, 107,* 9–42. An excellent summary of the methods. Start here for the basics.

CHAPTER 5

CONTENTS

The lesioned brain

Studies of humans who have been unfortunate enough to acquire brain damage have provided a rich source of information for cognitive neuroscientists. The basic premise behind the approach is that, by studying the abnormal, it is possible to gain insights into normal function. This is a form of "reverse engineering", in which one attempts to infer the function of a component (or region) by observing what the rest of the cognitive system can and can't do when that component (or region) is removed. In this way, lesions "carve cognition at its seams" (McCarthy & Warrington, 1990).

Patient-based neuropsychology has tended to take two broad forms. In one tradition, which I shall call *classical neuropsychology*, attempts have been made to infer the function of a given brain region by taking patients with lesions to that region and examining their pattern of impaired and spared abilities (e.g. the textbook by Kolb and Whishaw, 2002, is broadly in line with this approach). This type of research has benefited greatly from the development of imaging methods that enable more accurate lesion localization and quantification. It also provides an important source of constraint on functional imaging data. In the second tradition, which I shall call *cognitive neuropsychology*, the pattern of spared and impaired abilities in and of themselves has been used to infer the building blocks of cognition – irrespective of where they are located in the brain (e.g. the textbook by Ellis and Young, 1988, is broadly in line with this approach; it contains no pictures of the brain). This approach has been particularly informative for guiding the development of detailed information-processing models, and provides the cognitive framework that underpins much imaging research. The schism between these traditions has run deep. For example, many journals either tacitly or explicitly favor one approach over the other. Moreover, each tradition has tended to rely on its own methodology, with classical neuropsychology favoring **group studies** and cognitive neuropsychology favoring **single case studies**. The development of cognitive neuroscience has led to something of a reconciliation of these traditions, and this textbook discusses both. The key point that one needs to bear in mind is this: the method one chooses should be appropriate to the question one is asking. It will be argued in this chapter that group studies are more appropriate for establishing lesion-deficit associations, whereas single case studies are particularly helpful for establishing how cognitive processes might be subdivided.

Naturally occurring brain lesions are "accidents of nature" that occur because of stroke, tumor, head injury or other types of brain damage. A complementary approach, that in many ways resembles the logic of the lesion method, involves magnetic stimulation of the intact brain to produce what has been described as "virtual lesions" (e.g. Pascual-Leone, Bartres-Faz, & Keenan, 1999). This method is called **transcranial magnetic stimulation** (TMS). The method makes contact with the literature from the classical neuropsychology tradition with its emphasis on lesion location. However, it can also be used to test information-processing theories of cognition because it can provide information on the timing of cognitive processes. The method has a number of advantages over traditional lesion methods.

WAYS OF ACQUIRING BRAIN DAMAGE

Brain damage can be acquired in a number of ways, as summarized below.

Neurosurgery

Operations are occasionally performed in cases of severe epilepsy in which the focus of the epileptic seizure is surgically removed. One of the most famous cases in neuropsychology, HM, had dense amnesia after part of his medial temporal lobe was surgically removed (see Chapter 9). Another surgical procedure formerly used to reduce epileptic seizures spreading across the brain was to sever the fibers of the corpus callosum. This operation was referred to as the **split-brain** procedure. Patients who have undergone this intervention have only mild impairments in daily living but the impairments can be observed in laboratory conditions in which stimuli are presented briefly to each hemisphere (for a review, see Gazzaniga, 2000). Surgical intervention was also previously common in psychiatric patients (see the discussion on the prefrontal lobotomy in Chapter 14). In general, surgical procedures are only carried out in the absence of suitable pharmacological treatments.

Strokes (or cerebrovascular accident; CVA)

Disruptions to the blood supply of the brain (called **strokes** or cerebrovascular accidents; CVA) can result in global or local death of neurons. If an artery ruptures, this leads to a hemorrhage and an increase in intracranial pressure (typically relieved by surgery). People born with **aneurysms** are more susceptible to rupture. These are localized regions of over-elastic artery that may balloon and rupture. Blood vessels may also become blocked if, for example, a fatty clot gets pushed from a large vessel into a smaller one (an *embolism*) or a stationary clot becomes large enough to block the vessel (*thrombosis*). Other vascular disorders include *angiomas* (tangled and tortuous blood vessels liable to rupture) and arteriosclerosis (hardening of the vessel walls).

Traumatic head injuries

Whereas vascular disorders tend to affect older people, traumatic head injuries are the most common form of brain damage in people under 40 years of age. They are particularly common in young males as a result of road traffic accidents. Traumatic head injuries are classified in two ways, "open" or "closed", depending on whether or not the skull is fractured. Open head injuries often have more localized injuries, whereas closed head injuries have more widespread effects (as the brain ricochets in the skull) and often produce loss of consciousness.

Tumors

The brain is the second most common site for tumors (after the uterus), and brain tumors are often spread from other parts of the body (these are called metastatic tumors). Tumors are caused when new cells are produced in a poorly regulated manner. Brain tumors are formed from supporting cells such as the meninges and glia (termed meningioma and gliomas, respectively). Tumors adversely affect the functioning of the brain because the extra cellular material puts pressure on the neurons, disrupting functioning and possibly leading to cell death.

Viral infections

A number of viruses target specific cells in the brain. These include herpes simplex encephalitis (HSE), human immunodeficiency virus (HIV) and Creutzfeldt-Jakob disease (CJD).

Neurodegenerative disorders

Most western societies have a large ageing population that will, if anything, continue to get larger and older. In 1900, 4% of people were over the age of 65; in 2030, 20% of the population is estimated to be over 65. An increase in life expectancy is bringing about an increase in degenerative illnesses that affect the brain. By far the most common is dementia of the Alzheimer type (or DAT). This is associated with atrophy in a number of regions of the brain, with memory loss (amnesia) typically being the earliest noted symptom. Other neurodegenerative diseases include Parkinson's disease and Huntington's disease (see Chapter 8), Pick's disease (often the medical diagnosis in cases of "semantic dementia"), and multi-infarct dementia (caused by many small strokes that can be hard to distinguish from DAT).

DISSOCIATIONS AND ASSOCIATIONS

In 1990, two very unusual patients came to the attention of Roberto Cubelli (Cubelli, 1991). One patient, CF, was unable to write any vowel letters and left gaps in their place (e.g. "Bologna" → B L GN). Another patient, CW, made spelling errors selectively on vowels (e.g. "dietro" → diatro); equivalent errors were not found in his spoken language. By contrast, Kay and Hanley (1994) report a different patient who made spelling errors selectively on consonants (e.g. "record" → recorg). The basic logic behind the cognitive neuropsychological approach is that a difficulty in one domain relative to an absence of difficulty in another domain can be used to infer the independence of these domains. In the case of the patients just discussed, the implication was that the brain has separate neural resources for the processing of written vowels relative to consonants. These neural resources need not lie in different locations of the brain (at least on a millimeter or centimeter scale), but might reflect two different populations of interspersed neurons. Note, also, that it is not clear that one can conclude that the *only* function of these neurons is the coding of consonants and/or vowels. The difference could be relative and, indeed, without testing a whole range of other stimuli (e.g. digits), it is unwise to conclude exclusivity of function. Nonetheless, it is reasonable to conclude that there are some neural resources predominantly implicated in written vowel processing relative to consonants and vice versa.

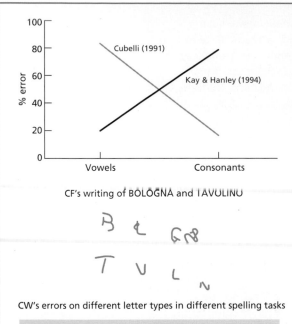

CF's writing of BOLOGNA and TAVOLINO

CW's errors on different letter types in different spelling tasks

Stimuli	Vowels	Consonants
Written spelling	42	16
Oral spelling	18	3
Delayed copying	35	7
Typing	25	15

Some patients produce spelling errors selectively on either consonants or vowels. This may imply separate neural resources for coding consonants and vowels. Data from Cubelli (1991).

If a patient is impaired on a particular task (task A) but relatively spared on another task (task B), this is referred to as a **single dissociation**. If the patient performs entirely normally on task B compared to a control group, this has been termed a *classical* single dissociation, whereas if the patient is impaired on both tasks but is significantly more impaired on one task, this is referred to as a *strong* single dissociation (Shallice, 1988). In either of these instances, one inference is that task A and task B utilize different cognitive processes with different neural resources. However, other inferences could also be made.

It could be the case that both task A and task B use exactly the same cognitive/neural resources as each other but task B requires more of this resource than task A (i.e. task B is harder). If brain damage depletes this resource, then task B may be relatively or selectively impaired. This has been referred to as a **task-resource artefact** (Shallice, 1988). Another explanation of a single dissociation is in terms of a **task-demand artefact** (Shallice, 1988). A task-demand artefact is when a single dissociation occurs because a patient performs one of the tasks suboptimally. For example, the patient may have misunderstood the instructions or have adopted an unusual strategy for performing the task. Task-demand artefacts can be minimized by assessing the patient's general intellectual functioning, giving clearer instructions or training, using ecologically valid tests, and repeating the same (or similar tests) on several occasions.

In general, almost all neuropsychological studies are aimed at proving that two or more tasks have different cognitive/neural resources and disproving the task-resource and task-demand explanations even if this is not explicitly stated in these terms. In the case of Cubelli's patients, a task-demand artefact can easily be ruled out because the same task (i.e. writing) was performed in both conditions. One of the most powerful ways of discounting a task-resource artefact is to document a **double dissociation**, which merely refers to two single dissociations that have a complementary profile of abilities. To remain with the current example, Kay and Hanley's patient could write vowels better than Cubelli's patient, whereas Cubelli's patient could write consonants better than Kay and Hanley's.

So far, the discussion has emphasized the importance of dissociations between deficits, but what about *associations* of deficits? For example, if for every patient that resembled Cubelli's there were 10, 20 or 100 times as many patients who had comparable **dysgraphia** for *both* consonants and vowels, then would this diminish the findings of the dissociation? Some researchers would suggest not. There are some theoretically uninteresting reasons why two symptoms may associate together, the main reason being that they are close together in the brain and so tend to be similarly affected by strokes (or whatever) in that region. For example, patients with difficulties in recognizing faces often have difficulties in perceiving colors but this probably reflects neuroanatomical proximity rather than suggesting a "super-module" that is specialized for both. It is the (double) dissociations between the two that count from a theoretical point of view.

Needless to say, this particular viewpoint has attracted controversy. It has been argued that it is important to know how common a particular dissociation is in order to rule out that it hasn't been observed by chance (Robertson, Knight, Rafal & Shimamura, 1993). For example, if brain damage affects some written letters more than others in a random fashion, then it would still be possible to find patients who appear to have selective difficulties in writing vowels but it would be a chance occurrence rather than meaningful dissociation. Other researchers have focused more on associations between symptoms (so-called **syndromes** rather than dissociations. The use of the double dissociation itself has been subject to criticism (see Dunn & Kirsner, 2003). Some have argued that the use of double dissociation implies an endorsement of the notion of "modularity" (e.g. as specified by Fodor, 1983; see Chapter 1). However, it need not. Shallice (1988) discusses why this argument is wrong by setting up the following thought trap: if modules exist, then double dissociations are a reliable way of uncovering them; double dissociations do exist, therefore modules exist. The way out of this trap, however, is to ask the question: can non-modular systems produce double dissociations? It has been demonstrated that other types of cognitive architecture, such as interactive connectionist models, can produce double dissociations (Plaut, 1995). The

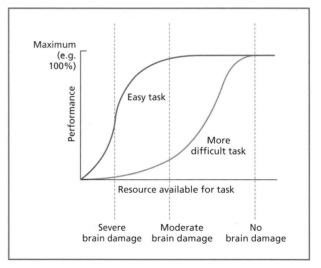

In a classical dissociation, performance on one task lies within the control range (shown by dotted lines). In a strong dissociation, both tasks fall outside the control range but one task is significantly more impaired than the other. From Shallice (1988). Copyright © Cambridge University Press. Reproduced with permission.

A task-resource artefact can arise because one task uses more of a cognitive/neural resource than the other (i.e. one task is harder). One could construe brain damage as depleting the amount of resource available. In this instance, at moderate brain damage the patient can still perform the easy task normally. A single dissociation need not reflect different cognitive/neural substrates for the tasks. Adapted from Shallice (1988).

KEY TERMS

Dysgraphia
Difficulties in spelling and writing.

Syndrome
A cluster of different symptoms that are believed to be related in some meaningful way.

reason why they do so is interesting. It reflects the fact that these systems also contain units that are functionally specialized for certain types of process/information, even though the system is interactive, and even though these units may respond (to a greater or lesser degree) to a range of stimuli.

Some have argued that the reliance on double dissociations is flawed because it requires the study of "pure" cases (Dunn & Kirsner, 2003). However, it need not (Shallice, 1979). First of all, one must be careful to state what is meant by a pure case. For example, imagine that the dysgraphic patients mentioned above also had amnesia. Would the fact that they were not "pure dysgraphic" exclude them from study? This might depend on the theoretical stance one adopts. If one's theoretical model assumes that writing and memory are independent (as most do), then studying spelling in isolation is entirely feasible.

It is worth stating that finding a double dissociation between two patients on two tasks is only part of the neuropsychologist's toolkit. To interpret their spared and impaired performance, one requires evidence from a range of other relevant tasks. For example, to fully interpret the dysgraphic patients' impairments it would be interesting to know if they could copy vowels and consonants, or recognize them visually. The types of error that patients produce can also be an important source of information, irrespective of their performance level (i.e. how good or bad they are). For example, the independence of consonants and vowels was initially inferred from the types of errors made in dysgraphia (Caramazza & Miceli, 1990) and not from the double dissociation logic. The double dissociation is useful, but it is not a panacea.

SINGLE CASE STUDIES

Caramazza's assumptions for theorizing in cognitive neuropsychology

Although the use of single cases of brain-damaged individuals to study normal cognitive/brain function began in the mid-nineteenth century, attempts to formalize the logic of this approach were lacking for many years. Caramazza provided one of the first serious attempts to do so in the 1980s (Caramazza, 1986; Caramazza, 1992; Caramazza & Badecker, 1989; Caramazza & McCloskey, 1988; McCloskey & Caramazza, 1988). He suggested that three underlying, and unstated, assumptions underpinned almost all neuropsychological studies to date:

1. *The fractionation assumption.* The first assumption is that damage to the brain can produce selective cognitive lesions. Note that the assumption is stated with reference to a lesion within a particular cognitive model and not to a lesion to a particular region of the brain (although the two may, of course, be correlated). Caramazza is principally interested in using observations of brain-damaged individuals to inform theories of cognition (cognitive neuropsychology), not to localize cognitive processes in the brain (classical neuropsychology).

2. *The transparency assumption.* The **transparency assumption** states that lesions affect one or more components within the pre-existing cognitive system but they do not result in a completely new cognitive system being created. This assumption

is needed because one wishes to study the abnormal in order to understand the normal, and not just to study the abnormal as an end in itself.

3. *The universality assumption.* The universality assumption is that all cognitive systems are basically identical.

Caramazza acknowledges that these assumptions may, under some situations, not hold true. It is a matter for empirical research to determine the extent to which they are true and, hence, the validity of any inference that can be drawn from the study of brain-damaged individuals. Critics have pointed to a number of potential difficulties with the assumptions. Kosslyn and van Kleek (1990) have suggested that whether or not selective cognitive impairments will be observed (the fractionation assumption) depends on the neural architecture. For example, selective deficits may be more likely if neurons performing a given operation are clustered together rather than distributed around the brain, and if the neurons are dedicated to one operation rather than shared by many operations. Nevertheless, selective cognitive impairments *can* be observed and so the fractionation assumption appears to hold true at one level, even if there are some cognitive processes that may be hard to uncover by the lesion method by virtue of an atypical neural architecture.

The transparency assumption is potentially the most problematic. Basically, one needs to assume that brain damage removes one component of cognition but does not create, from scratch, a rearranged or different cognitive system. Examples of brain plasticity, and rehabilitation and recovery after brain damage, might at first appear to be convincing arguments against transparency. But they need not be. For example, imagine that a patient has severe problems in speaking after a stroke (i.e. aphasia) but that these problems ameliorate over time. This could be taken as *prima facie* evidence that the brain has somehow reorganized itself after the stroke. However, it could be that the pre-existing cognitive model has just been reinstated rather than that a whole new way of performing the task has been created. As such, this would *not* be a violation of the transparency assumption. Plasticity at a neural level is a pervasive aspect of brain function (see also Chapter 9), and need not imply behavioral change or functional change. It is important to point out that the assumption is more likely to hold true for brain damage acquired during adulthood than childhood (Thomas & Karmiloff-Smith, 2002). It is also worth pointing out that the transparency assumption refers to the cognitive organization of the cognitive system and not necessarily its location. Consider the case of an epileptic child who has his left hemisphere removed and then learns to speak using the right hemisphere (Vargha-Khadem, Carr, Isaacs, Brett, Adams, & Mishkin, 1997a). Is that a violation of the transparency assumption? It could be, but it need not be. It depends on whether the new right hemisphere system is cognitively equivalent to the one in the left. The transparency assumption refers to the comparability between premorbid and post-morbid cognitive systems, and not on where such systems are located. Although the debate remains open about the validity of this assumption, a good rule of thumb is that the transparency assumption is less likely to be violated in adult relative to child cases, and when studied soon after injury relative to later in time (or if the cognitive profile after injury remains stable over time).

The universality assumption, that all cognitive systems are basically the same, may also be problematic to neuropsychology. But Caramazza has argued that it is equally problematic for other methods within cognitive neuroscience. Basically, one needs to assume that an individual (or individuals) are representative of the population at large in order to make generalizations to normal cognition. Individual

The use of single cases is not peculiar to neuropsychology. For example, it is the mainstay of archaeology and anthropology. In 1974, Donald Johanson discovered a partial skeleton of a single primate, Lucy, from 3.18 million years ago, which had walked upright and had a small brain. Previous theories had suggested that brain enlargement preceded the ability to walk upright. This single case proved this not to be so. Note that Johanson did not have to provide a group of "Lucys" for his findings to be acceptable to the scientific community. John Reader/Science Photo Library.

differences, such as they are, are attributable to "noise" (e.g. variations in performance related to time) or other factors that may be related to the efficiency of the cognitive system (e.g. expertise) but need not reflect qualitative differences in the way the task is performed. Of course, if there are individual qualitative differences, then this is theoretically interesting. Finding a framework to explore and account for these differences is a challenge for cognitive neuroscience in general, rather than patient-based neuropsychology in particular. Caplan (1988), however, has argued that individual differences are more of a problem for single case studies relative to other methods because this method gives exaggerated importance to exceptional findings. But this could be construed as the strength of this method rather than a weakness – assuming that the individual differences can be ascribed to something of theoretical interest rather than just "noise".

The case for single case studies

Caramazza and McCloskey (1988) have gone as far as to suggest that the single case study is the *only* acceptable method in cognitive neuropsychology. The titles of the papers debating this position tell a story of their own. The original paper, entitled "The case for single patient studies" (Caramazza & McCloskey, 1988), was interpreted as the case against group studies. A subsequent paper, "The case against the case against group studies" (Zurif, Gardner, & Brownell, 1989), defended group studies on the grounds that "syndromes [i.e. associations of symptoms] are what the world gives us". This provoked a paper with a particularly amusing title: "Clinical syndromes are not God's gift to cognitive neuropsychology: A reply to a rebuttal to an answer to a response to the case against syndrome-based research" (Caramazza & Badecker, 1991). To understand this heated debate, it is necessary to take a step back and consider the argument as initially laid out.

Consider first the logic of testing subjects in the non-brain-damaged population. One may recruit a sample of subjects (S_1 to S_n) and make the assumption, valid or not, that they have broadly equivalent cognitive systems (M). One may then conduct an experiment (E), making the further assumption that all participants carry it out in equivalent ways (i.e. no task-demand artefacts), and derive a set of observations (O_1 to O_n). In this instance, it is argued that it is quite feasible to average the observations of the group because it is assumed that the only difference between the subjects is "noise" (i.e. variations in performance over time, differences in speed or ability).

Consider next the situation in which one wishes to test a group of brain-damaged patients (P_1 to P_n). As before, it is assumed that each has (before their lesion) essentially the same cognitive system (M) and that each is given the same experiment (E) and complies with the experiment in the same way. However, each patient may have a different lesion to the cognitive system (L_1 to L_n) and so difference in observed performance may be attributable to differences in lesion rather than between-patient noise and, as such, averaging across patients is not possible. Determining where the lesion is in the cognitive system can only be determined on the basis of empirical observation of each case in turn. It is crucial to bear in mind the distinction between a lesion to a cognitive component (which is relevant to the discussion here) and an anatomical lesion. At present, there is no magic way of working out what the precise cognitive profile of a given patient will be from a structural lesion (except in the most general terms). Thus, establishing the cognitive impairment requires cognitive testing of individual patients.

What if one were to establish that a group of patients had identical lesions to the same component of the cognitive system, could one then average across the patients? Caramazza has argued that, although legitimate, the study becomes a series of single case studies, not a group study, and so the unit of interest is still the single case. To establish that they had the same lesion, one would have to carry out the same set of experiments on each individually. As such, one would not learn any more from averaging the set of patients than could be learned from a single case itself. The objection is not against the idea of testing more than one patient *per se*, but rather averaging the results of many patients assumed (but not proven) to be equivalent.

Some of the common objections against the use of the single case study are that one cannot create a theory based on observations from only a single case, or that it is not possible to generalize from a single case. The counterarguments are that nobody is trying to construct whole new theories of cognition based on a single case. Theories, in neuropsychology and elsewhere, must account for a wide range of observations from different sources, both normal and brain-damaged. For example, cognitive models of reading are able to account for different observations found in skilled readers and also account for the different types of acquired dyslexia (drawn from several different single cases). They must also account for the pattern of performance (e.g. the types of error made) as well as the level of performance (i.e. following the logic of dissociations). Although nobody wishes to construct a theory based on a single case, observations from single cases constitute valid data with which to test, amend and develop theory. As for the argument that it is not possible to generalize from a single case, the counterquestion would be "generalize to what?". It is entirely plausible to generalize from a single case to a model of normal cognition. It is, however, much harder to generalize from one single case to another single case. Two patients with a stroke may have very different cognitive profiles (i.e. one cannot generalize from one case to another), but it should nevertheless be possible for each particular case to generalize to some aspect of normal cognition.

In a non brain-damaged population…					
Subjects	S_1	S_2	S_3	S_4…	S_n
Cognitive system Experiment	M E	M E	M E	M E	M E
Observations	O_1	O_2	O_3	O_4…	O_n

In a brain-damaged population…					
Subjects	P_1	P_2	P_3	P_4…	P_n
Cognitive system Lesion Experiment	M L_1 E	M L_2 E	M L_3 E	M L_4 E	M L_n E
Observations	O_1	O_2	O_3	O_4…	O_n

Caramazza has argued that it is possible to average observations (O_1 to O_n) across different non-brain-damaged subjects (S_1 to S_n) because they are assumed to have the same cognitive system (M) that performs the experiment (E) in comparable ways. The same logic may not apply to brain-damaged patients (P_1 to P_n) because each patient will have a different cognitive lesion (L), which cannot be known a *prior* (Caramazza & McCloskey, 1988).

Evaluation

The argument presented above has emphasized the point that single case studies are a valid methodology and they may have a particularly important role to play in determining what the components of cognitive systems are. The discussion has also argued that the term "lesion" can be construed both in terms of disruption to a component in a cognitive model, as well as a region of organic brain damage. Does this mean that group studies have no role to play at all? It will be argued that group studies do have an important role to play, and that they may be particularly suited to addressing different types of question from the single case approach.

GROUP STUDIES AND LESION-DEFICIT ANALYSIS

The introduction to this chapter discussed the historical schism that exists between cognitive neuropsychology, which is aimed at developing purely cognitive accounts of cognition, and cognitive neuropsychology, which is aimed at developing brain-based accounts of cognition. Both approaches fit well within a cognitive neuroscience framework. The cognitive neuropsychology tradition enriches the conceptual framework and provides a testable hypothesis about what the likely neural components of cognition are (although not necessarily where they are). The classical neuropsychology tradition provides important contrastive data with functional imaging. There are several reasons why regions may appear active or inactive in functional imaging tasks, and a region of activity need not imply that a region is critically involved in that particular task. Studies of patients with lesions in that area do enable such conclusions to be drawn. The lesions of patients, however, are typically large and rarely restricted to the region of interest. Thus, to be able to localize which region is critical for a given task, several patients may need to be considered.

Ways of grouping patients

How does one decide the principle by which patients should be grouped in order to associate lesion sites with deficits? There are at least three approaches in the literature:

1. *Grouping by syndrome.* Patients are assigned to a particular group on the basis of possessing a cluster of different symptoms. This approach is particularly common in psychiatric studies (e.g. of schizophrenia) but there are equivalent approaches in neuropsychology (e.g. the aphasia subtypes identified by Goodglass and Kaplan, 1972).
2. *Grouping by cognitive symptom.* Patients are assigned to a particular group on the basis of possessing one particular symptom (e.g. auditory hallucinations; difficulty in reading non-words). They may also possess other symptoms but, assuming that the other symptoms differ from case to case, the method should be sensitive to the symptom under investigation.
3. *Grouping by anatomical lesion.* Patients are selected on the basis of having a lesion to a particular anatomical region. This region may have been identified as interesting by previous functional imaging studies. This method need not require that patients have damage exclusively to the region of interest. The patients may have additional damage elsewhere but, assuming that the other lesions differ from case to case, the method should be sensitive to the region in question (Damasio & Damasio, 1989).

There is no right or wrong way of deciding how to group patients, and to some extent it will depend on the precise question being addressed. The method of grouping cases by syndrome is likely to offer a more coarse level of analysis, whereas grouping according to individual symptoms may provide a more fine-grained level of analysis. In general, the syndrome-based approach may be more appropriate for understanding the neural correlates of a given disease pathology rather than developing theories concerning the neural basis of cognition.

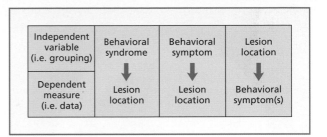

The method of grouping patients by symptom (2 in the list above) and then finding out what regions of damage they have in common is relatively new. This is made feasible by new techniques that compare the location of lesions from MRI scans of different patients on a voxel-by-voxel basis thus producing a fine-grained statistical map of the likely lesion 'hot spot' (Rorden & Karnath, 2004). For example, it has been used to separate out the different contributions of frontal regions in tests of executive function (e.g. Shammi & Stuss, 1999; Stuss et al., 2002). One advantage of working forward from a symptom to a lesion location is that it could potentially reveal more than one region as being critically involved. For example, let's assume that a deficit can arise from damage to either region X or region Y. If one were to initially group patients according to whether or not they have damage to region X and test for a deficit (3 in the list above), then one could falsely conclude that region X is the key region that gives rise to this deficit and the method would not detect the importance of region Y. The main situation in which one would group patients by lesion site and then test for the presence of a particular symptom (3 in the list above) is if one has a specific testable prediction about what the region is critical for (e.g. the region has been implicated by functional imaging studies).

There are at least three different ways of grouping patients to carry out a lesion-deficit analysis.

Caveats and complications

There are at least two caveats and complications that warrant further discussion. The first concerns the ability of current structural imaging techniques to identify lesions. The second concerns the inferences that can be drawn from lesion-deficit associations that can, if not articulated properly, lapse into neophrenology.

Damasio and Damasio (1989) discuss how certain types of neuropathology are more suited to lesion-deficit analysis than others, at least with current techniques. The most suitable lesions are those in which dead tissue is eventually replaced by cerebrospinal fluid. This is frequently the case in stroke (at least in the chronic rather than acute phase), in damage resulting from the herpes simplex encephalitis (HSE) virus and following neurosurgery. Identifying the site of a lesion caused by a tumor is particularly problematic when the tumor is *in situ*, but is less problematic once it has been excised. Certain tumors (e.g. gliomas) may infiltrate surrounding tissue and so have no clear boundary, and physical strain around the tumor may cause swelling (termed **odema**). This distorts the true size and shape of the brain tissue and may render neurons inoperative even if they are not destroyed. Similar arguments apply to the presence of leaked blood during hemorrhage, and the intracranial swelling associated with closed head injury. In general, reliable lesion images are best obtained three months after onset and when the neuropsychology testing is carried out at a similar time to the structural imaging (Damasio & Damasio, 1989).

On finding that a function (F) is disrupted following a lesion to region X, it is tempting to conclude that function F is located in region X or, worse still, that

KEY TERM

Odema
A swelling of the brain following injury.

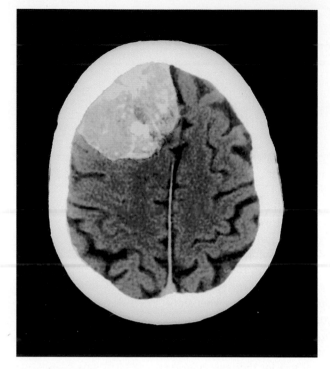

A tumor (here shown on a CT scan) can make it hard to estimate lesion size, and the distortion in the shape of the brain makes it hard to map onto a standard atlas. Sovereign, ISM/Science Photo Library.

the purpose of region X is to implement F. These conclusions, and the second one in particular, are tantamount to endorsing a neophrenological view of brain structure–function relationship. Before jumping to such a conclusion, one would need to consider a number of other questions. Is this the only function of region X? Do other regions contribute to the performance of function F, or is this the only region that does so? On finding that a function (F) is disrupted following a lesion to region X, a more cautious conclusion is that region X is critical for performing some aspect of function F. This assertion does not assume that region X has a single function, or that function F has a discrete location. It is also important to note that even a very discrete brain lesion can disrupt the functioning of distant brain regions that are structurally intact; this is termed **diaschisis**. For example, structural lesions to the left frontal lobe can result in markedly reduced PET activity in other distant regions (e.g. left inferior posterior temporal lobe) during a letter judgment task (Price, Warburton, Moore, Frackowiak, & Friston, 2001). This can occur even though this distant region is not lesioned and may function normally in other contexts. The implications are that damage to one region can disrupt the functioning of another, intact, region when these two regions work together to implement a particular cognitive function.

Evaluation

Group studies of patients can be important for establishing whether or not a given region is critical for performing a given task or tasks. Two broad methods are favored, depending on the hypothesis being addressed. The first method involves establishing (on a case by case basis) whether or not a patient is impaired on a given task and then determining the lesion location(s). The second method involves selecting the group on the basis of a lesion to a predefined area and then establishing what functional deficits the group has. This second method is important for testing predictions derived from functional imaging research.

ANIMAL MODELS IN NEUROPSYCHOLOGY

The two main methods that use non-human animals that are considered in this textbook are single-cell recordings (discussed in Chapter 3) and lesion methods. Both of these methods have been greatly assisted by structural MRI scanning enabling individual differences in each animal's brain anatomy to be taken into consideration when placing electrodes and lesions, and also for determining the extent of lesions in vivo. When non-human animals are used in this way, it is typically referred to as **behavioral neuroscience** rather than cognitive neuroscience.

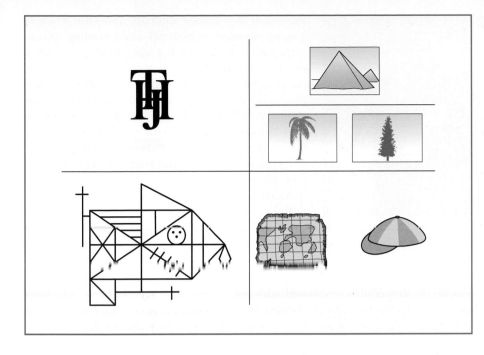

The purpose of a neuropsychological assessment is to ascertain a patient's level of functioning relative to that expected based on his or her premorbid functioning (e.g. Cipolotti & Warrington, 1995a). Some common neuropsychological tests are shown; clockwise from top left: patients with visual recognition problems find it hard to identify overlaid letters relative to non-overlaid ones (from BORB; Riddoch & Humphreys, 1995); patients with semantic memory impairments may find it hard to match the palm tree to the pyramid (Howard & Patterson, 1992); patients with aphasia may find it hard to decide whether things rhyme (from PALPA; Kay, Lesser, & Coltheart, 1992); patients with memory problems may be able to copy but not remember this figure (from Rey, 1964, © International Universities Press Inc.).

The implication of this difference in terminology is that humans think but animals behave or, rather, we know that humans think but we can't be so sure about other animals.

Although lesion methods in humans rely on naturally occurring lesions, it is possible – surgically – to carry out far more selective lesions on other animals. Unlike human lesions, each animal can serve as its own control by comparing performance before and after the lesion. It is also common to have control groups of animals that have undergone surgery but received no lesion, or a control group with a lesion in an unrelated area. There are various methods for producing experimental lesions in animals (Murray & Baxter, 2006):

1. *Aspiration*. The earliest methods of lesioning involved aspirating brain regions using a suction device and applying a strong current at the end of an electrode tip to seal the wound. These methods could potentially damage both gray matter and the underlying white matter that carries information to distant regions.
2. *Transection*. This involves cutting of discrete white matter bundles such as the corpus callosum (separating the hemispheres) or the fornix (carrying information from the hippocampus).
3. *Neurochemical lesions*. Certain toxins are taken up by selective neurotransmitter systems (e.g. for dopamine or serotonin) and once inside the cell they create chemical reactions that kill it. A more recent approach involves toxins that bind to receptors on the surface of cells, allowing for even more specific targeting of particular neurons.
4. *Reversible "lesions"*. Pharmacological manipulations can sometimes produce reversible functional "lesions". For example, scopolamine produces a temporary amnesia during the time in which the drug is active. Cooling of parts of the brain also temporarily suppresses neural activity.

A family of macaque monkeys.

Studies of non-human animals have also enabled a more detailed anatomical understanding of the brain and, in particular, the anatomical connectivity between regions. In non-human animals, injecting the enzyme horseradish peroxidase into axons carries a visible tracer back to the cell bodies that send them. The tracer can be visualized at post-mortem. This enables one to ascertain which regions project to a given region (Heimer & Robards, 1981).

Whilst the vast majority of neuroscience research is conducted on rodents, some research is still conducted on non-human primates. In many countries, including in the EU, neuropsychological studies of great apes (e.g. chimpanzees) are not permitted. More distant human relatives used in research include three species of macaque monkeys (rhesus monkey, cynomolgus monkey and Japanese macaque) and one species of New World primate, the common marmoset. There are a number of difficulties associated with the use of animal models in neuropsychology, not least the concern for the welfare of the animals. Scientists working with these species must provide a justification as to why the research requires primates rather than other animals or other methods, and they must justify the number of animals used. It is also important to have careful breeding programs to avoid having to catch animals from the wild and to protect the animals from viruses. It is important to give them adequate space and social contact. Another disadvantage of animal models is that there are some human traits that do not have obvious counterparts in other species. Language is the most obvious such trait; consciousness is a more controversial one (e.g. see Stoerig & Cowey, 1997).

TRANSCRANIAL MAGNETIC STIMULATION (TMS)

Attempts to stimulate the brain electrically and magnetically have a long history. Electric currents are strongly reduced by the scalp and skull and are therefore more suitable as an invasive technique on people undergoing surgery. In contrast, magnetic fields do not show this attenuation by the skull. However, the limiting factor in developing this method has been the technical challenge of producing large magnetic fields, associated with rapidly changing currents, using a reasonably small stimulator (for an historical overview, see Walsh and Cowey, 1998). Early attempts at magnetic stimulation were successful at eliciting phosphenes (e.g. Magnussen & Stevens, 1914), but this was probably due to stimulation of the retina rather than the brain (Barlow, Kohn, & Walsh, 1947). It was not until 1985 that adequate technology was developed to magnetically stimulate focal regions of the brain (Barker, Jalinous, & Freeston, 1985). Since then, the number of publications using this methodology has increased rapidly. Typically, the effects of TMS are small, such that they alter reaction time profiles rather than elicit an overt behavior. But there are instances of the latter. For example, if the coil is placed over the region of the right motor cortex representing the hand, then the subject may experience a sensation or involuntary movement in the left hand (given that the right motor cortex sends move-ment signals to the left part of the body). If the coil is placed over the right visual cortex, then the subject may report visual sensations or "phosphenes" on the left side (given that the right visual cortex represents the left side of space). Even more specific examples have been documented. Stewart, Battelli, Walsh and Cowey (1999) stimulated a part of the visual cortex dedicated to motion perception (area V5) and reported that these particular phosphenes tended to move. Stimulation in other parts of the visual cortex pro-duces static phosphenes.

How does TMS work?

TMS works by virtue of the principle of electro-magnetic induction that was first discovered by Michael Faraday. A change in electric current in a wire (the stimulating coil) generates a magnetic field. The greater the *rate of change* in electric current, the greater the magnetic field. The mag-netic field can then induce a secondary electric current to flow in another wire placed nearby. In the case of TMS, the secondary electric current is induced, not in a metal wire, but in the neurons below the stimulation site. The induced electric current in the neurons is caused by making them "fire" (i.e. generate action potentials) in the same way as they would when responding to stimuli in the environment. The use of the term "magnetic" is something of a misnomer as the magnetic field acts as a bridge between an electric current in the stimulating coil and the current induced in the brain. Pascual-Leone et al. (1999) suggest that "electrodeless, non-invasive electric stimulation" may be more accurate, although it is unlikely that this term will catch on.

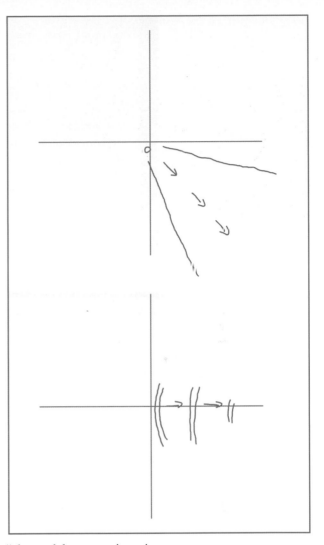

An example of two phosphenes produced by stimulating area V5. Left hemisphere V5 stimulation produces right visual field phosphenes moving away from the center. The first was described as "movement of a single point in a static field" and the second as "drifting right, not continuous". From Stewart et al. (1999). Copyright © 1999 Elsevier. Reproduced with permission.

A number of different designs of stimulating coil exist, and the shape of the coil determines how focused the induced current is. One of the most common designs is the figure-of-eight coil. Although the coil itself is quite big, the focal point of stimulation lies at the intersection of the two loops and is about 1 cm^2 in area. If you have access to TMS equipment, try holding the coil a few centimeters above your arm. When the pulse is released, you should feel a slight harmless twinge on a small area of skin that is representative of the area of direct stimulation of the brain.

The "virtual lesion"

TMS causes neurons underneath the stimulation site to be activated. If these neurons are involved in performing a critical cognitive function, then stimulating them artifi-cially will disrupt that function. Although the TMS pulse itself is very brief (less than 1 millisecond), the effects on the cortex may last for several tens of milliseconds. As

WHAT IS THE "VISUAL" CORTEX OF A BLIND PERSON USED FOR?

Could whole regions of the brain normally dedicated to one type of processing (e.g. vision) take on a completely different functional characteristic (e.g. touch)? A number of studies have investigated the functioning of the visual cortex (in the occipital lobes) in people who were blind from a very early age.

Sadato et al. (1996) conducted a PET study demonstrating that early blind Braille readers showed activity in their primary visual cortex (V1) during Braille reading. This was not found for late blind or sighted individuals with their eyes closed. However, functional imaging methods, such as PET, can reveal increases in activity that may not be functionally critical. It could be, for instance, that the blind readers are *trying* to use the visual cortex during Braille reading but that this activity is not actually contributing to task performance. To address this, lesion methods are appropriate. Given that early blind people with late brain damage restricted to occipital regions are rare (but see Hamilton, Keenan, Catala, & Pascual-Leone, 2000), TMS avails itself as the most appropriate method.

Cohen et al. (1997b) studied tactile identification of Braille letters in early blind individuals, and tactile identification of embossed letters in roman type in both early blind and (blindfolded) sighted individuals. When they placed their finger on the letter, a train of TMS pulses was delivered. The TMS was delivered to a number of sites, including the mid-occipital ("visual" cortex), the sensory-motor (tactile/motor cortex) and "air" as the control condition. The results are in the figure on the left. For the blind subjects, TMS over mid-occipital regions impaired tactile letter discrimination. This suggests that the "visual" cortex is used for touch in the early blind. Sighted people show disruption when TMS is applied over sensory-motor cortex. It is perhaps surprising that blind people don't additionally show an effect here. It could be that, because they are more skilled, they require a higher intensity of TMS for disruption to be induced. There is evidence for plasticity in somatosensory, as well as mid-occipital, regions in the blind as the region of the brain representing their reading fingers is enlarged by as much as two or three times (Pascual-Leone & Torres, 1993). Similar TMS studies have revealed cortical enlargements are found for skilled racquet players (Pearce, Thickbroom, Byrnes, & Mastaglia, 2000), and cortical reductions found for limb amputees (Cohen, Bandinelli, Findley, & Hallett, 1991). These suggest that level of use is critical for plasticity.

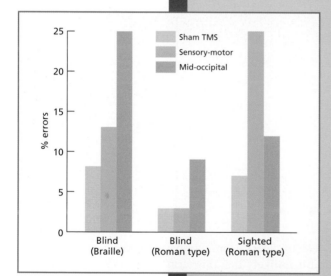

TMS over mid-occipital "visual" cortex impairs tactile identification in the blind but not in blindfolded sighted people, whereas TMS over sensory-motor (tactile) cortex impairs tactile discrimination in sighted individuals. From Cohen et al. (1997). Reprinted by permission of Macmillan Publishers Ltd. Copyright 1997.

Is it likely that any brain region can substitute for the function of another? In this instance, the function of the brain region is largely the same (i.e. it makes fine-grained spatial discriminations) even though in one instance it responds to vision and in another to touch. However, more recent research suggests that the occipital cortex in blind individuals can support tasks of a very different nature (e.g. verb generation; Amedi, Floel, Knecht, Zohary, & Cohen, 2004).

such, the effects of a single TMS pulse are quickly reversed. Although this process is described as a "virtual lesion" or a "reversible lesion", a more accurate description would be in terms of interference. In the cognitive psychology literature, **dual-task interference** paradigms are used to determine whether two tasks share cognitive resources. For example, it is hard to pat your head whilst rubbing your tummy (although it is easy to do each in isolation). This suggests they share some cognitive mechanisms. In contrast, it is easy to pat your head and read aloud, which suggests little sharing of cognitive mechanisms. TMS uses a comparable logic to infer whether a given brain region is critical. If a region is critical for a task, then there is likely to be interference because of the dual use of the region in terms of the computational demands of the task together with the activity ensuing from the applied stimulation.

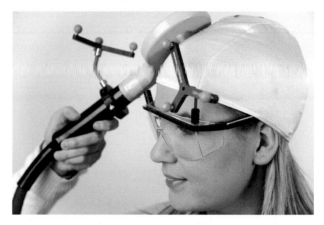

The coil is held against the participant's head, and a localized magnetic field is generated during performance of the task. University of Durham/ Simon Fraser/Science Photo Library.

TMS has a number of advantages over traditional lesion methods (Pascual-Leone et al., 1999). The first advantage is that real brain damage may result in a reorganization of the cognitive system (a violation of the "transparency assumption") whereas the effects of TMS are brief and reversible. This also means that within-subject designs (i.e. with and without lesion) are possible in TMS that are very rarely found with organic lesions (neurosurgical interventions are an interesting exception, but in this instance the brains are not strictly premorbidly "normal" given that surgery is warranted). In TMS, the location of the stimulated site can be removed or moved at will. In organic lesions, the brain injury may be larger than the area under investigation and may affect several cognitive processes.

Advantages of TMS over organic lesions	Advantages of organic lesions over TMS
• No reorganization/compensation • Can be used to determine timing of cognition • Lesion is focal • Lesion can be moved within the same participant • Can study "functional connectivity"	• Subcortical lesions can be studied • Lesions can be accurately localized with MRI (effects of TMS are less well understood spatially) • Changes in behavior/cognition are more apparent

KEY TERM

Dual-task interference
If there is a decrement in performance associated with doing two things at once, it suggests that these two tasks share cognitive processes.

Will TMS completely replace traditional neuropsychological methods? Probably not. For one thing, TMS is restricted in the sites that can be stimulated, i.e. those beneath the skull; stimulations elsewhere cannot be studied with TMS. Moreover, the spatial extent of the changes induced by TMS is not fully understood and it is possible that more distant brain structures receive stimulation if they are connected to the stimulation site (Paus, 1999). In contrast, organic lesion localization using MRI is more tried and tested. Another advantage of traditional neuropsychology is that the "accidents of nature" turn up some unexpected and bizarre patterns. For example, some patients can name body parts but not point to named parts of their body (Semenza & Goodglass, 1985) and some patients can draw a bicycle but not recognize a drawing of a bicycle (Behrmann, Moscovitch, & Winocur, 1994). Perhaps these sorts of pattern could also be observed with TMS, but nobody would think to look for them without the patient-based observations. Indeed, the effects of TMS "lesions" are often only observable through slowed reaction times and not through error rates, or the externally observable behavior that characterizes most neurological deficits.

FACILITATION, INTERFERENCE AND FUNCTIONAL INTEGRATION USING TMS

The previous sections argued that dissociations between spared and impaired performance form the cornerstone of much lesion-based research. TMS, as a method of "virtual lesions", is no exception. So far, the discussion of lesions – virtual and real – has focused on decrements in performance. More surprisingly, lesions can sometimes improve performance; this is called facilitation. In organic lesions, facilitation is generally very hard to observe because the patient is typically not assessed before the lesion and so the baseline level of performance can only be guessed at (but for a review, see Kapur, 1996). In TMS, the reversible nature of the lesion means that facilitation in performance following a virtual lesion can be easier to detect (Theoret, Kobayashi, Valero-Cabre, & Pascual-Leone, 2003). How could a lesion paradoxically improve performance? If there are different processes competing in the brain, then eliminating one process from the competition (using TMS) might have a beneficial effect on the other. Alternatively, if one region sends inhibition to another, then removing the source of the inhibition might facilitate the functioning of the other region. Understanding how the functioning of one region of the brain depends on the functioning of another is termed functional integration. A list of the functions of individual parts of the brain will only ever tell a partial story. One must also consider how the different regions cooperate and compete. TMS may provide a unique window onto these mechanisms.

The brain divides up the visual world into different attributes such as color, shape and motion and these different attributes are essentially represented in different regions of the brain (see Chapter 6 for discussion). One theoretical question is: "Do these regions compete with each other, and does attending to one attribute (e.g. motion) have positive or negative consequences for irrelevant attributes (e.g. color)?" To answer this question, Walsh, Ellison, Battelli and Cowey (1998b) presented subjects with arrays of different shapes made up of different colors that were either moving or static. The task of the subjects was to determine whether a pre-specified target (e.g. a moving cross, a static cross, a green cross) was present or absent in the array as quickly as possible. TMS was delivered at area V5 (specialized for visual

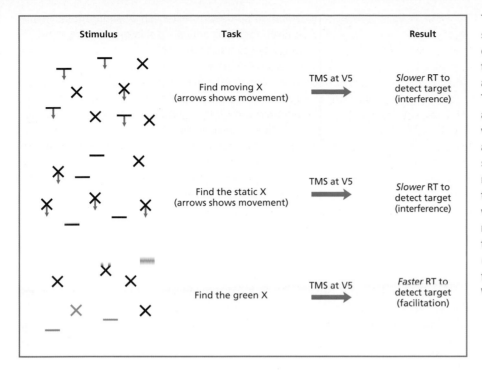

Stimulus	Task		Result
	Find moving X (arrows shows movement)	TMS at V5 →	*Slower* RT to detect target (interference)
	Find the static X (arrows shows movement)	TMS at V5 →	*Slower* RT to detect target (interference)
	Find the green X	TMS at V5 →	*Faster* RT to detect target (facilitation)

The participants must search for the presence or absence of a specified target (e.g. moving X) in an array of other items. TMS was applied over area V5 (involved in visual motion perception) at various points during search. If motion was relevant to the search task, then performance was impaired, but if motion was irrelevant to the search task, then performance was facilitated. Adapted from Walsh et al. (1998b).

motion perception) at a number of different time intervals but, for simplicity, the overall pattern across time only will be discussed here. In the first two examples, motion is needed to discriminate between targets and distractors because relying on shape alone will not help (some Xs move and some Xs are static). Unsurprisingly, a virtual lesion to V5 disrupts this visual search, as has been found for organic lesions to this area (McLoed, Heywood, Driver, & Zihl, 1989). The unexpected finding comes when there is no motion at all and the participants must find a target based on color and form (a green X). In this instance, a virtual lesion to V5 facilitates search efficiency. This suggests that different visual areas may compete with each other and eliminating an irrelevant visual area can improve the operation of relevant ones.

Practical aspects of using TMS

When designing experiments using TMS (or when evaluating other people's choice of design), there are three main considerations: when to deliver the pulses, where to deliver the pulses, and selection of appropriate control conditions (for a good overview, see Robertson, Theoret and Pascual-Leone, 2003). Finally, given that the brain is being stimulated, one must be fully aware of safety and ethical considerations when performing TMS experiments.

Timing issues – repetitive or single pulse?

The issue of when to deliver the pulse is crucial to the success, or otherwise, of a TMS experiment. On rare occasions, the time taken for a stimulus to be registered in a given brain region is known by previous research using other techniques. For example, single-cell recordings suggest that it takes 100 ms for a visual stimulus to be registered in the primary visual cortex (area V1), and TMS studies in which a

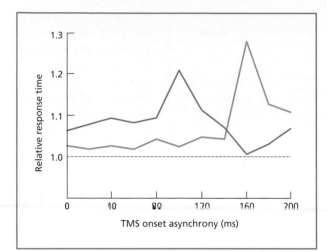

TMS can be used to establish *when* in a task a given region is critical. In this experiment, participants had to search for a visual target in an array that was either present or absent. TMS applied over the parietal lobes disrupted performance, but only in specific time windows, with present trials occurring earlier (100 ms; purple line) than absent trials (160 ms; green line). A temporal dissociation such as this could not be observed in patients with irreversible organic brain damage. From Ashbridge et al. (1997). Copyright © 1997 Elsevier. Reproduced with permission.

single pulse is delivered close to this critical window can render the subject effectively "blind" to the stimulus (Corthout, Uttle, Ziemann, Cowey, & Hallett, 1999). On most occasions, information such as this will not be known. In this situation, there are a number of options. First, one could make the time of pulse delivery a variable in its own right. For example, if a stimulus is presented for 500 ms, the TMS pulse (or pulses) could be delivered in different time windows (0–50 ms, 50–100 ms, ... 450–500 ms). This experimental design could thus provide important information about the timing of cognition, as well as providing information about the necessity of that region. An alternative solution is to use a train of pulses during the task (i.e. repetitive or rTMS). In this situation, the experiment becomes potentially more powerful in its ability to detect the necessity of a region but it would not be possible to draw conclusions about timing because it would be unclear which pulse (or pulses) was critical. Whether or not single pulse or rTMS is used is not only related to whether or not timing is an independent variable, but also to the nature of the task itself. Some tasks may require several pulses for TMS to exert interference. The reasons why this might be are not fully understood, but it is a general rule of thumb that TMS studies of perceptual processes have often used single pulse designs, whereas studies of "higher" cognition (e.g. memory, language) have often used rTMS (Walsh & Rushworth, 1999).

How to hit the spot?

To conduct a TMS experiment, one needs to make some assumptions about which regions of the brain would be interesting to stimulate. In some instances, functional resolution is all that is needed. Just as with the arguments concerning classical versus cognitive neuropsychology, one may wish to establish that a given task/behavior can be selectively disrupted (in which case, the location of the stimulation site is not relevant to the type of conclusion drawn).

Positions on the head can be defined relative to landmarks, such as those used in the EEG system of electrode placement. Skull landmarks include the inion (a bony protrusion at the back of the skull), the anion (the bony ridge between the eyebrows), and the vertex (midway between the anion and inion, and midway between the ears).

For example, one published way of approximately locating area V5 (dedicated to visual motion perception) is by marking a spot 5 cm in front of the inion, and 3 cm up from it (Walsh, Ashbridge, & Cowey, 1998a). The spot can be physically marked by placing an X on the skin, or by marking the position on a taut swimming cap. If a precise location is not known before the study, then one could stimulate, say, six different spots lying in a 2 × 3 cm grid, drawn on a swimming cap relative to a fixed skull landmark. Different adjacent positions could then serve as control conditions in the analysis.

Structural and functional MRI can also be used to locate candidate regions of stimulation taking into account individual differences in brain anatomy and skull shape (this is called *frameless stereotaxy*). A structural or functional MRI scan can be obtained prior to TMS and then online digital registration (using specialist software) enables the position on the skull to be identified. Alternatively, the TMS could be performed prior to a structural MRI scan in which the stimulation sites used have been marked in such a way as to render them visible on the scan. Cod liver oil tablets attached to the head have been used previously (e.g. Walsh, Ellison, Passingham, Jahanshahi, & Rothwell, 2001).

What is the appropriate control condition?

Two possible control conditions for TMS experiments have already been considered. First, one can compare performance when the same region is stimulated in critical and non-critical time windows. Second, one can compare stimulation in critical and non-critical regions. Some consideration needs to be given to the selection of the non-critical region. Using regions adjacent to the critical region can provide extra clues about the spatial size of the region of interest. In studies in which there is good reason to believe that the cognitive function is lateralized, one could use the same site on the opposite hemisphere as a control. A further advantage in using the control conditions mentioned above is that peripheral effects of TMS can be minimized. These include the loud sound of the pulse and twitches caused by inadvertent stimulation of the facial nerves and muscles. The latter can be more pronounced at some sites and so using adjacent regions or opposite hemisphere regions would minimize this. "Sham TMS", in which the coil is held in the air rather than against the head, is not an ideal control condition, and having no TMS at all as a control condition is also not desirable. Another control condition that can be used in TMS experiments is a task control. Thus, the same region can be stimulated at the same times but with some aspect of the task changed (e.g. the stimuli, the instructions).

Evaluation

TMS is an interesting addition to the cognitive neuroscientist's toolkit. It is able to ascertain the importance of a given region by stimulating that region during task performance. As such, it is related to other lesion methods that are used for establishing the importance of a given region but it has certain advantages over the organic lesion method. The main advantage lies in the fact that the interference is short-lived and reversible. It can also be used to explore how regions interact with each other (functional connectivity) and shed light on the timing of cognitive processes.

SAFETY AND ETHICAL ISSUES IN TMS RESEARCH

Researchers need to bear in mind a number of safety issues when conducting TMS experiments. It is essential to be aware of the local regulations that apply in your own institution but the following points are likely to be important:

- Whereas single pulse TMS is generally considered to be safe, repetitive-pulse TMS carries a very small risk of inducing a seizure (Wassermann, Cohen, Flitman, Chen, & Hallett, 1996). Given this risk, participants with epilepsy or a familial history of epilepsy are normally excluded. Participants with pacemakers and medical implants should also be excluded. Credit cards, computer discs and computers should be kept at least 1 meter away from the coil.
- The number of pulses that can be delivered to a participant in a given testing session has been established, by consensus (Pascual-Leone et al., 1993; Wassermann, 1996). Up-to-date information about safety is available on: http://pni.unibe.ch/MailList.htm (note that the web address is case sensitive). The intensity of the pulses that can be delivered is normally specified with respect to the "motor threshold"; that is, the intensity of the pulse, delivered over the motor cortex, that produces a just noticeable motor response (for a discussion of problems with this, see Robertson et al., 2003).
- During the experiment, some participants might experience minor discomfort due to the sound of the pulses and facial twitches. Although each TMS pulse is loud (~100 dB), the duration of each pulse is brief (1 ms). Nonetheless, it is mandatory to protect the ears with earplugs or headphones. When the coil is in certain positions, the facial nerves (as well as the brain) may be stimulated, resulting in involuntary twitches (e.g. blinking, jaw clamping). Participants should be warned of this and told they can exercise their right to withdraw from the study if it causes too much discomfort.
- It is generally believed that a single session of TMS has no long-term consequences. However, repeated participation in experiments could conceivably have longer-term effects – either positive or deleterious. A number of studies report an *improvement* in mood in depressed individuals following repeated frontal lobe stimulation (e.g. George et al., 1995). But this study involved repeated stimulation on a daily basis. Except in cases of therapeutic intervention, it is good practice not to test the same participants many times over a short interval.

SUMMARY AND KEY POINTS OF THE CHAPTER

- A double dissociation between two patients occurs when patient 1 is significantly better than patient 2 on task A, and patient 2 is significantly better than patient 1 on task B. The standard interpretation of this is that task A and task B utilize some different neural resources.

- The use of single cases has led to important insights into the way in which cognitive components are organized and may be fractionated.
- Group studies of patients are important for making links between lesion location and behavioral deficits, and provide an important source of converging evidence for functional imaging data.
- Transcranial magnetic stimulation (TMS) works by stimulating a region of cortex placed beneath a current-carrying coil. This stimulation temporarily interferes with ongoing cognitive activity in that region and, therefore, provides information about the necessity of that region for performing the task. This has been termed a "virtual lesion".

EXAMPLE ESSAY QUESTIONS

- What assumptions must one accept to be able to draw inferences about normal cognition from adults with brain damage? Are these assumptions plausible?
- Critically evaluate the role of group studies in neuropsychological research.
- What are the advantages and disadvantages of using single cases to draw inferences about normal cognitive functioning?
- How have TMS studies contributed to our knowledge of brain plasticity?
- Compare and contrast lesion methods arising from organic brain damage with TMS.

RECOMMENDED FURTHER READING

- A special edition of *Cognitive Neuropsychology* (1988), 5(5), is dedicated to methodological issues related to single case and group studies in neuropsychology.
- A special section of the journal *Cortex* (2003), 39(1), debates the use of dissociations in neuropsychology.
- Pascual-Leone, A., Davey, N. J., Rothwell, J., Wassermann, E. M., & Puri, B. K. (2002). *Handbook of transcranial magnetic stimulation*. London: Arnold. A detailed account of the methods and uses of TMS, with a strong clinical slant.
- Walsh, V. & Pascual-Leone, A. (2003). *Transcranial magnetic stimulation: A neurochronometrics of mind*. Cambridge, MA: MIT Press. A detailed account of the methods and uses of TMS, with a cognitive neuroscience slant.

CHAPTER 6

CONTENTS

The seeing brain

Students who are new to cognitive neuroscience might believe that the eyes do the seeing and the brain merely interprets the image on the retina. This is far from the truth. Although the eyes play an undeniably crucial role in vision, the brain is involved in actively constructing a visual representation of the world that is not a literal reproduction of the pattern of light falling on the eyes. For example, the brain divides a continuous pattern of light into discrete objects and surfaces, and translates the two-dimensional retinal image into a three-dimensional interactive model of the environment. In fact, the brain is biased to perceive objects when there is not necessarily an object there. Consider the Kanizsa illusion – it is quite hard to perceive the stimulus as three corners as opposed to one triangle. The brain makes inferences during visual perception that go beyond the raw information given. Psychologists make a distinction between **sensation** and **perception**. Sensation refers to the effects of a stimulus on the sensory organs, whereas perception involves the elaboration and interpretation of that sensory stimulus based on, for example, knowledge of how objects are structured. This chapter will consider many examples of the constructive nature of the seeing brain, from the perception of visual attributes, such as color and motion, up to the recognition of objects and faces.

Do you automatically perceive a white triangle that isn't really there? This is called the Kanizsa illusion.

FROM EYE TO BRAIN

The **retina** is the internal surface of the eyes that contains specialized photoreceptors that convert (or *transduce*) light into neural signals. The photoreceptors are made up of **rod cells**, which are specialized for low levels of light intensity, such as those found at night, and **cone cells**, which are more active during daytime and are specialized for detecting different wavelengths of light (broadly corresponding to color, although the brain's perception of color does not always correspond to what is on the retina). Information from the retina is transmitted to the brain via the *optic nerves*. The point at which the optic nerve leaves the eye is called the **blind spot** because there are no rods and cones present there. If you open only one of your eyes (and keep it stationary), there is a spot in which there is no visual information. Yet, one does not perceive a black hole in one's vision. This is another example of the brain filling in missing information. The highest concentration of cones is at a point called the *fovea*, and the level of detail that can be perceived (or visual acuity) is greatest at this point. Rods are more evenly distributed across the retina.

KEY TERMS

Sensation
The effects of a stimulus on the sensory organs.

Perception
The elaboration and interpretation of a sensory stimulus based on, for example, knowledge of how objects are structured.

Retina
The internal surface of the eyes containing photoreceptors that convert light to neural signals.

Rod cells
A type of photoreceptor specialized for low levels of light intensity, such as those found at night.

Cone cells
A type of photoreceptor specialized for high levels of light intensity, such as those found during the day, and specialized for the detection of different wavelengths.

Blind spot
The point at which the optic nerve leaves the eye. There are no rods and cones present there.

To find your blind spots, hold the image about 50 centimeters away. With your left eye open (right closed), look at the +. Slowly bring the image (or move your head) closer while looking at the +. At a certain distance, the dot will disappear from sight...this is when the dot falls on the blind spot of your retina. Reverse the process. Close your left eye and look at the dot with your right eye. Move the image slowly closer to you and the + should disappear.

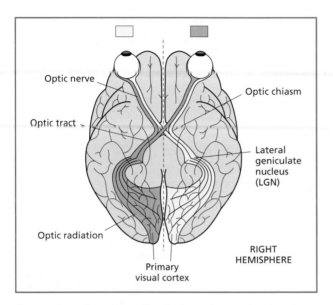

Connections from the retina to the primary visual cortex – the geniculostriate pathway. From Zeki (1993). Copyright © Blackwell Publishing. Reproduced with permission.

The primary visual cortex and geniculostriate pathway

There are a number of different pathways from the retina to the brain (for a review, see Stoerig and Cowey, 1997). The dominant visual pathway in the human brain travels to the **primary visual cortex** at the back, or posterior, of the brain, via a processing station called the lateral geniculate nucleus (LGN). The primary visual cortex is also referred to as V1, or as the striate cortex because it has a larger than usual stripe running through one layer that can be seen when stained and viewed under a microscope. This particular route is called the geniculostriate pathway.

The neural representation in the lateral geniculate nucleus divides up information on the retinal surface in a number of interesting ways. Objects in the right side of space (termed the right "visual field") fall on the left side of the retina of *both* eyes and project to the left lateral geniculate nucleus. The representation in the lateral geniculate nucleus thus contains information from both the left and right eyes. This information is segregated into the six different neuronal layers of this structure, three for each eye. The layers of the lateral geniculate nucleus are not only divided according to the eye (left or right) but contain a further subdivision. The upper four layers have small cell bodies and have been termed *parvocellular*, or P layers, whereas the lower two layers contain larger cell bodies and have been

KEY TERM

Primary visual cortex (or V1)
The first stage of visual processing in the cortex; the region retains the spatial relationships found on the retina and combines simple visual features into more complex ones.

EYE–BRAIN MYTH 1

Do not make the mistake of believing that the retina of the left eye represents just the left side of space, and the retina of the right eye represents just the right side of space. (If you are still confused, close one eye and keep it fixed – you should be able to see both sides of space with a minor occlusion due to the nose.) Rather, the left side of the left eye and the left side of the right eye both contain an image of objects on the right side of space. The right side of the left eye and the right side of the right eye both contain an image of objects on the left side of space.

termed *magnocellular*, or M layers. Parvocellular cells respond to detail and are concerned with color vision. Magnocellular cells are more sensitive to movement than color and respond to larger areas of visual field (e.g. Maunsell, 1987).

Most neurons in the lateral geniculate nucleus have a particular characteristic response to light that is termed a *center-surround* receptive field (similarly for ganglion cells in the retina). The term **receptive field** denotes the region of space that elicits a response from a given neuron. One intriguing feature of the receptive fields of these cells, and many others in the visual system, is that they do not respond to light as such (Barlow, 1953; Kuffler & Barlow, 1953). Rather, they respond to differences in light across their receptive field. Light falling in the center of the receptive field may excite the neuron, whereas light in the surrounding area may switch it off (but when the light is removed from this region, the cell is excited again). Light over the entire receptive field may elicit no net effect because the center and surround inhibit each other. These center-surround cells form the building blocks for more advanced processing by the primary visual cortex, enabling detection of, amongst other things, edges and orientations.

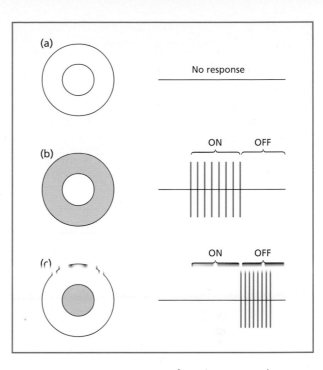

A center-surround receptive field of the lateral geniculate nucleus. Light over the entire receptive field yields no response (a). The *presence* of light over the center (b) yields excitation, whereas the surround responds to the *absence* of light (c). From Zeki (1993). Copyright © Blackwell Publishing. Reproduced with permission.

EYE–BRAIN MYTH 2

If you think that the response of neurons on the retina or in the brain is like the response of pixels in a television screen, then think again. Some visual neurons respond when light is taken away, or when there is a *change* in light intensity across the region that they respond to. Other neurons in extrastriate areas respond only to certain colors, or movement in certain directions. These neurons often have very large receptive fields that do not represent a very precise pixel-like location at all.

The properties of neurons in the primary visual cortex were elucidated by pioneering work by David Hubel and Torsten Wiesel (1959, 1962, 1965, 1968, 1970a), for which they were awarded the Nobel Prize in Medicine in 1981. The method they used was to record the response of single neurons in the visual cortex of cats and monkeys. Before going on to consider their work, it might be useful to take a step backwards and ask the broader question: "What kinds of visual information need to be coded by neurons?" First of all, neurons need to be able to represent how light or dark something is. In addition, neurons need to represent the color of an object to distinguish, say, between fruit and foliage of comparable lightness/darkness but complementary in color. Edges also need to be detected, and these might be defined as abrupt changes in brightness or color. These edges might be useful for perceiving the shape of objects. Changes in brightness or color could also reflect movement of

KEY TERM

Receptive field
The region of space that elicits a response from a given neuron.

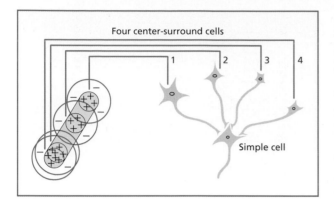

Four center-surround cells

1 2 3 4

Simple cell

A simple cell in V1 responds to lines of particular length and orientation. Its response may be derived from a combination of responses from different cells with center-surround properties such as those located in the lateral geniculate nucleus. From Zeki (1993). Copyright © Blackwell Publishing. Reproduced with permission.

an object, and it is conceivable that some neurons may be specialized for extracting this type of visual information. Depth may also be perceived by comparing the two different retinal images.

The neurons in the primary visual cortex (V1) transform the information in the lateral geniculate nucleus into a basic code that enables all of these types of visual information to be extracted by later stages of processing. As with many great discoveries, there was an element of chance. Hubel and Wiesel noted that an oriented crack in a projector slide drove a single cell in V1 wild, i.e. it produced lots of action potentials (cited in Zeki, 1993). They then systematically went on to show that many of these cells responded only to particular orientations. These were termed **simple cells**. The responses of these simple cells could be construed as a combination of the responses of center-surround cells in the lateral geniculate nucleus (Hubel & Wiesel, 1962). The cells also integrate information across both eyes and respond to similar input to either the left or right eye. Many orientation-selective cells were found to be wavelength-sensitive too (Hubel & Wiesel, 1968), thus providing a primitive code from which to derive color.

Just as center-surround cells might be the building blocks of simple cells, Hubel and Wiesel (1962) speculated that simple cells themselves might be combined into what they termed **complex cells**. These are orientation-selective too, but can be distinguished from simple cells by their larger receptive fields and the fact that complex cells require stimulation across their entire length, whereas simple cells will respond to single points of light within the excitatory region. Outside of V1, another type of cell, termed **hypercomplex cells**, which can be built from the responses of several complex cells, was observed (Hubel & Wiesel, 1965). These cells were also orientation-sensitive but the length was also critical. The receptive fields of hypercomplex cells may consist of adding excitatory complex cells, but with inhibitory complex cells located at either end to act as "stoppers". In sum, the response properties of cells in V1 enable more complex visual information (e.g. edges) to be constructed out of more simple information.

Cortical and non-cortical routes to seeing

To date, around ten different pathways from the eye to the brain have been discovered, of which the pathway via the (dorsal) lateral geniculate nucleus to V1 is the most well understood and appears to make the largest contribution to human visual perception (Stoerig & Cowey, 1997). The other routes are evolutionarily more ancient. Evolution appears not to have replaced these routes with "better" ones but has retained them and added new routes that enable finer levels of processing or that serve somewhat different functions. For example, a visual route to the suprachiasmatic nucleus (SCN) in the hypothalamus provides information about night and day that could be used to configure a biological clock (Klein, Moore, & Reppert, 1991). Other routes, such as via the superior colliculus and inferior pulvinar, seem to be important for orienting to

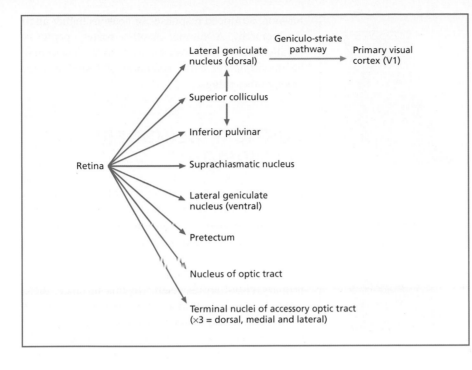

There are believed to be ten different routes from the retina to different regions of the brain.

stimuli (e.g. a sudden flash of light) by initiating automatic body and eye movements (e.g. Wurtz, Goldberg, & Robinson, 1982). These latter routes may be faster than the route via V1 and can thus provide an early warning signal to potentially threatening stimuli. This can explain how it is possible to unconsciously turn to look at something but without realizing its importance until after orienting.

EYE–BRAIN MYTH 3

The image on the retina and the representation of it in V1 are "upside down" with respect to the outside world. As such, one might wonder how the brain turns it the right way up. This question is meaningless because it presupposes that the orientation of things in the outside world is in some way "correct" and the brain's representation of it is in some way "incorrect". There is no "correct" orientation (all orientation is relative) and the brain does not need to turn things around to perceive things appropriately. The function of the seeing brain is to extract relevant information from the environment, not to create a carbon copy that preserves, among other things, the same relative top-to-bottom orientation.

Evaluation

The primary visual cortex (V1) contains cells that enable a basic detection of visual features, such as edges, that are likely to be important for segregating the scene into different objects. There is some evidence for a hierarchical processing of visual features such that responses of earlier neurons in the hierarchy form the building blocks

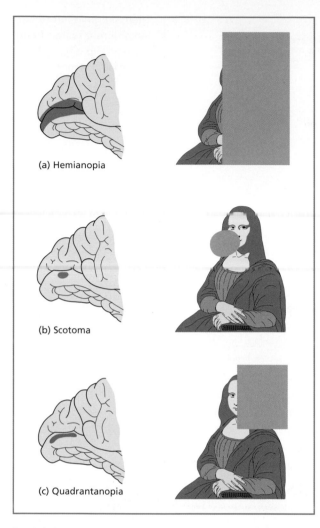

(a) Hemianopia

(b) Scotoma

(c) Quadrantanopia

Partial damage to the primary visual cortex (V1) can result in blindness in specific regions. This is because this region of the brain is retinotopically organized. Area V1 is at the back of the brain and on the middle surface between the two hemispheres. Adapted from Zeki (1993).

KEY TERMS

Hemianopia
Cortical blindness restricted to one half of the visual field (associated with damage to the primary visual cortex in one hemisphere).

Quadrantanopia
Cortical blindness restricted to a quarter of the visual field.

Scotoma
A small region of cortical blindness.

for more advanced responses of neurons higher up in the hierarchy. A number of other routes operate in parallel to the geniculostriate route to V1. These may be important for early detection of visual stimuli, among other things.

CORTICAL BLINDNESS AND "BLINDSIGHT"

Loss of one eye, or the optic nerve of that eye, results in complete blindness in that eye. The spared eye would still be able to perceive the left and right sides of space and transmit information to the left and right primary visual cortex. But what would be the consequences of *complete* damage to one side of the primary visual cortex itself? In this instance, there would be cortical blindness for one side of space (if the left cortex is damaged, then the right visual field would be blind, and vice versa). The deficit would be present when using either the left or right eye alone, or both eyes together. This deficit is termed **hemianopia** (or homonymous hemianopia). *Partial* damage to the primary visual cortex might affect one subregion of space. As the upper part of V1 (above a line called the calcarine fissure) represents the bottom side of space, and the lower part of V1 represents the top part of space – damage here can give rise to cortical blindness in a quarter of the visual field (so-called **quadrantanopia**). Blindness in a smaller region of space is referred to as a **scotoma**. Note that the layout of visual information in V1 parallels that found on the retina. That is, points that are close in space on the retina are also close in space in V1. Areas such as V1 are said to be *retinotopically organized*.

The previous section described how there are several visual routes from the eye to the brain. Each of these routes makes a different contribution to visual perception. Taking this on board, one might question whether damage to the brain (as opposed to the eyes) could really lead to total blindness unless each and every one of these visual pathways coincidentally happened to be damaged. In fact, this is indeed the case. Damage to the primary visual cortex does lead to an inability to report visual stimuli presented in the corresponding affected region of space and can be disabling for such a person. Nevertheless, the other remaining visual routes might permit some aspects of visual perception to be performed satisfactorily in exactly the same regions of space that are reported to be blind. This paradoxical situation has been referred to as "**blindsight**" (Weiskrantz, Warrington, Sanders, & Marshall, 1974).

Blindsight ≠ normal vision − awareness of vision
Blindsight = impaired vision + no awareness of vision

Patients exhibiting blindsight deny having seen a visual stimulus even though their behavior implies that the stimulus was in fact seen (for a review, see Cowey, 2004). For example, patient DB had part of his primary visual cortex (V1) removed to cure a chronic and severe migraine (this was reported in detail by Weiskrantz, 1986). When stimuli were presented in DB's blind field, he reported seeing nothing. However, if asked to point or move his eyes to the stimulus then he could do so with accuracy, while still maintaining that he saw nothing. DB could perform a number of other discriminations well above chance, such as orientation discrimination (horizontal, vertical or diagonal), motion detection (static or moving) and contrast discrimination (gray on black versus gray on white). In all these tasks DB felt as if he was guessing even though he clearly was not. Some form/shape discrimination was possible but appeared to be due to detection of edges and orientations rather than shape itself. For example, DB could discriminate between X and O but not between X and Δ and not between squares and rectangles that contain lines of similar orientation (but see Marcel, 1998).

How can the performance of patients such as DB be explained? First of all, one needs to eliminate the possibility that the task is being performed by remnants of the primary visual cortex. For example, there could be islands of spared cortex within the supposedly damaged region (Campion, Latto, & Smith, 1983). However, many patients have undergone structural MRI and it has been established that no cortex remains in the region corresponding to the "blind" field (Cowey, 2004). Another explanation is that light from the stimulus is scattered into other intact parts of the visual field and is detected by intact parts of the primary visual cortex. For example, some patients may be able to detect stimuli supposedly in their blind field because of light reflected on their nose or other surfaces in the laboratory (Campion et al., 1983). Evidence against this comes from the fact that performance is superior in the "blindsight" region to the natural blind spot (found in us all). This cannot be accounted for by scattered light (see Cowey, 2004). Thus, the most satisfactory explanation of blindsight is that it reflects the operation of other visual routes from the eye to the brain (such as that via the superior colliculus) rather than residual ability of V1.

This account raises important questions about the functional importance of conscious versus unconscious visual processes. If unconscious visual

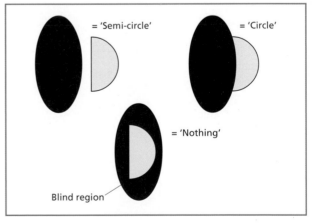

If a visually presented semi-circle abuts a cortical scotoma (the shaded area), then the patient might report a complete circle. Thus, rather than seeing a gap in their vision, patients with blindsight might fill in the gap using visual information in the spared field. If the semi-circle is presented inside the scotoma, it isn't seen at all, whereas if it is away from the scotoma, it is perceived normally. Adapted from Torjussen (1976).

processes can discriminate well, then why is the conscious route needed at all? As it turns out, such questions are misguided because the unconscious routes (used in blindsight) are not as efficient and are only capable of coarse discriminations in comparison to the finely-tuned discriminations achieved by V1 (see Cowey, 2004). At present, we do not have a full understanding of why some neural processes but not others are associated with conscious visual experiences. Nevertheless, studies of patients with blindsight provide important clues about the relative contribution and functions of the different visual pathways in the brain.

FUNCTIONAL SPECIALIZATION OF THE VISUAL CORTEX BEYOND V1

The neurons in V1 are specialized for detecting edges and orientations, wavelengths and light intensity. These form the building blocks for constructing more complex visual representations based on form (i.e. shape), color and movement. Some of the principal anatomical connections between these regions are shown in the figure below. The occipital cortex outside V1 is known as the *extrastriate cortex* (or prestriate cortex). The receptive fields in these extrastriate visual areas become increasingly broader and less coherently organized in space, with areas V4 and V5 having very broad receptive fields (Zeki, 1969). The extrastriate cortex also contains a number of areas that are specialized for processing specific visual attributes such as color (area **V4**) and movement (area **V5** or MT, standing for medial temporal). To some extent, the brain's strategy for processing information outside of V1 is to "divide and conquer". For example, it is possible to have brain damage that impairs color perception (cerebral **achromatopsia**) or movement perception (cerebral **akinetopsia**) that preserves other visual functions.

Information from V1 is sent in parallel to a number of other regions in the extrastriate cortex, some of which are specialized for processing particular visual attributes (e.g. V5/MT for movement). These extrastriate regions interface with the temporal cortex (involved in object recognition) and parietal cortex (involved in space and attention).

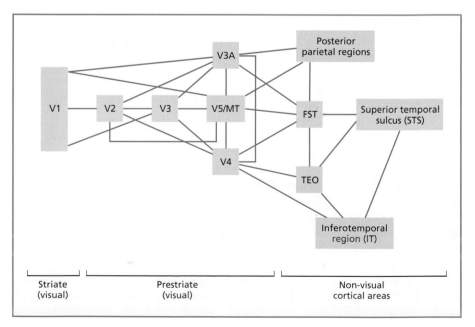

V4: The main color center of the brain

Area V4 is believed to be the main color center in the human brain because lesions to it result in a lack of color vision, so that the world is perceived in shades of gray (Heywood, Kentridge, & Cowey, 1998; Zeki, 1990). This is termed cerebral achromatopsia. It is not to be confused with color blindness in which people (normally men) have difficulty discriminating reds and greens because of a deficiency in certain types of retinal cells. Achromatopsia is rare because there are two V4 areas in the brain and it is unlikely that brain damage would symmetrically affect both hemispheres. Damage to one of the V4s would result in one side of space being seen as colorless (left V4 represents color for the right hemifield and vice versa). Partial damage to V4 can result in colors that appear "dirty" or "washed out" (Meadows, 1974). In people who have not sustained brain injury, area V4 can be identified by functional imaging by comparing viewing patterns of colored squares (so-called Mondrians, because of a similarity to the work of that artist) with their equivalent gray-scale picture (Zeki, Watson, Lueck, Friston, Kennard, & Frackowiak, 1991). The gray-scale pictures are matched for luminance such that if either image were viewed through a black and white camera they would appear identical to each other.

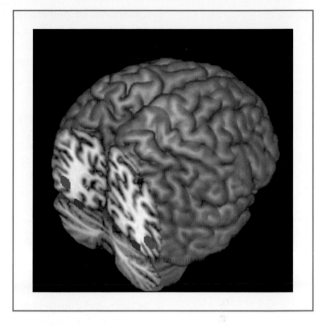

Area V5/MT (in red) lies near the outer surface of both hemispheres and is responsible for perception of visual motion. Area V4 (in blue) lies on the under surface of the brain, in each hemisphere, and is responsible for the perception of color. This brain is viewed from the back.

Why is color so important that the brain would set aside an entire region dedicated to it? Moreover, given that the retina contains cells that detect different wavelengths of visible light, why does the brain need a dedicated color processor at all? To answer both of these questions, it is important to understand the concept of **color constancy**. Color constancy refers to the fact that the color of a surface is perceived as constant even when illuminated in different lighting conditions and even though the physical wavelength composition of light reflected from a surface can be shown (with recording devices) to differ under different conditions. For example, a surface that reflects a high proportion of long-wave "red" light will appear red when illuminated with white, red, green or any other type of light. Color constancy is needed to facilitate recognition of, say, red tomatoes across a wide variety of viewing conditions.

The derivation of color constancy appears to be the function of V4 (Zeki, 1983). Neurons in V4 may achieve this by comparing the wavelength in their receptive fields with the wavelength in other fields. In this way it is possible to compute the color of a surface while taking into account the illuminating conditions (Land, 1964, 1983). Cells in earlier visual regions (e.g. V1) respond only to the local wavelength in their receptive field and their response would change if the light source were changed even if the color of the stimulus was not (Zeki, 1983). Achromatopsic patients with damage to V4 are able to use earlier visual processes that are based on wavelength discrimination in the absence of color experience. For example, patient MS could tell if two equiluminant colored patches were the same or different if they abutted to form a common edge but not if they were separated (Heywood, Cowey, & Newcombe, 1991). This occurs because wavelength comparisons outside of V4 are made at a local level.

It should be pointed out that V4 is not the only color-responsive region of the brain. For example, Zeki and Marini (1998) compared viewing of appropriately colored objects (e.g. red tomato) with inappropriate ones (e.g. blue tomato) and found activation in, amongst other regions, the hippocampus, which may code long-term memory representations.

V5/MT: The main movement center of the brain

If participants in a PET scanner view images of moving dots relative to static dots, a region of the extrastriate cortex called V5 (or MT) becomes particularly active (Zeki et al., 1991). Earlier electrophysiological research on the monkey had found that all cells in this area are sensitive to motion, and that 90% of them respond preferentially to a particular direction of motion and will not respond at all to the opposite direction of motion (Zeki, 1974). None were color-sensitive.

Patient LM lost the ability to perceive visual movement after bilateral damage to area V5/MT (Zihl, von Cramon, & Mai, 1983). This condition is termed akinetopsia (for a review, see Zeki, 1991). Her visual world consists of a series of still frames: objects may suddenly appear or disappear, a car that is distant may suddenly be seen to be near, and pouring tea into a cup would invariably end in spillage as the level of liquid appears to rise in jumps rather than smoothly.

More recent studies have suggested that other types of movement perception do not rely on V5/MT. For example, LM is able to discriminate biological from non-biological motion (McLoed, Dittrich, Driver, Perrett, & Zihl, 1996). The perception of **biological motion** is assessed by attaching light points to the joints and then recording someone walking/running in the dark. When only the light points are viewed, most people are still able to detect bodily movement (relative to a condition in which these moving lights are presented jumbled up). LM could discriminate biological from non-biological motion but could not perceive the overall direction of movement. Separate pathways for this type of motion have been implied by functional imaging (Vaina, Solomon, Chowdhury, Sinha, & Belliveau, 2001).

LM was able to detect movement in other sensory modalities (e.g. touch, audition), suggesting that her difficulties were restricted to certain types of visual movement (Zihl et al., 1983). However, functional imaging studies have identified supramodal regions of the brain that appear to respond to movement in three different senses – vision, touch and hearing (Bremmer et al., 2001). This suggests that V5 is specialized for visual movement.

When this array of dots is set in motion, most people can distinguish between biological and non-biological motion.

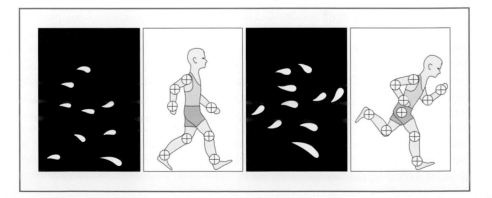

Evaluation

One emerging view of visual processing in the brain beyond V1 is that different types of visual information get parsed into more specialized brain regions. Thus, when one looks at a dog running across the garden, information about its color resides in one region, information about its movement resides in another and information about its identity (this is my dog rather than any dog) resides in yet another, to name but a few. The question of how these different streams of information come back together (if at all) is not well understood, but may require the involvement of non-visual processes related to attention (see Chapter 7).

HOW DOES THE BRAIN RESPOND TO VISUAL ILLUSIONS?

When you look at the top figure do you have a sense of motion in the circles even though the image is static? This image is called the Enigma illusion. When you look at the bottom image do you see one vase or two faces? Does this image appear to spontaneously flip between one interpretation and the other, even though the image remains constant? Examples such as these reveal how the brain's perception of the world can differ from the external physical reality. This is, in fact, a normal part of seeing. Visual illusions are in many respects the norm rather than the exception, even though we are not always aware of them as such.

A PET study has shown that parts of the brain specialized for detecting real movement (area MT/V5) also respond to the Enigma illusion (Zeki, Watson, & Frackowiak, 1993). A recent study suggests that the illusion is driven by tiny adjustments in eye fixation (Troncoso, Macknik, Otero-Millan, & Martinez-Conde, 2008). An fMRI study using stimuli such as the image has shown how different visual and non-visual brain structures cooperate to maintain perceptual stability. The momentary breakdown of activity in these regions is associated with when participants report a perceptual flip (Kleinschmidt, Buchel, & Zeki, 1998).

Do you see movement in the image on the top when you stare at the center? Do you see a vase or faces on the bottom? How does the brain interpret such ambiguities? Top image by Isia Levant, 1981, www. michaelbach. de/ot/mot_enigma/index.html

RECOGNIZING OBJECTS

For visual information to be useful it must make contact with knowledge that has been accumulated about the world. There is a need to recognize places that have been visited and people who have been seen, and to recognize other stimuli in the environment in order to, say, distinguish between edible and non-edible substances. All of these examples can be subsumed under the process of "object recognition". Although different types of object (e.g. faces) may recruit some different mechanisms, there will nevertheless be some common mechanisms shared by all objects, given that they are extracted from the same raw visual information.

The figure below describes four basic stages in object recognition that, terminology aside, bear a close resemblance to Marr's (1976) theory of vision:

1. The earliest stage in visual processing involves basic elements such as edges and bars of various lengths, contrasts and orientations. This stage has already been considered above.

2. Later stages involve grouping these elements into higher-order units that code depth cues and segregate surfaces into figure and ground. Some of these mechanisms were first described by the Gestalt psychologists and are considered below. It is possible that this stage is also influenced by top-down information based on stored knowledge. These visual representations, however, represent objects according to the observer's viewpoint and object constancy is not present.

3. The viewer-centered description is then matched onto stored three-dimensional descriptions of the structure of objects (**structural descriptions**). This store is often assumed to represent only certain viewpoints and thus the matching process entails the computation of object constancy (i.e. an understanding that objects remain the same irrespective of differences in viewing condition). There may be two different routes to achieving object constancy, depending on whether the view is "normalized" by rotating the object to a standard orientation.

4. Finally, meaning is attributed to the stimulus and other information (e.g. the name) becomes available. This will be considered primarily in Chapter 11.

Disorders of object recognition are referred to as visual agnosia, and these have been traditionally subdivided into **apperceptive agnosia** and **associative agnosia**, depending on whether the deficit occurs at stages involved in perceptual processing or stages involving stored visual memory representations (Lissauer, 1890). This classification is perhaps

KEY TERMS

Structural descriptions
A memory representation of the three-dimensional structure of objects.

Apperceptive agnosia
A failure to understand the meaning of objects due to a deficit at the level of object perception.

Associative agnosia
A failure to understand the meaning of objects due to a deficit at the level of semantic memory.

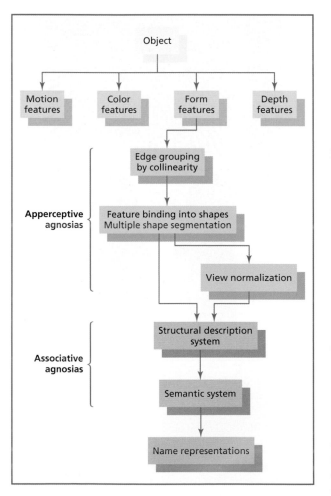

A simple model of visual object recognition. From Riddoch and Humphreys (2001).

too simple to be of much use in modern cognitive neuroscience. Models such as the one of Riddoch and Humphreys (2001) acknowledge that both perception and the stored properties of objects can be broken down into even finer processes. It is also the case that most contemporary models of object recognition allow for interactivity between different processes rather than discrete processing stages. This is broadly consistent with the neuroanatomical data (see earlier) of connections between early and late visual regions and vice versa.

Parts and wholes: Gestalt grouping principles

In the 1930s, Gestalt psychologists identified a number of principles that explain why certain visual features become grouped together to form perceptual wholes. These operations form a key stage in translating simple features into three-dimensional descriptions of the world, essential for object recognition. The process of segmenting a visual display into objects versus background surfaces is also known as **figure–ground segregation**. The Gestalt approach identified five basic principles to account for how basic visual features are combined:

1. *The law of proximity* states that visual elements are more likely to be grouped if they are closer together. For example, the dots in (a) in the figure tend to be perceived as three horizontal lines because they are closer together horizontally than vertically.
2. *The law of similarity* states that elements will be grouped together if they share visual attributes (e.g. color, shape). For example, (b) tends to be perceived as vertical columns rather than rows because elements in columns share both shape and color.
3. *The law of good continuation* states that edges are grouped together to avoid changes or interruptions; thus, (c) is two crossing lines rather than > and <.

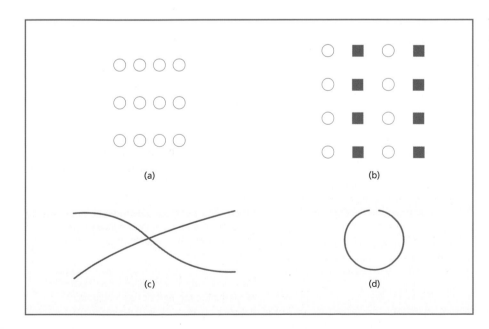

(a)

(b)

(c)

(d)

The Gestalt principles of (a) law of proximity, (b) law of similarity, (c) law of good continuation and (d) law of closure.

4. *The law of closure* states that missing parts are "filled in"; thus (d) has circular properties in spite of the gap. This law, and the previous one, is important for recognizing objects that are partly occluded.
5. *The law of common fate* states that elements that move together tend to be grouped together. A good example of this comes from studies of biological motion perception (e.g. Johansson, 1973). Light points attached to bodily joints are perceived as movement of a single human figure when viewed in the dark.

Case HJA: Seeing the parts but not the whole

Perhaps the most detailed study of visual agnosia in the literature is case HJA, which was reported in a number of studies by Humphreys, Riddoch and colleagues (e.g. Humphreys & Riddoch, 1987; Riddoch, Humphreys, Gannon, Blott, & Jones, 1999). HJA was a businessman who suffered a bilateral stroke that left him with severe difficulties in recognizing objects but with preserved sensory discriminations of length, orientation and position. A number of tests conducted on HJA support the conclusion that he has difficulty in integrating parts into wholes – a type of apperceptive agnosia on the simple model on p. 114. The evidence in support of this interpretation is summarized in the table below. These results support the conclusion that HJA has difficulties in using perceptual grouping mechanisms to translate his intact perception of lines into more complex visual descriptions required to access stored knowledge. His visual system does not permit him to take advantage of Gestalt-based grouping mechanisms that support normal object recognition. Humphreys and Riddoch have termed this **integrative agnosia**. It isn't the case that no grouping at all occurs. There is evidence that local contours may be grouped together but more global grouping mechanisms required for object recognition are compromised (Giersch, Humphreys, Boucart, & Kovacs, 2000). Functional imaging studies of healthy participants show that some local grouping of collinear elements does occur in V1 (spared in HJA) as well as in higher visual areas (Altmann, Bulthoff, & Kourtzi, 2003).

KEY TERM

Integrative agnosia
A failure to integrate parts into wholes in visual perception.

HJA's spared abilities	HJA's impaired abilities
• He is able to copy drawings of objects that he cannot recognize, suggesting that he can "see" them at some level.	• He is unable to recognize pictures but gives a reasonable description of their parts. For example, when shown a carrot: "The bottom point seems solid and the other bits are feathery. It does not seem logical unless it is some sort of brush."
• He is able to draw objects from memory, suggesting that he can access structural descriptions from memory but not vision.	• When shown degraded pictures he does not benefit from Gestalt principles in the same way as other people do (Boucart & Humphreys, 1992).
• He is able to recognize objects from modalities other than vision and has good verbal knowledge about them.	• He is unable to perform an object decision task in which "novel" objects are created by recombining the parts of real objects.

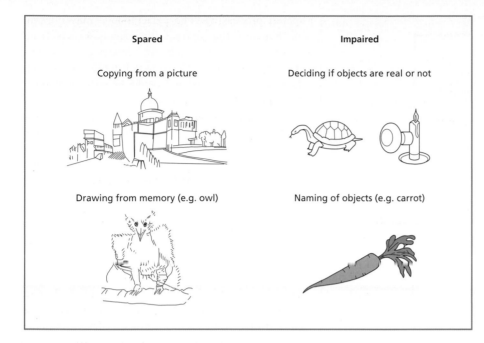

Spared	Impaired
Copying from a picture	Deciding if objects are real or not
Drawing from memory (e.g. owl)	Naming of objects (e.g. carrot)

HJA is impaired at deciding if objects are real or made up and naming objects. However, he can copy drawings and draw objects from memory. Adapted from Humphreys and Riddoch, (1987) and Riddoch and Humphreys (1995).

Accessing structural descriptions: Object constancy

One of the most important aspects of object recognition is to be able to recognize an object across different viewpoints and different lighting conditions – this is termed **object constancy**. It is generally agreed that object constancy is brought about by matching the constructed visual representation with a store of object descriptions in memory that carry information about the invariant properties of objects. One suggestion is that the brain stores only structural descriptions in the usual or canonical view, such that the principal axis is in view. Indeed, naming times for objects presented in usual views are faster (Palmer, Rosch, & Chase, 1981). Clinical tests of object constancy typically involve identifying (i.e. naming) objects drawn from different angles, or matching together different instances of the same object.

A number of different ways in which this matching to memory process might occur have been put forward. Some researchers have argued that object constancy is achieved by matching features or parts of objects to structural descriptions (Biederman, 1987; Warrington & Taylor, 1973). Others have argued that the most important mechanism is more holistic and involves extracting the principal axis of an object (e.g. Marr & Nishihara, 1978). For example, if the principal axis of a tennis racket is viewed from a foreshortened angle it is harder to recognize. Others have suggested that both processes play a role (e.g. Humphreys & Riddoch, 1984; Warrington & James, 1986). The latter seems the most plausible based on the evidence reviewed below.

Some visual agnosic patients are able to recognize and name objects from the usual view but are impaired at recognizing objects presented in unusual views (e.g. Humphreys & Riddoch, 1984; Warrington & Taylor, 1973). This typically occurs after damage to the right parietal lobe, which has a particularly important role in

KEY TERM

Object constancy
An understanding that objects remain the same, irrespective of differences in viewing condition.

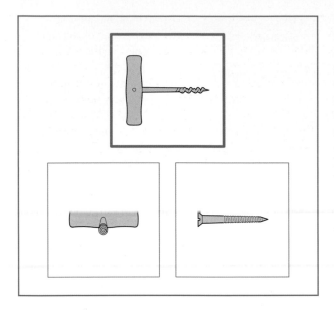

A test of object recognition that requires matching to an unusual view. From Riddoch and Humphreys (1995).

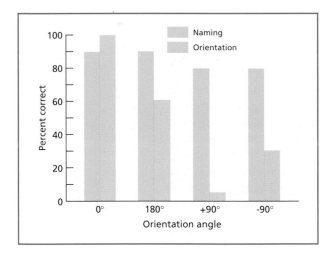

Patient EL could produce the names of items presented in various orientations (green bars), but could not correctly judge whether or not an object was in its correct orientation (purple bars). From Harris et al. (2001). Copyright © The MIT Press. Reproduced with permission.

spatial processing. The parietal lobe may contain mechanisms that extract the principal axis from an object and then rotate the object to a canonical view, thus facilitating matching. Patients with damage to this process would have to rely on a mechanism that is independent of the way that the object is viewed. Thus, in these patients, the route drawn on the right of the model is impaired and the one on the left is spared (p. 114). Other patients may have more subtle damage to this route such that they do not appear to be visually agnosic in tests of object naming or matching, yet they are unable to decide on the correct orientation for an object or even decide whether two simultaneously presented objects have the same orientation (e.g. Harris, Harris, & Caine, 2001; Turnbull, Della Sala, & Beschin, 2002). These striking cases of an inability to extract the orientation of an object despite adequate object recognition have been given the name **object orientation agnosia**. These patients appear to achieve object constancy by using a view-independent route that does not extract the orientation (or principal axis) of objects.

An alternative account for the advantage of usual views is that these are more familiar and have more robust neural representations (Karnath, Ferber, & Bulthoff, 2000; Perrett, Oram, & Wachsmuth, 1998), rather than suggesting two specialized routes. However, recent functional imaging evidence would appear to support the two-routes view, with different hemispheres implicated in each. This evidence is outlined below.

Neural substrates of object constancy

The infero-temporal cortex (IT) takes its input from the geniculostriate pathway and appears to code the type of information important for object constancy. For example, single-cell recordings show that these cells respond to very specific object attributes, and have large receptive fields that almost always cover the fovea and typically extend to both hemifields (Gross, 1992; Gross, Rocha-Miranda, & Bender, 1972). Thus, the neurons tend to code for specific visual information but are less concerned with the location of the object – an ideal condition for computing object constancy.

An fMRI study used pairs of stimuli of the same object that differed in size, viewpoint or exemplar in a similar vein to the clinical tests of object constancy discussed above (Vuilleumier, Henson, Driver, & Dolan, 2002a). The logic behind the experiment is that the response of neurons tends to decrease over time if the "same" stimulus is repeated (priming). Thus, one can correlate reductions in fMRI signal with repetition of particular object attributes (i.e. whether or not "same" refers to the same viewpoint, the same size or the same type of object). It was found that the left infero-temporal (or fusiform) region responds irrespective of viewpoint or size, whereas viewpoint (but not size) was important for the comparable region in the right hemisphere. This is convincing evidence that there are at least two routes to object constancy – one that is sensitive to viewpoint and one that is not.

CATEGORY SPECIFICITY IN VISUAL OBJECT RECOGNITION?

It has already been suggested that higher visual areas of the brain may be specialized for processing particular visual attributes such as color and motion. But are there higher visual areas of the brain that are specialized for recognizing different categories of object such as animals, faces, places, words and bodies? Chapter 1 outlined Fodor's (1983) theory that many cognitive functions are carried out by domain-specific modules. The term "domain-specific" refers to the fact that the module is hypothesized to process one, and only one, type of information (e.g. there may be a module that processes faces but not other types of stimuli). Evidence in favor of this strong position has been mustered from dissociations of spared and impaired performance in the recognition of different classes of object and from the observation that different regions of the brain are optimized for responding to certain classes of stimuli. The notion that the brain represents different categories in different ways is termed **category specificity**. A parallel debate exists in the literature concerning whether the semantic representation of objects is represented categorically (see Chapter 11), as well as for the structural descriptions of objects. The alternative to the domain-specific hypothesis is that different categories of stimuli require somewhat different kinds of processing (e.g. words are recognized by parts, and faces recognized holistically), and that such differences may be relative rather than absolute.

This chapter discusses the domain-specific hypothesis with regards to faces; Chapter 12 discusses a similar proposal with regards to recognizing visual words (e.g. Dehaene, Le Clec'H, Poline, Le Bihan, & Cohen, 2002; Petersen, Fox, Snyder, & Raichle, 1990). However, it is worth noting that functional imaging studies have recently identified other regions that appear to be relatively specialized for the visual recognition of particular categories. These include the *parahippocampal place area* (PPA), which responds to scenes more than objects (e.g. Epstein & Kanwisher, 1998), and the *extrastriate body area* (EBA), which responds to the human body more than to faces, scenes or objects (e.g. Downing, Jiang, Shuman, & Kanwisher, 2001). Although these studies argue in favor of some degree of category specificity, it is unclear whether they support domain-specificity in the strong form (i.e. that the regions are only involved in recognizing stimuli from one category). The strongest evidence for domain specificity in object recognition so far has come from face processing and this is considered next.

KEY TERM

Category specificity
The notion that the brain represents different categories in different ways (and/or different regions).

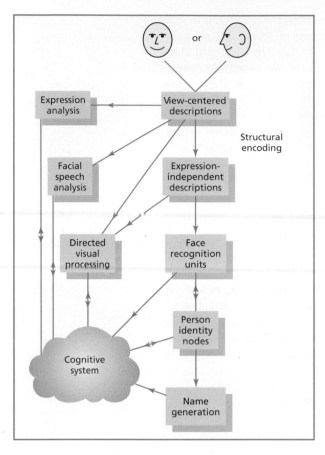

The Bruce and Young (1986) model of face recognition.
From Parkin (1996).

RECOGNIZING FACES

Although faces are a type of visual object like any other, there is some reason to believe that the process of face recognition may be different from other aspects of object recognition. First of all, the goal in face recognition is normally to identify one particular face (e.g. "that is Barack Obama!") rather than categorizing a face as such (e.g. "that visual object is a face!"). Second, researchers have suggested that faces might be "special" either because of the type of processing they require or because they are a distinct category. Although there is good evidence to suggest that faces do have a different neural substrate from most other objects and can be disproportionately spared or impaired, the reasons why this is so remain a matter of controversy.

A basic model of face processing

Bruce and Young (1986) proposed a cognitive model of face recognition that has largely stood the test of time. They assume that the earliest level of processing involves computation of a view-dependent structural description, as postulated for object recognition more generally. Following this, a distinction is made between the processing of familiar and unfamiliar faces. Familiar faces are recognized by matching to a store of face-based structural descriptions (which they term **face recognition units**). Following this, a more abstract level of representation, termed **person identity nodes**, accesses semantic (e.g. their occupation) and name information about that individual. A separate route (termed directed visual processing) was postulated to deal with unfamiliar faces. Benton and Van Allen (1968) devised a test of "face constancy" in which different images of the same unfamiliar face must be matched across lighting conditions and viewpoints. Some patients are able to perform this task but not recognize familiar faces, whereas others show the reverse pattern, suggesting different routes to "face constancy" – one based on matching to stored representations, and the other based – possibly – on processing of facial and external (e.g. hair) features (e.g. Malone, Morris, Kay, & Levin, 1982).

A number of other face-processing routes are postulated to occur in parallel to the route involved in recognizing familiar people. Evidence from neurological patients suggests that recognition of emotional expression, age and gender is independent of familiar face recognition (Tranel, Damasio; & Damasio; 1988 for electrophysiological data, see Hasselmo, Rolls, & Bayliss, 1989), as is the ability to use lip-reading cues (Campbell, Landis, & Regard, 1986).

Evidence that faces are special

The Bruce and Young (1986) model has a number of similarities with models of object recognition, including distinctions between "apperceptive" and "associative" stages, and distinctions between view-independent and view-dependent codes. However, in other respects faces may differ from other objects. Broadly speaking, two lines of evidence have been presented to back up the claim. First, that faces have a distinct neural substrate; second (and related to the first), that faces can thus be selectively impaired.

Impairments of face processing that do not reflect difficulties in early visual analysis are termed **prosopagnosia** (Bodamer, 1947). The term prosopagnosia is also sometimes used specifically to refer to an inability to recognize previously familiar faces. As such, care must be taken to describe the putative cognitive mechanism that is impaired rather than relying on simple labeling. The case study reported by De Renzi (1986) had profound difficulties in recognizing the faces of people close to him, including his family, but could recognize them by their voices or other non-facial

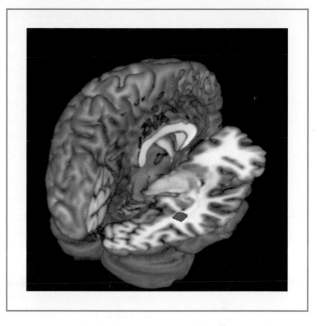

Approximate location of the fusiform face area in the right hemisphere, viewed from the back.

information. He once remarked to his wife: "Are you [wife's name]? I guess you are my wife because there are no other women at home, but I want to be reassured." In contrast, the patient could perform perceptual tests involving faces normally. Within the Bruce and Young (1986) model his deficit would be located at the face recognition unit stage. The patient's ability to recognize and name other objects was spared.

Functional imaging has also suggested that there could be an area of the brain specialized for faces: the so-called "fusiform face area" in the right hemisphere (Kanwisher, 2000; Kanwisher, McDermott, & Chun, 1997). There is still debate concerning whether this region responds to certain other stimuli (e.g. Chao, Martin, & Haxby, 1999) as is discussed in more detail below.

Why are faces special?

This section considers four accounts of why faces might be special. These accounts are not necessarily mutually exclusive and there might be several factors that contribute.

Task difficulty

Faces are complex visual stimuli that are very similar to each other (e.g. they all consist of mouth, nose, eyes, etc.), so are faces special simply by virtue of added task difficulty relative to other kinds of objects? A number of reports of patients with visual agnosia without prosopagnosia would appear to speak against this view (e.g. Rumiati, Humphreys, Riddoch, & Bateman, 1994). Farah, Levinson and Klein (1995a) attempted to address the issue of task difficulty directly by creating an object recognition task (using spectacle frames) of comparable difficulty to a face recognition task in controls (both tasks performed at 85% correct). They found that their prosopagnosic, LH, was impaired on the face task (62%) but not the frames task (92%), ruling out a task difficulty explanation.

Part-based versus holistic perceptual processing

Perhaps faces are treated differently from other types of object because they require a special type of processing, rather than being special because they are faces as such. The most influential theory along these lines has been proposed by Farah (1990; Farah, Wilson, Drain, & Tanaka, 1998). Her thesis is that *all* object recognition lies on a continuum between recognition by parts and recognition by wholes. Recognition of faces may depend more on holistic processing, whereas recognition of written words may depend on more part-based processing (e.g. identifying the sequence of letters in the word); recognition of most other objects lies somewhere in between. Farah's initial source of evidence came from a meta-analysis of cases with visual agnosia, prosopagnosia and difficulties in visual word recognition (pure alexia; see Chapter 12). She found no convincing cases of isolated object agnosia (without prosopagnosia or alexia) or prosopagnosia with alexia (without object agnosia), supporting the claim that these lie on a continuum (Farah, 1990).

Subsequent to this, there have been two reported cases of isolated object agnosia without prosopagnosia or alexia (Humphreys & Rumiati, 1998; Rumiati et al., 1994), a case of isolated object agnosia and alexia without prosopagnosia (Moscovitch, Winocur, & Behrmann, 1997) and a case of prosopagnosia and alexia without object agnosia (De Renzi & di Pellegrino, 1998). These cases support an alternative view in which there are separate stores of structural descriptions for objects, faces and words rather than a continuum between two types of underlying perceptual processes (but see Farah, 1997).

Visual expertise at within-category discrimination

A somewhat different account from that of Farah has been put forward principally by Gauthier and colleagues (Diamond & Carey, 1986; Gauthier & Logothetis, 2000;

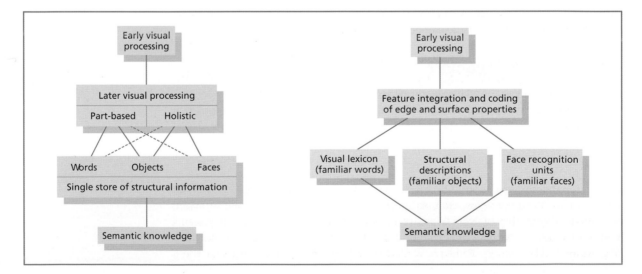

In Farah's model, differences between recognition of words, objects and faces reflects different weightings of part-based versus holistic perception (left). Other models have suggested, on the basis of dissociations between object agnosia, prosopagnosia and alexia, that there may be separate stores of structural knowledge for these categories (right).

Gauthier & Tarr, 1997; Gauthier, Tarr, Anderson, Skudlarski, & Gore, 1999). Their account has two key elements: (1) that faces require discrimination within a category (between one face and another), whereas most other object recognition requires a superordinate level of discrimination (e.g. between a cup and comb); and, consequently, that (2) we become "visual experts" at making these fine within-category distinctions through prolonged experience with thousands of exemplars. Like Farah's explanation, this account assumes that faces are special because of processing demands rather than because faces are a domain-specific category.

Examples of "Greebles". Greebles can be grouped into two genders and come from various families. To what extent does discriminating against greebies resemble discriminating against faces? Images provided courtesy of Michael J. Tarr (Carnegie Mellon University, Pittsburgh), see www. tarrlab.org

The evidence for this theory comes from training participants to become visual experts at making within-category discriminations of non-face objects, called "Greebles". As participants become experts they move from part-based to holistic processing, as has often been proposed for faces (Gauthier & Tarr, 1997). In addition, they have shown that Greeble experts activate the "fusiform face area" (Gauthier et al., 1999) and similar findings have been reported for experts on natural categories such as birds and cars (Gauthier, Skudlarski, Gore, & Anderson, 2000). In addition, Greeble recognition has a characteristic N170 ERP signal normally only found for faces (Rossion, Gauthier, Goffaux, Tarr, & Crommelinck, 2002). Gauthier and Logothetis (2000) conducted similar training studies in monkeys and found that certain cells (claimed to be analogous to face cells) became sensitive to the whole configuration after training even though non-facial stimuli were used.

Faces are a distinct category

Although it might indeed be the case that faces make different processing demands on certain perceptual mechanisms relative to other classes of stimuli, there is some evidence to suggest that these accounts are not sufficient to explain the whole picture. Some have argued that what is additionally required is the assumption that faces really are a distinct category and are represented as such in the adult brain. For example, there is evidence of dissociations between faces and other expert categories from ERP studies (Carmel & Bentin, 2002) and human neuropsychology (McNeil & Warrington, 1993; Sergent & Signoret, 1992). Sergent and Signoret (1992) reported a prosopagnosic patient, RM, who had a collection of over 5000 miniature cars. He was unable to identify any of 300 famous faces, or the face of himself or his wife, or match unfamiliar faces across viewpoints. Nevertheless, when shown 210 pictures of miniature cars he was able to give the company name, and for 172 he could give the model and approximate year of manufacture. Thus, although the "fusiform face area" may tend to represent within-category exemplars (Gauthier et al., 2000), there could still be scope for finer-grained categorical dissociations. McNeil and Warrington (1993) reported patient WJ, who was unable to distinguish previously familiar faces from unfamiliar ones. Following his stroke, he acquired a flock of 36 sheep, which testing revealed that he could distinguish from unfamiliar sheep. This case was taken to support the view that faces are a special category independent of the type of perceptual processing, but skeptics may argue that the sheep recognition task could be performed in different ways (e.g. recognizing markings rather than holistic configuration) or that the level of expertise is not matched (e.g. 36 sheep versus many thousands of faces).

Evaluation

There is good evidence to suggest that face recognition can be spared or impaired relative to the recognition of other objects. To account for this, it might be necessary to assume that faces engage different types of perceptual mechanism related to holistic versus part-based processing and might require expert within-category discriminations. Whereas these accounts might be necessary to explain the data, they might not be sufficient. There remains some evidence to suggest that there is indeed a separate store of structural descriptions for familiar faces.

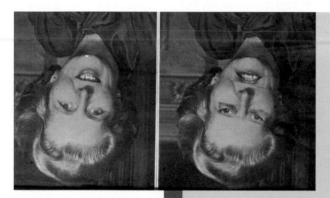

You should recognize this face instantly even if it is upside down. But what is wrong with the image? Turn it the right way up to find out. From Thompson, P. (1980). Copyright © Pion Limited, London. Reproduced with permission.

THE MARGARET THATCHER ILLUSION

What is wrong with this face? Turn it upside down and have a look. In the so-called "Thatcher illusion" the holistic configuration of the face, in its inverted orientation, disrupts the ability to detect local anomalies in the stimulus such as an inversion of the eyes and mouth (Thompson, 1980). The success of the illusion is based on two properties of the face recognition system. First, that faces usually have an upright orientation and may be stored in the brain as such. This explains why the anomaly is detected upon inversion. Second, that faces are processed largely on the basis of surface features and global shape rather than piecemeal from parts.

For most adults, inverted faces are much harder to identify (Yin, 1969). But, prosopagnosic patients such as LH may show no advantage of upright over inverted faces, suggesting this information is lost (Farah, Wilson, Drain, & Tanaka, 1995b). The "correct" upright orientation for a face emerges during the early stages of development rather than being present from birth (Diamond & Carey, 1986). This suggests a role of visual expertise. Indeed, "Greeble" experts also show such an inversion effect (Gauthier & Tarr, 1997).

VISION IMAGINED

Close your eyes and imagine a horse galloping left-to-right through a green field and jumping over a fence. To what extent is this "visual imagery" task achieved by using the same mechanisms used to visually perceive objects, color, movement and so on? At one extreme, imagining scenes such as these may not use any of the same mechanisms as seeing. But why would the brain develop separate mechanisms for seeing a horse and imagining the visual appearance of one? At the other extreme, imagining scenes could use exactly the same mechanisms as visual perception. This, of course, raises the question of how it is possible to distinguish between perception and imagination at all, and what prevents us from lapsing into hallucinatory delirium. As is often the case, the truth may lie somewhere between these extreme viewpoints.

A number of case studies have supported the conclusion that difficulties in visual imagery parallel difficulties in visual perception, such that selective impairments of color, objects, space and so on tend to be found both in perception and in mental imagery. For example, Levine, Warach and Farah (1985) document two patients. The first patient had both prosopagnosia and achromatopsia. This was accompanied by an inability to imagine previously known faces or the colors of objects. The other patient was impaired in spatial aspects of vision (e.g. poor visually guided reaching – optic ataxia). This was accompanied by difficulties in spatial imagery (e.g. poor descriptions of routes). Beauvois and Saillant (1985) also report a patient who could not imagine colors. Given visual imagery strategies (e.g. "imagine a beautiful snowy landscape – what color is the snow?") but could retrieve color "facts" from non-perceptual long-term memory (e.g. "what do people say when asked what color snow is?").

In contrast to these studies showing close imagery–perception parallels, Behrmann, Moscovitch and Winocur (1994) report a study of patient CK that suggests that visual imagery and visual perception can be dissociated. CK was unable to recognize or name objects from vision, although he could recognize them by other means (e.g. touch), and a number of studies suggested that, like HJA, he had integrative agnosia. In contrast to his poor object recognition he could produce detailed drawings of objects from memory and describe the visual appearance of objects. This imagery–perception dissociation can be accounted for by assuming that CK has access to object structural descriptions top-down (i.e. from memory) but not bottom-up (i.e. from visual perception). Similar findings were initially reported for HJA (Humphreys & Riddoch, 1987). However, a subsequent study on HJA some 16 years later suggests that caution is warranted in postulating a strong separation of vision and imagery (Riddoch et al., 1999). Although HJA could initially draw accurately from memory, this ability receded over time (but his memory, in general, remained intact). Presumably, visual input is needed to maintain the structural descriptions over longer periods of time.

The studies above suggest that visual imagery for properties such as color and object shape is normally related to the ability to perceive those characteristics, although the two may occasionally be disconnected. A more controversial claim that has been made about mental imagery is that the primary visual cortex (V1) is necessary for it (Kosslyn, Thompson, Kim, & Alpert, 1995; Kosslyn et al., 1999; Kosslyn, Ganis, & Thompson, 2001). Kosslyn et al. (1995) compared an imagery condition of visualizing objects of different sizes relative to a

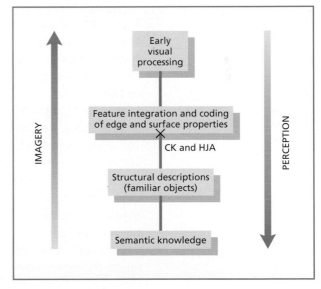

Imagery may involve some of the same structures as perception, but activated in the reverse ("top-down") direction. CK and HJA can use intact knowledge of object structure to perform the imagery task despite poor perceptual integration. But does imagery need to go back as far as early visual processing in V1?

non-imagery baseline. They found that there was activity in V1 and, moreover, that the locus of activity was related to the size of the imagined stimulus. (Recall that V1 is retinotopically organized so that images that cover a large area on the retina will cover a large area on V1.) To establish the functional necessity of V1 for imagery, Kosslyn et al. (1999) conducted a TMS study on participants who were making imagery judgments about a previously learned array of line gratings (e.g. parallel lines of different width, length and orientation). They found that TMS over V1 did indeed disrupt mental imagery.

How is it possible to reconcile the finding of Kosslyn and colleagues, suggesting that early perceptual processes are important for imagery, with other studies suggesting that later visual processes (e.g. those supporting color or object recognition) are the critical ones? The solution may lie in considering the *content* of the images. Kosslyn's experiments involved imagery for lines and retinal size for which V1 may be important, whereas other studies involved imagery for faces, objects, spatial location and colors, which are less likely to depend on V1 when activated top-down. Thus, the extent to which different perceptual regions are involved in imagery may be related to the different content of what is being imagined.

SUMMARY AND KEY POINTS OF THE CHAPTER

- The primary visual cortex (V1) contains a spatial map based on the retinal image and detects edges and boundaries within the visual scene.
- The primary visual cortex may be necessary for conscious awareness of vision. Damage to this area can lead to a condition called blindsight, in which conscious experiences of vision are abolished, although some visual processing in the "blind" region is still computed by routes that bypass V1.
- Later visual regions are specialized for analyzing particular visual attributes such as color (area V4) and motion (area V5/MT).
- The ability to recognize objects from a wide variety of views (object constancy) may arise from matching visual features to a stored representation of objects or from mentally rotating the seen object to a standard viewpoint. Basic categorical recognition of objects implicates inferotemporal processing, whereas recognizing the orientation may involve the parietal lobes.
- The processing of faces relative to other objects may, to some degree, utilize different neural substrates and cognitive resources. Faces may make more demands on holistic processes, and typically require individuation of particular exemplars. It is also possible that faces are special because they are an evolutionarily salient category.
- Mental imagery utilizes many of the same resources as actually perceiving and, like vision itself, different types of image (e.g. of color, objects, lines) may have different neural substrates.

EXAMPLE ESSAY QUESTIONS

- What is "blindsight"? What can studying blindsight tell us about the normal visual system?
- To what extent is the primary visual cortex (V1) necessary for visual perception?
- One function of the visual system is to extract constant properties of a stimulus independently from moment-to-moment fluctuations in viewing conditions. Explain how the brain achieves this, using the examples of color constancy and object constancy.
- Are faces "special"? If so, why?
- To what extent is visually imagining like visually perceiving?

RECOMMENDED FURTHER READING

- Farah, M. J. (2000). *The cognitive neuroscience of vision*. Oxford: Blackwell. This book provides excellent coverage of most topics covered in this chapter and a few vision-related topics covered elsewhere (e.g. space and attention; visual word recognition).

- Peterson, M. A. & Rhodes, G. (2003). *Perception of faces, objects and scenes: Analytic and holistic processes*. Oxford: Oxford University Press. An up-to-date collection of papers that will be of interest to students wanting to pursue more advanced reading.

- Zeki, S. (1993). *A vision of the brain*. Oxford: Blackwell. This is a thorough account of the neuroscience of vision from an historical and contemporary perspective. It is particularly strong on single-cell data and early stages of visual processing.

CHAPTER 7

CONTENTS

The spatial brain

Where is my left hand now? Where is the glass in relation to the plate? How far away from me is the plate? Where is the nearest bank? Questions such as these all involve some appreciation of where things are located in space. However, the computational demands placed on the brain in each of these instances is quite different. For example, knowing where objects are in immediate space and where body parts are currently located may place more reliance on sensory maps of space. These sensory maps of space are often coded relative to the position of the body (so-called **egocentric space**) or eye gaze (so-called **retinocentric space**). In contrast, knowing the way to the nearest bank may rely on more abstract memory maps of space. Finding the location of one object relative to another (so-called **allocentric space**) may involve a different computation from finding the location of one object relative to oneself (in egocentric space). One of the main take-home messages from this chapter will be that the brain represents space at different levels of abstraction and in different ways. Space, as far as the brain goes, is not a single continuous entity.

One other critical property of space, from the brain's point of view, is that it is a common dimension of most perceptual systems and also of our motor/action system. For example, imagine that a cat comes and sits on the table next to you. You may apprehend its location via sight, sound (if it purrs), touch (if you reach out to it) or even by smell. Space is a common dimension of all these systems and the brain uses this property of perceptual systems as a way of integrating information across sensory modalities (so-called **cross-modal perception**).

Space may be important not only for integrating information across the senses but also for prioritizing incoming information. Our perceptual systems are unable to process fully all the information that they receive at a given point in time. The problem is solved by selectively processing information in particular regions of space and filtering out other information. This process is referred to as spatial attention. As such, any discussion of the way that the brain represents space typically also involves a discussion of attentional mechanisms in the brain. Indeed, this shall be the starting point of our journey into space.

A SPOTLIGHT ON ATTENTION

Attention is the process by which certain information is selected for further processing and other information is discarded. Attention is needed to avoid sensory overload. The brain does not have the capacity to fully process all the information it receives. Nor would it be efficient for it to do so. As such, attention is often likened to a filter or a bottleneck in processing (e.g. Broadbent, 1958).

In terms of visual attention, one of the most pervasive metaphors is to think about attention in terms of a spotlight. The spotlight may highlight a particular location in space (e.g. if that location contains a salient object) it may move from one location to another (e.g. when searching) and it may even zoom in or out

WOULD WE NOTICE A GORILLA IN OUR MIDST?

Although most of us would confess to the occasional amnesia (forgetfulness) or aphasia (slips of the tongue), we often – erroneously – think of our visual system as infallible. The richness of our visual experiences leads us to believe that they will always be accurate. If we were watching a game of basketball and someone in a gorilla costume walked between the players, surely we would be aware of it? But if you were concentrating on your game, then there is a high probability (50%) that you would not notice it (Simons & Chabris, 1999). This phenomenon is termed **inattentional blindness**. There is a limited capacity of information that one can be aware of, and concentrating on the game utilizes much of this capacity. This limited capacity system is associated with attention. A related phenomenon is **change blindness**, in which participants fail to notice the appearance/disappearance of objects between two alternating images (Rensink, O'Regan, & Clark, 1997) or even when the person serving you in a shop briefly disappears from view and another person reappears to continue the interaction (Simons & Levin, 1998). Functional imaging suggests an involvement of non-visual parietal areas in change detection that is consistent with attentional effects (Beck, Rees, Frith, & Lavie, 2001).

When concentrating on counting the passes in a basketball game, many people fail to notice the arrival of the gorilla! This study shows that much visual processing can occur without awareness, particularly if our attention is focused on a demanding task. Figure provided by Daniel Simons. Copyright © 1999 Daniel J. Simons. Reproduced with permission of the author.

KEY TERMS

Inattentional blindness
A failure to consciously see something because attention is directed away from it.

Change blindness
Participants fail to notice the appearance/disappearance of objects between two alternating images.

(e.g. La Berge, 1983). The locus of the attentional spotlight need not necessarily be the same as the locus of eye fixation. It is possible, for example, to look straight ahead whilst focusing attention to the left or right (when "looking out of the corner of one's eyes"). However, there is a natural tendency for attention and eye fixation to go together because visual acuity (discriminating fine detail) is greatest at the point of fixation. It is important not to take the spotlight metaphor too literally. For example, there is evidence to suggest that attention can be split between two non-adjacent locations (Castiello & Umiltà, 1992). The most useful aspects of the spotlight metaphor are to emphasize the notion of limited capacity (not everything is illuminated), and to emphasize the spatial characteristics of attention.

Posner described a classic study to illustrate that attention operates on a spatial basis (Posner, 1980; Posner & Cohen, 1984). The participants were presented with three boxes on the screen in different positions: left, central and right. The task of the participants was simply to press a button when they detected a target in one

WHY DO ACTORS MAKE A HIDDEN ENTRANCE FROM STAGE RIGHT?

It is generally believed that the right hemisphere is more specialized for spatial processing than the left hemisphere, in that the right hemisphere represents left space and, to a lesser extent, right space, whereas the left hemisphere tends to represent right space alone (e.g. Mesulam, 1999). One consequence of this is that right-hemisphere lesions have severe consequences for spatial attention, particularly for the left of space (as in the condition of "neglect"). Another consequence of right-hemisphere spatial dominance is that, in a non-lesioned brain, there is *over-attention* to the left side of space (termed **pseudoneglect**). For example, there is a general tendency for everyone to bisect lines more to the left of center (Bowers & Heilman, 1980). This phenomenon may explain why actors enter from stage right when they do not wish their entrance to be noticed (Dean, 1946). It may also explain why pictures are more likely to be given titles referring to objects on the left, and why the left side of pictures feels nearer than the right side of the same picture when flipped (Nelson & MacDonald, 1971). The light in paintings is more likely to come from the left side and people are faster at judging the direction of illumination when the source of light appears to come from the left (Sun & Perona, 1998). Moreover, we are less likely to bump into objects on the left than the right (Turnbull & McGeorge, 1998). Thus, there is a general leftwards attentional bias in us all.

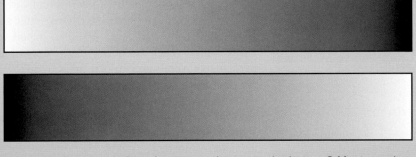

Which bar appears darker: the one on the top or the bottom? Most people perceive the bottom bar as being darker because of an attentional bias to the left caused by a right-hemisphere dominance for space/attention, even though the two images are identical mirror images. From Nicholls et al. (1999). Copyright © Elsevier. Reproduced with permission.

KEY TERM

Pseudoneglect
In a non-lesioned brain there is over-attention to the left side of space.

Attention has been likened to a spotlight that highlights certain information or a bottleneck in information processing. But how do we decide which information to select and which to ignore?

of the boxes. On "catch trials" no target appeared. At a brief interval before the onset of the target, a cue would also appear in one of the locations. The purpose of the cue was to summon attention to that location. On some trials the cue would be in the same box as the target and on others it would not. As such, the cue is completely uninformative with regards to the later position of the target. When the cue precedes the target by up to 150 ms, participants are significantly faster at detecting the target at that location. The cue captured the attentional spotlight and this facilitated subsequent perceptual processing at that location. At longer delays (above 300 ms) the reverse pattern is found: participants are slower at detecting a target in the same location as the cue. This can be explained by assuming that the spotlight initially shifts to the cued location but if the target does not appear, attention shifts to another location (called "disengagement"). There is a processing cost in terms of reaction time associated with going back to the previously attended location. This is called **inhibition of return**. More recent research has suggested that inhibition of return is partly related to the spatial location itself and partly related to the object that happens to occupy that location (e.g. Tipper, Driver, & Weaver, 1991). If the object moves, then the inhibition can also move with the object rather than remaining entirely at the initial location.

How does the spotlight know where to go? Who controls the spotlight? In the Posner spatial cueing task, the spotlight is attracted by a sudden change in the periphery. That is, attention is externally guided. This is referred to as **exogenous orienting**. However, it is also possible for attention to be guided, to some degree, by the goals of the perceiver. This is referred to as **endogenous orienting**. La Berge (1983) presented participants with words and varied the instructions. In one instance, they were asked to attend to the central letter and on another occasion they were asked to attend to the whole word. When attending to the central letter, participants were faster at making judgments about that letter but not other letters in the word. In contrast, when asked to attend to the whole word they were faster at making judgments about all the letters. Thus, the attentional focus can be manipulated by the demands of the task.

Another commonly used paradigm that uses endogenous attention is called **visual search**. In visual search experiments, participants are asked to detect the presence or absence of a specified target object (e.g. the letter F) in an array of other distracting objects (e.g. the letters E and T). One influential theory of how we find targets in a cluttered field is

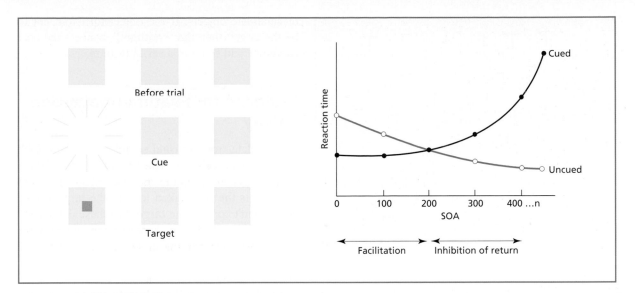

Subjects initially fixate at the central box. A brief cue then appears as a brightening of one of the peripheral boxes. After a delay (called the "stimulus onset asynchrony", or SOA), the target then appears in the cued or uncued box. Subjects are faster at detecting the target in the cued location if the target appears soon after the cue (facilitation) but are slower if the target appears much later (inhibition). From Posner and Cohen (1984). Reprinted with permission from Lawrence Erlbaum Associates, Inc.

referred to as Feature-Integration Theory, or FIT (e.g. Treisman, 1988; Treisman & Gelade, 1980). This theory is not only a theory of spatial (visual) attention but also a theory of how we combine the different attributes that make up objects (e.g. its form, color and location). This theory will be considered in the next section.

ATTENDING TO VISUAL OBJECTS: FEATURE-INTEGRATION THEORY

Look at the two arrays of letters in the figure overleaf. Your task is to try to find the blue "T" as quickly as possible. Was the letter relatively easy to find in the first array but hard to find in the second array? In the second case, did you feel as if you were searching each location in turn until you found it? In the first array, the target object (the blue T) does not share any features with the distractor objects in the arrays (red Ts and red Ls). The object can therefore be found from a simple inspection of the perceptual mechanism that supports color detection. According to Feature-Integration Theory (FIT), perceptual features such as color and shape are coded in parallel and prior to attention (Treisman, 1988; Treisman & Gelade, 1980). If an object does not share features with other objects in the array it appears to "**pop-out**". In the second array, the distractors are made up of the same features that define the object. Thus, the object cannot be detected by inspecting the color module alone (because some distractors are blue) or by inspecting the shape module alone (because some distractors are T shaped). To detect the target one needs to bring together information about several features (i.e. a conjunction of color *and* shape). FIT assumes that this occurs by allocating spatial attention to the location

KEY TERM

Pop-out
The ability to detect an object amongst distractor objects in situations in which the number of distractors presented is unimportant.

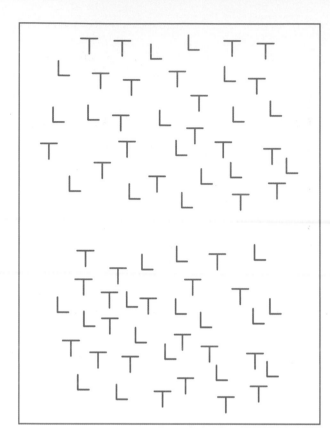

Try to find the blue "T" as quickly as possible. Why is one condition harder than the other? Feature-Integration Theory assumes that basic features are coded in parallel but that focused attention requires serial search. When the letter differs from others by a single feature, such as color, then it can be identified quickly by the initial stage of feature detection. When the letter differs from others by two or more features, then attention is needed to serially search.

of candidate objects. If the object turns out not to be the target, then the "spotlight" inspects the next candidate and so on in a serial fashion.

Evidence for Feature-Integration Theory

Typical data from a visual search experiment such as the one conducted by Treisman and Gelade (1980) is presented on the next page. The dependent measure is the time taken to find the target (some arrays don't contain the target but these data aren't presented here). The variables manipulated were the number of distractors in the array and the type of distractor. When the target can only be found from a conjunction of features, then the greater the number of distractors, the slower the search. This is consistent with the notion that each candidate object must be serially inspected in turn. When a target can be found from only a single feature, it makes very little difference how many distractors are present because it "pops out".

If attention is not properly deployed, then individual features may incorrectly combine. These are referred to as **illusory conjunctions**. For example, if displays of colored letters are presented briefly so that serial search with focal attention cannot take place, then subjects may incorrectly say that they had seen a red "H" when in fact they had been presented with a blue "H" and a red "E" (Treisman & Schmidt, 1982). This supports the conclusion arising from FIT that attention needs to be deployed to combine features of the same object correctly.

Evidence against Feature-Integration Theory

One difficulty with FIT is that there is no *a priori* way to define what constitutes a "feature". Features tend to be defined in a *post hoc* manner according to whether or not they elicit pop-out. In the example presented on the next page, it is generally assumed that the features consist of lines (e.g. vertical line, horizontal line) rather than letters (i.e. clusters of lines). However, some evidence does not support this assumption. For example, searching for an L amongst Ts is hard if the T is rotated at 180 or 270 degrees, and easier if the T is rotated at 0 or 90 degrees (Duncan & Humphreys, 1989). This occurs even though the basic features (horizontal and vertical lines) are equally present in them all. Duncan and Humphreys (1989) suggest that most of the data that FIT attempts to explain can also be explained in terms of how easy it is to perceptually group objects together rather than in terms of parallel feature perception followed by serial attention. They found that it is not just the similarity between the target and distractor that is important but also the similarity between different types of distractor. This implies that there is some feature binding prior to attention and this contradicts a basic assumption of FIT.

Finally, FIT is an example of what has been termed an **early selection** model of attention. Recall that the main reason for having attentional mechanisms is to select some information for further processing, at the expense of other information. According to early selection theories, information is selected according to perceptual attributes (e.g. color or pitch). This can be contrasted with **late selection** theories that assume that all incoming information is processed up to the level of meaning (semantics) before being selected for further processing (Styles, 2006, has a very accessible review of this debate). One of the most frequently cited examples of late selection is the **negative priming** effect (Tipper, 1985). Subjects must name the red object and ignore the blue one (see the figure overleaf). If the ignored object suddenly becomes the attended object, then participants are slower at naming it (called negative priming). The effect can also be found if the critical object is from the same semantic category. This suggests that the ignored object was, in fact, processed meaningfully rather than being excluded purely on the basis of its color as would be expected by early selection theories such as FIT.

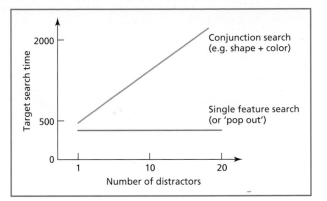

According to FIT, when a target is defined by a conjunction of features, search becomes slower when there are more items because the items are searched serially. When a target is defined by a single feature it may "pop out"; that is, the time taken to find it is not determined by the number of items in the array.

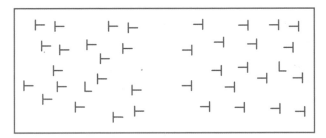

Searching for an L amongst Ts is hard if the T is rotated at 180 or 270 degrees (left), but easier if the T is rotated at 0 or 90 degrees (right). It suggests that features in visual search consist of more than oriented lines, or that some form of feature integration takes place without attention.

Evaluation

How can the evidence both for and against FIT be reconciled? The selection of objects for further processing may sometimes be early (i.e. based on perceptual features) and sometimes late (i.e. based on meaning), depending on the demands

---

KEY TERMS

Early selection
A theory of attention in which information is selected according to perceptual attributes.

Late selection
A theory of attention in which all incoming information is processed up to the level of meaning (semantics) before being selected for further processing.

Negative priming
If an ignored object suddenly becomes the attended object, then participants are slower at processing it.

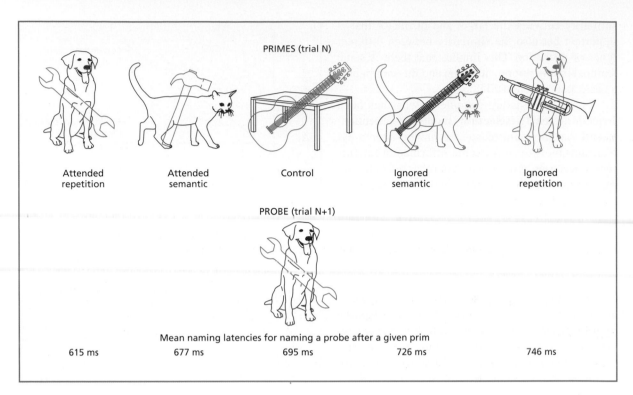

PRIMES (trial N)

| Attended repetition | Attended semantic | Control | Ignored semantic | Ignored repetition |

PROBE (trial N+1)

Mean naming latencies for naming a probe after a given prim

| 615 ms | 677 ms | 695 ms | 726 ms | 746 ms |

In this example, participants must name the red object and ignore the blue one. If an ignored object becomes an attended object on the subsequent trial, then there is cost of processing, which is termed negative priming.

of the task. Lavie (1995) has shown that, when there is a high perceptual load (e.g. the large arrays typically used for visual search), then selection may be early but in conditions of low load in which few objects are present (as in the negative priming task), then there is a capacity for all objects to be processed meaningfully consistent with late selection. Other findings have suggested that the process of feature binding may also operate at several levels (Humphreys, Cinel, Wolfe, Olson, & Klempen, 2000), with some forms of binding occurring prior to attention. This could account for the distractor similarity effects of Duncan and Humphreys (1989).

SPACE, ATTENTION AND THE PARIETAL LOBES

Having considered some of the main evidence for spatially-selective attentional mechanisms, this section will now go on to consider the neural basis of these processes. A number of regions are likely to be implicated in spatial behavior and attention, but the parietal lobes are considered to have a particularly important role.

From early visual processing in the occipital cortex, two important pathways can be distinguished that may be specialized for different types of information (e.g. Ungerleider & Mishkin, 1982). A ventral route (or "what" pathway) leading into the temporal lobes may be concerned with identifying objects. In contrast, a dorsal route (or "where" pathway) leading in to the parietal lobes may be specialized for locating objects in space. The latter route may also guide action towards objects and some researchers also consider it a "how" pathway as well as "where" (see Chapter 8).

Single-cell recordings from the parietal lobes of monkeys have identified neurons that combine visual spatial information with postural information (Andersen, Snyder, Li, & Stricanne, 1993). This is essential for locating objects in external space because a location on the retina can't be used to locate an object in space without taking into account the position of the eyes, head and body at the particular point in time. Moreover, parietal neurons tend to respond according to behavioral saliency of a stimulus (e.g. if it has an abrupt onset

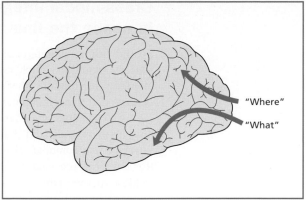

or is relevant to the task) rather than mere presence in the receptive field (Gottlieb, Kusunoki, & Goldberg, 1998). This is consistent with a role in selective attention. The left and right parietal lobes contain more neurons that selectively respond to right and left space, respectively (although it is not completely lateralized, the right hemisphere contains some right responding neurons and the left hemisphere has some left responding ones). In keeping with this, patients with lesions to the posterior parietal lobe can present with a syndrome called hemispatial **neglect**, in which they fail to attend to stimuli on the opposite side of space to the lesion. Neglect is normally far more severe following right hemisphere lesions, resulting in failure to attend to the left. This suggests that, in humans, there is likely to be a hemispheric asymmetry such that the right parietal lobe is more specialized for spatial representation than the left (e.g. Pouget & Driver, 2000).

With regards to the Posner spatial cueing task (see p. 133), it has been suggested that the parietal lobes are not critical for the initial orienting to the cue but are necessary to disengage attention (Posner & Petersen, 1990). When given a brief cue flashed to either the left or right side, the neglect patients may engage attention and move their eyes to the side normally. However, if the cue orients them to the right and then the target appears on the left (the neglected side), they may fail to detect it. The fact that patients can detect targets on the left when cued to the left suggests that the deficit is indeed related to shifting of attention rather than a problem of initial perception.

With regards to the Treisman-style visual search tasks (see p. 134), TMS applied over the parietal lobe slows conjunction searches but not single-feature searches (Ashbridge, Walsh, & Cowey, 1997; Ashbridge, Cowey, & Wade 1999) and a PET study has demonstrated parietal involvement in conjunction but not single-feature searches (Corbetta, Schulman, Miezin, & Petersen, 1995). Patients with parietal lesions often show a high level of illusory conjunction errors on these tasks (e.g. Friedman-Hill, Robertson, & Treisman, 1995). The precise role played by the parietal lobes in visual search tasks is hard to pinpoint because there are several candidate mechanisms, including spatial working memory, attentional engagement and disengagement and multi-sensory integration. Indeed, each of these mechanisms may depend on the parietal lobes to some extent. These will be considered in more detail in the light of neuropsychological data. Before turning to this, however, the next section considers how the parietal lobes and attentional mechanisms are involved in modalities other than vision.

After early visual processing, there are separate routes specialized for identifying objects (the "what" route) and locating objects (the "where" route). In some forms of brain damage, it is possible to perceive objects without knowing where they are.

KEY TERM

Neglect
A failure to attend to stimuli on the opposite side of space to the lesion.

Cross-modal integration:
Is space the final frontier?

Spatial frames of reference may be used to integrate information from different sensory modalities such as hearing, touch and vision. Mechanisms of selective attention that bind together different visual features (as in the FIT model) may also be extended to explain the binding of features across different senses (e.g. when listening to someone speak and watching their lip movements). Single-cell data from animals have indicated that regions in the parietal cortex act as a multi-sensory interface that combines visual, somatosensory (touch), auditory and postural signals (for a review, see Andersen, 1997). These multi-modal cells have similar receptive fields across modalities. So provided that a stimulus is at the critical location, it may not matter whether the stimulus itself is, say, visual or auditory in nature.

A number of experimental findings also suggest that different sensory modalities may tap a common attentional/spatial resource. Earlier research based on dual-task interference (i.e. the extent to which it is possible to do two things at once) suggested that there might be different attentional resources for each sense (Wickens, 1980). However, there can indeed be significant dual-task effects when spatial factors are considered. If one is attending to a visual target, then auditory distraction coming from the same location can affect performance (Driver & Spence, 1994).

HOW IS THE BRAIN FOOLED BY A VENTRILOQUIST?

In ventriloquism, there is a conflict between the actual source of a sound (the ventriloquist him or herself) and the apparent source of the sound (the dummy). In this instance, the sound appears to come from the dummy because the dummy has associated lip movements whereas the lip movements of the ventriloquist are suppressed. In other words, the spatial location of the visual cue "captures" the location of the sound. The same effect is found at cinemas in which the speakers are located at the sides but the sounds can subjectively appear to be coming out of the central screen.

This **ventriloquist effect** has been studied inside the laboratory and provides important clues about how the brain integrates information across modalities and creates a coherent sense of space. Witkin, Wapner and Leventhal (1952) found that sound localization was impaired in the presence of a visual cue in a conflicting location.

Why is it that sound tends to be captured by the visual stimulus but not vice versa? One explanation is that the ability to locate things in space is more accurate with vision than audition, so when there is a mismatch between them, the brain may default to the visual location. Driver and Spence (1994) found that people are able to repeat back a speech stream (or "shadow") more accurately when lip movements and the loudspeaker are on the same side of space than when they are on opposite sides.

KEY TERM

Ventriloquist effect
A tendency to mis-localize heard sounds onto a seen source of potential sounds.

In the brain, there are multi-sensory regions such as in the superior temporal sulcus and parietal regions that respond selectively to sound and vision when both occur at the same time in the same location (Calvert, 2001). The activity in response to sound and vision together may be greater than the sum of the individual responses to sound and vision in isolation (i.e. the effects are super-additive). These regions may be important for tasks such as lip reading, although they are not necessarily specialized for this purpose (they respond to a range of other stimuli and not just speech). When the sound and the visual cue are in different locations, as in ventriloquism, then right parietal regions are implicated (Macaluso, George, Dolan, Spence, & Driver, 2004).

More bizarrely, there is an analogue of the "ventriloquist effect" in the tactile modality. Botvinick and Cohen (1998) placed participants' hands under a table and out of sight and placed a rubber hand on top of the table and in view. Watching the rubber hand stimulated whilst their own (unseen) hand was stimulated could induce a kind of "out of body" experience. Participants report curious sensations such as, "I felt as if the rubber hands were my hands." In this instance, there is a conflict between visual and tactile location and the conflict is resolved by visual capture of the tactile sensation.

LOSING SPACE: SEEING ONE OBJECT AT A TIME

The idea that one could perceive an object but not its location is highly counter-intuitive, because it falls outside of the realm of our own experiences. However, there is no reason why the functioning of the brain should conform to our intuitions. Patients with **Balint's syndrome** typically have damage to both the left and the right parietal lobes and have severe spatial disturbances (Balint, 1909, translated 1995). Patients with Balint's syndrome may notice only one object at a time. For example, the patient may notice a window, then, all of a sudden, the window disappears and a necklace is seen, although it is unclear who is wearing it. After gazing for a while, a refreshing cup of tea may be observed but the patient may not be able to pick it up properly because he or she cannot adequately work out where it is. It is as if there is no "there" there (Robertson, 2004). The syndrome itself consists of several symptoms, and it is more helpful to consider these as being related to separate mechanisms within the parietal lobes even though they all involve some computation of space. In this section, **simultanagnosia** is primarily the symptom of interest. Optic ataxia is considered in Chapter 8.

Although the condition is rare, studies of individual cases have revealed important clues about how we all perceive space. For example, patient RM has been extensively studied by Robertson and colleagues (e.g. Robertson, 2004; Robertson, Treisman, Friedman-Hill, & Grabowecky, 1997). RM was unable to locate objects verbally, or by reaching or pointing. In contrast, his basic visual

KEY TERMS

Balint's syndrome
A severe difficulty in spatial processing normally following bilateral lesions of parietal lobe; symptoms include simultanagnosia, optic ataxia and optic apraxia.

Simultanagnosia
Inability to perceive more than one object at a time.

> ## THREE CLINICAL CHARACTERISTICS OF BALINT'S SYNDROME
>
> 1. Inability to perceive more than one object at a time (simultanagnosia)
> 2. Inability to reach in the proper direction for an object under visual guidance (optic ataxia)
> 3. Fixation of gaze without a primary deficit of eye movement (optic apraxia)

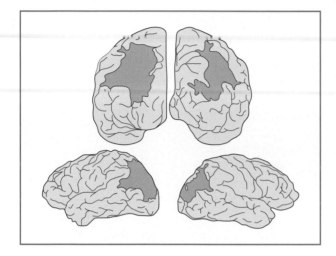

RM has extensive damage to both the left and right parietal lobes and severe difficulties in perceiving spatial relationships (top diagrams are viewed from the back of the brain; bottom diagrams are viewed from the side). Adapted from Robertson (2004).

abilities were normal (normal 20/15 visual acuity, normal color vision, contrast sensitivity, etc.). He was impaired at locating sounds, too. He was, however, able to state which parts of his body had been touched (e.g. left, right hand) and could follow commands to, say, touch his upper left arm with his right index finger. This suggests that spatial frames for the body had been preserved. The opposite dissociation has been reported in another patient with parietal damage (although not with Balint's syndrome; Stark, Coslett, & Saffran, 1996). The brain appears to contain different mechanisms for computing body space and external space.

To say that Balint's patients can recognize single objects but cannot compute spatial relationships leads to some potential ambiguities. Consider a face. Is a face a single object or a collection of several objects (eyes, nose, mouth, etc.) arranged in a particular spatial configuration? A number of factors appear to determine whether parts are grouped together or not. Humphreys et al. (2000) showed that in their Balint's patient, GK, parts are likely to be grouped into wholes if they share shape, if they share color or if they are connected together. This suggests that some early feature binding is possible prior to attention, and this may be related to Gestalt principles (see Chapter 6). Another factor that determines grouping of parts into wholes is the familiarity of the stimulus and how a given stimulus is interpreted (so-called top-down influences). Shalev and Humphreys (2002) presented GK with the ambiguous stimuli on the next page. When asked whether the two circles were at the top or bottom of the oval he was at chance (55%). He performed the task well (91%) when asked whether the eyes were at the top or bottom of the face.

Finally, it is a moot point as to whether these patients should be considered to have deficits of spatial attention or whether the medium of spatial representation itself has been lost. These two ways of thinking are clearly related because spatial representations may be the medium over which attention operates, so without the former there cannot be the latter. Indeed, Balint's patients show an interesting parallel to inattention errors exhibited by normal participants. Recall that if a blue H and a red E are presented very quickly to normal participants, then illusory conjunction errors may be reported (e.g. red H). Balint's patients show these errors even when they are free to view objects for as long as they like (e.g. Friedman-Hill et al., 1995). This suggests that a spatial representation is not only needed to appreciate the spatial relationship between objects but also to support the kinds of processes needed to bind individual object features together.

LOSING HALF OF SPACE: SPATIAL FRAMES AND NEGLECT

Patients with neglect (also called hemispatial neglect, visuospatial neglect or visual neglect) fail to attend to stimuli on the opposite side of space to their lesion – normally a right-sided lesion resulting in inattention to the left side of space. This could conceivably arise from disruption of a number of different mechanisms, including a loss of neurons dedicated to representing parts of space, a failure to shift attention to one side of space (the explanation favored by Posner & Petersen, 1990) or some combination of the two. To some extent, Balint's syndrome could be considered a double form of neglect (left + right), although this may be an oversimplification (see Robertson, 2004).

What is neglect?

There are a number of common ways of testing for neglect. Patients may omit features from the left side when drawing or copying. In tests of **line bisection**, patients tend to misplace the center of the line towards the right (because they underestimate the extent of the left side). The bias in bisection is proportional to the length of the line (Marshall & Halligan, 1990). **Cancellation tasks** are a variant of the visual search paradigms already discussed, in which the patients must search for targets in an array (normally

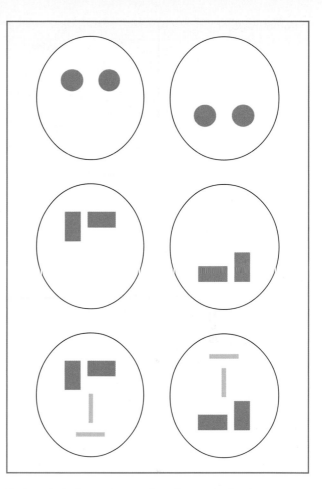

Under what circumstances is a face perceived as a whole or as a collection of parts? Patient GK can identify the location of the ovals when he is told that they are the eyes of a face but not if he thinks of them just as circles inside an oval. The former judgment may use his intact ventral route for identifying faces/objects, whereas the latter might use the impaired dorsal route for appreciating the location of the circles relative to another. GK was also better at making location judgments about the rectangles when other face-like features were added. From Robertson (2004).

Different ways of assessing neglect include copying, drawing from memory, finding the center of a line (line bisection) and crossing out targets in an array (cancellation).

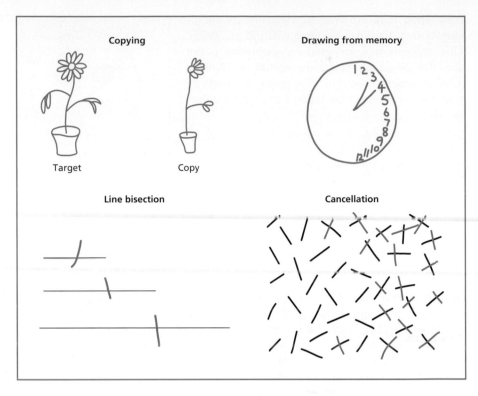

striking them through as they are found). They will typically not find ones on the right. Some of these tasks may be passed by some neglect patients but failed by others, the reasons for which have only recently started to become clear (Halligan & Marshall, 1992; Wojciulik, Husain, Clarke, & Driver, 2001). In extreme cases, neglect patients may shave only half of their face or eat half of their food on the plate.

Mort et al. (2003) examined the brain regions critical for producing neglect in 35 patients and concluded that the critical region was the right angular gyrus of the inferior parietal lobe. Functional imaging studies of healthy participants performing line bisection also point to an involvement of this area in that particular task (Fink et al., 2000); as do the results from a TMS study (Fierro et al., 2000). However, there are different types of spatial neglect that reflect different types of space. For example, neglect of the left side of objects (irrespective of whether the object is on the left or right of space) is associated with lesions of the right superior temporal gyrus, whereas neglect of the left side of space per se is linked to the right angular gyrus (Hillis, Newhart, Heidler, Barker, & Degaonkar, 2005).

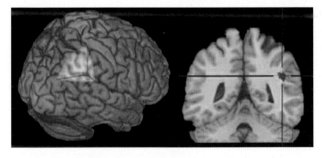

Neglect is associated with lesions to the right inferior parietal lobe. This photo shows the region of highest overlap of the lesions of 14 patients. From Mort et al. (2003). Reprinted by permission of Oxford University Press.

Is neglect a problem in low-level perception or attention?

It is important to stress that neglect is not a disorder of low-level visual perception. A number of lines of evidence support this conclusion. Functional imaging reveals that objects in the neglected visual field still activate visual regions in the occipital cortex (Rees, Wojciulik, Clarke, Husain, Frith, & Driver, 2000). Stimuli presented in the neglected field can often be detected if attention is first cued to that side of space (Riddoch & Humphreys, 1983). This also argues against a low-level perceptual deficit. The situations in which neglect patients often fare worse are those requiring *voluntary* orienting to the neglected side and those situations in which there are several stimuli competing for attention. One additional symptom of neglect that illustrates this point is called **extinction**. When a single stimulus is presented briefly to either the left or the right of fixation, the neglect patient will generally accurately report them (thus, the patient can "see" the left stimulus here). But when presented with two stimuli at the same time, the patient tends to report seeing the one on the right but not the one on the left. This can be conceptualized in terms of different perceptual representations competing for attention and visual awareness (e.g. Desimone & Duncan, 1995). With only one stimulus this is unproblematic because there are no competing stimuli, but with two stimuli the reduced attentional/spatial capacity means that only one stimulus tends to be reported and the left stimulus loses out in the competition.

"I see a frog"

"I see the sun"

"I see a sun" (extinction condition, frog not reported)

Neglect patients may fail to notice the stimulus on the left when two stimuli are briefly shown (called extinction) but notice it when it is shown in isolation. It suggests a reduced spatial–attentional capacity rather than a problem in low-level perception.

Neglect is not just restricted to vision, but can apply to other senses as well. This is consistent with the single-cell data noted above. Pavani, Ladavas and Driver (2002) have shown that neglect patients show a right-skewed bias in identifying the location of a sound (but note that they are not "deaf" to sounds on the left). Extinction can also cross sensory modalities. A tactile (or visual) sensation on the right will not be reported if accompanied by a visual (or tactile) stimulus on the left, but will be reported when presented in isolation (Mattingley, Driver, Beschin, & Robertson, 1997).

Different types of neglect and different types of space

By now it should be becoming clear that space is not represented in the brain as a single continuous entity. Cognitive neuroscientists refer to different spatial **reference frames** to capture the notion that space can operate over different dimensions. Different reference frames may exist for real and imagined space, near and far space, bodily versus external space, and space within versus between objects. Studying patients with neglect has provided a rich source of double dissociations between these different types of spatial representation.

Perceptual versus representational neglect

Bisiach and Luzzatti (1978) established that neglect can occur for spatial mental images and not just for spatial representations derived directly from perception. Patients were asked to imagine standing in and facing a particular location in a town square that was familiar to them (the Piazza del Duomo, in Milan). They were then asked to describe the buildings that they saw in their "mind's eye". The patients often

KEY TERMS

Extinction
When presented with two stimuli at the same time (one in each hemispace), then the stimulus on the opposite side of the lesion is not consciously perceived.

Reference frames
A representational system for coding space (e.g. near versus far space; imaginal versus external space)

La Piazza del Duomo. Image from http://en.wikipedia.org/wiki/File:Panor%C3%A1mica_Plaza_Duomo_ (Mil%C3%A1n).jpg

failed to mention buildings in the square to the left of the Duomo. Was this because of loss of spatial knowledge of the square or a failure to attend to it? To establish this, the patients were then asked to imagine themselves at the opposite end of the square, facing in, and describe the buildings. In this condition, the buildings that were on the left (and neglected) are now on the right and are reported, whereas the buildings that were on the right (and reported previously) are now on the left and get neglected. Thus, spatial knowledge of the square is not lost but is unavailable for report. Subsequent research has established that this so-called representational neglect forms a double dissociation with neglect of "real" space (Bartolomeo, 2002; Denis, Beschin, Logie, & Della Sala, 2002). The brain appears to contain different spatial reference frames for mental imagery and for perceptual events in external space. This suggests that perception and imagery can dissociate at higher levels of visual processing but in both cases information on the left side is compromised.

Near versus far space

Double dissociations exist between neglect of near space (Halligan & Marshall, 1991) versus neglect of far space (Vuilleumier, Valenza, Mayer, Reverdin, & Landis, 1998). This can be assessed by line bisection using a laser pen and stimuli in either near or far space, even equating for visual angles. Near space appears to be defined as "within reach" but it can get stretched! Berti and Frassinetti (2000) report a patient with a neglect deficit in near space but not far space. When a long stick was used instead of a laser pointer, the "near" deficit was extended. This suggests that tools quite literally become fused with the body in terms of the way that the brain represents the space around us. This is consistent with single-cell recordings from animals suggesting that visual-receptive fields for the arm get spatially stretched when the animal has been trained to use a rake tool (Iriki, Tanaka, & Iwamura, 1996).

Personal and peri-personal space

Patients might show neglect of their bodily space. This might manifest itself as a failure to groom the left of the body or failure to notice the position of the left limbs (Cocchini, Beschin, & Jehkonen, 2001). This can be contrasted with patients who show neglect of the space outside their body, as shown in visual search type tasks, but not the body itself (Guariglia & Antonucci, 1992).

The orientation of the body and the orientation of the world can have independent effects on neglect, suggesting that these are also coded separably. Calvanio, Petrone and Levine (1987) displayed words in four quadrants of a computer screen for the patients to identify. When seated upright, patients showed left neglect. However, when lying down on their side (i.e. 90 degrees to upright), the situation was more complex. Performance was determined both relative to the left–right dimension of the room and the left–right dimension of the body.

Within objects versus between objects (or object-based versus space-based)

Look at the figures to the right (from Robertson, 2004). Note how the patient has attempted to draw all of the objects in the room (including those on the left) but has distorted or omitted the left parts of the objects. Similarly, the patient has failed to find the 'A's on the left side of the two columns of letters even though the right side of the left column is further leftwards than the left side of the right column. This patient would probably be classed as having object-based neglect.

This distinction is not always as clear-cut as may first seem, as it is not straightforward to define what constitutes an object. As noted already, a face can be considered an object, but so can an eye or an eyelash. The object in question may be more dynamically defined according to the current spatial reference frame being attended. Driver and Halligan (1991) devised a task that pitted object-based coordinates with environmentally based ones. The task was to judge whether two meaningless objects were the same or not. On some occasions, the critical difference was on the left side of the object but on the right side of space and the patient did indeed fail to spot such differences.

Written words are an interesting class of object because they have an inherent left to right order of letters. Patients with left object-based neglect may make letter substitution errors in reading words and non-words (e.g. reading "home" as "come"), whereas patients with space-based (or between object) neglect may read individual words correctly but fail to read whole words on the left of a page. In one unusual case, NG, the patient made neglect errors in reading words that were printed normally but also made *identical* errors when the words were printed vertically, printed in mirror image (so that the neglected part of the word was on the opposite side

The patient makes omission errors on the left side of objects irrespective of the object's position in space. From Robertson (2004).

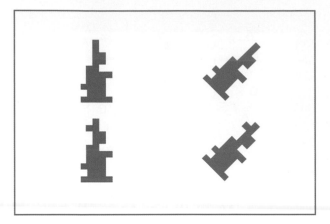

Are these objects the same or different? The critical difference lies on the left side of the object but, in the slanted condition, on the right side of space. From Driver and Halligan (1991).

of space) and even when the letters were dictated aloud one by one (Caramazza & Hillis, 1990a). This strongly suggests that it is the internal object frame that is neglected. Intriguingly, in patients with bilateral parietal damage it is possible to have two different types of neglect co-occurring, such as left neglect of objects, and right neglect of environmental space (Costello & Warrington, 1987; Humphreys & Riddoch, 1994).

In summary, studies of neglect have told us a great deal about how the brain represents space at many different levels. Different spatial reference frames may be evoked depending on the nature of the task (e.g. reaching for an object versus imagining a route). Whilst neglect patients typically have problems in attending to the right side, this will also depend on the particular reference frame that is evoked.

What happens to the neglected information?

Patients with neglect can be shown to process information in the neglected field to at least the level of object recognition. The ventral "what" route seems able to process information "silently" without entering awareness, whereas the dorsal "where" route to the parietal lobe is important for creating conscious experiences of the world around us. Vuilleumier, Schwartz, Clarke, Husain and Driver (2002b) presented brief pictures of objects in left, right or both fields. When two pictures were presented simultaneously the patients extinguished the one on the left and only reported the one

---

HOW IS "LACK OF AWARENESS" IN NEGLECT DIFFERENT FROM "LACK OF AWARENESS" IN BLINDSIGHT?

Neglect	Blindsight
• Lack of awareness is not restricted to vision and may be found for other sensory modalities	• Lack of awareness is restricted to the visual modality
• Whole objects may be processed implicitly	• Implicit knowledge is restricted to basic visual discriminations (e.g. direction of motion; but see Marcel, 1998)
• Lack of awareness can often be overcome by directing attention to neglected region	• Lack of awareness not overcome by directing attention to "blind" region
• Neglect patients often fail to voluntarily move their eyes into neglected region	• Blindsight patients do move their eyes into "blind" region
• Neglected region is egocentric	• Blind region is retinocentric

on the right and when later shown the neglected stimuli they claimed not to remember seeing them (a test of explicit memory). However, when later asked to identify a degraded picture of the object, their performance was facilitated, which suggests that the extinguished object was processed unconsciously. Other lines of evidence support this view. Marshall and Halligan (1988) presented a neglect patient with two depictions of a house that were identical on the non-neglected (right) side but differed on the left side such that one of the two houses had flames coming from a left window. Although the patients claimed not to be able to perceive the difference between them, they did, when forced to choose, state that they would rather live in the house without the flames! This, again, points to the fact that the neglected information is implicitly coded to a level that supports meaningful judgments being made.

REMEMBERING SPACE: DOES THE HIPPOCAMPUS STORE A LONG-TERM MAP OF THE ENVIRONMENT?

As noted, the ability to find one's way through the environment to reach an endpoint that is not in view (e.g. selecting the quickest route to the bank) may rely on different mechanisms to locating objects in the immediate environment. This task is likely to place more demand on structures relating to memory than perception, and it is perhaps unsurprising that the region of the brain that some believe may contain a "spatial map" is also crucial for human memory: the hippocampus.

Evidence that the rat hippocampus contains a spatial map

In the 1970s, a number of lines of evidence led to the hypothesis that the hippocampus contains a spatial map of the environment (O'Keefe & Nadel, 1978). This research was conducted on rats because it involved single-cell recordings and the creation of precise anatomical lesions. O'Keefe (1976) planted electrodes into the hippocampus of rats that subsequently explored an enclosed environment. The firing rate of the neuron was measured when the rat was located at various points in the

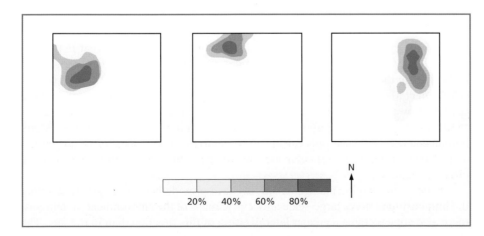

In this figure, the firing rate of three different cells is shown (the darker the shade, the more likely it is to respond). The data is obtained using single-cell recordings from the rat hippocampus. Adapted from Chakraborty, Anderson, Chaudhry, Mumford and Jeffery (2004).

box. It was found that a given neuron only responded strongly when the rat was at a particular location. Neurons showing this pattern of firing are referred to as **place cells**. Given that each neuron responds to a given place, when a collection of neurons are considered together they could function as a map of the environment.

Subsequent research has suggested that place cells are more complex than originally thought. The responses of place cell are often highly context sensitive. For example, if the environment is substantially changed (e.g. the box is white instead of black), then the place that the neuron codes can also change substantially (Anderson & Jeffery, 2003). In a black box, a place cell may respond maximally when the rat is in the north-west corner, but the same cell may respond maximally in a white box when the rat is in the south-east corner. This is termed "remapping". Thus, the firing of a given place cell cannot be used to unambiguously infer the rat's location in an environment without also knowing the wider context. One analogy to this could be to consider that we store multiple maps of the places we visit. It could be that the same neuron codes for one location in the "London map" and a different location in the "Paris map", and is able to flip between the two depending on the context.

Further evidence that the hippocampus stores a spatial map of the environment comes from lesion studies of rats using the Morris **water maze** (Morris, Garrud, Rawlins, & O'Keefe, 1982). If a rat is placed in a container filled with milky water in which there is a submerged platform, then the rat will, by trial and error, eventually find the platform (rats are good swimmers!). As the water is milky, the platform is not visible and the rat must learn the route. If the rat is placed in the environment again, it will remember the location and swim there directly without trial-and-error meandering. If, however, the hippocampus is lesioned, then the rat is unable to learn the location of the platform and relies once more on trial and error. There is good evidence to suggest that the hippocampus spatial map is allocentric in nature. The rat is able to find the submerged platform even if it is placed in a different starting point from the one that it previously learned from. Thus, the rat has acquired a map of where the platform is located that is independent of its own orientation and position.

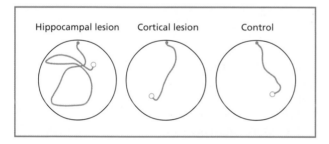

The route taken by a typical rat in the Morris water maze. The control rat and ones with cortical lesions can remember the location of the submerged platform and go directly there, whereas hippocampal-lesioned rats find the platform by trial and error. From Morris et al. (1982). Reprinted by permission from Macmillan Publishers Ltd, copyright © 1982.

Does the human hippocampus contain a spatial map?

Most of the evidence cited above comes from studies of rats. But what is the evidence, if any, that the human hippocampus contains a spatial map? Single-cell recordings in the primate (Rolls, Robertson, & Georges-Francois, 1997) and human (Ekstrom et al., 2003) hippocampus suggest that place cells are to be found in these species. However, there is at least one crucial difference from the rodent place cells. In rodents, the place cells respond when the animal is in that physical location. Many human and primate place cells can also respond to the mental location of the animal (e.g. if they attend to a particular location in space that differs from their current physical location).

Functional imaging and lesion studies have provided converging evidence that the hippocampus stores large-scale allocentric maps of the environment. In humans, there also appears to be a greater lateralization of this function than in rodents. The

DOES DRIVING A TAXI INCREASE YOUR GRAY MATTER?

London taxi drivers are required to sit an exam (called "the knowledge") in which they are given two locations within the city and must generate a plausible route. Maguire et al. (2000) studied the gray matter volume of cab drivers (using voxel-based morphometry) and found that the volume in the right hippocampus is greater than in IQ-matched individuals. Could it be that the taxi drivers choose their occupation because they have better spatial memories (and bigger hippocampi)? It turns out that the amount of time spent in the job correlates with the volume of the region. This suggests that this region may expand with usage and argues against a predisposition influencing the choice of occupation.

right hippocampus seems to be particularly important for spatial memory, whereas the left hippocampus appears to be more specialized for remembering and storing other contextual details. In a series of experiments, Burgess and colleagues have used a virtual reality environment in which subjects could roam freely, learn routes and encounter various objects, landmarks and people. Hartley, Maguire, Spiers and Burgess (2003) found that finding one's way through the virtual town activated the right hippocampus relative to a baseline task of following a visible trail. This may account for the observation that we tend to be good at remembering routes if we uncover them ourselves rather than are shown them by another person. Spiers et al. (2001a) used a similar paradigm in groups of patients with either left or right hippocampal damage. The patients had to learn to navigate through the town. During their exploration they would collect different objects from different characters in different locations. Their memory was assessed by map drawing, together with forced-choice recognition of locations, characters and objects. The patients with right hippocampal damage were impaired on navigation, map drawing and scene recognition. In contrast, the patients with left hippocampal damage had problems in remembering who gave them the objects, and the order and location in which they were received.

In summary, these results suggest that the hippocampus serves multiple memory functions and is not just a repository for spatial maps – although there is a degree of functional specialization in the right hippocampus for spatial context.

Reconciling the different roles of the hippocampus and parietal lobes in spatial cognition

This chapter has contrasted the different types of spatial processes performed in two key areas of the brain: the parietal lobes and hippocampus (although there are other relevant regions). To conclude the chapter, it is worthwhile to consider how these different processes may work together in a concerted fashion. The spatial functions of parietal lobes may be broadly characterized as transforming sensory-based maps of space (e.g. retinocentric coordinates) into various egocentric maps of space that facilitate interaction with the environment (e.g. reaching and grasping objects); enable information from the different senses to be integrated; and prioritize incoming information through spatial attention. The hippocampus, in contrast, is involved in the long-term storage of spatial maps of the environment that is largely invariant of the viewpoint of the observer (i.e. allocentric). Burgess (2002) considers how these two mechanisms could interact in a task such as the Piazza del Duomo imagery task: the hippocampus may store a long-term representation of the layout of the square and the function of the parietal lobe may be to superimpose a viewer-centered reference frame onto this map in order to inspect it.

Evaluation

There is good evidence that both humans and other animals have a long-term spatial representation of the environment that is stored in the hippocampus (lateralized in the right hippocampus in humans). However, the hippocampus and the "place cells" within it do not code only spatial information but also seem to be involved in representing and storing other types of contextual information that is critical for memory.

SUMMARY AND KEY POINTS OF THE CHAPTER

- Attention is the process by which certain information is selected for further processing and optimizes efficiency by preventing sensory overload.
- Attention may operate at particular locations (or on objects) and enable different attributes of an object (e.g. color and form) to be coherently bound together.
- The parietal lobes may transform sensory-based maps of space (e.g. retinocentric coordinates) into various egocentric (body-centered) maps of space.
- The functions of these spatial maps are to:
  - facilitate interaction with the environment (e.g. reaching and grasping objects).
  - enable information from the different senses to be integrated.
  - prioritize incoming information through spatial attention.
- Studies of neglect have been important for establishing that space is represented at many different levels within the brain.
- The hippocampus is involved in the long-term memory storage of spatial maps of the environment that is largely invariant of the viewpoint of the observer (i.e. allocentric).

EXAMPLE ESSAY QUESTIONS

- Discuss the evidence for and against the Feature-Integration Theory (FIT) of visual perception and attention.
- How is information from different sensory modalities brought together in the brain?
- How is it possible to recognize an object but not know its location in space?
- Is there a single representation of space in the brain, or does the brain represent space at several different levels? Discuss, using evidence from patients with neglect.
- Does the hippocampus contain a spatial map of the world?
- Compare and contrast the role of the hippocampus and the parietal lobes in terms of how the brain constructs representations of space.

RECOMMENDED FURTHER READING

- Farah, M. J. (2000). *The cognitive neuroscience of vision*. Oxford: Blackwell. This contains chapters on attention, neglect and awareness and describes studies from cell recording, patients and functional imaging.
- Posner, M. I. (2004). *The cognitive neuroscience of attention*. Hove: Psychology Press. An edited book with chapters at the cutting edge of research. Recommended for students who want to find out about more advanced topics.
- Robertson, L. C. (2004). *Space, objects, minds and brains*. Hove: Psychology Press. A very interesting and readable extended essay that focuses on findings from brain-damaged patients.
- Styles, E. A. (2006). *The psychology of attention*, 2nd edition. Hove: Psychology Press. This book is a good introduction to attention that explains difficult ideas in a straightforward way. It covers neglect, but otherwise does not focus on cognitive neuroscience findings.

CHAPTER 8

CONTENTS

The acting brain

Action is our way of interfacing with the world, and our means of putting all our goals and desires into practice. Action has traditionally been viewed as the endpoint of cognition. Having perceived an object and made a cognitive decision about what to do with it, we may then, depending on our goals, act towards it. Findings from cognitive neuroscience have radically shaken up this viewpoint. For example, in some situations it is possible to accurately act towards objects that have not been consciously seen. In addition, it has been claimed that not only is our action system equipped to produce our own actions, it may also be used to understand the actions of others – an important part of social cognition. Moreover, the processes that generate and control actions also appear to generate and control thought and cognition more generally. These ideas will also be explored in this chapter, together with an overview of more traditional areas of research on the "acting brain", such as Parkinson's disease, the role of the basal ganglia and tool use.

A BASIC COGNITIVE FRAMEWORK FOR MOVEMENT AND ACTION

A simple model of movement and action is presented below and is unpacked in more detail throughout the chapter. Note that the model is hierarchically organized.

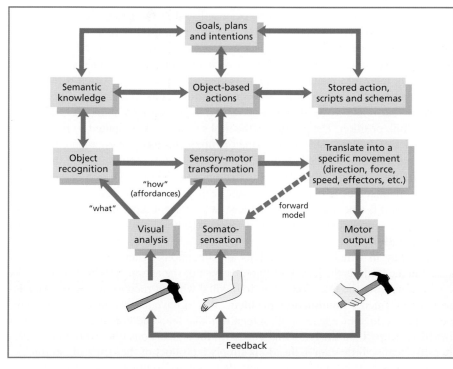

A very basic cognitive framework for understanding movement and action.

At the highest level, there is action planning based on the goals and intentions of the individual. At the lowest level, there are the perceptual and motor systems that interface with the external world. Action can be considered to be an outcome of all these processes that work together in a concerted fashion, combining the needs of the person with the current environmental reality. As such, the term "action" needs to be contrasted with the physical *movement* of the body that ensues. Movements can sometimes occur in the absence of cognition. A reflex movement generated, say, when a hand goes near a flame occurs in the absence of a centrally generated command.

There are a number of computational problems faced when performing an action. Imagine a task of turning off a light switch. There are potentially an infinite number of motor solutions for completing the task in terms of the angles of the joints and their trajectories through space. This has been termed the **degrees of freedom problem** (for a discussion, see Haggard, 2001). There are likely to be physical constraints on the solution (e.g. to minimize the torque on joints) but there could also be cognitive constraints too (e.g. to minimize the amount of planning). It is probably not the case that actions are calculated from scratch each time one needs to be performed. Most theories of action postulate the existence of generalized **motor programs** (Schmidt, 1975). This may simplify the computations (and computational speed) underlying movement. For example, in producing a tennis serve the different movement components may be linked together. Motor programs may code general aspects of the movement (e.g. the timing of different components) rather than the actual means of performing the movement (e.g. the joints and muscles). One commonly cited example is the fact that handwriting does not change when different effectors are used (e.g. writing with feet) or when the amplitude is changed (e.g. writing on a blackboard versus a notebook).

Most actions are directed towards externally perceived objects, particularly via vision. After early visual analysis, two routes diverge into different streams specialized for object recognition (the "what" or ventral stream) and object location (the "how", "where" or dorsal stream). This was covered in Chapter 7. One aspect that is particularly relevant to the present topic is how this visual information is integrated with somatosensory information. **Somatosensation** refers to a cluster of perceptual processes that relate to the skin and body, and includes touch, pain, thermal sensation and limb position. The position of the limbs in space is computed by receptors in the muscles and joints, and this is termed **proprioception**. Information concerning the location of objects coded on the surface of sensory receptors (e.g. on the retina) is insufficient to permit interaction with that object unless the position of the sensory receptors themselves is taken into account (e.g. gaze direction and head position). As such, there is a need to co-register these two different types of information into a common spatial reference frame. This process will be referred to as **sensory-motor transformation**.

The way in which the goals, plans and intentions of an individual are represented in the brain is the least understood aspect of the action system. The difficulty lies in explaining the intentions of an individual without recourse to what psychologists have termed a **homunculus problem**. We all have a sense in which "I" make a decision to go somewhere or "I" intend to make tea. The homunculus problem is that there is no "I" in the brain that makes all these decisions (the word homunculus literally means "little man"); the "I" is simply a product of the firing of neurons.

Note that, in this simple framework, there are bi-directional arrows to and from the "goals, plans and intentions". This implies that the system may also be used to observe and understand the actions and intentions of other people, as well as to generate one's own actions. This may be vital for learning skills by observation and may form an important component of comprehending actions.

THE ROLE OF THE FRONTAL LOBES IN MOVEMENT AND ACTION

The frontal lobes take up around a third of the cortical area and comprise a number of functionally and anatomically separate regions. Moving from the posterior to the anterior of the frontal lobes, their function becomes less specific to movement and action. The more anterior portions are involved in the control of behavior irrespective of whether it results in an overt action (i.e. in aspects of thought such as planning, reasoning and working memory).

Primary motor cortex and frontal eye fields

The **primary motor cortex** (in the precentral gyrus, Brodmann's area [BA] 4) is responsible for execution of all voluntary movements of the body. Most other frontal regions are related to action planning, irrespective of whether or not actions are actually executed. Different regions of the primary motor cortex represent different regions of the body – that is, it is *somatotopically organized*. The left hemisphere is specialized for movements of the right side of the body and the right hemisphere is specialized for movements of the left side of the body (although the division is not as

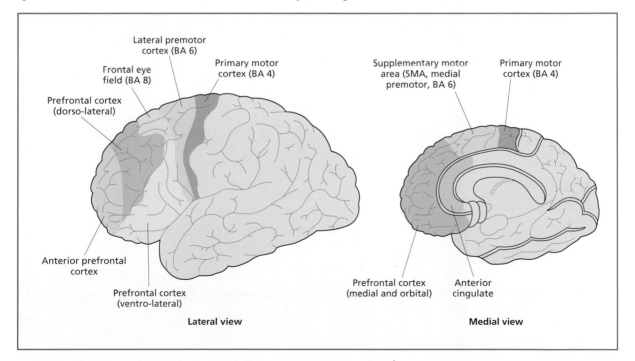

Anatomical and functional divisions of the frontal lobes. Broadly speaking, the primary motor cortex initiates voluntary movements, the premotor regions are involved in online coordination of movements; and the prefrontal regions plan and select actions according to goals.

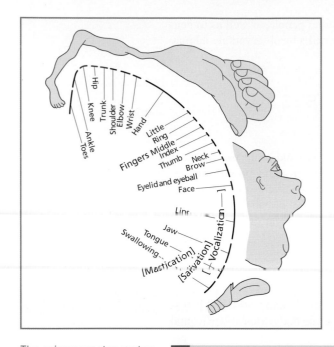

The primary motor cortex controls movement in different parts of the body. Areas governing different parts of the body are arranged spatially (somatotopic organization) but do not strictly reflect the spatial arrangement of the body. From Penfield and Rasmussen (1950).

strict as once believed; Tanji, Okano, & Sato, 1998). Thus, damage to one hemisphere as a result of, say, stroke could result in a failure to move the other side of the body – **hemiplegia**. Note that some parts of the body, such as the hands, have a particularly large representation because of the need for fine levels of movement control.

Voluntary movement of the eyes is not determined by the primary motor cortex but by a separate region of the frontal lobes known as the **frontal eye fields** (Brodmann's area 8). Stimulation of this region in monkeys with microelectrodes results in movement of the eyes (Bruce, Goldberg, Bushnell, & Stanton, 1985). The separation of body and eyes may reflect the different nature of the input signals that guide movement: eye movement is primarily guided by external senses (vision and hearing) whereas skeletal-based movements rely more heavily on proprioceptive information concerning position of the limbs (derived from parietal regions).

KEY TERMS

Hemiplegia
Damage to one side of the primary motor cortex results in a failure to voluntarily move the other side of the body.

Frontal eye fields
Responsible for voluntary movement of the eyes.

COULD NEURAL ACTIVITY IN THE PRIMARY MOTOR CORTEX BE USED TO GUIDE A PROSTHETIC LIMB?

The relationship between the activity of individual neurons and resultant limb movement is understood in some detail. This holds out the promise of being able to use this information to guide an artificial limb in patients with amputated or paralyzed limbs (Chapin, 2004). Studies of the firing of single cells in the primary motor cortex show that activity is highest for a given direction of movement (the "preferred direction") and it decreases gradually with directions further and further away (for reviews, see Georgopoulos, 1997; Georgopoulos, Schwartz, & Kettner, 1986). Different neurons prefer different directions, and the firing is genuinely related to the direction of movement rather than the spatial location of the endpoint. Thus, a neuron would fire equivalently with different starting and ending positions assuming the direction is the same (Georgopoulos, Kalaska, & Caminiti, 1985).

One computational issue raised by these findings is this: how do the neurons decide on a single movement to execute given that lots of different neurons with lots of different preferred movements will be active at a given point in time? One possible solution could be that the most active neuron(s) at that point in time is the one that dictates the actual movement (i.e. a "winner takes all" solution). This idea is unsatisfactory because movements tend to be very precise whereas the coding of preferred direction is broad (e.g. a neuron with a preferred direction of 70 degrees would still respond strongly at 60 and 80 degrees). This idea also turns out to be empirically incorrect. The direction of the resultant movement appears to be computed by summing together the vectors (i.e. degree of activity multiplied by preferred direction) of a whole population of neurons (the so-called "population vector"). Thus, each neuron contributes, to a greater or lesser degree, in determining the final movement. The direction can be computed from measurements in fewer than 100 cells (Salinas & Abbott, 1994), and preliminary results suggest that cell recordings from rats can accurately guide a robot arm (Chapin, 2004). However, there will undoubtedly be significant limitations in developing this method in humans. For example, equivalent population vectors are found in imagining as well as executing movements (Georgopoulos, Lurito, Petrides, Schwartz, & Massey, 1989) and it is unlikely that measurements of primary motor cortex alone can reveal the intentions of the individual to act or not to act.

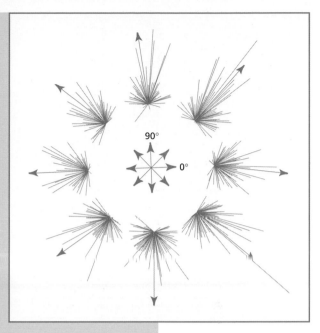

Each line represents the preferred direction of many neurons in the primary motor cortex, and their length represents the amount of firing. The population vector, calculated for eight different directions, is the gray line and this predicts the direction of movement. From Georgopoulos, Caminiti, Kalaska and Massey (1983), with kind permission of Springer Science and Business Media.

Different contributions of the lateral versus medial premotor cortex

The area immediately in front of the primary motor cortex is termed the **premotor cortex**. Many studies have drawn attention to the different roles played by the lateral premotor cortex and the medial premotor cortex also known as the **supplementary motor area (SMA)** (e.g. Goldberg, 1985; Passingham, 1988). Whereas the lateral premotor cortex has been associated with acting with objects in the environment (e.g. reaching for a coffee cup), the SMA has conversely been associated with dealing with spontaneous well-learned actions, particularly action sequences that do not place strong demands on monitoring the environment (e.g. playing a familiar tune on a musical instrument).

In one experiment, TMS was delivered to three frontal regions in three conditions: "simple" button presses (pressing the same key over and again), "scale" button presses (pressing consecutive buttons as in a musical scale) and "complex" button presses (as in playing a pre-learned musical piece). TMS over the SMA

KEY TERMS

Premotor cortex
The lateral area is important for linking action with objects in the environment; the medial area is known as the supplementary motor area and deals with well-learned actions and action sequences.

Supplementary motor area (SMA)
Deals with well-learned actions, particularly action sequences that do not place strong demands on monitoring the environment.

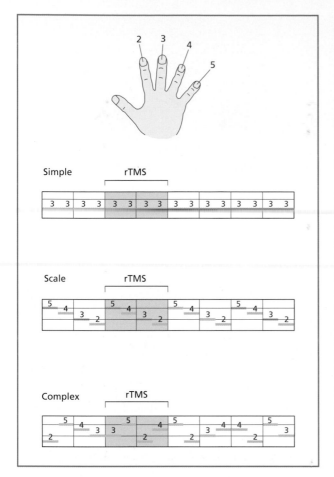

Gerloff, Corwell, Chen, Hallett and Cohen (1997) contrasted three different types of action sequence: repetitive movements of the same finger (top), a regular pattern of finger movements as in a scale (middle) and an irregular memorized pattern of finger movements (bottom). Only the latter condition was disrupted by TMS applied over the supplementary motor area. This suggests that this region is critical for coordinating complex learned movement patterns. From Gerloff et al. (1997). Reprinted by permission of Oxford University Press.

disrupted the sequence in the "complex" condition only, whereas TMS over the primary motor cortex affected both "complex" and "scale" action sequences; TMS over the lateral prefrontal cortex had no effects (Gerloff, Corwell, Chen, Hallett, & Cohen, 1997). Gerloff et al. (1997) suggested that the SMA has a critical role in organizing forthcoming movements in complex motor sequences that are rehearsed from memory and fit into a precise timing plan.

If the SMA is important for implementing internally generated actions, the lateral premotor region is more important for producing movements based on external contingencies (e.g. "pull a handle if the light is blue, rotate it if it is red"). In the monkey, lesions in this area prevent these kinds of associations being formed but without loss of basic sensory or motor abilities (Passingham, 1988). Single-cell recordings in the monkey also show that lateral premotor neurons respond when movement is required to an external cue but not to spontaneous movements from memory, whereas the opposite is true for the SMA (Halsband, Matsuzaka, & Tanji, 1994). Lateral premotor regions are also considered to contain a "vocabulary" of actions (e.g. tearing, grasping) that have both a sensory and motor component (Rizzolatti, Fadiga, Fogassi, & Gallese, 1996). These will be discussed later in terms of "mirror neurons" and sensory-motor transformation.

Different contributions of prefrontal versus premotor regions

Prefrontal regions lie to the front of premotor regions and are principally involved in planning and higher aspects of the control of action. Unlike premotor and motor regions, prefrontal regions are involved extensively in higher cognition more generally rather than action specifically. Premotor regions have a primary role in preparing actions (to internally or externally triggered events), while the prefrontal region mediates their selection and maintains the goal of the action. The prefrontal cortex is also involved in attending to actions, for example, in novel or difficult situations (Passingham, 1996). This has been termed *attention to action*.

The study of Frith, Friston, Liddle and Frackowiak (1991) provides a good illustration of prefrontal function. Participants were required to generate finger movements that were either predetermined (i.e. move the finger that is touched) or in which the participant could freely choose which finger to move. Note that the actual motor response is identical in both tasks. Nevertheless, the dorsolateral prefrontal cortex showed greater activation in the free choice task, suggesting that it is involved in "willed" or intentional aspects of action (for a review, see Jahanshahi and Frith, 1998). Its role may extend to the open-ended selection of responses more generally. Similar activation was found when subjects were asked to generate any word from a specified letter ("S" or "F") in contrast to producing a predetermined word (Frith et al., 1991).

The function of the prefrontal cortex is by no means specific to action. It is involved, for example, in manipulating and holding things "in mind" (this will be dealt with in Chapter 14, "The executive brain"). Nevertheless, one of the most influential models of executive function (the SAS model of Norman and Shallice, 1986) was initially put forward to explain action errors and, as such, will be introduced here.

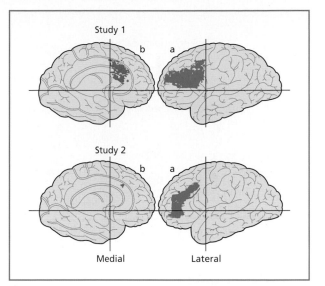

Activation in the (a) left dorsolateral prefrontal cortex and (b) anterior cingulate when participants generate words beginning with S or F relative to being given the words (top) and when participants choose which finger to move relative to being instructed which to move (bottom). These regions may be important for response selection and willed action. Redrawn from Frith et al. (1991), Royal Society of London.

Evaluation

The movement and action system of the frontal lobes is hierarchically organized. The *primary motor cortex* is essential for the execution of voluntary movements. The *premotor cortex* is important for the preparation of actions, and may be functionally subdivided into actions that are elicited by external cues (lateral premotor) or that are internally generated (medial premotor, SMA). The *prefrontal cortex* is involved in the selection of actions and their corresponding goals. This will be considered next.

PLANNING ACTIONS: THE SAS MODEL

Damage to prefrontal regions does not impair the movement or execution of actions *per se*. Rather, the actions themselves become poorly organized and do not necessarily reflect the goals and intentions of the individual. For example, a patient with damage to the prefrontal cortex may repeat an action that has already been performed and is no longer relevant (called **perseveration**), or might act impulsively on irrelevant objects in the environment (called **utilization behavior**). An example of this, in the acute phase of a stroke, was described by Shallice, Burgess, Schon and Baxter (1989, p. 1588):

...the patient was found early in the morning wearing someone else's shoes, not apparently talking or responding to simple commands, but putting coins into his mouth and grabbing imaginary objects. He went around the house, moving furniture, opening cupboards and turning light switches on and off.

KEY TERMS

Perseveration
Repeating an action that has already been performed and is no longer relevant.

Utilization behavior
Impulsively acting on irrelevant objects in the environment.

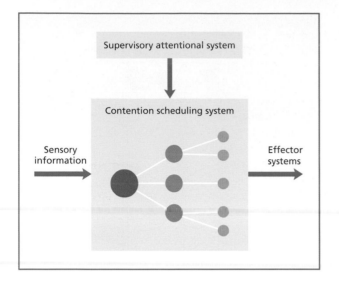

Supervisory attentional system

Contention scheduling system

Sensory information

Effector systems

In the supervisory attentional system (SAS) model, contention scheduling selects the most active schema. The activation of schemas depends partly on the environment (derived from sensory input) and partly on the biasing influence of current and future goals (derived from the SAS component). From Humphreys and Forde (1998).

Norman and Shallice (1986; see also Cooper & Shallice, 2000) proposed a model to explain goal-driven action. The model is called the SAS or "Supervisory Attentional System" and has subsequently been applied to explain the control of cognition more generally (discussed in Chapter 14). One of the key distinctions that they make is between actions that are performed automatically (with minimal awareness) versus actions that require attention and some form of online control. For example, when driving it may be possible to change gears, stop at traffic lights, turn corners and so on in a kind of "autopilot" mode. In fact, drivers often have no recollection of having gone through traffic lights, even though they know that they must have done so. These actions may be using well-learned **schemas** and are assumed not to require SAS control. By contrast, imagine that you are required to reverse into a narrow space, or that you are diverted down an unfamiliar route. Situations such as these may require an interruption of automatic behavior or setting up a novel action sequence and these are assumed to require intervention of the SAS.

The SAS model contains a number of different components. Familiar actions and action routines may be stored as schemas. For example, specific objects (e.g. chopsticks, hammer) may have their own action schema. Specific tasks (e.g. making tea) may be stored as a hierarchical collection of schemas (sometimes called scripts). In many respects, this organization of actions into abstract scripts and object-based schemas is akin to the distinction between syntax and word-based knowledge in language and, as with language, there is a debate about the extent to which they are separable (e.g. Patriot, Grafman, Sadato, Flitman, & Wild, 1996; Zanini, Rumiati, & Shallice, 2002).

Contention scheduling is the mechanism that selects one particular schema to be enacted from a host of competing schemas. The idea of competition between schemas is the key part of this model. Schemas can be activated by objects in the environment (e.g. a hammer will activate its own particular schema). Schemas also receive biasing top-down activation from the SAS system that represents information about the needs of the person. If these two sources of activation are summed, then the most appropriate schema (i.e. that satisfies the current needs and is consistent with the environmental reality) should have the highest activation. This schema will then be selected by the contention-scheduling mechanism and translated into a specific action. As such, there is no need for a special entity with decision-making powers (i.e. a homunculus) as the decision to act is directly determined by the activation levels of schemas.

The action errors made by patients with prefrontal lesions can be explained by this model if one assumes that there is an imbalance in the type of information that enters into the contention scheduling process. Utilization behavior can be accounted for by assuming that schemas are activated solely by environmental cues without any SAS regulation. Repetition of the same action (perseveration) is accounted for by assuming that activated schemas are not deactivated when they are no longer relevant to the current goal, or that the goal itself is not changed once it has been successfully accomplished.

KEY TERMS

Schema
An organized set of stored information (e.g. of familiar action routines).

Contention scheduling
The mechanism that selects one particular schema to be enacted from a host of competing schemas.

Damage to the frontal lobes can also lead to what some researchers have termed "**frontal apraxia**" (Schwartz, Montgomery, Fitzpatrick-DeSalme, Ochipa, Coslett, & Mayer, 1995), or "action disorganization syndrome" (Humphreys & Forde, 1998). This is characterized by failure in tasks of routine activity (e.g. making tea) that involve setting up and maintaining different subgoals (e.g. boil kettle, add sugar) but with no basic deficits in object recognition or gesturing the use of isolated objects. This disorder has been variously explained as damage to the scripts themselves (Humphreys & Forde, 1998), to the online maintenance of scripts (Sirigu, Zalla, Pillon, Grafman, Agid, & Dubois, 1995) or to some combination of these (Schwartz et al., 1995). In many ways, the errors of these patients reflect those associated with "lapses of attention" in us all. Reason (1984) documented many everyday action slips, including putting a match in the mouth and striking the cigarette instead of vice versa.

Evaluation

Damage to prefrontal regions does not prevent movement but instead can produce actions that are disorganized, inappropriate and/or unintentional. This set of behaviors has frequently been characterized as a "dysexecutive syndrome". The syndrome affects the control of thoughts as well as actions and can be accounted for within the SAS model. This model makes an important distinction between automatic actions and those requiring attention and online control.

OWNERSHIP AND AWARENESS OF ACTIONS

If all our actions, from those of a criminal to those of a world leader, are the product of the firing of neurons in our heads, then do we really have any responsibility for our actions? This is a deep question and it would be glib to assume that science will provide an easy answer. However, attempts to draw these sorts of issues into a scientific framework have been made.

Libet, Gleason, Wright and Pearl (1983) recorded EEG activity from the scalp above the primary motor cortex and the SMA when subjects simply pressed a key "whenever they felt the urge to". The exact time at which the key was pressed could be recorded from an electrical signal from the wrist movement. In addition, participants reported the time at which they were first aware of wanting to move. This was achieved by noting the position of a hand on a gradually rotating clock face. Libet and colleagues found that the EEG activity (or "readiness potential") started several hundred milliseconds before the participants reported an intention to act. The results appeared to suggest that the brain had made an unconscious commitment to act before subjects experienced a conscious intention to act. One strong interpretation is that "free will" (i.e. the feeling that "I" decide my own actions) is something of an illusion.

Haggard and Eimer (1999) identified which particular cognitive mechanism is likely to be associated with the conscious intention. In their variation of the experiment, the subject could "freely choose" either a left or right response, resulting in a lateralized readiness potential over the opposite hemisphere. Their results suggested

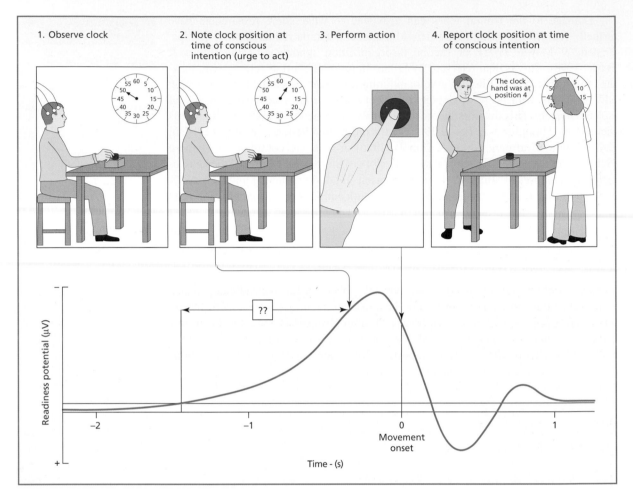

The motor cortex generates a readiness potential long before the participant declares an intention to act. This challenges the classical Cartesian view that the mind controls the brain. Redrawn from Haggard (2008). Reprinted by permission of Macmillion Publishers Ltd, copyright 2008.

that awareness of intentions is related to selection of a specific movement (left or right) rather than a generalized intention to act. This finding is also consistent with the data discussed above that suggest that willed action may be functionally related to response selection in conditions in which the response is essentially arbitrary (e.g. which finger to move) or is drawn from an open-ended set of responses (e.g. which word to say) (Frith et al., 1991; Jahanshahi & Frith, 1998). Even after an urge to move, however, the participant may not be fully committed to act and may still be able to suppress the action (Brass & Haggard, 2007). This suggests the operation of a late checking mechanism.

One way in which a sense of ownership over actions could be maintained is by predicting the sensory outcomes of our actions. One influential class of model, which links together action intention with action outcome, is **forward models** (e.g. Wolpert, Ghahramani, & Jordan, 1995). A simplistic example appears on p. 153 with respect to somatosensation (similar pathways may exist for other senses). The main assumption is that a representation of the motor command (a so-called "efference copy") is used to predict the sensory consequences of an action. For example, tickling oneself is less ticklish than being tickled by another person because we can use our own motor commands to predict what the sensation will feel like. The motor command when one tickles oneself can be used to predict what the sensation will feel like (and, hence, it is possible to compensate for it). Another example comes from eye movements. When we move our eyes the visual world appears static rather than moving, even though the image on the retina changes considerably. In this instance the motor command to move the eyes is used to predict (and compensate for) changes in visual input.

KEY TERM

Forward model
A representation of the motor command (a so-called "efference copy") is used to predict the sensory consequences of an action.

THE ANARCHIC (OR "ALIEN") HAND SYNDROME

...the pathological hand of these patients is seen to wander involuntarily, and to perform purposeless movements. Often the arm levitates spontaneously, sometimes with tentacular movements of the fingers...

(Marchetti & Della Sala, 1998)

...when G.C. had a genital itch, the right hand scratched it vigorously, in view of other people, causing considerable embarrassment to the patient, who tried to stop the right hand with her left....The patient considered the left hand to be the one she could trust...while the right hand was the untrustworthy one that "always does what it wants to do."

(Della Sala, Marchetti, & Spinnler, 1991, p. 1114)

In the "anarchic hand syndrome", the hand and arm of a patient may produce an action such as grasping an object or interfering with the activities of the other hand that the patient regards as *unintentional*. Although unintentional, the patient typically acknowledges that the arm and action belong to them. Della Sala et al. (1991) have suggested that patients who do not have such awareness might be better classified as having "*alien* hand syndrome" to distinguish it from anarchic hand.

The damage typically reflects the supplementary motor area (SMA) of one hemisphere together with tracts of the corpus callosum, which connects the two hemispheres together (Goldberg, Mayer, & Toglia, 1981). Thus, in the case of a left SMA lesion, the control of the right "anarchic" hand would be at the whim of the intact left lateral premotor regions (which may control more object-based action than the SMA).

The anarchic (or alien) hand syndrome. The eponymous protagonist of the film *Dr. Strangelove* is a type of "mad scientist", whose eccentricities include a severe case of alien hand syndrome – his right hand, clad in an ominous black leather glove, occasionally attempts to strangle him. © Sunset Boulevard/Corbis Sygma.

ACTION COMPREHENSION AND IMITATION

There are broadly two ways in which to reproduce the actions of another person. The first way involves a shallow level of analysis. It is possible to reproduce an action via sensory-motor transformations that do not make any inferences about the goals and intentions of the actor; this is *mimicry*. The second way involves observing the action, computing the goals and intentions of the actor and then reproducing the actions oneself based on the goal. This is **imitation** proper and it implies a deeper level of processing of the observed action. Aside from imitation, another situation in which goals are shared between individuals is in *joint action*; for example, when several people are lifting a heavy object or several people are operating different parts of a machine (Sebanz, Bekkering, & Knoblich, 2006).

There is evidence to suggest that humans tend to reproduce the actions of others by representing the goal state rather than by mimicry, particularly when the action is more complex. Wohlschlager, Gattis and Bekkering (2003) found that, when asked to "copy" the actions of another, there is a tendency to reproduce the goal of the action (e.g. putting an object in a cup) rather than the means of the action (e.g. which particular arm is used). Infants appear to imitate based on goals too (Gergely, Bekkering, & Kiraly, 2002). In this study, the infants watched an adult press a button on a table by using their forehead. In one condition, the adult's hands and arms are bound up under a blanket and in the other condition the adult's hands are free. When the adult's hands are free, the infants copy the action directly – they use their foreheads too. But when the adult's hands are not free, the infants imitate the goal but not the action, i.e. the infants use their hands rather than their head. The implication is that the infants understand that the goal of the action is to press the button and they assume that the adult would have used his or her hands had they been free.

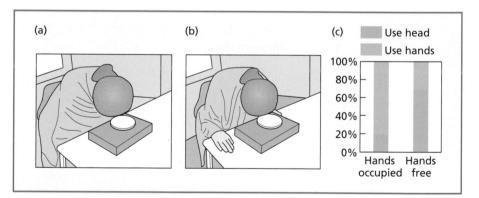

Infants imitate the goal of actions rather than the motor aspects of actions. If the experimenter presses a button with his or her head because their arms are occupied, the infants "copy" the action by using their hands rather than heads – i.e. they appear to infer that the experimenter would have used his or her hands to achieve the goal had they been free. From Gergely et al. (2002). Reprinted by permission of Macmillion Publishers Ltd, copyright 2002.

Mirror neurons

One of the most fascinating discoveries in cognitive neuroscience over the last decade has been of the **mirror neuron** system. Rizzolatti and colleagues found a group of neurons in the monkey premotor cortex (area F5) that respond both during the performance *and* the observation of the same action (e.g. di Pellegrino, Fadiga, Fogassi, Gallese, & Rizzolatti, 1992; Rizzolatti et al., 1996). Thus, the response properties of mirror neurons disregard the distinction between self and other. It responds to actions performed by the experimenter or another monkey as well as to actions performed by itself. The response properties of these neurons are quite specific. They are often tuned to precise actions (e.g. tearing, twisting, grasping) that are goal-directed. They do *not* respond to mimicked action in the absence of an object, or if the object moves robotically without an external agent. This suggests that it is the purposeful nature of the action rather than the visual/motoric correlates that is critical. By contrast, other regions such as superior temporal sulcus, also respond to specific movements of body parts but have a purely visual component (Perrett et al., 1989).

Moreover, mirror neurons respond if an appropriate action is implied as well as directly observed. Umiltà and colleagues (2001) compared viewing of a whole action versus viewing of the same action in which a critical part (the hand–object interaction) was obscured by a screen. These findings suggest that the premotor cortex contains abstract representations of action intentions that are used both for planning one's own actions and interpreting the actions of others.

The evidence above is derived from non-human primates. What is the evidence that humans possess such a system? The human analogue of area F5 is believed to be in Broca's area (specifically, in Brodmann's area 44) extending into the premotor area (Rizzolatti, Fogassi, & Gallese, 2002). This region is activated by the observation of hand movements, particularly when imitation is required (Iacoboni, Woods, Brass, Bekkering, Mazziotta, & Rizzolatti, 1999), and also the observation of lip movements within the human repertoire (e.g. biting and speaking but not barking) (Buccino et al., 2004). Moreover, TMS applied over the primary motor cortex increases the amplitude of motor evoked potentials elicited in the hands/arms when participants also observed a similar action (Strafella & Paus, 2000). This suggests that action observation biases activity in the primary motor area itself.

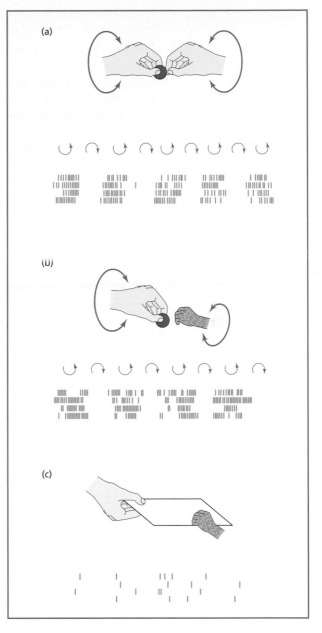

This neuron responds to the rotating action of an object in the experimenter's hands (a) or when the monkey rotates the object held by the experimenter (b) but not during grasping without rotation (c). Notice that the neuron is even sensitive to the direction of rotation (responding counter-clockwise, not clockwise). Adapted from Rizzolatti et al. (1996).

WIDER IMPLICATIONS OF THE MIRROR NEURON SYSTEM

- Did human language evolve from hand gestures? The human homologue of monkey area F5 is Broca's area (Rizzolatti & Arbib, 1998) – an area traditionally associated with language.
- Are mirror neurons important for being able to empathize with others, by internally simulating their behavior (Gallese, 2001)?
- Do individuals with particular difficulties in understanding others (e.g. autistic people) have impaired mirror neuron systems? Dapretto et al. (2006) present fMRI evidence to suggest that autistic people have lower activity in the mirror system when imitating and observing expressions, but others have questioned whether this can explain the range of autistic behaviors (Southgate & Hamilton, 2008).

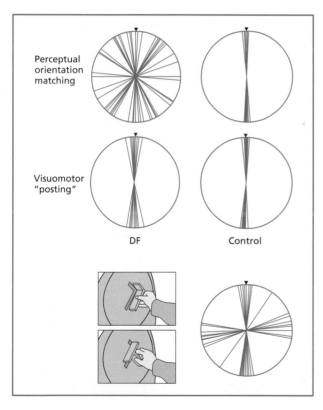

Can the hand "see" better than the eye? Patient DF can accurately post objects through slots even though she cannot report the orientation of the slots from vision. With more complex objects (e.g. T-shaped), she appears to use single orientations to guide action. Adapted from Milner et al. (1991a) and Goodale et al. (1994).

PARIETOFRONTAL CIRCUITS FOR SENSORY-MOTOR TRANSFORMATION

This chapter has, so far, only considered in detail the role of the frontal lobes in some of the highest levels of action processing – namely, action planning and organization, the intention to act and comprehending the actions and intentions of others. The remaining sections will deal with topics related to how specific actions are put into place and enacted. This involves, among other things, an appreciation of where things are in space and what certain objects (e.g. tools) can be used for. The parietal lobes appear to be specialized for this type of information.

"What" versus "how": The dorsal and ventral streams reconsidered

Ungerleider and Mishkin (1982) first described two routes of visual processing, which they labelled the "what" route (or ventral stream from occipital to temporal) and the "where" route (or dorsal stream from occipital to parietal). Goodale and Milner (1992; Milner & Goodale, 1995) have offered a somewhat different characterization of these routes in terms of "what" versus "how". In doing so, they placed an emphasis on output requirements (identification verses action) rather than input requirements (identity versus location). As they noted, we do not reach to locations in space but to objects. These arguments over labeling are not critical to the present discussion, and the term "sensory-motor" captures both the "how" and "where" nature of the dorsal stream adequately.

Damage to dorsal versus ventral streams has different consequences for action. First of all, consider damage to the ventral route, running along the inferior temporal lobes. Patient DF has visual agnosia that impairs her ability to recognize objects from vision, despite intact basic visual processes. Milner and colleagues (1991a) presented DF with a letter box in which the orientation of the slot could be rotated. DF had difficulty in matching the orientation of the slot to visually presented alternatives. However, when asked to post a letter she was able to reach towards the slot and orient her hand appropriately. This suggests a dissociation between visual perception (based on the impaired ventral stream) and visual control of action (using the spared dorsal stream). When DF was given a more complex T-shaped object and slot, she was still fairly accurate but she did make some errors, which tended to be at 90 degrees. This suggests that her action is driven by orientation of a single edge. Thus the dorsal route cannot adequately integrate different edges into whole objects (Goodale, Meenan, Bulthoff, Nicolle, Murphy, & Racicot, 1994).

Turning next to impairments of the dorsal stream – some patients with damage to the parietal lobe have deficits in acting towards objects in space. However they do not (unlike DF) have problems in recognizing single objects. **Optic ataxia** is a symptom arising from damage to the occipito-pariental junction (Karnath & Perenin, 2005). These patients are unable to accurately reach towards objects under visual guidance. Perenin and Vighetto (1988) argue that this reflects a failure to transform visual perceptual information into appropriate motor commands. For example, when acting towards an oriented slot their hands may be oriented incorrectly or they may miss the slot altogether (a double dissociation with DF). The deficits would sometimes be restricted to a particular hand (typically the hand opposite the side of the lesion) or even a particular hand when it was in a particular half of space.

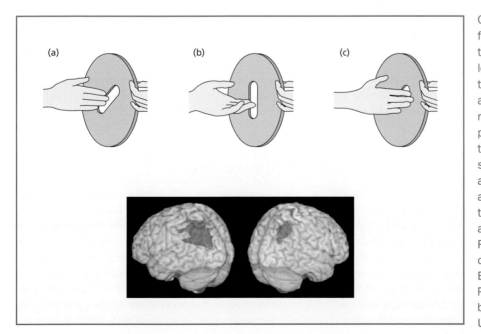

Optic ataxia may arise following lesions to either the left or right parietal lobe (often affecting the opposite hand), and results in both mis-reaching (c) and hand posture problems (b); the correct solution is shown in (a). It reflects an inability to link visual and motor information together. Top: from Perenin and Vighetto (1988). Reprinted by permission of Oxford University Press. Bottom: from Karnath and Perenin (2005). Reprinted by permission of Oxford University Press.

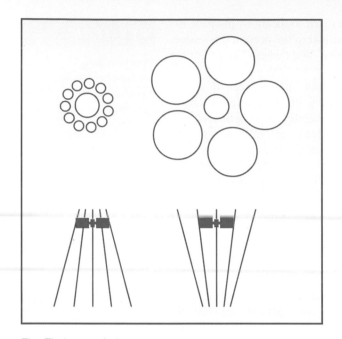

The Titchener circle (above) and Ponzo (railway track; below) illusions affect perception but not action. When a subject is asked to pick up the central circle or horizontal rod, the grip aperture more closely resembles the true rather than the distorted size.

The latter suggests that it is unlikely to be purely motoric (because the "bad" hand functions well in the "good" side of space) or purely visual (because the "good" hand functions well in the "bad" side of space) but due to a failure to integrate the two (when the "bad" hand is in the "bad" side of space).

Action deficits may depend on the type of action required. For example, grasping may require greater processing of object-based properties than reaching or pointing (e.g. Jeannerod, 1997). Neglect patients with damage to the dorsal stream may show a rightward bias when asked to point to the center of a rod but, if asked to pick the rod up between thumb and forefinger, they may do so in the center of the rod (Robertson, Nico, & Hood, 1995). In this instance, the act of grasping may lead to more efficient processing of the object coordinates than reaching.

Interestingly, dissociations between vision for action and visual perception have been found in the normal population. Certain *visual illusions*, such as the Ponzo or railway track illusion and the Titchener circles illusion, result in physically identical objects being perceived as different in size. If one is asked to pick up the size-distorted object (e.g. a poker chip in the Titchener illusion), then the grip aperture between thumb and finger is not influenced by the illusion (Aglioti, DeSouza, & Goodale, 1995; Jackson & Shaw, 2000).

In summary, evidence from brain-damaged individuals points to specialized visual mechanisms that guide action. Studies of single-cell recordings in primates shed light on the nature of the underlying mechanisms at the neural level.

Neural mechanisms of sensory-motor transformation

Different types of information need to be linked to enable sensory-motor transformation. This section will consider three broad ways in which neurons code information relevant to this process. Most of the evidence comes from primate single-cell recordings.

Neurons that code specific types of actions

The neurons located in area F5 are interesting not only for their "mirror" properties (i.e. they represent the actions of both self and others) but also for the specificity of the actions they represent. Rizzolatti and Luppino (2001) describe them in terms of an action "vocabulary", including grasping, holding and tearing. For example, a neuron that responds to performed finger movements for grasping may not discharge for scratching. Other neurons may be specialized for different types of hand shaping (e.g. precision grip, whole-hand prehension). The advantage of having a stored repertoire is that the brain does not have to compute certain aspects of the action each time, and may also enable certain types of action to become associated with familiar objects.

Neurons that code action-relevant properties of objects

Murata, Gallese, Luppino, Kaseda and Sakata (2000) studied neurons in an area of the parietal lobe, called anterior intraparietal area (AIP), in which neurons respond selectively to restricted shapes (e.g. cylinder, sphere, cube), sizes and orientations. Representations such as these provide a potentially suitable interface for the more general motor vocabulary in areas such as the frontal lobe. Similar neural mechanisms may be found in humans, although the situation is likely to be more complex because of the large range of man-made manipulable objects that we use. In this instance, use of familiar objects could be seen as "fixing of action parameters" within the parietal-frontal network (Wolpert & Ghahramani, 2000). An fMRI study in humans has also identified the AIP area as coding object shape for actions (Culham, 2004). The region shows greater activity for grasping relative to reaching and does not respond to two-dimensional object images.

Neurons that code sensory information across different modalities

Chapter 7 discussed how certain neurons, in the parietal lobes and elsewhere, respond to information from different senses, particularly when they represent the same region of space. With regards to action, it may be particularly important to integrate visual and proprioceptive information about the location of the body. Graziano (1999) identified neurons in the macaque premotor regions that respond to both the felt position of the arm (irrespective of whether the arm was covered or in view) and the visual position of the arm (irrespective of whether it was the monkey's own arm or a stuffed arm in that position). If the arm was moved, then the visual receptive field would move too. This suggests that vision was coded relative to the body. This facilitates interaction with the external world irrespective of changes in eye fixation.

The studies noted above provide the building blocks for a theory of how sensory and motor systems may be interfaced. But, of course, the *meaning* of objects is going to be as critical for determining how and when they are used. This is likely to be especially important for humans. Whereas other species may use objects found in their natural environments as tools, humans have created for themselves a wide range of manipulable objects to perform specific functions, each with specific associated actions. The next section considers how these may be represented in the brain.

HOW TO MOVE A PHANTOM LIMB

Almost everyone who has a limb amputated will experience a **phantom limb** – a vivid sensation that the limb is still present and, in some cases, painful (for a fascinating review, see Ramachandran and Hirstein, 1998). Phantom limbs can be explained by plasticity in the brain. The neurons in the brain that previously used to respond to stimulation of the limb may instead be stimulated by activation in nearby regions of cortex (perhaps representing other parts of the body). This gives rise to an illusory sensation that the limb has returned.

KEY TERM

Phantom limb
The feeling that an amputated limb is still present.

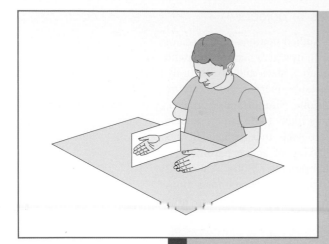

This patient has one real arm and a phantom limb that is immobile (i.e. the amputated arm feels as if it still exists and feels paralyzed). When the patient looks in the mirror it creates the illusion that the amputated arm has returned and can move again.

The nature of the phantom differs significantly from one patient to another. Some report being able to move the phantom (e.g. it may appear to be gesturing). The motor cortex presumably doesn't "know" that the limb is missing and continues to send commands. For other patients, the limb may be immobile and potentially painful (this may relate to whether the limb was paralyzed prior to amputation). Ramachandran and Rogers-Ramachandran (1996) report a clever experiment, based on visual feedback, which enables such patients to re-experience movement in the phantom and, in some cases, alleviate pain. The patient puts the intact arm into a box with a mirrored side so that a second hand can be seen reflected in the position where the phantom is felt. When asked to move both hands they can experience movement in the phantom based on the visual feedback. This study illustrates the point that sensory (touch and vision) and motor information is highly integrated in the brain.

USING OBJECTS AND TOOLS

A number of evolutionary developments appear to have facilitated the skilled use of tools found in modern man. First, there is the freeing of the hands by walking upright rather than on all fours that occurred 4–6 million years ago. Second, there is the development of the hands themselves in which the thumb appears to have become much longer in humans relative to chimps. This facilitates a precision grip, such as that used in picking up a peanut. Finally, there is the corresponding development of the brain in terms of the disproportionate amount of space dedicated to representing the hands. It is hard not to underestimate the impact that tool use has had in terms of human beings' mastery of the environment, from the deserts to the poles. Note that the term "**tool**" is used broadly, not only to encompass hammers and chisels but also cups, pencils and so on. These objects afford certain actions for specific goals.

Tools, like other classes of object, are represented in the brain at several levels, as noted previously. First, a three-dimensional structural description of the object is computed (based on grouping of parts, detection of edges and so on) and is matched to a store of visuospatial object descriptions in the brain. These descriptions may represent objects in their typical views (rather than the view as observed) and appear to be located in the *infero-temporal cortex* (or IT). To understand the object and access other kinds of information (e.g. its name, factual knowledge), the tool/object would also have a representation in semantic memory. What distinguishes tools from many other classes of object (e.g. cats, clouds, carpets) is the fact that they have specific gestures and functions associated with them.

A number of lines of evidence suggest that the store of object-based actions is located in the left inferior parietal lobe. Chao and Martin (2000) compared activity (fMRI) when viewing "manipulable man-made objects" relative to other classes of objects and found activity in both the left inferior parietal lobe and Broca's area, consistent with the monkey data discussed above. Rumiati and colleagues (2004) examined object-based action more directly by asking participants to generate actions in the scanner (they used PET, which is more suitable than fMRI if participants are required to move). They used the factorial design depicted below, in which participants were presented with either static objects or actions (without the object) and were required to either gesture the appropriate action or produce the name of it. Producing an action from a static picture of an object (called *pantomiming*) was found to be particularly associated with the left inferior parietal lobe and a left lateral premotor region, controlling for other factors (e.g. object recognition).

Consistent with the imaging data, some patients with damage to the left hemisphere may be unable to produce appropriate actions on command given either an object (e.g. an iron), a word or a command (e.g. intransitive gestures such as "waving goodbye"). These patients are traditionally classified as having **ideomotor apraxia** (e.g. Gonzalez Rothi, Ochipa, & Heilman, 1991; Liepmann, 1905). These studies are broadly consistent with the involvement of the left parietal lobe. It is important to establish whether or not the patient can copy meaningless actions (e.g. holding the left palm upwards) or produce them from verbal description. In such instances, this would imply a more general deficit of sensory-motor transformation that is not strictly related to object use (e.g. Schwoebel, Buxbaum, & Coslett, 2004).

An important debate in the literature concerns the extent to which semantic representations of objects are critical for the production of object-related gestures. Semantic representations specify abstract conceptual knowledge of words and objects that are neither sensory nor motoric in nature. Some studies have reported surprisingly good use of pantomiming or performance of routine actions in the face of poor semantic knowledge (Beauvois, 1982; Lauro-Grotto, Piccini, & Shallice, 1997). This poses a challenge to a simple model in which retrieval of actions is contingent on the retrieval of semantic knowledge because this would predict that loss of semantic knowledge of objects should produce a comparable difficulty in generating actions for those objects.

There are a number of ways of modifying this basic model to account for this. First, one could fractionate semantic knowledge itself into separate stores with a separate, impaired, store of functional knowledge in these patients (e.g. Beauvois, 1982). A second explanation is to suggest that there is a direct route from the

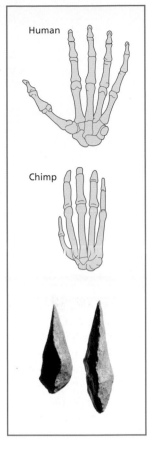

Acheulean tools dating from 1.5 million years ago found in central-East Africa. The thumb of humans has evolved to be considerably longer than that of the chimp's, enabling precision grip. Stone tools: John Reader/Science Photo Library.

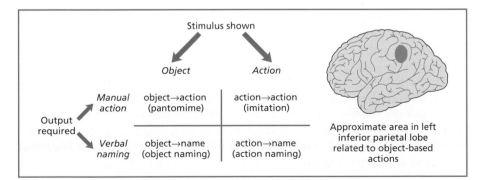

Rumiati et al. (2004) compared the brain activity when subjects were asked to generate actions or name actions from either an object or action. They found a region in the left inferior parietal lobe that appears specific to object-based action in their "pantomime" condition.

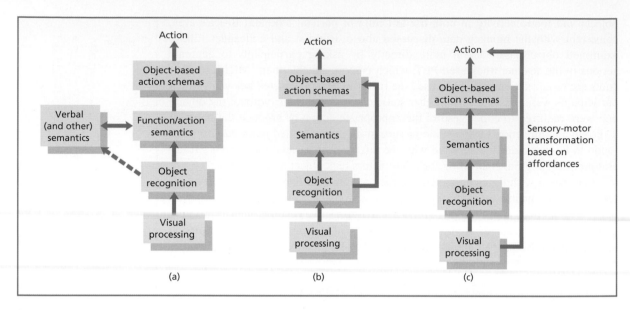

Some patients can gesture the use of objects despite poor understanding and naming ability for those objects. This can be explained in three ways: fractionated semantic knowledge (a), direct links between stored object and action representations (b) or affordances related to non-arbitrary correspondences between visual features and motor commands (c).

structural descriptions of objects to their actions that bypasses semantic memory altogether (Riddoch, Humphreys, & Price, 1989). A third explanation suggests that certain structural properties of objects imply certain usages that can be deduced independently of their conventional usage. For example, semi-spherical shapes may imply a container, a handle may imply grasping and a sharp edge may imply cutting. Gibson (1979) has referred to these as **affordances**. Evidence from semantic dementia favors the third account over the other two (Hodges, Bozeat, Lambon Ralph, Patterson, & Spatt, 2000). Hodges et al. found that the level of impairment in tool use was directly related to the degree of semantic impairment for those same items. This was assessed from tasks such as naming, and from various matching tasks (e.g. matching bottle and glass, bathroom and razor, scissors to knife). Many errors clearly implied use of affordances. For example, one patient correctly held the scissors by the handle rather than the blade but did so bimanually (plausibly correct) rather than unimanually (conventionally correct). The patients could copy actions performed by the experimenter and use novel tools (e.g. the test of Goldenberg and Hagmann, 1998). This suggests that the deficits were truly object related. These object-based affordances may account for the fact that many ideomotor apraxic patients perform better when given the actual objects rather than producing the actions simply from memory.

One unanswered question is why object-based actions should reside predominantly in the left hemisphere of humans (no such bias has been found in other primates). One possibility dating back to the work of Liepmann (1905) is that it reflects the fact that the majority of people are right-handed for tool use. At present there are too few studies of lefthanders with focal brain injuries who have also been appropriately assessed for object use. Perhaps the issue will be resolved with functional imaging of normal participants.

Evaluation

The human brain contains a store of object-dependent actions that may reside in the left inferior parietal lobe and may by impaired in ideomotor apraxia. These actions may normally be accessed from semantic representations of objects, but actions can often be inferred from the non-arbitrary relationship between the structures of tools and the functions they serve (affordances).

PREPARATION AND EXECUTION OF ACTIONS

Role of subcortical structures in movement and action

The chapter so far has concentrated on cortical influences on action and movement. However, subcortical structures have an important role to play particularly with regards to the preparation and execution of actions. These structures may be important for setting the particular parameters of the movement, such as the force and duration of movement and for controlling the movement in progress. One PET study that highlights the different roles of cortical and subcortical structures was conducted by Krams and colleagues (1998). In one condition, participants were shown a hand position, given three seconds to *prepare*, and were then asked to *execute* it (PE condition). In another condition, they were required to *execute* it as soon as it was shown (E condition), and in the final experimental condition they were asked to *prepare* but not to execute (P condition). (The baseline condition was viewing the hand movement without preparation or execution.) The cerebellum and basal ganglia were found to be more active when both preparation and execution were required (PE relative to P; also PE relative to E). In contrast, the prefrontal cortex including Broca's area was more active when merely preparing to produce copied movements (P relative to PE; also P relative to E).

The figure below summarizes the two main cortical-subcortical loops involved in the generation of movement. One loop passes through the basal ganglia and the other through the cerebellum. These loops have somewhat different functions. The *cerebellar loop* is involved in the coordination of movements. It may utilize a copy of the cortical motor commands to ensure that the desired movement occurs accurately and occurs at the desired time (Ohyama, Nores,

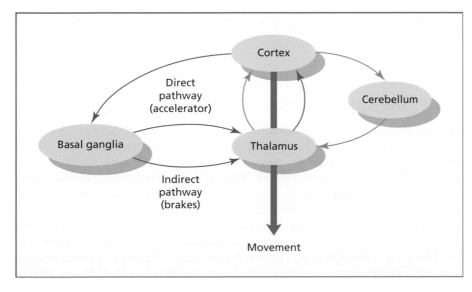

Two main subcortical loops are involved in movement generation. The cerebellar loop coordinates the timing and trajectory of movement using sensory and motor information. The basal ganglia loop regulates the excitability of frontal motor structures and biases the likelihood of movement and the nature of the movement (e.g. the force).

Murphy, & Mauk, 2003). For example, it is physiologically active during coordination tasks that require one movement to be synchronized with another (Ramnani, Toni, Passingham, & Haggard, 2001). Moreover, patients with cerebellum lesions produce tremulous movements that suggest that they are unable to use information about the progress of the movement to update the initiated motor program (Haggard et al., 1995). Given this role, it is perhaps not surprising that the cerebellum connects strongly with lateral premotor and parietal regions involved in sensory-motor transformation.

The *basal ganglia loop*, by contrast, is especially important for initiation and execution of internally generated movements and for linking one action to the next. The "loop" actually consists of around five different loops. Each loop has essentially the same architecture (a set of interconnected excitatory and inhibitory pathways) but projects to somewhat different structures in the basal ganglia and in the cortex (e.g. Alexander & Crutcher, 1990). There are strong connections to premotor areas, particularly the supplementary motor area (SMA). The basal ganglia appear to be important not only for movement initiation and execution, but are also implicated in cognitive functioning, reward-based learning and procedural learning (e.g. Saint-Cyr, 2003). To appreciate the function of the basal ganglia in more detail, it is helpful to consider the nature of motor disorders associated with basal ganglia pathology. It is to be noted that the basal ganglia do not generate the signals to execute a movement (this is achieved from connections from the primary motor cortex down the brainstem to the spinal cord). They function, instead, to modify activity in frontal motor structures and influence the probability of movement and the nature of the movement (e.g. its amplitude).

The spinal cord makes connections between the brain and the muscles and controls simple reflexive movements (e.g. to avoid sudden injury). Unlike the other actions considered so far, reflexes can't be construed as cognitively based. As well as these descending fiber tracts, the spinal cord also contains ascending fibers that provide sensory feedback about the state of the body and the fate of the executed movement. For example, Patient GO lost these pathways from a severe peripheral sensory disease (Rothwell, Traub, Day, Obeso, Thomas, & Marsden, 1982). Although he could make accurate quick movements with appropriate force, his lack of sensory feedback meant that he was unable to sustain motoric tasks. For example, when carrying a suitcase he would quickly drop it unless he continually looked down to see it was there.

Hypokinetic disorders of the basal ganglia: Parkinson's disease

Parkinson's disease affects about 0.15% of the total population and has a mean age of onset at around 60 years. It was first described by James Parkinson in 1817 in his "Essay on the shaking palsy". No single cause has yet been found, although in some cases a genetic link has been suggested. However, the neuropathological signs of the disease are fairly well understood. Dopaminergic brain cells are lost in the pathways linking the basal ganglia and substantia nigra (e.g. Brooks et al., 1990).

To understand the symptoms of Parkinson's disease it is necessary to understand the nature of the basal ganglia circuit in more detail. First of all, it is important to recall the nature of inhibitory and excitatory pathways. Imagine that two brain structures, "A" and "B", connect such that "A" connects to "B" (A → B). If the connection

Michael J. Fox was diagnosed with young-onset Parkinson's disease in 1991. Upon disclosing his condition to the public in 1998, he has since committed himself to the campaign for increased Parkinson's research in a bid to uncover a cure. © Lucas Jackson/Reuters/Corbis.

is inhibitory, then greater activity in "A" produces less activity in "B". If the connection is excitatory, then greater activity in "A" produces more activity in "B". The loops connecting the basal ganglia and thalamus consist of a mix of inhibitory and excitatory connections that combine together to form two complementary routes: a direct route that promotes action (increases activity in the cortex) and an indirect route that inhibits action (decreases activity in the cortex) (DeLong, 1990). These direct and indirect routes act like an accelerator and brake in the initiation of action. Lesions of the connections between the substantia nigra and the basal ganglia in Parkinson's disease have a net effect of increasing the output of the indirect pathway (the brakes) and decreasing the output on the direct pathway (the accelerator). The net result is a poverty of self-initiated movement.

Not all types of movement and action are affected equally in Parkinson's disease. For example, an ordinarily immobile patient may walk or run normally in situations of risk such as fire, and the shuffling gait can be improved by provision of lines on the floor over which the patients must step (Martin, 1967). This suggests that there is not a simple mechanical failure, but that there is a failure in self-initiating the action that can to some extent be overcome by external cues. The motor programs themselves also appear to be preserved. For example, signatures and handwriting style are preserved even though the kinematics are impaired such that writing is very slow and shrunken in size (a symptom called *micrographia*; McLennan, Nakano, Tyler, & Schwab, 1972). One common finding is that patients with Parkinson's disease are relatively spared at initiating actions in which the response is determined by some property of the stimulus (e.g. left finger if stimulus green, right finger if stimulus red) but significantly impaired on simple reaction time tasks (e.g. press a single button, or any button, when the stimulus appears) (e.g. Evarts, Teravainen, & Calne, 1981). How are we to account for the relatively spared actions? Recall that there is an additional subcortical route that bypasses the basal ganglia altogether and goes via the cerebellum (note: this is not to be confused with the direct and indirect pathways, both of which go through the basal ganglia). This route may be more involved in

KEY TERMS

Hypokinetic
A reduction in movement.

Hyperkinetic
An increase in movement.

Huntington's disease
A genetic disorder affecting the basal ganglia and associated with excessive movement.

MOTOR SYMPTOMS OF PARKINSON'S DISEASE

Symptoms include the following (e.g. Beradelli, Rothwell, Thompson, & Hallett, 2001):

- akinesia (lack of spontaneous movement)
- bradykinesia (slowness of movement)
- decay of movement sequences (walking degenerates to a shuffle)
- failure to scale muscle activity to movement amplitude
- failure to weld several movement components into a single action plan
- rigidity
- tremor (when stationary)

actions specified by environmental cues, whereas the routes through the basal ganglia are more involved with self-initiated actions associated with the supplementary motor area (SMA). PET studies have shown that patients with Parkinson's disease have reduced frontostriatal activation during self-initiated action but can show normal activation in externally triggered actions (Jahanshahi, Jenkins, Brown, Marsden, Passingham, & Brooks, 1995).

The pattern of spared and impaired action in patients with Parkinson's disease is also found in cognitive tasks with minimal motor requirements. This suggests a wider role of the basal ganglia in cognition. Patients with Parkinson's disease perform poorly on tasks of "executive function" (see Chapter 14) that involve the self-initiation of cognitive strategies (Taylor, Saint-Cyr, & Lang, 1986). Brown and Marsden (1988) used a variant of the Stroop test in which the subject must either name the INK color (e.g. say "red" when the written word *green* is printed in red ink) or the WORD color (e.g. say "green" when the written word *green* is printed in red ink). Participants would either have to spontaneously switch between naming the ink and naming the color or they would receive a written cue (INK or WORD) before each trial. The patients with Parkinson's disease were impaired on the uncued self-initiated trails but not the cued trials.

Hyperkinetic disorders of the basal ganglia: Huntington's disease and Tourette's syndrome

If Parkinson's disease is characterized as a poverty of spontaneous movement (**hypokinetic**), then a number of disorders exist that can be characterized as an excess of spontaneous movement (**hyperkinetic**). **Huntington's disease** is a genetic disorder with a well-characterized neuropathology (e.g. MacDonald, Gines, Gusella, & Wheeler, 2003). The symptoms consist of dance-like, flailing limbs (chorea) and contorted postures. The symptoms arise in mid-adulthood and degenerate over time. Many of those condemned in the Salem witch trials of 1692 are now believed to have suffered from the illness. Huntington's disease arises because of depletion of inhibitory neurons in the early part of the indirect pathway linking the basal ganglia with the thalamus (Wichmann & DeLong, 1996). The net effect of this lesion is that the output of the indirect pathway (the brakes) is reduced, whereas the output of the direct pathway (the accelerator) remains normal. This shift in the balance of power promotes movement in general.

Tourette's syndrome is also likely to involve disordered function of the basal ganglia (Mink, 2001) but the precise pathology is unclear. It is characterized by excessive and repetitive actions that can be simple (e.g. a head jerk) or more complex (e.g. cleaning routines). As such, the disorder can be characterized as a failure to inhibit or otherwise control the initiation of action, and it has similar characteristics to **obsessive-compulsive disorder**. The repetitive, and sometimes obsessive, nature of the actions may be an outcome of a somewhat different function of the basal ganglia – namely, its involvement in the learning of habits and procedures (Graybiel, 2008). This may set up a vicious cycle in which the production of an unwanted act paradoxically increases the chances that the act will be performed again and again.

KEY TERMS

Tourette's syndrome
A neuropsychiatric disorder with an onset in childhood characterized by the presence of motor and/or vocal tics.

Obsessive-compulsive disorder
An anxiety disorder characterized by repetitive thoughts and/or acts (e.g. counting, cleaning).

SYMPTOMS OF TOURETTE'S DISEASE

Symptoms include:

- motor tics (e.g. eye blinks, neck movements)
- echolalia (repeating someone else's words)
- palilalia (repeating one's own words)
- coprolalia (production of obscenities)

Evaluation

A number of circuits involving the cortex (notably frontal) and subcortical structures are critical for the initiation and execution of movement. One circuit, involving the cerebellum, is involved in coordinating the movement once initiated. Another circuit, involving the basal ganglia, is involved in establishing self-initiated movements. The basal ganglia have a role to play in cognition more generally and their role is by no means restricted to generating movements. These findings underscore an important point – action should not be viewed as the interface between "cognition" and "bodily movement"; rather, action is a cognitive process in its own right.

SUMMARY AND KEY POINTS OF THE CHAPTER

- Action can be considered an outcome of a number of processes working together in a concerted fashion. These processes include selection and maintenance of goals; the identification of objects in the environment and translation of their visuospatial properties into motor commands; preparing movements; and executing and online control of movements.

- The prefrontal cortex is involved in the highest stages of action planning and cognitive control in general. The SAS model provides a good account of action selection and its breakdown following frontal lobe damage.
- The lateral premotor cortex may be involved both in the preparation of action (particularly towards external objects) and in observing the actions of others (using "mirror neurons"). This may be important for imitation and skill learning.
- Visual processing of objects contains both a ventral stream (involved in explicit object recognition) and a dorsal stream. The dorsal stream codes action-relevant properties of objects (e.g. their absolute size, position in egocentric space).
- The dorsal stream terminates in the parietal lobes, and parietofrontal networks are responsible for developing action plans based on the current external reality and the goals of the individual (sensory-motor transformation).
- Humans use a vast range of tools. Tool use may be achieved by retrieving stored knowledge of objects and their actions via semantic memory, or may be partially achieved using "affordances" based on sensory-motor properties of objects. A difficulty in using objects is referred to as apraxia.
- The preparation and execution of action is influenced by two main subcortical circuits involving: (1) the cerebellum and (2) the basal ganglia. The cerebellar loop is involved in the online coordination of movement by comparing intended motor acts with sensory outcomes.
- The basal ganglia regulate action via a balance of action-promoting and action-inhibiting pathways, and are particularly involved in self-generated actions (prepared in the supplementary motor area). Parkinson's and Huntington's diseases can be explained as a disruption of this balance, leading to a poverty or excess of movement.

EXAMPLE ESSAY QUESTIONS

- What is the role(s) of the frontal lobes in action?
- What are mirror neurons and how has their discovery changed the way that people think about action?
- How are object-related actions stored and retrieved?
- How is it possible to accurately act towards an object that is apparently not visually perceived?
- How are vision and action integrated in the brain?
- Compare and contrast the role of the cerebellum and the basal ganglia in action.

RECOMMENDED FURTHER READING

- Goodale, M. A. & Milner, A. D. (2004). *Sight unseen*. Oxford: Oxford University Press. A very good and accessible account of the role of vision in action.

- Haggard, P., Rossetti, Y., & Kawato, M. (2008). *Sensory-motor foundations of higher cognition (attention and performance XXII)*. Oxford: Oxford University Press.

- Johnson-Frey, S. H. (2004). The neural bases of complex tool use in humans. *Trends in Cognitive Sciences, 8*, 71–78. An up-to-date summary of this literature.

- Rizzolatti, G., Sinigaglia, C., & Anderson, F. (2007). *Mirrors in the brain*. Oxford: Oxford University Press.

CHAPTER 9

CONTENTS

The remembering brain

9

The ability to learn and remember has several evolutionary advantages. It enables one to predict future outcomes on the basis of experience and adapt to new situations. One can learn to avoid situations previously associated with threat, or to return to locations where food has previously been found. **Plasticity** refers to the brain's ability to change as a result of experience and, whilst greatest during childhood, plasticity persists throughout life. At a neural level, plasticity occurs by changing the pattern of synaptic connectivity between neurons. Given that the whole brain is capable of such changes, one could regard learning and memory to be a feature of the brain as a whole rather than a specialized module or faculty. Indeed there are no instances in which memory is completely lost or abolished. Even amnesics can learn and remember certain things. Although the whole brain may make contributions to learning and memory, it is crucial to recognize that different regions contribute in different ways. Some regions may be specialized for learning and remembering words, other regions specialized for learning and remembering visual objects, and other regions may be especially important for recollecting episodes from one's life. The latter is the traditional sense in which the word "memory" is used, but there is far more to memory than that.

The general approach of this chapter is to consider different types of memory, how they are implemented in the brain and how they interact. The chapter begins by considering the distinction between long-term and short-term or working memory; a more detailed consideration of the role of executive functions in working memory is reserved for Chapter 14. The chapter then considers different types of long-term memory and discusses amnesia in terms of this theoretical framework. It then goes on to discuss whether the hippocampus has a time-limited role, whether there are separate neural substrates for familiarity and recollection and the cognitive/neural mechanisms of forgetting. Finally, the chapter discusses frontal lobe contributions to memory and distortions of memory.

SHORT-TERM AND WORKING MEMORY

The labels "short-term" and "long-term" appear to suggest that there could be different types of memory evoked for different periods of time with, perhaps, separate stores for things that happened a few days ago relative to several years ago. This is a popular misconception. It is not how psychologists distinguish between short- and long-term memory. **Short-term memory (STM)** is defined as memory for information currently held "in mind" and has limited capacity. **Long-term memory** refers to information that is stored. It need not be presently accessed or even consciously accessible. The long-term store is considered to have essentially unlimited capacity within the inherent confounds of the brain. According to this definition, memory for things that happened several hours, days or years ago are all stored within long-term memory.

KEY TERMS

Plasticity
The brain's ability to change as a result of experience.

Short-term memory
Memory for information currently held "in mind"; it has limited capacity.

Long-term memory
Memory for information that is stored but need not be consciously accessible; it has an essentially unlimited capacity.

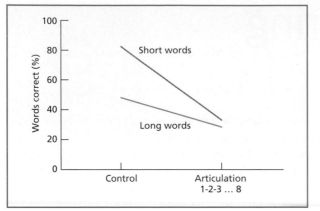

Recall of word lists from short-term memory is reduced for longer words and affected by articulatory suppression. Data from Baddeley (1975).

The capacity limit of phonological short-term memory

"Short-term memory" is often used as an abbreviated term for phonological short-term memory or verbal working memory. Other types of short-term memory may exist for other material, notably visuospatial material. The capacity limitation of phonological short-term memory is typically investigated with span tasks, in which participants are read a sequence of, say, digits, and must repeat them back immediately or after brief retention. Miller (1956) argued that humans have a span of seven items plus or minus two (i.e. between five and nine items). He argued that the seven items are meaningful "chunks" of information rather than words or syllables. For example, familiar dates such as "1812" may be one chunk but "5297" may be four single-digit chunks. However, others have argued that chunking is relying on long-term memory to recode information and that the true capacity limitation is lower (Cowan, 2001). Other evidence against Miller's proposal comes from evidence that the capacity limitation is related to phonological characteristics of the stimuli and not merely their meaningfulness. Span length is lower when lists of words are polysyllabic (e.g. "skeleton, binocular, ..."; Baddeley, Thomson, & Buchanan, 1975) or when they are phonologically similar (e.g. "map, can, cap, mat ..."; Baddeley, 1966b). Thus, the number of meaningful chunks cannot be the sole limitation. Another factor that may influence span is the opportunity to rehearse the material. Span is reduced if participants are asked to silently mouth irrelevant speech (e.g. saying "the, the, the ..." or "1, 2, 3 ...") while encoding a list (Baddeley, Lewis, & Vallar, 1984). This is termed **articulatory suppression**. Baddeley argues that span tasks involve at least two components: a phonological store and a rehearsal mechanism based on subvocal articulation that refreshes the store. Articulatory suppression impairs the latter. Collectively, he terms the store and rehearsal mechanism the "phonological loop" or the "articulatory loop" (e.g. Baddeley et al,. 1984). More brain-inspired models of this process consider the loop in terms of reciprocal activation between speech perception processes and mechanisms of speech production (e.g. Buchsbaum & D'Esposito, 2008; Jones, Macken, & Nicholls, 2004).

How do short-term and long-term memory interact?

KEY TERM

Articulatory suppression
Silently mouthing words while performing some other task (typically a memory task).

One of the most influential models of short-term memory is the "modal model" of Atkinson and Shiffrin (1968). This model divides memory into very short-lived sensory registers, a general-purpose short-term store and long-term memory. It is to be noted that Atkinson and Shiffrin did not regard their short-term store as a phonological system but rather as a control system that has more in common with Baddeley's central executive (see p. 183) than the phonological loop. In the modal model, information can only get into long-term memory, and get out of it again, via the short-term system. However, empirical evidence does not support this conclusion. First, neurological patients with reduced digit spans are capable of long-term learning. Patients with digit spans limited to one item are capable of learning and retaining lists of words, and learning paired associates (e.g. table–mouse, cabbage–money, cloud–banana) (Warrington & Shallice, 1969). Second, frequent exposure to a stimulus in short-term memory is not sufficient for learning. For example, participants are very bad at recalling the details of coins that they see many times per day (Nickerson & Adams, 1979).

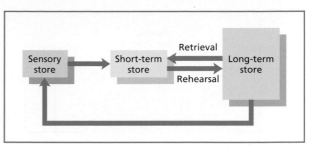

Although the modal model is incorrect, there is now good evidence that short-term memory is indeed important for long-term learning. Whereas the modal model assumed a central bottle-neck in processing (affecting all types of material), contemporary models assume that there are various short-term memory components and that each component is material-specific. Damage to a specific component will affect learning of that specific material rather than learning *per se*. Tasks such as learning of paired associates rely on forming new associations between words that have already been learned. Patients with phonological short-term memory impairments can do this (Warrington & Shallice, 1969); however, if unfamiliar words are used, such as when learning new vocabulary, these patients are impaired (Baddeley, 1993; Baddeley, Papagno, & Vallar, 1988). Moreover, individual differences in phonological short-term memory predict learning of toy names in children (Gathercole & Baddeley, 1990). There were no differences in their ability to attach familiar names (e.g. Michael, Peter) to toys but differences occurred for made-up names (e.g. Piekle, Meater).

Similarly, it has been suggested that there is a short-term memory capacity for visuospatial information (Logie, 1995). Hanley, Young, and Pearson (1991) report a patient with damage putatively to this component. The patient had difficulty with mental rotation tasks (e.g. deciding whether a rotated figure is the same as an upright one) and with memorizing visuospatial sequences (up 1, left 1, down 2, etc.). The patient could recall visual images of faces, scenes and so on from long-term memory provided they were acquired before the illness but not after the illness. This suggests a role of visuospatial short-term memory in long-term learning of visual information.

In the "modal model", short-term memory (STM) was regarded as essential for long-term learning: the greater the rehearsal in STM, the greater the learning. This idea is no longer generally accepted.

The concept of working memory

The concept of working memory is essentially an extension of the one already described for short-term memory. The key difference is that **working memory** emphasizes a wider role in cognition (reasoning, comprehension, etc.) whereas short-term memory is often taken to imply a more passive retention of material. One of the most influential models is that proposed by Baddeley and Hitch (Baddeley, 1986; Baddeley & Hitch, 1974). This model consists of three components. The phonological loop has already been described in detail and consists of a limited-capacity phonological store, together with a mechanism for refreshing it (based on subvocal rehearsal). A comparable system is postulated in the visual domain and termed the visuospatial sketchpad. Collectively, the phonological loop and visuospatial sketchpad are considered to be "slave systems". They can be contrasted with the third component: the central executive. The central executive coordinates the slave systems, and cognition in general, by retrieving things from memory, specifying task goals, initiating and terminating cognitive routines and so on. It is the interaction between

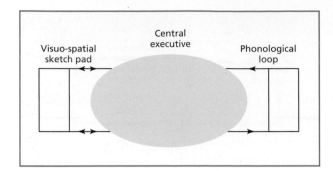

Baddeley and Hitch's (1974) model of working memory.

the flexible executive system and the more specific processing routines that is the essential characteristic of a working memory.

The working memory approach has lent itself to a number of cognitive neuroscience investigations, most of which will be considered in detail in Chapter 14 (The Executive Brain). In general, a network of regions are involved with conjoint activation of both frontal regions (involved in manipulating and retrieving information) and posterior regions (involved in storing of material).

AMNESIA AT THE MOVIES

Amnesia has been a favorite topic in Hollywood since the earliest days of cinema (no fewer than ten silent movies on the topic were made) and continues to inspire film-makers today (for a thorough review, see Baxendale, 2004). Rich socialites may become caring mothers after falling from a yacht (*Overboard*, 1987), trained assassins may forget their vocation and become stalked themselves (*The Bourne Identity*, 2002; *The Long Kiss Goodnight*, 1996), and others just require a second bump on the head to be restored to their former selves (*Tarzan the Tiger*, 1922).

Clinical amnesia tends to affect both memory for events that happened prior to injury (retrograde memory) and learning of new information (anterograde memory), although relatively selective impairments can be found. In movie amnesia, the extent of retrograde or anterograde amnesia is often very pure. For example, Leonard from the film *Memento* (2000) has total anterograde memory loss but no loss of retrograde memory (he can even remember sustaining the injury). The film vividly captures the fact that he is stuck in the present, relying purely on his retrograde memory and memory aids (notes, photos, tattoos). In one scene, he is trying to hold in mind a clue (in working memory) and searching for a pen to write it down. But, as soon as he is distracted and stops rehearsing, the clue disappears from his mind as if it was never there. Whereas the portrayal is generally accurate, his description of it as a "short-term memory problem" is not.

Selective difficulties in retrograde amnesia have been noted in the academic literature, but there is controversy as to whether these have organic or psychogenic origin related to extreme stress (Kopelman, 2000). Fortunately for Hollywood scriptwriters, psychogenic amnesia can arise after committing a violent crime (Schacter, 1986). *The Bourne Identity* (2002) offers one example of focal retrograde amnesia in the movies. It is not clear whether the character's amnesia is organic or psychogenic. According to one reviewer: "Its protagonist, who's found floating off the coast of Marseilles with two bullets in his back and the number of a Zurich safe-deposit box in some sort of laser body-implant, has no idea who he is. But he has somehow retained lightning martial-arts reflexes, fluency in a handful of languages, and the wired instincts of a superspy." These skills would indeed be expected to be preserved in amnesics.

Many films portraying amnesia show a loss of identity or a change in personality. This is not what is found in amnesia of neurological origin, in which one's sense of identity is preserved (although perhaps frozen in time). Personality changes can indeed arise from brain damage but are normally associated with a different pathology from amnesia (namely, orbitofrontal regions) or with psychiatric illness.

The 2001 film *Memento* chronicles the story of Leonard, an ex-insurance investigator who can no longer build new memories, as he attempts to find the perpetrator of a violent attack which caused his post-traumatic anterograde amnesia and left his wife dead. The attack is the last event he can recall. © Corbis Sygma.

DIFFERENT TYPES OF LONG-TERM MEMORY

So far, evidence has been presented in favor of the distinction between short-term and long-term memory. Just as short-term memory may have several components (e.g. visuospatial, phonological), long-term memory may consist of different components. This has been termed the multiple memory systems approach (e.g. Nyberg & Tulving, 1996).

One distinction that can be made is whether the memories are consciously accessible or not; termed **declarative memory** and **non-declarative memory**, respectively (Squire, Knowlton, & Musen, 1993) or, alternatively, **explicit memory** and **implicit memory**, respectively. Non-declarative memory can be thought of as consisting of several subdomains. **Procedural memory** refers to memory for skills such as riding a bike. It is not consciously accessible in the sense that the contents of the memory are not amenable to verbal report. Evidence suggests that the basal ganglia are important for the learning of procedural skills and habits (Packard & Knowlton, 2002).

Perceptual representation systems are those used for perceiving sounds, words, objects and so on (Schacter, 1987). They are memory systems in the sense that they store knowledge of the perceptual world and are capable of learning. Evidence for perceptual learning comes from priming studies. Priming refers to the fact that information is easier to access if it has recently been encountered. For example, people are more likely to complete a word fragment such as H__SE as HORSE if that word has recently been encountered. This is assumed to reflect the fact that the perceptual representation of the word is more accessible the second time around (Tulving & Schacter, 1990). Schacter, Cooper and Delaney, (1990) showed participants a sequence of unfamiliar objects. Although all objects were unfamiliar, some were plausible three-dimensional configurations whereas others were impossible configurations. When shown a second time, participants were

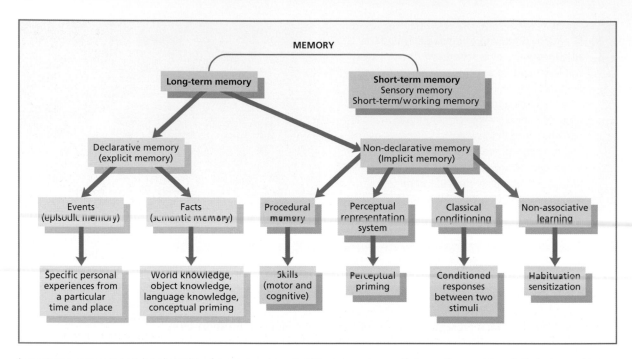

Long-term memory can be thought of as a number of different systems. But are the systems fully independent or do they depend on each other to some extent? From Gazzaniga et al. (2002). Copyright © 2002 W. W. Norton & Company, Inc. Reproduced with permission.

instructed to make a possible–impossible judgment. Priming was found (i.e. faster response times) only for the possible configurations, and not for the impossible configurations. This suggests that our perceptual systems have learned to distinguish plausible objects and that this is the source of priming in tests of implicit memory. The neural signature of priming appears to be reduced activity on the second presentation relative to the first (Schacter & Badgaiyan, 2001). Imaging studies (Schacter & Badgaiyan, 2001) and a report of a patient with occipital lobe lesion (Gabrieli, Fleischman, Keane, Reminger, & Morell, 1995) are consistent with the notion that priming involves brain regions involved in perception.

Within declarative or explicit memory, Tulving (1972) has proposed the influential distinction between episodic and semantic memory. **Semantic memory** is conceptually based knowledge about the world, including knowledge of people, places, the meaning of objects and words. It is culturally shared knowledge. By contrast, **episodic memory** refers to memory of specific events in one's own life. The memories are specific in time and place. For example, knowing that Paris is the capital of France is semantic memory, but remembering a visit to Paris or remembering being taught this fact is episodic memory. Episodic memory has a first-person characteristic to it, i.e. the memories involve oneself as an observer/participant. For this reason, it is also known as autobiographical memory. Facts about oneself (e.g. addresses, the name of your spouse) are normally regarded as semantic memory, and are usually called personal semantic memory.

There is good evidence for multiple memory systems but there is nevertheless likely to be some overlap between them. This will be outlined in subsequent sections.

AMNESIA

One of the most famous patients in the neuropsychological literature is HM (for reviews, see Corkin, 1984; Parkin, 1996). HM began to experience epileptic seizures at the age of ten and, by the time of leaving high school, his quality of life had deteriorated to a point where surgeons and family decided to intervene surgically. The procedure involved removing the medial temporal lobes, including the hippocampus, bilaterally (Scoville & Milner, 1957). What the surgeons did not foresee was that HM would develop one of the most profound amnesias on record. Several decades after the operation, it was observed that HM "does not know where he lives, who cares for him, or where he ate his last meal. His guesses as to the current year may be off by as much as 43 years.... In 1982 he did not recognize a picture of himself that had been taken on his fortieth birthday in 1966" (Corkin, 1984, p. 255).

Global amnesics have memory problems both in terms of learning new information (**anterograde memory** impairment) and remembering information prior to their brain damage (**retrograde memory** impairment). HM's retrograde deficit extends back to age 16 (11 years before his surgery) and his anterograde deficit is extremely severe (Sagar, Cohen, Corkin, & Growden, 1985). It is to be noted that amnesia is a heterogeneous disorder, with patients differing both in terms of severity and also in some qualitative respects (Spiers, Maguire, & Burgess, 2001b). This may reflect different sites of damage in and around the medial temporal lobe. It is also to be noted that HM's lesion affected several regions, not just the hippocampus.

HM's amnesia was a result of neurosurgery. However, in most people amnesia arises as a result of stroke, head injury or viral infection (notably herpes simplex encephalitis). One particularly common cause of amnesia ensues from long-term alcoholism and may be related to thiamine deficiency. This is termed **Korsakoff's syndrome**, or Korsakoff's amnesia. Korsakoff's syndrome is associated with pathology of the midline diencephalon, including the dorsomedial thalamus and the mamillary bodies (Parkin & Leng, 1993).

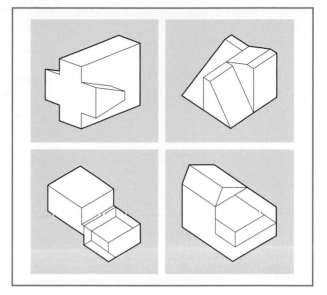

Possible and impossible objects used in the study by Schacter, Cooper and Delaney (1990). Only possible objects show priming effects, suggesting that priming taps a perceptual store of known objects. Copyright © 1990 American Psychological Association. Reproduced with permission.

KEY TERMS

Anterograde memory
Memory for events that have occurred after brain damage.

Retrograde memory
Memory for events that occurred before brain damage.

Korsakoff's syndrome
Amnesia arising from long-term alcoholism.

Damage to a number of regions in the medial temporal lobes and surrounding structures can produce an amnesic syndrome (marked with an asterisk). From Parkin (2001).

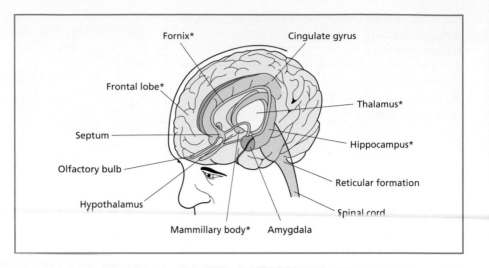

Preserved and impaired memory in amnesia

Within the framework of different types of memory outlined above, which type of memory appears to be disturbed in amnesia? Is it indeed possible to impair one particular aspect of long-term memory without there being consequences to the other systems? This section considers four different types of memory in turn.

Episodic memory

Amnesic patients are impaired on tests of episodic memory both for events related to their own lives (autobiographical memory) and other types of episode (e.g. learning lists of words). Learning of new material is normally assessed on test batteries such as the Wechsler Memory Scale (e.g. Wechsler, 1984). This contains tests of recall and recognition for verbal and visual material. Amnesia is clinically defined as poor performance on memory tests relative to that expected based on their IQ scores. Knowledge of events and facts pertaining to their life prior to the onset of amnesia (i.e. in the retrograde period) can be assessed with tests such as the Autobiographical Memory Interview (Kopelman, Wilson, & Baddeley, 1990). The degree of retrograde memory loss can vary significantly between patients (Kapur, 1999). It is debatable whether retrograde memory loss can exist without any anterograde impairment in cases of organic amnesia (Kopelman, 2000), although this pattern is reported in amnesia arising from psychiatric illness and "mental breakdown" (Kritchevsky, Chang, & Squire, 2004).

Amnesia normally consists of a severe impairment in anterograde memory, with a more variable impairment in retrograde memory (shading represents degree of impairment).

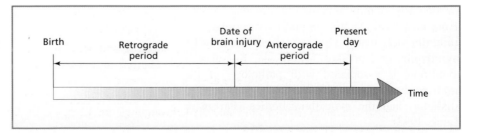

Short-term memory

One of the most consistent findings in the literature is that short-term memory in tasks such as digit span is spared (Baddeley & Warrington, 1970). Milner (1971) noted an occasion in which HM held on to a number for 15 minutes by continuously rehearsing it and using mnemonic strategies. A minute or so after stopping, he had no recollection of being asked to remember a number.

Procedural and perceptual (implicit) memory

When given new tasks requiring visuomotor coordination, such as drawing around a shape when the hand is viewed in a mirror, then performance is initially poor but improves with practice. The same is true of amnesic patients (Milner, 1966). Thus, procedural knowledge appears to be spared. The same is true of other implicit memory tasks that do not have a strong motor com-

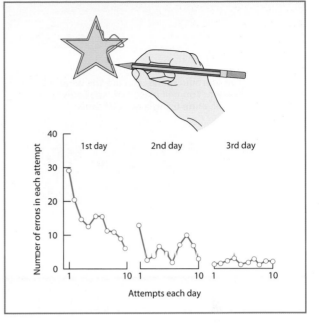

Patient HM is able to learn mirror drawing over a three-day period, despite no apparent memory for having performed the task before. From Blakemore (1977). Copyright © Cambridge University Press. Reproduced with permission.

ponent. Knowlton, Squire and Gluck (1994) devised a weather prediction game in which geometric shapes predict weather patterns with a partial degree of certainty (60–85% predictive). Participants often feel that they are guessing although they exhibit learning over 50–100 trials. That is, there is evidence of implicit learning. Amnesic patients also show normal learning despite poor declarative memory for the stimuli, whereas patients with Parkinson's disease show the reverse dissociation consistent with a role of the basal ganglia in learning of habitual responses (Knowlton, Mangels, & Squire, 1996).

Graf, Squire and Mandler (1984) tested implicit memory for words. The amnesics were given lists of words to read (e.g. DEFEND) and, at test, were presented with fragments (e.g. DEF___). They were asked either to recall the word previously shown or to generate the first word that came to mind. The latter was considered an implicit test of memory insofar as the participants were not directly asked a memory question. They found that amnesics performed normally under the implicit testing procedure (i.e. they showed priming) but not given explicit memory instructions. Within the framework proposed by Schacter (1987), this would be accounted for within the perceptual representation system for words.

Semantic memory

At first sight, amnesic patients appear to retain their knowledge of vocabulary and the world. This was initially taken as evidence that semantic memory is intact in amnesic patients (e.g. Parkin, 1982). However, a more complex picture has emerged over the years. One critical issue is the age at which the information was acquired. Most semantic knowledge is acquired within the first few years of life, whereas episodic memory develops later and is acquired throughout the lifespan. Given that amnesia tends to preserve relatively older memories (Ribot, 1882), could the

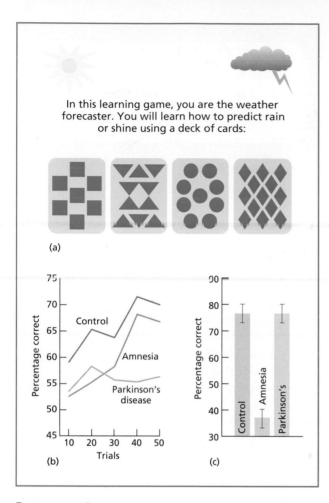

(a)

(b)

(c)

Four cue cards are presented in varying combinations and the participant must predict rain or shine (a). After repeated exposure, both controls and amnesics learn to predict but Parkinson's patients do not (b). When given a test of explicit memory about the test, the amnesic patients perform badly but the Parkinson's patients perform well (c). Adapted from Knowlton et al. (1996).

apparent sparing of semantic knowledge reflect its early acquisition? To address this question, a number of studies have investigated knowledge of vocabulary (Verfaellie, Reiss, & Roth, 1995) and famous people (Parkin, Montaldi, Leng, & Hunkin, 1990) that came into the public domain in the years prior to the onset of amnesia. These studies show amnesics to be impaired (see also Westmacott and Moscovitch, 2002). There is at least one case on record in which retrograde semantic memory is reported to be intact in the face of severe retrograde amnesia (Warrington & McCarthy, 1988). However, the patient was primarily assessed on tasks such as choosing the familiar name/face from an array, rather than supplying actual semantic details. As such, both semantic and episodic memory appear to be impaired in the retrograde period.

The discussion above pertains to the retention of previously learned semantic facts by amnesics. Can amnesics acquire new vocabulary after they become amnesic (i.e. in the anterograde period)? For patient HM (Gabrieli, Cohen, & Corkin, 1988) and many other amnesics (e.g. Manns, Hopkins, & Squire, 2003b), the answer appears to be "no". But this is by no means common to all amnesics. One amnesic is even reported to have learned a second language, Italian, following the onset of her anterograde amnesia (Hirst, Phelps, Johnson, & Volpe, 1988). Others have acquired information about famous people, public events and new vocabulary after becoming amnesic (Kitchener, Hodges, & McCarthy, 1998). However, there is one important caveat to bear in mind when considering these studies. Namely, it could be the case that both semantic and episodic memory are impaired but that semantic memory is less vulnerable because it can be learned through repetition and multiple events. There is evidence that new semantic memories may be acquired but perhaps at a slower rate (Holdstock, Mayes, Isaac, Gong, & Roberts, 2002). If tissue surrounding the hippocampus, such as the entorhinal cortex, is spared, then semantic learning may be possible although not necessarily normal (Vargha-Khadem, Gadian, Watkins, Connelly, Van Paesschen, & Mishkin, 1997b; Verfaellie, Koseff, & Alexander, 2000).

Amnesia as a deficit in consolidation

To summarize the preceding sections: amnesic patients have impaired episodic memory, typically in both retrograde and anterograde periods. In contrast they have spared short-term memory, procedural memory and perceptual priming (a type of implicit memory). Tulving and colleagues (1988) regard amnesia specifically as a difficulty with episodic memory. However, semantic memory is impaired in amnesia including after focal hippocampal lesions, even though it is often less vulnerable to damage than episodic memory (Holdstock et al., 2002; Manns et al., 2003b). New semantic memories may be formed by repetition learning that is not dependent on the hippocampus. As such, Squire and colleagues suggest that amnesia is a deficit in declarative memory (e.g. Manns et al., 2003b, Squire, 1992). This explanation offers the most satisfactory description of the pattern of preservation and impairment.

Accounts of amnesia purely in terms of damage to a memory system (whether it be declarative or episodic) are clearly insufficient, in that they offer no account of the function of that system or the underlying mechanisms. One common mechanistic explanation of amnesia is in terms of a deficit of **consolidation**. Consolidation is the process by which moment-to-moment changes in brain activity are translated into permanent structural changes in the brain (e.g. by forming new neural connections). On the surface, consolidation theory seems better equipped to explain deficits in forming new memories rather than retrograde memory impairments. However, consolidation theories have been used to account for retrograde memory loss by assuming that consolidation takes years to achieve and, thus, poorly consolidated memories for events prior to injury will be affected too (e.g. Squire, 1992). However, for consolidation theory to be true it is necessary to limit it to the consolidation of certain types of information, given that amnesics can learn some things.

Why is it that the medial temporal lobes require this process of consolidation when other learning mechanisms of the brain (e.g. those involved in implicit memory) apparently do not? Or, to put it another way, what is special about declarative memory? One suggestion is that this type of memory involves linking together lots of different types of information (perceptual, affective, semantic, cognitive) that are likely to be processed in very different regions of the brain. As such, many theories of medial temporal lobe function suggest that they implement an index or pointer system that link together diverse aspects of an event (e.g. Murre, Graham, & Hodges, 2001; Nadel & Moscovitch, 1997). Dudai (2004) argues that this consolidation mechanism takes longer and follows on from a more rapid synaptic consolidation. This may be the neurobiological correlate of context learning and one suggestion is that amnesia reflects a failure of context (e.g. Mayes, 1988). Memory for context closely relates to Tulving's (1972) definition of episodic memory as being specifiable in time ("when did the event occur?") and place ("where did the event occur?"), although context can incorporate other types of situational information too. Although semantic memories are normally defined as context-free, they also require different kinds of information (e.g. appearance, function, name) to be bound together.

Huppert and Piercy (1978) tested the context deficit hypothesis. They presented pictures on either one occasion or three occasions over a period of two days to Korsakoff amnesics. After presenting pictures on the second day, the patients were given a test: they were shown the pictures again and asked to decide whether they were seen today or yesterday. The pictures shown three times on the first day showed a striking tendency to be misjudged as being presented on the second day. That is, the amnesics confused frequency of presentation with how recently it was presented. This is consistent with the contextual deficit account.

Evaluation

Accounting for the learning and memory that amnesics *can* do is as important as understanding what they can't remember. The results support a "multiple memory systems" view of the brain in which declarative memory is particularly affected in amnesics. Episodic memories may be special by virtue of the fact that they contain

KEY TERM

Long-term potentiation (LTP)
An increase in the long-term responsiveness of a postsynaptic neuron in response to stimulation of a presynaptic neuron.

rich contextual detail. These contextual details may be linked together by structures in the medial temporal lobe, including the hippocampus, and may gradually be consolidated over time. Newly learned semantic facts may initially be context dependent but become less so over time. Although most contemporary researchers would concur with many of these points, it is worthwhile pointing out that this represents a rather simple view of memory and amnesia. Subsequent sections will delve more deeply into the different mechanisms that constitute remembering, and their neural basis.

In models that assume a time-limited role for the hippocampus in memory consolidation, the hippocampus initially acts to bind together different aspects of the memory (e.g. perceptual, affective, linguistic components) represented in disparate regions of the brain. Over time, these different aspects of the memory trace may be linked as part of a cortico-cortical network that is largely independent of the hippocampus. Active units/connections are shown in red. From Frankland and Bontempi (2005). Reprinted by permission from Macmillan Publishers Ltd, copyright 2005.

THE NEUROSCIENCE OF CONSOLIDATION

The initial formation of memories involves an increase in the probability that a postsynaptic neuron will fire in response to neurotransmitters released from presynaptic neurons. In the laboratory, this has been studied by applying brief, high-frequency stimulation to presynaptic neurons and the artificially induced change in responsiveness of the postsynaptic neuron is termed **long-term potentiation** (or LTP). In awake rats, the effects are sustained over weeks. This process is accompanied by rapid modification of existing synaptic proteins, followed by synthesis of new proteins at the modified synapse. The time course of this process can be assessed by injecting chemicals that inhibit protein synthesis at various stages after learning and is found to occur within an hour (e.g. Agranoff, David, & Brink, 1966). This synaptic consolidation is a universal property of the nervous system.

Dudai (2004) distinguishes between two types of consolidation: a fast *synaptic consolidation* that may occur anywhere in the nervous system, and a slower *system consolidation* that may be related particularly to the hippocampus and declarative memory. In rats, this can be studied by

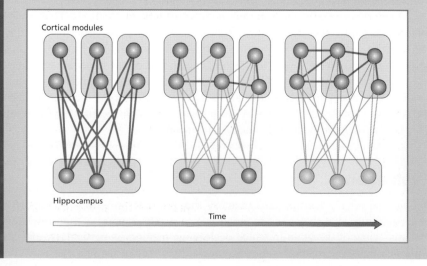

Cortical modules

Hippocampus

Time

lesioning the hippocampus at various stages after learning (e.g. Kim & Fanselow, 1992). These studies suggest that, in rats, it takes around one month for consolidation to be complete. In humans, evidence from retrograde amnesia suggests that the process may take years. This mechanism is not well understood but is assumed to involve the hippocampal formation sending synaptic messages to neocortical neurons that promote consolidation mechanisms in the neocortex itself. In effect, the memory is slowly transferred from the hippocampus to the cortex.

A number of connectionist models have been developed to mimic long-term consolidation of episodic and/or semantic memory. The model of McClelland, McNaughton and O'Reilly (1995) provides a computational motivation for having a slow learning mechanism. They argue that adding a new memory to the neocortex straightaway would significantly distort old memories by a process called "catastrophic interference". In their model, the hippocampus learns rapidly and then integrates this information gradually to enable efficient learning without disrupting existing memory structures.

MEMORY STORAGE AND CONSOLIDATION: A TIME-LIMITED ROLE FOR THE HIPPOCAMPUS?

It has been argued that one of the crucial functions of the hippocampus is the consolidation of memories, particularly episodic memory. But how long does it take for a memory to be fully consolidated? Moreover, is its role restricted to consolidation or does it store some aspect of the memory that is needed to enable efficient retrieval? Although most researchers argue that the content of a memory (who, what, where and when) is stored in the neocortex, it is unclear whether the hippocampus is needed to link these attributes together just during consolidation or in perpetuity.

One of the most consistently reported findings in the amnesia literature is that recall of events in the retrograde period shows a *temporal gradient* such that memories from earlier in life are easier to recall than those later in life. This has been termed **Ribot's law**, after its discoverer (Ribot, 1882). For example, Butters and Cermak (1986) reported the case of a college professor, PZ, who became amnesic a couple of years after writing his autobiography. When tested for his ability to recollect events from his life, a clear temporal gradient was found, with more remote memories spared. The most common explanation for this phenomenon is in terms of consolidation theory – namely, that the older the event, the more consolidated it is and the less dependent on the hippocampus it is (Squire, 1992). However, other explanations for the temporal gradient exist.

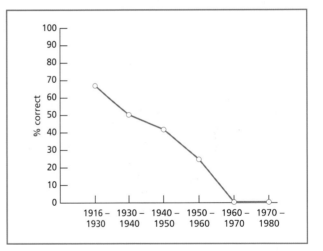

PZ was an eminent scientist (born 1914) who developed amnesia two years after writing his autobiography. His ability to recall events from his past life showed a clear temporal gradient. From Butters and Cermak (1986). Copyright © Cambridge University Press. Reproduced with permission.

FIVE DIFFERENT EXPLANATIONS FOR TEMPORAL GRADIENTS IN AMNESIA

1. The temporal gradient can arise because the stimuli are not carefully matched across decades (i.e. the stimuli for more remote decades are easier) (Sanders & Warrington, 1971).
2. The apparent loss of retrograde knowledge is anterograde amnesia in disguise. Alcoholics who subsequently go on to develop Korsakoff's amnesia may not have fully encoded the memories in the first instance. This cannot, of course, account for all cases but it may account for some.
3. Older memories become more semantic-like and less episodic with the passing of time because they get rehearsed more often. They become more like stories than memories (Cermak & O'Connor, 1983).
4. Each time an old event is remembered, this creates a new memory for that event. The older the event, the greater the number of traces and the more resilient to brain damage it will be (Nadel & Moscovitch, 1997).
5. The hippocampus has a time-limited role and the more consolidated the memory is, the less dependent on the hippocampus it is (Squire, 1992).

It is difficult to establish how long, in humans, the hippocampus is required before consolidation is complete. The extent of retrograde amnesia can vary from a few years to over 40 years (e.g. Cipolotti et al., 2001). Some have argued that there is no evolutionary advantage to having a system that takes so long to consolidate a memory and suggest, instead, that the hippocampus is involved in some permanent aspects of memory storage (Nadel & Moscovitch, 1997). In support of this view, a number of functional imaging studies have failed to find a difference in medial temporal lobe activity comparing recall of events from the recent past relative to the remote past (Gilboa, Winocur, Grady, Hevenor, & Moscovitch,

The different regions of the medial temporal lobe.

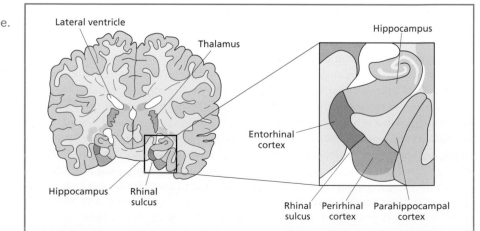

2004; Maguire, Henson, Mummery, & Frith, 2001). However, Haist, Bowden Gore and Mao (2001) did find evidence, using fMRI, of a remote versus recent difference in a famous faces test on older adults. They found evidence for two different consolidation mechanisms with somewhat different time courses. The hippocampus was believed to be important for several years, whereas the entorhinal cortex may be involved in consolidation for up to 20 years. The entorhinal cortex is the major input and output portal between the hippocampus and the neocortex. Some researchers have interpreted this region as being important for forming new semantic memories, as opposed to episodic memories (Vargha-Khadem, Isaacs, & Mishkin, 1994; Verfaellie et al., 2000), and it is interesting to note that the Haist et al. (2001) study also investigated retrograde semantic memory. Other research has suggested that the extent of retrograde amnesia is linked to the size of the entorhinal and parahippocampal lesion but not of the hippocampus itself (Yoneda, Mori, Yamashita, & Yamadori, 1994). In summary, on balance the evidence favors the notion of a time-limited role for the hippocampus, although surrounding brain structures may also contribute to this process and give rise to different profiles of amnesia when damaged.

Most of the lesion studies described so far have concerned amnesic patients with deficits believed to lie, minimally, in consolidation. A complementary approach is to study patients with damage to the lateral neocortex. This is assumed to be the storage site after memories have been consolidated. A number of studies involving semantic dementia patients have been carried out along these lines (with atrophy typically in the anterior temporal cortex). It has been demonstrated that these patients can use their relatively intact episodic/autobiographical knowledge to supplement their impoverished knowledge of objects and words. For example, some patients are better at naming objects (e.g. a toothbrush) when the object belongs to the patient and is in its familiar context (Snowden, Griffiths, & Neary, 1994). However, these patients do not have intact episodic memory across all time spans and show a *reversed* temporal gradient to that found in amnesia: namely, better recent than remote memory (e.g. Nestor, Graham, Bozeat, Simons, & Hodges, 2002). Although these patients have impoverished language as well as memory, they can be tested using the same cue words for different time periods (e.g. "think of a memory related to a *restaurant* in 2000–2005, or 1960–1970") or using famous faces (Hodges & Graham, 1998). How far back does their good episodic memory go? Nestor et al. (2002) argue that it is around four years and that this figure corresponds to the time-limited role of the hippocampus. The explanation is as follows. Patients with damage to the lateral neocortex of the temporal lobes have impaired memory storage for both semantic and episodic memories. However, memories for recent events have not yet been fully transferred from the hippocampus to the neocortex and so are relatively intact.

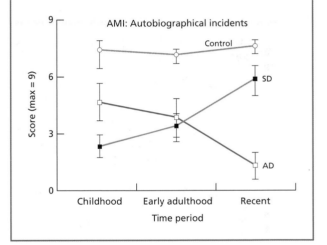

Semantic dementia patients (SD) show a reverse temporal gradient from that found in amnesics with Alzheimer's disease (AD). This has been used as evidence to support a time-limited role of the hippocampus in memory consolidation. Reprinted from Nestor, Graham, Bozeat, Simons and Hodges (2002). Copyright 2002, with permission from Elsevier.

KEY TERMS

Recognition memory
A memory test in which participants must decide whether a stimulus was shown on a particular occasion.

Recall
Participants must produce previously seen stimuli without a full prompt being given (compare recognition memory).

Familiarity
Context-free memory in which the recognized item just feels familiar.

Recollection
Context-dependent memory that involves remembering specific information from the study episode.

THEORIES OF REMEMBERING, KNOWING AND FORGETTING

Recall versus recognition and familiarity versus recollection

This chapter has, thus far, concentrated on different types of memory *systems*. But to what extent do different types of memory *tasks* use different memory systems? Within the domain of explicit tests of memory (i.e. in which participants are directly asked to remember), the main tasks used are tests of **recognition memory** and tests of **recall**. In typical tests of recall, participants may be shown a list of words and asked to recall them in any order (free recall), in the order given (serial recall) or given a prompt (e.g. "one of the words begins with W", cued recall). In typical tests of recognition memory, participants may be shown a list of words and then, at test, asked to decide whether a given word was previously presented on that list (single probe recognition) or shown two words and asked to decide which one was previously presented in the list (forced choice recognition). Some typical results are shown below.

Mandler (1980) proposed that recognition memory consists of two distinct mechanisms and that this could account for its general advantage over tests of recall. One mechanism, **familiarity**, is considered to be context free and the recognized item just feels familiar. The other mechanism, **recollection**, is context dependent and involves remembering specific information from the study episode. Tests of recall are considered almost exclusively to be dependent on recollection.

If amnesia reflects a deficit of contextual information, then it would be expected that they would be more reliant on familiarity and that recognition memory may be less impaired than recall. However, in most amnesics this is not the case (Kopelman & Stanhope, 1998). It is important to note that most amnesics have damage to several regions in and around the medial temporal lobes and if the mechanisms supporting familiarity and recollection are separate but nearby, then deficits in both could well be the norm. A number of recent reports of patients with very selective damage to the hippocampus do, however, support the notion that recollection can be specifically impaired (Aggleton & Brown, 1999; Bastin et al., 2004). Mayes and colleagues have documented the remarkable patient, YR (Mayes et al., 2001; Mayes, Holdstock, Isaac, Hunkin, & Roberts, 2002; Mayes et al., 2004). Not only was YR's recognition memory for single items (e.g. words, pictures) spared but she could recognize previously seen stimulus pairs provided they were of the same kind (e.g. word–word, object–object) but *not* if they were of a different kind (e.g. object–location, word–object, face–name). This supports the view that the hippocampus binds together different types of information to form memory traces.

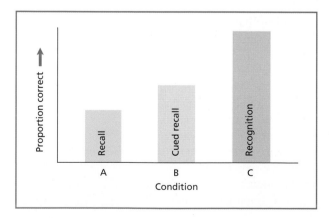

Typical results from different types of memory test. From Parkin (1999).

In contrast to the position that familiarity and recollection are different processes, some have argued that they are just stronger and weaker forms of the same process (e.g. Wixted & Stretch, 2004) or that the processes involved in familiarity are a subset of those involved in recollection. For example, recollection may require the additional use of frontal mechanisms (e.g. Manns, Hopkins, Reed, Kitchener, & Squire, 2003a; Squire, Stark, & Clark, 2004). There is some problematic evidence for these accounts. Ranganath et al. (2004) conducted an fMRI study that shows hippocampal activity in recollection, whereas familiarity selectively activated an adjacent region of cortex, called the perirhinal cortex. A more recent single case study of a human patient with a perirhinal lesion but spared hippocampus demonstrated impaired familiarity but spared recollection (Bowles et al., 2007). This supports the idea that familiarity and recollection have partly separable neural processes. Animal studies confirm the importance of the perirhinal region in recognition memory and stimulus–stimulus association memory (Murray & Bussey, 1999).

Aside from medial temporal regions, a number of cortical regions have been associated with recollection and familiarity: notably in the frontal lobes. Broadly speaking, there are two ways in which such activity can be interpreted: (1) in terms of different conscious experiences; and (2) in terms of different underlying processes. Of course, these two ideas need not be mutually exclusive and are probably related. Recollection and familiarity are associated with different "feelings" or conscious states. These have been called "remembering" and "knowing", respectively (Gardiner, 2000; Tulving, 1985). Recollection, in particular, has been described as "mental time travel", in which contextual detail is placed in a personal past (Wheeler, Stuss, & Tulving, 1997). In one recognition memory test using fMRI, participants were asked to judge whether they *remember* any context detail, or whether they *know* that they have seen it before but do not recollect context (Henson, Rugg, Shallice, Josephs, & Dolan, 1999a). A left anterior frontal region was associated with "remember" responses and explained as retrieval of contextual detail, whereas a right dorsolateral frontal region was associated with "know" responses and explained as greater memory monitoring due to lack of certainty.

Why do we forget things?

Forgetting may be important for efficient use of memory, rather than a design fault. Access to previous information needs to be prioritized so that the most relevant information is retrieved. One needs to remember where, for example, the car is parked today not where it was parked last week. It may be adaptive to lose information for some episodes, or to blend information from different episodes together (e.g. to be able to remember where one *tends* to park the car). Explanations of why we forget have tended to be divided into the stages of encoding, storage or retrieval (for a more unitary account of forgetting, see Wixted, 2004). Each of these may be relevant to some degree.

If information is not processed adequately at encoding it may be forgotten. The **levels-of-processing account** of memory states that information that is processed semantically is more likely to be remembered than information that is processed perceptually (Craik & Lockhart, 1972). For example, if participants are asked to generate an adjective for a list of words (e.g. house → big) relative to generating a rhyme (house → mouse) or counting letters (house → 5), they are much more able to later recall those words (Eysenck, 1974). Regions in the frontal lobes may be important for selecting the attributes to attend to at encoding (Kapur, Craik, Tulving, Wilson, Houle, & Brown, 1994). Some studies have examined forgetting due to encoding

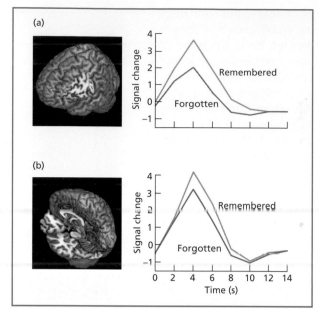

(a)

(b)

Activity at encoding in (a) left ventrolateral prefrontal cortex and (b) left parahippocampal region predicts whether or not the word is likely to be subsequently remembered or forgotten.

directly. Wagner et al. (1998b) scanned participants when they were studying a list of words that were subsequently tested in a recognition memory test. Following the test, they then went back and looked at the brain activity during encoding to ask the question: does the brain activity at encoding predict which items are later going to be recognized and which will be forgotten? Activity in left temporal (parahippocampal) and a left frontal site (Brodmann area 44) at encoding was predictive of later recognizing versus forgetting. The frontal activity may relate to selection of features to encode whereas the medial temporal activity reflects actual memory formation. An amnesic patient has been shown to demonstrate normal frontal activity at encoding despite having no subsequent memory (see Buckner, Kelley, & Petersen, 1999). In contrast, electrode recordings in epileptic patients undergoing surgery have also shown that synchronous firing of neurons in hippocampal and surrounding cortical regions predicts subsequent memory versus forgetting (Fell, Klaver, Lehnertz, Schaller, Elger, & Fernandez, 2001).

Distinguishing between forgetting due to loss from storage versus a failure of retrieval is very hard in practice. This is because information that appears inaccessible may subsequently be remembered (implying it was never really lost), or information may appear accessible when certain tests are used (e.g. implicit tests) but not others. If one accepts a multiple memory systems view, then it is conceivable that memories can be lost from one store but not other stores.

Tulving (1983) has argued that the extent to which there is contextual similarity between the retrieval attempt and the initial encoding phase predicts the likelihood of remembering versus forgetting. This has been termed the **encoding specificity hypothesis**. Godden and Baddeley (1975) taught people lists of words either on land or underwater (when diving), and tested their recall either on land or underwater. Recall was better when learning and test were in the same location (land–land, sea–sea) relative to when they differed (land–sea, sea–land). Similarly, alcoholics may hide objects when drunk, forget where they are when sober, but remember the location again on a subsequent binge (Goodwin, Powell, Bremer, Hoine, & Stern, 1969). In these experiments, forgetting appears to reflect retrieval difficulties rather than storage difficulties.

What type of mechanism gives way to forgetting things that have already been encoded? Two broad explanations exist: passive mechanisms such as trace decay (memories spontaneously weaken), or active mechanisms such as interference and inhibition (memories weaken through interactions with each other or with strategic control processes). Although trace decay is hard to rule out altogether, there is good evidence for more active forgetting mechanisms. Anderson, Bjork and Bjork (1994) devised a memory paradigm consisting of three phases. In the first phase, participants study lists of words associated with several different category labels (e.g. fruit–orange, fruit–banana). In the second phase, they rehearse some of the associations (e.g. fruit–orange) but not others (e.g. fruit–banana). In the test phase they are given the category labels (e.g. fruit–) and asked to generate the initial studied words.

KEY TERM

Encoding specificity hypothesis
Events are easier to remember when the context at retrieval is similar to the context at encoding.

Performance on unstudied exemplars (e.g. banana) was worse than for studied items in the second phase and, crucially, was worse than that expected if the second phase had been omitted altogether. Anderson et al. (1994) argue that the act of retrieval causes active inhibition of similar competing memories. This has been termed **retrieval-induced forgetting**. To return to the car analogy, remembering where one parked the car today may actively inhibit memories for where it was parked on other days.

The previous section suggested that in some situations memories can *automatically* be inhibited, leading to forgetting, but can memories be inhibited *voluntarily*? Can we choose to forget? Experiments

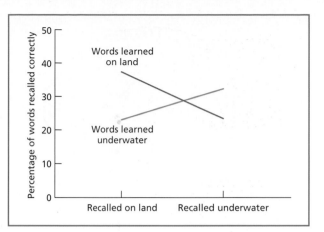

Words are better remembered if they are both learned and recalled in the same context. From Baddeley (1990).

using the **directed forgetting** paradigm suggest that it is possible. In directed forgetting experiments participants are read two lists of words. In the experimental condition, after the first list they are told that this was a practice block and the list can be forgotten. In the control condition, they are told that the first list needs to be remembered. After both lists have been presented they are instructed to recall from both lists even though they had previously been instructed to forget them. Recall is generally worse for the words given forget instructions (Bjork, 1998). Conway and Fthenaki (2003) found that lesions to the right frontal lobe disrupted the ability to do direct forgetting but retrieval induced forgetting remained intact. This demonstrates a dissociation between voluntary or strategic forgetting, on the one hand, and automatic or rehearsal-based forgetting, on the other. Anderson et al. (2004) conducted an fMRI study in which pairs of words (e.g. jaw–gum, steam–train) were learned and then, at test, cue words (e.g. jaw– steam–) were presented and participants were instructed either to remember the associate or not remember it. Controlling the unwanted memories increased left and right dorsolateral prefrontal cortex activation, but decreased hippocampal activation relative to the remembering condition.

THE ROLE OF THE PREFRONTAL CORTEX IN LONG-TERM MEMORY

The prefrontal cortex of the frontal lobes is traditionally viewed as having a controlling and organizing role in relation to cognition rather than a storage role. These "executive functions" are discussed in detail in another chapter, but will be briefly considered here in the context of the online control of memory-related processes. It is helpful to consider a number of different broad subdivisions within the frontal lobes. First, one can make a division between the outer (lateral) surface, on the one hand, and the under surface (orbitofrontal) and medial surface, on the other. The orbitofrontal and medial regions have strong connections with medial temporal and diencephalic regions. Lesions here can produce memory impairments, albeit of a different character from classical amnesia (e.g. Parkin, 1997). For example, the production of false and incoherent memories is often observed following lesions in this region, one extreme form of which is confabulation (considered later). Damage to the lateral frontal lobes does not produce memory dysfunction *per se*, but disrupts the control of cognition more generally, including some aspects of memory. Most of the insights into the roles of the lateral frontal lobes in

KEY TERMS

Retrieval-induced forgetting
Retrieval of a memory causes active inhibition of similar competing memories.

Directed forgetting
Forgetting arising because of a deliberate intention to forget.

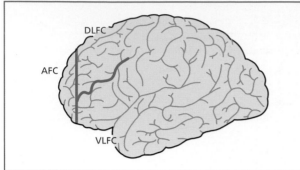

A number of researchers have made a distinction between the separate functions of the ventrolateral (VL), dorsolateral (DL) and anterior frontal (AF) cortex of the lateral frontal lobe. From Fletcher and Henson (2001). Reproduced with permission of Oxford University Press.

long-term memory have come from functional imaging studies. In their review of the literature, Fletcher and Henson (2001) identify dorsolateral and ventrolateral regions that appear to be associated with different functions (see also, Petrides, 1996).

Ventrolateral prefrontal region

This region is often activated during memory encoding. It is activated during incidental learning (Kapur et al., 1994), i.e. situations in which participants do not know that their memory will later be tested. Thus, whatever its function, it is not specific to long-term memory. Fletcher and Henson (2001) suggest that the left ventrolateral region is involved in maintaining and retrieving semantic memories. (See Chapter 12 for a discussion of Broca's area, which lies in the left ventrolateral frontal lobe.) This region is associated with levels-of-processing manipulations in which semantic versus shallow processing of a stimulus is compared using functional imaging (Kapur et al., 1994). Activity in this region predicts subsequent remembering versus forgetting (Wagner et al., 1998b). One earlier suggestion in the literature was that the left frontal lobe in general is specialized for encoding, and the right for retrieval (Tulving, Kapur, Craik, Moscovitch, & Houle, 1994). This was termed the HERA model, standing for Hemispheric Encoding/Retrieval Asymmetry. However, subsequent studies have shown this to be not strictly true. Although the left hemisphere may be important during verbal encoding, the right hemisphere may be important when pictures or faces are presented (Wagner, Poldrack, Eldridge, Desmond, Glover, & Gabrieli, 1998a).

Dorsolateral prefrontal region

The dorsolateral prefrontal cortex (particularly on the left hemisphere) has been associated with selecting from a range of alternatives and is by no means specific to memory tasks (Frith, 2000). In one encoding task, activity in this region increased when the list of words to be memorized became more disorganized (e.g. words thematically grouped versus random) (Fletcher, Shallice, & Dolan, 1998a). However, this region is more widely recognized for playing a role in memory retrieval. Retrieval demands can vary, depending on the type of retrieval cue provided (e.g. free recall, cued retrieval or recognition) and/or the amount of information that needs to be retrieved (e.g. the amount of contextual information). Activity in the dorsolateral region, particularly on the right, is greatest when the retrieval cue is minimal (e.g. free recall; Fletcher, Shallice, Frith, Frackowiak, & Dolan, 1998b) and is greatest when context must be recollected compared to simple recognition (Henson, Shallice, & Rugg, 1999b). Fletcher and Henson (2001) suggest that the specific function of the region is to evaluate what has been retrieved (or "monitoring").

CONSTRUCTIVE MEMORY AND MEMORY DISTORTIONS

One popular metaphor for memory is in terms of a store of memory traces, and the act of remembering involves the retrieval of traces from the store (see Roediger, 1980).

This metaphor is very misleading. The idea that the past is somehow represented directly in the brain independently from other aspects of cognition has been termed the "memory trace paradox" (Dalla Barba, 2001). The past is not, by and large, represented in different brain structures from those concerned with dealing with the present. Thus the act of remembering can be construed as making inferences about the past based on what is currently known and accessible. This general approach to memory stands in sharp contrast to the storehouse metaphor, and is termed the **constructive memory** approach (e.g. Schacter, Norman, & Koutstaal, 1998). Studies based on the constructive memory approach have tended to rely on evidence of memory distortions (i.e. mis-remembering an event) rather than forgetting.

Source memory

Source memory provides a good example of how remembering involves making an inference and attribution. **Source monitoring** is the process by which retrieved memories are attributed to their original context; for example, whether the event was seen or imagined, whether the story was told by Tim or Bob, whether the event happened in the morning or evening and so on. This is closely related to the process of *recollection* that has already been considered. However, Johnson and colleagues argue that placing an event in context involves an active evaluation process rather than directly retrieving information that specifies the origin of the memory (Johnson, 1988; Johnson, Hashtroudi, & Lindsay, 1993). Moreover, the evaluation is based on qualitative characteristics of the information retrieved, such as the level of perceptual, temporal, spatial, semantic and affective information.

Johnson, Foley and Leach (1988a) asked participants to distinguish between memories of heard and imagined words. One group of participants heard some words in the experimenter's voice and was asked to imagine another set of words in the *experimenter's voice*. These participants made more source confusions than another group who heard words in the experimenter's voice and were asked to imagine another set of words in their *own voice*. Encoding of more perceptually distinct features can aid source monitoring (deciding whether a word was heard or imagined) even if the perceptual features are imagined.

We do not just remember enacted or perceived events. We also remember mental events involving our thoughts, intentions, dreams and imaginations. How do we tell if a memory is for an external event or a mental event? It has been suggested that external events contain richer spatial, temporal, affective and perceptual detail than mental events, whereas mental events contain more detail about "cognitive operations" (Johnson & Raye, 1981; Johnson, Foley, Suengas, & Raye, 1988b). The latter refers to the strategies used to generate the thought, and this may also form part of the encoded memory. For example, source confusions are less common given a strategically more complex encoding task (e.g. exemplar generation, animal → "dog") relative to an easier one (e.g. antonym generation, hot → "cold") (Johnson, Raye, Foley, & Foley, 1981). Schizophrenics have difficulties with this aspect of source monitoring. They tend to classify self-generated words as having been externally generated by the experimenter (Brebion, Smith, Gorman, & Amador, 1997).

KEY TERMS

Constructive memory
The act of remembering construed in terms of making inferences about the past, based on what is currently known and accessible.

Source monitoring
The process by which retrieved memories are attributed to their original context.

How can we distinguish between memories for heard words and memories for imagined words? Source monitoring involves an active evaluation of the quality and content of the retrieved information.

Source monitoring has been associated with the lateral prefrontal cortex. Patients with lesions in this region have difficulties in putting memories in their spatial and temporal context despite having good general recognition memory (Janowsky, Shimamura, & Squire, 1989; Milner, Corsi, & Leonard, 1991b). Henson et al. (1999b) measured brain activity when healthy participants were required to judge the temporal context (first or second list) or spatial context (high or low) of previously presented words. When compared against a baseline of simple old/new recognition of words, bilateral dorsolateral prefrontal activation was found.

Try reading aloud these lists of words to a friend and then ask them to recall as many of them as possible. Do they misremember hearing the words "sleep", "foot" and "bread"? (Lists taken from Roediger and McDermott, 1995.)

bed	shoe	butter
rest	hand	food
awake	toe	eat
tired	kick	sandwich
dream	sandals	rye
wake	soccer	jam
snooze	yard	milk
blanket	walk	flour
doze	ankle	jelly
slumber	arm	dough
snore	boot	crust
nap	inch	slice
peace	sock	wine
yawn	smell	loaf
drowsy	mouth	toast

False memories

The notion that retrieval of memories is inherently variable implies that judgments about memory can also be inaccurate. Such inaccuracies may tend to be inconsequential or rare. However, in more extreme cases entire episodes that never existed may be recollected, as in the case of confabulation (discussed below). A **false memory** is a memory that is either partly or wholly inaccurate, but is accepted as a real memory by the person doing the remembering.

KEY TERM

False memory
A memory that is either partly or wholly inaccurate but is accepted as a real memory by the person doing the remembering.

Roediger and McDermott (1995) developed a paradigm that could induce high levels of false recall and false recognition in non-clinical populations. At study, participants are read lists of words (e.g. bed, night, tired . . .) that are semantically related to a critical word that is never presented (e.g. sleep). At test, participants claim to remember many of the critical words. They do so with high confidence and will attribute recollective experience to the false recognition (not just familiarity). If some of the lists are presented in male and female voices they will state that the critical word "sleep" was heard in a particular voice, even if the instructions encourage them not to guess (Payne, Elie, Blackwell, & Neuschatz, 1996).

How can these results be explained? One explanation is that the critical word is implicitly activated at encoding through a semantic network (Underwood, 1965). However, it is not clear why this would result in a conscious feeling of remembering as opposed to familiarity. Another explanation is that participants consciously think about the critical word, "sleep", at encoding and subsequently make a source confusion (mistaking thinking for hearing). One problem for this theory is that false recognition can be induced using abstract shapes presented at study that are based on a non-presented prototype (Koutstaal, Schacter, Verfaellie, Brenner, & Jackson, 1999). It is unlikely that participants would consciously generate other abstract shapes at study. A more satisfactory explanation is that false recognition/recall occurs because the features of the non-presented item reactivate the features in the "memory trace" of true memories (Schacter & Slotnick, 2004). Evidence for this comes from the observation of hippocampal activity in both true and false recognition observed by fMRI (Cabeza, Rao, Wagner, Mayer, & Schacter, 2001). However, there are some brain differences between true and false recognition. If words are initially presented on either the left or right side, then a contralateral ERP component is subsequently observed for true but not false memories (Fabiani, Stadler, & Wessels, 2000). Moreover, in an fMRI study involving abstract shapes, activity in early visual regions was found for true but not false memories (Slotnick & Schacter, 2004). Why don't participants use this sensory signal to avoid false recognition? It is possible that the difference between true and false memories lies within implicit memory systems and makes little contribution to the conscious memory evaluation.

Neuropsychology of confabulation

Confabulating patients provide memories and information that is false and sometimes self-contradictory without intending to lie (Gilboa & Moscovitch, 2002). For example, when one patient was asked about the Falklands war, she spontaneously described a fictitious holiday to the islands (Damasio, Graff-Radford, Eslinger, Damasio, & Kassell, 1985). She pictured herself strolling with her husband, and buying local trinkets in a store. When asked by the experimenter what language they speak there, she confidently replied: "Falklandese, what else?" Some confabulations may have an obvious relationship to events from the person's past, whereas others are harder to account for. Patients tend to believe in the false memory and even act upon it.

Although confabulating patients typically perform poorly on standard memory tests, they differ from amnesics in important ways. When recalling a story, amnesic patients may forget most of the information, whereas confabulating patients may embellish it or introduce new facts. Confabulation is associated with damage to different regions from amnesia, namely the orbitofrontal and ventromedial prefrontal cortex and often arises when the *anterior communicating artery* that lies beneath this region is ruptured (although the symptom is often transient). It is unlikely that it is due to filling in gaps to avoid social embarrassment because most confabulating patients are unaware or unconcerned about their problem.

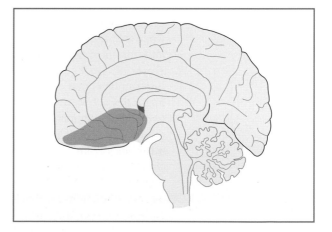

Confabulation is often associated with damage to the ventromedial frontal and orbitofrontal regions.

Moscovitch (1995) suggests that **confabulation** results from a failure of a particular type of retrieval operation. He argues that episodic memories tend to be retrieved by strategic search functions, whereas semantic knowledge tends to be retrieved by more automatic, associative search processes. Damage to the strategic search mechanisms in confabulators may result in the retrieval of memories and memory fragments that are inappropriate in the context of the current task. The fact that patients will confabulate across all time periods of their life supports the notion that the defective mechanism is in retrieval. Although strategic retrieval tends to be associated more with episodic memories, there are exceptions. The retrieval of certain types of semantic memories, such as describing historical events or fairytales, also tends to be impaired in confabulators (Delbecq-Derouesne, Beauvois, & Shallice, 1990; Moscovitch & Melo, 1997). These memories require strategic reconstruction of a complex narrative even though these memories lack the contextual aspect of recollection.

A number of related accounts of confabulation explain it in terms of source monitoring (Johnson, O'Connor, & Cantor 1997) or executive functions (Burgess & Shallice, 1996b). Burgess and Shallice identify a number of relevant mechanisms, including "description processes" that specify the type of memory required, "editing processes" that check whether the retrieved memory meets the task requirements, and "mediator processes" that trouble-shoot by resolving internal inconsistencies (e.g. of being in two places at the same time). Within this type of framework confabulation may arise from damage to several components either in isolation or perhaps in combination (see also, Kopelman, Ng, & Van Den Brouke, 1997). One difficulty faced by theories of strategic retrieval, source monitoring and executive functions is that the weight of evidence, particularly from functional imaging, suggests that the lateral frontal lobes are crucial for these operations. However, the lesion site in confabulation is the orbitofrontal and ventromedial frontal lobes and no confabulator has been reported with lesions solely of the lateral frontal lobes (Gilboa & Moscovitch, 2002). Moreover, not all patients with source memory deficits or executive deficits confabulate. This discrepancy could be resolved if the ventromedial/orbitofrontal regions initiate strategic retrieval operations and the lateral frontal lobe implements them (Savage et al., 2001).

An alternative explanation is that confabulators fail to suppress old memories when they are no longer relevant, and so these previously relevant memories intrude into current retrieval attempts (Schnider, 2003; Schnider & Ptak, 1999; Schnider, Treyer, & Buck, 2000). This has been termed temporal context confusion. The implication is that confabulated memories represent blends of information from real memories across different time periods. Although this sounds superficially similar to a source memory account, Schnider argues that the deficient mechanism is one of inhibiting irrelevant memories rather than context retrieval *per se*. Evidence from this comes from a number of studies in which confabulators are compared to non-confabulating amnesics. The task of the patients is to detect whether a word has previously been presented before in the *current* list. If patients producing spontaneous confabulations are given a word that was on a previous list but that is new to the current list, then they incorrectly state that it was in fact on the current list. In terms of lesion location, Schnider points out that the ventromedial/orbitofrontal cortex has long been implicated in suppressing responses that are no longer rewarded through connections with limbic structures (Jones & Mishkin, 1972). He argues that confabulation may be related to this general mechanism.

In most cases, the content of confabulations falls within the range of typical experiences. In some instances, however, confabulations are reported as "fantastic"

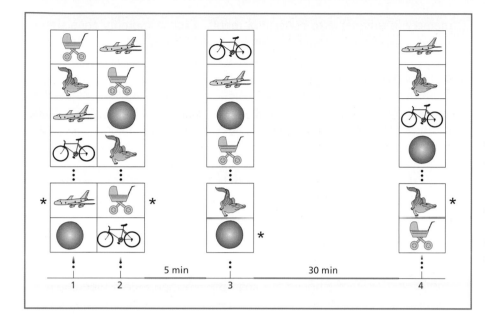

In the task devised by Schnider, participants must remember whether an item was previously presented in the *current* list (marked by *). However, some items are repeated between lists too (e.g. the crocodile appears on several lists) and confabulating patients have particular difficulties with these items. From Schnider and Ptak (1999). Reprinted by permission from Macmillan Publishers Ltd.

or "bizarre". In one frequently cited case, a patient believed he was a "space pirate" (Damasio et al., 1985). Some researchers have argued that damage to additional mechanisms may be needed to account for bizarre confabulations (e.g. semantic memory – Dalla Barba, 1993; or "mediator processes" – Burgess & Shallice, 1996b). However, even in the space pirate story the original authors note that the Columbia space shuttle mission was prominent in the news at the time, and that many of the patient's visual descriptions appeared to be from the film *Star Wars*. Thus memory for an observed event may be confused for an enacted event. Memories for events in which oneself has been an active participant may be more emotionally loaded, and one suggestion is that the region damaged in confabulation also stores the emotional content of memories (Damasio, 1996).

Evaluation

At present there is little consensus as to the nature of the mechanisms that can give rise to confabulations. The two most satisfactory accounts are that it reflects a failure to implement strategic retrieval, or that it reflects a failure to suppress irrelevant memories leading to temporal context confusion.

SUMMARY AND KEY POINTS OF THE CHAPTER

- Neuropsychology shows that short-term and long-term memory can be separately impaired and thus represent different systems. Phonological short-term memory may be important for learning new phonological material, but not necessary for long-term learning *per se*.
- Long-term memory can be divided into explicit and implicit memory (or declarative/non-declarative), according to whether the content of

memory is amenable to conscious report. Explicit memory consists of knowledge of facts (semantic memory) and events (episodic memory). Implicit memory consists primarily of skills and habits (procedural memory) and perceptual knowledge.

- Amnesia can arise from damage to medial temporal lobes, including the hippocampus and surrounding regions. It results in selective impairment of declarative memory, leaving implicit memory intact. Both semantic and episodic memory is impaired in amnesia, although the extent of semantic memory impairment is variable.

- Amnesia is typically explained as a deficit in consolidation (i.e. forming of permanent new connections) and produces difficulties in acquiring new declarative memories (anterograde impairment) and retrieving old memories that were not fully consolidated at time of injury (retrograde impairment). It is generally believed that the hippocampus has a time-limited role in consolidation that gives rise to a temporal gradient when damaged (remote memories are spared more than recent memories).

- Recognition memory is generally believed to have two components: recollection (context-dependent) and familiarity (context-independent). It is controversial whether these have separable neural substrates or whether familiarity is a weak form of recollection.

- Forgetting can occur because items are not processed deeply enough at encoding and/or because they fail to get consolidated. Forgetting can also occur because of retrieval failure. There is evidence that memory retrieval can actively inhibit other memories.

- The lateral frontal lobes have an important role to play in: (a) maintaining information in working memory; (b) selecting information in the environment to focus on (important for encoding); (c) providing cues and strategies to enable memory retrieval; and (d) evaluating the content of memories (as in "source monitoring").

- "Constructive memory" refers to the fact that memory processes can never be fully separate from other aspects of information processing (e.g. schemas, biases, current goals and percepts) and requires a process of attribution and inference. This can lead to memory distortions, such as confusing the source of a memory (e.g. confusing perceived and imagined events) or claiming that items were previously seen (false recognition). In certain brain-damaged patients, entire events that never happened may be recollected (confabulation).

EXAMPLE ESSAY QUESTIONS

- Is short-term memory distinct from long-term memory? Is short-term memory needed for long-term learning?
- What types of memory are typically impaired in amnesia?

- Are semantic and episodic memory separate memory systems?
- Does the hippocampus have a time-limited role in memory consolidation?
- What is the role of the frontal lobes in memory?
- How can memory distortions arise?

RECOMMENDED FURTHER READING

- Parker, A., Wilding, E. D., & Bussey, T. J. (2002). *The cognitive neuro-science of memory: Encoding and retrieval*. Hove: Psychology Press. An advanced text that focuses on human imaging studies and lesion studies in non-human animals.

- Squire, L. R. & Schacter, D. L. (2002). *Neuropsychology of memory, 3rd edition*. New York: Guilford Press. An advanced text that primarily focuses on lesion studies (in humans and other animals) but with some coverage of other methodologies.

- Baddeley, A., Eysenck, M. W., & Anderson, M. (2009). *Memory*. Hove: Psychology Press. A very good starting point, with a focus on cognition rather than neuroscience.

- Tulving, E. & Craik, F. I. M. (2005). *The Oxford Handbook of Memory*. Oxford: Oxford University Press. Good coverage in all areas.

CHAPTER 10

CONTENTS

The hearing brain

Sound originates from the motion or vibration of an object; for example, the vibration of the vocal chords, the plucking of a violin string or the passing of an overhead aircraft. This manifests itself in the surrounding medium, normally air, as changes in pressure in which molecules are alternately squeezed together and stretched apart. The human auditory system is capable of detecting a huge range of changes in air pressure, from around 0.00002 to over 100 Pascals. However, the role of the hearing brain is not merely to detect such changes. As with vision and other perceptual systems, the goal of hearing is not to create a literal depiction of the outside world, but rather to construct an internal model of the world that can be interpreted and acted upon. This model is constructed not only from ongoing sensory information but also from previous sensory experiences. In vision, a tomato will not be perceived to change color when it is moved from indoor lighting to outdoor lighting (even if the wavelength reflected from it has changed). Hearing operates on the same principles. The hearing brain is also concerned with extracting "constancy" out of an infinitely varying array of sensory input and it will actively interpret the sensory input. For

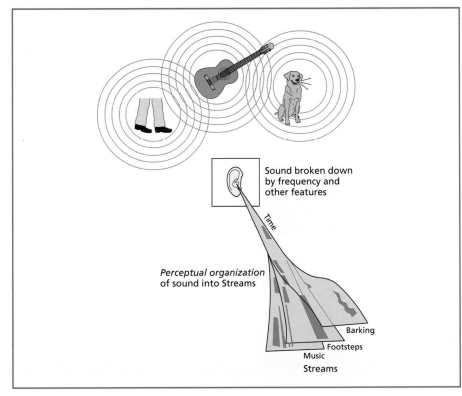

Sound broken down
by frequency and
other features

Time

*Perceptual organization
of sound into Streams*

Barking

Footsteps

Music

Streams

In our noisy environments, our ears often encounter several sounds at once. But, it is the job of the brain (not the ears!) to figure out how many different sound sources (or "streams") there are and what they correspond to. This will depend both on the incoming sensory information and learned knowledge about sounds (e.g. melodies of music, the pitch range of voices).

example, we recognize a familiar tune when presented in a different key and we can recognize a familiar voice in a wide range of acoustic environments (in person, on the telephone, shouting over a megaphone). The hearing brain also uses stored knowledge to supplement the auditory input. If one is listening to a familiar song, such as Don Maclean's "American Pie", but there are gaps of 2–5 seconds in the song ("Bye, bye Miss _____, Drove my chevy ..."), then auditory cortical areas are more active during the gaps, relative to unfamiliar songs (Kraemer, Macrae, Green, & Kelley, 2005). Our musical and lyrical knowledge can fill in silent gaps in heard songs (or almost silent, given that there is the scanner background noise).

One difference that does exist between the auditory and visual senses is their sensitivity to temporal and spatial information. The auditory system is exquisitely tuned to detect temporal information, such as rapid changes in frequency that characterize certain speech sounds, and in grouping information together over time, such as in extracting melody from music. The different time intervals associated with "dots" and "dashes" in Morse Code are much easier to process when heard than seen (Saenz & Koch, 2008). In contrast, it is generally much easier to locate an object in space with vision than with hearing (Bertelson & Aschersleben, 1998).

This chapter will start by considering how sounds are processed by the early auditory system up to the primary and secondary auditory cortex. It will then go on to consider in more detail how the brain extracts features from the auditory scene, and divides up the auditory world into different streams (e.g. corresponding to different sound sources), and different kinds of information (e.g. "what" versus "where"). The final part of the chapter will consider auditory perception for three different classes of stimuli: music, voices and speech.

THE NATURE OF SOUND

One of the simplest sounds has a sinusoid waveform (when pressure change is plotted against time) and these sounds are termed **pure tones**. Pure tones have a characteristic **pitch** that is related to the frequency of the sound wave (measured in Hertz, i.e. vibrations per second). The human auditory system responds to sound frequencies between 20 Hz and 20,000 Hz. The intensity of the sound (i.e. its amplitude when considered as a sine wave) is related to the subjective experience of **loudness**. In perception, it is crucial to make a distinction between the physical properties of a stimulus and their perceived characteristics. Thus, in vision, although there is a close relationship between the wavelength of light (a physical property) and color (a psychological property), the relationship isn't straightforward (it is possible to see color without its associated wavelength, as in after-images, and it is possible to process wavelength without perceiving color, as in cerebral achromatopsia). Similarly, in hearing, although pitch is related to the frequency of sounds and loudness is related to the intensity (or amplitude) of sounds, the relationship isn't straightforward. Pitch and loudness are regarded as psychological features of sounds, whereas frequency and intensity are physical properties. For example, the pitch of a low frequency sound appears to get lower if it is made louder and the pitch of a high frequency sound appears to get higher if it is made louder (Stevens, 1935). Although amplitude and frequency might be independent physical properties of sound waves, the subjective properties most closely associated with them (pitch and loudness) are not processed by the brain in a completely independent way.

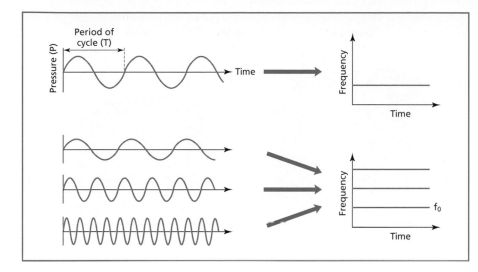

A pure tone (top) consists of sinusoidally varying pressure. Many naturally occurring sounds, such as musical tones (bottom), consist of a regular series of sinusoids of different frequencies. The perceived pitch is related to the lowest frequency in the series (the fundamental frequency, f_0). The relative amplitudes of the sinusoids can help to distinguish between different musical instruments.

In everyday life, pure tones are seldom heard. However, many sounds can be described in terms of combinations of superimposed sinusoids of different frequencies, intensities and phases. For example, musical notes typically contain a series of regularly spaced sinusoids. Thus, a piano note of 220 Hz can be described in terms of sinusoids at 220 Hz, 440 Hz, 660 Hz and so on. The lowest component (in this example 220 Hz), termed the **fundamental frequency** (f_0), typically determines the perceived pitch of a musical note. However, if the fundamental frequency is missing from the series (e.g. a tone made up of 440 Hz, 660 Hz, 880 Hz, etc.), then the pitch is still perceived as equivalent to 220 Hz. This is termed the **missing fundamental phenomenon** and is an example of pitch constancy, i.e. two notes with completely different physical characteristics (i.e. a single note of 220 Hz v. a series of sinusoids at 440 Hz, 660 Hz, 880 Hz, etc.) can have the same perceived pitch.

The relative intensity levels of the different sinusoid components of musical sounds are important for discriminating between the same notes played on different musical instruments i.e. **timbre** (pronounced "tamber"). Timbre, like pitch, is a psychological characteristic of a sound. White noise can be thought of as an infinite sum of sinusoids of every frequency.

FROM EAR TO BRAIN

The ear contains three main parts: the outer, middle and inner ear. The outer ear contains the pinna (pinnae in plural), or earlobes, and the auditory canal. Reflections of the sound wave within the folds of the pinna and within the auditory canal can amplify certain sounds and are important for locating a sound source. The middle ear converts airborne vibrations to liquid-borne vibrations with minimal loss of energy. A series of three tiny bones (malleus, incus and stapes; also called hammer, anvil and stirrup) transfers the mechanical pressure on the eardrum, at the end of the airborne auditory

KEY TERMS

Fundamental frequency
The lowest frequency component of a complex sound that determines the perceived pitch.

Missing fundamental phenomenon
If the fundamental frequency of a complex sound is removed, then the pitch is not perceived to change (the brain reinstates it).

Timbre
The perceptual quality of a sound enables us to distinguish between different musical instruments.

The structure of the outer, middle and inner ear.

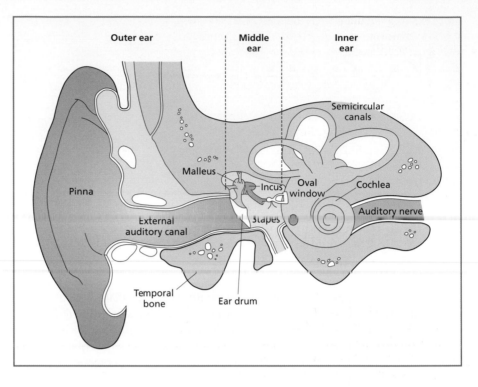

canal, to a smaller membrane, called the oval window, in the fluid-filled **cochlea**. The inner ear contains chambers that are important both for the senses of hearing (the cochlea) and balance (including the semicircular canals). The cochlea converts liquid-borne sound into neural impulses. A membrane within the cochlea, termed the **basilar membrane**, contains tiny hair cells linked to receptors. Sound induces mechanical movement of the basilar membrane and the hair cells on it. These movements induce electrochemical changes in the receptor cells, which stimulate associated auditory nerve fibers. The basilar membrane is not uniform but has different mechanical properties at either end (e.g. von Bekesy, 1960). The end nearest the oval window is narrower and stiffer, and shows a maximal deflection to high frequency sounds. The end nearest the center of its spiral shape is wider and more elastic and shows a maximal deflection to low frequency sounds.

There are four or five synapses in the auditory pathway from the ear to the brain, starting with projections from the auditory nerve to the cochlear nuclei in the brainstem, and ending with projections from the medial geniculate nucleus to the **primary auditory cortex**, also called A1 or the "core" region (the main cortical area to receive auditory-based thalamic input). The primary auditory cortex is located in Heschl's gyrus in the temporal lobes and is surrounded by adjacent secondary auditory cortical areas called the **belt** and **parabelt regions** (e.g. Kaas, Hackett, & Tramo, 1999). These secondary regions also receive some input from the medial geniculate nucleus and, hence, damage to the primary auditory cortex does not produce complete deafness but does lead to problems in identifying and locating sounds (Musiek, Baran, Shinn, Guenette, & Zaidan, 2007). This ascending pathway is not a passive transmission of information from the ear but, rather, is involved in the active extraction and synthesis of information in the auditory signal. For example, whilst the cochlear nucleus has 90,000 neurons, the medial geniculate nucleus has 500,000 and the auditory cortex has 100,000,000 (Worden, 1971). In addition, there are descending, top-down, pathways that go as far back as the cochlea itself (Rasmussen, 1953) and may be important in auditory attention.

The early auditory system can be said to have a **tonotopic organization**. Just as different parts of the basilar membrane respond maximally to different sound frequencies, neurons within the auditory nerve respond maximally to certain sound frequencies more than others. Moreover, the nerve bundle is orderly such that neurons responding to higher frequencies are located on the periphery and those responding to lower frequencies more centrally (Kiang, Watanabe, Thomas, & Clark, 1965). To some extent, this organization is carried upwards to the early cortical stages. In both humans (Formisano, Kim, Di Salle, van de Moortele, Ugurbil, & Goebel, 2003) and other animals (Merzenich, Knight, & Roth, 1973) there is evidence that the central region of the primary auditory cortex responds to lower frequencies and the outer regions, on both sides, to higher frequencies.

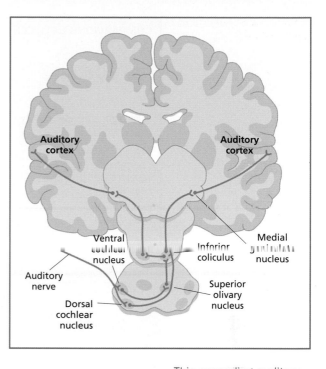

This ascending auditory pathway is not a passive transmission of information from the ear but, rather, is involved in the active extraction and synthesis of information in the auditory signal. From Gazzaniga et al. (2002). Copyright © 2002 W. W. Norton & Company Inc. Reproduced with permission.

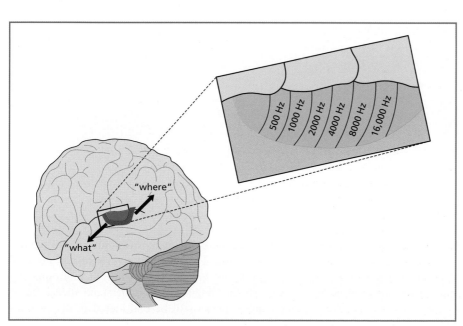

The primary auditory cortex lies on the medial surface of both the left and right temporal lobes and is organized tonotopically (i.e. different regions process different frequencies). It is surrounded by secondary auditory cortex (termed belt and parabelt) that processes more complex aspects of the sound and provide the starting point for separate "what" and "where" routes.

COMPARISONS BETWEEN THE AUDITORY AND VISUAL SYSTEMS

	Auditory system	Visual system
Thalamo-cortical route	Medial geniculate nucleus projects to primary auditory cortex	Lateral geniculate nucleus projects to primary visual cortex
Organizing principle of early neural processing	Tonotopic organization (orderly mapping between sound frequency and position on cortex)	Retinotopic organization (orderly mapping between position on retina and position on cortex)
Temporal and spatial sensitivity	Temporal > Spatial	Spatial > Temporal
Functional specialization of feature processing	Less well documented in the auditory domain	Well documented for color and movement
Higher-order context-dependent pathways	Evidence for separate auditory pathways for "what" versus "where"/"how"	Evidence for separate visual pathways for "what" versus "where"/"how"

DOING HEARING RESEARCH IN A NOISY MRI SCANNER

The noise from an MRI scanner is significant (up to 130 decibels, i.e. similar to a jet engine take-off). The scanner noise may not only mask the auditory stimulus of importance, it could also change the nature of the auditory task by requiring attentive strategies to actively filter out the background noise. One solution that is now commonly used is to use so-called **sparse scanning** (Hall et al., 1999). In this method, scanning is temporarily suspended for a few seconds so that an auditory stimulus can be displayed against a silent background and then scanning restarts. This method is possible because of the slow time it takes for the hemodynamic response function to reach a peak (about six seconds after stimulus onset).

BASIC PROCESSING OF AUDITORY INFORMATION

Beyond the early auditory cortical areas, there are many other routes and regions of the brain involved in auditory processing. The precise network of regions used depends on the stimulus content (e.g. human speech, voices, music, environmental noises) and the current context (e.g. whether one needs to understand speech, identify a speaker or locate a sound source). These will be considered in the sections below.

Feature processing in the auditory cortex

Just as visual perception involves the processing of different features (color, shape, movement, texture), so too does auditory perception, although the features differ

KEY TERM

Sparse scanning
In fMRI, a short break in scanning to enable sounds to be presented in relative silence.

(e.g. pitch, loudness, tempo). As with vision, there is some evidence of hierarchical processing of auditory feature information such that earlier cortical regions (e.g. the "core" region containing the primary auditory cortex) codes for more simple features and later cortical regions (e.g. the belt and parabelt) codes more complex information that could be thought of, to some extent, as conjunctions of simple features. Unlike vision, the evidence for modular-like organization of auditory features is less well established. But there is some evidence for a potential "pitch region" that responds to the psychological variable of pitch (i.e. how the note is perceived) as opposed to the physical properties of the sound (such as the frequency). This region, outside of primary auditory cortex, responds to perceived pitch, as in the "missing fundamental" illusion, rather than actual frequency (Bendor & Wang, 2005).

Kaas et al. (1999) present a summary of how more complex auditory features are constructed in a hierarchical fashion from core → belt → parabelt regions. Single cell recordings in primates show that the neurons in the core region respond to narrowly defined frequencies (e.g. responding maximally to a pure tone of 200 Hz), whereas cells in the belt region respond to a broader band of frequencies (e.g. responding to noise between 200 Hz and 300 Hz; Kosaki, Hashikawa, He, & Jones, 1997). This is consistent with the view that the neurons in the belt region sum together activity from many frequency-selective neurons in the core region; for example, by summing together activity from neurons tuned to respond to 200 Hz, 205 Hz, 210 Hz, 215 Hz and so on to 300 Hz. This can be considered analogous to the way that simple cells in vision sum together information from center-surround cells (see p. 106).

Neurons in the belt region will also respond to other more complex tones, such as vocalizations, more vigorously than with pure tones (Rauschecker, Tian, & Hauser, 1995). These sounds may be characterized by sudden shifts in frequency, such as abrupt onsets in speech (e.g. the /p/ phoneme) or warbling or twitter calls in other species. Indeed some neurons don't respond to fixed frequencies but only to changes in frequency and even the direction of change of frequency (Kajikawa et al., 2008; Whitfield & Evans, 1965). This could be considered analogous to complex cells in vision, which respond to movement and movement direction.

Neurons of the auditory cortex do not just respond to frequency-related information, they also respond to particular loudness levels and particular spatial locations. Clarey, Barone and Imig (1994) recorded from neurons in the cat primary auditory cortex using noise bursts but varying loudness and sound location. Some neurons respond only to particular loudness levels, and some neurons respond only to particular locations (typically contralaterally,

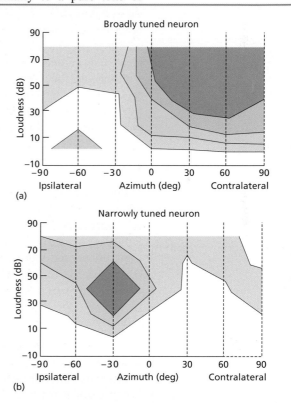

The density of shading represents the responsiveness of two different neurons in auditory cortex to sounds of different loudness levels presented in different regions of space. Neuron (a) responds to sounds over a broad range of loudness level and in various parts of space, whereas neuron (b) is more finely tuned to a particular loudness level and a particular part of space. From Clarey et al. (1994). Reprinted with permission of APS.

so sounds presented on the left of space are more strongly processed in the right auditory cortex and vice versa). Over a third of neurons respond to particular loudness levels *and* particular locations; for example, a neuron may produce a maximal response both if the sound is between 30 and 50 decibels and it is located between 20 and 40 degrees on a particular side of space.

"What" versus "where"

Within the auditory cortical areas, there is some degree of specialization for "what" versus "where". That is, some neurons/regions are relatively specialized for coding the content of the sound (irrespective of where it is coming from) and other neurons/regions are relatively specialized for coding where the sound is coming from (irrespective of what is heard). This may form the starting point for two separate routes to other non-auditory regions. Rauschecker and Tian (2000) found that neural responses in the anterior belt region showed a high degree of specialization for monkey calls (irrespective of their location), whereas the posterior belt region showed greatest spatial selectivity. They speculated that this may form the starting point for two routes: a dorsal route involving the parietal lobes that is concerned with locating sounds, and a ventral route along the temporal lobes concerned with identifying sounds. Functional imaging evidence from humans is largely consistent with this view (e.g. Barrett & Hall, 2006). For sounds that can be reproduced (e.g. speech in humans), one additional suggestion is that the auditory dorsal route acts as a "how" route – i.e. the auditory signal interfaces with motor representations in parietal and frontal cortex rather than spatial ones. This is considered later in the section on speech perception.

There are two broad solutions for identifying where a sound is located:

1. *Inter-aural differences.* If a sound is lateralized it will tend to arrive at one ear before the other (inter-aural time difference) and will be less intense at the farthest ear because it lies in the "shadow" of the head (inter-aural intensity difference). Frequency-selective neurons in the core and belt regions adjust their responsiveness according to the inter-aural loudness differences and inter-aural time differences (Brugge & Merzenich, 1973). For example, a neuron that is selective for a particular frequency may be more responsive, i.e. generate more action potentials, when the left ear is played the sound slightly before the right ear but may reduce its responsiveness if the right ear hears the sound first.

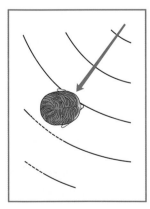

The sound arrives at the left ear first (inter-aural time difference) and is more intense in the incoming ear (inter-aural intensity difference).

2. *Distortions of the sound wave by the head and pinnae.* To test the role of the pinnae in sound localization, Batteau (1967) placed microphones into the "ear canal" of casts of actual pinnae whilst playing sounds to these artificial ears from different locations. When participants listen to these recordings, using headphones (i.e. so the sound isn't distorted by their own pinnae), they are able to localize the sounds. They cannot do so if the recordings were taken without the artificial ears attached. Moreover, performance is improved if sounds are recorded from participants' own ear shapes rather than a generic ear (Wenzel, Arruda, Kistler, & Wightman, 1993). The brain develops an internal model of how sounds get distorted by the unique shape of one's own ears and head (called a **head-related transfer function**, HRTF) and it is able to use this knowledge to infer the likely location. Griffiths and Warren (2002) propose that a region called the **planum temporale**, lying posterior to the primary auditory cortex, is involved in integrating the sensory input with the learned head-related

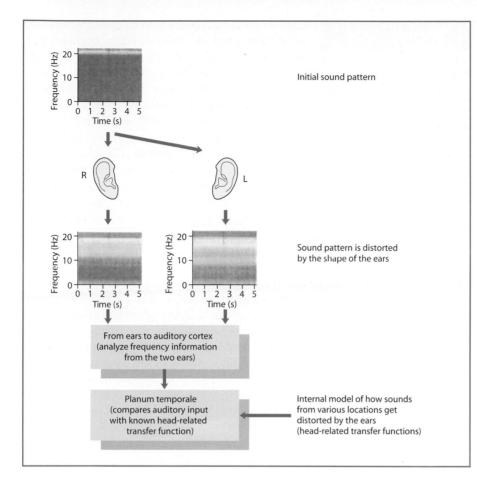

Initial sound pattern

Sound pattern is distorted by the shape of the ears

From ears to auditory cortex (analyze frequency information from the two ears)

Planum temporale (compares auditory input with known head-related transfer function)

Internal model of how sounds from various locations get distorted by the ears (head-related transfer functions)

The shape of the ears distorts incoming sounds in predictable ways that depend on the location of the sound. The brain contains an internal model of how the sounds get distorted (head-related transfer function) and it can link the model with the auditory input to infer the location of a sound. Adapted from Griffiths and Warren (2002).

transfer function for different parts of space. Whereas inter-aural differences only provide information about the left right (or azimuthal) location of a sound, distortions of the auditory input by the pinnae can be used to locate sounds in both the left–right direction and the top–bottom direction (Batteau, 1967).

The computations described above can be used to locate sounds relative to the head (i.e. an egocentric coding of space). However, to determine the actual location of the sound source (i.e. in allocentric space), one also needs to know the current orientation and tilt of the head. A sound that is 10 degrees to the left of the head could actually be directly in front of the person if the head happens to be oriented at 10 degrees to the right. As such, auditory information needs to be combined with bodily information, and it is perhaps not surprising that a fronto-parietal network is engaged in auditory localization.

Auditory memory and auditory stream segregation

Visual objects generally extend through time and are available for re-inspection. Auditory objects (e.g. a spoken word or musical phrase) tend not to hang around to be re-inspected. Most models of hearing postulate an important role of a sensory memory store to integrate auditory information over brief time intervals (a few seconds). This auditory memory is assumed to be tapped by all kinds of heard material, i.e. it should not be confused with the verbal short-term memory store that is considered speech-specific. Perhaps the best developed model of auditory memory is that proposed by Näätänen and colleagues (e.g. Näätänen, Tervaniemi, Sussman, Paavilainen, & Winkler, 2001), who regard the primary function of this memory system to lie in early **auditory stream segregation**. Complex auditory scenes such as a cocktail party or an orchestral performance can be divided into different streams (or "objects") according to, say, their pitch, melody, instrumentation or location in space. According to Näätänen et al. (2001), the auditory cortex itself (most likely the secondary auditory cortical areas) creates an auditory memory that facilitates, or indeed enables, this process.

Much of the evidence in this area comes from studies of a human ERP component termed the **mismatch negativity** (MMN). The mismatch negativity occurs when an auditory stimulus deviates from previously presented auditory stimuli (Näätänen, Gaillard, & Mantysalo, 1978). It occurs between 100–200 milliseconds after the onset of the deviant sound, and its main locus appears to be within the auditory cortex (Alho, 1995). The most simple example is a sequence of tones in which one tone has a deviant pitch (e.g. A-A-A-A-B where A = 1000 Hz, B > 1000 Hz). This is illustrated in the figure on the left. In one sense, the MMN can be considered as a "low level" phenomenon because it occurs in the absence of attention. It is found in some comatose patients several days before waking (Kane, Curry, Butler, & Cummins, 1993) and when the stimulus is presented to the unattended ear of healthy participants (Alho, Woods, & Algazi, 1994). However, the MMN is also found for more complex auditory patterns, suggesting a more sophisticated underlying mechanism. It is found if a descending tone sequence suddenly ascends in pitch or remains constant (Tervaniemi, Maury, & Näätänen, 1994), or if the repetitive stimulus consists of varying pairs of *descending* tones, so there is no physical standard, and the deviant stimulus consists of a pair of *ascending* tones (Saarinen, Paavilainen, Schoger, Tervaniemi, & Näätänen, 1992). Thus, the auditory memory must code rather abstract properties of the auditory stimuli.

Auditory stream segregation is unlikely to be limited to the auditory cortex. Griffiths and Warren (2002) suggest that the planum temporale, rather than auditory cortex, may be crucial for this role. Parietal regions may be important too. Cusack (2005) used

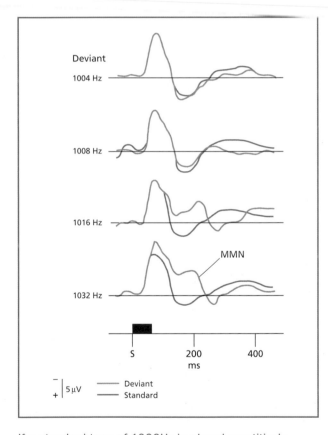

If a standard tone of 1000Hz is played repetitively (purple line) but with an occasional deviant tone that is >1000Hz (green lines), then there is a distinct EEG event-related potential detected at the scalp that is termed the mismatch negativity, MMN. This has been attributed to an auditory memory component and the MMN is also found for some more complex auditory patterns. Reprinted from Näätänen et al. (2001), Copyright 2001, with permission from Elsevier.

a perceptually ambiguous auditory stimulus of two alternating tones of different frequency that could either be interpreted as a single stream (like the "clip, clop, clip, clop" of a horse) or as two streams ("clip … clip …" overlaid on "… clop … clop"). That is, the stimuli in the two conditions were physically identical but associated with different percepts. This contrasts with the MMN approach, which always uses perceptually different repeated and deviant sounds that may be easier to segregate at a sensory level. This manipulation found activity in the right intra-parietal sulcus for two streams relative to one. This region has been implicated in binding different features together in vision (e.g. color and shape) and could possibly play a similar role in hearing. Indeed, patients with unilateral neglect (who typically have damage near this right parietal region) have difficulty in comparing auditory features if they are segregated into different auditory streams but not if they belong to the same stream (Cusack, Carlyon, & Robertson, 2000).

MUSIC PERCEPTION

Although music can rightfully be described as a form of art, this does not mean that it is purely a product of cultural learning. Many aspects of music perception have a biological basis and can be said to be "innate" in the same way as some argue language to be innate (e.g. Peretz, 2006). Namely, that it is a universal phenomenon (all known human cultures, past and present, have had it) and it emerges early in life without formal training (but with exposure to an appropriate environment). At this point, it is important to emphasize a distinction between music perception and music production. Music production typically requires many years of formal training (although it need not, as in singing or tapping/clapping a rhythm). In contrast, all of us, with the possible exception of those who are "tone deaf" (see later), are able to perceive and appreciate music and are avid consumers of music.

Music can be said to have a number of essential features (Dowling & Harwood, 1986). First, musical systems tend to be based on a discrete set of pitch levels. The infinite set of different pitches that the brain perceives become parsed into a finite set of musical notes. For example, the Western musical scale is made up of seven repeating notes (A to G, forming an octave when the first note is repeated), with intermediate semi-tones (the flats and sharps). Second, these different notes are combined to form perceptible groups and patterns. The way that these notes are grouped together is not arbitrary but depends on certain properties of the auditory system, such as those involved in auditory stream segregation. For example, notes that are similar in pitch or have similar time lengths may be grouped together. Some notes when played together "sound right" (consonance) or clash (dissonance) and this may depend on the physical relationship between the notes. For example, two notes that are double in fundamental frequency (e.g. 220 Hz and 440 Hz) have the lowest dissonance and this has a special status in musical systems. In the Western musical system, this doubling corresponds to the same note an octave apart.

Is the right hemisphere to music as the left hemisphere is to language? Although this hypothesis is interesting, it is also misleading as neither music nor language can be considered as single faculties. There is evidence that the right hemisphere may be more dominant for the processing of pitch-related information. However, the left hemisphere is also important for certain aspects of music.

The model of musical cognition by Peretz and Coltheart (2003) contains separate processes for the lyrics versus melody and rhythm of music, as well as a further sub-division between processes for temporal organization (such as rhythm) and pitch-based organization (including melody). From Peretz and Coltheart (2003), by permission of Macmillan Publishers Ltd.

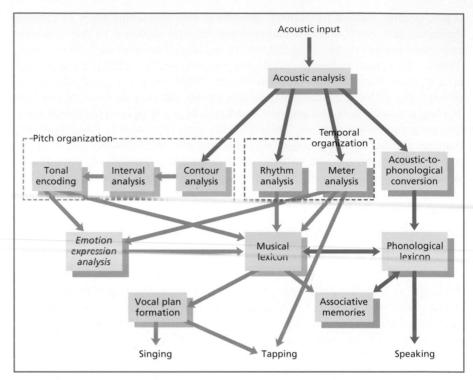

Alcock et al. (2000b) report that pitch abilities are more affected by right-hemispheric lesions but timing abilities are more affected by left-hemispheric lesions. Peretz and Coltheart (2003) outlined a basic cognitive model of music processing that emphasizes different components of musical processing. The first distinction that they make is between processes that are shared between music and speech (shown in the figure above in blue) and those that are potentially specific to music (shown in green). Thus, listening to someone singing "Happy Birthday" would evoke at least two routes: one concerned with the words and one concerned with the music. Within the domain of music, they then make a distinction between *pitch organization* (which includes pitch relations between notes) and *temporal organization*, including rhythm (the tempo of beats) and meter (the way beats are grouped). Much of the evidence for this model has come from people with an acquired or congenital **amusia**.

Memory for tunes

Some brain-damaged patients are unable to recognize previously familiar melodies despite being able to recognize songs from spoken lyrics, and being able to recognize voices and environmental sounds. For example, case CN was a non-musician who suffered bilateral temporal lobe damage (Peretz, 1996). Although she had some difficulties with pitch perception, her most profound difficulty was in identifying previously familiar tunes and, as such, her damage was attributed to a memory component of music (the "musical lexicon" in the model above). Subsequent studies show that CN can identify intonation from speech, which requires analysis of pitch contours but not knowledge of tunes (Patel, Peretz, Tramo, & Labrecque, 1998). In contrast to CN, some brain-damaged patients can lose the ability to recognize spoken words but are still able to recognize tunes (Mendez, 2001).

Rhythm

Disorders of rhythm can occur independently of disorders of pitch. Di Pietro Laganaro, Leeman and Schinder (2004) report a case of acquired amusia who could process pitch-based melody but could not identify rhythm from auditory input. He could do so from visual input, suggesting the problem wasn't in general time perception. Members of the KE family with a congenital speech disorder (see Chapter 16) also have problems in rhythm production and rhythm perception but perform as well as controls in pitch-based melody production and melody perception (Alcock et al., 2000a).

Pitch and pitch-related structural processing

Some people have good perception and production of rhythm but are impaired on pitch-based aspects of music. One recently studied group is those individuals who are said to be "**tone deaf**" or have so-called **congenital amusia** because there is no known neurological cause such as brain damage. This can occur in up to 4% of the population and is not associated with difficulties in other domains, such as general intelligence (Ayotte, Peretz, & Hyde, 2002). It is associated with right-hemisphere abnormalities in white and gray matter density, both in right the auditory cortex and the right inferior frontal gyrus (Hyde, Lerch, Zatorre, Griffiths, Evans, & Peretz, 2007). Hyde and Peretz (2004) presented participants with a series of five notes in which the fourth note was either out of pitch or out of time. Tone-deaf participants could detect the timing but not the pitch violations.

The model of Peretz and Coltheart (2003) contains different stages of pitch processing in music that are concerned with the general up–down structure (contour analysis), the precise relationship between successive notes (interval analysis) and, finally, the construction of **melody** (tonal encoding). In most music, the melody follows certain regularities in which only some notes are "allowed". Determining the set of possible notes for a given melody is what Peretz and Coltheart mean by "tonal encoding". As well as allowing certain notes and not others, some notes are more probable at certain points in the melody than others. This rule-like aspect of music has been referred to as "musical syntax" (Koelsch & Siebel, 2005). Whereas both random pitch sequences and tonal melodies activate the bilateral auditory cortex and surrounding temporal regions (Patterson, Uppenkamp, Johnsrude, & Griffiths, 2002), musical syntactic deviations are associated with activation of inferior frontal regions (Maess et al., 2001). This tends to be bilateral and stronger on the right but includes Broca's area on the left, which has, historically, been considered as specific to language.

Timbre

One notable omission from the model of Peretz and Coltheart (2003) is timbre. This perceptual quality of a sound enables us to distinguish between different musical instruments. The same note played on a cello and a saxophone will sound

very different even if they are matched for pitch and loudness. Different instruments can be distinguished partly on the basis of how the note evolves over time (e.g. the attack and decay of the note) and partly on the basis of the relative intensity of the different frequency components of the note. Timbre perception is particularly affected by lesions of the right temporal lobe and can be dissociated from some aspects of pitch-related perception such as melody (e.g. Samson & Zatorre, 1994).

Music and emotion

Music has a special ability to tap into our emotional processes. This may rely on certain musical conventions such as happy music tending to be a faster tempo than sad music; happy being in major keys, and sad being in minor keys; dissonance between notes to create tension; musical syntactic deviations to create "surprise"; and fast and regular to create scary music (think *Jaws*). It would be interesting to know to what extent these themes carry cross-culturally. Functional imaging shows that emotional music activates the same circuitry as other emotional stimuli and even the brain's reward circuitry (Blood & Zatorre, 2001; Koelsch, Fritz, von Cramon, Muller, & Friederici, 2006). This suggests that music can be a powerful motivator like sex, food and drugs, although the function of music, in evolutionary terms, remains unknown. Patients with acquired difficulties in emotion processing, such as in recognizing fearful faces, may show comparable deficits in recognizing scary music (Gosselin, Peretz, Johnsen, & Adolphs, 2007).

The music for movies such as *Jaws* and *Psycho* is designed to create a sense of fear. Would a patient with damage to the amygdala, who can't recognize fear from faces, be able to identify scary music? © DLILLC/Corbis.

WHAT IS THE FUNCTION OF MUSIC?

Unlike language, the function of music is less obvious. Music gives people a huge amount of enjoyment but, whilst humans prefer music over silence, the reverse is true of other primates (McDermott & Hauser, 2007). But enjoyment, in itself, does not explain its existence from a Darwinian point of view: namely, in what ways does music promote survival of our species? Darwin's (1871) own answer to this question is that human musical tendencies are derived from a system for attracting mates. Another answer to the problem is that music exists because it brings people together and creates social cohesion, both of which lead to survival benefits (e.g. Huron, 2001). A third suggestion, made in *The Singing Neanderthals* (Mithen, 2005), is that music is a precursor to language. Steven Pinker (1997) takes the contrary view by arguing that language was the precursor to music (rather than music the precursor to language) and that music, whilst being immensely enjoyable, does not have an adaptive function. As he puts it: "Music is auditory cheesecake. It just happens to tickle several important parts of the brain in a highly pleasurable way, as cheesecake tickles the palate." Whilst a resolution of this debate does not appear close, one promising new line of research that could bear on this issue is looking for music-like abilities in other species (e.g. McDermott & Hauser, 2007).

VOICE PERCEPTION

Voices, like faces, convey a large amount of socially relevant information about the people around us. It is possible to infer someone's sex, size, age and mood from their voice. Physical changes related to sex, size and age affect the vocal apparatus in systematic ways. Larger bodies have longer vocal tracts and this leads to greater dispersion of certain frequencies (the formants found, for example, in human vowels and dog growls are more dispersed in larger animals). Adult men have larger vocal folds (17–25 mm) than adult women (12.5–17.5 mm), resulting in a lower pitched male voice. One can also infer the current emotional state (angry, sad, etc.) from a voice even in an unfamiliar language (Scherer, Banse, & Wallbott, 2001). Familiar people can also be recognized from their voice but this is generally more difficult than recognizing them from

Every human culture, past and present, is believed to have had music. But what evolutionary function could music serve?

their face (Hanley, Smith, & Hadfield, 1998). Individual differences in the shape and size of the vocal apparatus (teeth, lips, etc.) and resonators (e.g. nasal cavity), together with learned speaking style (e.g. accent), create a unique voice signature.

One recent case study, of developmental origin, was unable to identify familiar voices of personal acquaintances or famous people despite being able to recognize their faces and despite being able to extract other important information from voices including their sex and emotional state (Garrido et al., 2009). Interestingly, fMRI of healthy participants shows that identifying a speaker from his or her voice activates face-selective regions, although interpreting what the speaker says does not (von Kriegstein, Kleinschmidt, Sterzer, & Giraud, 2005). Thus, although face and voice information is theoretically separable, the two are often activated together when the person is known.

Belin, Zatorre, Lafaille, Ahad and Pike (2000) claimed to have identified a voice-selective area in the human brain. They found three regions in the bilateral superior temporal sulcus that respond to vocal sounds (speech and non-speech such as laughs) more than non-vocal sounds of comparable acoustic complexity, and including other sounds produced by humans such as clapping. Other studies have suggested that these different regions may be sensitive to different aspects of voice. In particular, the right superior temporal region anterior to auditory cortex (i.e. in the auditory "what" pathway) appears to be important for speaker identity (Belin

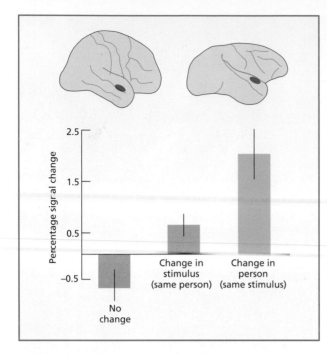

Approximate location of the voice-selective region in the right temporal lobe of humans (left) and macaques (right). This region responds more, in terms of fMRI BOLD signal, when the speaker changes (but the syllable/vocalization is the same) than when the syllable/vocalization changes (but the speaker is the same). Reprinted from Scott (2008), Copyright 2008, with permission from Elsevier.

& Zatorre, 2003; Warren, Scott, Price, & Griffiths, 2006). A recent fMRI study with macaque monkeys has identified a homologous region that responds not only to vocalizations from their own species but is also affected by changes in identity between different vocalizers (Petkov et al., 2008).

SPEECH PERCEPTION

At what stage of processing, if any, does the brain treat speech sounds differently from other kinds of auditory stimuli? This question often reduces to identifying the stage in speech processing that is left lateralized. Wernicke, one of the earliest researchers to consider this question, believed that sensory speech processing was bilateral but that the left advantage arose through connections with the left motor–speech system (cited in Hickok and Poeppel, 2004). Functional imaging studies have shown that the primary auditory cortex of both left and right hemispheres responds equally to speech and other types of auditory stimuli (Binder et al., 2000). This suggests divergence at a later cortical stage. Beyond auditory cortex, humans begin to show a greater left hemisphere responsiveness for speech relative to non-speech along the so-called "what" route of the temporal lobes. For example, Scott, Blank, Rosen and Wise (2000) report increased activity in a left temporal region in intelligible relative to unintelligible speech of comparable acoustic complexity. The right hemisphere homologue did not show this preference but was more responsive to dynamic pitch variation. This is consistent with the notion that the left hemisphere is specialized for processing rapid temporal change, and the right hemisphere extracts more melodic aspects (Zatorre, Belin, & Penhune, 2002). Moreover, a specific type of acquired auditory agnosia called **pure word deafness** is found following damage to the left hemisphere (e.g. Takahashi, Kawamura, Shinotou, Hirayama, Kaga, & Shindo, 1992). These patients are able to identify environmental sounds and music but not speech. The patients are able to produce speech but heard speech appears to be "too fast" or "distorted".

The nature of the speech signal

To appreciate the difficulties faced by the auditory system during speech perception, consider a typical **spectrogram** for the sentence "Joe took father's shoe bench out". A spectrogram plots how the frequency of sound (on the vertical y axis) changes over time (on the horizontal x axis) with the intensity of the sound represented by level of darkness. The first thing to notice is that, although there are gaps in the spectrogram, these typically correspond to the articulation of certain consonants (e.g. "t", "b", "f") rather than gaps occurring between words. Although we are used to seeing gaps between words in written language, they do not exist in speech (one famous example being "I scream" versus "ice-cream", which have the same sound). Thus, segmenting the speech stream into words will rely on stored knowledge of possible words as well as some auditory cues (e.g. stress patterns).

Another difficulty is that the same words can have very different acoustic properties depending on the person producing them. Male and female speakers have different pitch ranges, and speakers have different accents, talking speeds and so on. This is the familiar problem of extracting constant information from sensory input that can vary infinitely.

Looking again at the spectrogram, it appears as if some speech sounds have very different characteristics from others. The basic segments of speech are called phonemes and, perhaps surprisingly, fewer than 100 phonemes describe all the languages of the world. The International Phonetic Alphabet (IPA) contains one written symbol for each phoneme; English contains around 44 phonemes. It is important not to confuse phonemes with letters. For example, the TH and SH in "thin" and "shin" are single phonemes (θ and ʃ in IPA) that are typically represented by two letters. Phonemes are more formally defined as minimal contrastive units of spoken language. To understand what this means, hold your hand very close to your mouth and say the words "pin" and "peg". Did you notice that the "p" sound of pin was more associated with an outward expulsion of air (called aspiration)? These are two **allophones** of the single "p" phoneme. Although they are physically different, the difference is irrelevant for recognizing the words. In some languages, the presence or absence of aspiration may signify a change in meaning. In Thai, "paa" aspirated means to split, whereas "paa" unaspirated means forest. These are separate phonemes in Thai, but allophonic variants in English.

The different acoustic properties of phonemes can be related back to the way they are articulated. Vowels are produced with a relative free flow of air, modified by the shape (high, middle, low) and position (front, center, back) of the tongue. In the spectrogram (see next page), this free flow is represented as a series of horizontal stripes (called **formants**). Consonants typically place more constriction on the flow of air, sometimes blocking it completely as in phonemes such as "b" and "d". Other consonants differ by **voicing**. Hold your voice box when saying "zzzz" versus "ssss". In the first instance, you should feel your vocal chords vibrating. On a spectrogram, this can be seen as a series of closely spaced vertical lines.

One way in which the brain deals with variability in the acoustic input is by using **categorical perception**. Categorical perception refers to the fact that continuous changes in input are mapped on to discrete percepts. For example, the syllables "da" and "ta" are identical except that the phoneme "t" is unvoiced ("d" and "a" are voiced). It is possible to experimentally manipulate the onset of voicing along a continuum from 0 ms (perceived as "da") to 80 ms (perceived as "ta"). But what happens at intermediary values such as 30 ms? Is a third type of sound perceived? No, listeners will always perceive it as one phoneme or the other, albeit to varying degrees of certainty (Eimas, 1963). Categorical perception also provides one way of dealing with variability in the acoustic signal due to **co-articulation**. Co-articulation refers to the fact that the production of a phoneme (and, hence, the sound of that phoneme) is influenced by the preceding and proceeding phonemes.

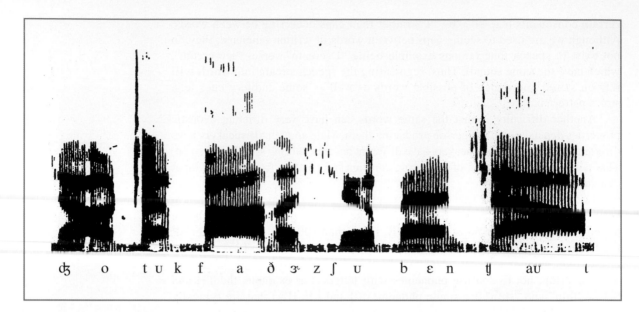

ʤ   o   t ʊ k f   a   ð ɝ z ʃ ʊ   b ɛ n ʧ   aʊ   ʇ

In the spectrogram, time is plotted along the *x*-axis and frequency along the *y*-axis, with intensity represented by darkness. There are no gaps between words but certain consonants (e.g. "b") block the flow of air and produce gaps. Vowels are represented by bands of horizontal stripes (called formants). The spectrogram represents "Joe took father's shoe bench out". From Tartter (1986). Copyright © Vivien Tartter. Reprinted with kind permission of the author.

The motor theory of speech perception

It has already been suggested that speech perception involves matching an infinitely varying acoustic signal to a finite number of stored representations in the brain. But what is the nature of these stored representations and how exactly does this process occur? One possibility is that the auditory signal is matched on to motor representations for producing one's own speech rather than matching to an acoustic template. This is the motor theory of speech perception (Liberman & Mattingly, 1985; Liberman & Whalen, 2000). In this account, phonemes are recognized by inferring the articulatory movements that would have been necessary to produce these sounds. The motor commands must be abstract insofar as one can understand speech without literally having to echo it back (for discussion of the notion of a motor program; see Chapter 8).

There is some evidence to support this theory. For example, for phonemes to come under the jurisdiction of the left hemisphere speech *perception* system (as opposed to production system), it is also necessary for one to have experience in producing such phonemes as part of one's natural language (Best & Avery, 1999). Watkins and Paus (2004) show that there is increased excitability of the motor system during speech perception tasks using PET and TMS. Studies such as these, however, do not show that this is the *only* way of perceiving speech but they do suggest a motor contribution. Many current models of speech postulate a mixture of both motor and auditory processing in the recognition of speech, as outlined in Chapter 11.

HEARING LIPS AND SEEING VOICES – THE MCGURK ILLUSION

Although we may not think of ourselves as good lip-readers, we all are capable of using this visual information to supplement what we hear. Visual cues from lip-reading are particularly important when the auditory input becomes less reliable, such as in noisy settings (Sumby & Pollack, 1954). Normally it is advantageous to combine information from two or more different senses. However, if the information contained in the two senses is discrepant, then the brain may generate a mis-perception or illusion based on its "best guess" solution. One striking example of this is the so-called **McGurk illusion** (McGurk & MacDonald, 1976). To create the illusion, one needs to dub together a separate auditory stream saying one thing (e.g. "baba") with visual lip-movements saying another thing (e.g. "gaga"). Participants often subjectively report hearing a third syllable – in this example, it is "dada". Close your eyes and you hear the correct auditory stimulus ("baba"), open them again and you hear the illusory stimulus ("dada"). At what point in the auditory or speech perception pathway does the illusion arise? A recent fMRI study by Skipper, van Wassenhove, Nusbaum and Small (2007) claims that the illusion arises because of convergence of the auditory and visual systems on the *motor* system for speech production (predominantly in the frontal lobes), which subsequently biases what is heard. They found that an illusory "da" stimulus (made up of auditory "ba" and visual "ga") initially resembles a real "da" stimulus (made up of auditory "da" and visual "da") in motor regions but not in auditory or visual regions.

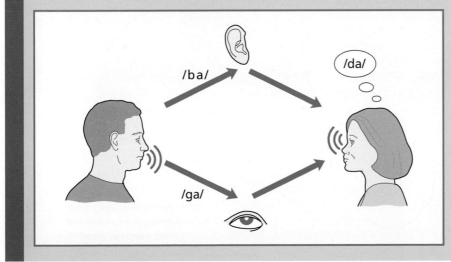

In the McGurk Illusion, the listener perceives a different syllable from that produced because of a mismatch between hearing and vision. At what stage in the auditory pathway might this illusion arise? Reprinted from Calvert, Campbell and Brammer (2000), Copyright 2000, with permission from Elsevier.

Auditory ventral and dorsal routes for "what" and "how"

A recent development in theories of speech recognition is attempting to make a reconciliation of acoustic and motor theories of speech perception. This has been achieved by suggesting that there are two routes for perceiving and producing speech: one that is based on lexical-semantic processing and one that is based on auditory-motor correspondence. These have been termed the ventral "what" route and the dorsal "how" route that is in many ways reminiscent of the one proposed for vision (Milner & Goodale, 1995). Others have termed the dorsal route as a "where" route, and it is likely that it is indeed involved in both locating the source of a sound as well as auditory-motor transformation.

Regions ventral to the left primary auditory cortex are considered by many to be specialized largely for speech (Scott & Wise, 2004). This processing is probably based on acoustic rather than motoric aspects of speech. Finally, this route is believed to make contact with structures critical for semantic memory, including the anterior temporal lobe (Scott & Wise, 2004) and possibly the medial and inferior temporal lobe (Hickok & Poeppel, 2004). This route is therefore specialized for identifying the conceptual content or the "what" of speech. The semantic system is believed to be a central processing stage in which speech recognition ends and speech production begins. As such, there are likely to be projections from the semantic system to frontal regions involved in word retrieval and articulation.

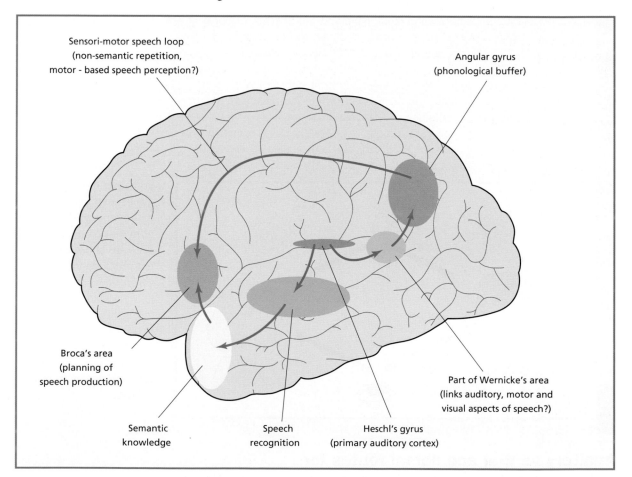

There may be two routes for perceiving and repeating speech: one that is based on lexical-semantic processing and one that is based on auditory-motor correspondence. These have been termed the ventral "what" route and the dorsal "how" route, respectively.

The dorsal or "how" route in many ways resembles the motor theory of speech perception. From the primary auditory cortex, there is a region at the interface of the superior temporal gyrus and the parietal lobe that acts as a computational hub linking together auditory, motor and possibly visual aspects of speech (Griffiths & Warren, 2002). Functional imaging studies show that the region responds to silently articulating a phrase relative to thinking about the phrase (Wise, Scott, Blank, Mummery, & Warbuton, 2001). Connections from parietal to frontal regions join the "how" speech circuit with the "what" pathway. Hickok and Poeppel (2004) have suggested that this sensory-motor "how" route between parietal and frontal lobes may be the neuroanatomical basis for the **articulatory loop** (or phonological loop) proposed by Baddeley (e.g. Baddeley, 1986; Baddeley, Lewis, & Vallar, 1984). This system is a short-term memory store for verbal material (see Chapter 9). The information in the store is refreshed by subvocal articulation, as in the case of retaining a phone number between looking it up in the directory and dialing. Indeed, left parietal regions have been implicated in implementing a phonological memory store in both human neuropsychology (Warrington & Shallice, 1969) and functional imaging (Jonides et al., 1998; Paulesu, Frith, & Frackowiak, 1993).

The existence of two routes also suggests that tasks such as repeating back speech can be accomplished in two ways. However, the "what" route should only be successful in the case of real words, whereas the "how" route can be used for novel and familiar words (as long as the speech consists of phonemes in the articulatory repertoire). Indeed, some unusual cases with acquired brain damage cannot repeat non-words but can repeat real words (Beauvois, Derouesne, & Bastard, 1981), suggesting selective difficulty of the "how" route. In contrast, patients with **deep dysphasia** cannot repeat non-words and make semantic errors in word repetition (e.g. they hear "dog" and say "cat"). This suggests that both routes are compromised and that repetition is based on poor semantic codes (Butterworth & Warrington, 1995; Martin, 1996).

KEY TERMS

Articulatory loop
A short-term memory store for verbal material that is refreshed by subvocal articulation.

Deep dysphasia
An inability to repeat non-words and the producion of semantic errors in word repetition.

SUMMARY AND KEY POINTS OF THE CHAPTER

- As with visual perception, hearing involves extracting features (e.g. loudness, pitch) out of the sensory signal that may be useful for segregating the input into different "objects" (e.g. separating out speakers in a noisy room).

- Cells within the (secondary) auditory cortex may have differing degrees of specialization for the content of the sound ("what") versus the location of the sound ("where"). This may be the starting point for an auditory dorsal/"where" pathway to the parietal lobes and a ventral/"what" pathway along the temporal lobes (predominantly left lateralized for speech).
- Music perception involves a number of different mechanisms: such as rhythm/timing, pitch perception, and melody (or pitch pattern perception). These different components have partially separate neural substrates as revealed by fMRI and lesion-based studies.
- There is some evidence for a specialized region in the (predominantly right) temporal lobe that is specialized for recognizing voices.
- Speech recognition involves extracting categorical information from sensory input that can vary infinitely (e.g. due to speaker differences in pitch, accent, articulation). This may be achieved via acoustic processing (matching the sounds on to stored auditory templates) and possibly via motor processing (matching the sounds on to stored articulation templates).
- Speech recognition (and speech repetition) may involve both a ventral "what" route (via semantics) and a dorsal "how" route for unfamiliar words and verbatim repetition (possibly corresponding to the use of the "articulatory loop").

EXAMPLE ESSAY QUESTIONS

- In what ways are the computational problems faced by the auditory system similar to and different from those faced by the visual system?
- What have studies using single-cell recordings contributed to our knowledge of how auditory information is represented in the brain?
- What is the evidence for separate "what", "where" and "how" routes in hearing?
- Does music perception rely on different brain mechanisms from the perception of other auditory stimuli?
- Why is speech perception different from music perception?
- What is the evidence for a motor component to speech perception?

RECOMMENDED FURTHER READING

- Moore, B. C. J. (2003). *Introduction to the psychology of hearing*, 5th edition. San Diego: Academic Press. This offers a good overview of basic processes in hearing, but for more recent studies based on neurophysiology, Kaas et al. (1999) is recommended.

- For music perception, a good overview paper is Stewart, L., von Kriegstein, K., Warren, J. D., & Griffiths, T. D. (2006). Music and the brain: Disorders of musical listening. *Brain*, *129*, 2533–2553. For more detailed articles, the following book is recommended: Peretz, I. & Zatorre, R. J. (2003). *The cognitive neuroscience of music*. Oxford: Oxford University Press.

- Moore, B. C. J, Tyler, L. K., & Marslen-Wilson, M. (2008). The perception of speech: From sound to meaning. Special issue of *Philosophical Transactions of the Royal Society of London B*, *363*, 917–921. A very good selection of papers on speech perception.

CHAPTER 11

CONTENTS

The speaking brain

The ability to produce, perceive and comprehend speech is a remarkable human achievement. In the most simplistic terms, spoken language is concerned with transferring ideas from one person's head to another person's head with the common physical link being the vibration of molecules in the air. It involves the transformation of thoughts into sentences and words and, ultimately, a series of articulatory commands sent to the vocal apparatus. These sound waves then produce mechanical changes on the cochlea (part of the inner ear) of the listener. These are perceived as speech and the words, sentences and meaning are inferred from this input. Speech recognition and speech production are often taught separately from each other, and it can be helpful to think about them as separate tasks. However, it is important to recognize that the driving force behind human language is to communicate ideas to the people around us. Outside of the laboratory, speech production normally only exists when someone else is around to engage in the complementary process of speech recognition. This social aspect of language implies that we are able to deduce what other people know, what they believe and what they don't know. It is highly questionable whether the vocalizations of other animals could be said to be "true language" in this sense.

The previous chapter considered early auditory processing of speech. This chapter will consider how familiar spoken words are recognized and how the meaning of words and sentences are derived before, finally, considering the process of speech production.

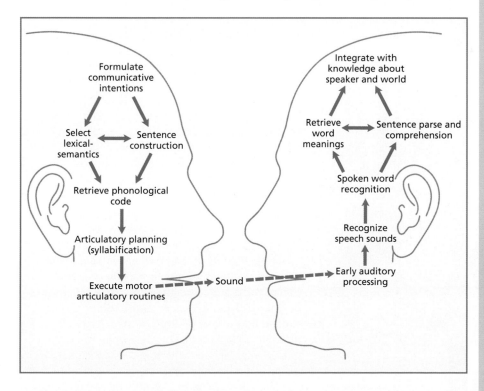

A simple schematic diagram showing some of the main stages in speech production (left) and speech comprehension (right).

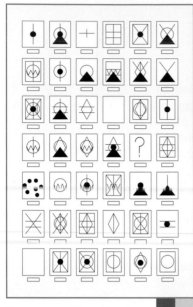

The pygmy chimp Kanzi learned to communicate using written "lexigrams". In what ways is this different from or similar to human language? Based on Savage-Rumbaugh et al. (1983).

DO NON-HUMAN ANIMALS HAVE LANGUAGE?

The idea of being able to talk to the animals, Dr Doolittle style, is a captivating one. Other species are clearly able to communicate with each other. For example, bees perform a dance that signals the location of nectar and vervet monkeys produce calls when faced with a threatening stimulus. But are these communication systems related to human language? The question of animal language is an important one because it focuses discussion on what language actually is and where it came from.

Other species do not have the same vocal tract as humans and are physically incapable of producing human-like speech. As such, attempts at teaching language to other animals have relied on training them to associate symbols with objects and actions. The main difficulty with these studies is that, although animals are capable of learning associations, it is not clear that they have a conceptual level of understanding. For example, pigeons can be trained to respond in different ways (pecking once or twice) to pictures of trees or water (Herrnstein, Lovelend, & Cable, 1977). But do they understand how trees relate to other concepts such as plants and bark, and could they use pecking to communicate the idea of a tree in the absence of a picture?

What about closer evolutionary neighbors, such as the chimpanzee? The chimp, Washoe, was taught American Sign Language and learned around 200 signs (Gardner, Gardner, & van Cantford, 1989). Moreover, there was evidence of overgeneralizations (e.g. using "hurt" for tattoo), and the combining of words for unfamiliar objects (e.g. "water bird" for duck). The system was also spontaneously acquired by Washoe's adopted son. The problem with these studies is that many signs are iconic rather than arbitrary (e.g. "give" is represented by an inward hand motion) and it is not clear how often Washoe produced random or inappropriate word combinations. Some have argued that the ability to generate an infinite number of meaningful word combinations is the uniquely human component of language (Hauser, Chomsky, & Fitch, 2002).

Savage-Rumbaugh and colleagues adopted a different approach with their bonobo or pygmy chimp, Kanzi (e.g. Savage-Rumbaugh, McDonald, Sevcik, Hopkins, & Rupert, 1986). Kanzi learned how to use arbitrary written symbols to communicate, and could select the symbols given human speech. There was evidence that the symbols were used flexibly (e.g. selecting "strawberry" to indicate wanting strawberries, the location of strawberries or the object itself) and

Kanzi using "lexigrams" to communicate. From Savage-Rumbaugh & Lewin, R. (1994).

evidence of appreciation of word order (e.g. "Kanzi chase X" versus "X chase Kanzi"). This research has, however, been criticized on the grounds that Kanzi's utterances were mainly food requests that may have been learned through reward and that would not be found in a natural setting (Seidenberg & Petitto, 1987). Thus, whilst non-human animals may have some of the basic cognitive prerequisites for language it is doubtful that they possess anything akin to the human capacity (Hauser et al., 2002).

SPOKEN WORD RECOGNITION

It is generally assumed that spoken word recognition entails matching some aspect of an acoustic form to a stored set of spoken words that comprise the set of known words in the speaker's vocabulary. This store of words is known as the **phonological lexicon** (or speech input lexicon), and the matching process itself is called **lexical access**. This process can be broken down in terms of a number of potentially distinct issues. First, what is the nature of the perceptual code that is used to access the stored set of words, and in what format are the stored speech forms themselves stored? Second, how is the matching process itself achieved? Are many different candidates considered together or one at a time? Is the process purely perceptual or does the semantic context matter?

Our brain contains a "mental lexicon", which, like a dictionary, specifies the properties of a word, such as how it is pronounced, its grammatical class (e.g. noun, verb) and its meaning(s).

What are the access units for spoken word forms?

Linguists have traditionally placed great emphasis on the importance of phonemes in the representation of speech. Some models of spoken word recognition also place great emphasis on the role of a phonemic code, as in the case of the motor theory of speech (Liberman & Mattingly, 1985; Liberman & Whalen, 2000). However, other cognitive neuroscientists have taken a more skeptical approach and have argued that phonemes may just be useful descriptions of the structure of language rather than something that is actually implemented in real cognitive/neural systems. For example, in some models acoustic features of speech (e.g. voicing, stops, formant frequencies) are considered to access the spoken word forms directly without an intermediate phonemic description (Marslen-Wilson & Warren, 1994).

The evidence for a phonemic level in lexical access is equivocal. Some patients with acquired speech recognition problems are able to comprehend spoken words but are poor at discriminating between phonemes (e.g. are "ta" and "da" different?), whereas others show the opposite dissociation (Miceli, Gainotti, Caltagirone, & Masullo, 1980). Indeed, the ability to explicitly segment speech into phoneme segments appears to be predicted by literacy levels, particularly for alphabetic scripts, rather than spoken language ability (Petersson, Reis, Askelof, Castro-Caldas, & Ingvar, 2000). This suggests that explicit phonemic awareness is not critical for speech recognition, although

LINGUISTIC TERMINOLOGY MADE SIMPLE

Phoneme A minimal unit of speech that serves to distinguish between meanings of words. In English, /r/ and /l/ are different phonemes because this sound difference can convey differences in word meaning (e.g. between "rip" and "lip"). In languages such as Japanese, this is not so and /r/ and /l/ are variants of a single phoneme.

Syllable Clusters of phonemes that are centered on a vowel sound. The vowel forms the *nucleus* of the syllable. The vowel may optionally be preceded by consonant sounds (termed the syllable *onset*), and may optionally be followed by more consonants (termed the syllable *coda*). The vowel and coda collectively make up the *rime* of the syllable. The words "mark", "market" and "marquetry" have one, two and three syllables, respectively.

Stress An increase in the activity of the vocal apparatus of a speaker that aids segmentation of the speech stream into words.

Morpheme The smallest meaningful unit in the grammar of a language. For example, "unladylike" has four syllables and three morphemes (un + lady+ like). "Dogs" has one syllable but two morphemes (dog+ s). Both "unladylike" and "dogs" are one word.

Word Words occupy an intermediate position in size between a morpheme and a phrase. A word is sometimes defined as being the minimal possible unit in a reply.

Syntax The rules (or grammar) that specify how words can be combined into sentences in a given language.

Semantics Broadly defined as the meaning of linguistic expressions, but also defined as the meaning of particular words (lexical-semantics) or the meaning of objects, words and other types of stimuli (semantic memory).

Pragmatics The way in which language is used in practice, such as implied or intended meaning (e.g. "can't you read?" may be used as a rhetorical question that does not require an answer).

Prosody Melodic aspects of spoken language such as stress, intonation (e.g. rising pitch to indicate a question) and emotion (e.g. slow and low to imply sadness).

Nouns "the" words that imply *things*, such as "the computer", "the idea".

Verbs "to" words, that imply an *action*, such as "to buy", "to think", "to eat".

Adjectives Words used descriptively such as "big", "soft", "easy".

Pronoun A word that can substitute for a noun (e.g. "I", "you" and "him"). In the sentence "Mr. Rice spoke to Tom and offered him a job", "him" is the pronoun; it takes the place of "Tom".

Preposition	Indicates a connection, between two other parts of speech, such as "to", "with", "by" or "from".
Function words (or closed class words)	Words that have little lexical meaning but instead serve to express grammatical relationships with other words within a sentence (e.g. pronouns, prepositions, "the", "and").

it remains to be determined whether such units are computed implicitly. In Hickok and Poeppel's (2004) model, explicit phoneme segmentation is captured by the dorsal route, whereas spoken word comprehension is performed by the ventral route. Recall from Chapter 10, that the ventral route is primarily concerned with speech comprehension, i.e. the process of translating between an acoustic input and a semantic output, whereas the dorsal route is concerned with more motoric aspects of speech (as well as locating sound sources), i.e. the process of translating an acoustic input into a motor output.

If not phonemes, then what are alternative perceptual access codes for spoken word recognition? Some researchers have argued that syllables may be critical (Mehler, Dommergues, Frauenfelder, & Segui, 1981), whereas others have empha- sized the importance of stress patterns (Cutler & Butterfield, 1992). In English, nouns tend to be stressed on the first syllable and this can be used by the speech recogni- tion system to infer likely word boundaries (consider the nouns *EN*voy and *DE*coy, and compare with verbs such as en*JOY* and de*CAY* in which stress is assigned to the second syllable). However, this is not the case in all languages. It is likely that the actual perceptual access code that is utilized is language specific and, in bilinguals, is governed by their dominant language (Cutler, Mehler, Norris, & Segui, 1992). The spoken word recognition system may select the most salient perceptual features to aid recognition, and in some languages (such as French) this may correspond to syllable structure whereas in others (such as English) it may correspond to stress patterns.

The cohort model

Although the precise nature of the mechanism by which spoken word recognition takes place is still debated, there is general consensus that it involves competition between similar sounding words (McQueen & Cutler, 2001). The most influen- tial model in this area is the **cohort model** of Marslen-Wilson and Tyler (1980; Marslen-Wilson, 1987). The acoustic information required to identify a word is revealed over time. The central idea of this model is that a large number of spoken words are, in parallel, initially considered as candidates but that words get elimi- nated as more evidence accumulates. For example, on hearing the sound "e" all words beginning with this sound would become active. This is termed the "cohort" of words. But as more information is revealed (e.g. "ele"), then the cohort gets whittled down to fewer words (e.g. "elephant", "electricity") until a point is reached ("eleph") in which the evidence is consistent with only a single word. This is termed the **uniqueness point**. Thus the start of a word, particularly the first syllable, has an exaggerated importance. Indeed, listeners are better at detecting speech distortions

KEY TERMS

Cohort model
In lexical access, a large number of spoken words are initially considered as candidates but words get eliminated as more evidence accumulates.

Uniqueness point
The point at which the acoustic input unambiguously corresponds to only one known word.

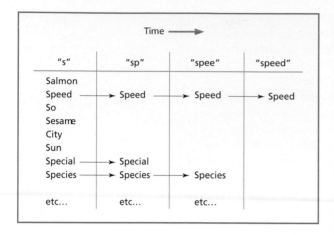

In the cohort model of spoken word recognition, all words that are initially consistent with the acoustic information become active in parallel. As more acoustic information is revealed, the size of the cohort is dwindled until a unique match can be made.

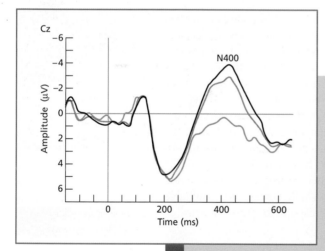

The N400 response to the critical word in three types of sentence: semantically coherent and correct ("the Dutch trains are *yellow*"; green line), semantically coherent but incorrect ("the Dutch trains are *white*"; brown line), semantically incoherent ("the Dutch trains are *sour*"; black line). From Hagoort et al. (2004). Reprinted with permission from AAAS.

when they occur prior to the uniqueness point, and the time taken to recognize a word depends on how early or late the uniqueness point occurs (e.g. Marslen-Wilson, 1987).

The uniqueness point is a structural property of the word, but do linguistic factors such as word frequency and semantic predictability influence recognition? Considering word frequency, it is the case that not all candidates in a cohort behave equivalently. For example, the ambiguous onset "spee" is compatible with "speed", "speech", "species" and so on. However, studies of reaction time priming show that infrequent words (e.g. "species") get activated less (Zwitserlood, 1989). This suggests an early effect of word frequency, but what about biasing effects of semantic context? For example, what would happen if "spee" were presented in the context of a sentence about highway driving (favoring "speed") or animal classification (favoring "species")? Initial versions of the cohort model permitted top-down activation whereby context could eliminate items in the cohort (e.g. Marslen-Wilson & Tyler, 1980). However, subsequent studies have

THE N400 AS AN INDEX OF SEMANTIC CONGRUITY

In electrophysiological studies, one component of the ERP waveform appears to be particularly sensitive to semantic anomalies and has been termed the N400 because it reflects a negative peak at around 400 ms after the onset of the critical word (Kutas & Hillyard, 1980). This peak probably reflects the integration of word meaning with the wider semantic context provided by other words or by knowledge of the world. Given that 400 ms is relatively slow in cognitive processing terms, the ERP data supports the general view that context exerts a late effect in word recognition (e.g. Zwitserlood, 1989). The N400 is found either when a word is semantically anomalous as in "the Dutch trains are *sour*" (trains cannot be tasted), or conflicts with known facts about the world as in "the Dutch trains are *white*" (Dutch people know they are yellow) (Hagoort, Hald, Bastiaansen, & Petersson, 2004). Words need not be presented in sentence form for the N400 to be elicited. For example, given a homographic word such as "bank", an N400 is elicited for the third word in triplets such as "river–bank–money" but not "finance–bank–money" (Titone & Salisbury, 2004). This result also suggests that the N400 reflects global context (operating over all three words) and not local context, given that the last two words are identical in both triplets.

challenged this view. The key to understanding this argument is that finding effects of context are not, in themselves, enough. One also needs to establish at which stage in processing context is important. Is it at the stage of selecting items from the cohort or at a later stage in which the selected information is thematically integrated? Reaction time studies suggest that perceptually ambiguous speech onsets do activate the full cohort, even though some words are contextually inappropriate (Zwitserlood, 1989). This suggests a late effect of context in spoken word recognition.

KEY TERM

Amodal
Not tied to one or more perceptual systems.

SEMANTIC MEMORY AND THE MEANING OF WORDS

How is the meaning of words represented?

On encountering a word such as "lion" one is able to retrieve many associated properties, such as the fact that it is an animal, has four legs, is a native of Africa and is a carnivore. Collectively, such properties are considered to comprise the meaning of the word. According to most theories, this same knowledge base is consulted irrespective of whether the spoken word is heard, the written word is seen or if a lion itself is seen, heard or just merely thought about. In other words, semantic memory is considered to be **amodal**. Another widely accepted principle is that similar concepts may be represented in similar ways, and similar concepts may share semantic features. The idea that similar concepts may be represented in similar ways also leads to the prediction that similar concepts may be represented in similar areas of the brain. There is an increasing amount of evidence that supports this view, although the precise nature of this organization is controversial.

A popular way of conceiving the representation of knowledge is in terms of an interconnected network of features. For example, the word "lion" may connect with features such as animal, carnivore, etc.; the feature "animal" may connect with eats, breathes, reproduces, etc.; "breathes" connects with lungs and so on. How are these features organized, if at all? The early influential model of Collins and Quinlan (1969) assumed a hierarchical organization. There is some evidence that supports

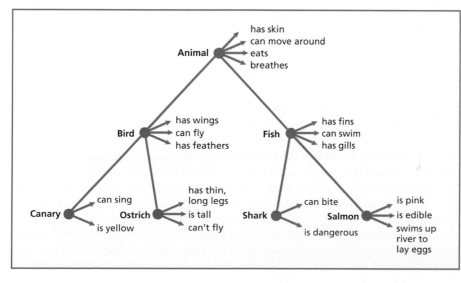

In the Collins and Quinlan (1969) model, semantic features are organized hierarchically with super-ordinate information accessed first. Subsequent models have retained the idea that knowledge may consist of a network of interconnected features but do not make the assumption of hierarchical organization. Reprinted from Collins and Quinlan (1969), Copyright 1969, with permission from Elsevier.

the model. Participants are faster at classifying a robin as a bird than an animal, because the latter requires going further up in the hierarchy. However, there are also many problems with the model. For example, not all concepts have clear hierarchies (e.g. the difference between truth, justice and law). Second, apparent effects of distance within the hierarchy could also be explained by how frequently two words or concepts co-occur (Wilkins, 1971). For example, robin and bird may co-occur together more than robin and animal. Most contemporary theories retain the basic idea that word meaning is represented via interconnected features but do not assume that the features are hierarchically organized.

Hierarchical or not, there is some evidence that these different kinds of super-ordinate and sub-ordinate information may have different neural substrates. Rogers et al. (2006) found that different parts of the ventral route for speech comprehension along the temporal lobes were activated depending on the specificity of the information. There was a posterior to anterior gradient for less specific information (e.g. animal), intermediate specificity (e.g. bird) and more specific information (e.g. robin). This may explain why some studies of lexical semantics have highlighted posterior regions (e.g. Hickock & Poeppel, 2004) whereas others implicate more anterior temporal regions (e.g. Mummery, Patterson, Price, Ashburner, Frackowiak, & Hodges, 2000). Both could be correct, depending on the type of information being evaluated.

Category specificity: The animate–inanimate debate

Two publications in the early 1980s triggered an enduring debate on the neural organization of semantic categories (for a review, see Capitani, Laiacona, Mahon, & Caramazza, 2003). Warrington and McCarthy (1983) documented a patient with acquired brain damage who had preserved knowledge for animals, foods and flowers relative to inanimate objects. The following year, Warrington and Shallice (1984) reported four patients with the opposite profile. These patients were impaired at comprehending pictures and words, in naming pictures and matching pictures and words. This is consistent with an impaired amodal knowledge system. To account for this pattern, Warrington and Shallice (1984) proposed the **sensory–functional distinction**. Rather than suggesting that the brain is organized categorically, they suggested that certain categories may depend critically on certain types of knowledge: animals and fruit and vegetables may be defined more by their sensory properties (color, shape, four legs, etc.), whereas inanimate objects, particularly tools, may be defined by their functions. This interpretation was favored because categories such as gemstones appeared to behave like animate kinds (= sensory) and body parts appeared to behave like inanimate kinds (= functional).

At this stage, it is worth clarifying the terms "sensory" and "functional". By sensory, it is generally meant that the knowledge is *about*, say, vision rather than knowledge being stored in a visual format. By functional, a restrictive definition would be "what it is used for", although some models have included all types of non-sensory knowledge (Farah & McClelland, 1991). Some contemporary accounts have adopted a more radical interpretation in claiming that "sensory" and "functional" may literally mean that conceptual knowledge is distributed over brain regions involved in perception and action, respectively (e.g. the "sensory-motor" account; Martin & Chao, 2001). The main motivation for these theories has come primarily from functional imaging. For example, different regions of temporal cortex show selective activity for tool movement versus human movement (Beauchamp, Lee, Haxby, & Martin, 2002). The same regions are implicated in naming tools versus animals (Beauchamp et al., 2002). Results such as these are intriguing but they can potentially be interpreted in different ways. For example, it could be the case that sensory-motor areas are activated top-down by other regions that form the core conceptual knowledge base (e.g. the "convergence zones" of Damasio, 1989), or that category-specific effects can arise at multiple levels within the cognitive system (e.g. at both modality-specific object recognition stages and amodal conceptual levels; Humphreys & Forde, 2001).

The sensory–functional account has been extensively challenged. First of all, to demonstrate a relative impairment in one domain relative to another it is important to be sure that the set of stimuli used are of equivalent difficulty (e.g. the words are equally common in the language). The earlier studies did not necessarily use the same stimuli on all patients or take into account all relevant factors. In some cases, an initial category-specific effect disappears when these factors are taken into consideration (Funnell & Sheridan, 1992; Parkin & Stewart, 1993), although this is not always the case (Capitani et al., 2003). A harder factor to control for is personal familiarity due to individual differences in exposure to categories. For example, it has been noted that all cases showing relative sparing of fruits and vegetables relative to animals have been female, and all cases showing relative sparing of animals relative to fruits and vegetables have been male (Albanese, Capitani, Barbarotto, & Laiacona, 2000).

More direct tests of the sensory–functional distinction have failed to provide strong support for the theory. For example, patients with animate category-specific deficits are not necessarily impaired at answering sensory relative to functional questions about animals or objects (e.g. Lambon Ralph, Howard, Nightingale, & Ellis, 1998). In fact, the same holds true in a follow-up study of patient JBR, one of Warrington and Shallice's original patients upon whom the initial theory was based (Funnell & DeMornay Davies, 1996). Conversely, some patients do present with selective difficulties in comprehending sensory properties but yet do not show the predicted category-specific impairments (Coltheart, Inglis, Cupples, Michie, Bates, & Budd, 1998).

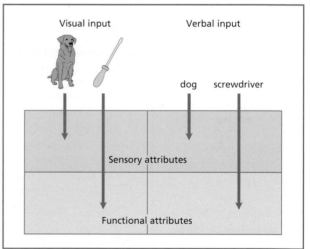

Are other theories more able to account for the data than the sensory–functional distinction? A number of other accounts explain category specificity according to the organization of more basic underlying features, but do not invoke the sensory–functional distinction (Caramazza & Hillis, 1990b; Devlin, Gonnerman, Andersen, & Seidenberg, 1998; Humphreys & Forde, 2001; Tyler & Moss, 2001). These models typically assume that correlated features (i.e. features that tend to co-occur) are represented together. For example, animals have more correlated features than other categories (e.g. eyes, mouth and fur tend to go together), whereas man-made objects can benefit from the fact that there are distinctive relations between their shape and function (e.g. sharp edges and cutting).

An alternative class of model altogether is to suggest that some concepts really are organized categorically in the brain. Caramazza and Shelton (1998) put forward an evolutionarily-based proposal that at least some categories are hard-wired. The categories proposed were animals, plant life (e.g. fruit and vegetables), conspecifics (other humans) and possibly tools. This theory can accommodate much of the data that

It has been argued that semantic memory may be organized along the lines of functional versus sensory features, rather than categorically along the lines of animals, tools, food, etc. From Humphreys and Forde (2001). Copyright © Cambridge University Press. Reproduced with permission.

is problematic for rival accounts, such as the sensory–functional distinction. It does have difficulty in explaining why category-specific deficits tend to be relative rather than absolute. Functional imaging studies show some selectivity of brain regions for certain categories, but the specialization is far from absolute (Joseph, 2001; Martin & Chao, 2001) and is by no means restricted to those categories considered to be innate (e.g. chairs; Ishai, Ungerleider, Martin, Schouten, & Haxby, 1999).

Category specificity in other domains of knowledge

Although the focus of attention has been on the animate–inanimate distinction, a consideration of other types of category is important for moving the debate forward and for considering the organization of knowledge more generally. In a later paper, Warrington and McCarthy (1987) extended their sensory–functional distinction to account for more fine-grained dissociations, and Allport (1985) presents another model along these lines (see below). In these models, concepts are distributed over many different domains of knowledge (such as action-based, shape-based, movement-based and so on) rather than being divided into a dichotomy (such as sensory-functional). This approach also resonates with the claim that conceptual processing overlaps with perceptual processing (Martin & Chao, 2001). As before, the central issues are whether apparent category specificity is truly category-based or feature-based.

Food

A number of studies have shown that impairments in understanding fruit and vegetables can dissociate from relative sparing of animals and man-made objects (e.g. Hart, Berndt,

In Allport's (1985) model, concepts are distributed over many different domains of knowledge rather than being divided into a dichotomy (e.g. functional, sensory). Reprinted from Allport (1985), Copyright 1985, with permission from Elsevier.

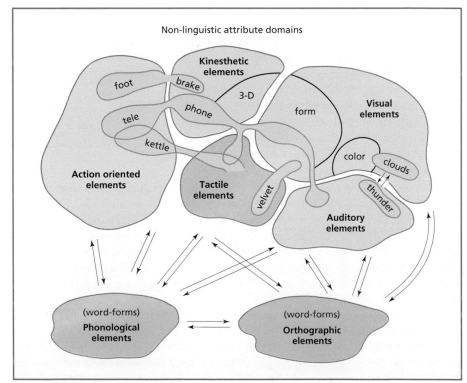

& Caramazza 1985; Samson & Pillon, 2003). In the case reported by Samson and Pillon (2003), the deficit extended to manufactured foods and the deficit was found in all comprehension tasks and when different types of semantic attribute were probed. The patient could choose the correct color given a black and white drawing, suggesting that there was no severe loss of sensory features (at least for color). They argued that food is represented categorically in support of Caramazza and Shelton (1998).

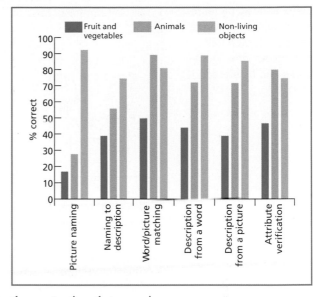

Colors

Luzzatti and Davidoff (1994) report a patient who was able to name colors but could not retrieve colors given black and white line drawings (e.g. of a tomato). The fact that the patient was able to name actual colors rules out a perceptual deficit, or a loss of the words themselves. Functional imaging also supports the contention that perceiving and knowing about colors are distinct (Chao & Martin, 1999). Another patient was impaired at comprehending the color of objects but had spared form, size and function knowledge (Miceli, Fouch, Capasso, Shelton, Tomaiuolo, & Caramazza, 2001). Interestingly, the patient showed no category specificity (e.g. for fruits and vegetables). Thus, it is possible to have selective difficulties in particular knowledge domains (e.g. color) that do not reveal themselves as other category effects.

Patient RS had a particular difficulty with fruit and vegetables relative to other categories in a wide range of tasks. From Samson and Pillon (2003).

Body parts

Are body parts animate? From a first principles point of view, the answer to this question is not obvious. Arms, eyes and so on are clearly key features of many animals but they are not animate in their own right. From an empirical point of view, some patients have relatively preserved knowledge of body parts relative to other living categories (Shelton, Fouch, & Caramazza, 1998). Conversely, other patients present with difficulties in understanding body parts. Patients with **autotopagnosia** are unable to localize body parts on themselves, on pictures or on others, and their errors appear to be conceptual (Semenza, 1988; Semenza & Goodglass, 1985). For example, they might point to their elbow instead of their knee or their ear instead of their eye. In this instance, the deficit is often restricted to one particular aspect of body-part knowledge – namely, their location. It is not due simply to an inability to localize *per se* or a sensory-motor deficit (e.g. they can demonstrate normal location of gloves and ties) or a gross loss of category knowledge (e.g. they can say that the mouth is used for eating, and name pictures of body parts). In the case of body parts, it seems as if different features are represented differently (e.g. bodily location versus function) rather than behaving as an isolatable category in which all the relevant features are affected.

Actions and verbs

Action concepts tend to map most closely on to the grammatical category of verbs. Logically, it appears possible to have action concepts that are not encoded with respect to a single word. For example, there is no single word for the action concept of "put the

KEY TERM

Autotopagnosia
An inability to localize body parts on oneself, on pictures or on others.

Some aphasic patients are impaired at naming verbs presented as pictorial actions. From Druks and Masterson (2000).

kettle on". Moreover, the meaning of verbs may encompass other types of information, such as the manner of execution (e.g. kicking done with the legs not arms), the type of object acted on (e.g. lifting implies an object acted on, but smiling does not), and intentions. Many verbs have no concrete action at all (e.g. to obey, to think). As such, it is helpful to think of action concepts as constituting part of semantic memory and verbs as constituting a grammatical property of words. The empirical evidence largely supports the distinction between grammatical and conceptual properties of verbs/actions (e.g. Druks, 2002; Shapiro & Caramazza, 2003). However, others have sought to explain differences in nouns and verbs purely in semantic terms. Bird, Howard and Franklin (2000) asked the question, "Why is a verb like an inanimate object?" The answer, according to this group, is that verbs and tools both load on to the functional side of the sensory–functional distinction. In support of this, lesion studies suggest an overlap in left parieto-frontal regions involved in both action and tool comprehension (Tranel, Kemmerer, Adolphs, Damasio, & Damasio, 2003). Moreover, event-related fMRI shows that verbs such as "lick", "pick" and "kick" activate regions that overlap with or are next to the corresponding part of the motor cortex – mouth, fingers and legs (Hauk, Johnsrude, & Pulvermuller, 2004). However, studies that directly compare action concepts against the noun/verb distinction do show independent contributions. One ERP study contrasted word attributes (abstract, high visual, high visual + motor) and grammatical class (noun, verb) and found independent effects with no interaction (Kellenbach, Wijers, Hovius, Mulder, & Mulder, 2002). TMS research has shown that retrieval of both nouns and verbs associated with actions is disrupted by stimulation of motor areas but the same does not apply to non-action words (Oliveri, Finocchiar, Shapiro, Gangitano, Caramazza, & Pascual-Leone, 2004). In summary, action concepts appear to be a relatively specialized category but this does not map on to the difference between nouns and verbs in a straightforward way.

Proper names

Proper names such as "Michael Jackson", "Paris" and "Lassie" denote particular instances, whereas corresponding common nouns such as "pop star", "city" and "dog" denote a class of entities. As with other categories, it is important to be clear whether any category specificity reflects damage to a conceptual system rather than word retrieval or grammatical mechanisms. Some patients have severe difficulties in retrieving proper names (called **proper name anomia**) but can comprehend them, suggesting the difficulty is not in semantics (e.g. Semenza & Zettin, 1988). However, other cases have been reported in which the deficit appears to reflect semantics (Bredart, Brennen, & Valentine, 1997). Ellis, Young and Critchley (1989) report a patient who, after a right temporal lobectomy, was unable to name or understand "singular objects" such as famous people, famous animals, famous buildings and brand names. There were no difficulties with animals *per se* or other categories. The opposite dissociation has been reported (Van Lancker & Klein, 1990). So are proper names represented categorically within the semantic system? This account seems too simplistic because dissociations within the domain of proper names have been reported. Some cases have impaired semantic knowledge of people but not places (Miceli, Capasso, Daniele, Esposito, Magarelli, & Tomaiuolo, 2000), whereas others have the opposite effect (Lyons, Hanley, & Kay, 2002).

Numbers

The conceptual representation of numbers is dealt with in Chapter 12. However, it is interesting to note at this juncture that there is a double dissociation between spared numbers and impairments of other concepts (Cappelletti, Kopelman, & Butterworth, 2002), and impaired numbers but spared knowledge of other concepts (Cipolotti, Butterworth, & Denes, 1991). It is often argued that the representation of number knowledge is a true categorical distinction (e.g. Dehaene, Piazza, Pinel, & Cohen, 2003).

Evaluation

That some semantic categories can be relatively spared or impaired relative to other categories is now well established empirically. Two broad types of explanation have been put forward to account for this: either that the brain is organized by categories, or that the brain is organized according to features, with different categories depending on different features to differing degrees. The most influential feature-based theory, namely the sensory–functional distinction, is found to be lacking. A consideration of various semantic categories reveals that, in some instances, conceptual features (e.g. relating to colors or actions) can be damaged without category specificity, and that apparent categories can be damaged (e.g. food or animals) without a disproportionate impairment of certain types of feature. This suggests that the organization of semantic memory is governed by multiple constraints. How these constraints develop (or have evolved) as a result of linguistic, perceptual and motor experience remains to be determined.

UNDERSTANDING AND PRODUCING SENTENCES

The preceding section has already introduced the notion that words carry not only information about meaning (semantics) but that they also carry information about syntactic roles (grammatical classes such as nouns, verbs and so on). The syntactic properties of words will determine the order and structure of the words within a sentence, i.e. **syntax**. This enables the listener to figure out who is doing what to whom. Consider the three sentences below. Sentences A and B have different meanings but the same syntax, whereas sentences A and C have the same meaning but different syntax.

A: The boy hit the girl.
B: The girl hit the boy.
C: The girl was hit by the boy.

KEY TERM

Syntax
The order and structure of the words within a sentence.

Is syntax (and parsing) independent from semantics?

The process of assigning a syntactic structure to words is termed **parsing**. One key debate in the literature concerns the extent to which parsing is based solely on the syntactic properties of words (so-called structure-driven parsing; Frazier & Rayner, 1982) or is additionally influenced by semantic properties of words (so-called discourse-driven parsing; MacDonald, Pearlmutter, & Seidenberg, 1994). Evidence in favor of single initial computation of sentence structure comes from **garden-path sentences**, in which the early part of a sentence biases a syntactic interpretation that turns out to be incorrect. The classic example of this is given by Bever (1970):

The horse raced past the barn fell.

In this example, the word "fell" comes as a surprise unless one parses the sentence as "The horse {THAT} raced past the barn {WAS THE ONE THAT} fell". The fact that there is any ambiguity at all suggests that not all possible sentence constructions are considered (consistent with a structure-driven parse). However, in some instances semantics does appear to bias the way that the sentence is parsed (consistent with a discourse-driven parse). For example, being led up the garden path can often be avoided if the ambiguous sentence is preceded by supporting context (Altmann, Garnham, & Henstra, 1994). Consider the following sentence:

The fireman told the man that he had risked his life for to install a smoke detector.

This sentence is less likely to lead down the garden path if preceded by context such as (Altmann et al., 1994):

A fireman braved a dangerous fire in a hotel. He rescued one of the guests at great danger to himself. A crowd of men gathered around him. The fireman told the man that he had risked his life for to install a smoke detector.

On balance, it seems that the setting up of a sentence structure is, to some degree, dependent on both syntactic and contextual factors.

Some researchers have taken this evidence as far as to state that syntactic and semantic processes are completely interwoven (McClelland, St John, & Taraban, 1989). However, studies of brain-damaged individuals and imaging/ERP methods speak against such a strong interpretation. It appears that certain aspects of syntax and lexical-semantics can be dissociated from each other. Patients with semantic dementia gradually lose the meaning of individual words but they still produce sentences that are grammatical, albeit lacking in content (e.g. "I've been worried to death thinking, trying, I am going to try and think with you today ... I think of things, I can't often say ... er ... say what to say"; Hodges, Patterson, & Tyler, 1994). Comprehension tests on semantic dementia patients also suggest that they can decide whether a sentence is grammatical or not even if it contains words that they apparently do not understand (e.g. is the following grammatical: "Are the boys fix the radio?"; Rochon, Kave, Cupit, Jokel, & Winocur, 2004). However, some aspects of syntax may depend on the integrity of the semantics of particular words; for example, when a word is grammatically singular but conceptually plural (e.g. "the *label* on the bottles" refers to more than one label; Rochon et al., 2004). Further evidence for a partial overlap between syntax and lexical semantics comes from the opposite dissociation – poor syntax but good single-word semantics. The patient reported by Ostrin and Tyler (1995) was unable to make grammaticality judgments or produce grammatical sentences but could use semantics to integrate words into phrases. ERP studies have also demonstrated different components associated with grammatical violations of (local) phrase structure versus (more global) syntactic structure (Friederici & Meyer, 2004). Thus, there is evidence to suggest that some aspects of syntax are independent of lexical semantics, whereas other aspects of syntax may depend on it.

The role of phonological short-term memory in sentence processing

It is well accepted that there is a phonological short-term memory store that appears to have a limited capacity and may be refreshed by subvocal rehearsal (e.g. Baddeley, Lewis, & Vallar, 1984). The function of the phonological store, aside from retaining telephone numbers whilst dialing, has been debated. One possibility is that it may assist syntactic parsing, particularly for long or syntactically complex sentences. For example, if the sentence is ambiguous and requires a change of parse, then the phonological trace in short-term memory may be consulted. Patients with markedly reduced digit spans can produce and comprehend many sentences adequately, which suggests that this component is not essential to all aspects of sentence processing (Caplan & Waters, 1990; Vallar & Baddeley, 1984). However, some patients show clear deficits in comprehension and grammaticality judgments when more complex sentences are presented. In the patient documented by Romani (1994), the deficit was abolished when written sentences were presented. A written record is permanent and can be re-inspected to enable a change in parse. Indeed, when written words were presented one by one, the deficit appeared again. This suggests a role of phonological short-term memory in parsing of syntactically demanding sentences presented in spoken form.

Is Broca's aphasia a syntactic disorder?

One controversial claim is that there is a dedicated syntactic processor that is involved in both sentence comprehension and sentence production and that this is associated with the syndrome of Broca's aphasia (and/or with damage to Broca's area). This particular aspect of Broca's aphasia is termed **agrammatism**, meaning "loss of grammar". The typical presenting symptoms are halting, "telegraphic" speech production that is devoid of function words (e.g. of, at, the, and), bound morphemes (e.g. –ing, –s) and often verbs. For example, given the "cookie theft" picture (see overleaf) to describe, one patient came out with "cookie jar ... fall over ... chair . .. water ... empty ..." (Goodglass & Kaplan, 1983). The standard nineteenth-century view of Broca's aphasia was in terms of a loss of motor forms for speech. This fails to explain the agrammatic characteristic that is observed. Moreover, subsequent studies show that articulatory deficits are caused by lesions elsewhere (Dronkers,

Sentence production abilities in aphasia have been assessed by giving patients complex pictures such as the "cookie theft" to describe. From Goodglass and Kaplan (1972).

1996) and even Broca's own cases had more extensive lesions, suggesting they may have had multiple deficits (Marie, 1906).

The nineteenth-century view that Broca's aphasics had better comprehension than production endured until the 1970s. However, many seemingly complex sentences such as "The bicycle that the boy is holding is broken" can be comprehended just from the content words and with minimal knowledge of syntax (bicycle...boy...hold...broke). It was only when these patients were given sentences in which syntax was crucial to comprehension that disorders became apparent. For example, "The boy is eating the ice-cream" is semantically constrained by the fact that ice-creams do not eat boys, whereas a sentence such as "The boy is chasing the girl" cannot be unambiguously interpreted by the semantics of constituent words alone. Caramazza and Zurif (1976) showed that Broca's aphasics are impaired on the latter type of sentence only.

Studies such as these hinge upon the assumption that different patients who all have the same classification of Broca's aphasia (or whatever label) have the same core deficit. However, this assumption may be incorrect. Some patients appear to be agrammatic in production only and are able to make grammaticality judgments and perform well on picture–sentence matching tasks in comprehension (Druks & Marshall, 1991; Linebarger, Schwartz, & Saffran, 1983). Other patients may have difficulties with function words rather than syntax, even though they meet the diagnostic criteria for Broca's aphasia (Miceli, Mazzucchi, Menn, & Goodglass, 1983). This

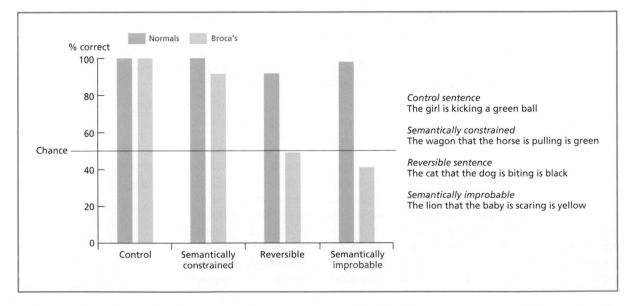

In a group study of so-called Broca's aphasics, Caramazza and Zurif (1976; data adapted from Figure 3) found that subjects had particular problems in comprehending sentences on a picture–sentence matching task when the subject and object of the verb were determined from syntax and not from semantics.

has led researchers such as Badecker and Caramazza (1985) to argue against grouping patients into syndromes such as "Broca's aphasia". While this does not disprove the notion of a central syntactic resource, it does undermine the methods on which the initial evidence is based. As an alternative approach, single cases studies suggest that "agrammatic" difficulties can be used to reveal a number of different aspects of language processing rather than reflecting a central syntactic mechanism. For example, some patients can produce syntax at the phrase level but not at the sentence level (Ostrin & Tyler, 1995), and some can produce sentences but have selective deficits with aspects of morphology such as –ing and –s (Miceli & Caramazza, 1988). Despite such intriguing single case findings, the debate concerning the use of group studies and aphasic patient classification still rumbles on (Caramazza, Capitani, Rey, & Berndt, 2001; Grodzinsky, Pinango, Zurif, & Drai, 1999).

Not only is there controversy about whether Broca's aphasia constitutes a reliable cluster of symptoms, there is also controversy concerning the role of Broca's area itself. Damage to the temporal lobes has been found to be more associated with sentence comprehension deficits than Broca's area (Dronkers, Wilkins, Van Valin, Redfern, & Jaeger, 2004). Patients with lesions in this area often have

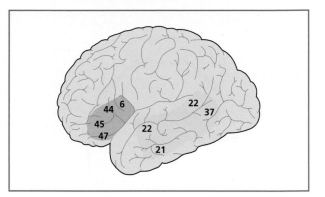

Areas of the brain important for sentence processing. Broca's area is traditionally defined as Brodmann areas 44 and 45. Reprinted from Friederici (2002), Copyright 2002, with permission from Elsevier.

LOOKING BACK ON NINETEENTH-CENTURY MODELS OF SPEECH AND APHASIA

Paul Broca (1861) is credited with providing the first scientific evidence that specific cognitive functions can be localized in the brain, although this idea had been around for some time (e.g. in the earlier phrenology movement). His patient, Leborgne, lost the ability to produce speech and his utterances consisted of "tan, tan, tan ...". Broca concluded that there is a dedicated language center in the brain.

Wernicke (1874) documented a different type of aphasia in which the patient was fluent but had difficulties comprehending speech. He divided the spoken forms of words into separate input and output centers termed "auditory images" and "motor images", respectively.

Damage to the auditory images was assumed to impair speech perception and was associated with **Wernicke's aphasia**. Damage to the motor images was assumed to impair speech production and was associated with **Broca's aphasia**. Perhaps the most influential model of speech and aphasia to derive from the classical nineteenth-century research is that of Lichtheim (1885). His basic idea survived at least 100 years in various guises (e.g. Goodglass & Kaplan, 1972). Lichtheim maintained Wernicke's distinction between auditory and motor centers and argued that they are linked by two routes: both directly and indirectly via a concept center (equivalent to semantic memory). These separate

KEY TERMS

Wernicke's aphasia
A type of aphasia traditionally associated with damage to Wernicke's area and associated with fluent but nonsensical speech, and poor comprehension.

Broca's aphasia
A type of aphasia traditionally associated with damage to Broca's area and linked to symptoms such as agrammatism and articulatory deficits.

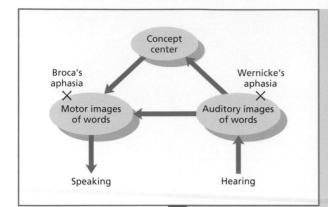

The Lichtheim model of speech and aphasia links together Wernicke's and Broca's area via direct and indirect routes.

routes were based on Lichtheim's observations that some aphasic patients have repetition disorders but adequate comprehension.

In some respects, the Lichtheim model still has a contemporary resonance. For example, the notion of separate speech input and output lexicons is still incorporated in most models (e.g. Shallice, 1988) as is the notion that there are both semantic and auditory-verbal routes to repetition (e.g. Butterworth & Warrington, 1995). The most significant challenges to the Lichtheim model have come from the observation that Broca's and Wernicke's aphasia are not well characterized as selective disorders of output and input. Broca's aphasics often have problems in comprehension as well as production (Caramazza & Zurif, 1976). Wernicke's aphasics also have difficulties in output as well as input. They tend to produce made-up words or neologisms: "A bun, bun (BULL)...a buk (BULL) is cherching (CHASING) a boy or skert (SCOUT)..." (Ellis, Miller, & Sin, 1983). In fact, some have argued that these are meaningless syndromes that have no real modern-day relevance (Badecker & Caramazza, 1985). Furthermore, the functions associated with the regions termed Broca's area and Wernicke's area tend to be manifold and do not always map on to the functions that one would expect from the aphasic subtypes. Articulation deficits are not associated with damage to Broca's area (Dronkers, 1996); this suggests it is not a speech motor store. Wernicke's area comprises a number of functional regions involved in perception of non-speech as well as speech, involved in translating acoustic into articulatory codes and involved in cross-modal integration (Wise, Scott, Blank, Mummery, & Warbuton, 2001).

difficulties with a wide range of sentences, but do not necessarily have difficulty in comprehending single words (in fact, they often meet the diagnostic criteria of Broca's aphasia!). Dronkers et al. did find that some left frontal regions are important for certain types of sentence, but these regions excluded Broca's area itself. This could reflect the working memory demands of processing longer and more complex sentences rather than syntax *per se*. Functional imaging studies also suggest an involvement of both left temporal and left frontal regions in sentence processing. Anterior Brodmann's area 22 is active in conditions that compare sentences with unstructured lists of words (e.g. Mayozer et al. 1993; Noppeney & Price, 2004).

So what is the function of Broca's area itself? While it has been shown to be active in some imaging studies of sentence processing (Caplan, 2001), this could arguably reflect aspects of working memory rather than syntax *per se* (Just, Carpenter, Keller, Eddy, & Thulborn, 1996). Indeed, the area is activated when processing single words in working memory tasks (Smith & Jonides, 1999), when processing words that are contextually inappropriate (Hagoort, Hald, Bastiaansen, & Petersson, 2004), when processing musical sounds that are contextually inappropriate (Maess, Koelsch, Gunter, & Friederici, 2001) and when perceiving the actions of others (Rizzolatti,

Fogassi, & Gallese, 2002). Of course, there is no necessary reason why it should have a single function. For example, it covers two Brodmann regions (areas 44 and 45). Some have argued that area 45 (and 47) may be more involved in working memory for semantic features and thematic structure, whereas area 44 is involved in "structure building" relevant to phonology and syntax but is not strictly language related (Friederici, 2002; Newman, Just, Keller, Roth, & Carpenter, 2003).

Evaluation

The study of syntactic mechanisms can be profitably studied by the methods of cognitive neuroscience. However, progress in this area and consensus amongst researchers has been hampered by disagreements concerning methodology, patient classification, and a persisting (but shaky) belief that the inferior left frontal region is crucial. It is suggested here that a reliance on the symptoms of individual patients may offer the most fruitful approach for exploring the cognitive mechanisms that contribute to sentence processing; whereas functional imaging data may have more relevance for informing debates concerning the specialization of anatomical regions. Broca's area may subserve a number of functions, only some of which are strongly related to language. Good candidates include establishing semantic and thematic coherence during comprehension and production; aspects of working memory; and linking action perception and production (including speech but not restricted to it). Less likely candidates include the actual motor plans for speech (Broca's original idea) and a central syntactic module (the dominant view from the 1970s).

RETRIEVING SPOKEN WORDS

Speech production, in natural situations, involves translating an intended idea into a sentence structure and retrieving and producing the appropriate words. To study this process in the laboratory, one standard method has been to study the retrieval of single words in isolation upon presentation of a picture or word definition. Both of these tasks are assumed to initiate semantic processes. A number of variables affect how easy a word is to retrieve as measured using naming reaction times or error rates (e.g. Barry, Morrison, & Ellis, 1997). These are summarized in the box overleaf. Most, if not all, of these variables can be construed as factors affecting not only spoken word retrieval but also processing of single words in other contexts (e.g. in speech recognition, and reading and spelling). A number of broad questions will be considered in this section. How many stages are there in retrieving spoken words,

EARLY SIGNS OF DEMENTIA IN THE LANGUAGE USE OF IRIS MURDOCH

Iris Murdoch's last novel, *Jackson's Dilemma,* was considered by both critics and her family to be something of a puzzle, in that it departed significantly in style from her previous novels. Whereas this could conceivably reflect a deliberate shift due to artistic motivations, a more likely scenario is that Murdoch was already in the early stages of Alzheimer's disease. This is known to

affect memory and result in word-finding difficulties. The novel was published in 1995, just before her diagnosis. To investigate the changes, text from the last novel was compared to two of her earlier ones. The results found that whereas the use of syntax and overall structure did not change, her vocabulary had changed such that she had a more restricted range of words, particularly relying more on higher frequency words than before (Garrard, Maloney, Hodges, & Patterson, 2005). Text analyses such as these, based on letters or diary entries, could possibly be developed in the future to lead to early diagnostic tools for diseases such as dementia of the Alzheimer's type.

Iris Murdoch; 1919–1999. © Sophie Bassouls/Sygma/Corbis.

PSYCHOLINGUISTIC PREDICTORS OF THE EFFICIENCY OF SINGLE WORD PROCESSING

Variable	Description	Possible explanation
Word frequency	More common words in the language are easier to retrieve and recognize	The strength of connections to words may be increased each time they are encountered (Jescheniak & Levelt, 1994) or the threshold for activating the word may be lowered by each experience (Morton, 1969)
Imageability (or concreteness)	Concrete words are easier to retrieve and recognize than abstract words	Concrete (or high imageability words) have richer semantic representations (e.g. Jones, 2002)
Age-of-acquisition	Words acquired earlier in life (e.g. doll) are at an advantage relative to late acquired words (e.g. wine)	Initially, a network will adjust itself to accommodate any pattern it encounters, but after adding more and more patterns the ability of the system to adjust further is diminished (reduced plasticity) (Ellis & Lambon Ralph, 2000)
Recency	More recently encountered words have an advantage	Exposure to a word may increase the strength of the connections to the word, or lower the threshold for activating the word. **Repetition priming** refers to the fact that a word seen previously will be identified faster on a subsequent occasion soon after (e.g. Wheeldon & Monsell, 1992)
Familiarity	More familiar items are at an advantage relative to less familiar ones	Related to the variables of word frequency and age-of-acquisition, but also dependent on the individual experience of the speaker

and are the stages discrete or interactive? What type of information is retrieved – syntactic, semantic, morphological, syllabic, phonemic and so on?

The type of information that needs to be retrieved in speech production is normally divided into three kinds. First, one must select a word based upon the meaning that one wishes to convey. This process is called **lexicalization**. This process is heavily constrained by knowledge of the listener (related to pragmatics). For example, the words "it", "horse", "stallion" and "animal" could, to some extent, all be used to convey the same concept. Second, at least in the context of producing sentences, the grammatical properties of a word must be retrieved and specified. This includes grammatical class (e.g. noun, verb, adjective) and, in many languages, the gender of the word. Finally, the actual form of the word in terms of its constituent syllables, phonemes and articulatory patterns needs to be retrieved. There is general consensus across different models that these are the kinds of information that need to be retrieved. However, individual models differ in terms of the nature of the mechanisms (e.g. whether different stages interact).

Studies of speech errors

Observations of everyday speech errors have been useful in constraining theories of word retrieval (e.g. Garrett, 1992). Speech errors tend to swap words for words, morphemes for morphemes, phonemes for phonemes and so on. This provides evidence for the psychological reality of these units. Considering the word level, it is possible to substitute words of similar meaning as in a semantic error, such as saying "dog" for cat. One variant of this error is the **Freudian slip**.

When Tony Blair referred to "weapons of mass distraction" (instead of destruction) during a debate on Iraq, what type of cognitive processes could have given rise to this mistake? © Richard Lewis/epa/Corbis.

Freud believed that speakers repress their true thoughts during conversation, and these could be revealed by inadvertent speech errors (Ellis, 1980). For example, the former British Prime Minister, Tony Blair, mistakenly referred to "weapons of mass *distraction*" (rather than destruction) in a parliamentary debate on the 2003 invasion of Iraq. It is also the case that word substitutions tend to preserve grammatical class, such that nouns swap for nouns, and verbs for verbs, as in the example "guess whose *mind* came to *name*?" (Garrett, 1992). Moreover, affixation of morphemes may occur independently of retrieval of word stems (Fromkin, 1971), as illustrated by the example "I random*ed* some sampl*y*" (instead of "I sampled some randomly"). In this instance, the suffix morphemes (–ed, –y) were stranded while the stem morphemes (random, sample) swapped.

A final type of word error is where the error has a similar phonological form to the intended word (e.g. historical → "hysterical") (Fay & Cutler, 1977). These are also called **malapropisms** after the character Mrs Malaprop (in Sheridan's play *The Rivals*, 1775) who made many such errors. These errors are typically used to support the notion that there is competition between similar words during normal word retrieval, rather than a single word selected immediately. Sometimes the exchange will be between phonemes, and it is generally the case that the exchanged phonemes will occupy the same position in the word (e.g. first consonants swap with each other, vowels swap with each other; Dell, Burger, & Svec, 1997). One example of this is **spoonerisms**, in which initial consonants are swapped (e.g. "you have *h*issed all my *m*ystery lectures").

Another common naturally occurring disruption of speech production is the **tip-of-the-tongue phenomenon** (Brown, 1991; Brown & McNeill, 1966). In a tip-of-the-tongue state the person knows, conceptually, the word that he or she wishes to say but is unable to retrieve the corresponding spoken form for output. It generally produces a "feeling of knowing" and can be intensely frustrating. These states can be elicited by giving people definitions or pictures of relatively infrequent words. For example, "a navigational instrument used in measuring angular distances, especially the altitude of the sun, moon and stars at sea" (the answer being *sextant*). Although the word may be elusive, other types of information may be available. For example, speakers of languages such as Italian often know the gender of a word (Vigliocco, Antonini, & Garrett, 1997), and speakers often know the approximate length of the word or the number of syllables (Brown & McNeill, 1966). These results suggest that words are not retrieved in an all-or-nothing manner but, rather, that different aspects of a word can become available at different stages and relatively independently from each other.

Patients with **anomia** as a result of brain damage have severe word-finding difficulties. This is strongly reminiscent of the normal tip-of-the-tongue state, but in pathological proportions. This symptom can arise from two very different types of impairment. First, it may be a result of a semantic difficulty that results in a failure to distinguish between different concepts and, consequently, a difficulty in specifying the precise word to be retrieved (Caramazza & Hillis, 1990b). Second, other patients may know exactly which word they want to produce but are unable to retrieve the associated phonological information to articulate it (e.g. Kay & Ellis, 1987).

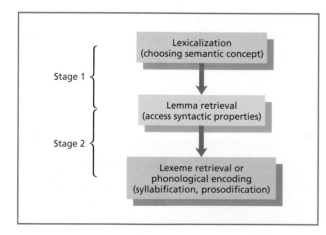

In Levelt's model, word retrieval takes place in two stages. The stages are discrete such that the second stage does not begin until the first stage is complete, and so phonological factors cannot influence word selection.

Discrete or interactive stages in spoken word retrieval?

The most influential models of spoken word retrieval divide the process of getting from a conceptual level of representation to a phonological word form into two steps. Further stages may be involved in translating this into motor commands. Consider the model put forward by Levelt and colleagues (for reviews, see Levelt, 1989, 2001). The first stage of their model involves retrieving a modality-independent word-level entry that specifies the syntactic components of the word (e.g. its grammatical class). These are termed **lemma** representations. Thus, this first stage involves lexicalization together with retrieval of syntactic features. The second stage involves retrieval of what they term a **lexeme** representation. Retrieval of the lexeme makes available the phonological code that drives articulation. This lemma–lexeme division accounts for some of the key findings in the speech production literature. First, it offers an account of the tip-of-the-tongue phenomenon by postulating that the lemma may be activated but the lexeme is not active (or is not fully active). Second, it offers a way of distinguishing between words with identical forms that differ in meaning (e.g. "bank" as in money or river) and/or grammatical class (the "watch"/to "watch"). These stimuli have different lemmas but a single lexeme. Using these stimuli, Jescheniak and Levelt (1994) found that word frequency effects are related to the frequency of lexemes and not lemmas.

The question of whether these stages are discrete or interact is a source of particular controversy. Levelt's model proposes that they are discrete in that lexeme retrieval does not begin until lemma selection is complete. In contrast, other models have assumed that partial phonological processing can occur prior to selection of a lemma being complete and, moreover, that this information can feed back up to influence lemma selection itself. Thus, if one is trying to say "sheep", then the process of lemma selection may activate a host of other semantic candidates, including "goat". If this information reaches the lexeme level, then one may expect activation of words such as "goal" because this is phonologically similar to the semantic associate "goat". But if "sheep" is completely selected and "goat" is completely unselected before the second stage begins, then no such priming of "goal" should occur. Indeed, it appears that "sheep" does not prime "goal" even

KEY TERMS

Lemma
A modality-independent word-level entry that specifies the syntactic components of the word.

Lexeme
The phonological code that drives articulation.

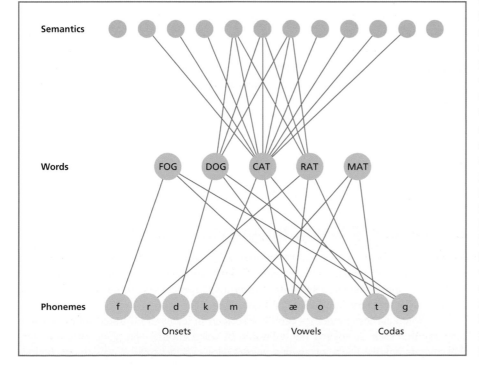

Dell's model contains three layers that are fully interactive: a layer of semantic features, a layer of words (or lemmas) and a phonological layer (in this version, it consists of different parts of the syllable). Mixed errors, such as cat → "rat" arise because of similarity both at the semantic and the phonological level. Models that do not allow interactive activation from phonology up to words have difficulty accounting for such errors. Reprinted from Levelt (1999), Copyright, 1999 with permission from Elsevier.

though it does prime "goat" (Levelt, Schriefers, Vorberg, Meyer, Pechmann, & Havinga, 1991). This evidence supports Levelt's discrete stages (but see Dell & O'Seaghdha, 1991).

However, there is some evidence that, on balance, is easier to account for with an interactive rather than discrete stage model. This includes the presence of so-called *mixed errors* that are both semantically and phonologically similar to the intended word (Dell & Reich, 1981). Examples of these include saying "rat" for cat, and "oyster" for lobster. If it were coincidental, then we would have to assume that "rat" is a semantic error for cat that just so happens to sound like it. However, these errors occur too often to be coincidences (Dell & Reich, 1981). In interactive models such as that of Dell's (1986), they occur because lemma selection arises out of both top-down semantic activation and bottom-up phonological activation. For the discrete stages model to account for this, it must assume that mixed errors are not generated more than expected by chance but they are just harder to detect and correct. These models assume that there is a monitoring device that checks for speech errors and that mixed errors are more likely to slip through the monitor. This explanation is plausible but *post hoc*.

The Levelt model has been criticized in other ways. Caramazza and Miozzo (1997) found that in tip-of-the-tongue states it is sometimes possible to report grammatical gender information without knowing the first phoneme (lemma access without lexeme access), but that it is also possible to know the first phoneme without knowing grammatical gender (lexeme access without lemma access). The latter should not be found if lemma retrieval were a prerequisite for access to phonological information. The authors argue in favor of the distinction between phonological and grammatical retrieval (similarly to Levelt and Dell) but argue against the idea that one is contingent upon the other. Futhermore, they present neuropsychological evidence to suggest that the organization of grammatical knowledge (putatively at a lemma level) is not amodal but is duplicated in both phonological and written modalities (Caramazza, 1997). For example, patient SJD had a selective difficulty in writing verbs relative to nouns but had no difficulty with producing spoken nouns and verbs (Caramazza & Hillis, 1991). Remarkably, the deficit was still found when the lexeme was the same. For example, SJD could write CRACK when dictated the spoken word and given the written sentence fragment *There's a ____ in the mirror* (noun form) but not *Don't ____ the nuts in here* (verb form). They suggest that grammatical information is independently represented in speaking and spelling, contrary to the notion of a single amodal lemma articulated by Levelt and colleagues.

In summary, there is good evidence for a separation between grammatical and phonological knowledge of single words but the precise organization of this knowledge is a matter of continued debate.

Articulation: Closing the communication loop

This chapter began with a simple model of spoken language in which ideas are shared between a speaker and a listener. Having started at the speech perception end of this loop, and considered semantic and syntactic processes, and word retrieval, the final stage to be considered is articulation itself.

As noted earlier, phonemes can be described in terms of a limited set of articulatory gestures such as voicing (i.e. vibration of vocal chords) and place of articulators (e.g. tongue against teeth, or against palate). However, in spite of this, many believe that the phoneme is not the basic unit of articulation. Others have argued that the basic unit of articulation is the syllable – at least for common syllables that may function as overlearned motor patterns (Levelt & Wheeldon, 1994). In connected speech there must be a mechanism that segments the phonological code into syllables across adjacent morphemes and adjacent words. This process has been called *syllabification*. For example, the phrase "he owns it" consists of three syllables ("he", "own", "zit") in which the final consonant of the word "owns" becomes the onset of the following syllable.

Broca's area was once thought to be critical for articulation. This is now disputed. Patients with articulation disorders typically have damage to the basal ganglia and/or the insula cortex but not necessarily Broca's area (Dronkers, 1996; but see Hillis, Work, Barker, Jacobs, Breese, & Maurer, 2004). Damage to the insula can result in difficulties in shaping the vocal tract, known as **apraxia for speech** (Dronkers, 1996). People with apraxia for speech know what it is that they want to say and have normal muscle tone of the speech articulators but distort the production of consonants, vowels and prosody. This is sometimes perceived by others as sounding like a foreign accent (Moen, 2000). The difficulties with prosody reflect poor coordination of the articulators rather than a primary deficit in prosody that is sometimes found following right hemisphere lesions (e.g. Pell, 1999). fMRI studies of articulation relative to speech perception show activity of the insula and frontal–motor regions but not Broca's area (Wise, Greene, Buchel, & Scott, 1999). However, others have suggested that Broca's area has an important role in the planning stages of syllabification in both overt and covert speech production, even if the motor commands themselves do not reside there (Indefrey & Levelt, 2004). The cerebellum and left basal ganglia lesions may also be crucial for efficient articulation. Damage to these regions can result in impaired muscular contractions known as **dysarthria** (Kent, Duffy, Slama, Kent, & Clift, 2001).

KEY TERMS

Apraxia for speech
Difficulties in shaping the vocal tract.

Dysarthria
Impaired muscular contractions of the articulatory apparatus.

SUMMARY AND KEY POINTS OF THE CHAPTER

- Recognizing spoken words involves a process of competition and selection between similar sounding words, as in the "cohort model".
- The meaning of words may be represented as a network of distributed semantic features, but there is controversy as to how these features are internally organized. The main theoretical positions are that they are organized by semantic category (e.g. semantic features pertaining to animals cluster together) or organized by domains of knowledge (e.g. semantic features pertaining to color or shape information cluster together).
- Deficits in syntax (word order) can occur largely, although perhaps not completely, independently from deficits in semantics (word meaning),

and vice versa. However, there is little evidence for a single "syntax module" that is disrupted in aphasic disorders, such as agrammatism or that arises specifically from lesions to Broca's area.

- Producing spoken words involves retrieving different kinds of information: semantic, grammatical and phonological. Evidence from tip-of-the-tongue, anomia and everyday speech errors suggests that some information can be retrieved in the absence of other types of information.
- There is controversy as to whether word-level (or "lemma") information and phonological-level (or "lexeme") information are retrieved as two discrete stages in time, or interactively such that the second stage begins before the first stage is complete.

EXAMPLE ESSAY QUESTIONS

- How is auditory input mapped on to our stored knowledge of spoken words?
- Does speech perception use mechanisms involved in speech production?
- Compare and contrast the "what" and "how" routes of speech perception with those proposed for vision.
- Are concepts organized categorically?
- Do the constructs of Wernicke's and Broca's aphasia have any useful validity in contemporary cognitive neuroscience?
- Do models of word retrieval require discrete stages corresponding to semantics, grammar and phonology?

RECOMMENDED FURTHER READING

- Harley, T. A. (2008). *The psychology of language: From data to theory*, 3rd edition. Hove: Psychology Press. A good place to start for more detailed background information about the cognitive psychology of language, but little focus on brain-based accounts.

- Hickok, G. & Poeppel, D. (2004). Towards a new functional anatomy of language. Special edition of *Cognition, 92*, 1–270. Elsevier Press. An excellent collection of papers that is particularly strong on speech recognition.

- Levelt, W. J. M. (2001). Spoken word production: A theory of lexical access. *Proceedings of the National Academy of Science USA, 98*, 13464–13471. A good summary paper of spoken word production.

- Martin, A. & Caramazza, A. (2003). The organisation of conceptual knowledge in the brain: Neuropsychological and neuroimaging perspectives. Special edition of *Cognitive Neuropsychology*. Hove: Psychology Press. A good collection of recent papers on the topic of category specificity in the organization of semantic memory.

CHAPTER 12

CONTENTS

The literate brain

The ability to read and write is essentially a cultural invention, albeit one of enormous significance. It enables humans to exchange ideas without face-to-face contact and results in a permanent record for posterity. It is no coincidence that our historical knowledge of previous civilizations is derived almost entirely from literate cultures. Literacy, unlike speaking, requires a considerable amount of formal tuition. As such, literacy provides cognitive neuroscience with an interesting example of an "expert system". Learning to read and write may involve the construction of a dedicated neural and cognitive architecture in the brain. But this is likely to be derived from a core set of other skills that have developed over the course of evolution. These skills include visual recognition, manipulation of sounds and learning and memory. However, it is inconceivable that we have evolved neural structures specifically for literacy, or that there is a gene specifically for reading (e.g. Ellis, 1993). Literacy is too recent an invention to have evolved specific neural substrates, having first emerged around 5000 years ago. Moreover, it is by no means universal. Even today perhaps almost half of the world's population is illiterate, and universal literacy has only occurred in Western societies over the last 100 years. Of course, the brain may acquire, through experience, a dedicated neural structure for literacy but this will be a result of *ontogenetic development* (of the individual) rather than *phylogenetic development* (of the species).

This chapter considers how skilled adult literacy relates to other cognitive domains such as visual recognition and spoken language; how a complex skill such as reading can be broken down into a collection of more basic mechanisms; and how the skills of reading and spelling may relate to each other. Evidence will be primarily drawn from adults who have already become experts at reading and spelling, including acquired disorders of reading and spelling.

THE ORIGINS AND DIVERSITY OF WRITING SYSTEMS

Writing has its historical origins in early pictorial representation. The point at which a picture ceases to be a picture and becomes a written symbol may relate to a transition between attempting to depict an object or concept versus representing units of language (e.g. words, phonemes, morphemes). For example, although Egyptian hieroglyphs consist of familiar objects (e.g. birds, hands), these characters actually denote the sounds of words rather than objects in themselves. As such, this is a true writing system that is a significant step away from the pictorial depictions of rock art.

Different cultures appear to have made this conceptual leap independently of each other (Gaur, 1987). This accounts for some of the great diversity of writing systems. The earliest writing system emerged between 4000 and 3000 BC, in what is now southern Iraq, and was based on the one-word–one-symbol principle. Scripts such as these are called **logographic**. Modern Chinese and Japanese **Kanji**

Logographs
Written languages based on the one-word–one-symbol principle.

Kanji
A Japanese writing system based on the logographic principle.

Balinese	ᬯᬦ᭄ᬓᬵᬭᬵ
Cyrillic	Кирилица
Etruscan	𐌀𐌔𐌕𐌖𐌂𐌆𐌆
Japanese (Kanji)	日本語
Japanese (Katakana)	カタカナ
Korean (Hangul)	한국어
Mayan	🐸🐵🐾
Sinhala	සිංහල

The diversity of written language.

are logographic, although they probably emerged independently from the Middle Eastern scripts. Individual characters may be composed of a number of parts that suggest meaning or pronunciation, but the arrangement of these parts is not linear like in alphabetic scripts.

Other types of script represent the sounds of words. Some writing systems, such as Japanese **Kana** and ancient Phoenician, use symbols to denote syllables. Alphabetic systems are based primarily on mappings between written symbols and spoken phonemes. All modern alphabets are derived from the one used by the Phoenicians; the Greeks reversed the writing direction to left–right at some point around 600 BC.

The term **grapheme** is normally used to denote the smallest meaningful unit of written language, analogous to the term "phoneme" in spoken language. In languages such as English, this corresponds to individual letters (Henderson, 1985), although the term is also often used to refer to letter clusters that denote phonemes (e.g. in the latter definition, the word THUMB would have three graphemes TH, U and MB corresponding to the phonemes "th", "u" and "m").

It is important to note that not all alphabetic scripts have a very regular mapping between graphemes and phonemes. Such languages are said to be **opaque**. Examples include English and French (consider the different spellings for the words COMB, HOME and ROAM). Not all irregularities are unhelpful. We write CATS and DOGS (and not CATS and DOGZ) and PLAYED and WALKED (not PLAY*ED* and WALK*T*) to preserve common morphemes for plural and past tense, respectively. However, other irregularities of English reflect historical quirks and precedents (Scragg, 1974). For example, KNIFE and SHOULD would have been pronounced with the "k" and "l" until the seventeenth century. Moreover, early spelling reformers changed spellings to be in line with their Greek and Latin counterparts (e.g. the spelling of DETTE was changed to DEBT to reflect the Latin "debitum"). Other languages, such as Italian and Spanish, have fully regular mappings between sound and spelling; these writing systems are said to be **transparent**.

KEY TERMS

Kana
A Japanese writing system in which each character denotes a syllable.

Grapheme
An abstract description that specifies letter identity.

Opaque orthography
A system of written language with an irregular (or semi-regular) correspondence between phonemes and graphemes.

Transparent orthography
A system of written language with a regular correspondence between phonemes and graphemes.

VISUAL WORD RECOGNITION

Cognitive mechanisms of visual word recognition

One of the earliest findings in the study of visual word recognition was the fact that there is little processing cost, in terms of reaction times, for recognizing long relative to short words (Cattell, 1886). Of course, reading a long word out loud will take longer than reading a short word aloud, and the preparation time before saying the word is also related to word length (Erikson, Pollack, & Montague, 1970). But the actual *visual* process of recognizing a word as familiar is not strongly affected by word length. This suggests a key principle in visual word recognition – namely, that the letter strings are processed in parallel rather than serially one by one. Recognizing printed words is thus likely to employ different kinds of mechanisms from recognizing spoken words. All the information for visual word recognition is instantly available to the reader and remains so over time (unless the word is unusually long and requires an eye movement), whereas in spoken word recognition the information is revealed piecemeal and must be integrated over time.

Visual word recognition also appears to be greater than the sum of its parts (i.e. its constituent letters) in so far as patterns across several letters are also important. If one is asked to detect the presence of a single letter (e.g. R) presented briefly, then performance is enhanced if the letter is presented in the context of a word (e.g. CARPET), or a nonsense letter string that follows the combinatorial rules of the language (e.g. HARPOT) than in a random letter string (e.g. CTRPAE) or even a single letter in isolation (Carr, Posner, Pollatsek, & Snyder, 1979; Reicher, 1969). This is termed the **word superiority effect**. It suggests that there are units of representation corresponding to letter clusters (or known letter clusters comprising words themselves) that influence the visual recognition of letters and words.

The evidence cited above is often taken to imply that there is a role of top-down information in visual word recognition. Stored knowledge of the structure of known words can influence earlier perceptual processes (McClelland & Rumelhart, 1981; Rumelhart & McClelland, 1982). Although this view is generally recognized, controversy still exists over the extent to which other higher-level processes, such as

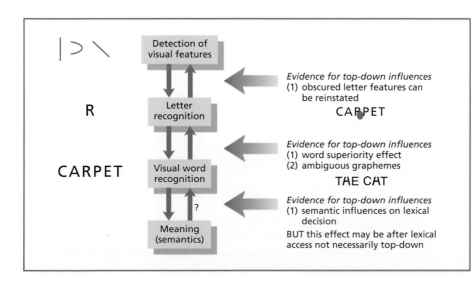

A basic model of visual word recognition showing potential evidence in favor of top-down influences.

meaning, can influence perceptual processing. One commonly used task to investigate word recognition is **lexical decision** in which participants must make a two-way forced choice judgment about whether a letter string is a word or not. Non-words (also called pseudo-words) are much faster to reject if they do not resemble known words (Coltheart, Davelaar, Jonasson, & Besner, 1977). For example, BRINJ is faster to reject than BRINGE.

According to many models, the task of lexical decision is performed by matching the perceived letter string with a store of all known letter strings that comprise words (Coltheart, 2004a; Fera & Besner, 1992; Morton, 1969). This store is referred to as the **visual lexicon** (also the orthographic lexicon, or the visual input lexicon, or orthographic input lexicon). Under this account, there is no reason to assume that meaning or context should affect tasks such as lexical decision. However, such effects have been reported and could potentially provide evidence for semantic influences on word recognition.

Meyer and Schvaneveldt (1971) used a modified lexical decision in which pairs of words were presented. Participants responded according to whether both letter strings were words or otherwise. Semantically related pairs (e.g. BREAD and BUTTER) were responded to faster than unrelated pairs (e.g. DOCTOR and BUTTER). A number of potential problems with this have been raised. The first concerns the nature of the lexical decision task itself. It is possible that it is not a pure measure of access to the visual lexicon but also entails a post-access checking or decision mechanism. This mechanism might be susceptible to semantic influences, rather than the visual lexicon itself being influenced by top-down effects (Chumbley & Balota, 1984; Norris, 1986). Moreover, it has been argued that these effects may not be truly semantic at all. If participants are asked to associate a word with, say, BREAD, they may produce BUTTER but are unlikely to produce the word CAKE, even though it is semantically related (similarly, ROBIN is more likely to elicit HOOD as an associate than BIRD). Shelton and Martin (1992) found that associated words prime each other in lexical decision but not other semantically related pairs. This suggests that the effect arises from inter-word association, but not top-down semantic influence.

A "visual word form area"

As already noted, most models of visual word recognition postulate a dedicated cognitive mechanism for processing known words (a visual lexicon). Although these models have been formulated in purely cognitive terms, it is a short logical step to assume that a dedicated cognitive mechanism must have a dedicated neural architecture. This was postulated as long ago as 1892 (Dejerine, 1892), although it is only in recent times that it has been accurately localized.

In recent years, a number of functional imaging studies have been reported that argue in favor of the existence of a so-called visual word form area (Cohen & Dehaene, 2004; Cohen, Lehericy, Chochon, Lemer, Rivaud, & Dehaene, 2002; Dehaene, Le Clec'H, Poline, Le Bihan, & Cohen, 2002; McCandliss, Cohen, & Dehaene, 2003; Petersen, Fox, Snyder, & Raichle, 1990). This area is located in the left mid occipitotemporal gyrus (or fusiform gyrus), anterior to other cortex dedicated to visual processing. Some of the response characteristics of this region to visual stimuli are listed on the next page. Meaningless shapes that are letter-like do not activate the region. This suggests that the neurons have

---

CHARACTERISTICS OF THE VISUAL WORD FORM AREA

- Responds to learned letters (or true fonts) compared to pseudo-letters (or false fonts) of comparable visual complexity (Price, Wise, & Frackowiak, 1996b)
- Repetition priming suggests that it responds to both upper and lower case letters even when visually dissimilar (e.g. "a" primes "A" more than "e" primes "A") (Dehaene et al., 2001)
- Subliminal presentation of words activates the area, which suggests that it is accessed automatically (Dehaene et al., 2001)
- Electrophysiological data comparing true and false fonts suggests that the region is activated early, at around 150–200 ms after stimulus onset (Bentin, Mouchetant-Rostaing, Giard, Echallier, & Pernier, 1999)

---

become tuned to the visual properties of known letters and common letter patterns (Cohen et al., 2002).

The visual word form area also responds to non-words made up of common letter patterns as well as to real words, although the degree of this activity may be task dependent (e.g. reading versus lexical decision; Mechelli, 2003; see also Fiebach, Friederici, Muller, & von Cramon, 2002). The responsiveness to non-words has cast some doubt over whether this region is actually implementing a visual lexicon (i.e. a store of known words). Dehaene and colleagues (2002) have argued that the region contains a prelexical representation of letter strings, whether known or unknown. However, the available functional imaging evidence is equivocal. This is because

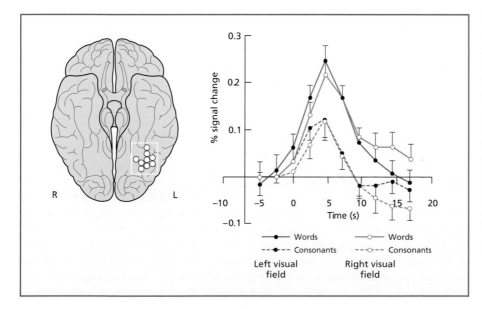

The visual word form area is located on the rear under-surface of the brain, primarily in the left hemisphere. It responds to written words more than consonant strings, and irrespective of whether they are presented in the left or right visual field. Reprinted from McCandliss et al. (2003), Copyright, 2003, with permission from Elsevier.

most cognitive models of visual word processing assume that non-words can only be so classified (e.g. in lexical decision) after a search of the visual lexicon has failed to find a match (Coltheart, 2004a). Thus, a neural implementation of a visual lexicon could be activated by the search process itself, irrespective of whether the search is successful or not (i.e. whether the stimulus is a word or non-word).

Other researchers have argued that the existence of the visual word form area is a myth because the region responds to other types of familiar stimuli, such as visually presented objects and Braille reading, and not just letter patterns (Price & Devlin, 2003; Price, Winterburn, Giraud, Moore, & Noppeney, 2003). These researchers argue that this region serves as a computational hub that links together different brain regions (e.g. vision and speech) according to the demands of the task. They, along with others, go so far as to say that there is no visual lexicon either at the cognitive or the neural level. To explain how participants are able to perform judgments such as lexical decision, they suggest that the decision takes place at a later semantic stage rather than at a visual lexicon (Plaut, 1997; Seidenberg & McClelland, 1989) or on the basis of how typical the letter patterns are rather than an exact match in a visual lexicon (Rogers, Lambon Ralph, Hodges, & Patterson, 2004).

This is a radical rethink of how visual word recognition takes place. Those who defend the notions of a visual word form area and/or a visual lexicon have cited a number of arguments in defense of their position. First, this particular anatomical region may contain different pockets of specialization (e.g. for words versus objects) that cannot be separately observed given the current resolution of functional imaging (Cohen & Dehaene, 2004). Second, at a cognitive level there exist patients who are able to recognize (by lexical decision) visual words and objects, but are selectively impaired at retrieving the meaning of visual words but *not* visual objects (Lambon Ralph, Sage, & Ellis, 1996). This could be interpreted as a disconnection between a functionally specialized visual word recognition system and the semantic system (Coltheart, 2004b). It has also been argued that damage to this region produces a specific difficulty with reading – namely, pure alexia or letter-by-letter reading (Cohen & Dehaene, 2004).

Evaluation

There is good evidence that an area of the left fusiform cortex in skilled readers is optimized for representing letters. The more familiar the letters/cluster/word, the greater the activation of this region. It may be located in the left hemisphere to enable close contact with other left-lateralized language regions.

Pure alexia or "letter-by-letter" reading

Imagine that a patient comes into a neurological clinic complaining of reading problems. When shown the word CAT, the patient spells the letters out "C", "A", "T" before announcing the answer – "cat". When given the word CARPET, the patient again spells the letters out, taking twice as long overall, before reading the word correctly. Whilst reading is often accurate, it appears far too slow and laborious to be of much help in everyday life. Historically, this was the first type of acquired dyslexia to be documented and it was termed **pure alexia** to emphasize the fact that reading was compromised without impairment of spelling, writing or verbal language (Dejerine, 1892). It has been given a variety of other names, including "letter-by-letter reading" (e.g. Patterson & Kay, 1982), "word form dyslexia" (e.g. Warrington & Shallice, 1980) and "spelling dyslexia" (e.g. Warrington & Langdon, 1994).

The defining behavioral characteristic of pure alexia is that reading time increases proportionately to the length of the word (the same is true of non-words), although not all patients articulate the letter names aloud. This is consistent with the view that each letter is processed serially rather than the normal parallel recognition of letters in visual word recognition. At least three reasons have been suggested for why a patient may show these characteristics:

1. It may be related to more basic difficulties in visual perception (Farah & Wallace, 1991).
2. It may relate to attentional/perceptual problems associated with perceiving more than one item at a time (Kinsbourne & Warrington, 1962a)
3. It may relate specifically to the processing of written stimuli within the visual word form system or "visual lexicon" (Cohen & Dehaene, 2004; Warrington & Langdon, 1994; Warrington & Shallice, 1980).

As for the purely visual account, it is often the case that patients have difficulty in perceiving individual letters even though single letter identification tends to out-perform word recognition (Patterson & Kay, 1982). Some patients do not have low-level visual deficits (e.g. Warrington & Shallice, 1980) but, even in these patients, perceptual distortions of the text severely affect reading (e.g. script or "joined-up" writing is harder to read than print). Deficits in simultaneously perceiving multiple objects are not always present in pure alexia, so this cannot account for all patients (Kay & Hanley, 1991). Other studies have argued that the deficit is restricted to the processing of letters and words. For example, some patients are impaired at deciding whether two letters of different case (e.g. E, e) are the same, but can detect real letters from made-up ones, and real letters from their mirror image (Miozzo & Caramazza, 1998). This suggests a breakdown of more abstract orthographic knowledge that is not strictly visual.

Many researchers have opted for a hybrid account between visual deficits and orthography-specific deficits. Disruption of information flow at various stages, from early visual to word-specific levels, can result in cessation of parallel letter reading and adoption of letter-by-letter strategies (e.g. Behrmann, Plaut, & Nelson, 1998; Bowers, Bub, & Arguin, 1996). These latter models have typically used "interactive activation" accounts in which there is a cascade of bottom-up and top-down processing (see the figure on p. 263). This interactive aspect of the model tends to result in similar behavior when different levels of the model are lesioned. Another line of evidence suggests that the flow of information from lower to higher levels is reduced rather than blocked. Many pure alexic patients are able to perform lexical decisions or even semantic categorizations (animal versus object) for briefly presented words that they cannot read (e.g. Bowers et al., 1996; Shallice & Saffran, 1986). For this

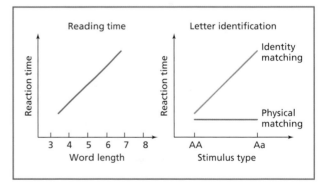

Some scripts are particularly difficult for letter-by-letter readers. Note the perceptual difficulty in recognizing "m" in isolation. From Warrington and Shallice (1980). Reproduced with permission of Oxford University Press.

In pure alexia (or letter-by-letter reading), reading time is slow and laborious and is strongly affected by word length (see graph on the left). Patients often have difficulty in determining whether two letters are the same when they differ by case (e.g. slow at judging that A-a have the same identity, but not at judging that A-a are physically different; see graph on the right). The disorder results in a difficulty in parallel processing of abstract letter identities but it is still debated whether the primary deficit is visual or reading-specific. Data adapted from Kay and Hanley (1991).

KEY TERMS

Attentional dyslexia
An inability to report the constituent letters of words that can be read (together with intact reading of isolated letters).

Neglect dyslexia
Reading errors that affect one side of a word.

to occur, one needs to assume that there is some partial parallel processing of the letter string that is able to access meaning and lexical representations, but that is insufficient to permit conscious visual word recognition.

Given the nature of the deficit, one may wonder how such patients are able to read anything at all, albeit very slowly. One suggestion is that these patients use a separate lexicon dedicated to spelling rather than reading (Warrington & Langdon, 1994; Warrington & Shallice, 1980). However, the existence of this separate lexicon is controversial (e.g. Behrmann & Bub, 1992; Coltheart & Funnell, 1987). An alternative explanation is that the same visual lexicon is used as in skilled reading but that it is accessed serially, rather than in parallel, either by the visual letters themselves (Patterson & Kay, 1982) or from letter names (Ward, 2003).

Spatial and attentional deficits in reading

Two other forms of acquired dyslexia should be mentioned at this stage: **attentional dyslexia** and **neglect dyslexia**. Unlike pure alexia, both attentional dyslexia and neglect dyslexia are linked to deficits in visuospatial attention rather than perceptual deficits or difficulties specific to visual language.

The first cases of attentional dyslexia were reported by Shallice and Warrington (1977). These patients had difficulty naming any item (letters, words, line drawings) when there was more than one of them in the visual field, and error rates increased with the number of items in the array. The patients were unable to report the constituent letters of words that they could read (the opposite pattern to pure alexia). The patients tended to make letter migration errors when pairs of words were presented (e.g. WIN FED read as "fin fed"). This deficit has been explained as disruption of an attentional control mechanism that selects information within a perceptual window, and attenuates other information. In attentional dyslexia, this mechanism is impaired, allowing intrusion of information from outside the window (Mozer & Behrmann, 1990; Shallice, 1988). What factors determine the focusing of the window? Visual information, prior to categorization of the stimulus, may be important. For example, increased spacing between words reduces migration errors (Mayall & Humphreys, 2002). However, the attentional window might be affected by categorical, non-visual factors. For example, reading of a letter flanked by numbers can be as good as reading a letter in isolation even though a letter flanked by other letters may severely disrupt performance (Shallice & Warrington, 1977).

Single letter	H	✓	(92%)
Flanked by numbers	65H43	✓	(88%)
Flanked by upper case	ITHJL	✗	(64%)
Flanked by lower case	ptHkd	✗	(70%)

In attentional dyslexia, patients are adversely affected by visual distractors. Patient FM could read single letters in isolation but was impaired if the letter was flanked by other letters but not numerals (Shallice & Warrington, 1977). The patient was required to name the colored letter (figures show percentage correct). The color could be perceived – FM could point to it.

Neglect dyslexia can also be characterized as a difficulty in attentional mechanisms. The problem appears to reflect a difficulty within a spatial reference frame for processing single words, rather than attentional competition between words (in attentional dyslexia). Patients with neglect dyslexia make reading errors that affect one side of a word. Left-neglect dyslexics may read LET as "wet", CLOCK as "block" and PREFERENTIAL as "deferential" (e.g. Riddoch, Humphreys, Cleton, & Fery, 1990). Right-neglect dyslexics may read HUMID as "human" and SPRINTER as "sprinkle" (e.g. Caramazza & Hillis, 1990a). Their responses typically consist of real word responses rather than non-words. This suggests that the neglected information is compensated for by using knowledge of familiar words. Neglect dyslexia appears to exist in several forms. This relates to the fact that spatial processing appears to occur at multiple levels within the brain (see Chapter 7). It is possible to distinguish between three different types of space: retinocentric, stimulus centered and object (or word) centered. For retinocentric neglect, whole words presented to one side of space may be neglected. Neglect dyslexia proper (i.e. neglect of letters within words) can either be stimulus centered (Haywood & Coltheart, 2001) or word/object centered (Caramazza & Hillis, 1990a; Miceli & Capasso, 2001). The key difference is that changes in presentation format (e.g. mirror-image, vertical writing or even oral presentation of letter names) alter the pattern of errors in stimulus-centered neglect dyslexia but not in the word/object-centered variety. Similarly, other perceptual manipulations such as letter spacing affect stimulus-centered (Hillis & Caramazza, 1991a) but not word/object-centered (Caramazza & Hillis, 1990a) neglect.

In summary, spatial attention may be allocated to words during reading in order to enable accurate word recognition. This mechanism can break down in at least two ways to give rise to attentional dyslexia and neglect dyslexia.

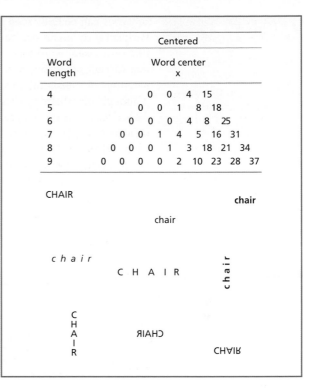

	Centered								
Word length				Word center x					
4				0	0	4	15		
5			0	0	1	8	18		
6		0	0	0	4	8	25		
7		0	0	1	4	5	16	31	
8	0	0	0	1	3	18	21	34	
9	0	0	0	0	2	10	23	28	37

NG tended to produce reading errors that affected letters to the right of the center of the word (top figure shows percent errors at each position). This occurred irrespective of the format in which the visual word was presented. This suggests that it is a word-centered type of neglect dyslexia. From Caramazza and Hillis (1990a).

Peripheral dyslexias

(1) Pure alexia (letter-by-letter reading)

- Reading time strongly related to word length
- Reading of single letters better than words
- Patients may sound out letter names

(2) Attentional dyslexia

- Unable to report constituent letters of words they can read
- Letter migration errors in reading pairs of words (e.g. WIN FED "fin fed")

(3) Neglect dyslexia

- Letter substitution errors on one half of the word (e.g. CLOCK → "block")

Central dyslexias

(1) Surface dyslexia

- Patients read regular words and non-words better than irregular words
- Irregular words pronounced phonetically

(2) Deep dyslexia

- Patients are able to read words but not non-words
- Semantic errors (e.g. CAT "dog")

(3) Phonological dyslexia

- Patients are able to read words better than non-words
- Absence of semantic errors

The distinction between acquired peripheral and central dyslexia

This chapter has so far discussed three types of acquired dyslexia – pure alexia, attentional dyslexia and neglect dyslexia. According to one classification, these three subtypes can be construed as varieties of **peripheral dyslexia** (e.g. Shallice, 1988). Peripheral dyslexias are believed to disrupt processing up to the level of computation of a visual word form. This stands in contrast to varieties of **central dyslexia** that disrupt processing after computation of a visual word form (e.g. in accessing meaning, or translating to speech). These will be considered later on in this chapter. Although this distinction is convenient, it is important to note that it may not be completely clear-cut. In particular, it has already been noted that there are semantic influences in peripheral dyslexia. Both patients with pure alexia and neglect dyslexia show evidence of being able to make simple semantic discriminations (e.g. animal or object) for words that they cannot read (e.g. Ladavas, Shallice, & Zanella, 1997; Shallice & Saffran, 1986). This suggests one of two interpretations. Either semantic influences can affect, top-down, stages prior to computation of a word form or there is a trickle of information (from the bottom up) beyond the visual word form that is sufficient to permit certain forced-choice judgments but insufficient to access word-specific semantic and phonological information. On balance, the evidence seems to favor the latter account.

WHAT DO STUDIES OF EYE MOVEMENT REVEAL ABOUT READING TEXT?

Eye movement is required when reading text because visual acuity is greatest at the fovea and words in the periphery are hard to recognize quickly and accurately. However, the control of eye movements in reading clearly has two masters: visual perception and text comprehension (Rayner & Juhasz, 2004; Starr & Rayner, 2001). The eyes move across the page in a series of jerks (called **saccades**) and pauses (called **fixations**). This stands in contrast to following a moving target, in which the eyes move smoothly. To understand this process in more detail, we can break it down into two questions: How do we decide where to land during a saccade? How do we decide when to move after a fixation?

First, reading direction affects both the movement of saccades and the extraction of information during fixation. English speakers typically have left-to-right reading saccades and absorb more information from the right of fixation. It is more efficient to consider upcoming words than linger on previously processed ones. The eyes typically fixate on a point between the beginning and middle of a word (Rayner, 1979), and take information concerning three or four letters on the left and 15 letters to the right (Rayner, Well, & Pollatsek, 1980). Hebrew readers do the opposite (Pollatsek, Bolozky, Well, & Rayner, 1981). The *landing position* within a word may be related to perceptual rather than linguistic factors. The predictability of a word in context does not influence landing position within the word (Rayner, Binder, Ashby, & Pollatsek, 2001), nor does morphological complexity (Radach, Inhoff, & Heller, 2004). Whether or not a word is *skipped* altogether seems to depend on how short it is (a perceptual factor) (Rayner &

McConkie, 1976) and how predictable it is (a linguistic factor) (Rayner et al., 2001). However, the frequency of a word and its predictability do influence the *length of time fixated* (Rayner & Duffy, 1986). Similarly, the length of time fixated seems to depend on morphological complexity (Niswander, Pollatsek, & Rayner, 2000).

In sum, eye movement studies are an important tool for studying visual perception in general and for studying language comprehension in particular.

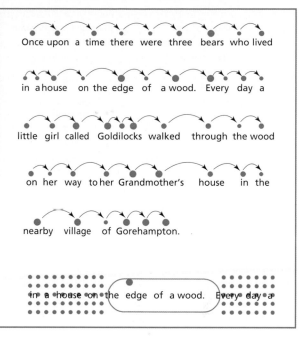

Top: not all words get fixated during reading and the duration of fixation varies from word to word (shown by the size of the dot). Bottom: in left-to-right readers, information is predominantly obtained from the right of fixation. From Ellis (1993).

DOES UNDERSTANDING TEXT REQUIRE PHONOLOGICAL MEDIATION?

When reading, even silently, there is a sense in which the words are heard in one's head, often called *inner speech*. This suggests that knowledge of the spoken word form often accompanies reading. However, there is a key difference between claiming that reading tends to trigger phonological processing and claiming that accessing the spoken forms of words is an obligatory component of understanding visually presented words. The latter is termed **phonological mediation**.

There is good evidence to suggest that just looking at written words can activate the corresponding phonology (e.g. Ferrand & Grainger, 2003). Moreover, this can occur very rapidly (Perfetti, Bell, & Delaney, 1988). Many of the studies conducted in this area have used as their stimuli **homophones** (words with the same phonology but different spelling; e.g. ROWS and ROSE) or pseudo-homophones (non-words that are pronounced like a real word; e.g. BRANE). Van Orden (1987; Van Orden, Johnston, & Hele, 1988) reported that normal participants are error-prone when making semantic categorizations when a stimulus is homophonic with a true category member (e.g. determining whether ROWS is a FLOWER). This was taken as evidence that mapping between visual words and their meaning requires phonological mediation.

It does not logically follow from these results that phonology is obligatory. For example, the homophonic interference effect may arise from response competition at a later stage of processing arising because both the visual word and spoken form have independent access to meaning. Evidence from neuropsychology strongly supports the position that the meaning of visual words can be accessed directly. For example, Hanley and McDonnell (1997)

KEY TERMS

Phonological mediation
The claim that accessing the spoken forms of words is an obligatory component of understanding visually presented words.

Homophone
Words that sound the same but have different meanings (and often different spellings); e.g. ROWS and ROSE.

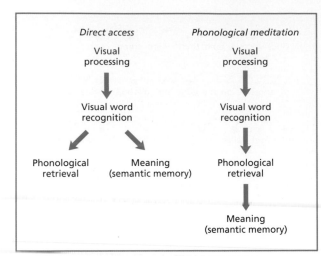

report an aphasic patient who made phonemic errors on tasks such as oral reading, picture naming, auditory repetition and spontaneous speech. Nevertheless, he could comprehend the meaning of written words. For example, he could provide the meaning of homophones even though he was no better than chance at deciding whether or not they would sound the same when read aloud. Other aphasic patients produce errors in spoken output (e.g. naming a BANANA as an "orange") but are able to write the name correctly (Rapp, Benzing, & Caramazza, 1997). Thus, there is evidence that written language is autonomous from spoken language in both input (reading) and output (writing).

Do we need to access the spoken forms of words in order to understand them? In the model on the left, phonological retrieval may accompany silent reading but is not essential for it. In the model on the right, phonological mediation is essential for comprehension of text.

READING ALOUD: ROUTES FROM SPELLING TO SOUND

The most influential models of reading aloud are based on a dual-route model of reading initially put forward by Marshall and Newcombe (1973). The key features of this model are: (1) a semantically-based reading route in which visual words are able to access semantics directly; and (2) a phonologically-based reading route that uses known regularities between spelling patterns and phonological patterns (e.g. the letters TH are normally pronounced as "th") to achieve reading.

Before going on to consider later developments of the model, it is important to state the key properties of the standard, traditional dual-route model (e.g. Morton, 1980; Patterson, 1981; Shallice, Warrington, & McCarthy, 1983). In the traditional model, the phonologically-based route is considered to instantiate a procedure called grapheme–phoneme conversion, in which letter patterns are mapped onto corresponding phonemes. This may be essential for reading non-words, which, by definition, do not have meaning or a stored lexical representation. Known words, by contrast, do have a meaning and can be read via direct access to the semantic system and thence via the stored spoken forms of words. Of course, many of these words could also be read via grapheme–phoneme conversion, although in the case of words with irregular spellings it would result in error (e.g. YACHT read as "yatched"). The extent to which each route is used may also be determined by speed of processing – the direct semantic access route is generally considered faster and more sensitive to how common a word is. Reading time data from skilled adult readers is broadly consistent with this framework. High-frequency words are fast to read, irrespective of the sound–spelling regularity. For low-frequency words, regular words are read faster than irregular ones (e.g. Seidenberg, Waters, Barnes, & Tanenhaus, 1984).

Profiles of acquired central dyslexias

The dual-route model predicts that selective damage to different components comprising the two routes should have different consequences for the reading of different types of written material. Indeed this appears to be so. Some patients are able to read non-words and regularly spelled words better than irregularly spelled words, which they tend to pronounce as if they were regular (e.g. DOVE pronounced "doove" like "move", and CHAOS pronounced with a "ch" as in "church"). These patients are called **surface dyslexics** (e.g. Patterson, Marshall, & Coltheart, 1985; Shallice et al., 1983). Within the dual-route system it may reflect reliance on grapheme–phoneme conversion arising from damage to the semantic system (e.g. Graham, Hodges, & Patterson, 1994; Ward, Stott, & Parkin, 2000) or visual lexicon itself (Coltheart & Funnell, 1987). This can be formally assessed with tests of semantic memory (see Chapter 11). These patients typically show a frequency × regularity interaction.

Another type of acquired dyslexia has been termed **phonological dyslexia**. These patients are able to read real words better than non-words, although it is to be noted that real word reading is not necessarily 100% correct (e.g. Beauvois & Derouesne, 1979). When given a non-word to read, they often produce a real word answer (e.g. CHURSE read as "nurse") and more detailed testing typically reveals that they have problems in aspects of phonological processing (e.g. auditory rhyme judgment) but that they can perceive the written word accurately (Farah, Stowe, & Levinson, 1996; Patterson & Marcel, 1992). As such, these patients are considered to have difficulties in the phonological route (grapheme–phoneme conversion) and are reliant on the lexical–semantic route.

Another type of acquired dyslexia exists that resembles phonological dyslexia in that real words are read better than non-words, but in which real word reading is more error-prone and results in a particularly intriguing type of error – a semantic error (e.g. reading CAT as "dog"). This is termed **deep dyslexia** (e.g. Coltheart, Patterson, & Marshall, 1980). The patients also have a number of other characteristics, including a difficulty in reading abstract relative to concrete words. Within the original 1973 dual-route model, this was explained as damage to grapheme–phoneme

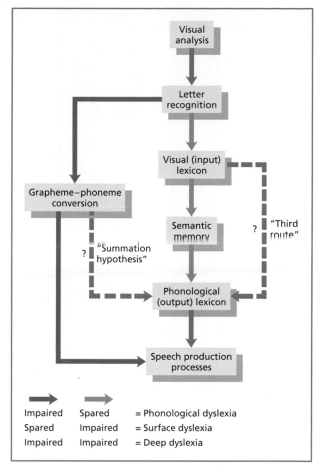

A dual-route model of reading. The standard lexical–semantic and grapheme–phoneme conversion routes are shown in solid lines (green and red respectively). Two alternative modifications to the model are shown with dashed lines.

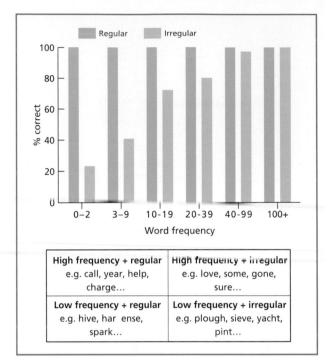

High frequency + regular	High frequency + irregular
e.g. call, year, help, charge...	e.g. love, some, gone, sure...
Low frequency + regular	**Low frequency + irregular**
e.g. hive, har ense, spark...	e.g. plough, sieve, yacht, pint...

Frequency × regularity interaction in the word reading of a semantic dementia patient and examples of words falling into these categories. Reprinted from Ward et al. (2000), Copyright 2000, with permission from Elsevier.

conversion and use of the intact semantic pathway (Marshall & Newcombe, 1973). However, this explanation is clearly inadequate because it predicts that the semantic route is normally very error-prone in us all, and it fails to predict that deep dyslexic patients have comprehension problems on tests of semantic memory that don't involve written material (Shallice, 1988). The most common way of explaining deep dyslexia is to assume that *both* reading routes are impaired (e.g. Nolan & Caramazza, 1982) (but see Coltheart, 1980; Saffran, Bogyo, Schwartz, & Marin, 1980). The lexical–semantic route is degraded such that similar concepts have effectively become fused together and cannot be distinguished from one another, and the absence of phoneme–grapheme conversion prevents an alternative means of output.

A number of studies have reported patients who can read words aloud accurately but have impaired non-word reading and impaired semantic knowledge (e.g. Cipolotti & Warrington, 1995b; Coslett, 1991; Funnell, 1983; Lambon Ralph, Ellis, & Franklin, 1995). So how are these patients able to read? The problem with non-words implies a difficulty in grapheme–phoneme conversion and the problem in comprehension and semantic memory implies a difficulty in the lexical–semantic route. One might predict the patients would be severely dyslexic – probably deep dyslexic. To accommodate these data, several researchers have argued in favor of a "third route" that links the visual lexicon with the phonological lexicon but does not go through semantics (e.g. Cipolotti & Warrington, 1995b; Coltheart, Curtis, Atkins, & Haller, 1993; Coslett, 1991; Funnell, 1983).

An alternative to the third route is provided by the *summation hypothesis* (Hillis & Caramazza, 1991b; Miceli, Capasso, & Caramazza, 1994; Ward et al., 2000). The summation hypothesis states that lexical representations in reading are selected by summing the activation from the semantic system and from grapheme–phoneme conversion. Thus patients with partial damage to one or both of these routes may still be able to achieve relatively proficient performance at reading, even with irregular words. For example, in trying to read the irregular word *bear*, a degraded semantic system may activate a number of candidates including bear, horse, cow, etc. However, the grapheme–phoneme conversion system will also activate, to differing degrees, a set of lexical candidates that are phonologically similar ("beer", "bare", "bar", etc.). By combining these two sources of information, the patient should be able to arrive at the correct pronunciation of *bear*, even though neither route may be able to select the correct entry by itself. This prediction was tested by Hillis and Caramazza (1991b). Their surface dyslexic/dysgraphic was able to read and spell irregular words for which he had partial understanding (e.g. superordinate category) but not irregular words for which no understanding was demonstrated.

Computational models of reading aloud

In the late 1980s, a more radical way of thinking about reading came about. This was motivated by the development of computational models of reading. The main model that will be considered is that of Seidenberg and McClelland (1989) and its successors (e.g. Plaut, McClelland, Seidenberg, & Patterson, 1996; Seidenberg, Plaut, Petersen, McClelland, & McRae, 1994). The first way in which these models could be said to differ from more traditional accounts is by having distributed representations of words. Rather than each word having its own entry in a lexicon, each node in a connectionist network may respond to several words. One word is distinguished from another word as a result of a collective pattern of responding over several nodes and the unique connections that they have to other regions. However, there are more substantial challenges to the dual-route model. It was argued that a single route from orthography to phonology was sufficient to read aloud all material – non-words, and both regularly and irregularly spelled words. This stands in contrast to the traditional view that lexical-semantics is needed to support irregular word reading. It is worth pointing out that these connectionist models were never intended to be single route only. A semantic route was also postulated, although not necessarily implemented, and deemed to be important in some situations (e.g. understanding what you read!), but the central claim was that both regular and irregular pronunciation could be derived from a single route.

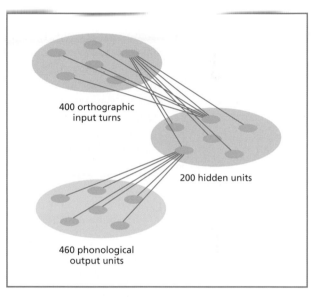

Showing that a computer simulation is capable of reading most English words via a single route is only interesting if one can further demonstrate that this is what humans do too. The ability of these models to reproduce a wide variety of normal and pathological reading patterns is critical for assessing the standing of these models. Interactions between frequency and regularity can arise from the operation of the single route because the weights between orthography and phonology are determined by how often spelling–sound patterns occur during training. This relates both to how often a word is encountered (a frequency effect) and to how often a particular spelling–sound pattern is encountered across many words (a regularity effect) (Seidenberg & McClelland, 1989). In some

400 orthographic input turns

200 hidden units

460 phonological output units

of the earlier connectionist models, non-word reading was poor relative to human performance (Besner, Twilley, McCann, & Seegobin, 1990). This was remedied in subsequent versions (Plaut et al., 1996), although, arguably, this was achieved by sacrificing some of the distributed representation principle (e.g. Zorzi, Houghton, & Butterworth, 1998). For example, separate nodes were used to represent different graphemic letter clusters even if these grapheme clusters were related (e.g. CH and TCH had separate nodes rather than sharing some nodes).

Later implementations of the model were able to reproduce characteristics of surface and phonological dyslexia when lesioned, but this required consideration of the additional semantic route (Plaut et al., 1996). Surface dyslexia was assumed to arise because of damage to the semantic route. Although there is good evidence for this, the problem is that the isolated single route has already been shown capable of reading irregular words, so why would a semantic lesion impair reading of these words in this model? To account for this, the model resorted to a division of labor between the two routes such that the semantic route takes on the onus of reading irregular words. Thus in order to account for the full range of data, the model needs to take on some (but by no means all) characteristics of traditional accounts.

The implemented part of the Seidenberg and McClelland model consists of orthographic and phonological units fully interconnecting with a mediating "hidden" layer. The representations are distributed in that the letter/phoneme string is related to activity spread across several units. From Coltheart et al. (1993). Copyright © American Psychological Association. Reproduced with permission.

Phonological dyslexia can be modeled by lesions to the phonological system itself or pathways to it (Plaut et al., 1996).

Other research groups have developed other models of reading that differ in important ways from the models inspired by Seidenberg and McClelland (1989). The dual-route cascaded model of reading (DRC) is essentially a computerized implementation of a more traditional reading model that contains a lexicon (i.e. nodes corresponding to words), lacks distributed representation but does contain other features characteristic of these models, such as interactivity between components (Coltheart, Curtis, Atkins, & Haller, 1993; Coltheart, Rastle, Perry, Langdon, & Ziegler, 2001). The model actually contains three routes because it implements a direct route between the visual lexicon and the phonological lexicon (see the discussion above). Arguably, the most satisfactory computational accounts of reading are those that contain a hybrid of aspects of the DRC and Seidenberg and McClelland model. For example, the model of Zorzi et al. (1998) claims that the pronunciation of non-words and exception words are computed by two different routes (as does the DRC), that these two routes interact, but there is no need for a third route (unlike DRC) and that grapheme–phoneme conversion operates by extracting statistical regularities during learning rather than implementing "rules" (similar to the Seidenberg and McClelland model).

In conclusion, connectionist models of reading have stimulated an important debate about the precise cognitive mechanisms underpinning reading. Although many issues remain to be resolved, it is clear that the most satisfactory models contain two routes. Moreover, claims that a single route can read all types of material (including non-words and irregularly spelled words) have particular difficulty in accounting for the data from acquired dyslexia.

Seidenberg and McClelland (1989)	Plaut, McClelland, Seidenberg and Patterson (1996)	Coltheart, Curtis, Atkins and Haller (1993) DRC
• Representation of orthography and phonology is fully distributed • No nodes corresponding to whole words (no lexicon) • Claims to be able to read all types of written material using a single route from spelling to sound (but some difficulty with non-words) • Unable to account for acquired dyslexias	• Localist representation of orthography and phonology (nodes represent individual letters or known letter clusters) • No nodes corresponding to whole words (no lexicon) • Suggests reading is a balance of two routes • Offers an account of acquired dyslexia	• Localist representation of orthography and phonology (nodes represent individual letters or known letter clusters) • Contains word nodes (i.e. a traditional lexicon) • Contains a "third route" • Offers an account of acquired dyslexia

What has functional imaging revealed about the existence of multiple routes?

The initial motivation for postulating two (or more) routes for reading was cognitive, not neuroanatomical. Nevertheless, functional imaging may provide an important source of converging evidence to this debate – at least in principle (for reviews, see Fiez & Petersen, 1998; Jobard, Crivello, & Tzourio-Mazoyer, 2003). Of course, functional imaging measures the activity of regions only in response to particular task demands, and so it does not provide any evidence for actual anatomical routes between brain regions. This activity itself can also be open to interpretation. A region may be active because it is successfully contributing to a task or it may be active because it is trying, but failing, to contribute. For example, brain activity associated with non-word processing is not straightforward to interpret for this reason. In spite of these difficulties, a number of studies have reported different brain regions to be responsive to different aspects of reading in ways that would be predicted by dual-route models.

Fiebach et al. (2002) report an event-related fMRI experiment of lexical decision in German speakers. A comparison of low-frequency words and non-words relative to high-frequency words revealed a pattern of activity that was interpreted as indicative of grapheme–phoneme conversion (high-frequency words are assumed to have efficient access to the lexical–semantic route and do not rely on this route so much). These included areas in the anterior insula and left inferior frontal gyrus (Brodmann area 44), considered to be important for phonology and articulation (e.g. Wise, Greene, Buchel, & Scott, 1999). By contrast, low-frequency words relative to non-words and high-frequency words activated an area implicated in lexical selection (left inferior frontal gyrus, Brodmann area 45). Lexical selection demands may be greatest for less common or semantically ambiguous words (for further discussion of these regions, refer to Chapters 11 and 14). Although German has a transparent spelling–sound mapping, studies of English reading aloud have shown that spelling–sound regularity (and its interaction with word frequency) engenders activity in those regions considered important for phonological processing and articulation (Fiez, Balota, Raichle, & Petersen, 1999).

In summary, functional imaging will undoubtedly be critical for establishing the neural basis of reading and has identified many regions that respond to different aspects of the task.

Is the same reading system universal across languages?

The dual-route model is an attractive framework for understanding reading in opaque languages such as English, in which there is a mix of regular and irregular spelling-to-sound patterns. But to what extent is this model likely to extend to languages with highly transparent mappings (e.g. Italian) or, at the other extreme, are logographic rather than alphabetic (e.g. Chinese)? The evidence suggests that the same reading system is indeed used across other languages but the different routes and components may be weighted differently according to the culture-specific demands.

Functional imaging suggests that reading uses similar brain regions across different languages, albeit to varying degrees. Italian speakers appear to activate more strongly areas involved in phonemic processing when reading words,

Although Chinese is not alphabetic, whole words and characters can nevertheless be decomposed into a collection of parts. There is evidence to suggest that there is a separate route that is sensitive to part-based reading of Chinese characters that is analogous to grapheme–phoneme conversion in alphabetic scripts.

whereas English speakers activate more strongly regions implicated in lexical retrieval (Paulesu et al., 2000). Studies of Chinese speakers also support a common network for reading Chinese logographs and reading Roman-alphabetic transcriptions of Chinese (the latter being a system, called pinyin, used to help in teaching Chinese; Chen, Fu, Iversen, Smith, & Matthews, 2002). Moreover, Chinese logographs resemble English words more than they do pictures in terms of the brain activity that is engendered, although reading Chinese logographs may make more demands on brain regions involved in semantics than reading English (Chee et al., 2000). The latter is supported by cognitive studies showing that reading logographs is more affected by word imageability than reading English words (Shibahara, Zorzi, Hill, Wydell, & Butterworth, 2003). Imageability refers to whether a concept is concrete or abstract, with concrete words believed to possess richer semantic representations. Thus, it appears that Chinese readers may be more reliant on reading via semantics but that the reading system is co-extensive with that used for other scripts.

Cases of surface dyslexia have been documented in Japanese (Fushimi, Komori, Patterson, Ijuin, & Tanabe, 2003) and Chinese (Weekes & Chen, 1999). Reading of Chinese logographs and Japanese Kanji can be influenced by the parts that comprise them. These parts have different pronunciations in different contexts, with degree of consistency varying. This is broadly analogous to grapheme–phoneme regularities in alphabetic scripts. Indeed, the degree of consistency of character–sound correspondence affecting reading of both words and non-words is particularly apparent for low-frequency words. The results suggest that there are non-semantic routes for linking print with sound even in scripts that are not based on the alphabetic principle. Conversely, phonological dyslexia has been observed in these scripts, adding further weight to the notion that the dual-route model may be universal (Patterson, Suzuki, & Wydell, 1996; Yin & Weekes, 2003). Similarly, surface dyslexia (Job, Sartori, Masterson, & Coltheart, 1983) and phonological dyslexia (De Bastiani, Barry, & Carreras, 1988) have been observed in Italian, even though this reading system is entirely regular and could, in principle, be achieved by grapheme–phoneme correspondence alone. As with English and Chinese, Italian also shows a word frequency $\times$ regularity interaction for reading aloud in skilled adult readers (Burani, Barca, & Ellis, 2006).

Evaluation

The dual-route model of reading presently remains the most viable model of reading aloud. It is able to account for skilled reading, for patterns of acquired dyslexia and for difference in regional activity observed in functional imaging when processing different types of written stimuli. The model also extends to written languages that are very different from English. However, the precise nature of the computations carried out still remains to be fully elucidated.

SPELLING AND WRITING

KEY TERM

Dysgraphia
Difficulties in spelling and writing.

Spelling has received less attention than the study of reading. For example, there is a paucity of functional imaging studies dedicated to the topic (but see Beeson et al., 2003). The reasons for this are unclear. Producing written language may be less common as a task for many people than reading; it may also be harder. For example, many adult developmental dyslexics can get by adequately at reading but only manifest their true difficulties when it comes to spelling (e.g. Frith, 1985). However, the study of spelling and its disorders has produced some intriguing insights into the organization of the cognitive system dedicated to literacy.

A model of spelling and writing

First, it is important to make a distinction between the process of selecting and retrieving a letter string to be produced, and the task of physically producing an output. The latter task may take various forms such as writing, typing and oral spelling. The term "spelling" can be viewed as an encompassing term that is neutral with respect to the mode of output. This distinction is, of course, reminiscent of the earlier distinction made between central and peripheral aspects of reading. Indeed, the terms central **dysgraphia** and peripheral dysgraphia have been used in the taxonomy of acquired disorders of spelling (Shallice, 1988).

As with reading, dual-route models of spelling have been postulated (for a review, see Barry, 1994). In spelling the task demands are reversed, in that one is attempting to get from a spoken word or a concept to an orthographic one (reading involves mapping an orthographic code to a spoken form and/or a concept). As such, the names of some of the components are changed to reflect this. For example, phoneme–grapheme conversion is a hypothesized component of spelling, whereas grapheme–phoneme conversion is the reading equivalent.

The principal line of evidence for this model comes from the acquired dysgraphias. In surface dysgraphia, patients are better at spelling to dictation regularly spelled words and non-words and are poor with irregularly spelled words (e.g. "yacht" spelled as YOT) (e.g. Beauvois & Derouesne, 1981; Goodman & Caramazza, 1986a). This is considered to be due to damage to the lexical–semantic route and reliance on phoneme–grapheme conversion. Indeed, these cases typically have poor comprehension characteristic of a semantic disorder (Graham, Patterson, & Hodges, 2000). In contrast, patients

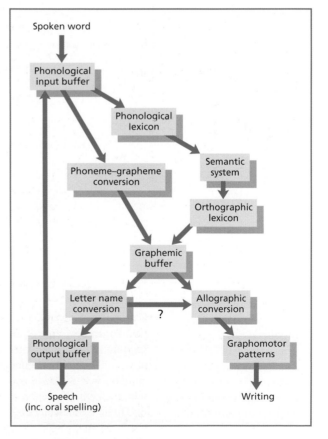

A dual-route model of spelling.

with phonological dysgraphia are able to spell real words better than non-words (e.g. Shallice, 1981). This has been explained as a difficulty in phoneme–grapheme conversion, or a problem in phonological segmentation itself. Deep dysgraphia (e.g. spelling "cat" as D-O-G) has been reported too (e.g. Bub & Kertesz, 1982). As with reading, there is debate concerning whether or not there is a "third route" that directly connects phonological and orthographic lexicons that bypasses semantics (e.g. Hall & Riddoch, 1997; Hillis & Caramazza, 1991b). It is important to note that all of these spelling disorders are generally independent of the modality of output. For example, a surface dysgraphic patient would tend to produce the same kinds of errors in writing, typing or oral spelling.

The graphemic buffer

The **graphemic buffer** is a short-term memory component that holds on to the string of abstract letter identities whilst output processes (for writing, typing, etc.) are engaged (e.g. Wing & Baddeley, 1980). The term "grapheme" is used in this context to refer to letter identities that are not specified in terms of case (e.g. B versus b), font (b versus b), or modality of output (e.g. oral spelling versus writing). Another important feature of the graphemic buffer is that it serves as the confluence of the phoneme–grapheme route and the lexical–semantic spelling route. As such, the graphemic buffer is used in spelling both words and non-words.

Wing and Baddeley (1980) analyzed a large corpus of spelling errors generated by candidates sitting an entrance exam for Cambridge University. They considered letter-based errors that were believed to reflect output errors ("slips of the pen") rather than errors based on lack of knowledge of the true spelling (e.g. the candidate had correctly spelled the word on another occasion). These errors consisted of letter transpositions (e.g. HOSRE for HORSE), substitutions (e.g. HOPSE for HORSE), omissions (e.g. HOSE for HORSE) and additions (HORESE for HORSE). These errors were assumed to arise from noise or interference between letters in the graphemic buffer. One additional characteristic of these errors is that they tended to cluster in the middle of words, giving an inverted U-shaped error distribution. Wing and Baddeley speculated that letters in the middle have more neighbors and are thus susceptible to more interference.

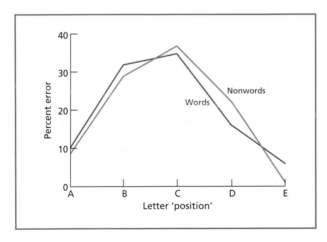

Patient LB had graphemic buffer damage and produced spelling errors with both words and non-words. The errors tended to cluster around the middle of the word. Reprinted from Caramazza et al. (1987), Copyright 1987 with permission from Elsevier.

The most detailed example of acquired damage to the graphemic buffer is patient LB (Caramazza, Hillis, Villa, & Romani, 1987; Caramazza & Miceli, 1990; Caramazza, Capasso, & Miceli, 1996). In some respects, the errors could be viewed as a pathological extreme of those documented by Wing and Baddeley (1980). For example, spelling mistakes consisted of single letter errors and were concentrated in the middle of words. In addition, equivalent spelling errors were found irrespective of whether the stimulus was a word or non-word, and irrespective of output modality. This is consistent with the central position of the graphemic buffer in the cognitive architecture of spelling. In addition, word length had a significant effect on the probability of an error. This is consistent with its role as a limited capacity retention system.

There is evidence to suggest that the information held in the graphemic buffer consists of more than just a linear string of letter identities (Caramazza & Miceli,

---

CHARACTERISTICS OF THE SPELLING ERRORS OF PATIENT LB WITH DAMAGE TO THE GRAPHEMIC BUFFER

- Errors consist of single letter substitutions, additions, omissions and transpositions
- Spelling errors clustered in the middle of words
- Longer words more likely to be mis-spelled than shorter ones
- Equivalent spelling errors on both words and non-words
- Equivalent spelling errors in different modalities of output

---

1990). In particular, it has been argued that consecutive double letters (e.g. the BB in RABDIT) have a special status. Double letters (also called geminates) tend to be mis-spelled such that the doubling information migrates to another letter (e.g. Tainturier & Caramazza, 1996). For example, RABBIT may be spelled as RABITT. However, errors such as RABIBT are conspicuously absent, even though they exist for comparable words that lack a double letter (e.g. spelling BASKET as BASEKT). This suggests that our mental representation of the spelling of the word RABBIT does not consist of R-A-B-B-I-T but consists of R-A-B[D]-I-T, where [D] denotes that the letter should be doubled. Why do double letters need this special status? One suggestion is that, after each letter is produced, it gets inhibited to prevent it getting produced again and to allow another letter to be processed (e.g. Shallice, Glasspool, & Houghton, 1995). When the same letter needs to be written twice in a row, a special mechanism is required to block this inhibition.

Output processes in writing and oral spelling

There is evidence for separate written versus oral letter name output codes in spelling. Some patients have damage to the letter names that selectively impairs oral spelling relative to written spelling (Cipolotti & Warrington, 1996; Kinsbourne & Warrington, 1965). The task of oral spelling is likely to be closely linked with other aspects of phonological processing (for a review, see Ward, 2003). In contrast, some patients are better at oral spelling than written spelling (Goodman & Caramazza, 1986b; Rapp & Caramazza, 1997). These peripheral dysgraphias take several forms and are related to different stages, from specification of the abstract letter to production of pen strokes.

Ellis (1979, 1982) refers to three different levels of description for a letter. The grapheme is the most abstract description that specifies letter identity, whereas an **allograph** refers to letters that are specified for shape (e.g. case, print versus script) but not motor output, and the **graph** refers to a specification of stroke order, size and direction. Damage to the latter two stages would selectively affect writing over oral spelling. Patients with damage to the allographic level may write in mIxeD CaSe, and have selective difficulties with either lower-case writing (Patterson & Wing, 1989) or upper-case writing (Del Grosso et al., 2000). They also tend to substitute a letter for one of similar appearance (Rapp & Caramazza, 1997). Although this could be taken as evidence for confusions

KEY TERMS

Allograph
Letters that are specified for shape (e.g. case, print versus script).

Graph
Letters that are specified in terms of stroke order, size and direction.

Patient IDT was unable to write letters to dictation, but could draw pictures on command and copy letters. This ability rules out a general apraxic difficulty. Reproduced from Baxter and Warrington (1986), copyright 1986, reproduced with permission from BMJ Publishing Group Ltd.

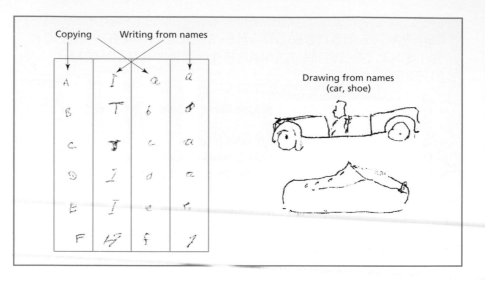

Patient VB is described as having "afferent dysgraphia", which is hypothesized to arise from a failure to utilize visual and motor feedback during the execution of motor tasks, such as writing. Similar errors are observed in normal subjects when feedback is disrupted by blindfolding and when producing an irrelevant motor response. From Ellis et al. (1987).

based on visual shape, it is also the case that similar shapes have similar graphomotoric demands. Some researchers have argued that allographs are simply pointers that denote case and style but do not specify the visual shape of the letter (Del Grosso Destreri et al., 2000; Rapp & Caramazza, 1997). Rapp and Caramazza (1997) showed that their patient, with hypothesized damage to allographs, was influenced by graphomotoric similarity and not shape when these were independently controlled for. Other dysgraphic patients can write letters far better than they can visually imagine them (Del Grosso Destreri et al., 2000) or can write words from dictation but cannot copy the same words from a visual template (Cipolotti & Denes, 1989). This suggests that the output codes in writing are primarily motoric rather than visuospatial.

The motor representations for writing themselves may be damaged ("graphs" in the terminology above). Some patients can no longer write letters but can draw, copy and even write numbers, which suggests that the difficulty is in stored motor representations and not action more generally (Baxter & Warrington, 1986; Zettin, Cubelli, Perino, & Rago, 1995).

Although the stored codes for writing may be motoric rather than visual, vision still has an important role to play in guiding the online execution of writing. Patients with **afferent dysgraphia** make many stroke omissions and additions in writing (Cubelli & Lupi, 1999; Ellis, Young, & Flude, 1987). Interestingly, similar error patterns are found when healthy individuals write blindfolded and have distracting motor activity (e.g. tapping with their non-writing hand) (Ellis et al., 1987). It suggests that these dysgraphic patients are unable to utilize sensory-motor feedback even though basic sensation (e.g. vision, proprioception) is largely unimpaired.

KEY TERM

Afferent dysgraphia
Stroke omissions and additions in writing that may be due to poor use of visual and kinesthetic feedback.

THE UNUSUAL SPELLING AND WRITING OF LEONARDO DA VINCI

The writing of Leonardo da Vinci is unusual in terms of both content and style. In terms of content, there are many spelling errors. This suggests that he may have been surface dyslexic/dysgraphic (Sartori, 1987). In terms of style, his handwriting is highly idiosyncratic and is virtually unreadable except to scholars who are familiar with his style. Da Vinci wrote in mirror-reversed script, such that his writing begins on the right side of the page and moves leftward. The letters themselves were mirror-image distortions of their conventional form. This has been variously interpreted as a deliberate attempt at code (to retain intellectual ownership over his ideas), as proof that he was no mere mortal (for either good or evil) or as being related to his left-handedness. It is well documented that da Vinci was a left-hander and a small proportion of left-handed children do spontaneously adopt such a style. An alternative is that he was born right-handed but sustained an injury that forced him to write with his left hand. Natural right-handers are surprised at how easy it is to write simultaneously with both hands, with the right hand writing

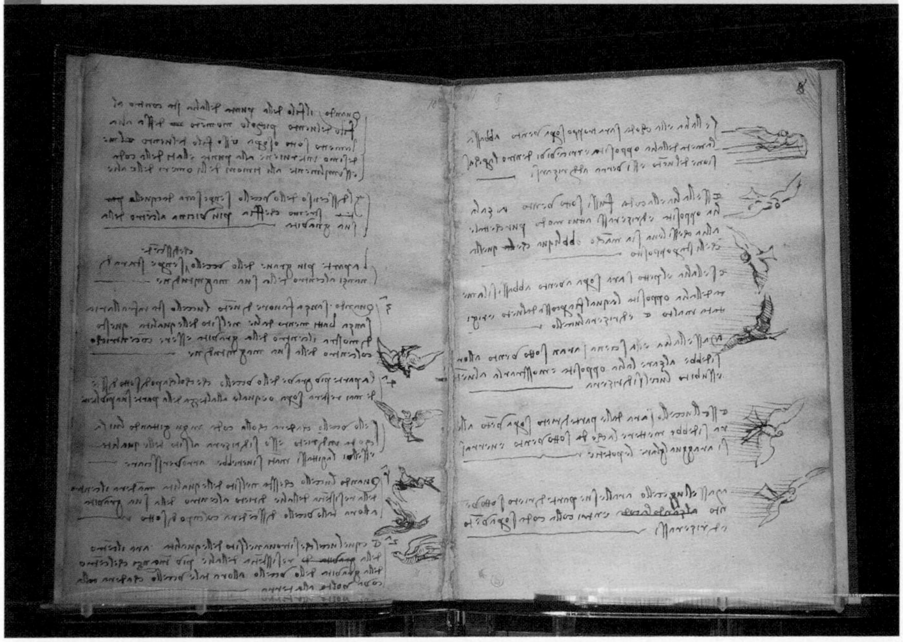

Was Leonardo da Vinci surface dysgraphic? Why did he write mirror-distorted letters from right to left? An example of this is shown here in his *Codex on the Flight of Birds*? (circa 1505). © Luc Viatour GFDL/CC.

normally and the left hand mirror-reversed (for discussion, see McManus, 2002).

As for his spelling errors, Sartori (1987) argues that da Vinci may have been surface dysgraphic. The cardinal feature of this disorder is the spelling of irregular words in a phonetically regular form. Although Italian (da Vinci's native language) lacks irregular words, it is nevertheless possible to render the same phonology in different written forms. For example, *laradio* and *l'aradio* are phonetically plausible, but conventionally incorrect, renditions of *la radio* (the radio). This type of error was commonplace in da Vinci's writings, as it is in modern-day Italian surface dysgraphics (Job, Sartori, Masterson, & Coltheart et al., 1983). It is, however, conspicuously absent in the spelling errors of normal Italian controls.

DOES SPELLING USE THE SAME MECHANISMS AS READING?

Given the inherent similarities between reading and spelling, one may wonder to what extent they share the same cognitive and neural resources. Many earlier models postulated the existence of separate lexicons for reading and spelling (e.g. Morton, 1980). However, the evidence in favor of this separation is not overwhelming. In fact, there is some evidence to suggest that the same lexicon may support both reading and spelling (Behrmann & Bub, 1992; Coltheart & Funnell, 1987). Both of these studies reported patients with surface dyslexia and surface dysgraphia who showed item-for-item consistency in the words that could and could not be read or spelled. These studies concluded that this reflects loss of word forms from a lexicon shared between reading and spelling.

There is also some evidence to suggest that the same graphemic buffer is employed both in reading and spelling (Caramazza et al., 1996; Tainturier & Rapp, 2003). However, graphemic buffer damage may have more dire consequences for spelling than reading because spelling is a slow process that makes more demands on this temporary memory structure than reading. In reading, letters may be mapped on to words in parallel and loss of information at the single letter level may be partially compensated for. For example, reading EL??HANT may result in correct retrieval of "elephant" despite loss of letter information (where the question marks represent degraded information in the buffer). However, attempting to spell from such a degraded representation would result in error. Patients with graphemic buffer damage are particularly bad at reading non-words because this requires analysis of all letters, in contrast to reading words in which partial information can be compensated for to some extent (Caramazza et al., 1996). Moreover, their errors show essentially the same pattern in reading and spelling, including a concentration at the middle of words. This suggests that the same graphemic buffer participates in both reading and spelling.

Functional imaging studies of writing activate a region of the left fusiform that is the same as the so-called "visual word form area" implicated in reading.

For example, this region is active when writing English words from a category examplar relative to drawing circles (Beeson et al., 2003), and when writing Japanese Kanji characters (Nakamura et al., 2000). Brain-damaged patients with lesions in this region are impaired at both spelling and reading for both words and non-words (Philipose et al., 2007). The functional interpretation of this region is controversial (see above) and may reflect a single lexicon for reading and spelling, a common graphemic buffer, or possibly a multi-modal language region. In each case, it appears that reading and spelling have something in common in terms of anatomy.

The above discussion suggests some overlap between reading and spelling in terms of "central" aspects of literacy, but what about input and output codes (e.g. letter names, allographs)? Cipolotti and Warrington (1996) document a patient who had impaired knowledge of letter names. This manifested itself not only in oral spelling relative to writing but also in recognizing words spelled out (e.g. "H", "O", "M", "E") relative to reading them. This suggests a common letter name code used for both input and output. However, there is some evidence for separate representations of allographs (letter forms or shapes) in reading versus writing, with the former being more visuospatial and the latter being more motoric in nature. For example, some patients are able to read and imagine letters (e.g. does "R" contain a curved segment?) but not write them (Baxter & Warrington, 1986), whilst other patients are able to write letters but not read or imagine them (Shuren, Maher, & Heilman, 1996).

Evaluation

Not only is the functional architecture of spelling very similar to that used for reading, there is also evidence to suggest that some of the cognitive components (and neural regions) are shared between the task. There is evidence to suggest sharing of the visual/orthographic lexicon and of the graphemic buffer. However, the evidence suggests that the representation of letters used in writing is primarily grapho-motoric and that this differs from the more visuospatial codes that support both reading and imagery of letters.

SUMMARY AND KEY POINTS OF THE CHAPTER

- The recognition of letters within words occurs automatically and in parallel, and is supported by knowledge of the structure of the language (i.e. which letters tend to go together).
- Evidence of top-down effects from semantics down to visual word recognition remains controversial. Most of the evidence that apparently supports this position is also consistent with post-access decision mechanisms and lexical–lexical priming.

- A region in the left fusiform gyrus responds to familiar letter strings more than false letters or consonant strings. This has been termed the "visual word form area", although it might also respond, to some degree, to other types of stimuli.
- Evidence from acquired dyslexia suggests that there are at least two routes used in reading words aloud: a sublexical route that translates graphemes into phonemes (impaired in phonological dyslexia) and a lexical–semantic route (impaired in surface dyslexia).
- There is evidence to suggest that many of the components involved in reading (e.g. graphemic buffer) are also involved in spelling.
- Letter representations used in spelling and writing exist at several levels: an abstract graphemic level, a level that specifies case and style (allograph) and a level that specifies the abstract motor commands (the graph level).

EXAMPLE ESSAY QUESTIONS

- Is there a "visual lexicon" or a "visual word form area" that is used to support visual word recognition?
- What is the evidence for top-down influences in visual word recognition?
- What factors influence the allocation of attention during reading? Discuss, using evidence from acquired peripheral dyslexia and eye movement studies in healthy participants.
- How many routes are there for reading a word aloud?
- To what extent is the cognitive/neural architecture for reading and spelling common to speakers of different languages?
- Does spelling use the same cognitive mechanisms as reading?

RECOMMENDED FURTHER READING

- Funnell, E. (2001). *Case studies in the neuropsychology of reading*. Hove: Psychology Press. A collection of papers based on acquired dyslexia.

- Sandak, R. & Poldrack, R. A. (2004). *The cognitive neuroscience of reading: a special issue of scientific studies of reading*. London: Taylor & Francis. A good collection of review papers.

- Snowling, M. & Hulme, C. (2005). *The science of reading: a handbook*. Oxford: Blackwell. Very thorough but also accessible. It also contains chapters on spelling. A strong recommendation.

CHAPTER 13

CONTENTS

The numerate brain

Numbers are everywhere. Signposts display prices, distances, percentages, bus routes and so on. Even most illiterate cultures have developed systems of trading and counting. This chapter is not concerned with algebra or calculus; it is concerned primarily with a core set of numerical abilities that seem to be common to almost all humans from infants to the elderly, from the unschooled to the mathematical prodigy. It is to be noted that a basic level of numerical competence is found in *almost all* individuals. Some people with a condition known as **dyscalculia** (or acalculia) lack a basic understanding of number. This difficulty may be a result of brain damage (i.e. numerical competence is lost) or may be of developmental origin (i.e. numerical competence is never gained). The study of dyscalculic individuals has led to important insights into numerical cognition.

Numerical ability can certainly be promoted, or held back, by cultural quirks and inventions. Surprisingly, the **place value** system of numerical notation was not introduced into Europe until the twelfth century, having been invented by Indian scholars and passed on to Arab traders (as was the notation for zero). The place value notation means that the quantity is determined by its place in the written string – thus the "1" in 41, 17 and 185 all mean something different. In our base-10 system, they refer to 1, 10, 100 or 10^0, 10^1, 10^2. Adding together two numbers (e.g. 41 + 17) basically involves little more than adding together the numbers in each place, carrying over if appropriate (7 + 1 is 8, and 4 + 1 is 5, so the answer is 58). Imagine performing multiplication or addition in Roman numerals that is not based on place value (e.g. XXXXI + XVII = LVIII). Scientific progress has undoubtedly benefited from cultural transmission of mathematical knowledge, such as place value, but there appears to be an aspect of numerical cognition that is independent of culture.

This chapter begins by summarizing the evidence that almost all humans and many other animals have a basic understanding of number. It then goes on to consider: how numbers are represented in the brain; where number meaning is represented in the brain; and the extent to which numerical cognition depends upon other cognitive systems (e.g. memory and language). Finally, the chapter contrasts two influential models from the literature and weighs up the evidence from cognitive neuroscience that speaks to these models.

UNIVERSAL NUMERACY?

Becoming skilled at mathematics in the modern world certainly requires learning of arbitrary notations and their meaning (e.g. +, −, >, Π, √), as well as specific procedures (e.g. for calculating the circumference of a circle). Over and above this acquired knowledge, humans and other species appear to have a more basic set of numerical abilities that enable them to estimate quantity and perform basic

An understanding of number is crucial for many day-to-day activities.

calculations. It is in this more fundamental sense that numeracy can be said to be universal.

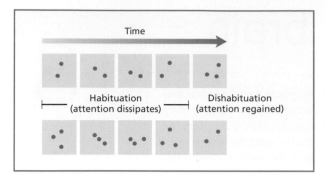

Babies lose interest when different displays are shown containing the same number (they habituate) but their interest increases when shown a display of a different number (dishabituation). This has been taken as evidence for an early appreciation of numbers.

Infants

Cognition in infants has often been studied by a procedure called **habituation**. Infants like to look at novel things and will become disinterested if they are given the same thing to look at (i.e. they habituate). Antell and Keating (1983) found that babies just a day old can discriminate between small numbers. If the babies are shown a series of three dots, in different configurations, they soon lose interest (they habituate). If they are then shown configurations of two dots, then their interest increases (they dishabituate). If two dots are shown for a while, and then three dots (or one dot), then the same type of pattern is found. Is this result really to do with number or any new stimulus? Strauss and Curtis (1981) found comparable results in slightly older infants if different objects are used in each array (three keys, three combs, three oranges, etc....changing to two objects, or vice versa). This suggests that it is the number of objects that they habituate to and not the objects themselves. Simple arithmetic in infants has been studied using a paradigm called *violation of expectancy*. Infants look longer at unexpected events. Wynn (1992) devised a puppet show using this principle to demonstrate simple addition and subtraction. For example, two puppets go behind a screen but when the screen is removed only one puppet is present (an unexpected event; 1 + 1 = 1) or two characters go behind the screen and when the screen is removed two puppets are present (an expected event; 1 + 1 = 2).

The unschooled

Nunes, Schliemann and Carraher (1993) studied the numerical abilities of street children in Brazil, who had little or no formal training in math. For example, one boy, when asked the cost of ten coconuts priced at 35 centavos, was able to come up with the correct answer, albeit using unusual methods: "Three will be one hundred and five; with three more it will be two hundred and ten; I need four more...that's three hundred and fifteen. I think it is three hundred and fifty." In this instance, the boy seems to decompose the multiplier (10 = 3 + 3 + 3 + 1), use stored facts ("3 × 35 = 105") and keep track of the sum. The idea of "adding zero" to 35 when multiplying by 10 may be meaningless in the world of coconuts (Butterworth, 1999).

Cavemen

Archaeological evidence suggests that Cro-Magnon man, around 30,000 years ago, kept track of the phases of the moon by making collections of marks on bones (Marshack, 1991).

Other species

Monkeys in the wild are able to compute 1 + 1 and 2 − 1, as demonstrated by a violation of expectancy paradigm (Hauser, MacNeilage, & Ware, 1996). After being

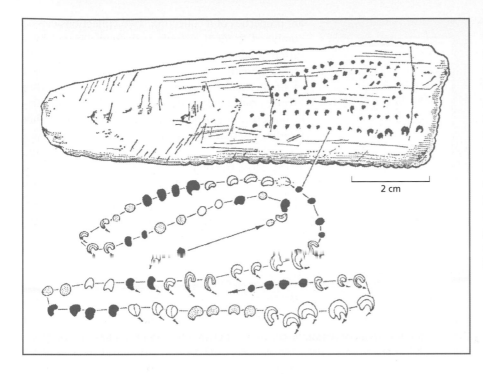

2 cm

In a bone plaque from Dordogne, France, there were 24 changes in the type of pitting made in the 69 marks. According to Marshack, the changes in technique may correspond to different phases of the moon (e.g. crescent-shaped, full or dark) (drawing after Marshack, 1970. *Notation dans les gravures du paléolithique supérieur*, Bordeaux, Delmas.).

trained to order sets of collections from 1 to 4, monkeys generalize this skill, without further training, to sets of 5 to 9 (Brannon & Terrace, 1998). Similarly, after basic training in responding to different quantities they are able to perform approximate addition (Cantlon & Brannon, 2007). For example, knowing that a set of 3 dots followed by a set of 5 dots should make 8 dots rather than 4 (they point to the correct answer). The skill that does require extensive training, however, is learning our arbitrary language-based symbols for numbers (Washburn & Rumbaugh, 1991). To give an example from a non-primate, lions will make a decision about whether to attack or withdraw on the basis of whether the size of their group is greater or smaller than the size of a rival group (McComb, Packer, & Pusey, 1994). The size of the rival group is manipulated experimentally by altering the number of roars made by a hidden loud speaker.

Having summarized the evidence for basic numerical abilities common to almost all humans and common to other species, the next section considers how number meaning is represented in the brain.

THE MEANING OF NUMBERS

A telephone number is a number (or, rather, a numerical label) but it is not a quantity. The phone number 683515 is not larger than the phone number 232854. The meaning of numbers has been variously referred to as magnitude, quantity (Dehaene, 1997) or numerosity (Butterworth, 1999). The distinction between these terms is subtle but it shall be returned to later. Number meaning is abstract. It is "threeness" that links together three animals, three oranges, three ideas and three events. Number meaning is also assumed to be independent of the format used to denote it (e.g. 3, III, "three", "trois" or three fingers). Integer numbers or whole numbers are properties of a collection. Two collections can be combined to yield a single collection denoted by a different number. Similarly, each collection (or each integer number) can be construed as being composed of smaller collections combined together. **Counting** involves putting each item in the collection in one-to-one correspondence with a number or some other internal/external tally ("one, two, three, four, five, six – there are 6 oranges!") (Gelman & Gallistel, 1978). Most fractions can be explained in terms of collections. Thus 6/7 refers to 6 parts of a collection of 7. Other types of number (e.g. zero, infinity, negative numbers) are harder to grasp and are learned later, if at all.

Accessing the meaning of numbers is automatic

When one looks at a number (e.g. *7* or *seven*) is the meaning automatically retrieved (i.e. that it refers to a collection larger than 6 but smaller than 8)? There is good evidence that it is. In reaction time experiments, interference is found if the numerical size of digits (i.e. their meaning) conflicts with the physical font size (Henik & Tzelgov, 1982). This is found both when participants must judge which is numerically larger and which is physically larger. An influence of numerical size on judgments of physical size implies that number meaning is accessed automatically even when it is not relevant to the task.

Moyer and Landauer (1967) conducted a seminal study investigating how number magnitude is represented. Participants had to judge which of two numbers was the larger (there was no conflict with physical size as both numbers were presented in the same font size). They noted two important effects on the pattern of response times. The **distance effect** refers to the fact that it is much easier (i.e. faster reaction time) to decide which number is larger when

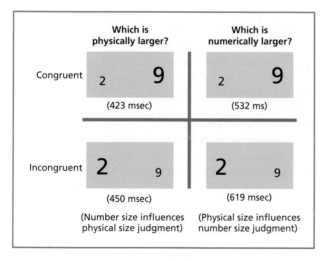

If physical size and numerical size are incongruent, then participants are slower at judging which number is physically or numerically larger. This is evidence that the meaning of a number is accessed automatically. Adapted from Girelli, Lucangeli and Butterworth (2000).

the distance between two numbers is large (e.g. 2 or 9) relative to small (e.g. 8 or 9). This suggests that number magnitude is retrieved, rather than, say, the relative order of numbers (since 2 and 8 both come before 9). The **size effect** refers to the observation that it is easier to judge which of two numbers is larger when the numbers are small (e.g. 3 or 5) compared to when they are large (e.g. 7 or 9), even when the distance between them is equal. The size effect has been taken as evidence to suggest that comparing numbers uses an analogous mechanism to comparing physical quantities (e.g. the length of two lines). In both cases, judging differences becomes harder as magnitude increases. This idea has been very influential and it will be returned to at a number of points in this chapter.

The evidence cited above suggests that the meaning of numbers is accessed automatically. But can number meaning be accessed subliminally? Koechlin,

Naccache, Block and Dehaene (1999b) asked participants to decide whether a stimulus was greater than or less than 5. The stimulus consisted of Arabic numerals (e.g. 7), number words (e.g. SEVEN) or dot patterns (which participants were asked to estimate not count). Crucially, before each trial a very brief (66 ms) additional stimulus was presented that the participants could not consciously report seeing – a prime. The prime was either greater or less than 5. If the prime and stimulus were on the same side of 5, then performance was enhanced. This suggests the involvement of a number meaning system that is independent of the particular notational format that is used (Arabic numerals, number names, dots).

Most of the discussion so far has been concerned with accessing the meaning of number symbols (Arabic numerals). Is the size of a collection retrieved automatically (e.g. arrays of three or six dots)? In the Koechlin

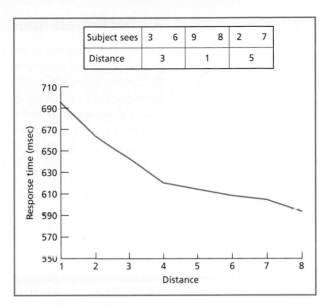

Subject sees	3	6	9	8	2	7
Distance		3		1		5

et al. (1999b) experiment, participants were asked not to count the dots. If, however, participants are asked to give exact answers to the size of a collection, then there do appear to be constraints on the automaticity of the process. People can estimate the size of a collection of up to four items rapidly. That is, people are just as fast at saying that there are one, two, three or four items in an array (called **subitizing**), but above that they slow down proportionally to the number of items in the collection as each one must be counted in turn (Mandler & Shebo, 1982). It is remarkable how similar this capacity limitation is to the abilities of infants and other species that were noted above.

In summary, there is good evidence that people access the meaning of number symbols automatically (although the effect is reduced for large numbers) and may access the exact size of small collections (up to four) automatically. The next section considers the neural basis of this number meaning system.

The ability to discriminate between two numbers increases as the numerical distance between them increases – the so-called "distance effect". From Butterworth (1999). Copyright © Palgrave-Macmillan. Reproduced with permission of the author.

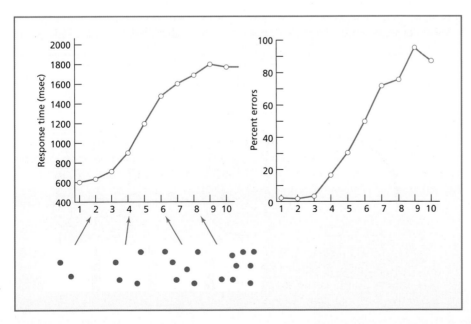

The ability to state how many objects are in an array may occur automatically for small arrays (< 4; called subitizing) but occurs serially for larger arrays (> 4; called counting). In this version of the experiment the arrays were presented briefly (200 ms).

A specialized neural region for number meaning?

There is now converging evidence for a region in the *intraparietal sulcus* (IPS) that is specialized for number meaning; functional imaging studies show activation of this region bilaterally, while lesion studies emphasize the importance of the left hemisphere in particular (this discrepancy will be returned to later). Functional imaging studies show that the IPS region is more active when people perform calculations relative to reading numerical symbols (Burbaud, Camus, Guehl, Biolac, Caille, & Allard, 1999), and in number comparison relative to number reading (Cochon, Cohen, van de Moortele, & Dehaene, 1999). The degree of activation of the region shows a distance effect for both digits and number words (Pinel, Dehaene, Riviere, & Le Bihan, 2001), and is sensitive to subliminal priming when the "unseen" prime and seen stimulus differ in quantity (Dehaene et al., 1998b). This suggests that the region is the anatomical locus for many of the cognitive effects already discussed.

Most of these studies used Arabic numbers or number names. Although this region does appear to respond to numbers more than, say, letters and colors (Eger, Sterzer, Russ, Giraud, & Kleinschmidt, 2003), fewer studies have looked at non-symbolic aspects of number. One study has argued that the region is responsible for representing "continuous quantities" because it was found to respond to comparisons of angles and line lengths as well as numbers (Fias, Lammertyn, Reynvoet, Dupont, & Orban, 2003). Another study with dot patterns showed habituation of the neural response to the number of items in an array, analogous to behavioral studies of human infants (Piazza, Izard, Pinel, Le Bihan, & Dehaene, 2004). But other researchers have questioned the specificity of this response. Shuman and Kanwisher (2004) compared discrimination of dot patterns with tasks such as color discrimination and found that the region was sensitive to both. They concluded that the intraparietal sulcus is not domain-specific for numbers. This does not necessarily mean that numbers do not have a specialized neural substrate, but rather that the region containing the neural substrate also contains neurons engaged in other types of task. Evidence from single-cell recordings in monkey parietal cortex supports this view. Nieder and Miller (2004) have identified neurons that respond to different sizes of dot array whilst the monkey performed a number discrimination task. Some

There is converging evidence from neuropsychology and functional imaging for the role of the parietal lobes in number meaning (particularly the left parietal lobe). Left figure from Cochon et al. (1999). Copyright © 1999 MIT Press. Reproduced with permission. Right figure reprinted from Dehaene et al. (1998a), Copyright 1998, with permission from Elsevier.

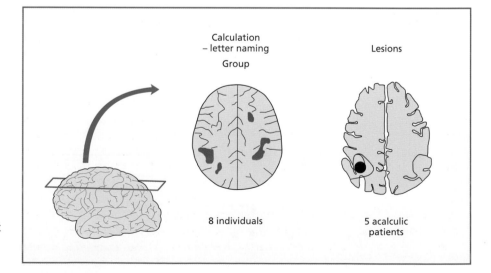

neurons may be tuned to respond to one dot, others to two dots, three dots and so on. The degree of response selectivity of the neuron is related to numerical size, and this may be a neural level equivalent of the size effect in reaction time studies that has already been discussed. For example, a neuron that responds maximally to four dots will respond very little to three or five dots but a neuron tuned to detect ten dots will respond quite strongly to nine or eleven dots. Of particular relevance to the present discussion is that as few as 20% of neurons in the region responded to array size. This suggests that the region as a whole is engaged in other activities.

Further evidence for a specialized neural substrate for number meaning comes from studies of patients with brain damage.

Can number meaning be selectively impaired?

Patient CG is one of the most remarkable cases of acquired dyscalculia that has been documented (Cipolotti, Butterworth, & Denes, 1991). This patient had effectively lost all number knowledge above the number 4. She could not count beyond 4, perform calculations beyond 4, read numbers beyond 4, and so on. In her daily life she could not give the right money in shops, use the phone, tell the time or catch a bus. She could, however, do simple sums up to 4, tell how many were in a collection up to 4 (which she did by counting not subitizing). She was aware that numbers beyond 4 existed, but could not say what they were. In contrast to this impairment, she had a normal IQ (= 99), normal spontaneous speech and normal long-term memory. Her knowledge of other categories (e.g. body parts, animals) was relatively preserved. Interestingly, CG's difficulties appeared to be in the domain of number rather than quantity. She could make size judgments (which object is bigger?), measure judgments (is a kilometer longer than a mile?) and judgments of more (e.g. could you get more coffee beans or salt grains into a cup?).

Dyscalculia refers to impairments of number processing and number knowledge that cannot be accounted for by difficulties in other faculties such as memory and language. Patient CG had poor number knowledge but good language. Can the opposite profile be observed? Rosser, Warrington and Cipolotti (1995) documented a severely aphasic patient, HAB, who was only able to utter a few phrases such as "I don't know" and "millionaire bub". He was unable to comprehend most spoken and written words. By contrast, he could accurately add, subtract and select the larger of two three-digit numbers. He did have some difficulty with multiplication, which is consistent with the suggestion that multiplication facts may be stored verbally (discussed below). In general, it seems as if number meaning can be preserved in the absence of the meaning of most other words in the language (see also Cappelletti, Kopelman, & Butterworth, 2002).

As for memory, there is undoubtedly a large *working memory* component involved in calculation that may depend on the complexity of the task (the number of stages) and the need to hold things "in mind" (e.g. when carrying over) (Furst & Hitch, 2000; Logie, Gilhooly, & Wynn, 1994). However, it seems unlikely that working memory deficits *alone* can account for acquired dyscalculia. Butterworth, Cipolotti and Warrington (1996) report a patient with a digit span of 2. That is, the patient can repeat back single digits, pairs of digits, but not triplets of digits (most people have a digit span of 7). This suggests that his impairment was in the articulatory loop component of working memory (see Chapters 9 and 11). However, he was in the top 37% of the population for mental arithmetic. These included questions such as adding together two three-digit numbers ("one hundred and twenty-eight plus one hundred and forty-nine"). This suggests that mental arithmetic is not strongly dependent on the articulatory loop.

The purpose of the above discussion has been to highlight dissociations of number knowledge from other aspects of cognition. Studies of numerical difficulties in brain-damaged individuals can also be used to explore more fine-grained predictions arising out of different theoretical models, as will be considered later.

Is number meaning exact or approximate? Left and right brain reconsidered

Most of the functional imaging experiments show a bilateral activation of the intra-parietal sulcus in number tasks (for a review, see Dehaene, Piazza, Pinel, & Cohen 2003). However, studies of both developmental dyscalculia (Isaacs, Edmonds, Lucas, & Gadian, 2001) and acquired dyscalculia (Grafman, Passafiume, Faglioni, & Boller, 1982) have emphasized the importance of the left hemisphere over the right. How can these differing results be reconciled? There are a number of possibilities. It could be that the right hemisphere has no functional role in numerical cognition and is just activated by virtue of being interconnected with its left counterpart. An alternative view, that appears to be supported by the weight of the evidence, is that the functional role of the right hemisphere is somewhat different (e.g. Langdon & Warrington, 1997).

Earlier in the chapter, it was mentioned that number meaning is typically thought of in terms of magnitude or numerosity. These terms convey somewhat different meanings. "Numerosity" refers to exact quantities that are potentially countable, whereas "magnitude" refers to a continuous dimension that is not necessarily countable. In the latter account, comparing two numbers is like comparing two lengths or two weights, and yields an approximate quantification. According to Dehaene (1997), the number meaning system of both hemispheres computes approximate quantities, and exact quantity information is only extracted through the additional use of language (in the left hemisphere) or other systems of symbolic notation (e.g. tally). Thus the left hemisphere number meaning system is special by virtue of its interconnections with language rather than the way it represents number. A different but related view put forward by Butterworth (1999) is that left and right hemispheres contain different types of number meaning systems. The right hemisphere system is assumed to represent approximate magnitude, whereas the left hemisphere system is assumed to represent exact numerosity. In Butterworth's model, both are considered to be largely independent of language.

In monkeys, who necessarily lack language, there is little evidence for a left–right difference in terms of the way that single neurons respond to quantities. Moreover, the same neurons appear to respond to both continuous and discrete quantities. Tudusciuc and Nieder (2007) showed monkeys either four lines of different length or arrays of one to four dots. They found that neurons in the intra-parietal sulcus that discriminate between length (continuous quantity) also discriminate between number of dots (as discrete quantities). As such, the meaning of numbers might be both discrete (at least for small numbers) and continuous.

Some patients with left hemisphere lesions are able to perform approximate calculations despite being clinically acalculic. Thus, the residual abilities of the right hemisphere may permit approximate quantification. Warrington (1982) reported a patient who could give estimates but not exact answers, saying, for example, that

5 + 7 is "13 roughly". Dehaene and Cohen (1991) document a patient with severe acalculia who could nevertheless perform approximate calculations. He could rapidly detect the falsehood of 2 + 2 = 9 but not 2 + 2 = 5, but the precision of his approximation decreased with increasing number size (43 + 21 = 69 was classed as correct but not 3 + 1 = 9).

Cohen and Dehaene (1996) presented digits to the left and right hemisphere of a *split-brain* patient. Severing of the fibers of the corpus callosum results in a lack of cortical transfer between the left and right hemispheres (but subcortical routes enable some transfer of information between hemispheres). By presenting stimuli briefly to the left or right of a centrally fixated point, it is possible to study the operation of each hemisphere in isolation. When digits were presented to the right hemisphere, the patient could not name them exactly but the answers were approximately correct (e.g. 5 → "six"). It suggests that the Arabic numeral is not transferred from right to left but, rather, that an approximate magnitude is.

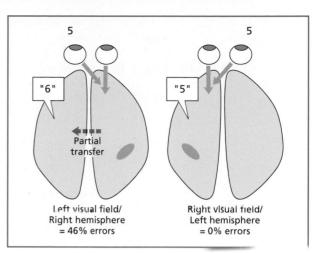

Cohen and Dehaene (1996) reported a "split-brain" patient who could accurately read digits presented briefly to the left hemisphere, but produced errors when they were presented to the right hemisphere. However, the errors were not random. They consisted of numerical approximations.

These studies support the contention that the right hemisphere contains approximate magnitude information. However, they do not shed light on whether the special status of the left hemisphere in representing exact quantities is attributable to language. If this were the case, then one would predict that cultures that lack number names would only be able to represent quantities approximately.

Some Amazonian cultures have only a handful of number names, equivalent to "one", "two" and "many". Are they able to understand and manipulate collections with magnitudes greater than 2 even though they are not differentiated linguistically? Two studies have recently confirmed that larger numbers than 2 can indeed be comprehended and simple arithmetic performed (e.g. adding two collections) (Gordon, 2004; Pica, Lemer, Izard, & Dehaene, 2004). However, the answers to larger calculations tended to be approximate rather than exact (e.g. five stones plus six stones may be ten, eleven or twelve stones). This suggests that, whereas some aspects of number meaning are independent of language, an understanding of larger exact numbers may require linguistic/symbolic representation.

COUNTING WITH FINGERS, BODIES AND BASES

To count beyond a small number of items, one may need a method to keep track of how many items have been counted so far. These may consist of external aids such as systems of tallying (e.g. the marks found on ancient bones) or internal aids such as linguistic symbols (written numerals and number names).

Given a large cultural diversity, humans appear to have developed a restricted number of ways of counting, in part, independently from each other. Two of the most common themes are (1) use of body parts and (2) use of base systems. Many cultures use fingers and other body parts

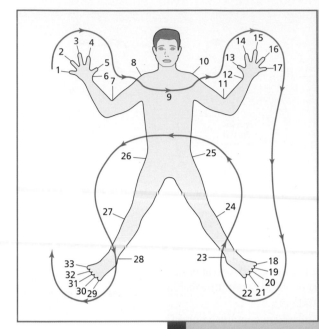

The number system of the Torres Strait islanders is based on body parts. Adapted from Ifrah (1985).

to keep track of how many items have been counted. It is probably no coincidence that the word "digit" can refer both to numbers and to fingers and toes. In other cultures, such as those found in Papua New Guinea, the relationship is more explicit (Lancy, 1983). The Yupno have no specialized number names, but use the names of body parts to count and represent numbers. Thus, "one" is the left little finger and "thirty-three" is the penis. In Kilenge, body parts can be combined and also act as bases. Thus 5 is "hand", 10 is "two hands" and 20 is "man". These terms can be combined such that 30 is "a man and two hands".

Many non-trading cultures have little practical need to represent large numbers. But the question of how large numbers are to be represented when, say, body parts are exhausted seems to have been solved using bases.

Bases are derived from a core property of numbers that is culturally independent – namely, that any given number (except 1 and 0) can be decomposed into a collection or collections. In our base-10 system, the number "35" refers to 3 collections of 10 and 5 collections of 1. Cultures such as the ancient Maya and the modern Basque language use base-20, with subunits of 5. Vestiges of a base-20 system can be heard in some European languages (77 in French is "soixante-dix-sept", literally "sixty and seventeen"). Base-60, with subdivisions of 10 units, was used by Babylonians and is retained in our measurement of angles and time.

Does a tendency to use body parts for counting have any brain-based explanation? Gerstmann (1940) observed that damage to the left parietal lobe can produce not just acalculia but also **finger agnosia** – an inability to identify individual fingers by touch (Kinsbourne & Warrington, 1962b). Together with agraphia and left–right disorientation, these were collectively called **Gerstmann's syndrome**. The different symptoms of this syndrome have now been shown to dissociate from each other (Benton, 1977). Nevertheless, the fact that evolution may have placed the representation of the body and fingers and number meaning close by may be evidence for a close evolutionary relationship (e.g. Rusconi, Walsh, & Butterworth, 2005).

MODELS OF NUMBER PROCESSING

A number of detailed models have been proposed that aim to capture much of the empirical data gathered on numerical cognition. In this section, two models will be considered in detail, although references to other models will be made when appropriate.

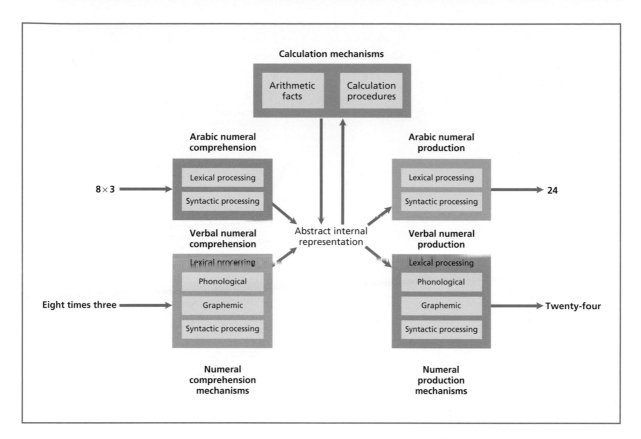

The first model is that proposed by McCloskey and colleagues (e.g. McCloskey, 1992; McCloskey, Caramazza, & Basili, 1985). This is the earlier of the two models and it offers a purely cognitive account of number processing without making specific claims about the neural architecture. A number of key features are worth noting. First, a distinction is made between specific number formats (both in input and output) and an abstract, internal, semantic representation. The format-specific codes are used for recognizing and producing numerical symbols. The semantic representation codes magnitude information. It also plays a critical role in transcoding and all forms of calculation. Calculation itself could be decomposed into different types of facts and procedures (e.g. separate stores and procedures for addition, subtraction, multiplication and division). **Transcoding** is the means by which one symbol is translated into another of a different type. It encompasses processes such as reading (written symbols to verbal ones), writing (verbal labels to written symbols) and others (e.g. from a written label to a hand gesture).

The second model to be considered is the Triple-Code Model proposed by Dehaene and colleagues (Dehaene, 1997; Dehaene & Cohen, 1995; Dehaene, Dehaene-Lambertz, & Cohen, 1998a). The "triple codes" refer to: (1) a semantic magnitude representation; (2) a verbal store of arithmetical facts; and (3) a visual representation for recognizing numerals and that acts as a "workbench" for performing certain calculations. Predictions are made at both a cognitive and neuroanatomical level. Considering each component in turn: the semantic magnitude representation is assumed to lie (bilaterally) in the intraparietal sulcus. The verbal store is used to

McCloskey's Model (1992) contains separate stores for calculation procedures, and separate stores for format-specific codes (e.g. Arabic numbers, number names). These are linked together via an amodal semantic representation of number. Reprinted from McCloskey (1992), Copyright 1992 with permission from Elsevier.

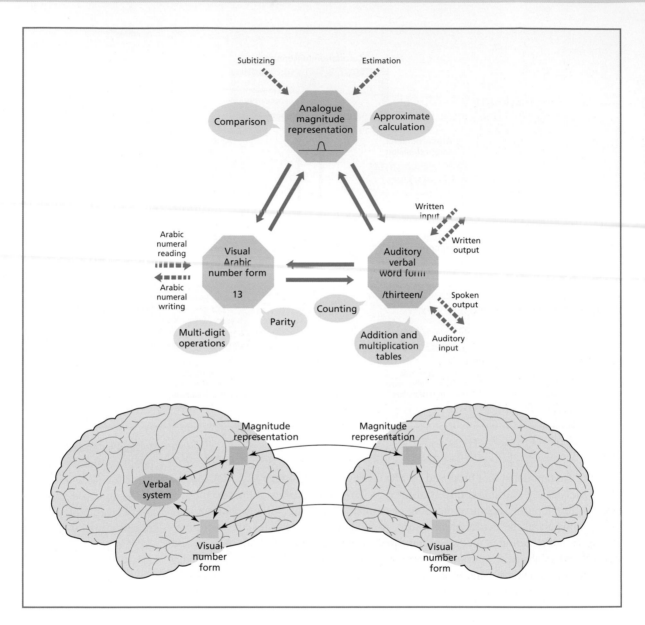

The three components of Dehaene's Triple-Code Model are: (a) a semantic magnitude representation; (b) a verbal store of arithmetical facts; and (c) a visual representation for recognizing numerals and a "workbench" for performing certain calculations. The two diagrams show the functional components (from Dehaene, 1992) and their approximate anatomical locations (Dehaene & Cohen, 1995).

comprehend and produce spoken number names and is also a repository for learned arithmetical facts and tables (e.g. "two and two is four"). This is assumed to be based in the left angular gyrus (Dehaene et al., 2003), which is in a separate region of the parietal lobe to number meaning. The visual code is used for recognizing and producing Arabic numerals, and may lie bilaterally in the fusiform gyrus (Dehaene, 1997). It also consists of a visuospatial workspace for conducting multi-digit operations (e.g. 256 + 142). Unlike the McCloskey Model, it is possible to produce verbal

The McCloskey Model	Dehaene's Triple-Code Model
• Cognitive model	• Cognitive and neuroanatomical model
• Number size is represented as base-10 units (divisible into 10s, 100s, 1000s, etc.)	• Number size is represented in a logarithmically compressed form (larger numbers harder to discriminate)
• Separate routines or stores for arithmetical operations (+, −, /, ×)	• No separate routines or stores for arithmetical operations (+, −, /, ×)
• Abstract (semantic) representations used for all calculations	• Some calculations are independent of number semantics (e.g. multiplication is verbal fact retrieval)
• Transcoding performed semantically	• Transcoding may be performed without semantics

numbers from visual numbers (3 → "three"), and vice versa ("three" → 3), without going through a central semantic bottle-neck. Dehaene's Triple-Code Model also suggests that not all calculations are carried out semantically. In particular, he argues that simple multiplications and additions may be retrieved as "facts" from the verbal code. More complicated sums (e.g. multi-digit addition) may be accomplished visually or using visual images. Both of these are residues of how the material was initially acquired; for example, the rote repetition of multiplication tables (for a more extreme variant of this proposal, see Campbell, 1994).

To contrast these two models, evidence will be drawn from three aspects of numerical cognition: the representation of number meaning (again), the nature of the processes that underpin different aspects of calculation (addition, subtraction, etc.) and mechanisms of transcoding between different numerical formats.

Base-10 units or linear-logarithmic semantics

Both models assume that there is a central semantic store of number magnitudes that is independent of specific number formats (e.g. numeral, number name, dots). However, the internal structure of this magnitude representation differs between the two models. The McCloskey Model assumes that the semantic number representation consists of separate representations for units (0–9), tens, hundreds, thousands and so on. Thus, the semantic representation mirrors the way that numbers are denoted in the place-value system. In the Dehaene Triple-Code Model, the semantic number representation consists of a single logarithmically compressed analogue scale. This is also referred to as a "mental number line". There is no division into tens, hundreds and so on. One of the main motivations for this proposal is the size effect that has already been discussed (i.e. it is harder to discriminate the magnitudes of two

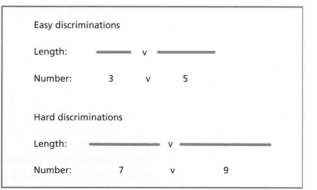

Is deciding which number is bigger equivalent to deciding which line is longer? A size effect is found for both, i.e. it is harder to decide which line/number is longer/larger as the line/number increases in size (even if the difference between lines/numbers is the same).

numbers that are large). The term "analogue" implies that number meanings (and other magnitudes) are represented on a continuous scale. Dehaene, Dupoux and Mehler (1990) asked participants to decide whether a two-digit number was smaller or larger than a reference number (e.g. 65). Participants were faster at rejecting 51 than 59, and the difference in reaction time was logarithmically determined. If the judgment had been made purely on comparing tens (i.e. fifty-something with sixty-something), then no difference would have been predicted. More recent studies using this paradigm have questioned these results. Nuerk, Weger and Willmes (2001) note that, in the 51 versus 65 comparison, both the digits representing tens and units lead to the same answer (5 < 6 and 1 < 5), whereas there is incompatibility in the case of 59 versus 65 (5 < 6 but 9 > 5). In a series of experiments, they propose that information about tens and units is independently available, in support of the McCloskey Model. They propose a hybrid model containing both logarithmic compression and separate tens and unit representations.

Calculation: Multiplication, addition, subtraction and division

According to Dehaene's Triple-Code Model, simple multiplication relies on retrieving facts from the verbal store just like any other word or phrase. Subtraction tends not to be learned in this rote fashion, and may make more demands on the number semantic representation. Addition can be performed in both ways – simple additions are likely to have been verbally learned by rote but can also be easily computed using the number semantic representation. In support of this, Delazer and Benke (1997) report a patient with a left parietal tumor who could recite and produce multiplication facts but had severely impaired knowledge of numbers (e.g. unable to add 13 + 9; unable to get 103 using poker chips with values of 100, 50, 10, 5, 1). By contrast, the severely aphasic patient, HAB (discussed above), could still perform many calculations but his multiplication (part of the verbal store in the Triple-Code Model) was performed atypically (Rosser et al., 1995). For example, 9×5 was done by converting it into an addition problem $18 + 18 + 9 = 45$ [i.e. $9 \times (2 + 2 + 1)$]. These studies support the conclusion that multiplication facts are stored in verbal form.

Other evidence has been brought to bear on this. First, difficulties in multiplication and subtraction form a double dissociation. Patients have been reported with greater difficulties in multiplication relative to subtraction (Cohen & Dehaene, 2000; Dehaene & Cohen, 1997; Van Harskamp & Cipolotti, 2001). The reverse dissociation has also been reported (Delazer & Benke, 1997; Van Harskamp & Cipolotti, 2001; Van Harskamp, Rudge, & Cipolotti, 2002). In healthy participants, Lee and Kang (2002) found that simultaneous phonological rehearsal delayed multiplication more than subtraction, and that holding a visuospatial image in mind delayed subtraction but not multiplication. In functional imaging experiments, the left angular gyrus (the putative "verbal code") shows more activity in multiplication than subtraction (Cochon et al., 1999), and is more involved in simple addition (below 10) than complex addition (above 10) (Stanescu-Cosson, Pinel, Van de Moortele, Le Bihan, Cohen, & Dehaene, 2000).

It is also important to stress that the McCloskey Model predicts dissociations between different aspects of calculation, but it does so in a different way. Calculation facts may be stored separately from procedural knowledge and number meaning, but no claims are made about whether some types of arithmetical operation are more "verbal" or "semantic" than others. Under the McCloskey Model, double dissociations between multiplication and subtraction merely reflect damage to distinct stores of knowledge (Dagenbach & McCloskey, 1992). There should be as many patterns of selective disruption as there are facts and operations.

As such, observation of addition and division impairments may critically distinguish between the models. Addition is, according to Dehaene's model, a combination of "verbal" (multiplication-like) and "semantic" (subtraction-like) processes and so it should never be selectively impaired relative to multiplication and subtraction. Addition is, in the McCloskey Model, merely a different operation and may be selectively impaired relative to other calculations. Van Harskamp and Cipolotti (2001) report a case of selectively impaired addition; patient FS was 96.3% correct for single-digit subtraction and multiplication but only 61.7% correct in single-digit addition. The authors suggest that this is more consistent with the McCloskey Model. Moreover, they have documented a patient with a selective impairment in performing division (Cipolotti & De Lacy Costello, 1995). Division is generally considered to be multiplication in reverse (e.g. 6/3 = ?, can be thought of as ? × 3 = 6), but the existence of this patient suggests this may not always be so. Again, this is more consistent with a separate stores account, such as in the McCloskey Model. Finally, it is claimed that subtraction (a semantic task according to Dehaene) can be impaired while the ability to comprehend and manipulate numerical quantities is intact (Van Harskamp et al., 2002).

McCloskey makes a distinction between "facts" and "procedures" that is not easily accommodated within the Triple-Code Model. For example, some patients appear to selectively lose the rule that multiplying by zero gives an answer of zero (see McCloskey, 1992) or lose the "borrowing rule" in multiplication (Sandrini, Miozzo, Cotelli, & Cappa, 2003). Another highly educated patient could not perform simple arithmetic with numbers (e.g. 2 + 3) but could do so with algebraic expressions, e.g. verifying whether $(a + b) × c = (a × c) + (b × c)$ (Hittmair-Delazer, Sailer, & Benke, 1995). Although the Triple-Code Model makes novel predictions and accounts for much data (particularly with regards to multiplication versus subtraction), some aspects of calculation aren't considered.

Transcoding: Reading, writing and saying numbers

Both the McCloskey and Dehaene models assume the existence of format-specific (and culturally dependent) codes for representing numbers, including Arabic numerals and written and spoken number names (8, "eight", EIGHT). These input and output codes may be selectively impaired. Anderson, Damasio and Damasio (1990) report a patient who could still read and write numbers but not letters or words, and Cipolotti (1995) reports the opposite dissociation. Ferro and Botelho (1980) report a patient who was unable to read (or use) mathematical operators (e.g. +) except when presented verbally (e.g. "plus"). On the spoken output side, McCloskey, Sokol and Goodman (1986) argue for a distinction between lexical and syntactic processes in number production. Patient HY's reading errors preserved the syntactic class (i.e. units, tens, hundreds...) but not the position within the class (e.g. 5 becomes "seven" but not "fifteen"), whereas patient JG's errors preserved the position in the class but not the syntactic class itself (e.g. 5 becomes "fifteen" but not "seven"). The production rules for writing Arabic numbers are somewhat different. Cipolotti, Butterworth and Warrington (1994) report a written "syntactic" deficit in which the patient failed to apply an overwriting-from-the-right rule. Thus, "one thousand nine hundred and forty-five" was written as 1000,945. Whilst these studies illuminate the workings of the number input and output processes, the key distinction between the models under consideration is whether these processes are directly connected (e.g. Triple-Code) or whether they must pass through a semantic bottle-neck (the McCloskey Model).

HY's reading of Arabic numbers	JG's reading of Arabic numbers
5 → *seven*	916 → *nineteen* hundred sixteen
17 → *thirteen*	912 → nine hundred *twenty*
317 → three hundred *fourteen*	620 → six hundred *two*

The two models make different predictions about transcoding (e.g. from Arabic digits to spoken number names). McCloskey (1992) regards the relationship between Arabic and verbal forms to be too irregular to be implemented by non-semantic transcoding procedures, at least for languages such as English (but for one account, see Power & Dal Martello, 1997). For example, the written digit 2 can be verbally rendered as "two", "twelve" or "twenty" depending on the context in which it is used (e.g. 2, 12, 20). The same cannot always be said of other languages. Chinese children must learn the numbers up to 10, but thereafter it is easy. Thus, 12 is literally translated as "ten-two" in Chinese and 21 is "two-ten-one". Not surprisingly, Chinese-speaking children outperform their English-speaking counterparts when learning to count (Miller & Stigler, 1987). In English, reading Arabic numbers does appear to use number semantics. For example, reading a digit aloud (e.g. 6) will facilitate reading of a similar-sized number (e.g. 5) relative to a more distant number (e.g. 9) (Brysbaert, 1995). However, the question is not whether transcoding *can* go via semantics (as this is uncontested) but rather whether it *must* go through semantics.

A number of studies have provided empirical evidence for a direct route between Arabic numeral recognition and verbal output that bypasses number semantics (Cipolotti, 1995; Cipolotti & Butterworth, 1995; Cipolotti, Warrington, & Butterworth, 1995; Seron & Noel, 1995). For example, the patient reported by Cipolotti and Butterworth (1995) could perform sums and subtractions up to six digits with 98% accuracy, but made errors on half of the Arabic numbers that he was asked to read. When asked to write "seventy thousand", he wrote 17,000, but when asked to add "56,748 + 13,252", he wrote 70,000. He read 4,070 as "four hundred thousand and seventy" and wrote "four thousand and seventy" as 1,070; yet, given 2,561 + 1,509, he could write 4,070. To explain this, Cipolotti and Butterworth added direct transcoding routes to the model of McCloskey, thus making it, in this respect, similar to that proposed in the Dehaene Triple-Code Model.

Why do Chinese-speaking children find learning to count easier than speakers of many other languages?

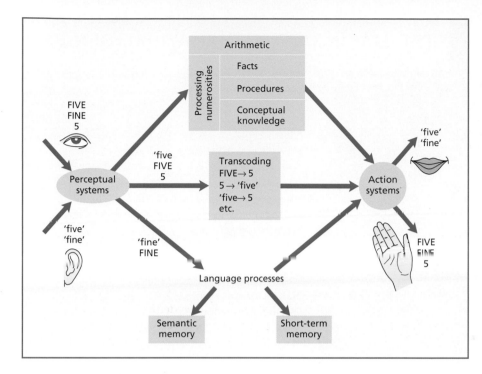

The model of Butterworth (1999) extends the model of McCloskey by adding separate transcoding routes that are independent of number meaning and calculation procedures. From Butterworth (1999), Copyright © Palgrave-Macmillan. Reproduced with permission of the author.

Evaluation

In summary, whereas some evidence from studies of number processing favors the Dehaene model over the McCloskey Model, other evidence favors the McCloskey Model over the Dehaene model. In terms of representation of number meaning, an analogical "mental number line" may be a necessary part of number meaning (as put forward by Dehaene), but may not be the only aspect of it. In terms of the representation of specific calculation procedures (addition, subtraction, multiplication, division), the McCloskey Model predicts that these different domains may be selectively impaired and evidence appears to support this over the suggestion that the operations differ solely according to the extent to which they are "semantic" or "verbal".

In terms of transcoding from Arabic to verbal forms, evidence favors both a semantic and an asemantic route (in line with the Dehaene model). Aside from the specific details and predictions of the models, it is worthwhile noting that the two models are conceptually different in the way that they approach numerical cognition. Dehaene's model attempts an explanatory account of *why* different types of numerical knowledge happen to be represented in a particular way (e.g. multiplication is different from subtraction because they tap different types of number-based representations). In contrast, the McCloskey Model offers a more descriptive account of different aspects of numerical cognition (e.g. multiplication and subtraction differ because they are assumed to be different in kind). Although the empirical evidence does not unequivocally support one model over the other, it is perhaps not surprising that the general approach taken by Dehaene has had far more influence in the field.

THE MAKING OF MATHEMATICAL GENIUS

Albert Einstein, 1879–1955 © Bettmann/Corbis.

Genius is ninety-nine percent perspiration and one percent inspiration.

(Albert Einstein)

Although many would be happy to label Einstein a genius, the extent to which this reflects hard work or innate skill could be debated endlessly. "Genius" is a notoriously difficult word to define, but some scientific progress has been made in understanding the neural basis of unusual ability. The mathematical prodigy, Gamm, was given a PET scan by Pesenti and colleagues (2001) whilst performing incredible calculations. For example, Gamm was able to divide prime numbers up to 60 decimal places (e.g. 31/61), and calculate the fifth root of numbers (e.g. $\sqrt[5]{8547799037}$). The regions of his brain that were activated included those involved in calculation *and* those involved in memory retrieval (control participants, given easier tasks, activated only the former). Gamm appears to have committed many number "facts" into long-term memory (he trained himself for six years for up to four hours per day) and uses these to reduce the high demands placed upon working memory during calculation. Observations of other prodigious calculators support this conclusion. Wim Klein can extract the thirteenth root of a 100-digit number in two minutes. To help him, he has learned the logarithm of all the integers up to 150 (Smith, 1983). Another prodigy, Aitken, solved the problem 777^2 by decomposing it to a simpler multiplication and a square: $[(777 + 23) \times (777 - 23)] + 23^2$. He had memorized all the squares from 1 to 100 (Gardner, 1990). In the case of Gamm and associates, it appears that their skills reflect perspiration more than inspiration. It is interesting to note that Einstein was almost certainly unable to perform these calculations and, conversely, it is a moot point as to whether Gamm is a "genius". Perhaps other factors are needed to explain the kind of ability possessed by Einstein (Witelson, Kigar, & Harvey, 1999).

It would be premature to state that there is no genetic contribution to numerical ability at all. Genetic factors may certainly contribute to numerical *disability* (e.g. Bruandet, Molko, Cohen, & Dehaene, 2003). The interaction between genes, environment and brain is likely to be complex. For example, autistic children may develop an unusual zeal for numbers that reflects a difficulty in socialization rather than a "gift" for numbers (Hermelin & O'Connor, 1986). Differences in motivation (as opposed to differences in some innate ability) can themselves be a product of genes and can result in a change in the environment that one creates for oneself.

ARE NUMBERS REPRESENTED IN A VISUOSPATIAL CODE?

One of the more general functions of the parietal lobes is in the representation of space, time and quantity (e.g. Walsh, 2003). Interestingly, the representation of number (another parietal function) appears also to have a strong spatial component. The evidence for this is summarized below:

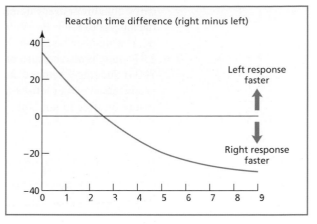

People are faster at making judgments about small numbers with their left hand and faster at making judgments about large numbers with their right hand. Adapted from Dehaene et al. (1993).

- When people are asked to make judgments about numbers (e.g. odd/even judgments), they are faster with their left hand for small numbers but faster with their right hand for larger numbers – the SNARC effect (Spatial Numerical Association of Response Codes; Dehaene, Bossini, & Giraux, 1993). It is as if they have a spatial number line running from left to right. The SNARC effect goes with the side of the response and not the responding hand. If the hands are crossed (so the left hand is on the right side of space, and vice versa), then smaller numbers are processed faster with a response on the left side of space (even when made with the right hand).
- Small numbers presented in the center of the screen (e.g. 1 and 2) orient attention to the left, but larger numbers (e.g. 8 and 9) orient attention to the right (Fischer, Castel, Dodd, & Pratt, 2003).
- Patients with visuospatial neglect (but who are not dyscalculic) show spatial biases in number bisection (e.g. "what number is midway between 11 and 19?...17") as if they are ignoring the left side of number space (e.g. Zorzi, Priftis, & Umiltà, 2002).
- Some people report being able to visualize numbers in particular visuospatial configurations, normally oriented from left to right (Sagiv, Simner, Collins, Butterworth, & Ward 2006).

Why are numbers represented in this particular way? There are, at least, two possible properties of numbers that lend themselves to this particular mode of representation. First of all, this type of representation could reflect the fact that numbers represent quantities (so-called cardinal numbers), perhaps in the form of a "mental number line". Alternatively, it could reflect the fact that numbers are an ordered set (ordinal numbers) and the fact that they refer to quantities is irrelevant. How is it possible to distinguish between these hypotheses? One way to address this is to consider other sequences such as the alphabet or the months of the year, which also form an ordered set but do not represent quantity. As it turns out, a response-side compatibility effect is found for these stimuli too (e.g. "January" is responded to faster by a left-sided response and "December" is responded to faster by a right-sided response) (Gevers, Reynvoet, & Fias, 2003). Moreover, people who consciously report number forms also tend to report them for other ordered sequences (Sagiv et al., 2006). This suggests that it is the ordinal property of numbers rather than magnitude (or "number meaning") that gives rise to this.

Evidence from neuropsychology suggests a separation between these different aspects of number representation. Delazer and Butterworth (1997) report a patient with impaired cardinal numbers but spared ordinal numbers. He used counting to carry out almost every number task. He could say what number came after 8, but not the answer to 8 + 1. By contrast, Dehaene and Cohen (1997) report a patient who was poor at number bisection, but not for other ordinal sequences (e.g. days). A recent ERP study is also consistent with this distinction (Turconi, Jemel, Rossion, & Seron, 2004). Judging whether a number was smaller or larger than 15 (a quantity judgment) produced an earlier left-lateralized signal, whereas judging whether a number comes before or after 15 (an order judgment) produced a later bilateral signal.

SUMMARY AND KEY POINTS OF THE CHAPTER

- Knowledge of numbers is a basic and near universal aspect of cognition. It is aided by language and cultural knowledge, but is not directly dependent on these.
- Number meanings can be selectively impaired by brain damage (dyscalculia) and may have a dedicated neural substrate (including the intraparietal sulcus).
- Whereas the right hemisphere enables approximate representation of number (e.g. about 10), the left hemisphere may enable exact, or countable, quantification (e.g. exactly 10). This is likely to be because the left hemisphere number–meaning system can interface with symbolic/linguistic representations.
- Different types of calculation procedure (subtraction, addition, multiplication, division) may be selectively impaired by brain damage.
- Transcoding between Arabic numerals and number names may be mediated both semantically and non-semantically.
- Numbers have a visuospatial component that may relate to the fact that they form an ordered set.

EXAMPLE ESSAY QUESTIONS

- To what extent is knowledge of number a product of innate endowment or cultural factors?
- Does knowledge of numbers have a separate neural substrate? Can it be selectively impaired?
- "Numerical cognition is performed by the left hemisphere." Discuss.
- Is language essential or helpful for understanding numbers?
- Does the brain contain separate systems for performing the arithmetical operations of multiplication, subtraction, addition and division?
- Compare and contrast the models of numerical cognition proposed by Dehaene versus McCloskey.
- What is the evidence that humans possess a "mental number line"?

RECOMMENDED FURTHER READING

- Campbell, J. I. D. (2005). *The handbook of mathematical cognition*. Hove: Psychology Press. An extensive set of papers on the topic written by different experts in the field. More advanced readings.

- Nieder, A. (2005). Counting on neurons: The neurobiology of numerical competence. *Nature Reviews Neuroscience*, 6, 177–190. An excellent summary of contemporary findings.

CHAPTER 14

CONTENTS

The executive brain

The "**executive functions**" of the brain can be defined as the complex processes by which an individual optimizes his or her performance in a situation that requires the operation of a number of cognitive processes (Baddeley, 1986). A rather more poetic metaphor is that the executive functions are the brain's conductor, which instructs other regions to perform, or be silenced, and generally coordinates their synchronized activity (Goldberg, 2001). As such, executive functions are not tied to one particular domain (memory, language, perception and so on) but take on a role that is meta-cognitive, supervisory or controlling. Executive functions have traditionally been equated with the frontal lobes, and difficulties with executive functioning have been termed as "frontal lobe syndrome". More accurately, executive functions are associated with the *prefrontal region* of the frontal lobes, and it is an empirically open question as to whether all aspects of executive function can be localized to this region.

The concept of executive functions is closely related to another distinction with a long history in cognitive science – namely, that between automatic and controlled behavior (e.g. Schneider & Shiffrin, 1977). This distinction has already been encountered in another context, namely, the production of actions. When driving a car, one may accelerate, change gear and so on, in an apparently "autopilot" mode. But if the traffic is diverted through an unfamiliar route, then one would need to override the automatic behavior and exert online control. This is often assumed to require the use of executive functions (Norman & Shallice, 1986). The same logic may also apply in situations that lack motor output, i.e. in the online control of thoughts and ideas. This provides humans (and possibly other species) with a remarkable opportunity; namely, to mentally simulate scenarios and think through problems "in the mind" without necessarily acting them out. It is hardly surprising, therefore, that some theories of executive function are effectively synonymous with aspects of *working memory* (Baddeley, 1996; Goldman-Rakic, 1992, 1996; Kimberg & Farah, 1993). The notion of working memory has been introduced elsewhere (see Chapter 9) and can be thought of as consisting of a network of both storage components (often related to the parietal lobes) and control processes (typically related to prefrontal cortex).

Two other general points are in need of mention in this preamble. First, the extent to which behavior is "automatic" (i.e. not requiring executive function) versus "controlled" (i.e. requiring executive function) may be a matter of degree rather than all or nothing. Even when generating words in fluent

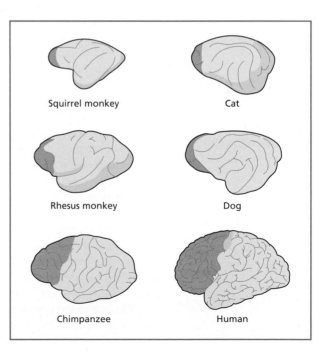

Enlargement of the prefrontal cortex shows an evolutionary progression (the brains are not drawn to scale). In humans, this region occupies almost a third of the cortical volume. Adapted from Fuster (1989).

conversation, some degree of executive control may be exerted. For example, one may need to select whether to say the word "dog", "doggy", "Fido" or "Labrador" depending on pragmatic context, rather than relying on, say, the most frequent word to be selected. Second, one must be cautious about falling into the trap of thinking that controlled behavior requires an autonomous controller (e.g. Monsell, 1995). Control may be a two-way, or many ways, street. Decisions may arise out of an interaction of environmental influences (bottom-up processes) and influences related to the motivation and goals of the person (top-down processes). The sight of a cream cake may trigger an "eat me" response, but whether or not one does eat it may depend on whether one is hungry or dieting.

The chapter begins with a consideration of the types of situation that require the involvement of executive functions and presents evidence from cognitive neuroscience for the role of the prefrontal cortex in these situations. The chapter then goes on to consider different cognitive and neuroanatomical models of executive functions. Finally, evidence for functional specialization of different brain regions is evaluated, with particular reference to the cognitive roles of the lateral prefrontal cortex and the anterior cingulate cortex. Before discussing executive functions, it is worthwhile to review the anatomy of the prefrontal cortex.

ANATOMICAL AND FUNCTIONAL DIVISIONS OF THE PREFRONTAL CORTEX

The most basic anatomical division within the prefrontal cortex is that between the three different cortical surfaces. The *lateral* surface of the prefrontal cortex lies anterior to the premotor areas (Brodmann's area 6) and the frontal eye fields (in Brodmann's area 8). This surface lies closest to the skull. The *medial* surface of the prefrontal cortex lies between the two hemispheres and to the front of the corpus collosum and the anterior cingulate cortex. In terms of anatomy, the anterior cingulate is not strictly part of the prefrontal cortex but it does have an important role to play in executive functions and as such will be considered in this chapter. The *orbital* surface of the prefrontal cortex lies above the orbits of the eyes and the nasal cavity. This is also called the *ventromedial* prefrontal or *orbitofrontal* cortex. The orbitofrontal cortex and parts of the medial prefrontal cortex are involved in the regulation of social behavior and utilization of emotional cues to guide behavior. Patients with lesions to this region typically exhibit socially disadvantageous behavior (sociopathy) but they may do well on other, purely cognitive, measures of executive function. Issues relating to social and emotional cognition are covered in Chapter 15; this chapter deals with non-social executive functions such as devising rules and plans, switching between tasks, manipulating information in working memory, avoiding habitual responses and so on.

The prefrontal cortex has extensive connections with virtually all sensory systems, the cortical and subcortical motor system and structures involved in affect and memory. There are also extensive connections between different regions of the prefrontal cortex. These extensive connections enable the coordination of a wide variety of brain processes. The lateral prefrontal cortex is more closely associated with sensory inputs than the orbitofrontal cortex. It receives visual, somatosensory and auditory information, as well as receiving inputs from multi-modal regions that integrate across senses. In contrast, the medial and orbital prefrontal cortex is

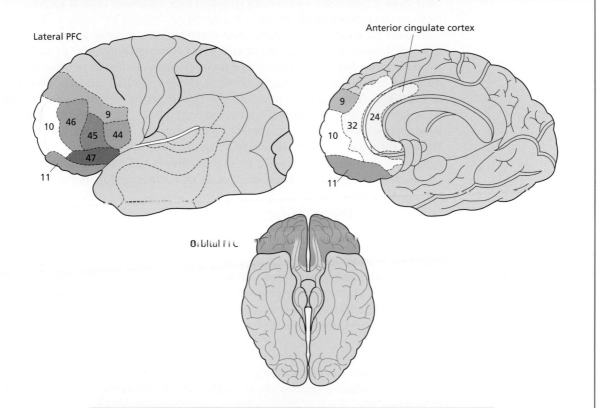

Brodmann's areas	Other names	Possible functions (left hemisphere)	Possible functions (right hemisphere)
45, 47, 44*	Ventro-lateral prefrontal cortex (VLPFC)	Retrieval and maintenance of semantic and/or linguistic information (Area 44 + 45 on left also called Broca's area)	Retrieval and maintenance of visual and/or spatial information
46,9	Dorso-lateral prefrontal cortex (DLPFC)	Selecting a possible range of responses, and suppressing inappropriate ones; manipulating the contents of working memory	Monitoring and checking of information held in mind, particularly in conditions of uncertainty; vigilance and sustained attention
10	Anterior prefrontal cortex; frontal pole; rostral prefrontal cortex	Multi-tasking; maintaining future intentions / goals whilst currently performing other tasks or sub-goals. (The medial portion has been implicated in "theory of mind" – see Chapter 15)	
24 (dorsal) 32 (dorsal	Anterior cingulate cortex (dorsal)	Monitoring in situations of response conflict and error detection	

* Parts of area 44 may have more in common with lateral premotor area 6, in that it is implicated in both the observation and production of action and speech.

The prefrontal cortex has three different surfaces: the lateral surface (top left), the medial surface (top right) and the orbitofrontal surface (bottom). The numbers refer to Brodmann areas that are discussed in the text.

more closely connected with medial temporal lobe structures critical for long-term memory and processing of emotion.

Aside from these gross anatomical divisions, a number of researchers have developed ways of dividing different regions into separate areas of functional specialization. These may correspond approximately, although not exactly, with different Brodmann areas (e.g. Fletcher & Henson, 2001; Petrides, 2000; Stuss et al., 2002). These include areas on the figure on the previous page as ventrolateral (including Brodmann's areas 44, 45 and 47), dorsolateral (including Brodmann's areas 46 and 9), the anterior prefrontal cortex (Brodmann's area 10) and the anterior cingulate. These terms are sufficient to capture most of the functional distinctions discussed in this chapter but it is to be noted that not all researchers regard the prefrontal cortex as containing functionally different subregions.

EXECUTIVE FUNCTIONS IN PRACTICE

This section considers some concrete scenarios in which executive functions may be needed. In their seminal paper, Norman and Shallice (1986) outline five types of situation in which automatic activation of behavior may be insufficient and in which executive functions may be needed to optimize performance:

1. Situations involving planning or decision making.
2. Situations involving error correction or trouble-shooting.
3. Situations where responses are not well learned or contain novel sequences of actions.
4. Situations judged to be dangerous or technically difficult.
5. Situations that require the overcoming of a strong habitual response or resisting temptation.

Taking each of these points in turn, it will be shown that studies of functional imaging and studies of brain-damaged individuals provide converging evidence for a role of the prefrontal cortex in executive functions.

Planning and decision making

The "Tower of London" task requires beads to be moved from an initial position to a specified end-point. Performance can be measured in terms of time to complete task or number of moves taken (relative to the optimal number of moves). From Shallice (1982), Royal Society of London.

Patients with lesions to the prefrontal cortex often show clinical symptoms of poor planning and decision making. To test this formally, a number of tests have been devised. Shallice (1982) reports a test called the "Tower of London", in which patients must move beads from one stake to another to reach a specified end-point. Patients with damage to the left anterior frontal lobe take significantly more moves.

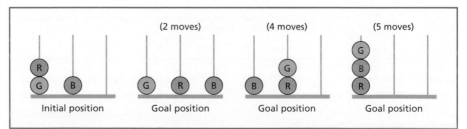

This implies that they perform by trial and error rather than planning their moves (see also Morris, Miotto, Feigenbaum, Bullock, and Polkey, 1997). Functional imaging studies suggest that the dorsolateral prefrontal cortex activity increases with the number of moves needed to reach the end-point (Rowe, Owen, Johnsrude, & Passingham, 2001). This is consistent with a role for this region in selecting and manipulating information in working memory during planning.

The "Tower of London" involves problem solving on a novel but rather artificial task. A more **ecologically valid** test was documented by Shallice and Burgess (1991). In the "Six Element Test" the patient is given six open-ended tasks to perform within a 15-minute period (e.g. arithmetic, writing out names of pictures). Critically, patients are instructed to attempt each task. However, they will be unable to complete all of them in the time allowed, and more points are awarded for earlier items. Constraints are placed on some of the ordering of tests. The patients would often fail to switch tasks, spend too long planning (e.g. taking notes) but never execute the plans and so on. The patients could easily perform the isolated tasks but their difficulties were only apparent when they had to coordinate between them.

The "Multiple Errand" test is similar but requires the patient to multi-task in a shopping precinct (e.g. finding the price of tomatoes, being in a certain place 15 minutes after starting). Social conventions as well as task rules were broken, such as asking the shopkeeper for a free birthday card (Shallice & Burgess, 1991).

KEY TERMS

Ecological validity
The extent to which a task relates to everyday situations outside of the laboratory.

Wisconsin Card Sorting Test
A test of executive functions involving rule induction and rule use.

Error correction and trouble-shooting

In the **Wisconsin Card Sorting Test**, patients with lesions of the prefrontal cortex often fail to correct errors that are pointed out to them and, instead, stick to a previously correct response (Milner, 1963; Nelson, 1976). This has been termed perseveration. In the test, a series of cards must be matched against reference cards. The cards can be matched according to one of three dimensions (which the patient must infer), namely color, number and shape. For example, in the color condition a blue card must be grouped with blue cards and red cards grouped with red cards (ignoring number and shape). After each trial, patients are told whether they are correct or not. Eventually, they are told that they are incorrect and they must then trouble-shoot, i.e. start sorting according to number or shape. Many patients fail to make this shift and continue to incorrectly sort according to the previous rule.

One event-related fMRI study compared trials in which healthy participants stick with the present rule versus trials in which they are told to change rule (Monchi, Petrides, Petre, Worsley, & Dagher, 2001). Dorsolateral prefrontal activity was associated with relating feedback (correct or incorrect) to the current rule; this was interpreted as monitoring. However, ventrolateral prefrontal and basal ganglia regions were associated with rule changes following feedback that the response was incorrect.

In the Wisconsin Card Sorting Test, patients are given a card that can be sorted by a number of rules (matching shape, number or color). Sometimes the rule unexpectedly changes and the patients must adjust their responses to the new rule. Based on Milner (1963).

Novelty

A number of clinical tests have been devised that require patients to develop strategies for dealing with novel situations. In the Cognitive Estimates Test (Shallice & Evans, 1978), patients with damage to the prefrontal cortex are impaired at producing estimates for questions in which an exact answer is unlikely to be known. For example, "How many camels are in Holland?" In the FAS Test (Miller, 1984), participants must generate a sequence of words (not proper names) beginning with a specified letter ("F", "A" or "S") in a one-minute period. This test is not as easy as it sounds (have a try) and involves generating novel strategies, selecting between alternatives and avoiding repeating previous responses. Patients with left lateral prefrontal lesions are often impaired (Stuss et al., 1998).

Dangerous or difficult situations

Wilkins, Shallice and McCarthy (1987) gave participants easy and difficult tasks involving the counting of clicks, in which the difficult condition involved sustained attention. Patients with lesions to the prefrontal cortex (particularly on the right) were impaired on the difficult but not the easy task. An appreciation of danger and risk is likely to involve the use of affective, reward-based cues. The ventromedial and orbitofrontal cortex may be particularly important for this aspect of executive functions and will be considered in Chapter 15.

Overcoming habitual response

The **Stroop Test** (Stroop, 1935) is a classic test of response interference that is based on the principle that reading words is more habitual than saying colors. If the word BLUE is printed in red ink and participants are asked to say the ink color (i.e. "red"), they are slowed relative to a control condition in which the printed word is not also a color name (Stroop used color-naming of Nazi swastikas as one of his control conditions; for a review, see MacLoed, 1991). Patients with lesions to the left prefrontal cortex show difficulties with this task (Perret, 1974) and functional imaging shows that the response conflict is associated with activation of the anterior cingulate (Bench, Frith, Grasby, Friston, Paulesu, & Frackowiak, 1993).

The Hayling Test requires patients to produce sensible or nonsense completions to sentences in which a prepotent response is available (Burgess & Shallice, 1996b). For example, "The captain wanted to stay with the sinking..." could elicit, in the sensible condition, the answer "ship" and, in the nonsense condition, "banana". Both patients with left and right prefrontal lesions are impaired on this task (Burgess & Shallice, 1996b), although one imaging study emphasized the role of the left dorsolateral prefrontal cortex (Nathaniel-James, Fletcher, & Frith, 1997).

Evaluation

The preceding section outlined the types of situation in which executive functions may be required. Much of this research has been motivated by the patterns of performance of patients with prefrontal lesions on a number of clinical tests and, more recently, by functional imaging studies based on such tests. Many of these tests involve multiple processes and deficits. As such, they are not always straightforward to interpret. Subsequent sections will examine in more detail the contribution of different processes to executive functioning.

THE FRONTAL LOBES AND INTELLIGENCE

Given the progressive enlargement of the frontal lobes with evolution, one would intuitively expect some relationship with intelligence. Although many non-specialists have a notion of what "intelligence" consists of, a precise definition in cognitive or neuroscientific terms is lacking. Many standard tests of IQ, such as the WAIS (Wechsler Adult Intelligence Scale; Wechsler, 1981) tap many different cognitive skills, e.g. calculation, factual knowledge, speed of processing, object recognition. The assumption, rightly or wrongly, is that some generic capacity in the brain is involved in all these tasks over and above the specific capacities for calculation, object recognition and so on. Jung and Haier (2007) conducted an extensive review of brain imaging studies of intelligence and argued that the integration between frontal and parietal regions was crucial. However, patients with lesions to the prefrontal cortex do not perform any worse on these tests of IQ than patients with lesions elsewhere (Warrington, James, & Maciejewski, 1986). However, these tests predominantly tap something called *crystallized intelligence*, which is based on previously acquired knowledge, rather than *fluid intelligence*, which may rely on current ability to solve problems (Cattell, 1971). To investigate this, Duncan, Burgess and Emslie (1995) selected patients with prefrontal cortex damage and high WAIS IQ (between 125 and 130; scale average is 100). Tests of fluid intelligence were administered. The patients were 22–38 points lower on this measure compared to their WAIS scores. They were also lower compared to a group of controls matched for WAIS IQ, sex, age and socioeconomic status. Thus, "intelligence" is compromised after frontal lobe damage but only in those situations in which novelty, flexible thinking and problem solving are implicated – that is, in those situations that putatively tap executive functions. An additional skill not captured by these tests is social intelligence – as exemplified by cooperation (the ability to work together to achieve common goals), empathy (understanding the thoughts and feelings of others), deception and so on. It has been suggested that the intelligence of primates evolved to solve social problems (Humphrey, 1976). This form of social intelligence appears to be dependent on the integrity of the prefrontal cortex (e.g. Stuss, Gallup, & Alexander, 2001b).

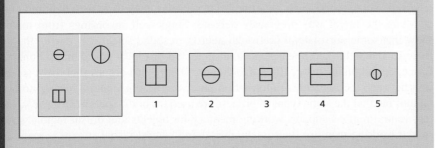

Patients with frontal lobe damage are impaired on tests of "fluid intelligence" such as this. Reprinted from Duncan et al. (1995), Copyright 1995, with permission from Elsevier.

MODELS OF EXECUTIVE FUNCTION

Although there are many different approaches to explaining executive functions, it is important to emphasize from the outset that there are some things that all models of executive functions appear to have in common. First, there is broad agreement as to what kinds of things that a model of executive functions needs to explain. As already outlined, this includes the ability to override automatic behavior in order to deal with novel situations, plan for the future rather than live for the moment and so on. Second, in order to account for this, the different models typically have a common set of core features. The type of processing must be inherently flexible in order to cope with changing tasks from moment to moment. It can implement a seemingly infinite range of "if-then" type mappings ("wink whenever I say bumblydoodle" to take an example from Miller and Cohen, 2001). Furthermore, almost all models assume that executive functions have a biasing influence (they make certain behaviors more or less likely) rather than dictating to the rest of the brain.

As for differences between models, one of the key distinctions is the extent to which different models assume that executive functions can be decomposed into several modular-like processes versus executive functions construed as a more unitary idea. Those that do argue for some degree of different specialization also differ in terms of whether the specialization is for different kinds of material (e.g. words versus scenes) or for different kinds of operations (e.g. manipulation versus maintenance) or both. This is not an all-or-nothing debate, as some models may assume relative degrees of specialization. It is also to be noted that different models have emerged to explain somewhat different sets of data. Some models have been largely derived from single-cell recordings (i.e. almost exclusively from non-humans), whereas others derive more from human lesion and imaging data. This can make it hard to know whether contradictory findings reflect true species differences or differences in tasks and methods.

The sections below will contrast four influential models of executive functions.

Goldman-Rakic's working memory model

Goldman-Rakic's (e.g. 1992, 1996) account is based primarily on animal lesion studies and single-cell recordings. Prefrontal activity may provide a refreshing mechanism for information stored in posterior regions of the brain. Lesions to the lateral prefrontal cortex can impair the ability to hold a stimulus/response in mind over a short delay, but not in responding *per se* or in long-term learning *per se* (Butters & Pandya, 1969). In one delayed response task, monkeys were presented with a box in a particular location on the screen. The box then disappeared and the monkey was required to hold the location "in mind". After a delay, they were then required to look at where the target was previously delayed. Single-cell recordings from monkeys show that some dorsolateral prefrontal neurons respond selectively during the delay period and that this is the neural mechanism for holding locations in mind (Funahashi, Bruce, & Goldman-Rakic, 1989). Goldman-Rakic (1996) argues that there is a division between the *content* of information processed in dorsolateral and ventrolateral regions but that the same types of process are used for both. Specifically, she suggests that ventral regions support working memory for objects and dorsal regions support spatial working memory (that is, the dorsal and ventral visual stream is manifested at the level of executive functions). Recent evidence is inconsistent with this view.

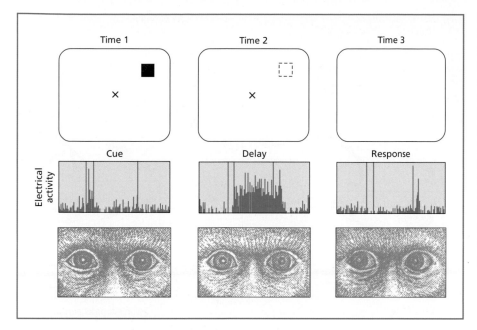

Single-cell recordings in the dorsolateral prefrontal cortex show that different neurons respond to (a) studying a target location, (b) holding it "in mind" during a delay, and (c) responding to the removal of a cue by moving the eyes to that location. From Goldman-Rakic (1992). Reprinted with permission of Patricia J. Wynne. www.patriciawynne.com

Rao, Rainer and Miller (1997) report that individual neurons can change their responsiveness from being object based to being location based as the demands of the task change, irrespective of whether they are located in dorsolateral or ventrolateral regions.

Petrides' model of maintenance versus manipulation

Petrides (1996, 2000, 2005) offers an alternative account of working memory to that of Goldman-Rakic. He argues that the dorsolateral and ventrolateral prefrontal regions should be distinguished by the fact that they are engaged in different types of process and not that they are specialized for different types of material (e.g. spatial versus object based). Like Goldman-Rakic and others (e.g. Baddeley, 1986), Petrides proposes that the main storage site of information is not within the frontal lobes themselves but in the posterior cortex.

This is a hierarchical model of working memory. In this model, the ventrolateral prefrontal cortex is responsible for activating, retrieving and maintaining information held in the posterior cortex. The dorsolateral prefrontal region is responsible when the information held within this system requires active manipulation (e.g. ordering of information). Petrides and Milner (1982) found that patients with prefrontal lesions were impaired on a **self-ordered pointing task**.

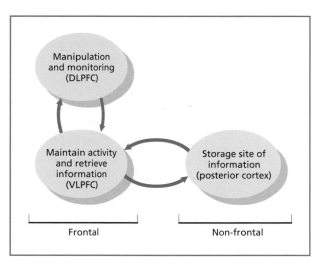

A hierarchical model of working memory in which ventrolateral prefrontal cortex (VLPFC) activates and maintains information, and the dorsolateral prefrontal cortex (DLPFC) manipulates that information.

A self-ordered pointing task based on Petrides and Milner (1982). Subjects are required to point to a new object on each trial and, as such, must keep an online record of previous selections.

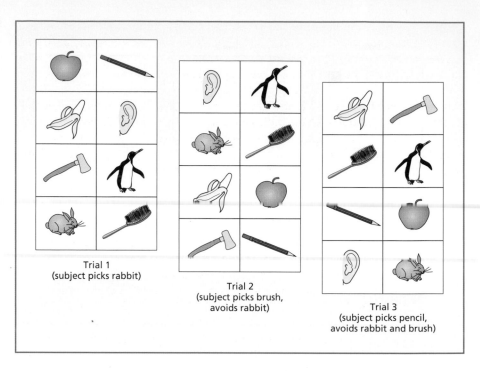

Trial 1
(subject picks rabbit)

Trial 2
(subject picks brush, avoids rabbit)

Trial 3
(subject picks pencil, avoids rabbit and brush)

The patients were presented with an array of eight words or pictures and, on the first trial, required to pick any one. On the second trial, they were asked to pick a different one from the first; on the third trial, they must pick a different one again and so on. As such, they must maintain and update an online record of chosen items. Similar studies on monkeys suggest the critical region to be the dorsolateral prefrontal cortex (Petrides, 1995). In a PET study, Owen, Evans and Petrides (1996) found that short-term retention of spatial locations was associated with ventrolateral prefrontal activity. However, if they had to maintain and update a record of which locations had been marked and avoid these, then dorsolateral prefrontal activity was found.

The original and revised SAS model

The original version of the SAS (Supervisory Attentional System) model consisted of a set of tasks and behaviors (termed schemas) and a biasing mechanism that activated/suppressed these schemas according to the individual's current goals (Norman & Shallice, 1986). The activation of schemas was conceptualized as a balance between bottom-up processes (cues in the environment, habits, etc.) and top-down processes (task instructions, long-term plans, etc.). Disruption of this balance, for example by a prefrontal lesion, would tend to result in recent or habitual responses being inappropriately elicited (e.g. in the Stroop Test, or Wisconsin Card Sort), poor planning and so on. This model was discussed in more detail with regards to action selection, but applies to selection of ideas and solutions too.

The revised version of the SAS model retains elements of the original model (i.e. biasing activation of schemas), but decomposes executive functions into several more modular-like processes. For example, the model of Shallice and Burgess (1996) contains no fewer than eight partially independent processes such as "goal setting", "control of monitoring and checking" and "rejection of schema". These eight different processes are grouped into three different stages: one for specifying a new schema, one for implementing it (this being akin to a working memory) and one for monitoring the results of schema implementation. Although the concept of distinct types of executive processes is controversial (e.g. Duncan & Owen, 2000), there is evidence from human brain lesions and functional imaging for some degree of relative specialization with the prefrontal cortex. For instance, the left prefrontal cortex may be particularly concerned with setting up schemas and the right prefrontal cortex may be particularly concerned with monitoring their effectiveness. This is considered in more detail in the remainder of the chapter.

Miller and Cohen's integrative model

Miller and Cohen's (2001) model has a number of similarities with the models discussed so far. Like the original SAS model, it considers the prefrontal cortex as providing biasing signals that enable novel and non-automatic mappings to be set up between sensory inputs, internal states and response outputs. Unlike the revised SAS model, it does not endorse a modular-like decomposition of executive functions. It does, however, allude to some possible functional differences. For example, Miller and Cohen suggest that emotional, social and appetitive stimuli may be harder to control, and perhaps require a different kind of mechanism, to less emotive, more cognitive associations (e.g. between color and shape).

The intellectual roots of Miller and Cohen's (2001) model lie more closely in the single-cell recordings tradition of Goldman-Rakic, rather than the human lesion studies of Shallice and colleagues. They emphasize that the prefrontal cortex maintains the goals and rules rather than the information itself. Prefrontal neurons respond primarily to the rules of the task rather than the specific stimulus or response (Asaad, Rainer, & Miller, 1998, 2000). For example, they may respond to a conjunction of a stimulus and response (e.g. "look left when I see object A") but not to the same stimulus out of context ("see object A") or the same response in a different context (e.g. "look left when I see object B"). However, the prefrontal cortex may implement more than just a working memory. For example, if one intends to buy a pen later in the day at the stationery store it is unlikely that this goal is actively held in mind all day. A more likely scenario is that the intention is laid down in long-term memory but there can be delayed re-activation of the task later in the day due to subsequent remembering or an environmental cue (e.g. seeing the store). This is termed **prospective memory**. Rainer, Rao and Miller (1999) identified single-cell recordings in monkey prefrontal cortex that appeared consistent with prospective coding of information rather than simple maintenance of sensory information (i.e. responding to the expectation of a stimulus).

Evaluation

Models of executive function differ according to the extent to which they propose the existence of specialized sub-routines (e.g. the Petrides' model, the SAS model), describe it in terms of a single working memory (e.g. Goldman-Rakic's model) or describe it as a temporary network of associations that are reconfigured from task to task (e.g. Miller and Cohen's model). However, all models assume that the prefrontal cortex has a biasing influence on more specialized routines in the brain and that this enables some control over behaviors that might be routine and automatic but not necessarily appropriate. The next section will consider evidence that different parts of the prefrontal cortex are specialized for somewhat different functions, as this is a key criterion for distinguishing between the models considered so far.

FUNCTIONAL SPECIALIZATION WITHIN THE LATERAL PREFRONTAL CORTEX?

The notion that executive functions may contain several distinct processes lends itself to the idea that these will have different neural substrates within the prefrontal cortex. A distinction has already been drawn between possible differences in function between the ventrolateral and dorsolateral prefrontal cortex. The following sections will consider whether differences in function also exist between the left and right hemispheres for these regions, and will then go on to consider other prefrontal regions. In general, both functional imaging (Fletcher & Henson, 2001) and lesion analysis (Stuss et al., 2002) suggest that there is some degree of functional specialization within prefrontal cortex. However, it is to be noted that the degree of functional specialization is likely to be relative rather than absolute (i.e. not strictly modular). Executive functions are, by their very nature, required for flexible behavior and so flexibility is likely to be a design specification at the neural level too. Nonetheless, different regions of the prefrontal cortex connect to different regions of the posterior cortex and so a degree of functional specialization may emerge for this reason.

Response selection and the left dorsolateral prefrontal cortex

Frith, Friston, Liddle and Frackowiak (1991) asked participants to freely select which of two fingers to move ("free choice"). In the control condition, the finger to move was specified by a touch ("no choice"). They found increased PET activity in the left dorsolateral prefrontal cortex (DLPFC) and the anterior cingulate cortex. These results are not specific to manual movements. They also found the same pattern of results in a comparison of "free" generation of words given a letter (e.g. hear "F", say "feather") relative to simple repetition of a word (e.g. hear "hot", say "hot"). Thus, the left lateralization is not material-specific. The region is also active when participants have to select *when* to make a response, rather than *which* response to make (Jahanshahi, Jenkins, Brown, Marsden, Passingham, & Brooks, 1995). In a review of the literature, Frith (2000) argues that the role of the left DLPFC is in "sculpting the response space". He suggests that the region is responsible for highlighting the range of possible responses and for suppressing inappropriate responses.

Producing sequences in a random order is cognitively demanding and is believed to rely heavily on executive functions (Baddeley, 1966a). If one is required to produce sequences of digits or letters at a fast rate, then randomness breaks down and participants start generating familiar sequences from memory, such as consecutive runs (4, 5, 6; X, Y, Z) or stored knowledge (e.g. acronyms, "B, B, C"; telephone numbers). Repetitive TMS over the left, but not right, DLPFC results in less random and more familiar sequences (Jahanshahi, Profice, Brown, Ridding, Dirnberger, & Rothwell, 1998). Moreover, activity in this region, as measured by PET, is associated with the ability to generate random sequences (Jahanshahi, Dirnberger, Fuller, & Frith, 2000). As randomness breaks down at fast rates, then so does activity in this region. (The study also found activity in the right dorsolateral region but the activity was not closely associated with performance of the task). The results of these studies are consistent with the view that left DLPFC is involved in specifying sets of responses.

This notion of suppressing inappropriate responses bears a clear relation to Petrides and Milner's (1982) self-ordered pointing task, in which participants must point to a new object on each trial, hence suppressing responses to old objects. It is interesting to note that patients with left frontal damage were reported to be severely impaired on all types of material (words, pictures, abstract designs), whereas right frontal patients had milder impairments restricted to pictures and designs (Petrides & Milner, 1982). However, the precise interpretation offered is of keeping track of what has happened (i.e. working memory) rather than suppressing inappropriate responses (e.g. Petrides, 2000). These two accounts are clearly related but attempts have been made to tease them apart. One study found that repetitive TMS over left DLPFC impairs "free choice" even in tasks with no working memory demands (Hadland, Rushworth, Passingham, Jahanshahi, & Rothwell, 2001). The previous responses were displayed on a monitor so they need not be held in mind.

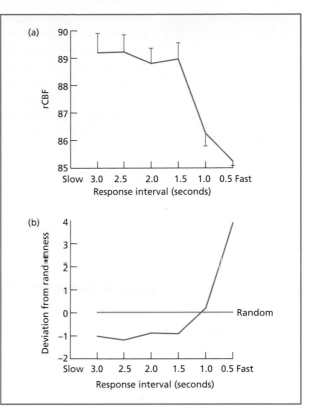

Activity in the left dorsolateral prefrontal cortex (a) is associated with ability to generate random sequences (b). When responses are required at a fast rate, the activity decreases and the responses start to deviate substantially from randomness. Reprinted from Jahanshahi et al. (2000), Copyright 2000 with permission from Elsevier.

Monitoring and the right dorsolateral prefrontal cortex

Monitoring is the process of relating information currently held in mind back to the task requirements. It is also a checking mechanism to ascertain whether retrieved or perceived information is valid. The region may be important both for monitoring the content of internally held information, such as monitoring the content of episodic or working memory (e.g. Habib, Nyberg, & Tulving, 2003), as well as for monitoring the content of externally presented information, as in tasks of **sustained attention** (e.g. Kanwisher & Wojciulik, 2000). Cabeza, Dolcos, Prince, Rice, Weissman and Nyberg (2003) directly compared fMRI activity in a memory retrieval task (word recognition) with a non-memory task of sustained attention (did the stimulus blip once, twice or never during a 12-second presentation). The study found common regions of right DLPFC activity between the two tasks. As such, it appears as if the region is related more to monitoring and attending than to memory or perception.

Monitoring demands may be greatest in conditions of uncertainty, and activity in this region

KEY TERMS

Monitoring
The process of relating information currently held in mind back to the task requirements.

Sustained attention
Retaining focus on the task requirements over a period of time.

tends to be greater during conditions of uncertainty. In episodic memory retrieval, activity in this region depends on how confident participants are in their judgment (low confidence, greater activity) irrespective of whether the stimulus was indeed old or new (Henson, Rugg, Shallice, & Dolan, 2000). This again suggests a role in monitoring rather than memory *per se*. Maril, Wagner and Schacter (2001) found that activity was greatest in the right DLPFC when subjects were in a tip-of-the-tongue state (induced by cues such as: Chinatown + director, Iraq + capital), relative to when they were certain that they did not know the answer, or when the solution was accessible to them. This suggests that activity in the region is related to uncertainty (in the tip-of-the-tongue state) rather than retrieval success or failure. Other regions were implicated too, including the anterior cingulate, and right ventrolateral prefrontal cortex (VLPFC). But the left DLPFC was not activated, suggesting some hemispheric differences.

One popular working memory task in the literature requires monitoring of a sequence of items in which the participant must decide whether the currently presented stimulus is the same as the one presented immediately before (1-back) or two items before (2-back) or three items before (3-back); the task is referred to as the **N-back task**. Performance can be contrasted with simple target detection (e.g. press a button if you see the letter "X"), which is also called 0-back. Cohen et al. (1997a) contrasted brain activity with fMRI in 3-back, 2-back, 1-back and 0-back. Activity in the right DLPFC showed a step function such that it was active only when judgments needed to be made for two or three back (i.e. 3 = 2 > 1 = 0). These conditions may be associated with greater uncertainty and require greater monitoring.

Reverberi, Lavaroni, Gigli, Skrap and Shallice (2005) devised a test of rule induction that appears to be sensitive to different prefrontal lesion sites in human patients (following Burgess & Shallice, 1996a). Patients are shown a sequence of cards containing ten numbered circles; one of the circles is colored blue. Their task is to decide which of the next circles will be colored in. The rules can change unexpectedly, and the rules themselves are more abstract than in the Wisconsin Card Sorting Test. Reverberi et al. found that patients with left lateral prefrontal lesions were impaired at inducing the rules, and that this difficulty was found irrespective of whether or not they had a working memory impairment (as assessed by their memory of successive spatial positions). They suggest that the difficulty lies

Different instructions in the N-back task alter the working memory load: is the present stimulus an X (0-back), is it the same as the one before (1-back), is it the same as the stimulus two before (2-back), is it the same as the stimulus three before (3-back)?

in synthesizing schemas, possibly related to Frith's (2000) notion of "sculpting the response space". In a second phase of the experiment, the sequence of blue circles was interspersed with sequences of red circles that followed a different rule. When red circles appeared, the task was simply to press that circle. When the blue circles appeared, the task was to predict the next in the sequence. Patients with right lateral prefrontal lesions and those with anterior cingulate lesions failed to revert back to the blue rule after the interfering red sequence, despite being instructed to do so. Reverberi et al. interpreted this as a failure to check or monitor their responses, consistent with a right frontal involvement in this function. Although this lesion study does not enable more specific anatomical predictions (e.g. concerning ventrolateral and dorsolateral regions), it provides strong evidence for different roles for left and right frontal cortex in executive functions.

Maintenance and the ventrolateral prefrontal cortex

The role of the ventrolateral prefrontal cortex has already been discussed in relation to the maintenance of information in working memory. It may be responsible for activating stored knowledge on the basis of current task demands to facilitate further decision making, or it may provide a refresher or rehearsal mechanism to sustain activity in posterior regions. In terms of the present discussion, one point to note is that there is evidence for material-specific differences between the left and right frontal lobes in these regions. Wagner, Poldrack, Eldridge, Desmond, Glover and Gabrieli (1998a) found left VLPFC activation (area 45/47) when participants were instructed to memorize words, and right DLPFC activation when participants were instructed to memorize colored visual textures. Manoach et al. (2004) report right VLPFC activity during spatial working memory. Finally, Kelley et al. (1998) extended this finding to words (left VLPFC), pictures of familiar objects (bilateral VLPFC) and unfamiliar faces (right VLPFC) given both memorizing and passive viewing instructions.

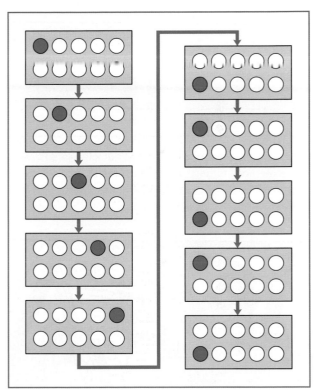

Patients are shown a sequence of cards containing ten numbered circles. One of the circles is colored blue. Their task is to decide which of the next circles will be colored in. The rules can change unexpectedly. In this example, the rule shifts from +1 to alternation (between circles 1 and 6).

One alternative account of the function of the *right* ventrolateral region is in terms of inhibition (Aron, Monsell, Sahakian, & Robbins, 2004). Inhibition can be understood in terms of reducing the likelihood of a particular behavior. As such, one would expect less inhibition after lesions in this area but greater brain activity (in normal participants) in situations that require inhibition relative to ones that don't. Indeed, patients with lesions in this region have particular difficulty in withholding a response when they receive a stop signal (Aron, Fletcher, Bullmore, Sahakian, & Robbins, 2003) and functional imaging data suggests that it is involved in both the inhibition of verbal and motor responses (Xue, Aron, & Poldrack, 2008).

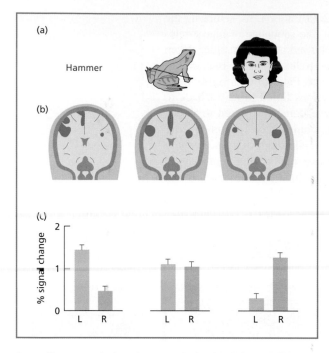

Attending to verbal and non-verbal stimuli has different consequences for left and right prefrontal activity. Reprinted from Kelley et al. (1998), Copyright 1998 with permission from Elsevier.

How do we perform multi-tasking? Could the anterior prefrontal region hold the key?

Further consideration of the role of the ventrolateral prefrontal cortex in memory and language (notably Broca's area) can be found in Chapters 9 and 11.

Multi-tasking and the anterior prefrontal cortex

Until recently, little was known about the function of the anterior-most part of the frontal lobes (also called rostral prefrontal cortex or the frontal pole). However, a number of recent studies and reviews have suggested that the region is specifically involved when multiple tasks need to be coordinated (Burgess, 2000; Christoff et al., 2001; Koechlin, Basso, Pietrini, Panzer, & Grafman, 1999a, Ramnani & Owen, 2004). Koechlin et al. (1999a) performed an fMRI experiment in which participants were required to hold in mind a main goal while concurrently performing subgoals. Neither holding in mind a goal by itself (working memory) nor switching between alternate goals was associated with activity in this region. Only when these two elements were combined was activity found in this region.

Similarly, Burgess, Scott and Frith (2003) conducted a prospective memory test in which participants had to hold in mind a future intention while performing an ongoing attention-demanding task, relative to a baseline in which no prospective memory was required. Anterior prefrontal activation was found only in the prospective memory condition. Given that it is impossible to do lots of things at the same time, all **multi-tasking** experiments can be regarded as having an element of maintaining future goals while current goals are being dealt with. Patients with lesions in this region may be particularly impaired at multi-tasking, even though each task in isolation may be successfully performed and even though they perform normally on other tests of executive function, including the Wisconsin Card Sorting Test and verbal fluency (Burgess, Veitch, Costello, & Shallice, 2000; Shallice & Burgess, 1991).

Evaluation

There is good evidence to suggest that different regions of the prefrontal cortex are implicated in different functions. This provides strong support for the notion that executive functions can be fractionated and do not consist of a unitary system. Some of the executive functions (e.g. in the DLPFC) may be largely lateralized according to the type of process, whereas others (e.g. in the VLPFC) may be largely lateralized according to the type of material being processed. The anterior prefrontal region may be important for coordinating goals and subgoals and is implicated in multi-tasking.

Many researchers would not fully endorse the view presented above and would favor a unitary/integrated account of prefrontal cortex function (as already discussed). Analyses showing that the same prefrontal regions are recruited by a wide variety of tasks (e.g. Duncan & Owen, 2000) and single-cell studies on monkeys demonstrating changes in the response properties of prefrontal neurons (e.g. Miller & Cohen, 2001) are cited as evidence against functional specialization. How can these two opposing views be reconciled? It will be for future researchers to decide how the different approaches can be linked together, if at all. However, the following points are worth bearing in mind:

- There could be inter-species differences between humans and other primates (most single-cell studies are conducted on the latter).
- Finding that a region is activated by many different types of task doesn't necessarily rule out functional specialization (e.g. monitoring may be used in diverse tasks such as sustained attention and episodic memory retrieval, to name but two).
- Functional specialization may be relative rather than absolute (e.g. the left DLPFC may be relatively specialized for selecting possible responses but may also be implicated in many other executive functions).
- It is not possible to find tasks that tap only executive functions or only one supposed type of executive function (this problem applies to all methodologies).

EGAS MONIZ AND THE PREFRONTAL LOBOTOMY

The career of Egas Moniz was an eventful one. In politics, he served as Portuguese Ambassador to Spain and was President of the Portuguese Delegation at the Paris Peace Conference in 1918, following the First World War. However, it is his contribution to neurology and neurosurgery that gained him fame and infamy. In the 1920s he developed cerebral angiography, enabling blood vessels to be visualized with radioactive tracers. In 1935, he developed the prefrontal lobotomy/leucotomy for the treatment of psychiatric illness. Between then and 1954, over 50,000 patients would have the procedure in the USA (Swayze, 1995) and over 10,000 in the UK (Tooth & Newton, 1961). This brought Moniz mixed fortunes. He was awarded the Nobel Prize for Medicine. However, he had to attend the ceremony in a wheelchair because, some years previously, he had been shot in the spine and partially paralyzed by one of his lobotomized patients.

Moniz's operation was designed to sever the connections between the prefrontal cortex and other areas, notably the limbic system (Moniz, 1937, 1954). This was often done in frighteningly simple ways. For instance, an icepick-type implement was inserted through the thin bony plate above the eyes and waggled from side to side.

At that point, there were no pharmacological treatments for psychiatric complaints. Lobotomy was used for a variety of disorders, including obsessive-compulsive disorder, depression and schizophrenia. The measurement of "improvement" in the patients was rather subjective, and the fact that the lobotomized patients tended to be duller and more apathetic than before was not sufficient to halt the appeal of the lobotomy. Formal assessments of cognitive function, if they had been carried out, would undoubtedly have revealed impairments in executive function.

Moniz died in 1955. By then, his surgical innovation had been phased out and its success has been left to history to judge.

THE ROLE OF THE ANTERIOR CINGULATE IN EXECUTIVE FUNCTIONS

Historically, the anterior cingulate cortex has been classified as belonging to the limbic lobe rather than the frontal lobes. However, a more detailed understanding of its neural connectivity has suggested that it may function as an interface between limbic and frontal regions. In their review, Bush, Luu and Posner (2000) distinguish between two functionally different regions of the anterior cingulate. A more dorsal region is termed the "cognitive division" and may be related to executive functions. It has strong interconnections with the DLPFC. This may explain why these regions tend to be activated together in functional imaging studies. It also has connections with parietal, premotor and supplementary motor areas. A more rostral "affective division" is connected with limbic and orbitofrontal regions. The remainder of this section will focus on the cognitive/executive region of the anterior cingulated, and further use of the term "anterior cingulate" in this chapter will be used to refer to this region unless stated otherwise. The affective division will be considered in Chapter 15, which covers the Social and Emotional Brain.

One postulated role of the anterior cingulate in executive functions is in the detection of errors (e.g. Carter, Braver, Barch, Botvinick, Noll, & Cohen, 1998). In human reaction time experiments, the trial immediately after an error (error + 1) tends to be slower and more accurate than after a correct trial (correct + 1) (Rabbitt, 1966). This implies the existence of some cognitive mechanism that monitors for errors and recalibrates task performance accordingly (e.g. slowing down to ensure greater accuracy). In macaque monkeys with anterior cingulate lesions, errors are more likely on "error + 1" trials than "correct + 1" trials

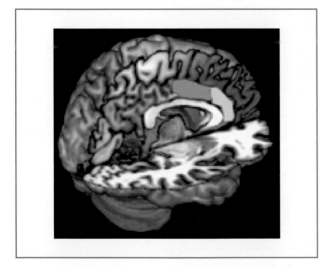

The anterior cingulate cortex lies above the corpus callosum on the medial surface of each hemisphere. It has been suggested that there are two broad divisions: a dorsal region implicated in executive functions (blue) and a ventral region implicated in emotional processing (green).

(Rushworth, Hadland, Gaffan, & Passingham, 2003). This suggests that no such adjustment is made following errorful behavior, and errors are more likely to follow errors. Moreover, when monkeys (Gemba, Sasaki, & Brooks, 1986) and humans (Dehaene, Posner, & Tucker, 1994) make errors an "error potential" can be detected at the scalp that appears to have its origins in the anterior cingulate. This response is called an **error-related negativity** and its onset is simultaneous with the error being made and peaks around 100 ms after the response (Gehring, Goss, Coles, Meyer, & Donchin, 1993). The studies cited above are ambiguous as to whether the anterior cingulate is important just for the detection of the error or also for the subsequent compensatory behavior. Event-related fMRI shows anterior cingulate activity on the error trial, with greater activity on the error + 1 trial in the lateral prefrontal cortex associated with behavioral adjustment (Kerns, Cohen, MacDonald, Cho, Stenger, & Carter, 2004). This suggests that the anterior cingulate's role is limited to error detection and not compensation, and the lateral prefrontal cortex is responsible for adjusting ongoing behavior.

A related role for the anterior cingulate may be in evaluating **response conflict**. The classic example of response conflict is provided by the Stroop Test (Stroop, 1935). In this task, participants must name the color of the ink and ignore reading the word (which also happens to be a color name). The standard explanation for the response conflict generated by this task is that reading of the word occurs automatically and can generate a response that is incompatible with that required (e.g. MacLoed & MacDonald, 2000). A number of functional imaging studies show activation of the anterior cingulate on incongruent trials, with high response conflict, relative to congruent trials (Bench et al., 1993; Carter et al., 2000; Pardo, Pardo, Janer, & Raichle, 1990). Patients with lesions in or around the anterior cingulate have difficulties in suppressing the prepotent response on incongruent Stroop trials (Stuss, Floden, Alexander, Levine, & Katz, 2001a).

Is a unitary cognitive account of the role of the anterior cingulate in executive functions (as opposed to in affective/social functions) possible? Carter and colleagues argue that it is (e.g. van Veen & Carter, 2002). They suggest that a role in error detection and conflict resolution are compatible with a more general role in evaluation of responses, whether correct or incorrect, and whether they are planned or already produced (but see Critchley et al., 2003; Swick & Turken, 1999).

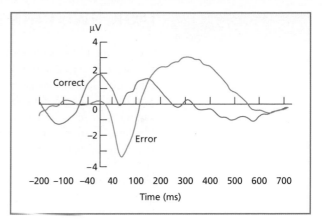

Error-related negativity is found at EEG scalp recordings following production of an incorrect response.

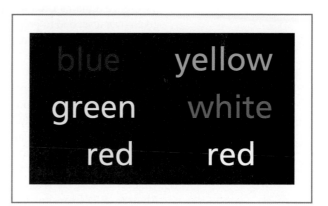

The Stroop Test involves naming the color of the ink and ignoring the written color name (i.e. "red, green, yellow, blue, yellow, white").

KEY TERMS

Error-related negativity
An electrical potential ("error potential") that can be detected at the scalp when an error is made.

Response conflict
A situation in which a prepotent incorrect response needs to be overcome to perform a task successfully (as in Stroop color naming).

TASK SWITCHING

Many of the tasks used to study executive functions are complex and are often based on tests that were initially developed to diagnose dysfunction of the prefrontal cortex rather than inform cognitive theory. One notable exception to this trend is the **task switching** paradigm (for a review, see Monsell, 2003). Every task requires its own configuration (or schema) that specifies the goal and the means to that goal. Task switching, therefore, involves discarding a previous schema and establishing a new one.

Imagine that you are a participant seated facing a computer screen, looking at a square 2 × 2 grid. A digit and/or number pair (e.g. L9) will appear in each part of the grid, moving clockwise, and you must make a response to each stimulus. When the stimulus is in the upper half of the grid, you must decide if the letter is a consonant or vowel. When the stimulus is in the lower half, you must decide if the digit is odd or even (some participants would get the complementary set of instructions). This produces two types of trial – those in which the task switches and those in which it does not. The reaction times for the switch trials are significantly slower, and this difference remains even though the change is predictable and even if the subject is given over a second to prepare before each stimulus is presented (Rogers & Monsell, 1995). This difference in reaction time between switch and non-switch trials is called the *switch cost*.

What is the cognitive process that gives rise to the switch cost? There are likely to be different contributions. It may involve deliberate retrieval from memory of the alternative goals and responses (Mayr & Kleigl, 2000). Previous schemas may also be triggered automatically. A previously used schema can slow down performance on the current task, even after several minutes, if the currently used stimuli remain compatible with the previous schema (Allport, Styles, & Hsieh, 1994). However, part of the switch cost must relate to presentation of the stimulus itself, because giving subjects as long as five seconds to prepare does not abolish the effect (Kimberg, Aguirre, & D'Esposito, 2000; Sohn, Ursu, Anderson, Stenger, & Carter, 2000).

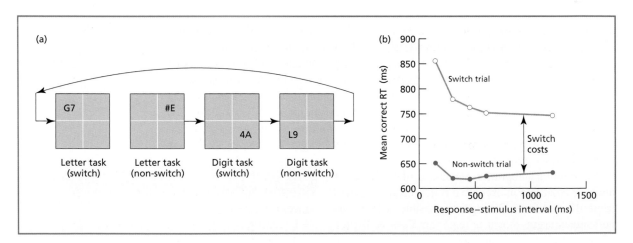

When the digit and/or letter pair is in the top half, the subject must decide whether the letter is a consonant or vowel. When it is in the bottom half, the digit must be classified as odd or even. This generates two types of trial – those in which the task switches and those in which it does not. Switch trials are significantly slower even though the switch is predictable and even if subjects are given over one second to prepare before the stimulus is shown. Reprinted from Monsell (2003), Copyright 2003 with permission from Elsevier.

The switch cost may either reflect suppressing the old task or reflect setting up the new task. This can be evaluated by considering switches between easy and hard tasks. Is it more difficult to switch from an easy to a hard task, or from a hard to an easy task? Surprisingly, perhaps, the switch cost is greater when switching from hard to easy. For example, bilinguals are faster at switching from their first to their second language than from their second to their first language in picture naming (Meuter & Allport, 1999). With Stroop stimuli, people are faster at switching from word naming to color naming (easy to hard) than color naming to word naming (hard to easy) (Allport et al., 1994). The switch cost may have more to do with suppressing the old task than setting up the new one.

Functional imaging studies reveal a variety of prefrontal regions together with the anterior cingulate cortex to be involved in task switching, by comparing switch trials with no-switch trials (e.g. Ravizza & Carter, 2008) or contrasting the switch preparation time (before the stimulus) with switch execution after the stimulus (e.g. Brass & von Cramon, 2002). However, it is not always straightforward to link specific regions with specific cognitive processes because there are often different types of switching mechanism. Most task-switching experiments involve both a switching of response rules as well as a switching of the stimulus selected. In the study described previously, for example, the left hand switches from responding "consonant" to responding "odd", and the stimulus selected switches from letter to digit (i.e. multiple aspects of the task are switched).

Bilingual speakers are faster at switching from their first to their second language, than from their second to their first language. How can this apparently paradoxical result be explained?

Rushworth, Hadland, Paus and Sipila (2002) attempted to control for these differences in a combined fMRI and TMS study. They note that TMS over the medial frontal lobes (in an area close to the anterior cingulate, called the pre-supplementary motor area) was found only to impair switch trials requiring a change in response mappings, but not a change in the stimulus that is responded to. They suggest that the medial frontal lobes are important for reassignment of stimulus–response pairings (e.g. which button to press), whereas lateral frontal regions may be involved in selection of the current rule (e.g. whether to respond to color or shape).

Dreher and Grafman (2003) conducted an interesting study that attempted to tease apart the different roles of the anterior cingulate versus lateral prefrontal cortex. They compared performing two tasks simultaneously (dual-tasking) versus performing two tasks successively (task switching). The anterior cingulate was more active in dual-tasking relative to task switching (increased response competition), but the left DLPFC was more active in task switching relative to dual-tasking (increased demands on setting up the schema).

The asymmetry of task switching (i.e. that it is easier to switch from easy to hard than vice versa) implies an important role of prefrontal inhibitory mechanisms that switch off the old task configuration. The same region in right ventrolateral cortex, assessed using fMRI, is involved in both task-switching on the Wisconsin Card Sort and in withholding responses on tasks in which there is an occasional stop signal (Konishi, Chikazoe, Jimura, Asari, & Miyashita, 1999). It is possible that, whilst the left prefrontal cortex is involved in setting up new task sets, the right prefrontal cortex is more concerned with inhibiting old ones. Patients with both left and right prefrontal lesions are impaired at task switching but for different reasons (e.g. Aron et al., 2004; Mayr, Diedrichsen, Ivry, & Keele, 2006). Specifically, damage to the right prefrontal cortex may result in difficulties in inhibiting the old task.

Evaluation

Task switching is a seemingly simple paradigm that can be useful for investigating different processes comprising executive functions. Although seemingly simple, it is unlikely that there is going to be anything akin to a "task-switching module" in the brain. Rather task switching may be an outcome of multiple processes (executive and non-executive) that depend on the nature of the task and what it is that is being switched (the response, the attended stimulus, or the whole task).

NEUROECONOMICS

The relatively new field of **neuroeconomics** uses brain-based methods and theories to account for economic decision making (for a review see, Loewenstein, Rick, & Cohen, 2008). The term "economic" can be construed in the broadest sense as referring not only to financial decisions (e.g. whether to spend, save or invest) but to other kinds of decisions that require allocation of a scarce resource (e.g. time) or an assignment of "value". Whereas much of theoretical economics describes how people *should* make decisions to achieve maximum benefits, the psychology of economics (and neuroeconomics) is concerned with how people actually *do* make decisions. For example, most people do not purchase clothing for purely utilitarian reasons (i.e. to keep warm) but for other reasons, including the need to advertise one's social status or personality, or, in some cases, because one simply enjoys the act of shopping. That is, the concept of value may have more to do with the perceived rewards to a given individual than the actual functional reward that may ultimately be obtained. There is also a strong social element as to how economic decisions are made. For example, in a financial sharing game (the "ultimatum game"; Guth, Schmittberger, & Schwarze, 1982), one player can choose to give money to another player, and that player can then choose whether to accept the offer (and the offer is then split) or reject the offer (both players leave with nothing). The person on the receiving end typically rejects offers that are less than 20% of the pot because they perceive the offer as unfair. However, this is at odds with a purely utilitarian approach (i.e. any offer of money is better than no money), suggesting that social and emotional rules (i.e. of fairness) are valued more than financial gain. Sanfey, Rilling, Aaronson, Nystron and Cohen (2003) studied this game using fMRI, in which people received either fair or unfair offers. Indeed, activity in a part of the brain that is linked with emotional processes (the insula) reliably predicts whether a player will reject an unfair offer.

Much of the emerging field of neuroecomics is concerned with the interaction between one's gut reactions (intuition or emotion) and one's goals and beliefs. It is no coincidence that this section appears at the end of the chapter on Executive Functions and before the chapter on Social and Emotional Processes. For example, one's brand loyalty (e.g. to Pepsi versus Coke) may sometimes be at odds with one's true taste preferences when they are assessed blind. Whereas the dorsolateral prefrontal cortex is associated with people's beliefs about which of two brands they are tasting (Pepsi versus Coke), the orbitofrontal cortex is associated with their actual ratings of how nice each drink is (McClure, Lee, Tomlin, Cypert, Montague, & Montague, 2004b).

Another example of a potential conflict between immediate rewards and long-term goals is the extent to which people are willing to forego immediate rewards for a potentially larger future reward. Do you want to go on holiday this year or invest the money for a better holiday in the future? Do you spend your money now or invest in a pension scheme? McClure, Laibson, Lowenstein and Cohen (2004a) argued that there were two different mechanisms for this kind of decision making, depending on whether an immediate reward was an option (i.e. a reward now v. at some future time) or not (i.e. different rewards at two future points in time). Whereas the former was associated with activation in regions related to emotional processes, the latter was more associated with executive functions including prefrontal and parietal regions.

SUMMARY AND KEY POINTS OF THE CHAPTER

- Executive functions are needed to optimize performance when: several cognitive processes need to be coordinated; a situation is novel or difficult; a situation does not require an automatic response (trouble-shooting, problem solving). The role of executive functions is typically described as "supervisory" or "controlling".
- Functional imaging studies and studies of brain-damaged patients point to a key role of the prefrontal cortex in executive functions. Patients with lesions here may have difficulties in problem solving, overcoming habitual responses, multi-tasking and so on.
- Working memory is an important aspect of executive functions and may consist of several subsystems, including maintenance (holding things in mind) and manipulation (e.g. re-ordering the content of information held in mind).
- A region in the left dorsolateral prefrontal cortex appears to be crucial

for setting up schemas and choosing a plausible set of responses. A region in the right dorsolateral prefrontal cortex appears to be important for monitoring when retrieved information is ambiguous or requires sustained attention.

- Ventrolateral prefrontal regions may be important for retrieving and maintaining information from posterior regions, and also (on the right side) in inhibition.
- The anterior prefrontal region may be critical for multi-tasking and maintaining goals.
- The dorsal anterior cingulate appears to be important for detecting errors and detecting response conflict, although lateral prefrontal regions may be needed to act on this information and modify behavior.

EXAMPLE ESSAY QUESTIONS

- Can executive functions be fractionated?
- What are the problems faced by clinical tests aimed to detect deficits in executive function?
- Is there an executive component to working memory? What is the evidence for it?
- Do the functions of the left prefrontal lobe differ from the right prefrontal lobe?
- How do we switch from one task to another?

RECOMMENDED FURTHER READING

- Goldberg, E. (2001). *The executive brain: Frontal lobes and the civilised mind*. Oxford: Oxford University Press. A good place to start for the uninitiated.

- Miller, E. K. & Cohen, J. D. (2001). An integrative theory of prefrontal cortex function. *Annual Review of Neuroscience, 24*, 167–202. A good overview of the neuroscientific evidence.

- Monsell, S. & Driver, J. (2000). *Control of cognitive processes: Attention and performance XVIII*. Cambridge, MA: MIT Press. A useful collection of papers at a more advanced level.

- Stuss, D. T. & Knight, R. T. (2002). *Principles of frontal lobe function*. Oxford: Oxford University Press. A useful collection of papers at a more advanced level.

CHAPTER 15

CONTENTS

The social and emotional brain

There is currently an unprecedented interest in the cognitive neuroscience of emotions. This interest has come about from research suggesting that emotions guide much of our ongoing behavior (contrary to the view that relying on emotions is the antithesis of behaving rationally; see Damasio, 1994) and, in particular, that emotions have a crucial role to play in shaping our social interactions. This has not always been the case in cognitive psychology. Cognitive psychology has tended to view the mind in terms of computer-inspired information processing models of cognition. It is entirely feasible to devise information-processing models of language, memory and even decision making that do not make reference to emotion. But, of course, computers don't mate or have predators. Nor do they socialize.

One contemporary view of **emotions** treats them as "action schemas" that prepare the organism for certain behaviors, particularly those with survival value (e.g. avoid threats, disease, mating; see Lane & Nadel, 2000). It is important to distinguish between conscious aspects of an emotion and the unconscious (or preconscious) aspects. The conscious aspects of emotion are the subjective feelings of that emotion. The preconscious aspects of emotion may concern, for example, detection of a potential threat. When stated in this way, the cognitive neuroscience of emotion differs little from the cognitive neuroscience of, say, vision or memory (e.g. vision has many different processes, both conscious and preconscious). It is also important to clarify the distinction between emotion and mood. A **mood** is used to refer to situations in which a particular emotion occurs frequently or continuously (e.g. fear is an emotion, and anxiety is a mood).

There are a number of reasons why the topics of emotion processing and social cognitive neuroscience have been placed together in this chapter. Recognizing the emotional state of others (e.g. in their faces) is likely to be an important component of social interactions. We may use our own emotional response or the perceived emotional response of another person to regulate our behavior, for example to terminate aggression, to console or to avoid contamination. Rather than studying individual brains in isolation, social cognitive neuroscience studies how the brain responds in the presence of other individuals.

This chapter begins by considering how the brain processes social and emotional cues that are derived from perceptual processing of stimuli, and faces in particular. It then considers the role that internal bodily responses (such as those associated with the skin conductance response) play in emotion processing, in decision making and in person recognition. Finally, it considers how the brain represents mental states, such as beliefs and desires. Most of us have an intuitive understanding of other people's mental states and this facilitates normal social interaction. However, a failure to represent the mental states of others may be a central feature of disorders such as autism.

KEY TERMS

Emotion
States/processes that prepare the organism for certain behaviors, particularly those with survival value.

Mood
Situations in which a particular emotion occurs frequently or continuously.

PROCESSING EMOTIONS AND SOCIAL CUES: READING FACES AND READING EYES

One of the first challenges faced by the empirical study of emotions is how to go about categorizing them or, indeed, whether it makes more sense to treat all emotions as a single entity. Are some types of emotion (e.g. happy, sad) more basic or primary than other types (e.g. love, jealousy)? Are emotional categories independent of language and culture? One of the most influential ethnographic studies of the emotions concluded that there are six basic emotional categories, which are independent of culture (Ekman & Friesen, 1976; Ekman, Friesen, & Ellsworth, 1972). These are: happy, sad, disgust, anger, fear and surprise. These studies were based on comparisons of the way that facial expressions are categorized and posed across diverse cultures. An alternative approach does not regard emotions as different categories but treats them instead as lying on particular dimensions (e.g. Rolls, 2000). For example, emotions can be defined according to their valence (whether they are pleasant or unpleasant) and their arousal (how intense the emotion is). If this type of theory were true, then one might expect to find different brain regions that selectively process negative or positive emotions, or patients with selective lesions to one of these dimensions. However, it will be shown that more fine-grained dissociations are found in practice (e.g. a selective difficulty with fear) and this is more consistent with the categorical than the dimensional approach to emotions.

Complex emotions such as jealousy, pride, embarrassment and guilt may be different from the basic emotions that can be easily recognized in another's face. They also imply awareness of another person's attitude to oneself, or awareness of oneself in relation to other people (Blakemore, Winston, & Frith, 2004). As such, they may involve a more complex attributional process, which is needed to represent the thoughts and beliefs of other people. Complex emotions may be modulated by cultural display rules more than basic emotions. For example, feelings of embarrassment come about by understanding that one's actions have met (or could meet with) the disapproval of other people. In such instances, a visual display of embarrassment can restore good relations with others following a social transgression (Semin & Manstead, 1982).

The neural substrates of emotion processing

One early and influential theory of emotion identified it with a circuit of predominantly limbic system structures that became known as the **Papez circuit**. These included the regions of the cingulate cortex, hippocampus, hypothalamus and anterior nucleus of the thalamus. The work of MacLean (1949) extended this idea to incorporate regions such as the amygdala and orbitofrontal cortex. The different regions were hypothesized to work together to produce an integrated "emotional brain". There are a number of reasons why these earlier views are no longer endorsed by contemporary cognitive neuroscience. First, some of the key regions of the Papez circuit can no longer be considered to carry out functions that relate primarily to the emotions (e.g. the role of the hippocampus in learning). Second, contemporary research places greater emphasis on different types of emotion (e.g. fear versus disgust). Each basic emotion may form part of its own circuit, and different parts of the circuit may make different cognitive contributions.

In the following sections, contemporary findings on the neural substrates of emotion are presented and the implications for behavior and social cognition text discussed.

KEY TERM

Papez circuit
A limbic-based circuit that was once thought to constitute a largely undifferentiated "emotional" brain.

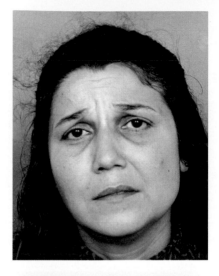

Paul Ekman tested a wide range of different cultures and concluded that there are six basic types of emotion expressed in faces: sad, happy, disgust, surprise, anger and fear. Copyright © Paul Ekman. Reproduced with permission.

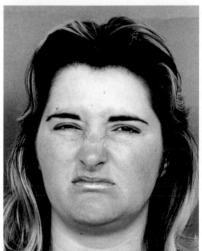

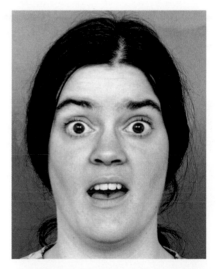

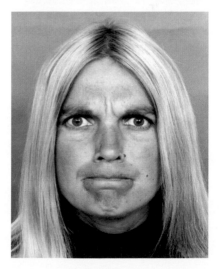

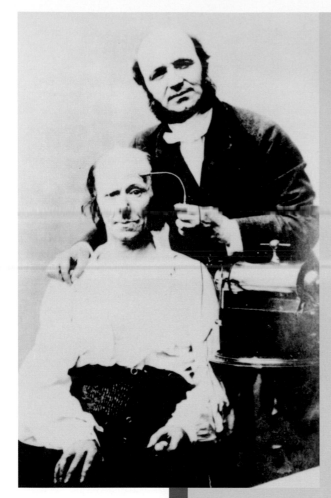

POSED VERSUS SPONTANEOUS EMOTIONAL DISPLAYS: CAN YOU TELL A SINCERE SMILE FROM AN INSINCERE SMILE?

Emotional displays are regulated by the social rules of one's culture. We may, from time to time, laugh at an unfunny joke, restrain our disappointment at an unwanted gift or avoid showing disgust to a well-intentioned culinary disaster. Different brain circuits are implicated in the production of controlled versus spontaneous emotional displays. Lesions to the basal ganglia, such as those found in Parkinson's disease, lead to better performance at producing posed emotional expressions than spontaneous ones (Smith, Smith, & Ellgring, 1996). The frontal cortex is likely to be important for representing goals to either show or suppress an emotional response (Hopf, Muller-Forrell, & Hopf, 1992). Kolb and Taylor (2000) report that patients with frontal lobe lesions are impaired at producing an appropriate expression given a hypothetical situation (e.g. a funeral).

Some aspects of emotional expression may be hard, if not impossible, to control. This appears to be the case in smiling, in which a posed smile does not produce wrinkles around the eyes. These are called the **Duchenne lines**. When looking at a smiling face, observers pay particular attention to this region (more so than for non-smiling faces) (Williams, Senior, David, Loughland, & Gordon, 2001). A non-Duchenne smile involves only the zygomatic major muscle that pulls the corner of the lips upwards. Non-Duchenne smiles should not necessarily be construed as a sign of deliberate insincerity. They can be observed in some natural emotional expressions. For example, a non-Duchenne smile together with gaze avoidance can be a sign of embarrassment (Keltner, 1995).

Dr. G. B. Duchenne mapped over 100 facial muscles using electrical stimulation of facial nerves. In 1862, he published "The Mechanism of Human Facial Expression" in which he noted that sincerely felt smiles involve contraction of eye muscles. Duchenne's principal photographic subject, "The Old Man", was afflicted with almost total facial anesthesia. National Library of Medicine/Science Photo Library.

KEY TERM

Duchenne lines
Wrinkles around the eyes associated with a sincere smile.

The amygdala and recognition of fear

The **amygdala** (from the Latin word for almond) is a small mass of grey matter that lies buried in the tip of the left and right temporal lobes. It lies to the front of the hippocampus and, like the hippocampus, is believed to be important for memory – particularly for the emotional content of memories (Richardson, Strange, & Dolan, 2004) and for learning whether a particular stimulus/response is rewarded or punished (Gaffan, 1992). In monkeys, bilateral lesions of the amygdala have been observed to produce a complex array of behaviors that have been termed the **Kluver–Bucy syndrome** (Kluver & Bucy, 1939; Weiskrantz, 1956). These behaviors include an unusual tameness and emotional blunting; a tendency to examine objects with the mouth; and dietary changes. This is explained in terms of objects losing their learned emotional value. The monkeys typically also lose their social standing. In humans, the effects of amygdala lesions are not as profound. This may reflect either a greater cortical influence on emotional and social behavior or the fact that the earlier monkey studies are likely to have produced lesions extending beyond the amygdala.

In humans, amygdala lesions can selectively impair the ability to recognize fear but not necessarily the other Ekman categories of emotion (e.g. Adolphs, Tranel, Damasio, & Damasio, 1994; Calder, Young, Rowland, Perrett, Hodges, & Etcoff, 1996). For example, patient DR suffered bilateral amygdala damage and subsequently displayed a particular difficulty with recognizing fear (Calder et al., 1996). She was also impaired to a lesser degree in recognizing facial anger and disgust. She could imagine the facial features of famous people, but not of emotional expressions. She could recognize famous faces and match different views of unfamiliar people, but could not match pictures of the same person when the expression differed (Young, Hellawell, Van de Wal, & Johnson, 1996). DR also shows comparable deficits in recognizing vocal emotional expressions, suggesting that the deficit is related to emotion processing rather than modality-specific perceptual processes (Scott,

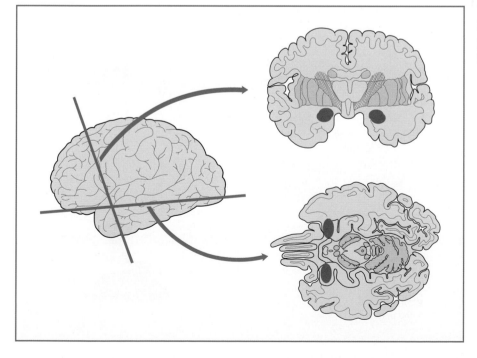

The amygdala is buried, bilaterally, in the anterior portion of the temporal lobes.

Young, Calder, Hellawell, Aggleton, & Johnson, 1997). Whilst it has been suggested that selective impairments in fear may arise because of a failure to attend closely to the eyes (Adolphs, Gosselin, Buchanan, Tranel, Schyns, & Damasio, 2005), this cannot account for the fact that some patients fail to recognize fear in speech (Scott et al., 1997) or music (Gosselin, Peretz, Johnsen, & Adolphs, 2007).

Functional imaging studies generally support, and extend, these conclusions. Morris et al. (1996) presented participants with morphed faces on a happy–neutral–fearful continuum (a parametric design; see Chapter 4). Participants were required to make male–female classifications (i.e. the processing of emotion was incidental). Left amygdala activation was found only in the fear condition; the happy condition activated a different neural circuit. Winston, O'Doherty and Dolan (2003) report that amygdala activation was independent of whether or not subjects engaged in incidental viewing or explicit emotion judgments. However, other regions, including the ventromedial frontal lobes, were activated only when making explicit judgments about the emotion. This was interpreted as reinstatement of the "feeling" of the emotion.

Some researchers have argued that the ability to detect threat is so important, evolutionarily, that it may occur rapidly and without conscious awareness (Le Doux, 1996). Ohman, Flykt and Esteves (2001) report that people are faster at detecting snakes and spiders amongst flowers and mushrooms than the other way around, and that search times are suggestive of pre-attentive "pop-out" (see Chapter 7). When spiders or snakes are presented subliminally to people with spider or snake **phobias**, then participants do not report seeing the stimulus but show a skin conductance response indicative of emotional processing (Ohman & Soares, 1994).

Le Doux has argued that the amygdala has a fast response to the presence of threatening stimuli such as snakes.

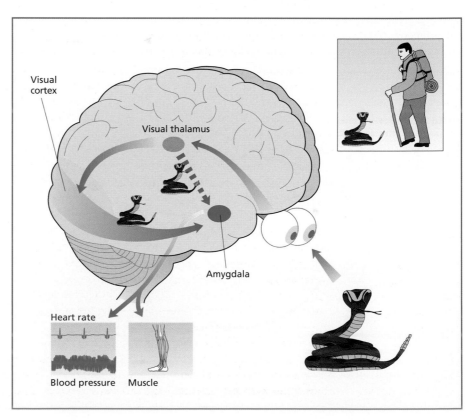

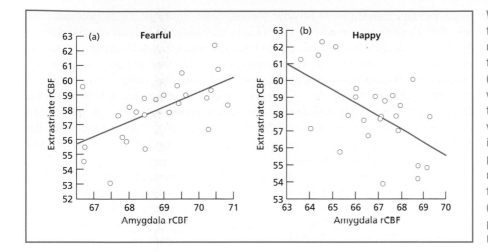

When shown fearful faces, increases in regional cerebral blood flow in the amygdala (rCBF) are associated with increases in blood flow in extrastriate visual regions involved in recognition of the potential threat. The reverse is true of happy faces. From Morris et al. (1998). Reprinted by permission of Oxford University Press.

In these experiments, arachnophobics show the response to spiders, not snakes; and ophidiophobics show a response to snakes but not spiders. In terms of neural pathways, it is generally believed that there is a fast subcortical route from the thalamus to the amygdala and a slow route to the amygdala via the primary visual cortex (e.g. Adolphs, 2002; Morris, Ohman, & Dolan, 1999). Functional imaging studies suggest that the amygdala is indeed activated by unconscious fearful expressions in both healthy participants (Morris et al., 1999) and in a "blindsight" patient with damage to primary visual cortex (Morris, de Gelder, Weiskrantz, & Dolan, 2001). This is consistent with a subcortical route to the amygdala, although it is to be noted that the temporal resolution of fMRI does not enable any conclusions to be drawn about processing speed.

Activation of a fear response by the amygdala may trigger changes elsewhere in the brain that enable the threat to be evaluated and responded to, if necessary. There are connections from the amygdala to the autonomic system (Le Doux, Iwata, Cicchetti, & Reis, 1988). These may help prepare the body for fight and flight by increasing heart and breathing rate. The anterior cingulate is believed to be involved in this process (Critchley et al., 2003). Functional imaging studies show that this region is selectively activated by fear relative to happiness (Morris et al., 1996). When the amount of fear in a facial expression is varied parametrically, then there is a strong relationship between the level of fear and increases in activity in regions of the visual cortex (Morris et al., 1998). The opposite is found when happiness is varied parametrically. Thus, the detection of potential threat by the amygdala may trigger more detailed perceptual processing of the threatening stimulus, enabling further evaluation. Other, more frontal, regions may also be important for deciding whether to act on this information. In conclusion, although the amygdala may be essential for the evaluation of potential danger, its role should be construed in terms of its influence upon a wider circuit of emotional processing.

Recognition of other emotional categories

Aside from fear, the other basic emotional category that has most clearly been shown to have a neural substrate that is largely independent of other emotions is *disgust*. The word disgust literally means "bad taste" and this category of emotion may be evolutionarily related to contamination and disease through ingestion, although its usage can be extended more broadly. Patients with Huntington's disease can show selective impairments in recognizing facial expressions of disgust (Sprengelmeyer et al., 1997) and relative impairments in vocal expressions of disgust (Sprengelmeyer et al., 1996). The degree of these impairments correlates with the amount of damage in a region called the insula (Kipps, Duggins, McCusker, & Calder, 2007). In healthy participants, facial expressions of disgust activate this region but not the amygdala (Phillips et al., 1997). The **insula** is a small region of cortex buried beneath the temporal lobes (it literally means "island"). It is involved in various aspects of bodily perception and also includes the primary gustatory cortex (the first cortical processing stage of taste after the thalamus).

Around half of all patients with amygdala lesions are also impaired at detecting facial expressions of sadness (Fine & Blair, 2000). A selective deficit in recognizing anger has recently been reported following damage to ventral regions of the basal ganglia and may be important for the recognition of signals of aggression (Calder, Keane, Lawrence, & Manes, 2004). Happiness may consist of a more distributed network that makes it difficult, if not impossible, for this emotional category to be selectively impaired.

Detecting and utilizing eye gaze information

The eye region distinguishes between many of the basic emotions, such as smiling or frowning. Making eye contact can be important for establishing one-to-one communication (dyadic communication), and the direction of gaze can be important for orienting attention to critical objects in the environment. Direct eye contact, in many primates, can be sufficient to initiate emotional behaviors. Macaques are more likely to show appeasement behaviors when shown a direct gaze relative to indirect or averted gazes (Perrett & Mistlin, 1990). Moreover, dominance struggles are often initiated with a mutual gaze and terminated when one animal averts its gaze (Chance, 1967).

Baron-Cohen argues that an *eye direction detector* is an innate and distinct component of human cognition (Baron-Cohen, 1995a; Baron-Cohen & Cross, 1992). Babies are able to detect eye contact from birth, suggesting that it is not a learned response (Farroni, Csibra, Simion, & Johnson, 2002). This ability is likely to be important for the development of social competence because the eyes code relational properties between objects and agents (e.g. "mummy sees daddy", "mummy sees the box"). The superior temporal sulcus contains many cells that respond to eye direction (Perrett et al., 1985) and lesions in this area can impair the ability to detect gaze direction (Campbell, Heywood, Cowey, Regard, & Landis, 1990). This region of the brain appears to be specialized for perception of biological motion and dynamic facial expression. It should not be confused with the fusiform region that is more specialized for facial identity.

Children with autism can detect whether the eyes of another person are directed at them and, as such, do not appear to be impaired in the perception of gaze (Baron-Cohen, Campbell, Karmiloff-Smith, Grant, & Walker, 1995). They do, however, have difficulties in using gaze information to predict behavior or infer desire. In the four sweets task, a cartoon face of Charlie directs his gaze to one of the sweets (Baron-Cohen et al., 1995). Children with autism are unable to decide: "which chocolate will Charlie take?" or "which one does Charlie want?". The difficulty in utilizing gaze information manifests itself as an absence of joint attention in the social interactions of autistic people (Sigman, Mundy, Ungerer, & Sherman, 1986).

Children with autism are able to detect which person is looking at them (top), but are unable to infer behavior or desires from eye direction (bottom). For example, they are impaired when asked "which chocolate will Charlie take?" or "which one does Charlie want?". Top photo from Baron-Cohen and Cross (1992). Reprinted with permission of Blackwell Publishing. Bottom panel from Baron-Cohen et al. (1995). Reproduced with permission from *British Journal of Developmental Psychology* © British Psychological Society.

Does emotion recognition have a communicatory function?

Charles Darwin (1872/1965) believed that emotions are an innate and automatic response. The findings from cognitive neuroscience are broadly consistent with this view. Darwin did not, apparently, believe that the function of emotional expression was communicatory (Blair, 2003). This may be partially true. Although the person expressing the emotion may not do so with intent to communicate, it is now very clear that other people readily pick up on and act on the emotional behavior of others.

Emotional expressions on the faces of other people can be important cues for guiding one's own behavior. These facial expressions can act as reinforcers in the classical conditioning framework (analogous to the famous experiments conducted by Pavlov).

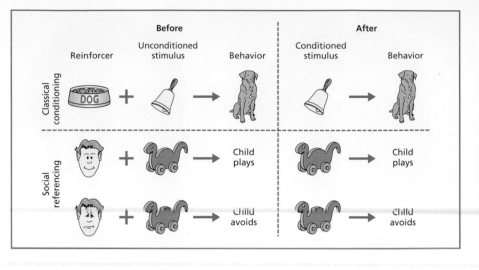

Facial expressions can act as **reinforcers** in classical conditioning experiments. A reinforcer is a stimulus that increases or decreases a particular pattern of behavior (termed positive and negative reinforcement, respectively). In Pavlov's famous experiments on dogs, a positive reinforcer (food) was paired with a neutral, unconditioned stimulus (a bell ring) to elicit a behavior (salivation). After repeated pairings of bell and food, the bell alone could elicit salivation (it had become a conditioned stimulus). If human infants are given a novel object, their behavior will be influenced by the response of their primary caregiver – a phenomenon termed **social referencing** (e.g. Klinnert, Campos, & Source, 1983). If the caregiver displays disgust, then the object will be avoided, but if the caregiver smiles, then the child will interact with the object. In this instance, the facial expression is the reinforcer (equivalent to the food), the novel object is the unconditioned stimulus (equivalent to the bell) and the behavior is avoidance or interaction. Learning may be rapid (single trial) and durable.

In adults, facial expressions of fear (Mineka & Cook, 1993), sadness (Blair, 1995) and disgust (Rozin, Haidt, & McCauley, 1993) can all be used as negative reinforcers. Happy expressions can be used as positive reinforcers (Matthews & Wells, 1999). Disgust expressions are often employed in the context of food. Sickness itself can also be a very powerful reinforcer for food. Novel food eaten during a period of illness, for example during chemotherapy (Fredrikson et al., 1993), may elicit a highly durable subsequent avoidance of that food called **conditioned taste aversion**. Anger, by contrast, tends not to act as an unconditioned stimulus but, rather, is used to curtail ongoing behavior by implying violation of social convention (Blair & Cipolotti, 2000).

Evaluation

The recognition of different basic emotions has largely different underlying neural substrates; the clearest examples being for fear and disgust in the amygdala and insula, respectively. These systems may have developed to enable quick and efficient processing of stimuli that are crucial for survival. They may trigger other cognitive processes in the organism that enable an appropriate response to the stimulus (e.g. fight or flight). Observing the facial expressions of others may enable us to interpret the feelings of others and react appropriately in social situations, and these expressions may enable us to learn the emotional valence of the objects around us. The eyes, in particular, may be used to direct attention to salient objects, and offer clues into other people's thoughts and desires.

PROCESSING EMOTIONS: A ROLE FOR SOMATIC RESPONSES?

So far, this chapter has considered the ability to process the emotional content of stimuli with a particular emphasis on faces given their importance as a social cue. This section considers the role that the internal bodily (or *somatic*) state has on the processing of emotions. The processing of emotional stimuli can result in changes in the body's physiological state such as increased heart rate and sweating. These responses form the basis of the traditional lie detector (or polygraph). In the laboratory, a common way of measuring the body's response is to monitor small changes in conductivity as a result of mild sweating. This is measured by applying a weak electrical current to the skin. This is termed the **skin conductance response** (SCR; or galvanic skin response, GSR). Tranel and Damasio (1995) report how the skin conductance response is affected by a number of brain lesions. Lesions to the ventromedial frontal lobes abolish SCR to psychological but not physical stimuli (e.g. bangs), whereas lesions to the anterior cingulate cortex abolish both. Functional imaging also points to a key role for the anterior cingulate in the production of the skin conductance response (Critchley, Elliott, Mathias, & Dolan, 2000).

Physiological changes to emotional stimuli clearly have a role to play in preparing the organism to respond to the situation. But do they also have a more cognitive role to play? The following sections consider three proposals. First, the James–Lange theory, which suggests that it is the bodily changes themselves that give rise to an emotion. Second, the somatic marker hypothesis, which suggests that emotional/bodily responses are implicated in decision making. Finally, the role of somatic responses in judging that a stimulus is familiar will be considered.

KEY TERM

Skin conductance response (SCR)
Changes in electrical conductivity on a person's skin, triggered by certain stimuli (e.g. emotional or familiar stimuli).

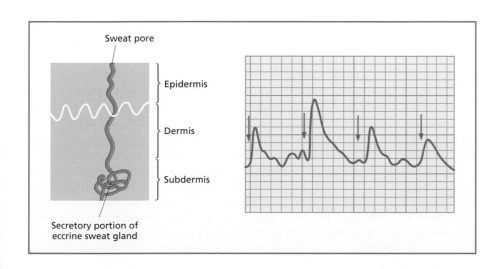

The skin conductance response (SCR) method involves recording changes in electrical conductivity on a person's skin on the hand. Heightened arousal can lead to more sweat even without overt sweating taking place. A person's SCR can be plotted as a continuous trace throughout the experiment. A peak SCR occurs between 1 and 5 seconds after face presentation.

The James–Lange theory of emotion

One of the founding fathers of psychology, William James (1890/1950), proposed a theory of emotion that placed the somatic response of the perceiver at its center. This theory later became known as the **James–Lange theory** of emotion. According to this theory, it is the self-perception of bodily changes that produces emotional experience. Thus, changes in bodily state precede the emotional experience rather than the other way around. We feel sad because we cry, rather than we cry because we feel sad. This perspective seems somewhat radical compared to the contemporary point of view elaborated thus far. For instance, it raises the question of what type of processing leads to the change in bodily states and whether or not this early process could itself be construed as a part of the emotion. There is good empirical evidence to suggest that changes in somatic state, in themselves, are not sufficient to produce an emotion. Schacter and Singer (1962) injected participants with epinephrine (also termed adrenaline), a drug that induces autonomic and visceral changes. They found that the presence of the drug by itself did not lead to self-reported experiences of emotion, contrary to the James–Lange theory. However, in the presence of an appropriate cognitive setting (e.g. an angry or happy man enters the room), the participants did self-report an emotion. A cognitive setting, without epinephrine, produced less intense emotional ratings. This study suggests that bodily experiences do not create emotions (contrary to James–Lange) but they can enhance conscious emotional experiences.

The somatic marker hypothesis

At least one current theory of emotions also emphasizes a role for bodily states. The key idea of the somatic marker hypothesis is that "somatic marker" signals have a direct influence on reasoning and decision making, either consciously or unconsciously (Damasio, 1994, 1996). In this theory, **somatic markers** form the link between previous situations stored throughout the cortex and the "feeling" of those situations stored in regions of the brain dedicated to emotion (e.g. the amygdala) and the representation of the body states (e.g. the insula). Decisions about current situations are taken on the basis of the retrieval of previously acquired knowledge about similar situations and reactivation of the physiological pattern that describes the appropriate emotion. The somatic markers are assumed to be stored in the ventromedial frontal cortex (including parts of the medial and orbitofrontal surface).

It is worth contrasting this hypothesis with those of the James–Lange theory. First, James–Lange theory is only concerned with conscious attribution of bodily states, whereas the somatic marker hypothesis also concerns unconscious biases. Second, the body proper is not critical to the somatic marker hypothesis as the body can be represented by an "as if" procedure in the brain. Thus, the brain simulates what the body might feel like in the absence of a literal experience of what the body does feel like. Finally, the somatic markers are assumed to play a direct and causal role in decision making; for example, those involving risks or social situations.

To investigate this hypothesis, the Iowa research group devised a gambling task that has been shown to distinguish between different lesion sites and cognitive profiles (Bechara, Damasio, Damasio, & Anderson, 1994; Bechara, Damasio, Tranel, & Damasio 1997; Bechara, Damasio, Tranel, & Anderson, 1998; Bechara, Damasio, Damasio, & Lee, 1999). Players are given four decks of cards (A to D), a "loan" of $2000 in fake US notes, and are instructed to play so that they win the most and lose the least. On turning each card, the player receives either a monetary penalty or gain. Playing mostly from packs A and B leads to a net loss, whereas playing mostly from packs C and D will lead to a net gain. Control subjects, without a brain lesion, learn to choose from C and D and to avoid A and B. Patients with lesions to the ventromedial frontal cortex do not (Bechara et al., 1994). Moreover, control subjects generate an anticipatory skin conductance response (SCR) *before* making a selection from a risky pile (A and B), whereas the patients do not (Bechara et al., 1994).

Patients with amygdala damage also have difficulties on this task but for different reasons (Bechara et al., 1999). Whereas neither ventromedial frontal nor amygdala damage patients showed an anticipatory SCR, only the ventromedial frontal patients produced a normal SCR after receiving a reward or punishment (i.e. monetary gain or loss). Thus, the amygdala may be more involved in emotional learning, whereas the ventromedial cortex may be implicated in using emotional information to guide behavior.

The results of the gambling task have been criticized on a number of grounds. Maia and McClelland (2004) argue that players do consciously know what the good decks are and are not relying on an unconscious SCR to guide decisions. In addition, the results of the ventromedial frontal patients can be explained by other theories such as a failure of **reversal learning** (that is, the ability to stop responding

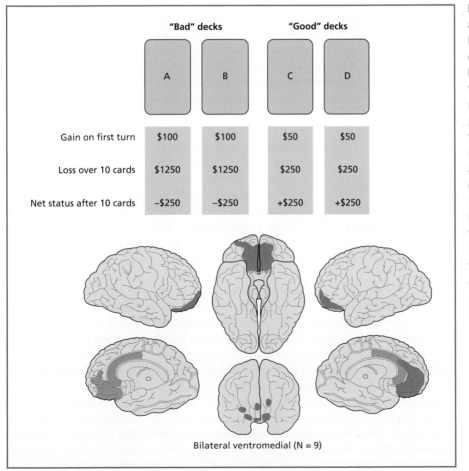

| | "Bad" decks | | "Good" decks | |
	A	B	C	D
Gain on first turn	$100	$100	$50	$50
Loss over 10 cards	$1250	$1250	$250	$250
Net status after 10 cards	−$250	−$250	+$250	+$250

Bilateral ventromedial (N = 9)

Players receive $2000 and must choose hidden cards from one of four packs, A to D. Playing preferentially from packs A and B will result in loss, whereas playing preferentially from packs C and D will result in gain. Players are not informed of this contingency. Will they learn to avoid A and B? Patients with damage to ventromedial frontal lobes are impaired on this task. From Bechara et al. (1998). Copyright © 1998 by the Society for Neuroscience.

to a previously rewarded stimulus that is no longer rewarded). This is because cards from bad decks A and B are rewarded with $100 dollars on the first turn, and cards from the good decks C and D are rewarded with only $50. Thus, patients must have to learn to avoid the previously advantageous decks, A and B. If there is initially no larger reward on the first trial of the bad decks, then patients with ventromedial frontal damage perform normally (Fellows & Farah, 2003).

In summary, there is good evidence to suggest that damage to the ventromedial cortex disrupts performance on the gambling task. However, there is only equivocal evidence in support of the use of somatic markers as opposed to a failure of reversal learning.

Electrodermal activity as an index of familiarity

One general finding is that familiar stimuli, relative to unfamiliar stimuli, have an emotional component that reveals itself as an SCR. This has been used in a number of ingenious studies to provide an objective hallmark of familiarity that does not always correspond to subjective reports of familiarity based on other sources of information (e.g. the availability of semantic or episodic memories). Tranel, Damasio and Damasio (1995) report a double dissociation between overt and covert recognition of familiar faces. Patients with ventromedial lesions have impaired SCR to familiar faces but can recognize and identify the faces accurately. By contrast, patients with prosopagnosia have impaired recognition of previously familiar faces but show an intact SCR to them. This raises the question of why prosopagnosics don't make use of this information to help them. Perhaps the response is too small for them to detect it consciously, or perhaps the absence of other confirmatory information dominates their decision.

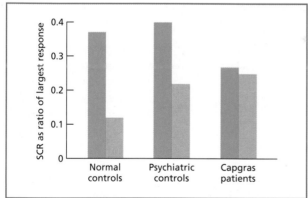

A dissociation between emotional content and factual content has been put forward to account for a fascinating delusional symptom called **Capgras syndrome**. In the Capgras syndrome, people report that their acquaintances (spouse, family, friends and so on) have been replaced by "body doubles" (Capgras & Reboul-Lachaux, 1923; Ellis & Lewis, 2001). They will acknowledge that their husband/wife looks like their husband/wife. Indeed, they are able to pick out their husband/wife from a line-up while maintaining all along that he/she is an imposter. To account for this, Ellis and Young (1990) suggest that these patients are the opposite of prosopagnosia. Thus, they can consciously recognize the

Most people produce a greater skin conductance response (SCR) to personally familiar faces, but patients with Capgras delusion do not. Reprinted from Ellis and Lewis (2001), Copyright 2001 with permission from Elsevier.

person/face but they lack an emotional response to them. As such, the person/face is interpreted as an imposter. This explains why the people who are doubled are those closest to the patient, as these would be expected to produce the largest emotional reaction. This theory "makes the clear prediction that Capgras patients will not show the normally appropriate skin conductance responses to familiar faces" (Ellis & Young, 1990, p. 244). Subsequent research has confirmed this prediction (e.g. Ellis, Young, Quayle, & DePauw, 1997). However, the findings of Tranel et al. (1995) are problematic. Their ventromedial frontal patients had abolished skin conductance to familiar faces but reported *no* signs of Capgras delusion. Thus, a lack of emotional response may well be necessary but it is unlikely to be sufficient. Perhaps some mechanism involved in decision making itself is compromised. If so, this points to a more complex relationship between decision making and emotional response than simply relying on the presence or absence of an SCR.

Evaluation

The relationship between emotions and bodily responses is more complex than previously envisaged. It is certainly possible to have strong bodily responses without consciously reporting an emotion (Schacter & Singer, 1962). Bodily responses such as the skin conductance response can be produced irrespective of whether an emotion is consciously perceived or not, and can thus be a useful objective index of emotional processing.

READING MINDS

Empathy and "simulation theory"

Empathy refers to the ability to appreciate others' points of view and share their experiences. **Simulation theory** is based on the assumption that *perceiving* the actions and emotional expressions of others uses the same neural and cognitive resources that are also used for *producing* actions and emotional expressions in oneself (e.g. Gallese, 2001, 2003; Gallese & Goldman, 1998). According to such a view, empathy is an emergent property of a sophisticated set of cognitive processes dedicated to action and emotion perception and production, rather than reflecting the operation of a dedicated mechanism specialized for empathy.

Simulation theories extend the notion of a mirror neuron (see Chapter 8) not only to action, but also to sensation and emotion. The term **mirror systems** is used to convey the idea of neural resources that disregard the distinction between self and others. For example, the insula region is activated both when we are disgusted and when we look at someone else scrunching up their face in an expression of disgust (Phillips et al., 1997). Moreover, people who score higher on certain measures of empathy show greater activation of their own disgust regions when watching other people being disgusted (Jabbi, Swart, & Keysers, 2007). This suggests that we may, in some literal sense, share the emotions of the people around us.

Imagine the scene from the James Bond film, in which a tarantula slowly crawls on Sean Connery's arm. Does it make *your* skin crawl? It has been shown that watching another person being touched activates some of the same neural mechanisms in the somatosensory cortex involved when we ourselves get physically touched (Blakemore, Bristow, Bird, Frith, & Ward, 2005; Keysers, Wicker, Gazzola, Anton, Fogassi, & Gallese, 2004). In a similar study, Singer and colleagues (2004) investigated empathy for pain. The brain was scanned when anticipating and watching a loved-one suffer a mild electric shock. There was an overlap between regions activated by expectancy of another person's pain and experiencing pain oneself, including the anterior cingulate cortex and the insula. In a follow-up to this study, participants in an fMRI scanner watched electric shocks delivered to people who were considered either good or bad on the basis of whether they had played fairly or unfairly in a game (Singer, Seymour, O'Doherty, Stephan, Dolan, & Frith, 2006). Whilst participants empathically activated their own pain regions

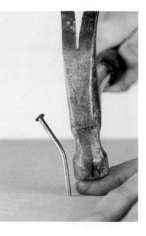

Do you empathize with someone by simulating how you would feel in their situation? © Image Source/Corbis.

when watching the "goodie" receive the electric shock, this response was attenuated when they saw the "baddie" receiving the shock. In fact, male participants often activated their pleasure and reward circuits when watching the baddie receive the shock – i.e. the exact opposite of simulation theory. This brain activity correlated with their reported desire for revenge. This suggests that, although simulation may tend to operate automatically, it is not protected from our higher order beliefs.

Simulation theory has a lot to recommend it: it is simple, elegant and testable. However, it is debatable whether it can be extended to explain not only the sensations and emotions of others but also theory of mind. **Theory of mind** refers to the ability to represent the mental states of others, i.e. their thoughts, desires, beliefs and intentions. Defendants of simulation theory argue that these mental states are continuous with sensations and emotions, and do not require some "higher" mechanism (Gallese, 2003). Many cognitive neuroscientists disagree. The challenge for simulation theory may be to account for **false beliefs** (rather than beliefs *per se*) and **deception**. Someone may hold a belief that differs from one's own belief and that differs from the true state of the world. Moreover, someone may hold a belief that is contradicted by deceptive behavior. This requires not simulation but a kind of "meta-simulation" that separates behaviors from beliefs, and in which mental states can be represented but need not be shared (e.g. Dennett, 1978; Wimmer & Perner, 1983). This type of representation is often considered the hallmark of "theory of mind" (Leslie, 1987) or "mentalizing" (Frith & Frith, 2003).

Mind reading in autism

He wandered about smiling, making stereotyped movements with his fingers, crossing them about in the air. He shook his head from side to side, whispering or humming the same three-note tune. He spun with great pleasure anything he could seize upon to spin... When taken into a room, he completely disregarded the people and instantly went for objects, preferably those that could be spun... He angrily shoved away the hand that was in his way or the foot that stepped on one of his blocks.

(This description of Donald, aged five, was given by Leo Kanner (1943), who also coined the term autism. The disorder was independently noted by Hans Asperger (1944), whose name now denotes a variant of autism).

Autism has been formally defined as "the presence of markedly abnormal or impaired development in social interaction and communication and a markedly restricted repertoire of activities and interests" (the American Psychiatric Association, 1994, *Diagnostic and statistical manual*; DSM-IV). It is a severe developmental condition that is evident before three years of age and lasts throughout life. There are a number of difficulties in diagnosing autism. First, it is defined according to behavior because no specific biological markers are known (for a review, see Hill & Frith, 2003). Second, the profile and severity may be modified during the course of development. It can be influenced by external factors (e.g. education, temperament), and may be accompanied by other disorders (e.g. attention deficit and hyperactivity disorder, psychiatric disorders). As such, autism is now viewed as a spectrum of conditions spanning all degrees of severity. It is currently believed to affect more than 0.6% of people, and is three times as common in males (Hill & Frith, 2003). **Asperger syndrome** falls within this spectrum, and is often considered a special subgroup. The diagnosis of Asperger syndrome requires that there is no significant delay in early language and cognitive development. However, the validity of these criteria has been questioned because it does not appear to be predictive of later functioning (Prior et al., 1998). A more useful distinction may be made between high- and low-functioning autism. Mental retardation, defined as an IQ lower than 70, is present in around 40% of cases of autism (Baird et al., 2000). Confusingly, the term "Asperger syndrome" is also often used to denote high-functioning autism.

IS AUTISM AN EXTREME FORM OF THE MALE BRAIN?

Baron-Cohen (2002) argues that the characteristics of all individuals can be classified according to two dimensions: "empathizing" and "systemizing". Empathizing allows one to predict a person's behavior and to care about how others feel. Systemizing requires an understanding of lawful, rule-based systems and requires an attention to detail. Males tend to have a brain type that is biased towards systemizing (S > E) and females tend to have a brain type that is biased towards empathizing (E > S). However, not all men and women have the "male type" and "female type", respectively. Autistic people appear to have an extreme male type (S >> E), characterized by a lack of empathizing (this would account for the mentalizing difficulties) and a high degree of systemizing (this would account for their preserved abilities and unusual interests). A questionnaire study suggests that these distinctions hold true (e.g. Baron-Cohen et al., 2003). However, it remains to be shown whether these distinctions are merely descriptive or indeed do reflect two real underlying mechanisms at the cognitive or neural level.

One observation that needs to be accounted for is the fact that autism is more common in males. The "male brain hypothesis" offers a simple explanation: males are more likely to have a male-type brain. An alternative, but potentially related, account may be in terms of genetic factors. Whereas it is likely that multiple genes confer autistic susceptibility (Maestrini, Paul, Monaco, & Bailey, 2000), one of them may lie on the sex-linked X chromosome. Evidence for this comes from **Turner's syndrome**. Most men have one X chromosome from their mother and a Y chromosome from their father (XY). Most women have two X chromosomes (XX), one from each parent. Women with Turner's syndrome have only a single X chromosome (XO) from either their father or mother. If the X chromosome has a maternal origin, then the woman often falls on the autistic spectrum; she does not if it has a paternal origin (Creswell & Skuse, 1999). It is suggested that the paternal X chromosome may have a preventive effect on autistic tendencies. An absence of this chromosome in some Turner's women and all normal males (who get their X chromosome from their mother) may leave them susceptible to autism.

KEY TERM

Turner's syndrome
A genetic disorder in which there is whole or partial deletion of one X chromosome.

Much of the behavioral data has been obtained from high-functioning individuals in an attempt to isolate a specific core of deficits. On a purely theoretical level, one reason why researchers have been interested in the study of autism is the belief that it might reveal something fundamental about social interactions in us all. Maybe autistic individuals lack some of the prerequisite skills that support socialization. One candidate deficit is the ability to represent mental states (e.g. Baron-Cohen, 1995b; Fodor, 1992). The first empirical evidence in favor of this hypothesis came with the development of a test of false belief devised by Wimmer and Perner (1983) and tested on autistic children by Baron-Cohen, Leslie and Frith (1985). In the version used with autistic children, the *Sally–Anne task*, the child is introduced to two characters, Sally and Anne. Sally puts a marble in a basket so that Anne can see. Anne then leaves the room, and Sally moves the marble to a box. When Anne enters the room, the child is asked "where will Anne look for the marble?" or "where does Anne think the marble is?". Children with autism reply "in the box", whereas normal children (aged 4+) and mentally retarded controls reply "in the basket". The erroneous reply is not due to a failure of memory, because the children can remember the initial location. It is as if they fail to understand that Anne has a belief that differs from physical reality – that is, a failure to represent mental states. This has also been called "mind-blindness" (Baron-Cohen, 1995b). Autistic children are still impaired when the false belief was initially their own. For example, in the *Smarties task*, the child initially expects to find chocolates in the chocolate packet and is surprised to find a pencil, but when asked what other people will think is in the packet, they reply "pencil" (Perner, Frith, Leslie, & Leekam, 1989).

A number of other studies have pointed to selective difficulties in mentalizing, compared to carefully controlled conditions. For example, people with autism can understand false photographs but not false beliefs (Leekam & Perner, 1991); can sequence behavioral pictures but not mentalistic pictures (Baron-Cohen, Leslie, &

The Sally–Anne task requires an understanding of "false belief" and tends to be failed by children with autism. Adapted from Wimmer and Perner (1983).

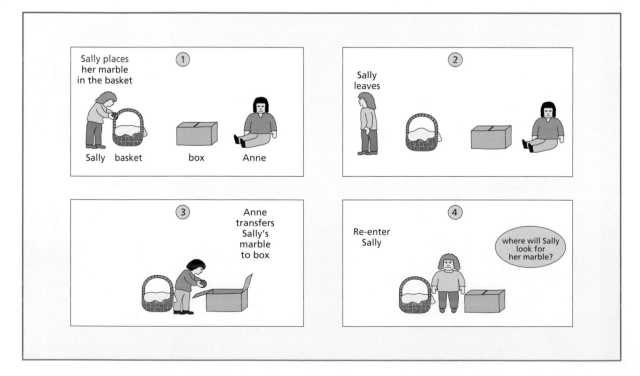

Frith, 1986); are good at sabotage but not deception (Sodian & Frith, 1992); and tend to use desire and emotion words but not belief and idea words (Tager-Flusberg, 1992). In all instances, the performance of people with autism is compared to mental-age controls to establish that the effects are related to autism and not general level of functioning.

The mentalizing or "theory of mind" account of autism has not been without its critics. These criticisms generally take two forms: either that other explanations can account for the data without postulating a difficulty in mentalizing (e.g. Russell, 1997; Stone & Gerrans, 2006), or that a difficulty with mentalizing is necessary but insufficient to explain all of the available evidence (e.g. Frith, 1989).

A number of studies have argued that the primary deficit in autism is one of executive functioning (e.g. Hughes, Russell, & Robbins, 1994; Ozonoff, Pennington, & Rogers, 1991; Russell, 1997). For example, the incorrect answer might be chosen on false belief tasks because of a failure to suppress the strongly activated "physical reality" alternative. However, it is not clear that this explanation can account for all the studies relating to mentalizing (e.g. picture sequencing). Moreover, high-functioning autistic people often have normal executive functions (e.g. Baron-Cohen, Wheelwright, Stone, & Rutherford, 1999) and early brain lesions can selectively disrupt theory of mind abilities without impairing executive functions (e.g. Fine, Lumsden, & Blair, 2001).

One difficulty with the theory-of-mind explanation is that it fails to account for cognitive strengths as well as weaknesses. One popular notion of autistic people is that they have unusual gifts or "savant" skills, as in the film *Rain Man*. In reality, these skills are found only in around 10% of the autistic population (Hill & Frith, 2003). Nevertheless, some account of them is needed for a full explanation of autism. The unusual skills of some autistic people may be partly an outcome of their limited range of interests. Perhaps one reason why some individuals are good at memorizing dates is that they practice it almost all the time. However, there is also evidence for more basic differences in processing style. For example, people on the autistic spectrum are superior at detecting embedded figures (Shah & Frith, 1983). One explanation for this is in terms of "weak central coherence" (Frith, 1989; Happe, 1999). This is a cognitive style, assumed to be present in autism, in which processing of parts (or local features) takes precedent over processing of wholes (or global features). A different explanation describes *all* individuals as having a mix of two different processing styles termed "empathizing" and "systemizing" (e.g. Baron-Cohen, Richler, Bisarya, Gurunathan, & Wheelwright, 2003). Most non-autistic people would lie near the middle and possess a mix of both. People with autism would lie at the extreme systemizing end and lack empathizing (Baron-Cohen, 2002). Empathizing allows one to predict another person's behavior, and care about how others feel. Thus, a lack of empathizing would account for the mentalizing difficulties. Systemizing requires an understanding of lawful, rule-based systems and requires an attention to detail. This would account for their preserved abilities and unusual interests (e.g. in calendar systems).

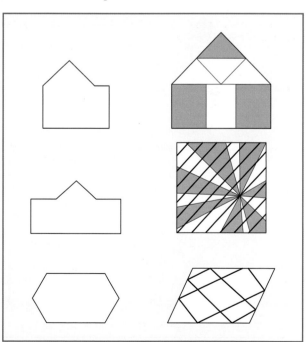

People with autism may be faster at spotting embedded figures similar to the ones shown here.

Neural basis of "theory of mind"

Evidence for the neural basis of theory of mind has come from two main sources: functional imaging studies of normal participants and behavioral studies of patients with brain lesions. Numerous tasks have been used, including directly inferring mental states from stories (e.g. Fletcher et al., 1995), from cartoons (e.g. Gallagher, Happé, Brunswick, Fletcher, Frith, & Frith, 2000) or when interacting with another person (e.g. McCabe, Houser, Ryan, Smith, & Trouard, 2001). A review and meta-analysis of the functional imaging literature was provided by Frith and Frith (2003), who identified three key regions involved in mentalizing.

Temporal poles

This region is normally activated in tasks of language and semantic memory. Frith and Frith (2003) suggest that this region is involved with generating schemas that

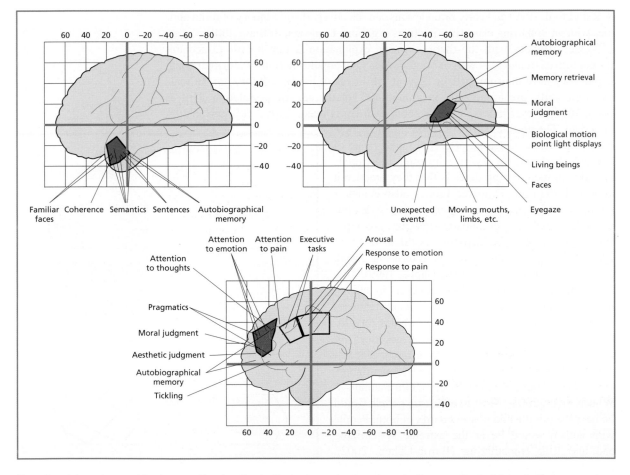

Functional imaging and lesion studies implicate three important regions in theory of mind (shaded): temporal poles (top left), temporal-parietal junction (top right) and the medial frontal lobes including a portion of the anterior cingulate (bottom; note the anterior cingulate is drawn as divided into functionally separate areas). From Frith and Frith (2003): Reprinted by permission of Royal Society of London and the author.

specify the current social or emotional context, as well as in semantics more generally. Zahn, Moll, Krueger, Huey, Garrido and Grafman (2007) report an fMRI study suggesting that this region responds to comparisons between social concepts (e.g. brave–honorable) more than matched non-social concepts (e.g. nutritious–useful). Also, not all the tests of mentalizing that activated this region involved linguistic stimuli. For example, one study used triangles that appeared to interact by, say, chasing or encouraging each other (Castelli, Happé, Frith, & Frith, 2000).

Medial prefrontal cortex

Frith and Frith (2003) report that this region is activated in all functional imaging tasks of mentalizing to date, and is the only region to be activated in a game-playing task in which participants must choose to cooperate or not with another player (e.g. McCabe et al., 2001). Some studies of frontal-lobe patients have suggested that the medial prefrontal regions are necessary for theory of mind (e.g. Stuss, Gallup, & Alexander, 2001b) but by no means all (Bird, Casteli, Malik, Frith, & Husain, 2004). The region lies in front of the anterior cingulate cortex proper and, according to the functional divisions of Bush, Luu and Posner (2000), the mentalizing region overlaps with the region dedicated to representing and attending to emotions (see Chapter 14). This region is different from the "executive" region of the anterior cingulate that appears to be involved in tasks such as Stroop (Barch, Braver, Akbudak, Conturo, Ollinger, & Snyder, 2001; Duncan & Owen, 2000). However, the "mentalizing region" also seems to be implicated in the pragmatics of language such as irony ("Peter is well read. He has even heard of Shakespeare") and metaphor ("your room is a pigsty"; Bottini et al., 1994). Interestingly, people with autism have difficulties with this aspect of language (Happé, 1995). In such instances, the speaker's *intention* must be derived from the ambiguous surface properties of the words (e.g. the room is not literally a pigsty). Functional imaging suggests that this region is involved both in theory of mind and in establishing the pragmatic coherence between ideas/sentences, including those that do not involve mentalizing (Ferstl & von Cramon, 2002).

Temporal-parietal junction

This region tends not to be only activated in tests of mentalizing but also in studies of the perception of biological motion, eye gaze, moving mouths and living things in general. These skills are clearly important for detecting other "agents" and processing their observable actions. Simulation theories argue that mentalizing need not involve anything over and above action perception. However, it is also conceivable that this region goes beyond the processing of observable actions, and is also concerned with representing mental states. Patients with lesions in this region fail theory of mind tasks that can't be accounted for by difficulties in body perception (Samson, Apperly, Chiavarino, & Humphreys, 2004). Saxe and Kanwisher (2003) found activity in this region, on the right, when comparing false belief tasks (requiring mentalizing) with false photograph tasks (not requiring mentalizing but entailing a conflict with reality). The result was also found when the false photograph involved people and actions, consistent with a role in mentalizing beyond any role in action/person perception.

Evaluation

Performance on tasks of theory of mind typically requires the use of several non-specialized (i.e. domain general) processes, including language processing, executive functions and action perception. The controversy lies in whether these mechanisms are the *only* ones that are needed to account for theory of mind (in some forms of simulation theory) or whether there is additionally the need for a specialized (i.e. domain-specific) mechanism that is specific to representing the mental states of others. Functional imaging and brain-lesion studies highlight the importance of several key regions in theory of mind, but the extent to which these regions are specific to theory of mind is controversial. Autism still offers the most convincing evidence for a specialized mechanism.

ANTISOCIAL BEHAVIOR

Certain individuals exhibit persistent behaviors that violate social or moral conventions. There are likely to be many different causes for such behavior. In a few instances the cause can be linked to a brain injury, particularly in the orbitofrontal region, which produces a pattern termed "acquired sociopathy". Another pattern that will be considered here is developmental psychopathy, in which aggression tends to be goal-directed. One cognitive account for psychopathic behavior is in terms of a failure to process distress cues in others.

In contrast people with autism are rarely knowingly cruel or hurtful. Their behavior could perhaps be considered as asocial rather than antisocial. Leslie, Mallon and Di Corcia (2006) found that autistic children pass tests of moral reasoning. For example, they identify it as bad to steal someone else's cookie when it makes them cry but that it isn't bad to eat one's own cookie even if the other person (who greedily wants two cookies) starts to cry. Their interest in rules may even give them a strong sense of social justice.

Acquired sociopathy following orbitofrontal cortex damage

When testing a number of their patients with frontal lobe lesions, Damasio and colleagues (1990) made an interesting observation, namely, that many of their patients met a published American Psychiatric Association (APA) criterion for **sociopathy**. Sociopaths exhibit irresponsible and unreliable behavior that is not personally advantageous; an inability to form lasting commitments or relationships; egocentric thinking; and a marked degree of impulsivity (Mealey, 1995). Sociopaths comprise around 3–4% of the male population and less than 1% of the female population (Robins, Tipp, & Przybeck, 1991). The term *acquired sociopathy* is used to refer to those individuals who did not exhibit such symptoms prior to their brain injury. Damage to certain regions of the frontal lobes not only disrupts personality, but it does so in a way that is systematic across individuals. It also does so in a way that has important implications for understanding the neural basis of human social interaction.

One of the earliest and most famous neurological cases in the literature is that of Phineas Gage (see Macmillan, 1986). After a lesion to the left frontal lobe, Gage was noted to be "irreverent, indulging at times in grossest profanity". Patient MGS is described as a modern case of Phineas Gage (Dimitrov, Phipps, Zahn, & Grafman, 1999). He had been decorated for service in Vietnam, with more than ten medals and a Purple Heart. Following a head injury, he was demoted for incompetent behavior. After an honorary discharge, he was noted to be sarcastic, lacking in tact (e.g. inappropriate disclosure of sexual history), moody and unable to manage his own finances.

THE EXTRAORDINARY CASE OF PHINEAS GAGE

One of the most famous cases in the neuropsychological literature is that of Phineas Gage (Harlow, 1993; Macmillan, 1986). On 13 September 1848, Gage was working on the Rutland and Burlington railroad. He was using a large metal rod (a tamping iron) to pack explosive charges into the ground when the charge accidentally exploded, pushing the tamping iron up through the top of his skull; it landed about 30 meters behind him. The contemporary account noted that Gage was momentarily knocked over but that he then walked over to an ox-cart, made an entry in his time book and went back to his hotel to wait for a doctor. He sat and waited half an hour for the doctor and greeted him with, "Doctor, here is business enough for you!" (Macmillan, 1986).

Not only was Gage conscious after the accident, he was able to walk and talk. Although this is striking in its own right, it is the cognitive consequences of the injury that have led to Gage's notoriety. Before the injury, Gage held a position of responsibility as a foreman and was described as shrewd and smart. After the injury, he was considered unemployable by his previous company; he was "no longer Gage" (Harlow, 1993). Gage was described as "irreverent, indulging at times in grossest profanity... manifesting but little deference for his fellows, impatient of restraint or advice when it conflicts with his desires... devising many plans of future operation, which are no sooner arranged than they are abandoned in turn for others" (Harlow, 1993). After various temporary jobs, including a stint in Barnum's Museum, he died of epilepsy (a secondary consequence of his injury) in San Francisco, some 12 years after his accident.

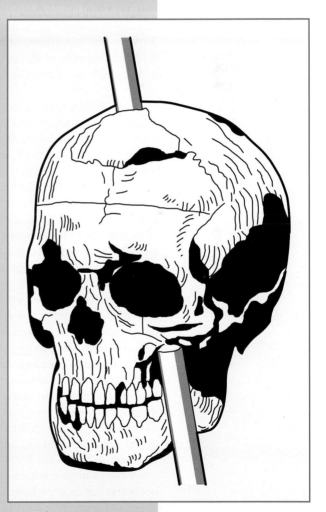

The skull of Phineas Gage, with tamping iron *in situ*.

Where was Phineas Gage's brain lesion? This question was answered recently by an MRI reconstruction of Gage's skull, which found damage restricted to the frontal lobes, particularly the left orbitofrontal/ventromedial region and the left anterior region (Damasio, Grabowski, Frank, Galaburda, & Damasio, 1994). Research suggests that this region is crucial for certain aspects of decision making, planning and social regulation of behavior, all of which appeared to have been disrupted in Gage. Other areas of the lateral prefrontal cortex are likely to have been spared.

How might we account for such behavior within the cognitive neuroscience framework presented in this chapter? There are at least four different explanations:

1. Loss of schemas pertaining to social knowledge.
2. A general impairment of executive functions.
3. An impairment of theory of mind.
4. Impaired use of emotional information to control online behavior.

One explanation for acquired sociopathy is that the knowledge structures (or schemas) for social and moral conventions have been lost or disrupted (e.g. Grafman, 1994; Grafman, Schwab, Warden, Pridgen, Brown, & Salazar, 1996). Some support for this comes from a sentence verification study concerning social and moral judgments that showed activation of the orbitofrontal cortex (Moll, Oliveira-Souza, Bramati, & Grafman, 2002). However, direct assessments of social knowledge in acquired sociopaths have generally not supported this position (Blair & Cipolotti, 2000; Saver & Damasio, 1991). Instead, it appears to be the case that *intact* social knowledge fails to be implemented. One exception to this rule may be in orbito-frontal lesions acquired during childhood. This may result in a failure to develop adequate social knowledge in the first place (Anderson, Bechara, Damasio, Tranel, & Damasio, 1999).

Executive functions are involved in the online control of behavior and would appear to be an attractive candidate for explaining acquired sociopathy. However, many patients who present with this behavioral profile pass most, if not all, of the conventional tests of executive function, including patient MGS discussed above (see also, Eslinger & Damasio, 1985). Of course, it could be argued that the tests being used are not sensitive enough, or that impairments of executive function might be hard to detect in individuals with a high premorbid intelligence. Evidence against this view comes from reports of double dissociations between sociopathy and executive functions (Bechara, Damasio, Tranel, & Anderson, 1998), and also the different neural substrates that are implicated (orbitofrontal in sociopathy and lateral frontal in executive functions; Rahman, Sahakian, Hodges, Rogers, & Robbins, 1999).

Perhaps acquired sociopathy arises from a deficit in understanding the minds of others; that is, they have a specific deficit in theory of mind? Some research has suggested a key role for the medial prefrontal cortex in theory of mind, whereas others have not. A link between theory of mind and acquired sociopathy has rarely been tested, but at least one acquired sociopathic patient with intact theory of mind is on record (Blair & Cipolotti, 2000).

The most convincing accounts of acquired sociopathy are those that postulate a role for emotions in the online control of social behavior. Several different accounts along these lines have been proposed and the empirical evidence, as yet, does not distinguish unequivocally between them. As already discussed, the somatic marker hypothesis states that acquired sociopathy arises because of absent links between emotional/somatic representations and memories and knowledge of prior events (Damasio, 1994, 1996). Many patients with acquired sociopathy have been shown to fail the Iowa Gambling task, which was designed to detect such an impairment, but by no means all fail it (Blair & Cipolotti, 2000; Manes et al., 2002). Rolls, Hornak, Wade and McGrath (1994) propose a different model. They argue that the function of the orbitofrontal cortex is to *reverse* stimulus-reinforcement associations (such as those formed on the early trials in the Iowa Gambling task), rather than retrieve them from memory. A difficulty in reversal learning was correlated with a questionnaire measuring socially inappropriate behavior. Blair and Cipolotti (2000) also prefer a reversal learning explanation to account for their single case study, JS. They argue that the orbitofrontal cortex is important for using expectations of others' emotions to suppress inappropriate behavior.

Developmental psychopathy

Developmental psychopathy contrasts with acquired sociopathy in a number of ways (Blair, 2003). Psychopathic individuals show aggression that is self-initiated and aimed towards specific goals. By contrast, acquired sociopathy is associated with aggression in situations of threat or frustration. For example, in a study of penetrating head injuries in Vietnam veterans, patients with frontal lesions scored highly on ratings of "gets annoyed easily" and "argues back" but not "argues" *per se* and not "gets angry and breaks things" (Grafman et al., 1996). Psychopaths show an early onset of extremely aggressive behavior that is not tempered by any sense of guilt or empathy with the victim (Hare, 1980). According to the cognitive developmental model of Blair (1995), psychopathic individuals represent the developmental case where sad and fearful expressions do not act as aversive unconditioned stimuli. That is, they do not use (or recognize) distress cues in others that would normally suppress violent behavior. In support of this position, it has been found that psychopaths show reduced autonomic responses to distress cues, but not to threatening stimuli (Blair, Jones, Clark, & Smith, 1997), and they fail to make the distinction between moral and conventional transgressions (Blair, 1995). Conventional transgressions refer to violations of societal rules (e.g. "talking during class"), whereas moral rules refer to the rights and welfare of others (e.g. "hitting someone") and may require empathy.

What type of cognitive deficit may be a feature of psychopathy? © Sunset Boulevard/Corbis.

Evaluation

The most satisfactory account of sociopathic tendencies following acquired lesions to orbitofrontal cortex is in terms of a failure to use emotional cues to guide current and future behavior. Similarly, in developmental psychopathy there may be a failure to use distress cues in order to modify behavior.

SUMMARY AND KEY POINTS OF THE CHAPTER

- Different categories of emotion have different neural substrates (the clearest examples being disgust and fear). These may have evolved for different reasons.
- Faces carry important social and emotional information that may be used to transfer emotional valence to neutral objects (social referencing) and be used to infer others' feelings and desires.
- The conscious and unconscious processing of an emotional stimulus will produce somatic responses (e.g. skin conductance response), and this is hypothesized to be linked to various aspects of cognition (e.g. in decision making).
- Understanding other people's mental states may require a specialized system. This has been termed "theory of mind" or "mentalizing".
- People with autism may lack a theory of mind mechanism, but impaired theory of mind alone cannot explain the full pattern of strengths and weaknesses in autism.
- The orbitofrontal cortex is important for using emotional cues to guide current and future behavior, and damage to this region can produce "sociopathic" tendencies.

EXAMPLE ESSAY QUESTIONS

- Do emotions have a function?
- Are there dedicated neural substrates for the recognition of different emotions?
- Can autism be explained as "mind-blindness"?
- To what extent can empathy and theory of mind be explained by a process of simulation?
- What is the evidence to suggest that the processing of emotional stimuli elicits somatic responses? What role, if any, might these responses play in cognitive processing?
- What cognitive/neural mechanisms are implicated in "acquired sociopathy"?

RECOMMENDED FURTHER READING

- Frith, C. D. & Wolpert, D. M. (2004). The *neuroscience of social interaction: Decoding, imitating and influencing the actions of others*. Oxford: Oxford University Press (also published as an issue of *Philosophical Transactions of the Royal Society of London B* (2003), *358*, 429–602).

- Harmon-Jones, E. & Winkielman, P. (2007). *Social Neuroscience*. New York: Guilford Press. An up-to-date collection including both emotional and social processes.

- Hill, E. L. & Frith, U. (2004). *Autism: Mind and brain*. Oxford: Oxford University Press (also published as an issue of *Philosophical Transactions of the Royal Society of London* B (2003), *358*, 277–427).

- Lane, R. D. & Nadel, L. (2000). *Cognitive neuroscience of emotion*. Oxford: Oxford University Press. A collection of papers covering many of the issues related to the first half of this chapter.

- Saxe, R. & Baron-Cohen, S. (2006). *Theory of mind*. Hove: Psychology Press (also published as an issue of *Social Neuroscience, 1*, 135–416).

CHAPTER 16

CONTENTS

The developing brain

Many people are drawn into a subject like psychology because of one nagging question: what makes us who we are? Were we predestined to become the person we are today as a result of our genetic endowment? If so, could a parent of the late twenty-first century be reading their child's genetic blueprint to figure out their cognitive strengths and weaknesses, their personality and disposition? Or are we shaped by our experiences and circumstances during life and during our formative years of development? These questions are central to the **nature–nurture debate**, i.e. the extent to which cognition and behavior can be attributed to genes or environment. Whilst the nature–nurture debate still has contemporary relevance and continues to excite both scientists and lay people, this chapter will consider how many of the commonly held assumptions surrounding this debate are misguided. For example, genes do not provide a predetermined "blueprint" but are themselves switched on and off by the environment, and the contemporary notion of "environment" is far broader than is commonly understood. It includes biological circumstances (e.g. diet, exposure to toxins), as well as personal and social circumstances.

Historically, the pendulum has swung between opposing extremes of this debate. For example, in 1874, Francis Galton published *English Men of Science: Their Nature and Nurture*, arguing that geniuses are born and not made. As well as coining the phrase "nature or nurture", he was the first person to realize that heredity could be estimated by comparing identical and non-identical twins. Galton's advocacy of nature over nurture would become associated with the discredited eugenics movement, which promoted selective breeding of the more cognitively able (although in practice this was often implemented by sterilization of the "feeble-minded").

In the early twentieth century, the pendulum had swung to the other extreme. Freudian theory, for example, emphasized the importance of early experiences and parenting style in development. The Russian psychologist, Lev Vygotsky (1896–1934), also emphasized the role of culture and interpersonal communication in development. Behaviorist theories, such as those put forward by B. F. Skinner (1904–1990), argued that all behavior was a product of learning as a result of rewards and punishments.

Jean Piaget (1896–1980) is regarded as the founding father of modern Western developmental psychology. Piaget took a middle ground with regards to the nature–nurture debate. He regarded development as a cyclical process of interactions between the child and

In Piaget's sensorimotor stage (0–2 years), a child learns about the nature of objects (e.g. that they still exist when hidden) and about the nature of cause and effect (e.g. that actions have consequences on the objects around). The child then passes through other stages (pre-operational, concrete and formal operational) with greater degrees of abstraction. Although the stages can be regarded as fixed and pre-determined, Piaget stressed the role of the environment to successfully develop the cognitive processes required for the next stage. © Brooke Fasani/Corbis.

his or her environment. In his view, the genetic contribution consists of developing a brain that is ready to learn in certain ways, but progression through the stages involves assimilating evidence from the environment and then developing new mechanisms in light of the feedback obtained. Whilst many of Piaget's experimental studies have not stood the test of time (e.g. children show evidence of reasoning long before Piaget suggested they should), his basic approach to development has been more enduring.

Following on from the developmental psychology tradition, developmental cognitive neuroscience has focused on brain-based explanations of developmental change (Johnson, 2005). One particular current approach is termed **neuroconstructivism** (Westermann, Mareschal, Johnson, Sirois, Spratling, & Thomas, 2007). Like Piaget's approach, this assumes constant interaction between environment and genetic factors, with a mature cognitive system emerging out of transformations of earlier ones. Unlike Piaget's approach, the predetermined aspect of development is construed in terms of multiple brain-based constraints (developmental changes in synapse formation, myelination, etc.) rather than the less well-defined notion of predetermined "stages".

This chapter will first consider the structural development of the brain, both prenatally and postnatally. It will then go on to consider the nature of developmental change, including evidence for critical/sensitive periods and innate knowledge. An overview of the origin of genetic differences and behavioral genetics will then go on to consider some specific examples of genetic influences in developmental cognitive neuroscience. Together with the advances made in molecular genetics, it is now becoming possible to understand how genetic influences and experience create changes in the structure and function of the brain. This is leading to an exciting rethink of the nature–nurture debate.

ADAPTING THE METHODS OF COGNITIVE NEUROSCIENCE FOR INFANTS AND CHILDREN

Methods such as fMRI and EEG are generally considered suitable for infants and children. One advantage of using these methods in younger people is that they don't necessarily require a verbal or motor response to be made.

Functional MRI

Gaillard, Grandon and Xu (2001) provide an overview of some of the considerations needed. If one wants to compare across different ages, then the most significant problem is that the structural properties of the brain change during development. Although the volume of the brain is stable by about five years of age, there are differences in white and gray matter volumes until adulthood (Reiss, Abrams, Singer, Ross, & Denckla, 1996). The hemodynamic response function is relatively stable after seven years of age but differs below this age (Marcar, Strassle, Loenneker, Schwarz, & Martin, 2004). Both the differences in brain structure and blood flow make it harder to compare activity in the same region across different ages. Younger children also find it harder to keep still in the scanner and this motion can disrupt the reliability of the MR signal.

ERP/EEG

When working with young subjects using ERP/EEG, a limiting factor is the child's willingness to tolerate the electrodes, the task and the time commitment required (Thomas & Casey, 2003). Children and adults can show quite different patterns of ERP (e.g. in terms of latency, amplitude or scalp distribution), even for tasks that both groups find easy (Thomas & Nelson, 1996). These could either reflect age-related cognitive differences (i.e. the same task can be performed in different ways at different ages) or non-cognitive differences (e.g. the effects of skull thickness, cell packing density or myelination).

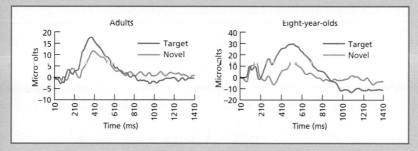

Adults and children show very different visual ERP waveforms despite having equivalent behavioral performance. Adapted from Thomas and Nelson (1996).

TMS

Current ethical and safety guidelines (Wassermann, 1996) do not recommend *repetitive* TMS to children except for compelling therapeutic purposes (e.g. treatment of depression).

STRUCTURAL DEVELOPMENT OF THE BRAIN

Gottlieb (1992) discusses different ideas about development. In *predetermined develop-ment*, genes dictate the structure of the brain, which enables the particular functions of the brain, which determines the kinds of experiences we have. This is a traditional view of how genes affect cognition. In contrast, Gottlieb also outlines a *probabilistic devel-opmental* perspective in which brain structure, and even the expression of genes, can be influenced by experience as well as vice versa. This represents the dominant view in modern developmental cognitive neuroscience. Even environmental influences in the womb, such as the diet of the mother and the presence of viruses or toxic agents, could alter brain structure and, hence, function. Following birth, all of our every-day experiences result in tiny changes to the structure of our brain, in the form of altering the pattern of syn-aptic connections. Sometimes these changes are even visible at the macroscopic level. Adults who learn to juggle with three balls over a three-month period show increased gray matter density, assessed with MRI, in

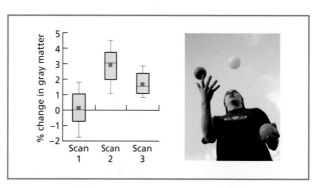

MRI scans were obtained at three time intervals: before learning to juggle; after three months of training; and after a further three months of no practice. The graph shows increases in gray matter density in an area associated with visual motion perception, area V5/MT (Reprinted by permission from Macmillan Publishers Ltd: Draganski et al., 2004, copyright 2004).

a region specialized for detecting visual motion (Draganski, Gaser, Busch, Schurierer, Bogdahn, & May, 2004). This example illustrates a central concept of this chapter – namely, *plasticity*. Plasticity refers to experience-dependent changes in neural functioning. However, even here there may be a role of genetic factors that, for instance, increase the brain's capability for plastic change at particular time points (sensitive periods) for different regions.

> GOTTLIEB'S (1992) DIFFERENT
> VIEWS OF DEVELOPMENT
>
> Predetermined development:
> Genes › Brain structure › Brain function › Experience
>
> Probabilistic development:
> Genes ⟷ Brain structure ⟷ Brain function ⟷ Experience

The structural development of the brain can be conveniently divided into the periods before and after birth (i.e. prenatal and postnatal, respectively).

Prenatal development

The human gestation period is around 38 weeks from conception. The newly formed embryo undergoes a rapid process of cell division, followed by a process of differentiation during which the different cells become increasingly specialized. The nervous system derives from a set of cells arranged in a hollow cylinder, the **neural tube**. By around five weeks, the neural tube has organized into a set of bulges and convolutions that will go on to form various parts of the brain (e.g. the cortex, the thalamus and hypothalamus, the midbrain, etc.). Closer to the hollow of the neural tube are several proliferative zones in which neurons and glial cells are produced by division of proliferating cells (**neuroblasts** and glioblasts). Purves (1994) estimates that the fetal brain must add 250,000 neurons per minute at certain periods in early development.

The newly formed neurons must then migrate outwards towards the region where they will be employed in the mature brain. This occurs in two ways. Passively, older cells tend to be pushed to the surface of the brain. Structures such as the hippocampus are formed this way. There is also an active mechanism by which newer cells are guided to particular destinations, pushing past the older cells. Rakic (1988) identified **radial glial cells** that act like climbing ropes, ensuring that newly formed neurons are guided to their final destination. The convoluted surface of the brain, the neocortex, is formed in this way.

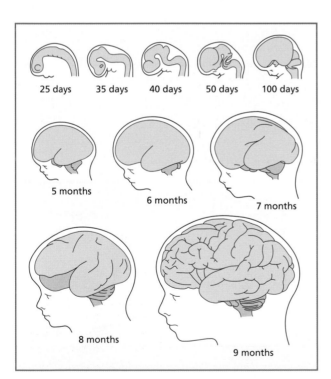

25 days   35 days   40 days   50 days   100 days

5 months

6 months

7 months

8 months

9 months

The embryonic and fetal development of the human brain. Cortical asymmetries between the left and right hemispheres, implicated in language acquisition, are present at 24 weeks. From Cowan (1979). Copyright © 1979 by Scientific American, Inc. All rights reserved.

Postnatal development

At birth, the head makes up around a quarter of the length of the infant. Although the brain itself is small (450g) relative to adult human size (1400g), it is large in comparison to remote human ancestors and living primates (a newborn human brain is about 75% of that of an adult chimpanzee). The vast majority of neurons are formed prior to birth, so the expansion in brain volume during postnatal development is due to factors such as the growth of synapses, dendrites and axon bundles; the proliferation of glial cells; and the myelination of nerve fibers.

Huttenlocher and Dabholkar (1997) measured the synaptic density in various regions of human cortex. This is a measure of the degree to which neurons are connected to each other and is unrelated to number of neurons *per se* or how active the synapses are. In all cortical areas studied to date, there is a characteristic rise and then fall in synapse formation (synaptogenesis). In primary visual and primary auditory cortex, the peak density is between 4 and 12 months, at which point it is 150% above adult levels, but falls to adult levels between 2 and 4 years. In prefrontal cortex, the peak is reached after 12 months but does not return to adult levels until 10 to 20 years old. PET studies of glucose metabolism in developing brains show a similar rise and fall to studies of synaptogenesis, although peaking time tends to be somewhat later (Chugani, Phelps, & Mazziotta, 1987). Glucose metabolism may be a measure of actual neural activity rather than neural structural changes. Why does the number of synapses fall during the course of development? It is not necessarily the case that more synapses reflects more efficient functioning. During development a process of fine-tuning the brain to the needs of the environment renders some connections redundant.

Myelination refers to the increase in the fatty sheath that surrounds axons and increases the speed of information transmission. In structural MRI, the increase in white matter volume over the first two decades of life may reflect the time course of myelination (Giedd et al., 1999). Again, the prefrontal cortex is one of the last areas to achieve adult levels of myelination and this, together with the late fine-tuning and elimination of synapses in this region, may contribute to the development of mature social behavior during adolescence and the control of behavior in general.

KEY TERM

Myelination
An increase in the fatty sheath that surrounds axons and increases the speed of information transmission.

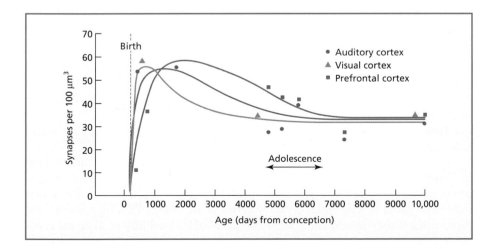

Synapse formation has a rise and fall pattern. It peaks soon after birth, although different cortical regions differ greatly in the time taken to fall again to adult synaptic levels. From Huttenlocher and Dabholkar (1997). Reprinted with permission of John Wiley & Sons Inc.

Protomap and Protocortex theories of brain development

Different regions of the cortex have structural differences. This is manifest in terms of the grouping of cell types in the different layers and also in terms of the patterns of their input–output connections, which ultimately determine the type of function they are likely perform. But how does this regional organization come about, and when? Specifically, to what extent is it a product of prenatal or postnatal brain development? The Protomap (Rakic, 1988) and Protocortex (O'Leary, 1989) theories of brain development provide different answers to these same questions.

The Protomap theory argues that the regional layout of the cortex is established at the prenatal stages of development. The early proliferating zone is assumed to specify the ultimate layout of different cortical regions. This may be achieved through the radial glial fibers that carry new neurons away from the proliferation zone (Rakic, 1988) and through regional differences in various molecular signals (called transcription factors) that affect the neurons' structure, migration and survival (see Sur & Rubenstein, 2005). Different doses of these signals determine the dimensions of the various lobes of the brain, such that, for example, a dose above a certain threshold may instruct a new neuron to develop features characteristic of a frontal lobe neuron (e.g. in terms of its connectivity) but below that dose it may resemble a parietal neuron (Fukuchi-Shimogori & Grove, 2001). This suggests a simple mechanism for creating individual differences in brain structure and also for evolutionary development (e.g. a shifting dose could enable an evolutionary jump in frontal lobe enlargement).

The Protocortex theory, on the other hand, argues that different regions of the cortex are initially equivalent but become specialized as a result of projections from the thalamus (O'Leary, 1989). This is assumed to be influenced by postnatal sensory experience. What would happen if part of the developing visual cortex were transplanted into parts of the brain normally specialized for touch or hearing? The Protocortex theory predicts that regions of cortex can initially be interchanged and that the transplanted visual cortex would now respond to touch or sound because it would be innervated by somatosensory or auditory projections from the thalamus. To some extent, this is indeed what happens. Visual cortex transplanted into somatosensory cortex responds to touch on a mouse's whiskers and reconnects to the somatosensory region of the thalamus (Schlagger & O'Leary, 1991). If visual information from the eyes is re-routed to the auditory cortex of a ferret (by re-wiring from the retina to auditory regions of the thalamus that then project to auditory cortex), then the auditory cortex takes on visual properties. The "auditory" neurons respond to particular visual orientations and movement directions (Sharma, Angelucci, & Sur, 2000; Sur Garraghty, & Roe, 1988).

How can the two theories be reconciled? In their review, Sur and Rubenstein (2005) conclude that, "the Protomap/Protocortex controversy no longer remains" (p. 809). The Protomap theory never completely excluded a role of environmental inputs. Conversely, visually re-wired "auditory" cortex still retains vestiges of normal auditory cortex connections and the visual representations are poorer than those found in true visual cortex (Sharma et al., 2000). This suggests that the Protocortex theory should not assume complete exchangeability of different cortical regions.

Evaluation

The section began with Gottlieb's (1992) distinction between predetermined development, in which brain structure is predetermined by genes, and probabilistic development, in which brain structure is determined by both genes and experiences. Evidence from studies of brain development supports the latter view.

FUNCTIONAL DEVELOPMENT OF THE BRAIN: SENSITIVE PERIODS AND INNATE KNOWLEDGE?

Having considered how brain *structure* is changed during development, the present section is primarily concerned with how brain *function* (i.e. different types of ability and knowledge) changes developmentally. In particular, two broad issues will be considered. First, the role of critical/sensitive periods in development and, second, the extent to which any kind of knowledge or ability can be said to be innate.

Critical and sensitive periods in development

In 1909, a young Austrian boy named Konrad Lorenz and his friend (and later wife), Gretl, were given two newly hatched ducklings by a neighbor. The ducklings followed them everywhere, apparently mistaking them for their parents. This process, now termed **filial imprinting**, was studied intensively by the adult Lorenz using goslings and earned him a Nobel Prize (see Tinbergen, 1951). Lorenz observed that there was a narrow window of opportunity, between 15 hours and 3 days, for a gosling to imprint. Once imprinted, the gosling is unable to learn to follow a new foster parent. The movement of a stimulus was deemed to be crucial for determining what object the gosling will imprint to. A region of the chick

These goslings follow the Austrian professor, Konrad Lorenz, as if he is their mother! This process is called filial imprinting. © Science Photo Library.

forebrain known as IMHV (intermediate and medial of the hyperstriatum ventral), which may correspond to mammalian cortex, is critical for enabling imprinting (Horn & McCabe, 1984).

The studies above suggest that there is a **critical period** for imprinting. A critical period has two defining features: first, learning can only take place within a limited time window and, second, the learning is hard to reverse in the face of later experience. Subsequent evidence suggests that the window of opportunity can be extended by lack of suitable early experience (e.g. to a moving object), and that learning can be reversed in certain circumstances. As such, many researchers prefer the more moderate terminology of a **sensitive period**. For instance, a chick imprinted to one object will often generalize to other objects of similar appearance (e.g. color and shape). By gradually changing the features of the objects to which it is exposed, the chick's final preference can be different from its initial preference, even after the end of the "critical" period (Bolhuis, 1990).

The development of visual abilities also shows evidence of a sensitive period. For example, Hubel and Wiesel (1970b) took single-cell recordings from the primary visual cortex of cats in whom one eye had been deprived of visual input in early life (by sewing it shut). They found that the cells responded to input from the sighted eye only, whereas normally reared cats possess cells that respond to inputs from both eyes. During a sensitive period between four and five weeks after birth, eye closure for three–four days leads to a sharp decline in the number of cells that will respond to input from both eyes.

What of "higher" cognitive abilities, such as language? Lenneburg (1967) initially argued that language acquisition has a critical period that ends abruptly at puberty. However, the ability to comprehend and produce language is likely to depend on other skills such as hearing, motor ability, working memory capacity and so on. Each of these basic skills may have its own sensitive period, which means that different components of language may have their own sensitive period rather than a fixed cut-off point at puberty. For example, the sensitive period for making phonemic discriminations such as the distinction between r/l, occurs during infancy and is resistant to subsequent exposure (McCandliss, Fiez, Protopapas, Conway, & McClelland, 2002). In contrast, accents are more fluid during childhood but become notoriously hard to change from the onset of adulthood.

Studies of feral children offer some support to Lenneburg's idea. Genie had been locked away by her mentally unstable family from the age of 20 months to 13 years when she was discovered in Los Angeles in 1970 (Curtiss, 1977). During this period she was severely maltreated and was not allowed to speak or be spoken to. On being rescued she was almost entirely mute, with a vocabulary of around 20 words. Within the first 18 months of being placed with a foster parent her language was reported to have developed well on all fronts, including both vocabulary and grammar, and this was cited as evidence *against* a sensitive period (Fromkin, Krashen, Curtiss, Rigler, & Rigler, 1974). However, subsequent studies are more consistent with a sensitive period and have revealed that her language acquisition remained very poor compared with young children, although it remains debated as to the extent to which her grammar was specifically affected or whether all aspects of language were affected (Jones, 1995).

Thankfully, research in which exposure to a first language is withheld from a child is limited to a tiny number of cases. However, second language acquisition offers a richer source of evidence to test for the existence of a sensitive period. Rather than a fixed point at which the sensitive period closes, the evidence suggests that second language attainment decreases linearly with age (Birdsong, 2006). Many adults are able to become fluent in a second language, but they may do so in different ways from children (e.g. more explicit strategy use). fMRI studies of bilinguals who have learned their second language at different ages suggest that it is the level of proficiency in the second language that determines how similar the second language is to the first language (in terms of neural resources used), rather than the age of acquisition (Abutalebi, Cappa, & Perani, 2005).

What general properties of the nervous system give rise to sensitive periods in development? Thomas and Johnson (2008) provide one recent overview. One possibility is that there is a strict maturational timetable in which a set of neurons are readied for learning (e.g. by synaptogenesis) and are then later "fossilized" (e.g. reducing plasticity, removing weaker connections) according to a strict timetable. A second possibility is that a set of neurons are readied for learning but that the process is self-terminating to some extent, i.e. the sensitive period will "wait" for suitable exposure. For example, in filial imprinting there is evidence that a particular gene is switched on at the start of the sensitive period but is switched off again ten hours after imprinting has occurred (Harvey, McCabe, Solomonia, Horn, & Darlison, 1998). In human infants born with dense cataracts over both eyes, there is a rapid increase in visual acuity when the cataracts are surgically removed, even as late as nine months after birth (Maurer, Lewis, Brent, & Levin, 1999). This suggests that the development of visual acuity will, to some extent, "wait" for an appropriate environment. However, this is only partly true, as nine-year-old children who had cataracts removed in the first six months of life have some difficulties in visual processing of faces (Le Grand, Mondloch, Maurer, & Brent, 2001).

RECOVERY OF FUNCTION AFTER EARLY BRAIN DAMAGE

Although strokes are rare in infancy and childhood, they do occur. Typically, however, the long-term effects on cognition are neither as severe nor as specific as those arising from strokes in adulthood. This is consistent with the view that plasticity is greatest earlier in life. Several studies have found that children who had strokes around the time of birth go on to develop intellectual and language skills in the normal range (e.g. Aram & Ekelman, 1986; Ballantyne, Spilkin, Hesselink, & Trauner, 2008). With regards to language, it is often found that early lesions to the left hemisphere can result in later right hemisphere language as assessed using fMRI (Liegeois et al., 2004). In this study, even lesions outside of "classical" language areas (e.g. Broca's area) were just as likely to result in right hemispheric language consistent with the view that functional specialization of regions emerges gradually and in a way that is not completely predetermined. Given that the brain has very limited scope to grow new neurons, one may wonder whether accommodating language in the right hemisphere would have a detrimental outcome on traditional right hemispheric functions (e.g. visuo-spatial skills). There is some evidence for this.

Lidzba, Staudt, Wilke and Krageloh-Mann (2006) report that the extent of right hemispheric language (assessed by fMRI) resulting from early stroke correlated negatively with performance on visuo-spatial tasks (i.e. greater right hemisphere language is associated with poorer visuo-spatial skills). This suggests that, whilst early plasticity can aid recovery, this may not be completely without a cost.

Innate knowledge?

Perhaps the most controversial topic in developmental cognitive neuroscience is the extent to which any form of knowledge or ability can be said to be innate (e.g. Karmiloff-Smith, 2006; Spelke, 1998). This division has a long historical and philosophical tradition between so-called **empiricists** (who believed that the mind is a blank slate) and **nativists** (who believed that at least some forms of knowledge are innate).

The word innate itself conjures up somewhat different connotations to different researchers. For some, the word is synonymous with the idea that behavior is a product of natural selection (Ridley, 2003). The word **instinct** is often used in this context and suitable examples would be filial imprinting in birds (Tinbergen, 1951) or even language in humans (Pinker, 1994). In this usage of the word "innate", there is still a role for experience to play, perhaps within a sensitive period of development. A chick will only imprint if it is exposed to a suitable stimulus in the environment and a child will only learn sophisticated language given suitable inputs. However, in both examples the particular content of the behavior cannot be said to be innate. The chick will as happily imprint to an Austrian professor as to its mother, and a child is capable of learning a diverse range of vocabulary and syntax, and not even the manner of production (e.g. speaking versus sign language) is strongly predetermined. In this sense of the word "innate", there is a readiness for certain knowledge to be acquired but the knowledge itself is not strictly innate.

This leads to a consideration of the second way in which the word innate is applied: namely, that knowledge or behavior can be said to be innate if it comes about in the absence of appropriate experience. It is this particular usage of the term that has attracted much controversy (Spelke, 1998). The very early development of the primary visual cortex of the cat can, in this sense, be said to be innate because it make no difference whether the cat has visual experience or not (Blakemore & Vansluyters, 1975). Both normally developing cats and cats that have been visually deprived in *both* eyes have cells that respond to lines of particular orientations up to around three weeks after birth (Blakemore & Vansluyters, 1975). However, experience is needed for a mature system to form. In the presence of complex visual experience, these cells become more finely tuned and resemble those of an adult by four weeks but in the absence of appropriate visual experience the blind cats lose this specificity.

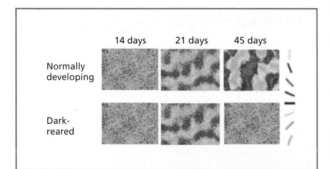

Orientation selectivity at 14, 21 and 45 days in the primary visual cortex of cats reared in a normal visual environment (top) and a dark-reared environment (bottom). The dark-reared cats show normal development up to 21 days but then show a decrease. The different colors represent the extent to which neurons respond to particular orientations. Adapted from Crair et al. (1998).

Similar conclusions arise when one considers the development of phobias. Humans can easily learn to become fearful of certain stimuli such as snakes (e.g. by pairing with an electric shock) but it is hard to become fearful of stimuli such as flowers – a phenomenon that has been termed **prepared learning** (Seligman, 1971). In a series of studies, Mineka and colleagues studied fear conditioning in monkeys (for a review, see Ohman & Mineka, 2001). Whereas monkeys born in captivity to wild-born monkeys show fear of snakes, monkeys who were born from mothers raised in captivity do not. The fearless monkeys could acquire fear of snakes by watching videos of other monkeys reacting with fear to snakes, but they could not acquire fear of flowers using the same method. This suggests that fear of snakes does require suitable experience, even if that fear is transmitted vicariously via other monkeys rather than through contact with snakes. That is, this behavior can be said to be innate in the sense of being a product of natural selection, but not in the sense of developing without experience.

Some preferences could, arguably, be said to be innate in the sense that they don't appear to depend on experience. Newborn infants prefer sweet tastes over neutral and sour ones (Desor, Maller, & Andrews, 1975) and they prefer some visual patterns over others. Harlow (1958) reported a series of ethically dubious experiments in which newborn monkeys were isolated from their natural mothers but "reared" by artificially created mothers such as a stuffed toy monkey or a metal wire monkey. The monkeys preferred to cling to the furry stuffed toy rather than the metal one, even if the metal one provided the monkey with milk. This went against the standard behaviorist doctrine at the time that maternal love was merely a learned reward for satisfying basic needs such as hunger (in which case the monkey should show affection to the wire mother).

Harlow, in his famous article "The Nature of Love", argues that monkeys have an innate preference for a soft versus wire "mother" even if the wire "mother" provides the infant with milk. From Harlow, 1958. Reproduced with kind permission of Harlow Primate Laboratory, University of Wisconsin.

Some abilities could also, arguably, be said to be innate in the sense that they don't appear to depend on experience. Newborn infants will imitate tongue protrusion (Meltzoff & Moore, 1977, 1983). That is, they demonstrate an understanding that a seen tongue being protruded corresponds to their own, unseen, motor ability to do the same. They concluded that, "the ability to use intermodal equivalences is an innate ability of humans" (1977, p. 78).

The studies above suggest that certain dispositions (e.g. to fear certain types of thing), preferences (e.g. sweet), abilities (e.g. to detect edges, intermodal

---

KEY TERM

Prepared learning
The theory that common phobias are biologically determined from evolutionary pressures.

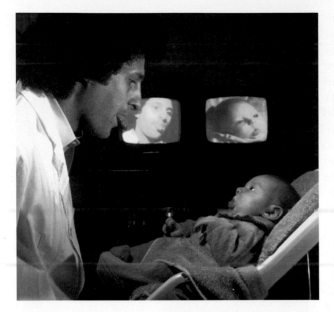

matching) can – in some sense of the word – be said to be innate. However, the issue of whether the specific content of knowledge (or so-called representations) is innate is much harder to substantiate. For example, newborn infants prefer to look at real faces relative to faces with the parts rearranged, but this could reflect a tendency to prefer certain symmetrical patterns (Johnson, Dziurawiec, Ellis, & Morton, 1991). ERP studies suggest that the ability to distinguish between upright and inverted faces, and to distinguish between monkey and human faces, occurs gradually and, presumably, via experience (Halit, de Haan, & Johnson, 2003). This makes it hard to argue that the specific *knowledge* of what a face looks like is innate, although one could still reasonably claim that a preference for particular kinds of pattern is an evolutionary adaptation.

This 23-day-old infant imitates the tongue protrusion of the experimenter, suggesting an understanding of the link between seen actions of another and their own, unseen, actions. Photo by Andrew N. Meltzoff and E. Ferorelli, with permission from Andrew N. Meltzoff.

KEY TERMS

Chromosome
An organized package of DNA bound up with proteins; each chromosome contains many genes.

Allele
Different versions of the same gene.

THE ORIGINS OF GENETIC DIFFERENCES

The human genetic code is organized on to 23 pairs of **chromosomes**, making a total of 46 chromosomes. One of the chromosomes of each pair comes from the maternal line and one from the paternal line. In each individual there are two copies of each gene normally present, one on each chromosome. However, genes may exist in different forms, termed **alleles**. The different alleles represent changes (or mutations) in the sequence of the gene that is propagated over many generations, unless natural selection intervenes. Many different allelic forms are common and benign but they account for the individual differences that are found between humans as well as differences between species. For example, two different alleles of a single gene determine whether or not the earlobes will be hanging or attached. In other instances single gene mutations are not benign, as in the case of Huntington's disease (see Chapter 8). A different allele may mean that the end-product encoded by the gene (such as enzymes) works less efficiently, more efficiently or not at all. Alternatively, it may mean that the gene works in an entirely novel way by, for example, altering the expression of other genes. Most behavioral traits will be an outcome of the concerted action of many genes. Even though a given gene may exist in only a small number of discrete allelic types, when many such genetic variants are combined together they may produce an outcome that is continuously distributed – such as the normal distribution found for height or IQ. Disorders such as autism, dyslexia and schizophrenia also appear to be polygenic in nature (see Tager-Flusberg, 2003).

As well as differences in alleles, individuals differ in the spacing of genes on the chromosomes (most of the genome contains non-gene segments). Whilst it is unclear whether this contributes to observable individual differences, an analysis of the spacing of various genomic markers is central to techniques such as genetic "finger-printing" and attempts to locate candidate genes on the basis of behavioral markers (e.g. presence of schizophrenia).

During production of eggs and sperm the genes from the maternal and paternal chromosomes are "shuffled" so that a single new chromosome is created that is a combination of the original two. This mechanism prevents the number of chromosomes doubling in each generation. This provides one mechanism leading to genetic variation through producing different combinations of a finite set of alleles. This process can also go wrong if segments of DNA get deleted or duplicated. Some relatively common genetic disorders formed in this way are summarized below. The relationship between cognition and genes tends to be complex insofar as various aspects of intellectual function are affected, albeit to somewhat different degrees.

Genetic disorder	Origins	Cognitive developmental characteristics
Down's syndrome	A duplicated copy of chromosome 21	General learning difficulties (IQ < 70), poor fine motor control, delayed and impaired expressive language
Turner syndrome	A missing copy of the X-chromosome (or deletion of part of it)	Not associated with mental retardation, but verbal IQ tends to be higher than non-verbal; some difficulties in executive functions and social skills (Ross, Zinn, & McCauley, 2000)
William's syndrome	A deleted segment of chromosome 7	General intellectual impairment but with some tendency for language abilities to be better than spatial abilities; high sociability but not necessarily high social intelligence (Karmiloff-Smith, 2007)

BEHAVIORAL GENETICS

Behavioral genetics is concerned with studying the inheritance of behaviors and cognitive skills. The approach has traditionally been applied to psychiatric disorders such as depression and schizophrenia but more recently it has been used to investigate specific aspects of cognition such as reading ability and memory ability (Plomin, DeFries, McClearn, & McGuffin, 2001). The classic methods of behavioral genetics are twin studies and adoption studies. These provide ways of disentangling nature and nurture.

Identical twins look the same but do they think the same?

Twin studies and adoption studies

Most behaviors run in families but it is hard to know to what extent this reflects shared environment or shared genes. When a child is placed into an adopted home, he or she will effectively have two sets of relatives: biological relatives with whom the child no longer shares any environment, and adopted relatives with whom the child shares an environment but not genes. Will the child more closely resemble the biological or adoptive family, thus emphasizing a role of nature or nurture, respectively? In many cases, it is not possible to contact or test the biological relatives but the genetic contribution can still be estimated by comparing the adopted child with non-adopted siblings in the household (i.e. both the adopted and non-adopted siblings share family environment but not genes).

Twin studies follow a similar logic. Twins are formed either when a single fertilized egg splits in to two (monozygotic or **MZ twins**) or when two eggs are released at the same time and separately fertilized (dizygotic or **DZ twins**). MZ twins are genetically identical; they share 100% of their genes. DZ twins are non-identical and share only 50% of their genes (i.e. the same as non-twin siblings). Given that both are assumed to share the same family environment, any difference between MZ and DZ twins is assumed to reveal genetic influences. Studies of twins reared apart combine the advantages of the standard twin study and adoption study.

There are a number of ifs and buts to the usefulness of these study designs. With regards to twin studies, it is assumed that MZ and DZ twins experience similar environments. However, MZ twins could be treated more similarly by others. Also, MZ twins often have more similar prenatal environments: many MZ twins share the same sac (called chorion) within the placenta, but DZ twins never do. As such, MZ twins may be more likely to be exposed to the same viruses prenatally. With regards to adoption studies, selective placement could mean that children tend to get adopted into similar environments (e.g. with regard to race or socioeconomic status). Another issue is whether families who adopt or who give up their children for adoption are representative of the general population. Plomin et al. (2001) provides an assessment of this debate and argues that the main findings are relatively robust to these potential drawbacks.

The concept of heritability

Twin studies and adoption studies are ways of establishing whether there is genetic influence. **Heritability** is an estimate of *how much* genetics contributes to a trait. In particular, heritability is the proportion of variance in a trait, in a given population, that can be accounted for by genetic differences amongst individuals. It can be estimated from the correlations for relatives on a given measure, such as IQ. If the correlation between IQ scores for biological parents and their adopted-away children is zero, then heritability is zero. If the correlation between biological parents and their adopted-away children is 0.50, then heritability is 100%, because biological parents and their children have 50% of their genes in common (as do all full siblings, and DZ

KEY TERMS

MZ twins (monozygotic)
Genetically identical twins caused when a fertilized egg splits in two.

DZ twins (dizygotic)
Twins who share half of their genes, caused when two eggs are fertilized by two different sperm.

Heritability
The proportion of variance in a trait, in a given population, that can be accounted for by genetic differences amongst individuals.

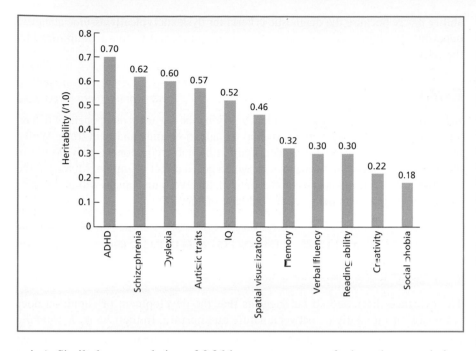

The approximate heritability of various psychological abilities and conditions: Attention Deficit and Hyperactivity Disorder, ADHD (Eaves, et al., 1997); schizophrenia (Gottesman, 1991); dyslexia (Hawke et al., 2006); autistic traits (Hoekstra, Bartels, Verweij, & Boosma, 2007); IQ (Bouchard & McGue, 1981); spatial visualization, memory, verbal fluency (Nichols, 1978); reading ability in elementary school (Thompson et al., 1991); creativity (Nichols, 1978); and social phobia (Kendler, Neale, Kessler, Heath, & Eaves, 1992).

twins). Similarly, a correlation of 0.26 between two sets of adopted-away relatives who share half their genes suggests a heritability of 52%.

In twin studies, if MZ twins correlate with each other by 1.00 and if DZ twins correlate with each other by 0.50, then heritability is 100%. A rough estimate of heritability in a twin study can be made by doubling the difference between the MZ and DZ correlations (Plomin et al., 2001).

The concept of heritability, although useful, is easily misunderstood. It measures how much variability is due to genetic factors within a given population, not the contribution it makes in a given individual. If the heritability of height is around 0.90, it doesn't mean that 90% of a person's height has come from their genes and 10% from the environment. It means that 90% of the differences in height between different people are due to their genes. To give another example, most people have ten fingers and this is genetically specified. However, the heritability measure for number of fingers is low because the *variability* in the number of fingers is due primarily to environmental reasons – industrial accidents, etc. (the example is from Ridley, 2003).

To consider a cognitive example, the fact that heritability for reading ability in elementary school pupils is 0.30 (Thompson, Detterman, & Plomin, 1991) does not mean that 30% of a child's ability is due to genes and 70% due to environment. Reading requires an appropriate environment (i.e. living in a literate culture) otherwise literacy will not exist at all. It also requires an appropriate brain architecture that will support reading. Both are equally essential. The measure of heritability may also vary according to the population studied. If one were to measure reading ability in a country in which education was not universal, then heritability would almost certainly be lower because reading ability would be an outcome of opportunity, i.e. an environmental factor. It is curious, but true, that the more that we become a meritocracy based upon equal opportunities the more that genetic differences will matter. Similarly, the heritability for reading disability, or dyslexia, in Western societies is higher, at 0.60 (Hawke, Wadsworth, & DeFries, 2006), than for reading ability *per se* because the diagnostic criteria for dyslexia typically assume adequate opportunity and intellect; i.e. variability in environmental factors is minimized by the selection criteria.

Evaluation

Behavioral genetics is concerned with quantifying the heritable component of behavior and cognition. It uses methods such as the adoption study and twin study. Whilst these methods are successful in identifying a heritable component, they do not in themselves elucidate the mechanism by which genes affect cognition. Moreover, the "heritability" of a trait depends on the environmental circumstances within the sample selected rather than being a pure measure of "nature".

BEYOND NATURE VERSUS NURTURE: GENE–ENVIRONMENT INTERPLAY

The evidence discussed so far suggests that the development of cognition does not neatly fit into a divide between nature and nurture. In their book, *Rethinking Innateness*, Elman and colleagues (1996) put it this way: "The answer is not Nature *or* Nurture; it's Nature *and* Nurture. But to say that is to trade one platitude for another; what is necessary is to understand the nature of the interaction" (p. 357). The advances made in identifying genes and in understanding genetic mechanisms at the molecular level are now being used to inform theories in developmental cognitive neuroscience. In particular, one is now in a position to investigate whether there are indeed genes for specific cognitive functions (a gene for grammar, a gene for schizophrenia, etc.). Whilst behavioral genetics may show that there is a genetic contribution to individual differences in cognitive traits, it is now possible to explore what that contribution consists of in more mechanistic terms.

Rutter, Moffitt and Caspi (2006) provide an overview of mechanisms of gene–environment interplay. Their review highlights four types of mechanism:

1. Environmental influences can alter the effects of genes. Although the sequence of DNA is normally fixed in a given individual and across all cells in his or her body, the timing and the degree of functioning of genes in the DNA can be affected by the environment (so-called epigenetic events). For example, increased maternal nurturing by a rat affects expression of a stress-reducing gene in its offspring that persists throughout their lifetime (Weaver et al., 2004)

2. Heritability varies according to environmental circumstances. As noted previously, the amount of variation in a population that is due to genetic factors is dependent on the environmental context. In an "equal opportunities" environment heritability tends to be maximized, but in populations with a large environmental risk (e.g. to certain pathogens) or high social control (e.g. on acceptable behavior) heritability will be minimized.

3. **Gene–environment correlations** (rGE) are genetic influences on people's exposure to different environments (Plomin, DeFries, & Loehlin, 1977). For example, people will seek out different environments (e.g. drug taking and novelty seeking) depending on their genotype (Benjamin, Li, Patterson, Greenberg, Murphy, & Hamer,

1996; Kotler et al., 1997). Also, the environment that a parent creates for raising his or her children will depend on the parent's own dispositions (intellect, personality, mental illnesses), which are partly genetic in origin.

4. **Gene X–environment interactions** (G x E) occur when susceptibility to a trait depends on a particular combination of a gene and environment. The effects of the gene and environment together exceed what would be expected from the sum of the parts.

Collectively, these four factors make it less plausible that there will be a "gene for" any given cognitive ability or behavior, as most genes do not appear to have a deterministic (all or nothing) role (Kendler, 2005). In the sections below, I will consider a few illustrative examples from cognitive neuroscience in detail. I shall discuss evidence for the role of the gene FOXP2 in language acquisition and ask whether it is a "gene for grammar". I'll consider how a purely cultural skill, reading, can have a genetic component, and I'll consider how cannabis use may reflect a gene X environment interaction in the onset of schizophrenia.

FOXP2, speech and grammar

In 1990, a remarkable family came to the attention of the scientific community. Around half of the members of the so-called KE family had problems in producing speech and language and, moreover, the pattern of inheritance was consistent with a single gene mutation. Affected family members would come out with sentences like "The boys eat four cookie" and "Carol is cry in the church". Indeed, early reports of the family suggested that they may have problems in specific aspects of grammar (Gopnik, 1990; Gopnik & Crago, 1991), i.e. a potential "gene for grammar". Since then, the affected mutation in the FOXP2 gene has been identified, the nature of the speech problems have been described in more detail and the neural substrates have been explored in both humans and other species (for a review, see Vargha-Khadem, Gadian, Copp, & Mishkin, 2005).

Whilst the core deficit in the family remains debated, the deficits are certainly not limited to grammar. Affected KE family members, relative to unaffected ones, score poorly on tests of pronunciation, grammar, semantics, verbal IQ and even non-verbal IQ, although the scores from the two groups overlap (Vargha-Khadem, Watkins, Alcock, Fletcher, & Passingham, 1995). Tests of oral praxis and orofacial praxis (e.g. copying tongue protrusions or lip pouting) do produce non-overlapping test scores, suggesting that **orofacial dyspraxia** is a core deficit. There is reduced volume in the basal ganglia (caudate nucleus) that correlates with their level of orofacial dyspraxia (Watkins et al., 2002). The basal ganglia have a key role in the control of voluntary movement. The basal ganglia, and the caudate in particular, have also been linked to implicit rule learning in artificial grammars (Lieberman, Chang, Chiao, Bookheimer, & Knowlton, 2004) suggesting a possible link to the grammatical deficits. Other families with Specific Language Impairment (SLI) of developmental origin don't appear to have the FOXP2 gene affected (Newbury et al., 2002), although some of them do perform poorly on grammar in the absence of orofacial dyspraxia (Falcaro et al., 2008). As such, there are likely to be multiple genes that affect grammar and, at present, there are no known genes that specifically affect only grammar.

KEY TERMS

Gene X–environment interactions
Susceptibility to a trait depends on a particular combination of a gene and environment.

Orofacial dyspraxia
An impaired ability to perform the coordinated movements that are required for speech.

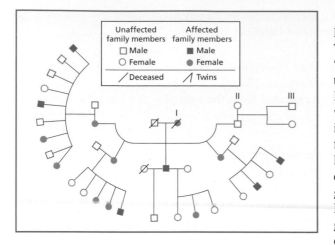

The family tree of three generations of the KE family shows that around half of the members have significant problems in speech and language. This problem has now been linked to a mutation in a single gene called FOXP2. Does this gene have a role to play in the evolution of human language? Reprinted by permission from Macmillan Publishers Ltd: Watkins et al. (2002), copyright 2004.

What do studies of the *normal* version of the FOXP2 gene reveal about its possible function? The product of the FOXP2 gene is what is called a "transcription factor", i.e. its molecular function is to affect the expression of other genes (see Vargha-Khadem et al., 2005). As such, its effects may be wide ranging and it is expressed in various tissues in the body, not just the brain. Haesler et al. (2004) found that FOXP2 expression in birds who need to learn their vocalization (e.g. canaries) had greater expression in the avian equivalent of the basal ganglia during song learning than song production. Intriguingly, the FOXP2 proteins of chimpanzee, gorilla and rhesus macaque are identical to each other but differ from humans' in terms of two small sequence changes, one of which is likely to be functional and has been dated to 200,000 years ago, about the time that anatomically modern humans emerged (Enard et al., 2002). The final word concerning the function of this gene has yet to be written.

Developmental dyslexia

The ability to read is a cultural invention. It is perhaps surprising to discover that a skill that is, by definition, a product of "nurture" should show an influence of "nature". However, learning to read will place demands on basic cognitive processes involved in visual recognition, phonological encoding and so on, and it is entirely likely that there are genetically-mediated differences in these abilities. Although culture is by definition environmental/non-genetic, the brain's ability to create and absorb cultural knowledge will be under genetic influence and be a product of evolution.

With regards to reading, different cultures have adopted different solutions for mapping between spelling and sound. For example, English and French have a high proportion of irregular mappings (e.g. compare the different pronunciations of MINT and PINT), whereas Italian has very few of these. One consequence of this is that learning to read and write in English and French is harder than in Italian, and rates of developmental dyslexia are higher in countries who speak those languages (Lindgren, De Renzi, & Richman, 1985). There could be several different "core" difficulties which vary from dyslexic to dyslexic (e.g. Castles, Datta, Gayan, & Olson, 1999), but that nevertheless transcend cultural differences in reading systems. One candidate core deficit is in phonological processing. Paulesu et al. (2001) compared English, French and Italian dyslexics and normally-reading controls matched for IQ and education level. The English and French dyslexics had received a formal diagnosis. Given that it is very unusual for Italian adults to receive a diagnosis of dyslexia, a large sample was screened and those falling in the bottom 10% of a number of speed-reading tasks were considered dyslexic. (Note: the Italian "dyslexics" were better readers than their English and French counterparts given the nature of their reading system, but were nevertheless poor readers with respect to their Italian controls.) All three groups of dyslexics showed evidence of poor performance in a number of verbal skills, suggesting a core deficit in this area. Brain activity when reading, measured using PET, was consistently reduced in the left posterior temporal

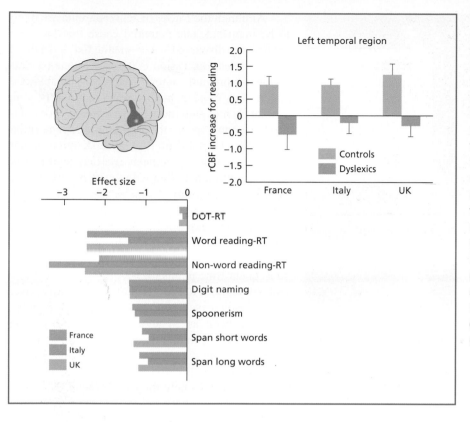

English, French and Italian dyslexics show less activation in a left temporal region relative to controls. English, French and Italian dyslexics show normal reaction time to a dot appearing, but have difficulties on word and non-word reading, and other non-reading tasks including digit naming, spoonerisms ("lucky duck" to "ducky luck") and span tasks (repeating back lists of short or long words). From Paulesu et al. (2001). Reprinted with permission from AAAS.

region in dyslexics relative to controls, suggesting a common neural mechanism independent of the reading system involved.

Schizophrenia and cannabis use

Schizophrenia is a severe disturbance of thought and affect characterized by a loss of contact with reality (i.e. a **psychosis**). The key symptoms include **hallucinations** (e.g. hearing voices), **delusions** (e.g. of being persecuted), disorganized thought and behavior (e.g. incoherence) and emotional disturbances (e.g. blunting of emotions, or inappropriate emotional responses). Some symptoms may be more pronounced in different individuals or in the same individual over time. In order to receive a formal diagnosis, one also needs social and/or occupational dysfunction (e.g. an inability to hold down a job or relationship) and the symptoms must be persisting for at least six months (American Psychiatric Association, 1994). The symptoms often appear in early adulthood and it is equally common in males and females but with an earlier onset in males (Castle, Wesseley, Der, & Murray, 1991). Typically, there is no known precipitating event such as a head injury or family trauma. Longitudinal studies suggest that adults with symptoms of schizophrenia are more likely to report psychotic symptoms at 11 years of age (e.g. in response to questions such as, "Have you ever had messages sent just to you through the television or radio?"), although these early differences are not diagnostic insofar as they do not uniquely predict who will and will not go on to develop it (Poulton, Caspi, Moffitt, Cannon, Murray, & Harrington, 2000).

KEY TERMS

Schizophrenia
A severe disturbance of thought and affect characterized by a loss of contact with reality.

Psychosis
Loss of contact with reality.

Hallucinations
Illusory percepts not shared by others (e.g. hearing voices).

Delusions
Fixed beliefs that are false or fanciful (e.g. of being persecuted).

Is smoking cannabis linked to schizophrenia?

Although the causes of schizophrenia are likely to be manifold, one potential cause that has been extensively discussed in the media and is pertinent to the present discussion is the role of one particular environmental factor – namely, cannabis use. Given that most cannabis users do not become schizophrenic and most schizophrenics have not used cannabis prior to the symptoms emerging, a possible mechanism is a gene X environment interaction. That is, cannabis use may tend to lead to schizophrenia in individuals with a particular genetic susceptibility. Caspi et al. (2005) provide evidence for this conclusion. Over the last 30 years a remarkable experiment has been conducted in Dunedin, New Zealand, in which over 1000 consecutive births have been systematically studied at subsequent time points (3, 5, 7, 9, 11, 13, 15, 18, 21 and 26 years). At age 11, participants were given a childhood psychiatric assessment that included questions about psychosis. They have been asked about cannabis usage from the age of 13. At age 26, participants were formally assessed for schizophrenia. Participants who reported some symptoms but did not meet the full diagnostic criteria (schizophreniform disorder) were also considered. In addition, the presence of a particular genetic variant was assessed, namely the COMT gene. The product of this gene is involved in the metabolism of the neurotransmitter **dopamine** released into synapses. Disturbances in dopamine pathways have long been implicated in schizophrenia (see Kapur, 2003). In particular, a common mutation at one place in the gene leads to the substitution of an amino acid (from valine, Val, to methionine, Met), such that those with two copies of the Val allele (Val/Val) are more efficiently able to break down dopamine, those with two copies of the Met allele (Met/Met) are least able to break down dopamine and those with a copy of both (Val/Met) are intermediate.

The results of Caspi et al.'s study showed a significant relationship between the COMT genotype and cannabis use, such that those with a Val allele (i.e. more efficient metabolism of dopamine) were more likely to show symptoms of schizophrenia, particularly if they had used cannabis (Caspi et al., 2005). Moreover, they found that there was a sensitive period during adolescence in which this gene X environment was important. The elevated risk of psychotic symptoms was not found in cannabis users who started smoking it after 21 years of age. Given the fact that the participants had been assessed throughout childhood, it was possible to exclude other factors such as childhood cognitive deficits, previous use of other drugs and conduct disorder at school. It was also possible to rule out the possibility that those with the Val allele were more likely to develop schizophrenia because they were more inclined to try cannabis (a possible gene–environment correlation). Those with the Met allele were just as likely to use it as those with the Val allele, but only those with the Val allele showed the increased risk.

The explanation involving the COMT gene and cannabis use may explain only a small, but significant, part of schizophrenia. Genetic linkage studies have identified potential "schizophrenia genes" on almost every chromosome, often with poor replications in different samples (Levinson, 2003). As such, it is possible that different schizophrenics have entirely different causes in terms of the genetic and environmental contributions, despite having equivalent symptoms. It still remains possible that a single brain pathway is being disrupted in multiple ways. It is also possible, if not probable, that there aren't strictly any "genes for" schizophrenia (i.e. in the deterministic sense that this set of genes will inevitably result in schizophrenia). The Val allele of COMT is *not* a gene for schizophrenia. But this doesn't mean that there isn't a genetic component. The Val allele of COMT is a normal gene that is present in a large proportion of the population that conveys susceptibility. The example of the COMT gene and cannabis use offers an important insight into how the tired nature–nurture debate can move forward. Instead of concluding that a given aspect of cognition is "part nature and part nurture", we can begin to understand what that could mean in terms of an underlying brain mechanism.

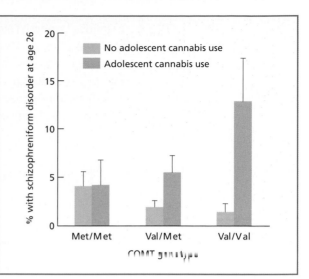

The COMT gene is involved in the metabolism of the neurotransmitter dopamine and the gene exists in two main forms (termed Val and Met). Each person has two copies of the gene. If you have a Val copy of the gene *and* you smoke cannabis during adolescence, then there is an increased risk of displaying symptoms of schizophrenia at age 26 – a gene X–environment interaction. Reprinted from Caspi et al. (2005) Copyright 2005, with permission from Elsevier.

SUMMARY AND KEY POINTS OF THE CHAPTER

- Structural changes in the brain occur throughout life. Genes not only influence prenatal development (e.g. the formation of large numbers of synapses around birth) but have a lifelong influence. Environmental influences can switch genes on or off, and can also influence brain structure (e.g. determining whether connections are used or lost).
- There is good evidence from both animal studies and human research for sensitive periods in development in which the brain is optimally readied to acquire certain skills or knowledge. However, these periods may be more flexible than were first thought.
- The word "innate" can mean at least two different things: either referring to instincts that have been shaped by natural selection (language being one candidate); or referring to knowledge/skills/resources acquired in the absence of experience (candidates include certain preferences and dislikes, and the existence of orientation-selective cells in visual cortex).
- Twin and adoption studies provide one way of showing that there is a genetic contribution for a given trait. However, the concept of "heritability" is not a pure measure of genetics because the amount of variance in a trait that is due to genetic factors will also depend on the amount of variance that is due to non-genetic factors.
- Genetic disorders can often affect some cognitive abilities more than others. However, genes are rarely highly specific for psychological/

cognitive traits. This is because genes interact with other genes, and there is a complex interplay between genes and environment. Sometimes a gene makes certain environments more likely to be sought out (a gene–environment correlation), and sometimes a gene leads to a susceptibility that also depends crucially on environmental circumstance (a gene–environment interaction).

EXAMPLE ESSAY QUESTIONS

- Evaluate the Protomap and Protocortex theories of brain development.
- What is the evidence for critical periods in development and what kinds of neural mechanism could give rise to them?
- To what extent can any kind of behavior be said to be innate?
- What is meant by the term heritability and how can it be measured?
- How might gene–environment interplay contribute to developmental and psychiatric disorders?

RECOMMENDED FURTHER READING

- Goswami, U. (2008). *Cognitive development: The learning brain*. Hove: Psychology Press. An introductory textbook on all aspects of development, including evidence from developmental cognitive neuroscience.

- Johnson, M. H. (2005). *Developmental cognitive neuroscience:* An introduction, 2nd edition. Oxford: Blackwell. A good introductory overview.

- Nelson, C. A. & Luciana, M. (2008). *Handbook of developmental cognitive neuroscience*, 2nd edition. Boston, MA: MIT Press. A comprehensive selection of advanced topics.

References

Abell, F., Krams, M., Ashburner, J., Passingham, R., Friston, K., Frackowiak, R., Happe, F., Frith, C., & Frith, U. (1999). The neuroanatomy of autism: A voxel-based whole brain analysis of structural scans. *NeuroReport*, *10*, 1647–1651.

Abutalebi, J., Cappa, S. F., & Perani, D. (2005). What can functional neuroimaging tell us about the bilingual brain? In J. F. Kroll, & A. M. B. de Groot (eds.), *Handbook of bilingualism*. Oxford: Oxford University Press.

Adolphs, R. (2002). Neural systems for recognizing emotion. *Current Opinion in Neurobiology*, *12*, 169–177.

Adolphs, R., Gosselin, F., Buchanan, T. W., Tranel, D., Schyns, P., & Damasio, A. R. (2005). A mechanism for impaired fear recognition after amygdala damage. *Nature*, *433*, 68–72.

Adolphs, R., Tranel, D., Damasio, H., & Damasio, A. (1994). Impaired recognition of emotion in facial expressions following bilateral damage to the human amygdala. *Nature*, *372*, 669–672.

Aggleton, J. P., & Brown, M. W. (1999). Episodic memory, amnesia, and the hippocampal-anterior thalamic axis. *Behavioral and Brain Sciences*, *22*, 425–489.

Aglioti, S., DeSouza, J. F. X., & Goodale, M. A. (1995). Size-contrast illusions deceive the eye but not the hand. *Current Biology*, *5*, 679–685.

Agranoff, B. W., David, R. E., & Brink, J. J. (1966). Chemical studies on memory fixation in goldfish. *Brain Research*, *1*, 303–309.

Aguirre, G. K., Zarahn, E., & D'Esposito, M. (1998). The variability of human BOLD hemodynamic response. *NeuroImage*, *8*, 360–369.

Albanese, E., Capitani, E., Barbarotto, R., & Laiacona, M. (2000). Semantic category dissociations, familiarity and gender. *Cortex*, *36*, 733–746.

Alcock, K. J., Passingham, R. E., Watkins, K., & Vargha-Khadem, F. (2000a). Pitch and timing abilities in inherited speech and language impairment. *Brain and Language*, *75*, 34–46.

Alcock, K. J., Wade, D., Anslow, P., & Passingham, R. E. (2000b). Pitch and timing abilities in adult left-hemisphere-dysphasic and right-hemisphere-damaged subjects. *Brain and Language*, *75*, 47–65.

Alexander, G. E., & Crutcher, M. D. (1990). Functional architecture of basal ganglia circuits: Neural substrates of parallel processing. *Trends in Neurosciences*, *13*, 266–271.

Alho, K. (1995). Cerebral generators of mismatch negativity (MMN) and its magnetic counterpart (mMMN) elicited by sound changes. *Ear and Hearing*, *16*, 38–51.

Alho, K., Woods, D. L., & Algazi, A. (1994). Processing of auditory-stimuli during auditory and visual attention as revealed by event-related potentials. *Psychophysiology*, *31*, 469–479.

Allport, D. A. (1985). Distributed memory, modular systems and dysphasia. In S. K. Newman, & R. Epstein (eds.), *Current perspectives in dysphasia*. Edinburgh: Churchill Livingstone.

Allport, D. A., Styles, E. A., & Hsieh, S. (1994). Shifting intentional set: Exploring the dynamic control of tasks. In C. Umiltà & M. Moscovitch (eds.), *Attention and performance XV: Conscious and nonconscious information processing*. Cambridge, MA: MIT Press.

Altmann, C. F., Bulthoff, H. H., & Kourtzi, Z. (2003). Perceptual organization of local elements into global shapes in the human visual cortex. *Current Biology*, *13*, 342–349.

Altmann, G. T., Garnham, A., & Henstra, J. A. (1994). Effects of syntax in human sentence parsing: Evidence against a structure-based parsing mechanism. *Journal of Experimental Psychology: Learning, Memory, and Cognition*, *20*, 209–216.

Amedi, A., Floel, A., Knecht, S., Zohary, E., & Cohen, L. G. (2004). Transcranial magnetic stimulation of the occipital pole interferes with verbal processing in blind subjects. *Nature Neuroscience*, *7*, 1266–1270.

American Psychiatric Association (1994). *Diagnostic and statistical manual of mental disorders*, 4th edition. (*DSM-IV*). American Psychiatric Association: Washington, DC.

Andersen, R. A. (1997). Multimodal integration for the representation of space in the posterior parietal cortex. *Philosophical Transactions of the Royal Society of London B*, *352*, 1421–1428.

Andersen, R. A., Snyder, L. H., Li, C. S., & Stricanne, B. (1993). Coordinate transformations in the representation of spatial information. *Current Opinion in Neurobiology*, *3*, 171–176.

Anderson, M. C., Bjork, R. A., & Bjork, E. L. (1994). Remembering can cause forgetting: Retrieval dynamics in long-term memory. *Journal of Experimental Psychology: Learning, Memory and Cognition*, *20*, 1063–1087.

Anderson, M. C., Ochsner, K. N., Kuhl, B., Cooper, J., Robertson, E., Gabrieli, S. W., Glover, G. H., & Gabrieli, J. D. E. (2004). Neural systems underlying the suppression of unwanted memories. *Science*, *303*, 232–235.

Anderson, M. I., & Jeffery, K. J. (2003). Heterogeneous modulation of place cell firing by changes in context. *Journal of Neuroscience*, *23*, 8827–8835.

Anderson, S. W., Bechara, A., Damasio, H., Tranel, D., & Damasio, A. R. (1999). Impairment of social and moral behavior related to early damage in human prefrontal cortex. *Nature Neuroscience*, 2, 1032–1037.

Anderson, S. W., Damasio, A. R., & Damasio, H. (1990). Troubled letters but not numbers. *Brain*, *113*, 749–766.

Antell, S. E., & Keating, D. P. (1983). Perception of numerical invariance in neonates. *Child Development*, *54*, 695–701.

Aram, D., & Ekelman, B. L. (1986). Cognitive profiles of children with unilateral brain lesions. *Developmental Neuropsychology*, *2*, 155–172.

Aron, A. R., Fletcher, P. C., Bullmore, E. T., Sahakian, B. J., & Robbins, T. W. (2003). Stop-signal inhibition disrupted by damage to right inferior frontal gyrus in humans. *Nature Neuroscience*, *6*, 115–116.

Aron, A. R., Monsell, S., Sahakian, B. J., & Robbins, T. W. (2004). A componential analysis of task-switching deficits associated with lesions of left and right frontal cortex. *Brain*, *127*, 1561–1573.

Aron, A. R., Robbins, T. W., & Poldrack, R. A. (2004). Inhibition and the right inferior frontal cortex. *Trends in Cognitive Sciences*, *8*, 170–177.

Asaad, W. F., Rainer, G., & Miller, E. K. (1998). Neural activity in the primate prefrontal cortex during associative learning. *Neuron*, *21*, 1399–3407.

Asaad, W. F., Rainer, G., & Miller, E. K. (2000). Task-specific neural activity in the primate prefrontal cortex. *Journal of Neurophysiology*, *84*, 451–459.

Ashbridge, E., Cowey, A., & Wade, D. (1999). Does parietal cortex contribute to feature binding? *Neuropsychologia*, *37*, 999–1004.

Ashbridge, E., Walsh, V., & Cowey, A. (1997). Temporal aspects of visual search studied by transcranial magnetic stimulation. *Neuropsychologia*, *35*, 1121–1131.

Ashburner, J., & Friston, K. J. (2000). Voxel-based morphometry: The methods. *NeuroImage*, *11*, 805–821.

Asperger, H. (1944). "Autistic psychopathy" in childhood. In U. Frith (ed.), *Autism and Asperger syndrome*. Cambridge: Cambridge University Press.

Atkinson, R. C., & Shiffrin, R. M. (1968). Human memory: A proposed system and its control processes. In K. W. Spence, & J. T. Spence (eds.), *The psychology of learning and motivation: Advances in research and theory* (Vol. 2). New York: Academic Press.

Attwell, D., & Iadecola, C. (2002). The neural basis of functional brain imaging signals. *Trends in Neurosciences*, *25*, 621–625.

Ayotte, J., Peretz, I., & Hyde, K. (2002). Congenital amusia: A group study of adults afflicted with a music-specific disorder. *Brain*, *125*, 238–251.

Baddeley, A. D. (1966a). The capacity for generating information by randomization. *Quarterly Journal of Experimental Psychology*, *18*, 119–129.

Baddeley, A. D. (1966b). Short-term memory for word sequences as a function of acoustic, semantic and formal similarity. *Quarterly Journal of Experimental Psychology*, *18*, 334–365.

Baddeley, A. D. (1986). *Working memory*. Oxford: Oxford University Press.

Baddeley, A. D. (1990). *Human memory: Theory and practice*. Hove: Psychology Press.

Baddeley, A. D. (1993). Short-term phonological memory and long-term learning: A single case study. *European Journal of Cognitive Psychology*, *5*, 129–148.

Baddeley, A. D. (1996). Exploring the central executive. *Quarterly Journal of Experimental Psychology*, *49A*, 5–28.

Baddeley, A. D., & Hitch, G. (1974). Working memory. In G. A. Bower (ed.), *Recent advances in learning and motivation* (Vol. 8). New York: Academic Press.

Baddeley, A. D., & Warrington, E. K. (1970). Amnesia and the distinction between long- and short-term memory. *Journal of Verbal Learning and Verbal Behavior*, *9*, 176–189.

Baddeley, A. D., Lewis, V., & Vallar, G. (1984). Exploring the articulatory loop. *Quarterly Journal of Experimental Psychology*, *36*, 233–252.

Baddeley, A. D., Papagno, C., & Vallar, G. (1988). When long-term learning depends on short-term storage. *Journal of Memory and Language*, *27*, 586–595.

Baddeley, A. D., Thomson, N., & Buchanan, M. (1975). Word length and the structure of short-term memory. *Journal of Verbal Learning and Verbal Behavior*, *9*, 176–189.

Badecker, W., & Caramazza, A. (1985). On considerations of method and theory governing the use of clinical categories in neurolinguistics and cognitive neuropsychology. *Cognition*, *20*, 97–125.

Baird, G., Charman, T., Baron-Cohen, S., Cox, A., Swettenham, J., Wheelwright, S., & Drew, A. (2000). A screening instrument for autism at 18 months of age: A 6-year follow-up study. *Journal of the American Academy of Child Adolescent Psychiatry*, *39*, 694–702.

Balint, R. (1909, trans. 1995). *Cognitive Neuropsychology*, *12*, 265–281.

Ballantyne, A. O., Spilkin, A. M., Hesselink, J., & Trauner, D. A. (2008). Plasticity in the developing brain: Intellectual, language and academic functions in children with ischaemic perinatal stroke. *Brain*, *131*, 2975–2985.

Barch, D. M., Braver, T. S., Akbudak, E., Conturo, T., Ollinger, J., & Snyder, A. (2001). Anterior cingulate cortex and response conflict: Effects of response modality and processing domain. *Cerebral Cortex*, *11*, 837–848.

Barker, A. T., Jalinous, R., & Freeston, I. L. (1985). Non-invasive magnetic stimulation of human motor cortex. *Lancet*, *1*, 1106–1107.

Barlow, H. B. (1953). Summation and inhibition in the frog's retina. *Journal of Physiology*, *119*, 69–88.

Barlow, H. B., Kohn, H. I., & Walsh, E. G. (1947). Visual sensations aroused by magnetic fields. *American Journal of Physiology*, *148*, 372–375.

Baron-Cohen, S. (1995a). The Eye-Direction Detector (EDD) and the Shared Attention Mechanism (SAM): Two cases for evolutionary psychology. In C. Moore, & P. Dunham (eds.), *The role of joint attention in development*. Hillsdale, NJ: Lawrence Erlbaum.

Baron-Cohen, S. (1995b). *Mindblindness: An essay on autism and theory of mind*. Cambridge, MA: MIT Press.

Baron-Cohen, S. (2002). The extreme male brain theory of autism. *Trends in Cognitive Sciences*, *6*, 248–254.

Baron-Cohen, S., & Cross, P. (1992). Reading the eyes: Evidence for the role of perception in the development of theory of mind. *Mind and Language*, *6*, 166–180.

Baron-Cohen, S., Campbell, R., Karmiloff-Smith, A., Grant, J., & Walker, J. (1995). Are children with autism blind to the mentalistic significance of eyes? *British Journal of Developmental Psychology*, *13*, 379–398.

Baron-Cohen, S., Leslie, A., & Frith, U. (1985). Does the autistic child have a "theory of mind"? *Cognition*, *21*, 37–46.

Baron-Cohen, S., Leslie, A. M., & Frith, U. (1986). Mechanical, behavioural and intentional understanding of picture stories in autistic children. *British Journal of Developmental Psychology*, *4*, 113–125.

Baron-Cohen, S., Richler, J., Bisarya, D., Gurunathan, N., & Wheelwright, S. (2003). The systemizing quotient: An investigation of adults with Asperger syndrome or high-functioning autism, and normal sex differences. *Philosophical Transactions of the Royal Society of London B*, *358*, 361–374.

Baron-Cohen, S., Wheelwright, S., Stone, V., & Rutherford, M. (1999). A mathematician, a physicist and a computer scientist with Asperger syndrome: Performance on psychology and folk physics tests. *Neurocase*, *5*, 475–483.

Barrett, D. J., & Hall, D. A. (2006). Response preferences for "what" and "where" in human non-primary auditory cortex. *Neuroimage*, *32*, 968–977.

Barry, C. (1994). Spelling routes (or roots or rutes). In G. D. A. Brown, & N. C. Ellis (eds.), *Handbook of spelling: Theory, process and intervention*. London: Wiley.

Barry, C., Morrison, C. M., & Ellis, A. W. (1997). Naming the Snodgrass and Vanderwart pictures: Effects of age of acquisition, frequency and name agreement. *Quarterly Journal of Experimental Psychology*, *50A*, 560–585.

Bartels, A., & Zeki, S. (2000). The neural basis of romantic love. *NeuroReport*, *11*, 3829–3834.

Bartley, A. J., Jones, D. W., & Weinberger, D. R. (1997). Genetic variability of human brain size and cortical gyral patterns. *Brain*, *120*, 257–269.

Bartolomeo, P. (2002). The relationship between visual perception and visual mental imagery: A reappraisal of the neuropsychological evidence. *Cortex*, *38*, 357–378.

Bastin, C., Van der Linden, M., Charnallet, A., Denby, C., Montaldi, D., Roberts, N., & Mayes, A. R. (2004). Dissociation between recall and recognition memory performance in an amnesic patient with hippocampal damage following carbon monoxide poisoning. *Neurocase*, *10*, 330–344.

Batteau, D. W. (1967). The role of the pinna in human localization. *Proceedings of the Royal Society of London B*, *168*, 158–180.

Baxendale, S. (2004). Memories aren't made of this: Amnesia at the movies. *British Medical Journal*, *329*, 1480–1483.

Baxter, D. M., & Warrington, E. K. (1986). Ideational agraphia: A single case study. *Journal of Neurology, Neurosurgery and Psychiatry*, *49*, 369–374.

Bayliss, G. C., Rolls, E. T., & Leonard, C. M. (1985). Selectivity between faces in the responses of a population in the superior temporal sulcus of the monkey. *Brain Research*, *342*, 91–102.

Beauchamp, M. S., Lee, K. E., Haxby, J. V., & Martin, A. (2002). Parallel visual motion processing streams for manipulable objects and human movements. *Neuron*, *34*, 149–159.

Beauvois, M.-F. (1982). Optic aphasia: A process of interaction between vision and language. *Philosophical Transactions of the Royal Society of London*, *298*, 35–47.

Beauvois, M.-F., & Derouesne, J. (1981). Lexical or orthographic agraphia. *Brain*, *104*, 21–49.

Beauvois, M.-F., & Derouesne, L. (1979). Phonological alexia: Three dissociations. *Journal of Neurology, Neurosurgery and Psychiatry*, *42*, 1115–1124.

Beauvois, M.-F., & Saillant, B. (1985). Optic aphasia for colours and colour agnosia: A distinction between visual and visuo-verbal impairments in the processing of colours. *Cognitive Neuropsychology*, *2*, 1–48.

Beauvois, M.-F., Derouesne, J., & Bastard, V. (1981). Auditory parallel to phonological alexia. *International Journal of Neuroscience*, *12*, 236–237.

Bechara, A., Damasio, A. R., Damasio, H., & Anderson, S. W. (1994). Insensitivity to future consequences following damage to human prefrontal cortex. *Cognition*, *50*, 7–15.

Bechara, A., Damasio, H., Damasio, A. R., & Lee, G. P. (1999). Different contributions to the human amygdala and ventromedial prefrontal cortex to decision making. *Journal of Neuroscience*, *19*, 5437–5481.

Bechara, A., Damasio, H., Tranel, D., & Anderson, S. W. (1998). Dissociation of working memory from decision making within the human prefrontal cortex. *Journal of Neuroscience*, *18*, 428–437.

Bechara, A., Damasio, H., Tranel, D., & Damasio, A. R. (1997). Deciding advantageously before knowing the advantageous strategy. *Science*, *275*, 1293–1295.

Beck, D. M., Rees, G., Frith, C. D., & Lavie, N. (2001). Neural correlates of change detection and change blindness. *Nature Neuroscience, 4,* 645–650.

Beeson, P. M., Rapcsak, S. Z., Plante, E., Chargualaf, J., Chung, A., Johnson, S. C., & Trouard, T. P. (2003). The neural substrates of writing: A functional magnetic resonance imaging study. *Aphasiology, 17,* 647–666.

Behrmann, M., & Bub, D. (1992). Surface dyslexia and dysgraphia: Dual routes, single lexicon. *Cognitive Neuropsychology, 9,* 209–251.

Behrmann, M., Moscovitch, M., & Winocur, G. (1994). Intact visual imagery and impaired visual perception in a patient with visual agnosia. *Journal of Experimental Psychology: Human Perception and Performance, 20,* 1068–1087.

Behrmann, M., Plaut, D. C., & Nelson, J. (1998). A literature review and new data supporting an interactive activation account of letter-by-letter reading. *Cognitive Neuropsychology, 15,* 7–51.

Bekesy, G. von (1960). *Experiments in hearing.* New York: McGraw-Hill.

Belin, P., & Zatorre, R. J. (2003). Adaptation to speaker's voice in right anterior temporal lobe. *NeuroReport, 14,* 2105–2109.

Belin, P., Zatorre, R. J., Lafaille, P., Ahad, P., & Pike, B. (2000). Voice-selective areas in human auditory cortex. *Nature, 403,* 309–312.

Bench, C. J., Frith, C. D., Grasby, P. M., Friston, K. J., Paulesu, E., & Frackowiak, R. S. J. (1993). Investigations of the functional anatomy of attention using the Stroop test. *Neuropsychologia, 31,* 907–922.

Bendor, D., & Wang, X. Q. (2005). The neuronal representation of pitch in primate auditory cortex. *Nature, 436,* 1161–1165.

Bengtsson, S. L., Nagy, Z., Skare, S., Forsman, L., Forssberg, H., & Ullen, F. (2005). Extensive piano practicing has regionally specific effects on white matter development. *Nature Neuroscience, 8,* 1148–1150.

Benjamin, J., Li, L., Patterson, C., Greenberg, B. D., Murphy, D. L., & Hamer, D. H. (1996). Population and familial association between the D4 dopamine receptor gene and measures of novelty seeking. *Nature Genetics, 12,* 81–84.

Bentin, S., & Deouell, L. Y. (2000). Structural encoding and identification in face processing: ERP evidence for separate mechanisms. *Cognitive Neuropsychology, 17,* 35–54.

Bentin, S., Allison, T., Puce, A., Perez, E., & McCarthy, G. (1996). Electrophysiological studies of face perception in humans. *Journal of Cognitive Neuroscience, 8,* 551–565.

Bentin, S., Mouchetant-Rostaing, Y., Giard, M. H., Echallier, J. F., & Pernier, J. (1999). ERP manifestations of processing printed words at different psycholinguistic levels. *Journal of Cognitive Neuroscience, 11,* 235–260.

Bentin, S., Sagiv, N., Mecklinger, A., Friederici, A., & von Cramon, Y. D. (2002). Priming visual face-processing mechanisms: Electrophysiological evidence. *Psychological Science, 13,* 190–193.

Benton, A. L. (1977). Reflections on the Gerstmann syndrome. *Brain and Language, 4,* 45–62.

Benton, A. L., & Van Allen, M. W. (1968). Impairment in facial recognition in patients with cerebral disease. *Cortex, 4,* 344–358.

Beradelli, A., Rothwell, J. C., Thompson, P. D., & Hallett, M. (2001). Pathophysiology of bradykinesia in Parkinson's disease. *Brain, 124,* 2131–2146.

Berger, H. (1929). Über das elektroenkephalogramm des menschen *Archiv für Psychiatrie und Nervenkrankheiten, 87,* 527–570.

Bertelson, P., & Aschersleben, G. (1998). Automatic visual bias of perceived auditory location. *Psychonomic Bulletin and Review, 5,* 482–489.

Berti, A., & Frassinetti, F. (2000). When far becomes near: Remapping of space by tool use. *Journal of Cognitive Neuroscience, 12,* 415–420.

Besner, D., Twilley, L., McCann, R. S., & Seegobin, K. (1990). On the association between connectionism and data: Are a few words necessary? *Psychological Review, 97,* 432–446.

Best, C. T., & Avery, R. A. (1999). Left-hemisphere advantage for click consonants is determined by linguistic significance and experience. *Psychological Science, 10,* 65–70.

Bever, T. G. (1970). The cognitive basis for linguistic structures. In J. R. Hayes (ed.), *Cognition and the development of language.* New York: Wiley.

Beyerstein, B. L. (1999). Whence cometh the myth that we only use 10% of our brains? In S. D. Salla (ed.), *Mind myths.* Chichester: Wiley.

Biederman, I. (1987). Recognition by components: A theory of human image understanding. *Psychological Review, 94,* 115–145.

Binder, J. R., Frost, J. A., Hammeke, T. A., Bellgowan, P. S., Springer, J. A., Kaufman, J. N., & Possing, E. T. (2000). Human temporal lobe activation by speech and non-speech sounds. *Cerebral Cortex, 10,* 512–528.

Bird, C. M., Casteli, F., Malik, O., Frith, U., & Husain, M. (2004). The impact of extensive medial frontal lobe damage on "theory of mind" and cognition. *Brain, 127,* 914–928.

Bird, H., Howard, D., & Franklin, S. (2000). Why is a verb like an inanimate object? Grammatical category and semantic category deficits. *Brain and Language, 72,* 246–309.

Birdsong, D. (2006). Age and second language acquisition and processing: A selective overview. *Language Learning, 56,* 9–49.

Bisiach, E., & Luzzatti, C. (1978). Unilateral neglect of representational space. *Cortex, 14,* 129–133.

Bjork, E. L. (1998). Intentional forgetting perspective: Comments, conjectures and some directed remembering. In J. M. Golding, & C. M. MacLoed (eds.), *Intentional forgetting: Interdisciplinary approaches.* Mahwah, NJ: Lawrence Erlbaum.

Blair, R. J. R. (1995). A cognitive developmental approach to morality: Investigating the psychopath. *Cognition, 57,* 1–29.

Blair, R. J. R. (2003). Facial expressions, their communicatory functions and neuro-cognitive substrates. *Philosophical Transactions of the Royal Society of London B, 358,* 561–572.

Blair, R. J. R., & Cipolotti, L. (2000). Impaired social response reversal: A case of acquired "sociopathy". *Brain, 123,* 1122–1141.

Blair, R. J. R., Jones, L., Clark, F., & Smith, M. (1997). The psychopathic individual: A lack of responsiveness to distress cues? *Psychophysiology, 34,* 192–198.

Blakemore, C. (1977). *Mechanics of the mind.* Cambridge: Cambridge University Press.

Blakemore, C., & Vansluyters, R. C. (1975). Innate and environmental factors in development of kittens' visual-cortex. *Journal of Physiology, 248,* 663–716.

Blakemore, S.-J., Bristow, D., Bird, G., Frith, C., & Ward, J. (2005). Somatosensory activations during the observation of touch and a case of vision-touch synesthesia. *Brain, 128,* 1571–1583.

Blakemore, S.-J., Rees, G., & Frith, C. D. (1998). How do we predict the consequences of our actions? A functional imaging study. *Neuropsychologia, 36,* 521–529.

Blakemore, S.-J., Winston, J., & Frith, U. (2004). Social cognitive neuroscience: Where are we heading? *Trends in Cognitive Sciences, 8,* 216–222.

Blood, A. J., & Zatorre, R. J. (2001). Intensely pleasurable responses to music correlates with activity in brain regions implicated in reward and emotion. *Proceedings of the National Academy of Science, USA, 98,* 11818–11823.

Bodamer, J. (1947). Die prosopagnosie. *Archiv für Psychiatrie und Zeitschrift für Neurologie, 179,* 6–54.

Bolhuis, J. J. (1990). Mechanisms of avian imprinting: A review. *Biological Reviews, 66,* 303–345.

Bottini, G., Corcoran, R., Sterzi, R., Paulesu, E., Schenone, P., Scarpa, P., Frackowiak, R. S. J., & Frith, C. D. (1994). The role of the right hemisphere in the interpretation of figurative aspects of language: A positron emission tomography activation study. *Brain, 117,* 1241–1253.

Botvinick, M., & Cohen, J. (1998). Rubber hands "feel" touch that eyes see. *Nature, 391,* 756.

Boucart, M., & Humphreys, G. W. (1992). The computation of perceptual structure and closure: Normality and pathology. *Neuropsychologia, 30,* 527–546.

Bouchard, T. J. J., & McGue, M. (1981). Familial studies of intelligence: A review. *Science, 212,* 1055–1059.

Bowers, D., & Heilman, K. M. (1980). Pseudoneglect: Effects of hemispace on a tactile line bisection task. *Neuropsychologia, 18,* 491–498.

Bowers, J. S., Bub, D., & Arguin, M. (1996). A characterisation of the word superiority effect in pure alexia. *Cognitive Neuropsychology, 13,* 415–441.

Bowles, B., Crupi, C., Mirsattari, S. M., Pigott, S. E., Parrent, A. G., Pruessner, J. C., Yonelinas, A. P., & Kohler, S. (2007). Impaired familiarity with preserved recollection after anterior temporal-lobe resection that spares the hippocampus. *Proceedings of the National Academy of Sciences, USA, 104,* 16382–16387.

Brammer, M. J. (2001). Head motion and its correction. In P. Jezzard, P. M. Matthews, & S. M. Smith (eds.), *Functional MRI.* Oxford: Oxford University Press.

Brannon, E. M., & Terrace, H. S. (1998). Ordering of the numerosities 1 to 9 by monkeys. *Science, 282,* 746–749.

Brass, M., & Haggard, P. (2007). To do or not to do: The neural signature of self-control. *Journal of Neuroscience, 27,* 9141–9145.

Brass, M., & von Cramon, D. Y. (2002). The role of the frontal cortex in task preparation. *Cerebral Cortex, 12,* 908–914.

Brebion, G., Smith, M. J., Gorman, J. M., & Amador, X. (1997). Discrimination accuracy and decision biases in different types of reality monitoring in schizophrenia. *Journal of Nervous and Mental Disease, 185,* 247–253.

Bredart, S., Brennen, T., & Valentine, T. (1997). Dissociations between the processing of proper and common names. *Cognitive Neuropsychology, 14,* 209–217.

Bremmer, F., Schlack, A., Shah, N. J., Zafiris, O., Kubischik, M., Hoffmann, K. P., Zilles, K., & Fink, G. R. (2001). Polymodal motion processing in posterior parietal and premotor cortex: A human fMRI study strongly implies equivalencies between humans and monkeys. *Neuron, 29,* 287–296.

Broadbent, D. E. (1958). *Perception and communication.* London: Pergamon Press.

Broca, P. (1861). Remarques sur le siège de la faculté du langagé articule, suivies d'une observation d'aphémie. *Bulletin et Mémoires de la Société Anatomique de Paris, 2,* 330–357.

Brooks, D. J., Ibanez, V., Sawles, G. V., Quinn, N., Lees, A. J., Mathias, C. J., Banniseter, R., Marsden, C. D., & Frackowiak, R. S. J. (1990). Differing patterns of striatal 18F-dopa uptake in Parkinson's disease, multiple system atrophy, and progressive supranuclear palsy. *Annals of Neurology, 28,* 547–555.

Brown, A. S. (1991). A review of the tip-of-the-tongue experience. *Psychological Bulletin, 109,* 204–223.

Brown, R., & McNeill, D. (1966). The "tip of the tongue" phenomenon. *Journal of Verbal Learning and Verbal Behavior, 5,* 325–337.

Brown, R. G., & Marsden, C. D. (1988). Internal versus external cues and the control of attention in Parkinson's disease. *Brain, 111*, 323–345.

Bruandet, M., Molko, N., Cohen, L., & Dehaene, S. (2003). A cognitive characterisation of dyscalculia in Turner syndrome. *Neuropsychologia, 42*, 288–298.

Bruce, C. J., Goldberg, M. E., Bushnell, M. C., & Stanton, G. B. (1985). Primate frontal eye fields: II. Physiological and anatomical correlates of electrically evoked eye movements. *Journal of Neurophysiology, 54*, 714–734.

Bruce, V., & Valentine, T. (1986). Semantic priming of familiar faces. *Quarterly Journal of Experimental Psychology, 38A*, 125–150.

Bruce, V., & Young, A. W. (1986). Understanding face recognition. *British Journal of Psychology, 77*, 305–327.

Brugge, J. F., & Merzenich, M. M. (1973). Responses of neurons in auditory cortex of the macaque monkey to monaural and binaural stimulation. *Journal of Neurophysiology, 36*, 1138–1158.

Brysbaert, M. (1995). Arabic number reading: On the nature of the numerical scale and the origin of phonological recoding. *Journal of Experimental Psychology: General, 124*, 434–452.

Bub, D., & Kertesz, A. (1982). Deep agraphia. *Brain and Language, 17*, 146–165.

Buccino, G., Lui, F., Canessa, N., Patteri, I., Lagravinese, G., Benuzzi, F., Porro, C. A., & Rizzolatti, G. (2004). Neural circuits involved in the recognition of actions performed by nonconspecifics: An fMRI study. *Journal of Cognitive Neuroscience, 16*, 114–126.

Buchsbaum, B. R., & D'Esposito, M. (2008). The search for the phonological store: From loop to convolution. *Journal of Cognitive Neuroscience, 20*, 762–778.

Buckner, R. L., Kelley, W. M., & Petersen, S. E. (1999). Frontal cortex contributes to human memory formation. *Nature Neuroscience, 2*, 311–314.

Burani, C., Barca, L., & Ellis, A. W. (2006). Orthographic complexity and word naming in Italian: Some words are more transparent than others. *Psychonomic Bulletin, & Review, 13*, 346–352.

Burbaud, P., Camus, O., Guehl, D., Biolac, B., Caille, J. M., & Allard, M. (1999). A functional magnetic resonance imaging study of mental subtraction in human subjects. *Neuroscience Letters, 273*, 195–199.

Burgess, N. (2002). The hippocampus, space, and viewpoints in episodic memory. *Quarterly Journal of Experimental Psychology, 55A*, 1057–1080.

Burgess, P. W. (2000). Strategy application disorder: The role of the frontal lobes in human multitasking. *Psychological Research, 63*, 279–288.

Burgess, P. W., & Shallice, T. (1996a). Bizarre responses, rule detection and frontal lobe lesions. *Cortex, 32*, 241–259.

Burgess, P. W., & Shallice, T. (1996b). Confabulation and the control of recollection. *Memory, 4*, 359–411.

Burgess, P. W., & Shallice, T. (1996c). Response suppression, initiation and strategy use following frontal lobe lesions. *Neuropsychologia, 34*, 263–273.

Burgess, P. W., Scott, S. K., & Frith, C. D. (2003). The role of the rostral frontal cortex (area 10) in prospective memory: A lateral versus medial dissociation. *Neuropsychologia, 41*, 906–918.

Burgess, P. W., Veitch, E., Costello, A., & Shallice, T. (2000). The cognitive and neuroanatomical correlates of multitasking. *Neuropsychologia, 38*, 848–863.

Bush, G., Luu, P., & Posner, M. I. (2000). Cognitive and emotional influences in anterior cingulate cortex. *Trends in Cognitive Sciences, 4*, 215–222.

Butters, N., & Cermak, L. S. (1986). A case study of the forgetting of autobiographical knowledge: Implications for the study of retrograde amnesia. In D. C. Rubin (ed.), *Autobiographical memory*. Cambridge: Cambridge University Press.

Butters, N., & Pandya, D. N. (1969). Retention of delayed-alternation: Effect of selective lesion of sulcus principalis. *Science, 165*, 1271–1273.

Butterworth, B. (1999). *The mathematical brain*. London: Macmillan.

Butterworth, B., & Warrington, E. (1995). Two routes to repetition: Evidence from a case of "deep dysphasia". *Neurocase, 1*, 55–66.

Butterworth, B., Cipolotti, L., & Warrington, E. K. (1996). Short-term memory impairments and arithmetical ability. *Quarterly Journal of Experimental Psychology, 49A*, 251–262.

Cabeza, R., Dolcos, F., Prince, S. E., Rice, H. J., Weissman, D. H., & Nyberg, L. (2003). Attention-related activity during episodic memory retrieval: A cross-function fMRI study. *Neuropsychologia, 41*, 390–399.

Cabeza, R., Rao, S. M., Wagner, A. D., Mayer, A. R., & Schacter, D. L. (2001). Can medial temporal lobe regions distinguish true from false? An event-related functional fMRI study of veridical and illusory recognition memory. *Proceedings of the National Academy of Science, USA, 98*, 4805–4810.

Calder, A. J., Keane, J., Lawrence, A. D., & Manes, F. (2004). Impaired recognition of anger following damage to the ventral striatum. *Brain, 127*, 1958–1969.

Calder, A. J., Young, A. W., Rowland, D., Perrett, D. I., Hodges, J. R., & Etcoff, N. L. (1996). Facial emotion recognition after bilateral amygdala damage: Differentially severe impairment of fear. *Cognitive Neuropsychology, 13*, 699–745.

Calvanio, R., Petrone, P. N., & Levine, D. N. (1987). Left visual spatial neglect is both environment-centred and body-centred. *Neurology, 37*, 1179–1183.

Calvert, G. A. (2001). Crossmodal processing in the human brain: Insights from functional neuroimaging studies. *Cerebral Cortex, 11*, 1110–1123.

Calvert, G. A., Campbell, R., & Brammer, M. J. (2000). Evidence from functional magnetic resonance imaging of crossmodal binding in the human heteromodal cortex. *Current Biology*, *10*, 649–657.

Campbell, J. I. (1994). Architectures for numerical cognition. *Cognition*, *53*, 1–44.

Campbell, R., Heywood, C., Cowey, A., Regard, M., & Landis, T. (1990). Sensitivity to eye gaze in prosopagnosic patients and monkeys with superior temporal sulcus ablation. *Neuropsychologia*, *28*, 1123–1142.

Campbell, R., Landis, T., & Regard, M. (1986). Face recognition and lip reading: A neurological dissociation. *Brain*, *109*, 509–521.

Campion, J., Latto, R., & Smith, Y. M. (1983). Is blindsight an effect of scattered light, spared cortex, and near-threshold vision? *Behavioral and Brain Sciences*, *6*, 423–486.

Cantlon, J. F., & Brannon, E. M. (2007). Basic math in monkey and college students. *PLoS Biology*, *5*, 2912–2919.

Capgras, J., & Reboul-Lachaux, J. (1923). L'illusion des sosies dans un delire systematisé chronique. *Bulletin de la Société Clinique de Médecine Mentale*, *2*, 6–16.

Capitani, E., Laiacona, M., Mahon, B., & Caramazza, A. (2003). What are the facts of semantic category-specific deficits? A critical review of the clinical evidence. *Cognitive Neuropsychology*, *20*, 213–261.

Caplan, D. (1988). On the role of group studies in neuropsychological and pathopsychological research. *Cognitive Neuropsychology*, *5*, 535–548.

Caplan, D. (2001). Functional neuroimaging of syntactic processing. *Journal of Psycholinguistic Research*, *30*, 297–320.

Caplan, D., & Waters, G. S. (1990). Short-term memory and language comprehension: A critical review of the neuropsychology literature. In G. Vallar, & T. Shallice (eds.), *Neuropsychological impairments of short-term memory*. Cambridge: Cambridge University Press.

Cappelletti, M., Kopelman, M., & Butterworth, B. (2002). Why semantic dementia drives you to the dogs (but not to the horses): A theoretical account. *Cognitive Neuropsychology*, *19*, 483–503.

Caramazza, A. (1986). On drawing inferences about the structure of normal cognitive systems from the analysis of patterns of impaired performance: The case for single-patient studies. *Brain and Cognition*, *5*, 41–66.

Caramazza, A. (1992). Is cognitive neuropsychology possible? *Journal of Cognitive Neuroscience*, *4*, 80–95.

Caramazza, A. (1997). How many levels of processing are there in lexical access? *Cognitive Neuropsychology*, *14*, 177–208.

Caramazza, A., & Badecker, W. (1989). Patient classification in neuropsychological research. *Brain and Cognition*, *10*, 256–295.

Caramazza, A., & Badecker, W. (1991). Clinical syndromes are not God's gift to cognitive neuropsychology: A reply to a rebuttal to an answer to a response to the case against syndrome-based research. *Brain and Cognition*, *16*, 211–227.

Caramazza, A., & Hillis, A. E. (1990a). Levels of representation, co-ordinate frames, and unilateral neglect. *Cognitive Neuropsychology*, *7*, 391–445.

Caramazza, A., & Hillis, A. E. (1990b). Where do semantic errors come from? *Cortex*, *26*, 95–122.

Caramazza, A., & Hillis, A. E. (1991). Lexical organisation of nouns and verbs in the brain. *Nature*, *349*, 788–790.

Caramazza, A., & McCloskey, M. (1988). The case for single-patient studies. *Cognitive Neuropsychology*, *5*, 517–528.

Caramazza, A., & Miceli, G. (1990). The structure of graphemic representations. *Cognition*, *37*, 243–297.

Caramazza, A., & Miozzo, M. (1997). The relation between syntactic and phonological knowledge in lexical access: Evidence from the "tip-of-the-tongue" phenomenon. *Cognition*, *64*, 309–343.

Caramazza, A., & Shelton, R. S. (1998). Domain-specific knowledge systems in the brain: The animate–inanimate distinction. *Journal of Cognitive Neuroscience*, *10*, 1–34.

Caramazza, A., & Zurif, E. B. (1976). Dissociation of algorithmic and heuristic processes in language comprehension. *Brain and Language*, *3*, 572–582.

Caramazza, A., Capasso, R., & Miceli, G. (1996). The role of the graphemic buffer in reading. *Cognitive Neuropsychology*, *13*, 673–698.

Caramazza, A., Capitani, E., Rey, A., & Berndt, R. S. (2001). Agrammatic Broca's aphasia is not associated with a single pattern of comprehension performance. *Brain and Language*, *76*, 158–184.

Caramazza, A., Hillis, A. E., Rapp, B. C., & Romani, C. (1990). Multiple semantics or multiple confusions? *Cognitive Neuropsychology*, *7*, 161–168.

Caramazza, A., Hillis, A. E., Villa, G., & Romani, C. (1987). The role of the graphemic buffer in spelling: Evidence from a case of acquired dysgraphia. *Cognition*, *26*, 59–85.

Carmel, D., & Bentin, S. (2002). Domain specificity versus expertise: Factors influencing distinct processing of faces. *Cognition*, *83*, 1–29.

Carr, T. H., Posner, M. I., Pollatsek, A., & Snyder, C. R. (1979). Orthography and familiarity effects in word processing. *Journal of Experimental Psychology: General*, *108*, 389–414.

Carter, C. S., Braver, T. S., Barch, D. M., Botvinick, M. M., Noll, D., & Cohen, J. D. (1998). Anterior cingulate cortex, error detection, and the online monitoring of performance. *Science*, *280*, 747–749.

Carter, C. S., MacDonald, A. M., Botvinick, M., Ross, L. L., Stenger, V. A., Noll, D., & Cohen, J. D. (2000). Parsing executive processes: Strategic vs.

evaluative functions of the anterior cingulate cortex. *Proceedings of the National Academy of Science, USA, 97,* 1944–1948.

Caspi, A., Moffitt, T. E., Cannon, M., McClay, J., Murray, R. M., Harrington, H. L., Taylor, A., Arseneault, L., Williams, B., Braithwaite, A., Poulton, R., & Craig, I. W. (2005). Moderation of the effect of adolescent-onset cannabis use on adult psychosis by a functional polymorphism in the catechol-o-methyltransferase gene: Longitudinal evidence for a gene X–environment interaction. *Biological Psychiatry, 57,* 1117–1127.

Castelli, F., Happé, F., Frith, U., & Frith, C. D. (2000). Movement and mind: A functional imaging study of perception and interpretation of complex intentional movements. *NeuroImage, 12,* 314–325.

Castiello, U., & Umiltà, C. (1992). Splitting focal attention. *Journal of Experimental Psychology: Human Perception and Performance, 18,* 837–848.

Castle, D., Wesseley, S., Der, G., & Murray, R. M. (1991). The incidence of operationally defined schizophrenia in Camberwell 1965–84. *British Journal of Psychiatry, 159,* 790–794.

Castles, A., Datta, H., Gayan, J., & Olson, R. K. (1999). Varieties of developmental reading disorder: Genetic and environmental influences. *Journal of Experimental Child Psychology, 72,* 73–94.

Cattell, J. M. (1886). The inertia of the eye and brain. *Brain, 8,* 295–312.

Cattell, R. B. (1971). *Abilities: Their structure, growth and action.* Boston: Houghton Mifflin.

Cermak, L. S., & O'Connor, M. (1983). The anterograde and retrograde retrieval ability of a patient with amnesia due to encephalitis. *Neuropsychologia, 21,* 213–234.

Chakraborty, S., Anderson, M. I., Chaudhry, A. M., Mumford, J. C., & Jeffery, K. J. (2004). Context-independent directional cue learning by hippocampal place cells. *European Journal of Neuroscience, 20,* 281–292.

Chance, M. (1967). The interpretation of some agonistic postures: The role of "cut-off" acts and postures. *Symposium of the Zoological Society of London, 8,* 71–89.

Chao, L. L., & Martin, A. (1999). Cortical regions associated with perceiving, naming and knowing about colours. *Journal of Cognitive Neuroscience, 11,* 25–35.

Chao, L. L., & Martin, A. (2000). Representation of manipulable man-made objects in the dorsal stream. *NeuroImage, 12,* 478–484.

Chao, L. L., Martin, A., & Haxby, J. V. (1999). Are face-responsive regions selective only for faces? *Neuroreport, 10,* 2945–2950.

Chapin, J. K. (2004). Using multi-neuron population recordings for neural prosthetics. *Nature Neuroscience, 7,* 452–455.

Chee, M. W. L., Weekes, B., Lee, K. M., Soon, C. S., Schreiber, A., Hoon, J. J., & Chee, M. (2000). Overlap and dissociation of semantic processing of Chinese characters, English words, and pictures: Evidence from fMRI. *NeuroImage, 12,* 392–403.

Chen, Y. P., Fu, S. M., Iversen, S. D., Smith, S. M., & Matthews, P. M. (2002). Testing for dual brain processing routes in reading: A direct contrast of Chinese character and pinyin reading using fMRI. *Journal of Cognitive Neuroscience, 14,* 1088–1098.

Christoff, K., Prabhakaran, V., Dorfman, J., Zhao, Z., Kroger, J. K., Holyoak, K. J., & Gabrieli, J. D. E. (2001). Rostrolateral prefrontal cortex involvement in relational integration during reasoning. *NeuroImage, 14,* 1136–1149.

Chugani, H. T., Phelps, M. E., & Mazziotta, J. C. (1987). Positron emission tomography study of human brain functional development. *Annals of Neurology, 22,* 487–497.

Chumbley, J. I., & Balota, D. A. (1984). A word's meaning affects the decision in lexical decision. *Memory and Cognition, 12,* 590–606.

Churchland, P. M. (1995). *The engine of reason, the seat of the soul.* Cambridge, MA: MIT Press.

Churchland, P. S., & Sejnowski, T. J. (1988). Perspectives on cognitive neuroscience. *Science, 242,* (4879), 741–745.

Cipolotti, L. (1995). Multiple routes for reading words, why not numbers? Evidence from a case of Arabic numeral dyslexia. *Cognitive Neuropsychology, 12,* 313–342.

Cipolotti, L., & Butterworth, B. (1995). Toward a multi-route model of number processing: Impaired number transcoding with preserved calculation skills. *Journal of Experimental Psychology: General, 124,* 375–390.

Cipolotti, L., & De Lacy Costello, A. (1995). Selective impairment for simple division. *Cortex, 31,* 433–449.

Cipolotti, L., & Denes, G. (1989). When a patient can write but not copy: Report of a single case. *Cortex, 25,* 331–337.

Cipolotti, L., & Warrington, E. K. (1995a). Neuropsychological assessment. *Journal of Neurology, Neurosurgery and Psychiatry, 58,* 655–664.

Cipolotti, L., & Warrington, E. K. (1995b). Semantic memory and reading abilities: A case report. *Journal of the International Neuropsychological Society, 1,* 104–110.

Cipolotti, L., & Warrington, E. K. (1996). Does recognizing orally spelled words depend on reading? An investigation into a case of better written than oral spelling. *Neuropsychologia, 34,* 427–440.

Cipolotti, L., Butterworth, B., & Denes, G. (1991). A specific deficit for numbers in a case of dense acalculia. *Brain, 114,* 2619–2637.

Cipolotti, L., Butterworth, B., & Warrington, E. K. (1994). From "one thousand nine hundred and forty-five" to 1000,945. *Neuropsychologia, 32,* 503–509.

Cipolotti, L., Shallice, T., Chan, D., Fox, N., Scahill, R., Harrison, G., Stevens, J., & Rudge, P. (2001). Long-term retrograde amnesia: The crucial role of the hippocampus. *Neuropsychologia, 39,* 151–172.

Cipolotti, L., Warrington, E. K., & Butterworth, B. (1995). Selective impairment in manipulating Arabic numerals. *Cortex*, *31*, 73–86.

Clarey, J. C., Barone, P., & Imig, T. J. (1994). Functional organization of sound direction and sound pressure level in primary auditory cortex of the cat. *Journal of Neurophysiology*, *72*, 2383–2405.

Cocchini, G., Beschin, N., & Jehkonen, M. (2001). The fluff test: A simple task to assess body representational neglect. *Neuropsychological Rehabilitation*, *11*, 17–31.

Cochon, F., Cohen, L., van de Moortele, P. F., & Dehaene, S. (1999). Differential contributions of the left and right inferior parietal lobules to number processing. *Journal of Cognitive Neuroscience*, *11*, 617–630.

Cohen, J. D., Noll, D. C., & Schneider, W. (1993). Functional magnetic resonance imaging: Overview and methods for psychological research. *Behavioral Research Methods, Instruments, & Computers*, *25*, 101–113.

Cohen, J. D., Peristein, W. M., Braver, T. S., Nystrom, L. E., Noll, D. C., Jonides, J., & Smith, E. E. (1997a). Temporal dynamics of brain activation during a working memory task. *Nature*, *386*, 604–607.

Cohen, L., & Dehaene, S. (1996). Cerebral networks for number processing: Evidence from a case of posterior callosal lesion. *Neurocase*, *2*, 155–174.

Cohen, L., & Dehaene, S. (2000). Calculating without reading: Unsuspected residual abilities in pure alexia. *Cognitive Neuropsychology*, *17*, 563–583.

Cohen, L., & Dehaene, S. (2004). Specialization within the ventral stream: The case for the visual word form area. *NeuroImage*, *22*, 466–476.

Cohen, L., Lehericy, S., Chochon, F., Lemer, C., Rivaud, S., & Dehaene, S. (2002). Language-specific tuning of visual cortex functional properties of the Visual Word Form Area. *Brain*, *125*, 1054–1069.

Cohen, L. G., Bandinelli, S., Findley, T. W., & Hallett, M. (1991). Motor reorganization after upper limb amputation in man: A study with focal magnetic stimulation. *Brain*, *114*, 615–627.

Cohen, L. G., Celnik, P., Pascual-Leone, A., Corwell, B., Faiz, L., Dambrosia, J., Honda, M., Sadato, N., Gerloff, C., Catala, M. D., & Hallett, M. (1997b). Functional relevance of cross-modal plasticity in blind humans. *Nature*, *389*, 180–183.

Collins, A. M., & Quinlan, M. R. (1969). Retrieval time from semantic memory. *Journal of Verbal Learning and Verbal Behavior*, *8*, 240–247.

Collins, D., Neelin, P., Peters, T., & Evans, A. (1994). Automatic 3D intersubject registration of MR volumetric data in standardized Talairach space. *Journal of Computer Assisted Tomography*, *18*, 192–205.

Coltheart, M. (1980). Deep dyslexia: A right hemisphere hypothesis. In M. Coltheart, K. E. Patterson, & J. C. Marshall (eds.), *Deep dyslexia*. London: Routledge.

Coltheart, M. (2004a). Are there lexicons? *Quarterly Journal of Experimental Psychology*, *57A*, 1153–1171.

Coltheart, M. (2004b). Brain imaging, connectionism and cognitive neuropsychology. *Cognitive Neuropsychology*, *21*, 21–26.

Coltheart, M., & Funnell, E. (1987). Reading and writing: One lexicon or two? In A. Allport, D. Mackay, W. Prinz, & E. Scheerer (eds.), *Language perception and production: Relationships between listening, speaking, reading and writing*. London: Academic Press.

Coltheart, M., Curtis, B., Atkins, P., & Haller, M. (1993). Models of reading aloud. Dual-route and parallel distributed approaches. *Psychological Review*, *4*, 589–608.

Coltheart, M., Davelaar, E., Jonasson, J. T., & Besner, D. (1977). Access to the internal lexicon. In S. Dornic (ed.), *Attention and performance VI*. Hillsdale, NJ: Lawrence Erlbaum.

Coltheart, M., Inglis, L., Cupples, L., Michie, P., Bates, A., & Budd, B. (1998). A semantic subsystem specific to the storage of information about visual attributes of animate and inanimate objects. *Neurocase*, *4*, 353–370.

Coltheart, M., Patterson, K. E., & Marshall, J. C. (1980). *Deep dyslexia*. London: Routledge.

Coltheart, M., Rastle, K., Perry, C., Langdon, R., & Ziegler, J. (2001). DRC: A dual route cascaded model of visual word recognition and reading aloud. *Psychological Review*, *108*, 204–256.

Conway, M. A., & Fthenaki, A. (2003). Disruption of inhibitory control of memory following lesions to the frontal and temporal lobes. *Cortex*, *39*, 667–686.

Cooper, R., & Shallice, T. (2000). Contention scheduling and the control of routine activities. *Cognitive Neuropsychology*, *17*, 297–338.

Corbetta, M., Schulman, G., Miezin, F., & Petersen, S. (1995). Superior parietal cortex activation during spatial attention shifts and visual feature conjunctions. *Science*, *270*, 802–805.

Corkin, S. (1984). Lasting consequences of bilateral medial temporal lobectomy: Clinical course and experimental findings in HM. *Seminars in Neurology*, *4*, 249–259.

Corthout, E., Uttle, B., Ziemann, U., Cowey, A., & Hallett, M. (1999). Two periods of processing in the (circum)striate visual cortex as revealed by transcranial magnetic stimulation. *Neuropsychologia*, *37*, 137–145.

Coslett, H. B. (1991). Read but not write "Idea": Evidence for a third reading mechanism. *Brain and Language*, *40*, 425–443.

Costello, A., & Warrington, E. K. (1987). The dissociation of visuospatial neglect and neglect dyslexia. *Journal of Neurology, Neurosurgery, and Psychiatry*, *50*, 1110–1116.

Cowan, N. (2001). The magical number 4 in short-term memory: A reconsideration of mental storage capacity. *Behavioral and Brain Sciences*, *24*, 87–185.

Cowey, A. (2004). Fact, artefact and myth about blindsight. *Quarterly Journal of Experimental Psychology, 57A*, 577–609.

Craik, F. I. M., & Lockhart, R. S. (1972). Levels of processing: A framework for memory research. *Journal of Verbal Learning and Verbal Behavior, 11*, 671–684.

Crair, M. C., Gillespie, D. C., & Stryker, M. P. (1998). The role of visual experience in the development of columns in cat visual cortex. *Science, 279*, 566–570.

Creswell, C. S., & Skuse, D. H. (1999). Autism in association with Turner syndrome: Genetic implications for male vulnerability to pervasive developmental disorders. *Neurocase, 5*, 511–518.

Crick, F. (1994). *The astonishing hypothesis: The scientific search for the soul.* New York: Charles Scribner's Sons.

Critchley, H. D., Elliott, R., Mathias, C. J., & Dolan, R. J. (2000). Neural activity relating to generation and representation of galvanic skin conductance responses: A functional magnetic resonance imaging study. *Journal of Neuroscience, 20*, 3033–3040.

Critchley, H. D., Mathias, C. J., Josephs, O., O'Doherty, J., Zanini, S., Dewar, B. K., Cipolotti, L., Shallice, T., & Dolan, R. J. (2003). Human cingulate cortex and autonomic control: Converging neuroimaging and clinical evidence. *Brain, 126*, 2139–2152.

Cubelli, R., & Lupi, G. (1999). Afferent dysgraphia and the role of vision in handwriting. *Visual Cognition, 6*, 113–128.

Cubelli, R. (1991). A selective deficit for writing vowels in acquired dysgraphia. *Nature, 353*, 258–260.

Culham, J. (2004). Human brain imaging reveals a parietal area specialized for grasping. In N. Kanwisher, & J. Duncan (eds.), *Functional neuroimaging of visual cognition.* Oxford: Oxford University Press.

Curtiss, S. (1977). *Genie: A psycholinguistic study of a modern-day "wild child".* New York: Academic Press.

Cusack, R. (2005). The intraparietal sulcus and perceptual organization. *Journal of Cognitive Neuroscience, 17*, 641–651.

Cusack, R., Carlyon, R. P., & Robertson, I. H. (2000). Neglect between but not within auditory objects. *Journal of Cognitive Neuroscience, 12*, 1056–1065.

Cutler, A., & Butterfield, S. (1992). Rhythmic cues to speech segmentation: Evidence from juncture misperception. *Journal of Memory and Language, 25*, 385–400.

Cutler, A., Mehler, J., Norris, D., & Segui, J. (1992). The monolingual nature of speech segmentation in bilinguals. *Cognitive Psychology, 24*, 381–410.

Dagenbach, D., & McCloskey, M. (1992). The organisation of arithmetic facts in memory: Evidence from a brain-damaged patient. *Brain and Cognition, 20*, 345–366.

Dalla Barba, G. (1993). Different patterns of confabulation. *Cortex, 29*, 567–581.

Dalla Barba, G. (2001). Beyond the memory-trace paradox and the fallacy of the homunculus. *Journal of Consciousness Studies, 8*, 51–78.

Damasio, A. R. (1989). The brain binds entities and events by multiregional activation from convergence zones. *Neural Computation, 1*, 123–132.

Damasio, A. R. (1994). *Descartes' error: Emotion, reason and the human brain.* New York: G. P. Putnam, & Sons.

Damasio, A. R. (1996). The somatic marker hypothesis and the possible functions of the prefrontal cortex. *Philosophical Transactions of the Royal Society of London B, 351*, 1413–1420.

Damasio, A. R., Graff-Radford, N. R., Eslinger, P. J., Damasio, H., & Kassell, N. (1985). Amnesia following basal forebrain lesions. *Archives of Neurology, 42*, 263–271.

Damasio, A. R., Tranel, D., & Damasio, H. (1990). Individuals with sociopathic behavior caused by frontal damage fail to respond autonomically to social stimuli. *Behavioral Brain Research, 41*, 81–94.

Damasio, H., & Damasio, A. (1989). *Lesion analysis in neuropsychology.* New York: Oxford University Press.

Damasio, H., Grabowski, T., Frank, R., Galaburda, A. M., & Damasio, A. R. (1994). The return of Phineas Gage: Clues about the brain from the skull of a famous patient. *Science, 264*, 1102–1105.

Dapretto, M., Davies, M. S., Pfeifer, J. H., Scott, A. A., Sigman, M., Bookheimer, S. Y., & Iacoboni, M. (2006). Understanding emotions in others: Mirror neuron dysfunction in children with autism spectrum disorders. *Nature Neuroscience, 9*, 28–30.

Darwin, C. J. (1871). *The descent of man and selection in relation to sex.* London: John Murray.

Darwin, C. J. (1872/1965). *The expression of the emotions in man and animals.* Chicago: University of Chicago Press.

De Bastiani, P., Barry, C., & Carreras, M. (1988). Mechanisms for reading non-words: Evidence from a case of phonological dyslexia in an Italian reader. In C. Semenza, & G. Denes (eds.), *Perspectives on cognitive neuropsychology.* Hillsdale, NJ: Lawrence Erlbaum.

De Renzi, E. (1986). Prosopagnosia in two patients with CT scan evidence of damage confined to the right hemisphere. *Neuropsychologia, 24*, 385–389.

De Renzi, E., & di Pellegrino, G. (1998). Prosopagnosia and alexia without object agnosia. *Cortex, 34*, 403–415.

Dean, A. (1946). *Fundamentals of play directing.* New York.

Dehaene, S. (1992). Varieties of numerical abilities. *Cognition, 44*, 1–42.

Dehaene, S. (1997). *The number sense.* New York: Oxford University Press.

Dehaene, S., & Cohen, L. (1991). Two mental calculation systems: A case study of severe acalculia with preserved approximation. *Neuropsychologia, 29*, 1045–1074.

Dehaene, S., & Cohen, L. (1995). Towards an anatomical and functional model of number processing. *Mathematical Cognition, 1*, 83–120.

Dehaene, S., & Cohen, L. (1997). Cerebral pathways for calculation: Double dissociation between rote and quantitative knowledge of arithmetic. *Cortex*, *33*, 219–250.

Dehaene, S., Bossini, S., & Giraux, P. (1993). The mental representation of parity and numerical magnitude. *Journal of Experimental Psychology: General*, *122*, 371–396.

Dehaene, S., Dehaene-Lambertz, G., & Cohen, L. (1998a). Abstract representations of numbers in the animal and human brain. *Trends in Neurosciences*, *21*, 355–361.

Dehaene, S., Dupoux, E., & Mehler, J. (1990). Is numerical comparison digital? Analogical and symbolic effects in two-digit number comparison. *Journal of Experimental Psychology: Human Perception and Performance*, *16*, 626–641.

Dehaene, S., Le Clec'H, G., Poline, J.-B., Le Bihan, D., & Cohen, L. (2002). The visual word form area: A prelexical representation of visual words in the fusiform gyrus. *NeuroReport 13*, 321–325.

Dehaene, S., Naccache, L., Cohen, L., Le Bihan, D., Mangin, J. F., Poline, J.-B., & Riviere, D. (2001). Cerebral mechanisms of word masking and unconscious repetition priming. *Nature Neuroscience*, *4*, 752–758.

Dehaene, S., Naccache, L., Le Clec'H, G., Koechlin, E., Mueller, M., Dehaene-Lambertz, G., Van de Moortele, P. F., & Le Bihan, D. (1998b). Imaging unconscious semantic priming. *Nature*, *395*, 597–600.

Dehaene, S., Piazza, M., Pinel, P., & Cohen, L. (2003). Three parietal circuits for number processing. *Cognitive Neuropsychology*, *20*, 487–506.

Dehaene, S., Posner, M. I., & Tucker, D. M. (1994). Localisation of a neural system for error detection and compensation. *Psychological Science*, *5*, 303–305.

Dejerine, J. (1892). Contribution a l'étude anatomoclinique et clinique des différentes variétés de cécité verbale. *Mémoires de la Société de Biologie*, *4*, 61–90.

Del Grosso Destreri, N., Farina, E., Alberoni, M., Pomati, S., Nichelli, P., & Mariani, C. (2000). Selective uppercase dysgraphia with loss of visual imagery of letter forms: A window on the organization of graphomotor patterns. *Brain and Language*, *71*, 353–372.

Delazer, M., & Benke, T. (1997). The arithmetic facts without meaning. *Cortex*, *33*, 697–710.

Delazer, M., & Butterworth, B. (1997). A dissociation of number meanings. *Cognitive Neuropsychology*, *14*, 613–636.

Delbecq-Derouesne, J., Beauvois, M. F., & Shallice, T. (1990). Preserved recall versus impaired recognition. *Brain*, *113*, 1045–1074.

Dell, G. S. (1986). A spreading activation theory of retrieval in sentence production. *Psychological Review*, *93*, 283–321.

Dell, G. S., & O'Seaghdha, P. G. (1991). Mediated and convergent lexical priming in language production: A comment on Levelt et al. (1991). *Psychological Review*, *98*, 604–614.

Dell, G. S., & Reich, P. A. (1981). Stages in sentence production: An analysis of speech error data. *Journal of Verbal Learning and Verbal Behavior*, *20*, 611–629.

Dell, G. S., Burger, L. K., & Svec, W. R. (1997). Language production and serial order: A functional analysis and a model. *Psychological Review*, *104*, 123–147.

Della Sala, S., Marchetti, C., & Spinnler, H. (1991). Right-sided anarchic (alien) hand: A longitudinal study. *Neuropsychologia*, *29*, 1113–1127.

DeLong, M. R. (1990). Primate models of movement disorders of basal ganglia origin. *Trends in Neurosciences*, *13*, 281–285.

Denis, M., Beschin, N., Logie, R. H., & Della Sala, S. (2002). Visual perception and verbal descriptions as sources for generating mental representations: Evidence from representational neglect. *Cognitive Neuropsychology*, *19*, 97–112.

Dennett, D. C. (1978). Beliefs about beliefs. *Behavioral and Brain Sciences*, *1*, 568–570.

Desimone, R., & Duncan, J. (1995). Neural mechanisms of selective visual-attention. *Annual Review of Neuroscience*, *18*, 193–222.

Desor, J. A., Maller, O., & Andrews, K. (1975). Ingestive responses of human newborns to salty, sour and bitter stimuli. *Journal of Comparative Physiological Psychology*, *89*, 966–970.

Devlin, J. T., Gonnerman, L. M., Andersen, S. E., & Seidenberg, M. S. (1998). Category-specific semantic deficits in focal and widespread brain damage: A computational account. *Journal of Cognitive Neuroscience*, *10*, 77–94.

Di Pietro, M., Laganaro, M., Leeman, B., & Schinder, A. (2004). Receptive amusia: Temporal auditory processing deficit in a professional musician following a left tempero-parietal lesion. *Neuropsychologia*, *42*, 868–877.

Diamond, M. C., Scheibel, A. B., & Elson, L. M. (1986). *The Human Brain Coloring Book*. New York: HarperCollins.

Diamond, R., & Carey, S. (1986). Why faces are and are not special: An effect of expertise. *Journal of Experimental Psychology: General*, *115*, 107–117.

Dimitrov, M., Phipps, M., Zahn, T. P., & Grafman, J. (1999). A thoroughly modern Gage. *Neurocase*, *5*, 345–354.

Donchin, E. (1981). Surprise! ... Surprise? *Psychophysiology*, *18*, 493–513.

Dowling, W. J., & Harwood, D. L. (1986). *Music cognition*. Orlando: Academic Press.

Downing, P. E., Jiang, Y. H., Shuman, M., & Kanwisher, N. (2001). A cortical area selective for visual processing of the human body. *Science*, *293*, 2470–2473.

Draganski, B., Gaser, C., Busch, V., Schurierer, G., Bogdahn, U., & May, A. (2004). Neuroplasticity: Changes in grey matter induced by training. *Nature*, *427*, 311–312.

Dreher, J. C., & Grafman, J. (2003). Dissociating the roles of the rostral anterior cingulate and the lateral prefrontal cortices in performing two tasks simultaneously or successively. *Cerebral Cortex, 13*, 329–339.

Driver, J., & Halligan, P. W. (1991). Can visual neglect operate in object centred co-ordinates? An affirmative case study. *Cognitive Neuropsychology, 8*, 475–496.

Driver, J., & Spence, C. J. (1994). Spatial synergies between auditory and visual attention. In C. Umiltà, & M. Moscovitch (eds.), *Attention and Performance XV: Conscious and nonconscious information processing*, 311–331, Cambridge, MA: MIT Press.

Dronkers, N. F. (1996). A new brain region for coordinating speech articulation. *Nature, 384*, 159–161.

Dronkers, N. F., Wilkins, D. P., Van Valin, R. D., Redfern, B. B., & Jaeger, J. J. (2004). Lesion analysis of the brain areas involved in language comprehension. *Cognition, 92*, 145–177.

Druks, J. (2002). Verbs and nouns: A review of the literature. *Journal of Neurolinguistics, 15*, 289–315.

Druks, J., & Marshall, J. C. (1991). Agrammatism: An analysis and critique, with new evidence from four Hebrew-speaking aphasic patients. *Cognitive Neuropsychology, 8*, 415–433.

Druks, J., & Masterson, J. (2000). *An object and action naming battery.* Hove: Psychology Press.

Dudai, Y. (2004). The neurobiology of consolidations, or, how stable is the engram? *Annual Review of Psychology, 55*, 51–86.

Duncan, J. (1995). Attention, intelligence and the frontal lobes. In M. S. Gazzaniga (ed.), *The cognitive neurosciences.* Cambridge, MA: MIT Press.

Duncan, J., & Humphreys, G. W. (1989). Visual search and visual similarity. *Psychological Review, 96*, 433–458.

Duncan, J., & Owen, A. M. (2000). Common regions of the human frontal lobe recruited by diverse cognitive demands. *Trends in Neurosciences, 23*, 475–483.

Duncan, J., Burgess, P. W., & Emslie, H. (1995). Fluid intelligence after frontal lobe damage. *Neuropsychologia, 33*, 261–268.

Dunn, J. C., & Kirsner, K. (2003). What can we infer from double dissociations? *Cortex, 39*, 1–7.

Dusoir, H., Kapur, N., Byrnes, D. P., McKinstry, S., & Hoare, R. D. (1990). The role of diencephalic pathology in human-memory disorder – evidence from a penetrating paranasal brain injury. *Brain, 113*, 1695–1706.

Eaves, L. J., Silberg, J. L., Meyer, J. M., Maes, H. H., Simonoff, E., Pickles, A., Rutter, M., Neale, M. C., Reynolds, C. A., Erikson, M. T., Heath, A. C., Loeber, R., Truett, K. R., & Hewitt, J. K. (1997). Genetic and developmental psychopathology: 2. The main effects of genes and environment on behavioral problems in the Virginia twin study of adolescent development. *Journal of Child Psychology and Psychiatry, 38*, 965–980.

Eberhardt, J. L. (2005). Imaging race. *American Psychologist, 60*, 181–190.

Eger, E., Schyns, P. G., & Kleinschmidt, A. (2004). Scale invariant adaptation in fusiform face-responsive regions. *NeuroImage, 22*, 232–242.

Eger, E., Sterzer, P., Russ, M. O., Giraud, A. L., & Kleinschmidt, A. (2003). A supramodal number representation in human intraparietal sulcus. *Neuron, 37*, 719–725.

Eimas, P. D. (1963). The relation between identification and discrimination along speech and nonspeech continua. *Language and Speech, 6*, 206–217.

Ekman, P., & Friesen, W. V. (1976). *Pictures of facial affect.* Palo Alto, CA: Consulting Psychologists Press.

Ekman, P., Friesen, W. V., & Ellsworth, P. (1972). *Emotion in the human face: Guidelines for research and an integration of findings.* New York: Pergamon.

Ekstrom, A. D., Kahana, M. J., Caplan, J. B., Fields, T. A., Isham, E. A., Newman, E. L., & Fried, I. (2003). Cellular networks underlying human spatial navigation. *Nature, 425*, 184–187.

Ellis, A. W. (1979). Slips of the pen. *Visible Language, 13*, 265–282.

Ellis, A. W. (1980). On the Freudian theory of speech errors. In V. A. Fromkin (ed.), *Errors in linguistic performance.* New York: Academic Press.

Ellis, A. W. (1982). Spelling and writing (and reading and speaking). In A. W. Ellis (ed.), *Normality and pathology in cognitive functions.* London: Academic Press.

Ellis, A. W. (1993). *Reading, writing and dyslexia: A cognitive analysis.* Hillsdale, NJ: Lawrence Erlbaum.

Ellis, A. W., & Lambon Ralph, M. A. (2000). Age of acquisition effects in adult lexical processing reflect loss of plasticity in maturing systems: Insights from connectionist networks. *Journal of Experimental Psychology: Learning, Memory and Cognition, 26*, 1103–1123.

Ellis, A. W., & Young, A. W. (1988). *Human cognitive neuropsychology.* Hove: Psychology Press.

Ellis, A. W., Miller, D., & Sin, G. (1983). Wernicke's aphasia and normal language processing: A case study in cognitive neuropsychology. *Cognition, 15*, 111–144.

Ellis, A. W., Young, A. W., & Critchley, E. M. R. (1989). Loss of memory for people following temporal lobe damage. *Brain, 112*, 1469–1483.

Ellis, A. W., Young, A. W., & Flude, B. M. (1987). "Afferent dysgraphia" in a patient and in normal subjects. *Cognitive Neuropsychology, 4*, 465–486.

Ellis, H. D., & Lewis, M. B. (2001). Capgras delusion: A window on face recognition. *Trends in Cognitive Sciences, 5*, 149–156.

Ellis, H. D., & Young, A. W. (1990). Accounting for delusional misidentifications. *British Journal of Psychiatry, 157*, 239–248.

Ellis, H. D., Young, A. W., Quayle, A. H., & DePauw, K. W. (1997). Reduced autonomic responses to faces in Capgras delusion. *Proceedings of the Royal Society of London B, 264*, 1085–1092.

Ellis, R., & Humphreys, G. W. (1999). *Connectionist psychology: A text with readings*. Hove: Psychology Press.

Elman, J., Bates, E., Johnson, M. H., Karmiloff-Smith, A., Parisi, D., & Plunkett, K. (1996). *Rethinking innateness: a connectionist perspective on development*. Cambridge, MA: MIT Press.

Enard, W., Przeworski, M., Fisher, S. E., Lai, C. S. L., Wiebe, V., Kitano, T., Monaco, A. P., & Paabo, S. (2002). Molecular evolution of FOXP2, a gene involved in speech and language. *Nature, 418*, 869–872.

Engel, A. K., Konig, P., & Singer, W. (1991). Direct physiological evidence for scene segmentation by temporal encoding. *Proceedings of the National Academy of Science, USA, 88*, 9136–9140.

Engel, A. K., Moll, C. K. E., Fried, I., & Ojemann, G. A. (2005). Invasive recordings from the human brain: Clinical insights and beyond. *Nature Reviews Neuroscience, 6*, 35–47.

Epstein, R., & Kanwisher, N. (1998). A cortical representation of the local visual environment. *Nature, 392*, 598–601.

Erikson, C. W., Pollack, M. D., & Montague, W. E. (1970). Implicit speech: Mechanisms in perceptual encoding? *Journal of Experimental Psychology, 84*, 502–507.

Eslinger, P. J., & Damasio, A. R. (1985). Severe disturbance of higher cognition after bilateral frontal ablation: Patient EVR. *Neurology, 35*, 1731–1741.

Evarts, E. V., Teravainen, H., & Calne, D. B. (1981). Reaction time in Parkinson's disease. *Brain, 104*, 167–186.

Eysenck, M. W. (1974). Age differences in incidental learning. *Developmental Psychology, 10*, 936–941.

Eysenck, M. W., & Keane, M. T. (2005). *Cognitive psychology: A student's handbook*. 5th edn. Hove: Psychology Press.

Fabiani, M., Stadler, M. A., & Wessels, P. M. (2000). True but not false memories produce a sensory signature in human lateralised brain potentials. *Journal of Cognitive Neuroscience, 12*, 941–949.

Falcaro, M., Pickles, A., Newbury, D. F., Addis, L., Banfield, E., Fisher, S. E., Monaco, A. P., Simkin, Z., & Conti-Ramsden, G. (2008). Genetic and phenotypic effects of phonological short-term memory and grammatical morphology in specific language impairment. *Genes, Brain and Behavior, 7*, 393–402.

Farah, M. J. (1990). *Visual agnosia*. Cambridge, MA: MIT Press.

Farah, M. J. (1994). Neuropsychological inference with an interactive brain: A critique of the "locality" assumption. *Behavioral and Brain Sciences, 17*, 43–104.

Farah, M. J. (1997). Distinguishing perceptual and semantic impairments affecting visual object recognition. *Visual Cognition, 4*, 199–206.

Farah, M. J., & McClelland, J. L. (1991). A computational model of semantic memory impairment: Modality specificity and emergent category specificity. *Journal of Experimental Psychology: General, 120*, 339–357.

Farah, M. J., & Wallace, M. (1991). Pure alexia as a visual impairment: A reconsideration. *Cognitive Neuropsychology, 8*, 313–334.

Farah, M. J., Levinson, K. L., & Klein, K. L. (1995a). Face perception and within-category discrimination in prosopagnosia. *Neuropsychologia, 33*, 661–674.

Farah, M. J., Stowe, R. M., & Levinson, K. L. (1996). Phonological dyslexia: Loss of a reading-specific component of the cognitive architecture? *Cognitive Neuropsychology, 13*, 849–868.

Farah, M. J., Wilson, K. D., Drain, H. M., & Tanaka, J. W. (1998). What is special about face perception? *Psychological Review, 105*, 482–498.

Farah, M. J., Wilson, K. D., Drain, H. M., & Tanaka, L. W. (1995b). The inverted inversion effect in prosopagnosia: Evidence for mandatory, face-specific perceptual mechanisms. *Vision Research, 35*, 2089–2093.

Farroni, T., Csibra, G., Simion, G., & Johnson, M. H. (2002). Eye contact detection in humans from birth. *Proceedings of the National Academy of Science, USA, 99*, 9602–9605.

Fay, D., & Cutler, A. (1977). Malapropisms and the structure of the mental lexicon. *Linguistic Inquiry, 8*, 505–520.

Fell, J., Klaver, P., Lehnertz, G., T., Schaller, C., Elger, C. E., & Fernandez, G. (2001). Human memory formation is accompanied by rhinal-hippocampal coupling and decoupling. *Nature Neuroscience, 4*, 1259–1264.

Fellows, L. K., & Farah, M. J. (2003). Ventromedial frontal cortex mediates affective shifting in humans: Evidence from a reversal learning paradigm. *Brain, 126*, 1830–1837.

Fera, P., & Besner, D. (1992). The process of lexical decision: More words about a parallel distributed processing model. *Journal of Experimental Psychology: Learning, Memory and Cognition, 18*, 749–764.

Ferrand, L., & Grainger, J. (2003). Homophone interference effects in visual word recognition. *Quarterly Journal of Experimental Psychology, 56A*, 403–419.

Ferro, J. M., & Botelho, M. A. S. (1980). Alexia for arithmetical signs: A case of disturbed calculation. *Cortex, 16*, 175–180.

Ferstl, E. C., & von Cramon, D. Y. (2002). What does the frontomedian cortex contribute to language processing: Coherence or theory of mind? *NeuroImage, 17*, 1599–1612.

ffytche, D. H., Howard, R. J., Brammer, M. J., David, A., Woodruff, P., & Williams, S. (1998). The anatomy of conscious vision: An fMRI study of visual hallucinations. *Nature Neuroscience, 1*, 738–742.

Fias, W., Lammertyn, J., Reynvoet, B., Dupont, P., & Orban, G. A. (2003). Parietal representation of symbolic and nonsymbolic magnitude. *Journal of Cognitive Neuroscience, 15*, 47–56.

Fiebach, C. J., Friederici, A. D., Muller, K., & von Cramon, D. Y. (2002). fMRI evidence for dual routes to the mental lexicon in visual word recognition. *Journal of Cognitive Neuroscience, 14*, 11–23.

Fierro, B., Brighina, F., Oliveri, M., Piazza, A., La Bua, V., Buffa, D., & Bisiach, E. (2000). Contralateral neglect induced by right posterior parietal rTMS in healthy subjects. *NeuroReport, 11*, 1519–1521.

Fiez, J. A., & Petersen, S. E. (1998). Neuroimaging studies of word reading. *Proceedings of the National Academy of Science, USA, 95*, 914–921.

Fiez, J. A., Balota, D. A., Raichle, M. E., & Petersen, S. E. (1999). Effects of lexicality, frequency, and spelling-to-sound consistency on the functional anatomy of reading. *Neuron, 24*, 205–218.

Fine, C., & Blair, R. J. R. (2000). Mini review: The cognitive and emotional effects of amygdala damage. *Neurocase, 6*, 435–450.

Fine, C., Lumsden, J., & Blair, R. J. R. (2001). Dissociation between "theory of mind" and executive functions in a patient with early left amygdala damage. *Brain, 124*, 287–298.

Finger, S. (2000). *Minds behind the brain: A history of the pioneers and their discoveries.* New York: Oxford University Press.

Fink, G. R., Marshall, J. C., Shah, N. J., Weiss, P. H., Halligan, P. W., Grosse-Ruyken, M., Ziemons, K., Zilles, K., & Freund, H. J. (2000). Line bisection judgments implicate right parietal cortex and cerebellum as assessed by fMRI. *Neurology, 54*, 1324–1331.

Fischer, M. H., Castel, A. D., Dodd, M. D., & Pratt, J. (2003). Perceiving numbers causes spatial shifts of attention. *Nature Neuroscience, 6*, 555–556.

Fletcher, P. C., & Henson, R. N. A. (2001). Frontal lobes and human memory: Insights from functional neuroimaging. *Brain, 124*, 849–881.

Fletcher, P. C., Happé, F., Frith, U., Baker, S. C., Dolan, R. J., Frackowiak, R. S. J., & Frith, C. D. (1995). Other minds in the brain: A functional imaging study of "theory of mind" in story comprehension. *Cognition, 57*, 109–128.

Fletcher, P. C., Shallice, T., & Dolan, R. J. (1998a). The functional roles of prefrontal cortex in episodic memory: I. Encoding. *Brain, 121*, 1239–1248.

Fletcher, P. C., Shallice, T., Frith, C. D., Frackowiak, R. S. J., & Dolan, R. J. (1998b). The functional roles of prefrontal cortex in episodic memory: II. Retrieval. *Brain, 121*, 1249–1256.

Flourens, M. J. P. (1824). *Recherches expérimentales sur les propriétés et les fonctions du systéme nerveux dans les animaux vertébrés.* Paris: J. B. Ballière.

Fodor, J. A. (1983). *The modularity of mind.* Cambridge, MA: MIT Press.

Fodor, J. A. (1992). A theory of the child's theory of mind. *Cognition, 44*, 283–296.

Fodor, J. A. (1998). *In critical condition: Polemical essays on cognitive science and the philosophy of mind.* Cambridge, MA: Bradford Books.

Formisano, E., Kim, D. S., Di Salle, F., van de Moortele, P. F., Ugurbil, K., & Goebel, R. (2003). Mirror-symmetric tonotopic maps in human primary auditory cortex. *Neuron, 40*, 859–869.

Forster, K. I. (1976). Accessing the mental lexicon. In R. J. Wales, & C. T. Walker (eds.), *New approaches to language mechanisms.* Amsterdam: North Holland.

Frankland, P. W., & Bontempi, B. (2005). The organization of recent and remote memories. *Nature Reviews Neuroscience, 6*, 119–130.

Frazier, L., & Rayner, K. (1982). Making and correcting errors in the analysis of structurally ambiguous sentences. *Cognitive Psychology, 14*, 178–210.

Fredrikson, M., Hursti, T., Salmi, P., Bojeson, S., Furst, C., Peterson, C., & Steineck, G. (1993). Conditioned nausea after cancer chemotherapy and autonomic system conditionability. *Scandanavian Journal of Psychology, 34*, 318–327.

Friederici, A. (2002). Towards a neural basis of auditory sentence processing. *Trends in Cognitive Sciences, 6*, 78–84.

Friederici, A. D., & Meyer, M. (2004). The brain knows the difference: Two types of grammatical violations. *Brain Research, 1000*, 72–77.

Friedman-Hill, S., Robertson, L. C., & Treisman, A. (1995). Parietal contributions to visual feature binding: Evidence from a patient with bilateral lesions. *Science, 269*, 853–855.

Friston, K. J. (1997). Imaging cognitive anatomy. *Trends in Cognitive Sciences, 1*, 21–27.

Friston, K. J. (2002). Beyond phrenology: What can neuroimaging tell us about distributed circuitry? *Annual Review of Neuroscience, 25*, 221–250.

Friston, K. J., & Frith, C. D. (1995). Schizophrenia: A disconnection syndrome? *Clinical Neuroscience, 3*, 89–97.

Friston, K. J., Price, C. J., Fletcher, P., Moore, C., Frackowiak, R. S. J., & Dolan, R. J. (1996). The trouble with cognitive subtraction. *NeuroImage, 4*, 97–104.

Frith, C. D. (2000). The role of dorsolateral prefrontal cortex in the selection of action, as revealed by functional imaging. In S. Monsell, & J. Driver (eds.), *Attention and performance XVIII: Control of cognitive performance,* Cambridge, MA: MIT Press.

Frith, C. D., Friston, K., Liddle, P. F., & Frackowiak, R. S. J. (1991). Willed action and the prefrontal cortex in man: A study with PET. *Proceedings of the Royal Society of London, 244*, 241–246.

Frith, U. (1985). Beneath the surface of developmental dyslexia. In K. Patterson, & J. Marshall (eds.), *Surface dyslexia: Neuropsychological and cognitive studies of phonological reading.* Hillsdale, NJ: Lawrence Erlbaum.

Frith, U. (1989). *Autism: Explaining the enigma.* Oxford: Blackwell.

Frith, U., & Frith, C. D. (2003). Development and neurophysiology of mentalising. *Philosophical Transactions of the Royal Society of London B, 358,* 459–472.

Fritsch, G. T., & Hitzig, E. (1870). On the electrical excitability of the cerebrum. In: G. Von Bonin (1960) (trans.), *Some papers on the cerebral cortex.* Springfield IL: Charles C. Thomas.

Fromkin, V. A. (1971). The non-anomalous nature of anomalous utterances. *Language, 51,* 696–719.

Fromkin, V., Krashen, S., Curtiss, S., Rigler, D., & Rigler, M. (1974). The development of language in Genie: A case of language acquisition beyond the "critical period". *Brain and Language 1,* 81–107.

Fukuchi-Shimogori, T., & Grove, E. A. (2001). Neocortex patterning by the secreted signalling molecule FGF8. *Science, 294,* 1071–1074.

Funahashi, S., Bruce, C. J., & Goldman-Rakic, P. S. (1989). Mnemonic coding of visual space in the monkey's dorsolateral prefrontal cortex. *Journal of Neurophysiology, 61,* 1–19.

Funnell, E. (1983). Phonological processes in reading: New evidence from acquired dyslexia. *British Journal of Psychology, 74,* 159–180.

Funnell, E., & DeMornay Davies, P. (1996). JBR: A reassessment of concept familiarity and a category-specific disorder for living things. *Neurocase, 2,* 461–474.

Funnell, E., & Sheridan, J. (1992). Categories of knowledge? Unfamiliar aspects of living and nonliving things. *Cognitive Neuropsychology, 9,* 135–153.

Furst, A. J., & Hitch, G. J. (2000). Separate roles for executive and phonological components of working memory in mental arithmetic. *Memory and Cognition, 28,* 774–782.

Fushimi, T., Komori, K., Patterson, K., Ijuin, M., & Tanabe, H. (2003). Surface dyslexia in a Japanese patient with semantic dementia: Evidence for similarity-based orthography-to-phonology translation. *Neuropsychologia, 41,* 1644–1658.

Fuster, J. M. (1989). *The prefrontal cortex: Anatomy, physiology, and neuropsychology of the frontal lobe,* 2nd edition. New York: Raven Press.

Gabrieli, J. D. E., Cohen, N. J., & Corkin, S. (1988). The impaired learning of semantic knowledge following bilateral medial temporal-lobe resection. *Brain, 7,* 157–177.

Gabrieli, J. D. E., Fleischman, D., Keane, M., Reminger, S., & Morell, F. (1995). Double dissociation between memory systems underlying explicit and implicit memory in the human brain. *Psychological Science, 6,* 76–82.

Gaffan, D. (1992). Amygdala and the memory of reward. In J. P. Aggleton (ed.), *The amygdala: Neurobiological aspects of emotion, memory and mental dysfunction.* New York: Wiley-Liss.

Gaillard, W. D., Grandon, C. B., & Xu, B. (2001). Developmental aspects of pediatric fMRI: Considerations for image acquisition, analysis and interpretation. *NeuroImage, 13,* 239–249.

Gall, F. J., & Spurzheim, J. C. (1810). *Anatomie et physiologie du système nerveux.* Paris: Schoell.

Gallagher, H. L., Happé, F., Brunswick, N., Fletcher, P. C., Frith, U., & Frith, C. D. (2000). Reading the mind in cartoons and stories: An fMRI study of "theory of mind" in verbal and nonverbal tasks. *Neuropsychologia, 38,* 11–21.

Gallese, V. (2001). The "shared manifold" hypothesis: From mirror neurons to empathy. *Journal of Consciousness Studies, 8,* 33–50.

Gallese, V. (2003). The manifold nature of interpersonal relations: The quest for a common mechanism. *Philosophical Transactions of the Royal Society of London B, 358,* 517–528.

Gallese, V., & Goldman, A. (1998). Mirror neurons and the simulation theory of mind-reading. *Trends in Cognitive Sciences, 2,* 493–501.

Ganis, G., Kosslyn, S. M., Stose, S., Thompson, W. L., & Yurgelun-Todd, D. A. (2003). Neural correlates of different types of deception: An fMRI investigation. *Cerebral Cortex, 13,* 830–836.

Gardiner, J. M. (2000). On the objectivity of subjective experiences and autonoetic and noetic consciousness. In E. Tulving (ed.), *Memory, consciousness and the brain: The Tallinn conference* (pp. 159–172). Philadelphia: Psychology Press.

Gardner, M. (1990). *Mathematical carnival.* London: Penguin.

Gardner, R. A., Gardner, B. T., & van Cantford, T. E. (1989). *Teaching sign language to chimpanzees.* Albany, NY: SUNY Press.

Garrard, P., Maloney, L. M., Hodges, J. R., & Patterson, K. (2005). The effects of very early Alzheimer's disease on the characteristics of writing by a renowned author. *Brain, 128,* 250–260.

Garrett, M. F. (1992). Disorders of lexical selection. *Cognition, 42,* 143–180.

Garrido, L., Eisner, F., McGettigan, C., Stewart, L., Sauter, D., Hanley, R., Schweinberger, S., Warren, J., & Duchaine, B. (2009). Developmental phonagnosia: A selective deficit of vocal identity recognition. *Neuropsychologia, 47,* 123–131.

Gathercole, S. E., & Baddeley, A. D. (1990). The role of phonological memory in vocabulary acquisition: A study of young children learning arbitrary names of toys. *British Journal of Psychology, 81,* 439–454.

Gaur, A. (1987). *A history of writing.* London: British Library.

Gauthier, I., & Logothetis, N. K. (2000). Is face recognition not so unique after all? *Cognitive Neuropsychology, 17,* 125–142.

Gauthier, I., & Tarr, M. J. (1997). Becoming a "Greeble" expert: Exploring mechanisms for face recognition. *Vision Research*, *37*, 1673–1682.

Gauthier, I., Skudlarski, P., Gore, J. C., & Anderson, A. W. (2000). Expertise for cars and birds recruits brain areas involved in face recognition. *Nature Neuroscience*, *3*, 191–197.

Gauthier, I., Tarr, M. J., Anderson, A. W., Skudlarski, P., & Gore, J. C. (1999). Activation of middle fusiform "face area" increases with expertise in recognizing novel objects. *Nature Neuroscience*, *2*, 568–573.

Gazzaniga, M. S. (2000). Cerebral specialization and inter-hemispheric communication: Does the corpus callosum enable the human condition? *Brain*, *123*, 1293–1326.

Gazzaniga, M. S., Mangun, G., & Ivry, R. (2002). Cognitive Neuroscience: The new biology of the mind. New York: W. W. Norton.

Gehring, W. J., Goss, B., Coles, M. G. H., Meyer, D. E., & Donchin, E. (1993). A neural system for error detection and compensation. *Psychological Science*, *4*, 385–390.

Gelman, R., & Gallistel, C. R. (1978). *The child's understanding of number.* Cambridge, MA: Harvard University Press.

Gemba, H., Sasaki, H., & Brooks, V. B. (1986). "Error" potentials in limbic cortex (anterior cingulate area 24) of monkeys during motor learning. *Neuroscience Letters*, *70*, 223–227.

George, M. S., Wassermann, E. M., Williams, W. A., Callahan, A., Ketter, T. A., Basser, P., Hallett, M., & Post, R. M. (1995). Daily repetitive transcranial magnetic stimulation improves mood in depression. *NeuroReport*, *6*, 1853–1856.

Georgopoulos, A. P. (1997). Voluntary movement: Computational principles and neural mechanisms. In M. D. Rugg (ed.), *Cognitive neuroscience.* Hove: Psychology Press.

Georgopoulos, A. P., Caminiti, R., Kalaska, J. F., & Massey, J. T. (1983). Spatial coding of movement: A hypothesis concerning the coding of movement direction by motor cortical populations. *Experimental Brain Research, Supplement*, *7*, 327–336.

Georgopoulos, A. P., Kalaska, J. F., & Caminiti, R. (1985). Relations between two-dimensional arm movements and single cell discharge in motor cortex and area 5: Movement direction versus movement endpoint. *Experimental Brain Research Supplement*, *10*, 176–183.

Georgopoulos, A. P., Lurito, J. P., Petrides, M., Schwartz, A. B., & Massey, J. T. (1989). Mental rotation of the neuronal population vector. *Science*, *243*, 234–236.

Georgopoulos, A. P., Schwartz, A. B., & Kettner, R. E. (1986). Neuronal population coding of movement direction. *Science*, *233*, 1416–1419.

Gergely, G., Bekkering, H., & Kiraly, I. (2002). Rational imitation in preverbal infants. *Nature*, *415*, 755–755.

Gerloff, C., Corwell, B., Chen, R., Hallett, M., & Cohen, L. G. (1997). Stimulation over the human supplementary motor area interferes with the organisation of future elements in complex motor sequences. *Brain*, *120*, 1587–1602.

Gerstmann, J. (1940). Syndrome of finger agnosia, disorientation for right and left, agraphia and acalculia. *Archives of Neurology and Psychiatry*, *44*, 398–408.

Gevers, W., Reynvoet, B., & Fias, W. (2003). The mental representation of ordinal sequences is spatially organized. *Cognition*, *87*, B87–B95.

Gibson, J. J. (1979). *The ecological approach to visual perception.* London: Houghton Mifflin.

Giedd, J. N., Blumenthal, J., Jeffries, N. O., Castellanos, F. X., Liu, H., Zijdenbos, A., Paus, T., Evans, A. C., & Rapoport, J. L. (1999). Brain development during childhood and adolescence: A longitudinal MRI study. *Nature Neuroscience*, *2*, 861–863.

Giersch, A., Humphreys, G. W., Boucart, M., & Kovacs, I. (2000). The computation of occluded contours in visual agnosia: Evidence for early computation prior to shape binding and figure-ground coding. *Cognitive Neuropsychology*, *17*, 731–759.

Gilboa, A., & Moscovitch, M. (2002). The cognitive neuroscience of confabulation: A review and a model. In A. D. Baddeley, M. D. Kopelman, & B. A. Wilson (eds.), *Handbook of memory disorders.* London: Wiley.

Gilboa, A., Winocur, G., Grady, C. L., Hevenor, S. J., & Moscovitch, M. (2004). Remembering our past: Functional neuroanatomy of recollection of recent and very remote personal events. *Cerebral Cortex*, *14*, 1214–1225.

Girelli, L., Lucangeli, D., & Butterworth, B. (2000). The development of automaticity in accessing number magnitude. *Journal of Experimental Child Psychology*, *76*, 104–122.

Godden, D., & Baddeley, A. D. (1975). Context-dependent memory in two natural environments: On land and under water. *British Journal of Psychology*, *66*, 325–331.

Goff, L. M., & Roediger, H. L. (1998). Imagination inflation for action events: Repeated imaginings lead to illusory recollections. *Memory and Cognition*, *26*, 20–33.

Goldberg, E. (2001). *The executive brain: Frontal lobes and the civilised mind.* Oxford: Oxford University Press.

Goldberg, G. (1985). Supplementary motor area structure and function: Review and hypotheses. *Behavioral and Brain Sciences*, *8*, 567–616.

Goldberg, G., Mayer, N. H., & Toglia, J. U. (1981). Medial frontal cortex infarction and the alien hand sign. *Archives of Neurology*, *38*, 683–686.

Goldenberg, G., & Hagmann, S. (1998). Tool use and mechanical problem solving in apraxia. *Neuropsychologia*, *36*, 581–589.

Goldman-Rakic, P. S. (1992). Working memory and mind. *Scientific American*, *267*, 73–79.

Goldman-Rakic., P. S. (1996). The prefrontal landscape: Implications of functional architecture for understanding human mentation and the central executive. *Philosophical*

Transactions of the Royal Society of London B, *351*, 1445–1453.

Gonzalez Rothi, L. J., Ochipa, C., & Heilman, K. M. (1991). A cognitive neuropsychological model of limb apraxia. *Cognitive Neuropsychology*, *8*, 443–458.

Goodale, M. A., & Milner, A. D. (1992). Separate visual pathways for perception and action. *Trends in Neurosciences*, *15*, 20–25.

Goodale, M. A., Meenan, J. P., Bulthoff, H. H., Nicolle, D. A., Murphy, K. J., & Racicot, C. I. (1994). Separate neural pathways for the visual analysis of object shape in perception and prehension. *Current Biology*, *4*, 604–610.

Goodglass, H., & Kaplan, E. (1972). *The assessment of aphasia and related disorders*. Philadelphia: Lea and Febiger.

Goodglass, H., & Kaplan, E. (1983). *The Boston diagnostic aphasia examination*. Philadelphia: Lea and Febiger.

Goodman, R. A., & Caramazza, A. (1986a). Aspects of the spelling process. Evidence from a case of acquired dysgraphia. *Language and Cognitive Processes*, *1*, 263–296.

Goodman, R. A., & Caramazza, A. (1986b). Dissociation of spelling errors in written and oral spelling: The role of allographic conversion in writing. *Cognitive Neuropsychology*, *3*, 179–206.

Goodwin, D. W., Powell, B., Bremer, D., Hoine, H., & Stern, J. (1969). Alcohol and recall: State dependent effects in man. *Science*, *163*, 1358.

Gopnik, M. (1990). Genetic basis of grammar defect. *Nature*, *347*, 25.

Gopnik, M., & Crago, M. (1991). Familial aggregation of developmental language disorder. *Cognition*, *39*, 1–50.

Gordon, P. (2004). Numerical cognition without words: Evidence from Amazonia. *Science*, *306*, 496–499.

Gosselin, N., Peretz, I., Johnsen, E., & Adolphs, R. (2007). Amygdala damage impairs emotion recognition from music. *Neuropsychologia*, *45*, 236–244.

Gottesman, I. I. (1991). *Schizophrenia genes: The origins of madness*. New York: Freeman.

Gottlieb, G. (1992). *Individual development and evolution*. New York: Oxford University Press.

Gottlieb, J. P., Kusunoki, M., & Goldberg, M. E. (1998). The representation of visual salience in monkey parietal cortex. *Nature*, *391*, 481–484.

Graf, P., Squire, L. R., & Mandler, G. (1984). The information that amnesic patients do not forget. *Journal of Experimental Psychology: Learning, Memory and Cognition*, *10*, 164–178.

Grafman, J. (1994). Alternative frameworks for the conceptualisation of prefrontal lobe functions. In F. Boller, & J. Grafman (eds.), *Handbook of neuropsychology*. Amsterdam: Elsevier.

Grafman, J., Passafiume, D., Faglioni, P., & Boller, F. (1982). Calculation disturbances in adults with focal hemispheric damage. *Cortex*, *18*, 37–50.

Grafman, J., Schwab, K., Warden, D., Pridgen, A., Brown, H. R., & Salazar, A. M. (1996). Frontal lobe injuries, violence, and agression: A report of the Vietnam head injury study. *Neurology*, *46*, 1231–1238.

Graham, K. S., Hodges, J. R., & Patterson, K. (1994). The relationship between comprehension and oral reading in progressive fluent aphasia. *Neuropsychologia*, *32*, 299–316.

Graham, N. L., Patterson, K., & Hodges, J. R. (2000). The impact of semantic memory impairment on spelling: Evidence from semantic dementia. *Neuropsychologia*, *38*, 143–163.

Graybiel, A. M. (2008). Habits, rituals, and the evaluative brain. *Annual Review of Neuroscience*, *31*, 359–387.

Graziano, M. S. A. (1999). Where is my arm? The relative role of vision and proprioception in the neuronal representation of limb position. *Proceedings of the National Academy of Sciences of the United States of America*, *96*, 10418–10421.

Griffiths, T. D., & Warren, J. D. (2002). The planum temporale as a computational hub. *Trends in Cognitive Sciences*, *25*, 348–353.

Griffiths, T. D., Rees, A., & Green, G. G. R. (1999). Disorders of human complex sound processing. *Neurocase*, *5*, 365–378.

Grodzinsky, Y., Pinango, M. M., Zurif, E., & Drai, D. (1999). The critical role of group studies in neuropsychology: Comprehension regularities in Broca's aphasia. *Brain and Language*, *67*, 134–147.

Gross, C. G. (1992). Representation of visual stimuli in inferior temporal cortex. *Philosophical Transactions of the Royal Society of London B*, *335*, 3–10.

Gross, C. G. (2000). Neurogenesis in the adult brain: death of a dogma. *Nature Reviews Neuroscience*, *1*, 67–73.

Gross, C. G. (2002). Genealogy of the "grandmother cell". *Neuroscientist*, *8*, 512–518.

Gross, C. G., Rocha-Miranda, C. E., & Bender, D. B. (1972). Visual properties of neurons in the inferotemporal cortex of the macaque. *Journal of Neurophysiology*, *35*, 96–111.

Guariglia, C., & Antonucci, G. (1992). Personal and extrapersonal space: A case of neglect dissociation. *Neuropsychologia*, *30*, 1001–1009.

Guth, W., Schmittberger, R., & Schwarze, B. (1982). An experimental analysis of ultimatum bargaining. *Journal of Economics, Behavior, & Organizations*, *3*, 367–388.

Habib, R., Nyberg, L., & Tulving, E. (2003). Hemispheric asymmetries of memory: The HERA model revisited. *Trends in Cognitive Sciences*, *7*, 241–245.

Hadland, K. A., Rushworth, M. F. S., Passingham, R. E., Jahanshahi, M., & Rothwell, J. (2001). Interference with performance of a response selection task has no working memory component: An rTMS comparison of the dorsolateral prefrontal and medial frontal cortex. *Journal of Cognitive Neuroscience*, *13*, 1097–1108.

Haesler, S., Wada, K., Nshdejan, A., Morrisey, E. E., Lints, T., Jarvis, E. D., & Scharff, C. (2004). FoxP2 expression in avian vocal learners and non-learners. *Journal of Neuroscience, 24,* 3164–3175.

Haggard, P. (2001). The psychology of action. *British Journal of Psychology, 92,* 113–128.

Haggard, P. (2008). Human volition: Towards a neuroscience of will. *Nature Reviews Neuroscience, 9,* 934–946.

Haggard, P., & Eimer, M. (1999). On the relation between brain potentials and conscious awareness. *Experimental Brain Research, 126,* 128–133.

Haggard, P., Miall, R. C., Wade, D., Fowler, S., Richardson, A., Anslow, P., & Stein, J. (1995). Damage to cerebellocortical pathways after closed head injury: A behavioural and magnetic resonance imaging study. *Journal of Neurology, Neurosurgery and Psychiatry, 58,* 433–438.

Hagoort, P., Hald, L., Bastiaansen, M., & Petersson, K. M. (2004). Integration of word meaning and world knowledge in language comprehension. *Science, 304,* 438–441.

Haist, F., Bowden Gore, J., & Mao, H. (2001). Consolidation of human memory over decades revealed by functional magnetic resonance imaging. *Nature Neuroscience, 4,* 1139–1145.

Halit, H., de Haan, M., & Johnson, M. H. (2003). Cortical specialisation for face processing: Face-sensitive event-related potential components in 3- and 12-month old infants. *NeuroImage, 19,* 1180–1193.

Hall, D. A., & Riddoch, M. J. (1997). Word meaning deafness: Spelling words that are not understood. *Cognitive Neuropsychology, 14,* 1131–1164.

Hall, D. A., Haggard, M. P., Akeroyd, M. A., Palmer, A. R., Summerfield, A. Q., Elliott, M. R., Gurney, E. M., & Bowtell, R. W. (1999). "Sparse" temporal sampling in auditory fMRI. *Human Brain Mapping, 7,* 213–223.

Halligan, P. W., & Marshall, J. C. (1991). Left neglect for near but not far space. *Nature, 350,* 498–500.

Halligan, P. W., & Marshall, J. C. (1992). Left unilateral neglect: A meaningless entity. *Cortex, 28,* 525–535.

Halligan, P. W., & Marshall, J. C. (1997). The art of visual neglect. *Lancet, 350,* 139–140.

Halsband, U., Matsuzaka, Y., & Tanji, J. (1994). Neuronal activity in the primate supplementary, pre-supplementary and premotor cortex during externally and internally instructed movement sequences. *Neuroscience Research, 20,* 149–155.

Hamilton, L. W. (1976). *Basic limbic system anatomy of the rat.* New York: Plenum Press.

Hamilton, R., Keenan, J. P., Catala, M., & Pascual-Leone, A. (2000). Alexia for Braille following bilateral occipital stroke in an early blind woman. *NeuroReport, 11,* 237–240.

Hanley, J. R., & McDonnell, V. (1997). Are reading and spelling phonologically mediated? Evidence from a patient with a speech production impairment. *Cognitive Neuropsychology, 14,* 3–33.

Hanley, J. R., Smith, S. T., & Hadfield, J. (1998). I recognise you but I can't place you: An investigation of familiar-only experiences during tests of voice and face recognition. *Quarterly Journal of Experimental Psychology, 51,* 179–195.

Hanley, J. R., Young, A. W., & Pearson, N. A. (1991). Impairment of visuo-spatial sketchpad. *Quarterly Journal of Experimental Psychology, 43A,* 101–125.

Happé, F. G. E. (1995). Understanding minds and metaphors: Insights from the study of figurative language in autism. *Metaphor and Symbolic Activity, 10,* 275–295.

Happé, F. G. E. (1999). Autism: cognitive deficit or cognitive style? *Trends in Cognitive Sciences, 3,* 216–222.

Hare, R. D. (1980). A research scale for the assessment of psychopathy in criminal populations. *Personality and Individual Differences, 1,* 111–119.

Harley, T. A. (2004). Does cognitive neuropsychology have a future? *Cognitive Neuropsychology, 21,* 3–16.

Harlow, H. F. (1958). The nature of love. *American Psychologist, 13,* 673–685.

Harlow, J. M. (1993). Recovery from the passage of an iron bar through the head. *History of Psychiatry, 4,* 271–281 (original work published in 1848 in *Publications of the Massachusetts Medical Society*).

Harris, I. M., Harris, J. A., & Caine, D. (2001). Object orientation agnosia: A failure to find the axis? *Journal of Cognitive Neuroscience, 13,* 800–812.

Hart, J., Berndt, R. S., & Caramazza, A. (1985). Category-specific naming deficit following cerebral infarction. *Nature, 316,* 439–440.

Hartley, T., Maguire, E. A., Spiers, H. J., & Burgess, N. (2003). The well-worn route and the path less travelled: Distinct neural bases of route following and wayfinding in humans. *Neuron, 37,* 877–888.

Harvey, R. J., McCabe, B. J., Solomonia, R. O., Horn, G., & Darlison, M. G. (1998). Expression of the GABA(A) receptor gamma 4-subunit gene: Anatomical distribution of the corresponding mRNA in the domestic chick forebrain and the effect of imprinting training. *European Journal of Neuroscience, 10,* 3024–3028.

Hasselmo, M. E., Rolls, E. T., & Bayliss, G. C. (1989). The role of expression and identity in the face-selective responses of neurons in the temporal visual cortex of the monkey. *Experimental Brain Research, 75,* 417–429.

Hauk, O., Johnsrude, I., & Pulvermuller, F. (2004). Somatotopic representation of action words in human motor and premotor cortex. *Neuron, 41,* 301–307.

Hauser, M. D., Chomsky, N., & Fitch, W. T. (2002). The faculty of language: what is it, who has it, and how did it evolve? *Science, 298,* 1569–1579.

Hauser, M. D., MacNeilage, P., & Ware, M. (1996). Numerical representations in primates. *Proceedings of the National Academy of Science, USA, 93,* 1514–1517.

Hawke, J. L., Wadsworth, S. J., & DeFries, J. C. (2006). Genetic influences on reading difficulties in boys and girls: The Colorado twin study. *Dyslexia, 12,* 21–29.

Haxby, J. V., Gobbini, M. I., Furey, M. L., Ishai, A., Schouten, J. L., & Pietrini, P. (2001). Distributed and overlapping representations of faces and objects in ventral temporal cortex. *Science, 293*, 2425–2430.

Haynes, J. D., & Rees, G. (2006). Decoding mental states from brain activity in humans. *Nature Reviews Neuroscience, 7*, 523–534.

Haywood, M., & Coltheart, M. (2001). Neglect dyslexia with a stimulus-centred deficit and without visuospatial neglect. *Cognitive Neuropsychology, 18*, 577–615.

Heimer, L., & Robards, M. J. (1981). *Neuroanatomical tract tracing methods.* New York: Plenum Press.

Henderson, L. (1985). On the use of the term "grapheme". *Language and Cognitive Processes, 1*, 135–148.

Henik, A., & Tzelgov, J. (1982). Is 3 greater than 5: The relation between physical and semantic size in comparison tasks. *Memory, & Cognition, 10*, 389–395.

Henson, R. A. (2005). What can functional neuroimaging tell the experimental psychologist? *Quarterly Journal of Experimental Psychology, 58A*, 193–233.

Henson, R. N. A., Rugg, M. D., Shallice, T., & Dolan, R. J. (2000). Confidence in recognition memory for words: Dissociating right prefrontal roles in episodic retrieval. *Journal of Cognitive Neuroscience, 12*, 913–923.

Henson, R. N. A., Rugg, M. D., Shallice, T., Josephs, O., & Dolan, R. J. (1999a). Recollection and familiarity in recognition memory: An event-related functional magnetic resonance imaging study. *Journal of Neuroscience, 19*, 3962–3972.

Henson, R. N. A., Shallice, T., & Rugg, M. D. (1999b). Right prefrontal cortex and episodic memory retrieval: A functional MRI test of the monitoring hypothesis. *Brain, 122*, 1367–1381.

Hermelin, B., & O'Connor, N. (1986). Idiot savant calendrical calculators: Rules and regularites. *Psychological Medicine, 16*, 1–9.

Herrnstein, R., Lovelend, D., & Cable, C. (1977). Natural concepts in pigeons. *Journal of Experimental Psychology: Animal Learning and Memory, 2*, 285–302.

Herzmann, G., Schweinberger, S. R., Sommer, W., & Jentzsch, I. (2004). What's special about personally familiar faces? A multimodal approach. *Psychophysiology, 41*, 688–701.

Heywood, C. A., Cowey, A., & Newcombe, F. (1991). Chromatic discrimination in a cortically color-blind observer. *European Journal of Neuroscience, 3*, 802–812.

Heywood, C. A., Kentridge, R. W., & Cowey, A. (1998). Cortical color blindness is not "blindsight for color". *Consciousness and Cognition, 7*, 410–423.

Hickok, G., & Poeppel, D. (2004). Dorsal and ventral streams: a framework for understanding aspects of the functional anatomy of language. *Cognition, 92*, 67–99.

Hill, E. L., & Frith, U. (2003). Understanding Autism: Insights from mind and brain. *Philosophical Transactions of the Royal Society of London B, 358*, 281–289.

Hillis, A. E., & Caramazza, A. (1991a). Deficit to stimulus-centred, letter shape representation in a case of unilateral neglect. *Neuropsychologia, 29*, 1223–1240.

Hillis, A. E., & Caramazza, A. (1991b). Mechanisms for accessing lexical representations for output: Evidence from a category-specific semantic deficit. *Brain and Language, 40*, 106–144.

Hillis, A. E., Newhart, M., Heidler, J., Barker, P. B., & Degaonkar M. (2005). Anatomy of spatial attention: Insights from perfusion imaging and hemispatial neglect in acute stroke. *Journal of Neuroscience, 25*, 3161–3167.

Hillis, A. E., Work, M., Barker, P. B., Jacobs, M. A., Breese, E. L., & Maurer, K. (2004). Re-examining the brain regions crucial for orchestrating speech articulation. *Brain, 127*, 1479–1487.

Hirst, W., Phelps, E. A., Johnson, M. K., & Volpe, B. T. (1988). Amnesia and second language learning. *Brain and Cognition, 8*, 105–116.

Hittmair-Delazer, M., Sailer, U., & Benke, T. (1995). Impaired arithmetic facts but intact conceptual knowledge: A single case study of dyscalculia. *Cortex, 31*, 139–147.

Hodges, J. R., & Graham, K. S. (1998). A reversal of the temporal gradient for famous person knowledge in semantic dementia: Implications for the neural organisation of long-term memory. *Neuropsychologia, 36*, 803–825.

Hodges, J. R., Bozeat, S., Lambon Ralph, M. A., Patterson, K., & Spatt, J. (2000). The role of conceptual knowledge in object use: Evidence from semantic dementia. *Brain, 123*, 1913–1925.

Hodges, J. R., Patterson, K., & Tyler, L. K. (1994). Loss of semantic memory: Implications for the modularity of mind. *Cognitive Neuropsychology, 11*, 505–542.

Hodges, J. R., Patterson, K., Oxbury, S., & Funnell, E. (1992). Semantic dementia. *Brain, 115*, 1783–1806.

Hodgkin, A. L., & Huxley, A. F. (1939). Action potentials recorded from inside a nerve fibre. *Nature, 144*, 710–712.

Hoekstra, R. A., Bartels, M., Verweij, C. J. H., & Boosma, D. I. (2007). Heritability of autistic traits in the general population. *Archives of Pediatrics and Adolescent Medicine, 161*, 372–377.

Hoge, R. D., & Pike, G. B. (2001). Quantitative measurement using fMRI. In P. Jezzard, P. M. Matthews, & S. M. Smith (eds.), *Functional MRI.* Oxford: Oxford University Press.

Holdstock, J. S., Mayes, A. R., Isaac, C. L., Gong, Q., & Roberts, N. (2002). Differential involvement of the hippocampus and temporal lobe cortices in rapid and slow learning of new semantic information. *Neuropsychologia, 40*, 748–768.

Hopf, H. C., Muller-Forrell, W., & Hopf, N. J. (1992). Localization of emotional and volitional facial paresis. *Neurology, 42*, 1918–1923.

Horn, G., & McCabe, B. J. (1984). Predispositions and preferences: Effects on imprinting of lesions to the chick brain. *Brain Research, 168*, 361–373.

Horwitz, B., Tagamets, M.-A., & McIntosh, A. R. (1999). Neural modelling, functional brain imaging, and cognition. *Trends in Cognitive Sciences, 3*, 91–98.

Hounsfield, G. N. (1973). Computerized transverse axial scanning (tomography). Part I: Description of system. Part II: Clinical applications. *British Journal of Radiology, 46*, 1016–1022.

Howard, D., & Patterson, K. E. (1992). *The pyramids and palm trees test.* Bury St Edmunds, UK: Thames Valley Test Corporation.

Hubel, D. H., & Wiesel, T. N. (1959). Receptive fields of single neurones in the cat's striate cortex. *Journal of Physiology, 148*, 574–591.

Hubel, D. H., & Wiesel, T. N. (1962). Receptive fields, binocular interaction and functional architecture in the cat's visual cortex. *Journal of Physiology, 160*, 106–154.

Hubel, D. H., & Wiesel, T. N. (1965). Receptive fields and functional architecture of monkey striate cortex. *Journal of Neurophysiology, 28*, 289–299.

Hubel, D. H., & Wiesel, T. N. (1968). Receptive fields and functional architecture of monkey striate cortex. *Journal of Physiology, 195*, 215–243.

Hubel, D. H., & Wiesel, T. N. (1970a). Cells sensitive to binocular depth in area 18 of the macaque monkey cortex. *Nature, 225*, 41–42.

Hubel, D. H., & Wiesel, T. N. (1970b). The period of susceptibility to the physiological effects of unilateral eye closure in kittens. *Journal of Physiology, 206*, 419–436.

Hughes, C., Russell, J., & Robbins, T. W. (1994). Evidence for executive dysfunction in autism. *Psychological Medicine, 27*, 209–220.

Humphrey, N. K. (1976). The social function of intellect. In P. Bateson, & R. A. Hinde (eds.), *Growing points in ethology.* Cambridge: Cambridge University Press.

Humphreys, G. W., & Forde, E. M. E. (1998). Disorder action schema and action dysorganisation syndrome. *Cognitive Neuropsychology, 15*, 771–811.

Humphreys, G. W., & Forde, E. M. E. (2001). Hierarchies, similarity, and interactivity in object recognition: "Category-specific" neuropsychological deficits. *Behavioral and Brain Sciences, 24*, 453–509.

Humphreys, G. W., & Riddoch, M. J. (1984). Routes to object constancy: Implications from neurological impairments of object constancy. *Quarterly Journal of Experimental Psychology, 36A*, 385–415.

Humphreys, G. W., & Riddoch, M. J. (1987). *To see but not to see: A case of visual agnosia.* Hove: Psychology Press.

Humphreys, G. W., & Riddoch, M. J. (1994). Attention to within-object and between-object spatial representations: Multiple sites for visual selection. *Cognitive Neuropsychology, 11*, 207–241.

Humphreys, G. W., & Rumiati, R. I. (1998). Agnosia without prosopagnosia or alexia: Evidence for stored visual memories specific to objects. *Cognitive Neuropsychology, 15*, 243–277.

Humphreys, G. W., Cinel, C., Wolfe, J., Olson, A., & Klempen, N. (2000). Fractionating the binding process: Neuropsychological evidence distinguishing binding of form from binding of surface features. *Vision Research, 40*, 1569–1596.

Huppert, F. A., & Piercy, M. (1978). The role of trace strength in recency and frequency judgements by amnesic and control subjects. *Quarterly Journal of Experimental Psychology, 30*, 346–354.

Huron, D. (2001). Is music an evolutionary adaptation? In R. J. Zatorre, & I. Peretz (eds.), *The biological foundations of music.* New York: New York Academy of Sciences.

Huttenlocher, P. R., & Dabholkar, A. S. (1997). Regional differences in synaptogenesis in human cerebral cortex. *Journal of Comparative Neurology, 387*, 167–178.

Hyde, K. L., & Peretz, I. (2004). Brains that are out of tune but in time. *Psychological Science, 15*, 356–360.

Hyde, K. L., Lerch, J. P., Zatorre, R. J., Griffiths, T. D., Evans, A. C., & Peretz, I. (2007). Cortical thickness in congenital amusia: When less is better than more. *Journal of Neuroscience, 27*, 13028–13032.

Hyman, I. E., Husband, T. H., & Billings, F. J. (1995). False memories of childhood experiences. *Applied Cognitive Psychology, 9*, 181–187.

Iacoboni, M., Woods, R., Brass, M., Bekkering, H., Mazziotta, J. C., & Rizzolatti, G. (1999). Cortical mechanisms of human imitation. *Science, 286*, 2526–2528.

Ifrah, G. (1985). *From one to zero: A universal history of numbers* (L. Blair trans.). New York: Viking (original work published 1981).

Indefrey, P., & Levelt, W. J. M. (2004). The spatial and temporal signatures of word production components. *Cognition, 92*, 101–144.

Iriki, A., Tanaka, M., & Iwamura, Y. (1996). Coding of modified body schema during tool use by macaque postcentral neurons. *NeuroReport, 7*, 2325–2330.

Isaacs, E. B., Edmonds, C. J., Lucas, A., & Gadian, D. G. (2001). Calculation difficulties in children of very low birth weight. *Brain, 124*, 1701–1707.

Ishai, A., Ungerleider, L. G., Martin, A., Schouten, J. L., & Haxby, J. V. (1999). Distributed representation of objects in the human ventral visual pathway. *Proceedings of the National Academy of Science, USA, 96*, 9379–9384.

Jabbi, M., Swart, M., & Keysers, C. (2007). Empathy for positive and negative emotions in gustatory cortex. *NeuroImage, 34*, 1744–1753.

Jackson, S. R., & Shaw, A. (2000). The Ponzo illusion affects grip-force but not grip-aperture scaling during prehension movements. *Journal of Experimental Psychology: Human Perception and Performance, 26*, 418–423.

Jahanshahi, M., & Frith, C. D. (1998). Willed action and its impairments. *Cognitive Neuropsychology, 15*, 483–533.

Jahanshahi, M., Dirnberger, G., Fuller, R., & Frith, C. D. (2000). The role of dorsolateral prefrontal cortex in random number generation: A study with positron emission tomography. *NeuroImage, 12,* 713–725.

Jahanshahi, M., Jenkins, I. H., Brown, R. G., Marsden, C. D., Passingham, R. E., & Brooks, D. J. (1995). Self-initiated versus externally triggered movements: An investigation using measurement of regional cerebral blood flow with PET and movement-related potentials in normal and Parkinson's disease subjects. *Brain, 118,* 913–933.

Jahanshahi, M., Profice, P., Brown, R. G., Ridding, M. C., Dirnberger, G., & Rothwell, J. C. (1998). The effects of transcranial magnetic stimulation over dorsolateral prefrontal cortex on suppression of habitual counting during random number generation. *Brain, 112,* 1533–1544.

James, W. (1890/1950). *The principles of psychology.* New York: Dover Publications.

Janowsky, J. S., Shimamura, A. P., & Squire, L. R. (1989). Source memory impairment in patients with frontal lobe lesions. *Neuropsychologia, 27,* 1043–1056.

Jasper, H. A. (1958). The ten-twenty system of the international federation. *Electroencephalography and Clinical Neurophysiology, 10,* 371–375.

Jeannerod, M. (1997). *The cognitive neuroscience of action.* Oxford: Blackwell.

Jescheniak, J. D., & Levelt, W. J. M. (1994). Word frequency effects in speech production: Retrieval of syntactic information and of phonological form. *Journal of Experimental Psychology: Learning, Memory and Cognition, 20,* 824–843.

Job, R., Sartori, G., Masterson, J., & Coltheart, M. (1983). Developmental surface dyslexia in Italian. In R. N. Malatesha, & M. Coltheart (eds.), *Dyslexia: A global issue.* The Hague: Martinus Njihoff Publishers.

Jobard, G., Crivello, F., & Tzourio-Mazoyer, N. (2003). Evaluation of the dual route theory of reading: A metanalysis of 35 neuroimaging studies. *NeuroImage, 20,* 693–712.

Johansson, G. (1973). Visual perception of biological motion and a model for its analysis. *Perception and Psychophysics, 14,* 201–211.

Johnson, M. H. (2005). *Developmental cognitive neuroscience: An introduction,* 2nd edition. Oxford: Blackwell.

Johnson, M. H., Dziurawiec, S., Ellis, H. D., & Morton, J. (1991). Newborns' preferential tracking of face-like stimuli and its subsequent decline. *Cognition, 40,* 1–19.

Johnson, M. K. (1988). Reality monitoring: An experimental phenomenological approach. *Journal of Experimental Psychology: General, 117,* 390–394.

Johnson, M. K., & Raye, C. L. (1981). Reality monitoring. *Psychological Review, 88,* 67–85.

Johnson, M. K., Foley, M. A., & Leach, K. (1988a). The consequences for memory of imagining in another person's voice. *Memory and Cognition, 16,* 337–342.

Johnson, M. K., Foley, M. A., Suengas, A. G., & Raye, C. L. (1988b). Phenomenal characteristics of memories for perceived and imagined autobiographical events. *Journal of Experimental Psychology: General, 117,* 371–376.

Johnson, M. K., Hashtroudi, S., & Lindsay, D. S. (1993). Source monitoring. *Psychological Bulletin, 114,* 3–28.

Johnson, M. K., O'Connor, M., & Cantor, J. (1997). Confabulation, memory deficits and frontal dysfunction. *Brain and Cognition, 34,* 189–206.

Johnson, M. K., Raye, C. L., Foley, H. J., & Foley, M. A. (1981). Cognitive operations and decision bias in reality monitoring. *American Journal of Psychology, 94,* 37–64.

Jones, B., & Mishkin, M. (1972). Limbic lesions and the problem of stimulus reinforcement associations. *Experimental Neurology, 36,* 362–377.

Jones, D. M., Macken, W. J., & Nicholls, A. P. (2004). The phonological store of working memory: Is it phonological and is it a store? *Journal of Experimental Psychology: Learning, Memory and Cognition, 30,* 656–674.

Jones, G. V. (2002). Predictability (ease of predication) as semantic substrate of imageability in reading and retrieval. *Brain and Language, 82,* 159–166.

Jones, P. E. (1995). Contradictions and unanswered questions in the Genie case: A fresh look at the linguistic evidence. *Language and Communication, 15,* 261–280.

Jonides, J., Schumacher, E. H., Smith, E. E., Koeppe, R. A., Awh, E., Reuter-Lorenz, P. A., Marscheutz, C., & Willis, C. R. (1998). The role of parietal cortex in verbal working memory. *Journal of Neuroscience, 18,* 5026–5034.

Joseph, J. E. (2001). Functional neuroimaging studies of category specificity in object recognition: A critical review and meta-analysis. *Cognitive, Affective and Behavioral Neuroscience, 1,* 119–136.

Josephs, O., & Henson, R. N. A. (1999). Event-related functional magnetic resonance imaging: Modelling, inference and optimization. *Philosophical Transactions of the Royal Society B, 354,* 1215–1228.

Jueptner, M., & Weiller, C. (1995). Does measurement of regional cerebral blood flow reflect synaptic activity? Implications for PET and fMRI. *NeuroImage, 2,* 148–156.

Jung, R. E., & Haier, R. J. (2007). The Parieto-Frontal Integration Theory (P-FIT) of intelligence: Converging neuroimaging evidence. *Behavioral and Brain Sciences, 30,* 135.

Just, M. A., Carpenter, P. A., Keller, T. A., Eddy, W. F., & Thulborn, K. R. (1996). Brain activation modulated by sentence comprehension. *Science, 274,* 114–116.

Kaas, J. H., & Hackett, T. A. (1999). "What" and "where" processing in auditory cortex. *Nature Neuroscience, 2,* 1045–1047.

Kaas, J. H., Hackett, T. A., & Tramo, M. J. (1999). Auditory processing in primate cerebral cortex. *Current Opinion in Neurobiology, 9,* 164–170.

Kajikawa, Y., de la Mothe, L. A., Blumell, S., Sterbing-D'Angelo, S. J., D'Angelo, W., Camalier, C. R., & Hackett, T. A. (2008). Coding of FM sweep trains and twitter calls in area CM of marmoset auditory cortex. *Hearing Research, 239,* 107–125.

Kane, N. M., Curry, S. H., Butler, S. R., & Cummins, B. H. (1993). Electrophysiological indicator of awakening from coma. *Lancet, 341,* 688–688.

Kanner, L. (1943). Autistic disturbances of affective contact. *Nervous Child, 2,* 217–250.

Kanwisher, N. (2000). Domain specificity in face perception. *Nature Neuroscience, 3,* 759–763.

Kanwisher, N., & Wojciulik, E. (2000). Visual attention: Insights from brain imaging. *Nature Reviews Neuroscience, 1,* 91–100.

Kanwisher, N., McDermott, J., & Chun, M. M. (1997). The fusiform face area: A module in human extrastriate cortex specialised for face perception. *Journal of Neuroscience, 17,* 4302–4311.

Kapur, N. (1996). Paradoxical functional facilitation in brain–behaviour research. *Brain, 119,* 1775–1790.

Kapur, N. (1999). Syndromes of retrograde amnesia: A conceptual and empirical synthesis. *Psychological Bulletin, 125,* 800–825.

Kapur, S. (2003). Psychosis as a state of abnormal salience: A framework linking biology, phenomenology, and pharmacology in schizophrenia. *American Journal of Psychiatry, 160,* 13–23.

Kapur, S., Craik, F. I. M., Tulving, E., Wilson, A. A., Houle, S., & Brown, G. M. (1994). Neuroanatomical correlates of encoding in episodic memory: Levels of processing effect. *Proceedings of the National Academy of Science, USA, 91,* 2008–2011.

Karmiloff-Smith, A. (1992). *Beyond modularity: A developmental perspective on cognitive science.* Cambridge, MA: MIT Press.

Karmiloff-Smith, A. (2006). Modules, genes, and evolution: What have we learned from atypical development? *Attention and Performance XXI,* 563–583.

Karmiloff-Smith, A. (2007). Williams syndrome. *Current Biology, 17,* R1035–R1036.

Karnath, H.-O., & Perenin, M.-T. (2005). Cortical control of visually guided reaching: Evidence from patients with optic ataxia. *Cerebral Cortex, 15,* 1561–1569.

Karnath, H.-O., Ferber, S., & Bulthoff, H. (2000). Neuronal representation of object orientation. *Neuropsychologia, 38,* 1235–1241.

Kaufmann, J. M., & Schweinberger, S. R. (2008). Distortions in the brain? ERP effects of caricaturing familiar and unfamiliar faces. *Brain Research, 1228,* 177–188.

Kay, J., & Ellis, A. W. (1987). A cognitive neuropsychological case study of anomia. *Brain, 110,* 613–629.

Kay, J., & Hanley, R. (1991). Simultaneous form perception and serial letter recognition in a case of letter-by-letter reading. *Cognitive Neuropsychology, 8,* 249–273.

Kay, J., & Hanley, R. (1994). Peripheral disorders of spelling: The role of the graphemic buffer. In G. D. A. Brown, & N. C. Ellis (eds.), *Handbook of spelling: Theory, process and intervention.* London: Wiley.

Kay, J., Lesser, R., & Coltheart, M. (1992). *Psycholinguistic assessments of language processing in aphasia.* Hove: Psychology Press.

Kellenbach, M. L., Wijers, A. A., Hovius, M., Mulder, J., & Mulder, G. (2002). Neural differentiation of lexico-syntactic categories or semantic features? Event-related potential evidence for both. *Journal of Cognitive Neuroscience, 14,* 561–577.

Kelley, W. M., Miezin, F. M., McDermott, K. B., Buckner, R. L., Raichle, M. E., Cohen, N. J., Ollinger, J. M., Akbudak, E., Conturo, T. E., Snyder, A. V., & Petersen, S. E. (1998). Hemispheric specialization in human dorsal frontal cortex and medial temporal lobe for verbal and nonverbal memory encoding. *Neuron, 20,* 927–936.

Keltner, D. (1995). Signs of appeasement: Evidence for the distinct displays of embarrassment, amusement and shame. *Journal of Personality and Social Psychology, 68,* 441–454.

Kendler, K. S. (2005). "A gene for…." The nature of gene action in psychiatric disorders. *American Journal of Psychiatry, 162,* 433–440.

Kendler, K. S., Neale, M. C., Kessler, R. C., Heath, A. C., & Eaves, L. J. (1992). The genetic epidemiology of phobias in women: The interrelationship of agoraphobia, social phobia, situational phobia and simple phobia. *Archives of General Psychiatry, 49,* 273–281.

Kent, R. D., Duffy, J. R., Slama, A., Kent, J. F., & Clift, A. (2001). Clinicoanatomic studies in dysarthria: Review, critique, and directions for research. *Journal of Speech, Language and Hearing Research, 44,* 535–551.

Kerns, J. G., Cohen, J. D., MacDonald, A. W., Cho, R. Y., Stenger, V. A., & Carter, C. S. (2004). Anterior cingulate conflict monitoring and adjustments in control. *Science, 303,* 1023–1026.

Keysers, C., Wicker, B., Gazzola, V., Anton, J. L., Fogassi, L., & Gallese, V. (2004). A touching sight: SII/PV activation during the observation and experience of touch. *Neuron, 42,* 335–346.

Kiang, N. Y.-S., Watanabe, T., Thomas, E. C., & Clark, L. F. (1965). *Discharge patterns of single fibres in the cat's auditory nerve.* Cambridge, MA: MIT Press.

Kim, J. J., & Fanselow, M. S. (1992). Modality-specific retrograde amnesia for fear. *Science, 256,* 675–677.

Kimberg, D. Y., Aguirre, G. K., & D'Esposito, M. (2000). Modulation of task-related neural activity in task-switching: An fMRI study. *Cognitive Brain Research, 10,* 189–196.

Kinsbourne, M., & Warrington, E. K. (1962a). A disorder of simultaneous form perception. *Brain, 85,* 461–486.

Kinsbourne, M., & Warrington, E. K. (1962b). A study of finger agnosia. *Brain, 85,* 47–66.

Kinsbourne, M., & Warrington, E. K. (1965). A case showing selectively impaired oral spelling. *Journal of Neurology, Neurosurgery and Psychiatry, 28*, 563–566.

Kipps, C. M., Duggins, A. J., McCusker, E. A., & Calder, A. J. (2007). Disgust and happiness recognition correlate with anteroventral insula and amygdala volume respectively in preclinical Huntington's disease. *Journal of Cognitive Neuroscience, 19*, 1206–1217.

Kitchener, E. G., Hodges, J. R., & McCarthy, R. (1998). Acquisition of post-morbid vocabulary and semantic facts in the absence of episodic memory. *Brain, 121*, 1313–1327.

Klein, D. C., Moore, R. Y., & Reppert, S. M. (1991). *Suprachiasmatic nucleus: The mind's clock.* Oxford: Oxford University Press.

Kleinschmidt, A., Buchel, C., & Zeki, S. (1998). Human brain activity during spontaneously reversing perception of ambiguous figures. *Proceedings of the National Academy of Science, USA, 265*, 2427–2433.

Klinnert, M. D., Campos, J. J., & Source, J. (1983). Emotions as behavior regulators: Social referencing in infancy. In R. Plutchik, & H. Kellerman (eds.), *Emotions in early development.* New York: Academic Press.

Kluver, H., & Bucy, P. C. (1939). Preliminary analysis of functions of the temporal lobes in monkeys. *Archives of Neurology and Psychiatry, 42*, 979–1000.

Knight, R. T. (1996). Contribution of human hippocampal region to novel detection. *Nature, 383*, 256–259.

Knowlton, B. J., Mangels, J. A., & Squire, L. R. (1996). A neostriatal habit learning system in humans. *Science, 273*, 1399–1402.

Knowlton, B. J., Squire, L. R., & Gluck, M. A. (1994). Probabilistic category learning in amnesia. *Learning and Memory, 1*, 106–120.

Koechlin, E., Basso, G., Pietrini, P., Panzer, S., & Grafman, J. (1999a). The role of the anterior prefrontal cortex in human cognition. *Nature, 399*, 148–151.

Koechlin, E., Naccache, L., Block, E., & Dehaene, S. (1999b). Primed numbers: Exploring the modularity of numerical representations with masked and unmasked semantic priming. *Journal of Experimental Psychology: Human Perception and Performance, 25*, 1882–1905.

Koelsch, S., & Siebel, W. A. (2005). Towards a neural basis of music perception. *Trends in Cognitive Sciences, 9*, 578–584.

Koelsch, S., Fritz, T. V., von Cramon, D. Y., Muller, K., & Friederici, A. D. (2006). Investigating emotion with music: An fMRI study. *Human Brain Mapping, 27*, 236–250.

Kolb, B., & Taylor, L. (2000). Facial expression, emotion and hemispheric organisation. In R. D. Lane, & L. Nadel (eds.), *Cognitive neuroscience of emotion.* Oxford: Oxford University Press.

Kolb, B., & Whishaw, I. Q. (2002). *Fundamentals of human neuropsychology*, 5th edition. New York: Worth/Freeman.

Konishi, S., Chikazoe, J., Jimura, K., Asari, T., & Miyashita, Y. (1999). Neural mechanism in anterior prefrontal cortex for inhibition of prolonged set interference. *Proceedings of the National Academy of Sciences, USA, 102*, 12584–12588.

Kopelman, M. D. (2000). Focal retrograde amnesia: An exceptionally critical review. *Cognitive Neuropsychology, 17*, 585–621.

Kopelman, M. D., & Stanhope, N. (1998). Recall and recognition memory in patients with focal frontal, temporal lobe and diencephalic lesions. *Neuropsychologia, 36*, 785–795.

Kopelman, M. D., Ng, N., & Van Den Brouke, O. (1997). Confabulation extending across episodic, personal and general semantic memory. *Cognitive Neuropsychology, 14*, 683–712.

Kopelman, M. D., Wilson, B. A., & Baddeley, A. D. (1990). *The autobiographical memory interview.* Bury St Edmunds, UK: Thames Valley Test Company.

Kosaki, H., Hashikawa, T., He, J., & Jones, E. G. (1997). Tonotopic organization of auditory cortical fields delineated by parvalbumin immunoreactivity in Macaque monkeys. *Journal of Comparative Neurology, 386*, 304–316.

Kosslyn, S. M. (1999). If neuroimaging is the answer, what is the question? *Philosophical Transactions of the Royal Society of London B, 354*, 1283–1294.

Kosslyn, S. M., & Van Kleek, M. H. (1990). Broken brains and normal minds: Why Humpty-Dumpty needs a skeleton. In E. L. Schwartz (ed.), *Computational neuroscience.* Cambridge, MA: MIT Press.

Kosslyn, S. M., Ganis, G., & Thompson, W. L. (2001). Neural foundations of imagery. *Nature Reviews Neuroscience, 2*, 635–642.

Kosslyn, S. M., Pascual-Leone, A., Felician, O., Camposano, S., Keenan, J. P., Thompson, W. L., Ganis, G., Sukel, K. E., & Alpert, N. M. (1999). The role of area 17 in visual imagery: Convergent evidence from PET and rTMS. *Science, 284*, 167–170.

Kosslyn, S. M., Thompson, W. L., Kim, I. J., & Alpert, N. M. (1995). Topographical representations of mental images in primary visual cortex. *Nature, 478*, 496–498.

Kotler, M., Cohen, H., Segman, R., Gritsenko, I., Nemanov, L., Lerer, B., Kramer, I., ZerZion, M., Kletz, I., & Ebstein, R. P. (1997). Excess dopamine D4 receptor (D4DR) exon III seven repeat allele in opioid-dependent subjects. *Molecular Psychiatry, 2*, 251–254.

Koutstaal, W., Schacter, D. L., Verfaellie, M., Brenner, C., & Jackson, E. M. (1999). Perceptually based false recognition of novel objects in amnesia: Effects of category size and similarity to category prototypes. *Cognitive Neuropsychology, 16*, 317–341.

Kraemer, D. J. M., Macrae, C. N., Green, A. E., & Kelley, W. M. (2005). Musical imagery: Sound of silence activates auditory cortex. *Nature, 434*, 158–158.

Krams, M., Rushworth, M. F. S., Deiber, M. P., Frackowiak, R. S. J., & Passingham, R. E. (1998). The preparation, execution and suppression of copied movements. *Experimental Brain Research*, *120*, 386–398.

Kriegstein, K. von, Kleinschmidt, A., Sterzer, P., & Giraud, A. L. (2005). Interaction of face and voice areas during speaker recognition. *Journal of Cognitive Neuroscience*, *17*, 367–376.

Kritchevsky, M., Chang, J., & Squire, L. R. (2004). Functional amnesia: Clinical description and neuropsychological profile of 10 cases. *Learning and Memory*, *11*, 213–226.

Kuffler, S. W., & Barlow, H. B. (1953). Discharge patterns and functional organization of mammalian retina. *Journal of Neurophysiology*, *16*, 37–63.

Kutas, M., & Hillyard, S. (1980). Reading senseless sentences: Brain potentials reflect semantic incongruity. *Science*, *207*, 203–205.

La Berge, D. (1983). Spatial extent of attention to letters and words. *Journal of Experimental Psychology: Human Perception and Performance*, *9*, 371–379.

Ladavas, E., Shallice, T., & Zanella, T. (1997). Preserved semantic access in neglect dyslexia. *Neuropsychologia*, *35*, 257–270.

Lambon Ralph, M. A., Ellis, A. W., & Franklin, S. (1995). Semantic loss without surface dyslexia. *Neurocase*, *1*, 363–369.

Lambon Ralph, M. A., Howard, D., Nightingale, G., & Ellis, A. W. (1998). Are living and non-living category-specific deficits causally linked to impaired perceptual or associative knowledge? Evidence from a category-specific double dissociation. *Neurocase*, *4*, 311–338.

Lambon Ralph, M. A., Sage, K., & Ellis, A. W. (1996). Word meaning blindness: A new form of acquired dyslexia. *Cognitive Neuropsychology*, *13*, 617–639.

Lancy, D. F. (1983). *Cross-cultural studies in cognition and mathematics*. New York: Academic Press.

Land, E. H. (1964). The retinex. *Scientific American*, *52*, 247–264.

Land, E. H. (1983). Recent advances in retinex theory and some implications for cortical computations. *Proceedings of the National Academy of Science, USA*, *80*, 5163–5169.

Lane, R. D., & Nadel, L. (2000). *Cognitive neuroscience of emotion*. Oxford: Oxford University Press.

Langdon, D. W., & Warrington, E. K. (1997). The abstraction of numerical relations: A role for the right hemisphere in arithmetic? *Journal of International Neuropsychological Society*, *3*, 260–268.

Langleben, D. D., Schroeder, L., Maldjian, J. A., Gur, R. C., McDonald, S., Ragland, J. D., O'Brien, C. P., & Childress, A. R. (2002). Brain activity during simulated deception: An event-related functional magnetic resonance study. *NeuroImage*, *15*, 727–732.

Lashley, K. S. (1929). *Brain mechanisms and intelligence*. Chicago: Chicago University Press.

Lauro-Grotto, R., Piccini, C., & Shallice, T. (1997). Modality-specific operations in semantic dementia. *Cortex*, *33*, 593–622.

Lauterbur, P. C. (1973). Image formation by induced local interactions: Examples employing Nuclear Magnetic Resonance. *Nature*, *242*, 190–191.

Lavie, N. (1995). Perceptual load as a necessary condition for selective attention. *Journal of Experimental Psychology: Human Perception and Performance*, *21*, 451–468.

Le Bihan, D., Mangin, J. F., Poupon, C., Clark, C. A., Pappata, S., Molko, N., & Chabriat, H. (2001). Diffusion tensor imaging: Concepts and applications. *Journal of Magnetic Resonance Imaging*, *13*, 534–546.

Le Doux, J. E. (1996). *The emotional brain*. New York: Simon and Schuster.

Le Doux, J. E., Iwata, J., Cicchetti, P., & Reis, D. (1988). Differential projections of the central amygdaloid nucleus mediate autonomic and behavioral correlates of conditioned fear. *Journal of Neuroscience*, *8*, 2517–2529.

Le Grand, R., Mondloch, C., Maurer, D., & Brent, H. P. (2001). Neuroperception: Early visual experience and face processing. *Nature*, *410*, 890.

Lee, K. M., & Kang, S.-Y. (2002). Arithmetic operation and working memory: Differential suppression in dual tasks. *Cognition*, *83*, B63–B68.

Leekam, S. R., & Perner, J. (1991). Does the autistic child have a metarepresentational deficit? *Cognition*, *40*, 203–218.

Lenneberg, E. (1967). *Biological foundations of language*. New York: Wiley.

Leslie, A. M. (1987). Pretence and representation: The origins of "Theory of Mind". *Psychological Review*, *94*, 412–426.

Leslie, A. M., Mallon, R., & Di Corcia, J. A. (2006). Transgressors, victims and cry babies: Is basic moral judgment spared in autism? *Social Neuroscience*, *1*, 270–283.

Levelt, W. J. M. (1989). *Speaking: From intention to articulation*. Cambridge, MA: MIT Press.

Levelt, W. J. M. (1999). Models of word production. *Trends in Cognitive Sciences*, *3*, 223–232.

Levelt, W. J. M. (2001). Spoken word production: A theory of lexical access. *Proceedings of the National Academy of Science, USA*, *98*, 13464–13471.

Levelt, W. J. M., & Wheeldon, L. (1994). Do speakers have access to a mental syllabary? *Cognition*, *50*, 239–269.

Levelt, W. J. M., Schriefers, H., Vorberg, D., Meyer, A. S., Pechmann, T., & Havinga, J. (1991). The time course of lexical access in speech production: A study of picture naming. *Psychological Review*, *98*, 122–142.

Levine, D. N., Warach, J., & Farah, M. (1985). Two visual systems in mental imagery: Dissociation of "what" and "where" in imagery disorders due to bilateral posterior cerebral lesions. *Neurology, 35,* 1010–1018.

Levinson, D. F. (2003). Molecular genetics of schizophrenia: A review of the recent literature. *Current Opinion in Psychiatry, 16,* 157–170.

Liberman, A. M., & Mattingly, I. G. (1985). The motor theory of speech perception revised. *Cognition, 21,* 1–36.

Liberman, A. M., & Whalen, D. H. (2000). On the relation of speech to language. *Trends in Cognitive Sciences, 4,* 187–196.

Libet, B., Gleason, C. A., Wright, E. W., & Pearl, D. K. (1983). Time of conscious intention to act in relation to onset of cerebral activity (readiness potential): The unconscious initiation of a freely voluntary act. *Brain, 102,* 623–642.

Lichtheim, L. (1885). On aphasia. *Brain, 7,* 433–484.

Lidzba, K., Staudt, M., Wilke, M., & Krageloh-Mann, I. (2006). Visuospatial deficits in patients with early left-hemispheric lesions and functional reorganization of language: Consequence of lesion or reorganization? *Neuropsychologia, 44,* 1088–1094.

Lieberman, M. D., Chang, G. Y., Chiao, J., Bookheimer, S. Y., & Knowlton, B. J. (2004). An event-related fMRI study of artificial grammar learning in a balanced chunk strength design. *Journal of Cognitive Neuroscience, 16,* 427–438.

Liegeois, F., Connelly, A., Cross, J. H., Boyd, S. G., Gadian, D. G., Vargha-Khadem, F., & Baldeweg, T. (2004). Language reorganization in children with early-onset lesions of the left hemisphere: An fMRI study. *Brain, 127,* 1229–1236.

Liepmann, H. (1905). Die linke hemisphere und das handeln. *Munchner Medizinische Wochenschrift, 49,* 2322–2326.

Lindgren, S. D., De Renzi, E., & Richman, L. C. (1985). Cross-national comparisons of developmental dyslexia in Italy and the United States. *Child Development, 56,* 1404–1417.

Linebarger, M. C., Schwartz, M. F., & Saffran, E. M. (1983). Sensitivity to grammatical structure in so-called agrammatic aphasics. *Cognition, 13,* 361–392.

Lissauer, H. (1890). A case of visual agnosia with a contribution to theory. *Archiv für Psychiatrie und Nervenrankheiten, 21,* 222–270.

Loewenstein, G., Rick, S., & Cohen, J. D. (2008). Neuroeconomics. *Annual Review of Psychology, 59,* 647–672.

Logie, R. H. (1995). *Visuospatial working memory.* Hove: Psychology Press.

Logie, R. H., Gilhooly, K. J., & Wynn, V. (1994). Counting on working memory in arithmetic problem solving. *Memory and Cognition, 22,* 395–410.

Logothetis, N. K., Pauls, J., Augath, M., Trinath, T., & Oeltermann, A. (2001). Neurophysiological investigation of the basis of the fMRI signal. *Nature, 412,* 150–157.

Luck, S. J. (2005). Ten simple rules for designing ERP experiments. In T. C. Handy (ed.), *Event-related potentials: A methods handbook.* Cambridge, MA: MIT Press.

Luders, E., Narr, K. L., Thompson, P. M., Rex, D. E., Jancke, L., Steinmetz, H., & Toga, A. W. (2004). Gender differences in cortical complexity. *Nature Neuroscience, 7,* 799–800.

Luzzatti, C., & Davidoff, J. (1994). Impaired retrieval of object-colour knowledge with preserved colour naming. *Neuropsychologia, 32,* 933–950.

Lyons, F., Hanley, J. R., & Kay, J. (2002). Anomia for common names and geographical names with preserved retrieval of people: A semantic memory disorder. *Cortex, 38,* 23–35.

Macaluso, E., George, N., Dolan, R., Spence, C., & Driver, J. (2004). Spatial and temporal factors during processing of audiovisual speech: A PET study. *NeuroImage, 21,* 725–732.

MacDonald, M. C., Pearlmutter, N. J., & Seidenberg, M. S. (1994). Lexical nature of syntactic ambiguity resolution. *Psychological Review, 101,* 676–703.

MacDonald, M. E., Gines, S., Gusella, J. F., & Wheeler, V. C. (2003). Huntington's disease. *Neuromolecular Medicine, 4,* 7–20.

MacLean, P. D. (1949). Psychosomatic disease and the "visceral brain": Recent developments bearing on the Papez theory of emotion. *Psychosomatic Medicine, 11,* 338–353.

MacLeod, C. M. (1991). Half a century of research on the Stroop effect: An integrative review. *Psychological Bulletin, 109,* 163–203.

MacLeod, C. M., & MacDonald, P. A. (2000). Interdimensional interference in the Stroop effect: Uncovering the cognitive and neural anatomy of attention. *Trends in Cognitive Sciences, 4,* 383–391.

Macmillan, M. B. (1986). A wonderful journey through skull and brains: The travels of Mr. Gage's tamping iron. *Brain and Cognition, 5,* 67–107.

Maess, B., Koelsch, S., Gunter, T. C., & Friederici, A. D. (2001). Musical syntax is processed in Broca's area: An MEG study. *Nature Neuroscience, 4,* 540–545.

Maestrini, E., Paul, A., Monaco, A. P., & Bailey, A. (2000). Identifying autism susceptibility genes. *Neuron, 28,* 19–24.

Magnussen, C. E., & Stevens, H. C. (1914). Visual sensation caused by a magnetic field. *Philosophical Magazine, 28,* 188–207.

Maguire, E. A., Gadian, D. G., Johnsrude, I. S., Good, C. D., Ashburner, J., Frackowiak, R. S. J., & Frith, C. D. (2000). Navigation-related structural change in the hippocampi of taxi drivers. *Proceedings of the National Academy of Science, USA, 97,* 4398–4403.

Maguire, E. A., Henson, R. N. A., Mummery, C. J., & Frith, C. D. (2001). Activity in prefrontal cortex, not hippocampus, varies parametrically with the increasing remoteness of memories. *NeuroReport, 12,* 441–444.

Maia, T. V., & McClelland, J. L. (2004). A re-examination of the evidence for the somatic marker hypothesis: What participants really know in the Iowa gambling task. *Proceedings of the National Academy of Science, USA, 101,* 16075–16080.

Malone, D. R., Morris, H. H., Kay, M. C., & Levin, H. S. (1982). Prosopagnosia: A dissociation between the recognition of familiar and unfamiliar faces. *Journal of Neurology, Neurosurgery and Psychiatry, 45,* 820–822.

Mandler, G. (1980). Recognising: The judgement of a previous occurrence. *Psychological Review, 27,* 252–271.

Mandler, G., & Shebo, B. J. (1982). Subitizing: An analysis of its component processes. *Journal of Experimental Psychology: General, 11,* 1–22.

Manes, F., Sahakian, B., Clark, L., Rogers, R., Antoun, N., Aitken, M., & Robbins, T. (2002). Decision-making processes following damage to the prefrontal cortex. *Brain, 125,* 624–639.

Manns, J. R., Hopkins, R. O., & Squire, L. R. (2003b). Semantic memory and the human hippocampus. *Neuron, 38,* 127–133.

Manns, J. R., Hopkins, R. O., Reed, J. M., Kitchener, E. G., & Squire, L. R. (2003a). Recognition memory and the human hippocampus. *Neuron, 37,* 171–180.

Manoach, D. S., White, N. S., Lindgren, K. A., Heckers, S., Coleman, M. J., Dubal, S., & Holzman, P. S. (2004). Hemispheric specialization of the lateral prefrontal cortex for strategic processing during spatial and shape working memory. *NeuroImage, 21,* 894–903.

Marcar, V. L., Strassle, A. E., Loenneker, T., Schwarz, U., & Martin, E. (2004). The influence of cortical maturation on the BOLD response: An fMRI study of visual cortex in children. *Pediatric Research, 56,* 967–974.

Marcel, A. J. (1998). Blindsight and shape perception: Deficit of visual consciousness or of visual function? *Brain, 121,* 1565–1588.

Marchetti, C., & Della Sala, S. (1998). Disentangling alien and anarchic hand. *Cognitive Neuropsychiatry, 3,* 191–207.

Marie, P. (1906). Révision de la question sur l'aphasie: La troisième convolution frontale gauche ne joue aucun role spéciale dans la fonction du langage. *Semaine Medicale, 21,* 241–247.

Maril, A., Wagner, A. D., & Schacter, D. L. (2001). On the tip of the tongue: An event-related fMRI study of semantic retrieval failure and cognitive control. *Neuron, 31,* 653–660.

Marr, D. (1976). Early processing of visual information. *Philosophical Transactions of the Royal Society of London B, 275,* 483–524.

Marr, D., & Nishihara, H. K. (1978). Representation and recognition of the spatial organisation of three-dimensional shapes. *Proceedings of the Royal Society of London B, 200,* 269–294.

Marshack, A. (1970). *Notation dans les gravures du paléolithique supérieur.* Bordeaux: Delmas.

Marshack, A. (1991). *The roots of civilization,* 2nd edition. London: Moyer Bell.

Marshall, J. C., & Halligan, P. W. (1988). Blindsight and insight in visuo-spatial neglect. *Nature, 336,* 766–767.

Marshall, J. C., & Halligan, P. W. (1990). Line bisection in a case of visual neglect: Psychophysical studies with implications for theory. *Cognitive Neuropsychology, 7,* 107–130.

Marshall, J. C., & Newcombe, F. (1973). Patterns of paralexia: A psycholinguistic approach. *Journal of Psycholinguistic Research, 2,* 175–199.

Marslen-Wilson, W., & Warren, P. (1994). Levels of perceptual representation and process in lexical access: Words, phonemes and features. *Psychological Review, 101,* 653–675.

Marslen-Wilson, W. D. (1987). Functional parallelism in spoken word recognition. *Cognition, 25,* 71–102.

Marslen-Wilson, W. D., & Tyler, L. K. (1980). The temporal structure of spoken language understanding. *Cognition, 8,* 1–71.

Martin, A., & Chao, L. L. (2001). Semantic memory and the brain: Structure and processes. *Current Opinion in Neurobiology, 11,* 194–201.

Martin, J. P. (1967). *The basal ganglia and posture.* London: Pitman.

Martin, N. (1996). Models of deep dysphasia. *Neurocase, 2,* 73–80.

Mather, G. (2000) *Foundations of perception.* Hove: Psychology Press.

Matthews, G., & Wells, A. (1999). The cognitive science of attention and emotion. In T. Dalgleish, & M. J. Power (eds.), *Handbook of cognition and emotion.* New York: Wiley.

Mattingley, J. B., Driver, J., Beschin, N., & Robertson, I. H. (1997). Attentional competition between modalities: Extinction between touch and vision after right hemisphere damage. *Neuropsychologia, 35,* 867–880.

Maunsell, J. H. R. (1987). Physiological evidence for two visual subsystems. In L. M. Vaina (ed.), *Matters of intelligence.* Dordrecht: Reidel.

Maurer, D. Lewis, T. L., Brent, H. P., & Levin, A. V (1999). Rapid improvement in the acuity of infants after visual input. *Science, 286,* 108–110.

Mayall, K., & Humphreys, G. W. (2002). Presentation and task effects on migration errors in attentional dyslexia. *Neuropsychologia, 40,* 1506–1515.

Mayall, K., Humphreys, G. W., & Olson, A. (1997). Disruption to word or letter processing? The origins of case-mixing effects. *Journal of Experimental Psychology: Learning, Memory and Cognition, 23,* 1275–1286.

Mayes, A. R. (1988). *Human organic memory disorders.* Cambridge: Cambridge University Press.

Mayes, A. R., Holdstock, J. S., Isaac, C. L., Hunkin, N. M., & Roberts, N. (2002). Relative sparing of item recognition memory in a patient with adult-onset damage limited to the hippocampus. *Hippocampus, 12,* 325–340.

Mayes, A. R., Holdstock, J. S., Isaac, C. L., Montaldi, D., Grigor, J., Gummer, A., Cariga, P., Downes, J. J., Tsivilis, D., Gaffan, D., Gong, Q. Y., & Norman, K. A. (2004). Associative recognition in a patient with selective hippocampal lesions and relatively normal item recognition. *Hippocampus, 14,* 763–784.

Mayes, A. R., Isaac, C. L., Holdstock, J. S., Hunkin, N. M., Montaldi, D., Downes, J. J., MacDonald, C., Cezayirli, E., & Roberts, J. N. (2001). Memory for single items, word pairs, and temporal order of different kinds in a patient with selective hippocampal lesions. *Cognitive Neuropsychology, 18,* 97–123.

Mayozer, B. M., Tzourio, N., Frak, V., Syrota, A., Murayama, N., Levrier, O., Salamon, G., Dehaene, S., Cohen, L., & Mehler, J. (1993). The cortical representation of speech. *Journal of Cognitive Neuroscience, 5,* 467–479.

Mayr, U., & Kleigl, R. (2000). Task-set switching and long-term memory retrieval. *Journal of Experimental Psychology: Learning, Memory and Cognition, 26,* 1124–1140.

Mayr, U., Diedrichsen, J., Ivry, R., & Keele, S. W. (2006). Dissociating task-set selection from task-set inhibition in the prefrontal cortex. *Journal of Cognitive Neuroscience, 18,* 14–21.

McCabe, K., Houser, D., Ryan, L., Smith, V., & Trouard, T. (2001). A functional imaging study of cooperation in two-person reciprocal exchange. *Proceedings of the National Academy of Sciences, USA, 98,* 11832–11835.

McCandliss, B. D., Cohen, L., & Dehaene, S. (2003). The visual word form area: Expertise for reading in the fusiform gyrus. *Trends in Cognitive Sciences, 7,* 293–299.

McCandliss, B. D., Fiez, J. A., Protopapas, A., Conway, M., & McClelland, J. L. (2002). Success and failure in teaching the [r]–[l] contrast to Japanese adults: Tests of a Hebbian model of plasticity and stabilization in spoken language perception. *Cognitive, Affective, & Behavioural Neuroscience, 2,* 89–108.

McCarthy, R. A., & Warrington, E. K. (1990). *Cognitive neuropsychology: A clinical introduction.* London: Academic Press.

McClelland, J. L., & Rumelhart, D. E. (1981). An interactive activation model of context effects in letter perception: Part 1. An account of the basic findings. *Psychological Review, 88,* 375–407.

McClelland, J. L., McNaughton, B. L., & O'Reilly, R. C. (1995). Why there are complementary learning systems in the hippocampus and neocortex: Insights from the successes and failures of connectionist models of learning and memory. *Psychological Review, 102,* 419–457.

McClelland, J. L., Rumelhart, D. E., & Group, T. P. R. (1986). *Parallel distributed processing: Volume 2. Psychological and biological models.* Cambridge, MA: MIT Press.

McClelland, J. L., St John, M., & Taraban, R. (1989). Sentence comprehension: A parallel distributed processing approach. *Language and Cognitive Processes, 4,* 287–335.

McCloskey, M. (1992). Cognitive mechanisms in numerical processing: Evidence from acquired dyscalculia. *Cognition, 44,* 107–157.

McCloskey, M., & Caramazza, A. (1988). Theory and methodology in cognitive neuropsychology: A response to our critics. *Cognitive Neuropsychology, 5,* 583–623.

McCloskey, M., Caramazza, A., & Basili, A. (1985). Cognitive mechanisms in number processing and calculation: Evidence from dyscalculia. *Brain and Cognition, 4,* 171–196.

McCloskey, M., Sokol, S. M., & Goodman, R. A. (1986). Cognitive processes in verbal-number production: Inferences from the performance of brain-damaged subjects. *Journal of Experimental Psychology: General, 115,* 307–330.

McClure, S., Laibson, D., Lowenstein, G., & Cohen, J. D. (2004a). Separate neural systems value immediate and delayed rewards. *Science, 306,* 503–507.

McClure, S., Lee, J., Tomlin, D., Cypert, K., Montague, L., & Montague, P. R. (2004b). Neural correlates of behavioural preferences for culturally familiar drinks. *Neuron, 44,* 379–387.

McComb, K., Packer, C., & Pusey, A. (1994). Roaring and numerical assessment in contests between groups of female lions, *Panthera leo. Animal Behaviour, 47,* 379–387.

McDermott, J., & Hauser, M. D. (2007). Nonhuman primates prefer slow tempos but dislike music overall. *Cognition, 104,* 654–668.

McGurk, H., & MacDonald, J. (1976). Hearing lips and seeing voices. *Nature, 264,* 746–748.

McLennan, J. E., Nakano, K., Tyler, H. R., & Schwab, R. S. (1972). Micrographia in Parkinson's disease. *Journal of Neurological Science, 15,* 141–152.

McLoed, P., Dittrich, W., Driver, J., Perrett, D., & Zihl, J. (1996). Preserved and impaired detection of structure from motion by a "motion-blind" patient. *Visual Cognition, 3,* 363–391.

McLoed, P., Heywood, C. A., Driver, J., & Zihl, J. (1989). Selective deficits of visual search in moving displays after extrastriate damage. *Nature, 339,* 466–467.

McManus, I. C. (2002). *Right hand, left hand.* London: Weidenfield, & Nicolson.

McNeil, J. E., & Warrington, E. K. (1993). Prosopagnosia: A face-specific disorder. *Quarterly Journal of Experimental Psychology, 46A,* 1–10.

McQueen, J. M., & Cutler, A. (2001). Spoken word access processes: An introduction. *Language and Cognitive Processes, 16,* 469–490.

Meadows, J. C. (1974). Disturbed perception of colours associated with localised cerebral lesions. *Brain*, *97*, 615–632.

Mealey, L. (1995). The sociobiology of sociopathy: An integrated evolutionary model. *Behavioral and Brain Sciences*, *18*, 523–541.

Mechelli, A., Gorno-Tempini, M. L., & Price, C. J. (2003). Neuroimaging studies of word and pseudoword reading: Consistencies, inconsistencies, and limitations. *Journal of Cognitive Neuroscience*, *15*, 260–271.

Mehler, J., Dommergues, J. Y., Frauenfelder, U. H., & Segui, J. (1981). The syllable's role in speech segmentation. *Journal of Verbal Learning and Verbal Behavior*, *20*, 298–305.

Meltzoff, A. N., & Moore, M. K. (1977). Imitation of facial and manual gestures by human neonates. *Science*, *198*, 75–78.

Meltzoff, A. N., & Moore, M. K. (1983). Newborn infants imitate adult facial gestures. *Child Development*, *54*, 702–709.

Mendez, M. (2001). Generalized auditory agnosia with spared music recognition in a left-hander: Analysis of a case with right temporal stroke. *Cortex*, *37*, 139–150.

Merzenich, M. M., Knight, P. L., & Roth, G. L. (1973). Cochleotopic organization of primary auditory cortex in the cat. *Brain Research*, *63*, 343–346.

Mesulam, M. M. (1999). Spatial attention and neglect: parietal, frontal and cingulate contributions to the mental representation and attentional targeting of salient extrapersonal events. *Philosophical Transactions of the Royal Society of London B*, *354*, 1325–1346.

Meuter, R. F. I., & Allport, A. (1999). Bilingual language-switching in naming: Asymmetrical costs of language selection. *Journal of Memory and Language*, *40*, 25–40.

Meyer, D. E., & Schvaneveldt, R. W. (1971). Facilitation in recognising pairs of words: Evidence of a dependence between retrieval operations. *Journal of Experimental Psychology*, *90*, 227–234.

Miceli, G., & Capasso, R. (2001). Word-centred neglect dyslexia: Evidence from a new case. *Neurocase*, *7*, 221–237.

Miceli, G., & Caramazza, A. (1988). Dissociation of inflectional and derivational morphology. *Brain and Language*, *35*, 24–65.

Miceli, G., Capasso, R., & Caramazza, A. (1994). The interaction of lexical and sublexical processes in reading, writing and repetition. *Neuropsychologia*, *32*, 317–333.

Miceli, G., Capasso, R., Daniele, A., Esposito, T., Magarelli, M., & Tomaiuolo, F. (2000). Selective deficit for people's names following left temporal damage: An impairment of domain-specific conceptual knowledge. *Cognitive Neuropsychology*, *17*, 489–516.

Miceli, G., Fouch, E., Capasso, R., Shelton, J. R., Tomaiuolo, F., & Caramazza, A. (2001). The dissociation of color from form and function knowledge. *Nature Neuroscience*, *4*, 662–667.

Miceli, G., Gainotti, G., Caltagirone, C., & Masullo, C. (1980). Some aspects of phonological impairment in aphasia. *Brain and Language*, *11*, 159–169.

Miceli, G., Mazzucchi, A., Menn, L., & Goodglass, H. (1983). Contrasting cases of Italian agrammatic aphasia without comprehension disorder. *Brain and Language*, *19*, 65–97.

Miller, E. (1984). Verbal fluency as a function of a measure of verbal intelligence and in relation to different types of pathology. *British Journal of Clinical Psychology*, *23*, 359–369.

Miller, E. K., & Cohen, J. D. (2001). An integrative theory of prefrontal cortex function. *Annual Review of Neuroscience*, *24*, 167–202.

Miller, G. A. (1956). The magical number seven, plus or minus two: Some limits on our capacity for processing information. *Psychological Review*, *63*, 81–97.

Miller, K. F., & Stigler, J. W. (1987). Counting in Chinese: Cultural variation in a basic skill. *Cognitive Development*, *2*, 279–305.

Milner, A. D., & Goodale, M. A. (1995). *The visual brain in action*. Oxford: Oxford University Press.

Milner, A. D., Perrett, D. I., Johnston, R. S., Benson, P. J., Jordan, T. R., Heeley, D. W., Bettucci, D., Mortara, F., Mutani, R., Terazzi, E., & Davidson, D. L. W. (1991a). Perception and action in visual form agnosia. *Brain*, *114*, 405–428.

Milner, B. (1963). Effects of brain lesions on card sorting. *Archives of Neurology*, *9*, 90–100.

Milner, B. (1966). Amnesia following operation on the medial temporal lobes. In C. W. Whitty, & O. L. Zangwill (eds.), *Amnesia*. London: Butterworth.

Milner, B. (1971). Interhemispheric differences in the location of psychological processes in man. *British Medical Bulletin*, *27*, 272–277.

Milner, B., Corsi, P., & Leonard, G. (1991b). Frontal lobe contribution to recency judgements. *Neuropsychologia*, *29*, 601–618.

Mineka, S., & Cook, M. (1993). Mechanisms involved in the observational conditioning of fear. *Journal of Experimental Psychology: General*, *122*, 23–38.

Mink, J. W. (2001). Basal ganglia dysfunction in Tourette's syndrome: A new hypothesis. *Pediatric Neurology*, *25*, 190–198.

Miozzo, M., & Caramazza, A. (1998). Varieties of pure alexia: The case of failure to access graphemic representations. *Cognitive Neuropsychology*, *15*, 203–238.

Mithen, S. (2005). *The singing Neanderthal: The origins of music, language, and body*. London: Weidenfield and Nicolson.

Moen, I. (2000). Foreign accent syndrome: A review of contemporary explanations. *Aphasiology*, *14*, 5–15.

Moll, J., Oliveira-Souza, R., Bramati, I. E., & Grafman, J. (2002). Functional networks in emotional, moral and nonmoral social judgments. *NeuroImage, 16*, 696–703.

Monchi, O., Petrides, M., Petre, V., Worsley, K., & Dagher, A. (2001). Wisconsin card sorting revisited: Distinct neural circuits participating in different stages of the task identified by event-related functional magnetic resonance imaging. *Journal of Neuroscience, 21*, 7733–7741.

Moniz, E. (1937). Prefrontal leucotomy in the treatment of mental disorders. *American Journal of Psychiatry, 93*, 1379–1385.

Moniz, E. (1954). How I succeeded in performing the prefrontal leucotomy. *Journal of Clinical and Experimental Psychopathology, 15*, 373 379.

Monsell, S. (1995). Control of mental processes. In V. Bruce (ed.), *Unsolved mysteries of the mind*. Hove: Psychology Press.

Monsell, S. (2003). Task switching. *Trends in Cognitive Sciences, 7*, 134–140.

Morris, J. S., de Gelder, B., Weiskrantz, L., & Dolan, R. J. (2001). Differential extra-geniculostriate and amygdala responses to presentation of emotional faces in a cortically blind field. *Brain, 124*, 1241–1252.

Morris, J. S., Friston, K. J., Buechel, C., Frith, C. D., Young, A. W., Calder, A. J., & Dolan, R. J. (1998). A neuromodulatory role for the human amygdala in processing emotional facial expressions. *Brain, 121*, 47–57.

Morris, J. S., Frith, C. D., Perrett, D., Rowland, D., Young, A. W., Calder, A. J., & Dolan, R. J. (1996). A differential neural response in the human amygdala to fearful and happy facial expressions. *Nature, 383*, 812–815.

Morris, J. S., Ohman, A., & Dolan, R. (1999). A sub-cortical pathway to the right amygdala mediating "unseen" fear. *Proceedings of the National Academy of Science, USA, 96*, 1680–1685.

Morris, R. G., Miotto, E. C., Feigenbaum, J. D., Bullock, P., & Polkey, C. E. (1997). The effect of goal-subgoal conflict on planning ability after frontal- and temporal-lobe lesions in humans. *Neuropsychologia, 35*, 1147–1157.

Morris, R. G. M., Garrud, P., Rawlins, J. N. P., & O'Keefe, J. (1982). Place navigation impaired in rats with hippocampal lesions. *Nature, 297*, 681–683.

Mort, D. J., Malhotra, P., Mannan, S. K., Rorden, C., Pambajian, A., Kennard, C., & Husain, M. (2003). The anatomy of visual neglect. *Brain, 126*, 1986–1997.

Morton, J. (1969). Interaction of information in word recognition. *Psychological Review, 76*, 165–178.

Morton, J. (1980). The logogen model and orthographic structure. In U. Frith (ed.), *Cognitive processes in spelling*. London: Academic Press.

Moscovitch, M. (1995). Confabulation. In D. L. Schacter (ed.), *Memory distortion*. Cambridge, MA: Harvard Press.

Moscovitch, M., & Melo, B. (1997). Strategic retrieval and the frontal lobes: Evidence from confabulation and amnesia. *Neuropsychologia, 35*, 1017–1034.

Moscovitch, M., Winocur, G., & Behrmann, M. (1997). What is special about face recognition? Nineteen experiments on a person with visual object agnosia and dyslexia but normal face recognition. *Journal of Cognitive Neuroscience, 9*, 555–604.

Moyer, R. S., & Landauer, T. K. (1967). Time required for judgements of numerical inequality. *Nature, 215*, 1519–1520.

Mozer, M. C., & Behrmann, M. (1990). On the interaction of selective attention and lexical knowledge: A connectionist account of neglect dyslexia. *Journal of Cognitive Neuroscience, 2*, 96–123.

Mummery, C. J., Patterson, K., Price, C. J., Ashburner, J., Frackowiak, R. S. J., & Hodges, J. R. (2000). A voxel-based morphometry study of semantic dementia: Relationship between temporal lobe atrophy and semantic memory. *Annals of Neurology, 47*, 36–45.

Murata, A., Gallese, V., Luppino, G., Kaseda, M., & Sakata, H. (2000). Selectivity for the size, shape and orientation of objects for grasping in neurons of monkey parietal area AIP. *Journal of Neurophysiology, 83*, 2580–2601.

Murray, E. A., & Baxter, M. G. (2006). Cognitive neuroscience and nonhuman primates: Lesion studies. In C. Senior, T. Russell, & M. S. Gazzaniga (eds.), *Methods in mind*. Cambridge, MA: MIT Press.

Murray, E. A., & Bussey, T. J. (1999). Perceptual-mnemonic functions of the perirhinal cortex. *Trends in Cognitive Sciences, 3*, 142–151.

Murre, J. M. J., Graham, K. S., & Hodges, J. R. (2001). Semantic dementia: Relevance to connectionist models of long-term memory. *Brain, 124*, 647–675.

Musiek, F. E., Baran, J. A., Shinn, J. B., Guenette, L., & Zaidan, E. (2007). Central deafness: An audiological case study. *International Journal of Audiology, 46*, 433–441.

Näätänen, R., Gaillard, A. W. K., & Mantysalo, S. (1978). Early selective-attention effect on evoked-potential reinterpreted. *Acta Psychologica, 42*, 313–329.

Näätänen, R., Tervaniemi, M., Sussman, E., Paavilainen, P., & Winkler, I. (2001). "Primitive intelligence" in the auditory cortex. *Trends in Neurosciences, 24*, 283–288.

Nadel, L., & Moscovitch, M. (1997). Memory consolidation, retrograde amnesia and the hippocampal complex. *Current Opinion in Neurobiology, 7*, 217–222.

Nakamura, K., Honda, M., Okada, T., Hankawa, T., Toma, K., Fukuyama, H., Konishi, J., & Shibasaki, H. (2000). Participation of the left posterior inferior temporal cortex in writing and mental recall of Kanji orthography: A functional MRI study. *Brain, 123*, 954–967.

Nathaniel-James, D. A., Fletcher, P., & Frith, C. D. (1997). The functional anatomy of verbal initiation and suppression using the Hayling test. *Neuropsychologia, 35*, 559–566.

Nelson, E. L., & Simpson, P. (1994). First glimpse: An initial examination of subjects who have rejected their recovered visulisations as false memories. *Issues in Child Abuse Accusations, 6,* 123–133.

Nelson, H. E. (1976). A modified card sorting test sensitive to frontal lobe deficits. *Cortex, 12,* 313–324.

Nelson, M. E., & Bower, J. M. (1990). Brain maps and parallel computers. *Trends in Neurosciences, 13,* 403–408.

Nelson, T. M., & MacDonald, G. A. (1971). Lateral organization, perceived depth and title preference in pictures. *Perceptual and Motor Skills, 33,* 983–986.

Nestor, P. J., Graham, K. S., Bozeat, S., Simons, J. S., & Hodges, J. R. (2002). Memory consolidation and the hippocampus: Further evidence from studies of autobiographical memory in semantic dementia and frontal variant frontotemporal dementia. *Neuropsychologia, 40,* 633–654.

Newbury, D. F., Bonora, M., Lamb, J. A., Fisher, S. E., Lai, C. S. L., Baird, G., Jannoun, L., Slonims, V., Stott, C. M., Merricks, M. J., Bolton, P. F., Bailey, A. J., & Monaco, A. P. (2002). FOXP2 is not a major susceptibility gene for autism or specific language impairment. *American Journal of Human Genetics, 70,* 1318–1327.

Newman, S. D., Just, M. A., Keller, T. A., Roth, J., & Carpenter, P. A. (2003). Differential effects of syntactic and semantic processing on the subregions of Broca's area. *Cognitive Brain Research, 16,* 297–307.

Nicholls, M. E. R., Bradshaw, J. L., & Mattingley, J. B. (1999). Free-viewing perceptual asymmetries for the judgement of brightness, numerosity and size. *Neuropsychologia, 37,* 307–314.

Nichols, R. C. (1978). Twin studies of ability, personality and interests. *Homo, 29,* 158–173.

Nickerson, R. S., & Adams, M. J. (1979). Long-term memory for a common object. *Cognitive Psychology, 11,* 287–307.

Nieder, A., & Miller, E. K. (2004). A parieto-fronto network for visual numerical information in the monkey. *Proceedings of the National Academy of Science, USA, 101,* 7457–7462.

Niswander, E., Pollatsek, A., & Rayner, K. (2000). The processing of derived and inflected suffixed words during reading. *Language and Cognitive Processes, 15,* 389–420.

Nolan, K. A., & Caramazza, A. (1982). Modality-independent impairments in word processing in a deep dyslexia patient. *Brain and Language, 16,* 237–264.

Noppeney, U., & Price, C. J. (2004). An fMRI study of syntactic adaptation. *Journal of Cognitive Neuroscience, 16,* 702–713.

Norman, D. A., & Shallice, T. (1986). Attention to action. In R. J. Davidson, G. E. Schwartz, & D. Shapiro (eds.), *Consciousness and self regulation.* New York: Plenum Press.

Norris, D. (1986). Word recognition: Context effects without priming. *Cognition, 22,* 93–136.

Nuerk, H.-C., Weger, U., & Willmes, K. (2001). Decade breaks in the mental number line? Putting the tens and units back in different bins. *Cognition, 82,* B25-B33.

Nunes, T., Schliemann, A. D., & Carraher, D. W. (1993). *Street mathematics and school mathematics.* Cambridge: Cambridge University Press.

Nunez, P. L. (1981). *Electric fields of the brain: The neurophysics of EEG.* London: Oxford University Press.

Nyberg, L., & Tulving, E. (1996). Classifying human long-term memory: Evidence from converging dissociations. *European Journal of Cognitive Psychology, 8,* 163–183.

O'Craven, K. M., & Kanwisher, N. (2000). Mental imagery of faces and places activates corresponding stimulus-specific brain regions. *Journal of Cognitive Neuroscience, 12,* 1013–1023.

O'Keefe, J. (1976). Place units in the hippocampus of the freely moving rat. *Experimental Neurology, 51,* 78–109.

O'Keefe, J., & Nadel, L. (1978). *The hippocampus as a cognitive map.* Oxford: Oxford University Press.

O'Leary, D. D. M. (1989). Do cortical areas emerge from a protocortex? *Trends in Neurosciences, 12,* 400–406.

Ogawa, S., Lee, T. M., Kay, A. R., & Tank, D. W. (1990). Brain magnetic resonance imaging with contrast dependent on blood oxygenation. *Proceedings of the National Academy of Science, USA, 87,* 9862–9872.

Ohman, A., & Mineka, S. (2001). Fears, phobias, and preparedness: Toward an evolved module of fear and fear learning. *Psychological Review, 108,* 483–522.

Ohman, A., & Soares, J. J. F. (1994). Unconscious anxiety: Phobic responses to masked stimuli. *Journal of Abnormal Psychology, 102,* 121–132.

Ohman, A., Flykt, A., & Esteves, F. (2001). Emotion drives attention: Detecting the snake in the grass. *Journal of Experimental Psychology: General, 130,* 466–478.

Ohyama, T., Nores, W. L., Murphy, M., & Mauk, M. D. (2003). What the cerebellum computes. *Trends in Neurosciences, 26,* 222–227.

Oliveri, M., Finocchiar, C., Shapiro, K., Gangitano, M., Caramazza, A., & Pascual-Leone, A. (2004). All talk and no action: A transcranial magnetic stimulation study of motor cortex activation during action word production. *Journal of Cognitive Neuroscience, 16,* 374–381.

Ostrin, R. K., & Tyler, L. K. (1995). Dissociations of lexical function: Semantics, syntax and morphology. *Cognitive Neuropsychology, 12,* 345–389.

Otten, L. J., & Rugg, M. D. (2005). Interpreting event-related brain potentials. In T. C. Handy (ed.), *Event-related potentials: A methods handbook.* Cambridge, MA: MIT Press.

Owen, A. M., Evans, A. C., & Petrides, M. P. (1996). Evidence of a two-stage model of spatial working memory processing within lateral prefrontal cortex: A positron emission tomography study. *Cerebral Cortex, 6,* 31–38.

Ozonoff, S., Pennington, B. F., & Rogers, S. J. (1991). Executive function deficits in high-functioning autistic individuals: Relationship to theory of mind. *Journal of Child Psychology and Psychiatry, 32*, 1081–1105.

Packard, M. G., & Knowlton, B. J. (2002). Learning and memory functions of the basal ganglia. *Annual Review of Neuroscience, 25*, 563–593.

Pakkenberg, B., & Gundersen, H. J. G. (1997). Neocortical neuron number in humans: effect of sex and age. *Journal of Comparative Neurology, 384*, 312–320.

Palmer, S. E., Rosch, E., & Chase, P. (1981). Canonical perspective and the perception of objects. In J. Long, & A. D. Baddeley (eds.), *Attention and performance IX*. Hillsdale, NJ: Lawrence Erlbaum.

Papanicolaou, A. C. (1995). An introduction to magnetoencephalography with some applications. *Brain and Cognition, 27*, 331–352.

Pardo, J. V., Pardo, P. J., Janer, K. W., & Raichle, M. E. (1990). The anterior cingulate cortex mediates processing selection in the Stroop attentional conflict paradigm. *Proceedings of the National Academy of Science, USA, 87*, 256–259.

Parkin, A. J. (1982). Residual learning capacity in organic amnesia. *Cortex, 18*, 417–440.

Parkin, A. J. (1996). H.M.: The medial temporal lobes and memory. In C. Code, C.-W. Wallesch, Y. Joanette, & A. R. Lecours (eds.), *Classic cases in neuropsychology*. Hove: Psychology Press.

Parkin, A. J. (1997). The long and winding road: Twelve years of frontal amnesia. In A. J. Parkin (ed.), *Case studies in the neuropsychology of memory*. Hove: Psychology Press.

Parkin, A. J. (1999) *Memory and amnesia*. Hove: Psychology Press.

Parkin, A. J. (2001). The Structure and mechanisms of memory. In B. Rapp (ed.), *The handbook of cognitive neuropsychology: What deficits reveal about the human mind*. New York: Psychology Press.

Parkin, A. J., & Leng, N. R. C. (1993). *Neuropsychology of the amnesic syndrome*. Hove: Psychology Press.

Parkin, A. J., & Stewart, F. (1993). Category-specific impairments? No. A critique of Sartori et al. *Quarterly Journal of Experimental Psychology, 46A*, 505–509.

Parkin, A. J., Montaldi, D., Leng, N. R. C., & Hunkin, N. M. (1990). Contextual cueing effects in the remote memory of alcoholic Korsakoff patients and normal subjects. *Quarterly Journal of Experimental Psychology, 42A*, 585–596.

Parkman, J. M., & Groen, G. (1971). Temporal aspects of simple additions and comparison. *Journal of Experimental Psychology, 92*, 437–438.

Pascual-Leone, A., & Torres, F. (1993). Plasticity of sensorimotor cortex representation of the reading finger in Braille readers. *Brain, 116*, 39–52.

Pascual-Leone, A., Bartres-Faz, D., & Keenan, J. P. (1999). Transcranial magnetic stimulation: Studying the brain-behaviour relationship by induction of "virtual lesions". *Philosophical Transactions of the Royal Society of London B, 354*, 1229–1238.

Pascual-Leone, A., Houser, C., Reeves, K., Shotland, L. M., Grafman, J., Sato, S., Valls-Sole, J., Brasil-Neto, J. P., Wassermann, E. M., & Cohen, L. G. (1993). Safety of rapid-rate transcranial magnetic stimulation in normal volunteers. *Electroencephalogy and Clinical Neurophysiology, 89*, 120–130.

Passingham, R. E. (1988). Premotor cortex and preparation for movement. *Experimental Brain Research, 70*, 590–596.

Passingham, R. E. (1996). Attention to action. *Philosophical Transactions of the Royal Society of London B, 351*, 1473–1479.

Patel, A. D., Peretz, I., Tramo, M., & Labrecque, R. (1998). Processing prosodic and musical patterns: A neuropsychological investigation. *Brain and Language, 61*, 123–144.

Patriot, A., Grafman, J., Sadato, N., Flitman, S., & Wild, K. (1996). Brain activation during script event processing. *Journal of Cognitive Neuroscience, 7*, 761–766.

Patterson, K. E. (1981). Neuropsychological approaches to the study of reading. *British Journal of Psychology, 72*, 151–174.

Patterson, K. E., & Kay, J. (1982). Letter-by-letter reading: Psychological descriptions of a neurological syndrome. *Quarterly Journal of Experimental Psychology, 34A*, 411–441.

Patterson, K. E., & Marcel, A. (1992). Phonological ALEXIA or PHONOLOGICAL alexia? In J. Alegria, D. Holender, J. J. de Morais, & M. Radeus (eds.), *Analytic approaches to human cognition*. Amsterdam: Elsevier.

Patterson, K. E., & Wing, A. M. (1989). Processes in handwriting: A case for case. *Cognitive Neuropsychology, 6*, 1–23.

Patterson, K. E., Marshall, J. C., & Coltheart, M. (1985). *Surface dyslexia: Neuropsychological and cognitive studies of phonological reading*. Hove: Psychology Press.

Patterson, K. E., Suzuki, T., & Wydell, T. N. (1996). Interpreting a case of Japanese phonological alexia: The key is in phonology. *Cognitive Neuropsychology, 13*, 803–822.

Patterson, R. D., Uppenkamp, S., Johnsrude, I. S., & Griffiths, T. D. (2002). The processing of temporal pitch and melody information in auditory cortex. *Neuron, 36*, 767–776.

Paulesu, E., Demonet, J. F., Fazio, F., McCrory, E., Chanoine, V., Brunswick, N., Cappa, S. F., Cossu, G., Habib, M., Frith, C. D., & Frith, U. (2001). Dyslexia: Cultural diversity and biological unity. *Science, 5511*, 2165–2167.

Paulesu, E., Frith, C. D., & Frackowiak, R. S. J. (1993). The neural correlates of the verbal component of working memory. *Nature, 362*, 342–345.

Paulesu, E., McCrory, E., Fazio, F., Menoncello, L., Brunswick, N., Cappa, S. F., Cotelli, M., Cossu, G., Corte, F., Lorusso, M., Pesenti, S., Gallagher, A., Perani, D., Price, C., Frith, C. D., & Frith, U. (2000). A cultural effect on brain function. *Nature Neuroscience*, *3*, 91–96.

Paus, T. (1999). Imaging the brain before, during and after transcranial magnetic stimulation. *Neuropsychologia*, *37*, 207–217.

Pavani, F., Ladavas, E., & Driver, J. (2002). Selective deficit of auditory localisation in patients with visuospatial neglect. *Neuropsychologia*, *40*, 291–301.

Payne, D. G., Elie, C. J., Blackwell, J. M., & Neuschatz, J. S. (1996). Memory illusions: Recalling, recognising and recollecting events that never occurred. *Journal of Memory and Language*, *35*, 261–285.

Pearce, A. J., Thickbroom, G. W., Byrnes, M. L., & Mastaglia, F. L. (2000). Functional reorganisation of the corticomotor projection to the hand in skilled racquet players. *Experimental Brain Research*, *130*, 238–243.

Pell, M. D. (1999). The temporal organisation of affective and non-affective speech in patients with right-hemisphere infarcts. *Cortex*, *35*, 455–477.

Pellegrino, G. di, Fadiga, L., Fogassi, L., Gallese, V., & Rizzolatti, G. (1992). Understanding motor events: A neurophysiological study. *Experimental Brain Research*, *91*, 176–180.

Penfield, W., & Rasmussen, T. L. (1950). *The cerebral cortex of man: A clinical study of localisation of function.* New York: Macmillan.

Perenin, M.-T., & Vighetto, A. (1988). Optic ataxia: A specific disruption in visuomotor mechanisms. I. Different aspects of the deficit in reaching for objects. *Brain*, *111*, 643–674.

Peretz, I., & Coltheart, M. (2003). Modularity of music processing. *Nature Neuroscience*, *6*, 688–691.

Peretz, I. (1996). Can we lose memories for music? The case of music agnosia in a nonmusician. *Journal of Cognitive Neuroscience*, *8*, 481–496.

Peretz, I. (2006). The nature of music from a biological perspective. *Cognition*, *100*, 1–32.

Perfetti, C. A., Bell, L. C., & Delaney, S. M. (1988). Automatic (prelexical) phonemic activation in silent reading: Evidence from backward masking. *Journal of Memory and Language*, *27*, 59–70.

Perner, J., Frith, U., Leslie, A. M., & Leekam, S. R. (1989). Exploration of the autistic child's theory of mind: Knowledge, belief and communication. *Child Development*, *60*, 689–700.

Perret, E. (1974). The left frontal lobe in man and the suppression of habitual responses in verbal categorical behaviour. *Neuropsychologia*, *12*, 323–330.

Perrett, D. I., & Mistlin, A. (1990). Perception of facial characteristics by monkeys. In W. Stebbins, & M. Berkley (eds.), *Comparative perception. Volume 2: Complex signals.* New York: Wiley.

Perrett, D. I., Harries, M. H., Bevan, R., Thomas, S., Benson, P. J., Mistlin, A. J., Chitty, A. J., Hietanen, J. K., & Ortega, J. E. (1989). Frameworks of analysis for the neural representation of animate objects and actions. *Journal of Experimental Biology*, *146*, 87–113.

Perrett, D. I., Hietanen, J. K., Oram, M. W., & Benson, P. J. (1992). Organisation and functions of cells responsive to faces in the temporal cortex. *Philosophical Transactions of the Royal Society London B*, *335*, 23–30.

Perrett, D. I., Oram, M. W., & Wachsmuth, E. (1998). Evidence accumulation in cell populations responsive to faces: An account of generalisation of recognition without mental transformations. *Cognition*, *67*, 111–145.

Perrett, D. I., Smith, P., Potter, D., Mistlin, A., Head, A., Milner, A., & Jeeves, M. (1985). Visual cells in the temporal cortex sensitive to face view and gaze direction. *Proceedings of the Royal Society of London B*, *223*, 293–317.

Pesenti, M., Zago, L., Crivello, F., Mellet, E., Samson, D., Duroux, B., Seron, X., Mazoyer, B., & Tzourio-Mazoyer, N. (2001). Mental calculation in a prodigy is sustained by right prefrontal and medial temporal areas. *Nature Neuroscience*, *4*, 103–107.

Petersen, S. E., Fox, P. T., Posner, M. I., Mintun, M., & Raichle, M. E. (1988). Positron emission tomographic studies of the cortical anatomy of single-word processing. *Nature*, *331*, 585–589.

Petersen, S. E., Fox, P. T., Snyder, A. Z., & Raichle, M. (1990). Activation of extrastriate and frontal cortical areas by visual words and word-like stimuli. *Science*, *249*, 1041–1044.

Petersson, K. M., Nichols, T. E., Poline, J.-B., & Holmes, A. P. (1999a). Statistical limitations in functional neuroimaging I: Non-inferential methods and statistical models. *Philosophical Transactions of the Royal Society of London B*, *354*, 1239–1260.

Petersson, K. M., Nichols, T. E., Poline, J.-B., & Holmes, A. P. (1999b). Statistical limitations in functional neuroimaging II: Signal detection and statistical inference. *Philosophical Transactions of the Royal Society of London B*, *354*, 1261–1281.

Petersson, K. M., Reis, A., Askelof, S., Castro-Caldas, A., & Ingvar, M. (2000). Language processing modulated by literacy: A network analysis of verbal repetition in literate and illiterate subjects. *Journal of Cognitive Neuroscience*, *12*, 364–382.

Petkov, C. I., Kayser, C., Steudel, T., Whittingstall, K., Augath, M., & Logothetis, N. K. (2008). A voice region in the monkey brain. *Nature Neuroscience*, *11*, 367–374.

Petrides, M. (1995). Impairments on nonspatial self-ordered and externally ordered working memory tasks after lesions of the mid-dorsal part of the lateral frontal cortex in monkey. *Journal of Neuroscience*, *15*, 359–375.

Petrides, M. (1996). Specialised systems for the processing of mnemonic information within the primate frontal cortex. *Philosophical Transactions of the Royal Society of London B*, *351*, 1455–1462.

Petrides, M. (2000). Middorsolateral and midventrolateral prefrontal cortex: Two levels of executive control for the processing of mnemonic information. In S. Monsell, & J. Driver (eds.), *Attention and performance XVIII: Control of cognitive performance*. Cambridge, MA: MIT Press.

Petrides, M. (2005). Lateral prefrontal cortex: Architectonic and functional organization. *Philosophical Transactions of the Royal Society B*, *360*, 781–795.

Petrides, M., & Milner, B. (1982). Deficits on subject-ordered tasks after frontal and temporal lesions in man. *Neuropsychologia*, *20*, 249–262.

Phelps, E. A., O'Connor, K. J., Cunningham, W. A., Funayama, E. S., Gatenby, J. C., Gore, J. C., & Banaji, M. R. (2000). Performance on indirect measures of race evaluation predicts amygdala activation. *Journal of Cognitive Neuroscience*, *12*, 729–738.

Philipose, L. E., Gottesman, R. F., Newhart, M., Kleinman, J. T., Herskovits, E. H., Pawlak, M. A., Marsh, E. B., Davis, C., Heidler-Gary, J., & Hillis, A. E. (2007). Neural regions essential for reading and spelling of words and pseudo words. *Annals of Neurology*, *62*, 481–492.

Phillips, M. L., Young, A. W., Senior, C., Brammer, M., Andrews, C., Calder, A. J., Bullmore, E. T., Perrett, D. I., Rowland, D., Williams, S. C. R., Gray, J. A., & David, A. S. (1997). A specific neural substrate for perceiving facial expressions of disgust. *Nature*, *389*, 495–498.

Phillips, W. A., Zeki, S., & Barlow, H. B. (1984). Localisation of function in the cerebral cortex: past, present and future. *Brain*, *107*, 327–361.

Piazza, M., Izard, V., Pinel, P., Le Bihan, D., & Dehaene, S. (2004). Tuning curves for approximate numerosity in the human intraparietal sulcus. *Neuron*, *44*, 547–555.

Pica, P., Lemer, C., Izard, V., & Dehaene, S. (2004). Exact and approximate arithmetic in an Amazonion indigene group with a reduced number lexicon. *Science*, *306*, 499–503.

Picton, T. W., Bentin, S., Berg, P., Donchin, E., Hillyard, S. A., Johnson, R., Miller, G. A., Ritter, W., Ruchkin, D. S., Rugg, M. D., & Taylor, M. J. (2000). Guidelines for using human event-related potentials to study cognition: Recording standards and publication criteria. *Psychophysiology*, *37*, 127–152.

Pinel, P., Dehaene, S., Riviere, D., & Le Bihan, D. (2001). Modulation of parietal activation by semantic distance in a number comparison task. *NeuroImage*, *14*, 1013–1026.

Pinker, S. (1994). *The language instinct*. London: Penguin.

Pinker, S. (1997). *How the mind works*. New York: Norton.

Pinker, S., & Prince, A. (1988). On language and connectionism: Analysis of a parallel distributed processing model of language acquisition. *Cognition*, *28*, 73–193.

Plaut, D. C. (1995). Double dissociation without modularity: Evidence from connectionist neuropsychology. *Journal of Clinical and Experimental Neuropsychology*, *17*, 291–321.

Plaut, D. C. (1997). Structure and function in the lexical system: Insights from distributed models of word reading and lexical decision. *Language and Cognitive Processes*, *12*, 765–805.

Plaut, D. C., McClelland, J. L., Seidenberg, M. S., & Patterson, K. (1996). Understanding normal and impaired word reading: Computational principles in quasi-regular domains. *Psychological Review*, *103*, 56–115.

Plomin, R., DeFries, J. C., & Loehlin, J. C. (1977). Genotype-environment interaction and correlation in the analysis of human behavior. *Psychological Bulletin*, *84*, 309–322.

Plomin, R., DeFries, J. C., McClearn, G. E., & McGuffin, P. (2001). *Behavioral genetics*, 4th edition. New York: Worth Publishers.

Pollatsek, A., Bolozky, S., Well, A. D., & Rayner, K. (1981). Asymmetries in the perceptual span for Israeli readers. *Brain and Language*, *14*, 174–180.

Posner, M. I. (1978). *Chronometric explorations of mind*. Hillsdale, NJ: Lawrence Erlbaum.

Posner, M. I. (1980). Orienting of attention: The VIIth Sir Frederic Bartlett Lecture. *Quarterly Journal of Experimental Psychology*, *32*, 3–25.

Posner, M. I., & Cohen, Y. (1984). Components of visual orienting. In H. Bouma, & D. G. Bouwhuis (eds.), *Attention and performance X: Control of language processes*. Philadelphia: Lawrence Erlbaum Inc.

Posner, M. I., & Petersen, S. E. (1990). The attentional system of the human brain. *Annual Review of Neuroscience*, *13*, 25–42.

Pouget, A., & Driver, J. (2000). Relating unilateral neglect to the neural coding of space. *Current Opinion in Neurobiology*, *10*, 242–249.

Poulton, R., Caspi, A., Moffitt, T. E., Cannon, M., Murray, R. M., & Harrington, H. L. (2000). Children's self-reported psychiatric symptoms predict adult schizophreniform disorders: A 15-year longitudinal study. *Archives of General Psychiatry*, *57*, 1053–1058.

Power, R., & Dal Martello, M. F. (1997). From 834 to eighty thirty four: The reading of Arabic numerals by seven-year-old children. *Mathematical Cognition*, *3*, 63–85.

Price, C. J., & Devlin, J. T. (2003). The myth of the visual word form area. *NeuroImage*, *19*, 473–481.

Price, C. J., Moore, C. J., Humphreys, G. W., Frackowiak, R. S. J., & Friston, K. J. (1996a). The neural regions sustaining object recognition and naming. *Proceedings of the Royal Society of London B*, *263*, 1501–1507.

Price, C. J., Warburton, E. A., Moore, C. J., Frackowiak, R. S. J., & Friston, K. J. (2001). Dynamic diaschisis: Anatomically remote and context-sensitive human brain lesions. *Journal of Cognitive Neuroscience, 13,* 419–429.

Price, C. J., Winterburn, D., Giraud, A. L., Moore, C. J., & Noppeney, U. (2003). Cortical localisation of the visual and auditory word form areas: A reconsideration of the evidence. *Brain and Language, 86,* 272–286.

Price, C. J., Wise, R. J. S., & Frackowiak, R. S. J. (1996b). Demonstrating the implicit processing of words and pseudowords. *Cerebral Cortex, 6,* 62–70.

Price, C. J., Wise, R., Ramsay, S., Friston, K., Howard, D., Patterson, K., & Frackowiak, R. (1992). Regional response differences within the human auditory-cortex when listening to words. *Neuroscience Letters, 146,* 179–182.

Prior, M., Eisenmajer, R., Leekam, S., Wing, L., Gould, J., Ong, B., & Dowe, D. (1998). Are there subgroups within the autistic spectrum? A cluster analysis of a group of children with autistic spectrum disorder. *Journal of Child Psychology and Psychiatry, 39,* 893–902.

Purkinje, J. E. (1837). Bericht ufiber die Versammlung deutscher. *Naturforscher und Arzte. Anat Physiologische, 3,* 177–180.

Purves, D. (1994). *Neural activity and the growth of the brain.* Cambridge: Cambridge University Press.

Quiroga, R. G., Reddy, L., Kreiman, G., Koch, C., & Fried, I. (2005). Invariant visual representation by single neurons in the human brain. *Nature, 435,* 1102–1107.

Rabbitt, P. M. A. (1966). Errors and error-correction in choice-response tasks. *Journal of Experimental Psychology, 71,* 264–272.

Radach, R., Inhoff, A., & Heller, D. (2004). Orthographic regularity gradually modulates saccade amplitudes in reading. *European Journal of Cognitive Psychology, 16,* 27–51.

Rahman, S., Sahakian, B. J., Hodges, J. R., Rogers, R. D., & Robbins, T. W. (1999). Specific cognitive deficits in mild frontal variant frontotemporal dementia. *Brain, 122,* 1469–1493.

Raichle, M. E. (1987). Circulatory and metabolic correlates of brain function in normal humans. In F. Plum, & V. Mountcastle (eds.), *Handbook of physiology: The nervous system.* Baltimore: Williams and Wilkins.

Raichle, M. E. (1998). Behind the scenes of functional brain imaging: A historical and physiological perspective. *Proceedings of the National Academy of Science, USA, 95,* 765–772.

Rainer, G., Rao, S. C., & Miller, E. K. (1999). Prospective coding for objects in the primate prefrontal cortex. *Journal of Neuroscience, 19,* 5493–5505.

Rakic, P. (1988). Specification of cerebral cortical areas. *Science, 241,* 170–176.

Ramachandran, V. S., & Hirstein, W. (1998). The perception of phantom limbs. *Brain, 121,* 1603–1630.

Ramachandran, V. S., & Rogers-Ramachandran, D. (1996). Synaesthesia in phantom limbs induced with mirrors. *Proceedings of the Royal Society of London B, 263,* 377–386.

Ramnani, N., & Owen, A. M. (2004). Anterior prefrontal cortex: Insights into function from anatomy and neuroimaging. *Nature Reviews Neuroscience, 5,* 184–194.

Ramnani, N., Toni, I., Passingham, R. E., & Haggard, P. (2001). The cerebellum and parietal cortex play a specific role in coordination: A PET study. *NeuroImage, 14,* 899–911.

Ranganath, C., Yonelinas, A. P., Cohen, M. X., Dy, C. J., Tom, S. M., & D'Esposito, M. (2004). Dissociable correlates of recollection and familiarity within the medial temporal lobes. *Neuropsychologia, 42,* 2–13.

Rao, S. C., Rainer, G., & Miller, E. K. (1997). Integration of what and where in the primate prefrontal cortex. *Science, 276,* 821–824.

Rapp, B., & Caramazza, A. (1997). From graphemes to abstract letter shapes: Levels of representation in written spelling. *Journal of Experimental Psychology: Human Perception and Performance, 25,* 1130–1152.

Rapp, B., Benzing, L., & Caramazza, A. (1997). The autonomy of lexical orthography. *Cognitive Neuropsychology, 14,* 71–104.

Rasmussen, G. L. (1953). Further observations of the efferent cochlear bundle. *Journal of Comparative Neurology, 99,* 61–74.

Rauschecker, J. F., & Tian, B. (2000). Mechanisms and streams for processing "what" and "where" in auditory cortex. *Proceedings of the National Academy of Science, USA, 97,* 11800–11806.

Rauschecker, J. F., Tian, B., & Hauser, M. D. (1995). Processing of complex sounds in the macaque nonprimary auditory cortex. *Science, 268,* 111–114.

Ravizza, S. M., & Carter, C. S. (2008). Shifting set about task switching: Behavioral and neural evidence for distinct forms of cognitive flexibility. *Neuropsychologia, 46,* 2924–2935.

Rayner, K. (1979). Eye guidance in reading: Fixation locations within words. *Perception, 8,* 21–30.

Rayner, K., & Duffy, S. A. (1986). Lexical complexity and fixation times in reading: Effects of word frequency, verb complexity, and lexical ambiguity. *Memory and Cognition, 14,* 191–201.

Rayner, K., & Juhasz, B. J. (2004). Eye movements in reading: Old questions and new directions. *European Journal of Cognitive Psychology, 16,* 340–352.

Rayner, K., & McConkie, G. W. (1976). What guides a reader's eye movements? *Vision Research, 16,* 829–837.

Rayner, K., Binder, K. S., Ashby, J., & Pollatsek, A. (2001). Eye movement control in reading: Word predictability has little influence on initial landing positions in words. *Vision Research, 41*, 943–954.

Rayner, K., Well, A. D., & Pollatsek, A. (1980). Asymmetry of the effective visual field in reading. *Perception and Psychophysics, 27*, 537–544.

Reason, J. T. (1984). Lapses of attention in everyday life. In R. Parasuraman, & D. R. Davies (eds.), *Varieties of attention*. Orlando, FL: Academic Press.

Rees, G., Wojciulik, E., Clarke, K., Husain, M., Frith, C., & Driver, J. (2000). Unconscious activation of visual cortex in the damaged right hemisphere of a parietal patient with extinction. *Brain, 123*, 1624–1633.

Reicher, G. M. (1969). Perceptual recognition as a function of meaningfulness of stimulus materials. *Journal of Experimental Psychology, 81*, 274–280.

Reiss, A. L., Abrams, M. T., Singer, H. S., Ross, J. L., & Denckla, M. B. (1996). Brain development, gender and IQ in children. A volumetric imaging study. *Brain, 119*, 1763–1774.

Rensink, R. A., O'Regan, J. K., & Clark, J. J. (1997). To see or not to see: The need for attention to perceive changes in scenes. *Psychological Science, 8*, 368–373.

Reverberi, C., Lavaroni, A., Gigli, G. L., Skrap, M., & Shallice, T. (2005). Specific impairments of rule induction in different frontal subgroups. *Neuropsychologia, 43*, 460–472.

Rey, A. (1964). *L'examen clinique en psychologie*. Paris: Presses Universitaires de France.

Rhodes, G. (1996). *Superportraits: Caricatures and recognition*. Hove: Psychology Press.

Rhodes, G., & Tremewan, T. (1993). The Simon then Garfunkel effect: Semantic priming, sensitivity, and the modularity of face recognition. *Cognitive Psychology, 25*, 147–187.

Rhodes, G., Brennan, S., & Carey, S. (1987). Identification and ratings of caricatures: Implications for mental representation of faces. *Cognitive Psychology, 19*, 473–497.

Ribot, T. (1882). *Diseases of memory*. New York: Appleton.

Richardson, M. P., Strange, B. A., & Dolan, R. J. (2004). Encoding of emotional memories depends on amygdala and hippocampus and their interactions. *Nature Neuroscience, 7*, 278–285.

Riddoch, M. J., & Humphreys, G. W. (1983). The effect of cueing on unilateral neglect. *Neuropsychology, 21*, 589–599.

Riddoch, M. J., & Humphreys, G. W. (1995). *Birmingham object recognition battery*. Hove: Psychology Press.

Riddoch, M. J., & Humphreys, G. W. (2001). Object recognition. In B. Rapp (ed.), *Handbook of cognitive neuropsychology*. Hove: Psychology Press.

Riddoch, M. J., Humphreys, G. W., & Price, C. J. (1989). Routes to action: Evidence from apraxia. *Cognitive Neuropsychology, 6*, 437–454.

Riddoch, M. J., Humphreys, G. W., Cleton, P., & Fery, P. (1990). Interaction of attentional and lexical processes in neglect dyslexia. *Cognitive Neuropsychology, 7*, 479–518.

Riddoch, M. J., Humphreys, G. W., Gannon, T., Blott, W., & Jones, V. (1999). Memories are made of this: The effects of time on stored visual knowledge in a case of visual agnosia. *Brain, 122*, 537–559.

Ridley, M. (2003). *Nature via nurture*. London: Fourth Estate.

Rizzolatti, G., & Arbib, M. A. (1998). Language within our grasp. *Trends in Neuroscience, 21*, 188–194.

Rizzolatti, G., & Luppino, G. (2001). The cortical motor system. *Neuron, 31*, 889–901.

Rizzolatti, G., Fadiga, L., Fogassi, L., & Gallese, V. (1996). Premotor cortex and the recognition of motor actions. *Cognitive Brain Research, 3*, 131–141.

Rizzolatti, G., Fogassi, L., & Gallese, V. (2002). Motor and cognitive functions of the ventral premotor cortex. *Current Opinion in Neurobiology, 12*, 149–154.

Robertson, E. M., Theoret, H., & Pascual-Leone, A. (2003). Studies in cognition: The problems solved and created by transcranial magnetic stimulation. *Journal of Cognitive Neuroscience, 15*, 948–960.

Robertson, I. H., Nico, D., & Hood, B. (1995). The intention to act improves unilateral neglect: Two demonstrations. *Neuroreport, 7*, 246–248.

Robertson, L. C. (2004). *Space, objects, minds and brains*. New York: Psychology Press.

Robertson, L. C., Knight, R. T., Rafal, R., & Shimamura, A. P. (1993). Cognitive neuropsychology is more than single-case studies. *Journal of Experimental Psychology: Learning, Memory and Cognition, 19*, 710–717.

Robertson, L. C., Treisman, A., Friedman-Hill, S., & Grabowecky, M. (1997). The interaction of spatial and object pathways: Implications from a patient with Balint's syndrome. *Journal of Cognitive Neuroscience, 9*, 295–317.

Robins, L. N., Tipp, J., & Przybeck, T. (1991). Antisocial personality. In L. N. Robins, & D. A. Reiger (eds.), *Psychiatric disorders in America*. New York: Free Press.

Rochon, E., Kave, G., Cupit, J., Jokel, R., & Winocur, G. (2004). Sentence comprehension in semantic dementia: A longtitudinal case study. *Cognitive Neuropsychology, 21*, 317–330.

Roediger, H. L. (1980). Memory metaphors in cognitive psychology. *Memory and Cognition, 8*, 231–246.

Roediger, H. L., & McDermott, K. B. (1995). Creating false memories: Remembering words not presented in lists. *Journal of Experimental Psychology: Learning, Memory and Cognition, 21*, 803–814.

Rogers, R. D., & Monsell, S. (1995). Costs of a predictable switch between simple cognitive tasks. *Journal of Experimental Psychology: General, 124*, 207–231.

Rogers, T. T., Hocking, J., Noppeney, U., Mechelli, A., Gorno-Tempini, M. L., Patterson, K., & Price, C. J.

(2006). Anterior temporal cortex and semantic memory: Reconciling findings from neuropsychology and functional imaging. *Cognitive Affective, & Behavioral Neuroscience, 6*, 201–213.

Rogers, T. T., Lambon Ralph, M. A., Hodges, J. R., & Patterson, K. (2004). Natural selection: The impact of semantic impairment on lexical and object decision. *Cognitive Neuropsychology, 21*, 331–352.

Rolls, E. T. (2000). Precis of the brain and emotion. *Behavioral and Brain Sciences, 23*, 177–234.

Rolls, E. T., & Deco, G. (2002). *Computational neuroscience of vision*. Oxford: Oxford University Press.

Rolls, E. T., & Tovee, M. J. (1995). Sparseness of the neuronal representation of stimuli in the primate temporal visual cortex. *Journal of Neurophysiology, 73*, 713–726.

Rolls, E. T., Hornak, J., Wade, D., & McGrath, J. (1994). Emotion-related learning in patients with social and emotional changes associated with frontal damage. *Journal of Neurology, Neurosurgery and Psychiatry, 57*, 1518–1524.

Rolls, E. T., Robertson, R. G., & Georges-Francois, P. (1997). Spatial view cells in the primate hippocampus. *European Journal of Neuroscience, 9*, 1789–1794.

Romani, C. (1994). The role of phonological short-term memory in syntactic parsing: A case study. *Language and Cognitive Processes, 9*, 29–67.

Rorden, C., & Karnath, H. O. (2004). Using human brain lesions to infer function: A relic from a past era in the fMRI age? *Nature Reviews Neuroscience, 5*, 813–819.

Ross, J., Zinn, A., & McCauley, E. (2000). Neurodevelopmental and psychosocial aspects of Turner syndrome. *Mental Retardation and Developmental Disabilities Research Reviews, 6*, 135–141.

Rosser, M. N., Warrington, E. K., & Cipolotti, L. (1995). The isolation of calculation skills. *Journal of Neurology, 242*, 78–81.

Rossion, B., Gauthier, I., Goffaux, V., Tarr, M. J., & Crommelinck, M. (2002). Expertise training with novel objects leads to left-lateralized facelike electrophysiological responses. *Psychological Science, 13*, 250–257.

Rothwell, J. C., Traub, M. M., Day, B. L., Obeso, J. A., Thomas, P. K., & Marsden, C. D. (1982). Manual motor performance in a deafferented man. *Brain, 105*, 515–542.

Rousselet, G. A., Mace, M. J.-M., & Thorpe, M. F. (2004). Animal and human faces in natural scenes: How specific to human faces is the N170 ERP component? *Journal of Vision, 4*, 13–21.

Rowe, J. B., Owen, A. M., Johnsrude, I. S., & Passingham, R. E. (2001). Imaging the mental components of a planning task. *Neuropsychologia, 39*, 315–327.

Rozin, P., Haidt, J., & McCauley, C. R. (1993). Disgust. In M. Lewis, & J. M. Haviland (eds.), *Handbook of emotions*. New York: Guilford Press.

Rumelhart, D. E., & McClelland, J. L. (1982). An interactive activation model of context effects in letter perception: Part 2. The contextual enhancement effect and some tests and extensions of the model. *Psychological Review, 89*, 60–94.

Rumiati, R. I., Humphreys, G. W., Riddoch, M. J., & Bateman, A. (1994). Visual object agnosia without prosopagnosia or alexia: Evidence for hierarchical theories of visual recognition. *Visual Cognition, 1*, 181–225.

Rumiati, R. I., Weiss, P. H., Shallice, T., Ottoboni, G., Noth, J., Zilles, K., & Fink, G. R. (2004). Neural basis of pantomiming the use of visually presented objects. *NeuroImage, 21*, 1224–1231.

Rusconi, E., Walsh, V., & Butterworth, B. (2005). Dexterity with numbers: rTMS over left angular gyrus disrupts finger gnosis and number processing. *Neuropsychologia, 43*, 1609–1624.

Rushworth, M. F. S., Hadland, K. A., Gaffan, D., & Passingham, R. E. (2003). The effect of cingulate cortex lesions on task switching and working memory. *Journal of Cognitive Neuroscience, 15*, 338–353.

Rushworth, M. F. S., Hadland, K. A., Paus, T., & Sipila, P. K. (2002). Role of the human medial frontal cortex in task switching: A combined fMRI and TMS study. *Journal of Neurophysiology, 87*, 2577–2592.

Russell, J. (1997). *Autism as an executive disorder*. Oxford: Oxford University Press.

Rutter, M., Moffitt, T. E., & Caspi, A. (2006). Gene–environment interplay and psychopathology: Multiple varieties but real effects. *Journal of Child Psychology and Psychiatry, 47*, 226–261.

Saarinen, J., Paavilainen, P., Schoger, E., Tervaniemi, M., & Näätänen, R. (1992). Representation of abstract stimulus attributes in human brain. *NeuroReport, 3*, 1149–1151.

Sadato, N., Pascual-Leone, A., Grafman, J., Ibanez, V., Deiber, M.-P., Dold, G., & Hallett, M. (1996). Activation of primary visual cortex by Braille reading in blind subjects. *Nature, 380*, 526–528.

Saenz, M., & Koch, C. (2008). The sound of change: Visually-induced auditory synesthesia. *Current Biology, 18*, R650–R651.

Saffran, E. M., Bogyo, L. C., Schwartz, M. F., & Marin, O. S. M. (1980). Does deep dyslexia reflect right-hemisphere reading? In M. Coltheart, K. E. Patterson, & J. C. Marshall (eds.), *Deep dyslexia*. London: Routledge.

Sagar, J. H., Cohen, N. J., Corkin, S., & Growden, J. H. (1985). Dissociations among processes in remote memory. *Annals of the New York Academy of Science, 444*, 533–535.

Sagiv, N., & Bentin, S. (2001). Structural encoding of human and schematic faces: Holistic and part based processes. *Journal of Cognitive Neuroscience, 13*, 1–15.

Sagiv, N., Simner, J., Collins, J., Butterworth, B., & Ward, J. (2006). What is the relationship between synaesthesia and visuo-spatial number forms? *Cognition, 101*, 114–128.

Saint-Cyr, J. A. (2003). Frontal-striatal circuit functions: Context, sequence, and consequence. *Journal of the International Neuropsychological Society, 9*, 103–127.

Salinas, E., & Abbott, L. F. (1994). Vector reconstruction from firing rates. *Journal of Computational Neuroscience, 1*, 89–107.

Samson, D., & Pillon, A. (2003). A case of impaired knowledge for fruit and vegetables. *Cognitive Neuropsychology, 20*, 373–400.

Samson, D., Apperly, I. A., Chiavarino, C., & Humphreys, G. W. (2004). Left temporoparietal junction is necessary for representing someone else's belief. *Nature Neuroscience, 7*, 499–500.

Samson, S., & Zatorre, R. J. (1994). Contribution of the right temporal lobe to musical timbre discrimination. *Neuropsychologia, 32*, 231–240.

Sanders, H. I., & Warrington, E. K. (1971). Memory for remote events in amnesic patients. *Brain, 94*, 661–668.

Sandrini, M., Miozzo, A., Cotelli, M., & Cappa, S. F. (2003). The residual calculation abilities of a patient with severe aphasia: Evidence for a selective deficit of subtraction procedures. *Cortex, 39*, 85–96.

Sanfey, A., Rilling, J., Aaronson, J., Nystron, L., & Cohen, J. (2003). Probing the neural basis of economic decision-making: An fMRI investigation of the ultimatum game. *Science, 300*, 1755–1758.

Sartori, G. (1987). Leonardo da Vinci, omo sanza lettere: A case of surface dysgraphia? *Cognitive Neuropsychology, 4*, 1–10.

Savage, C. R., Deckersbach, T., Heckers, S., Wagner, A. D., Schacter, D. L., Alpert, N. M., Fischman, A. J., & Rauch, S. L. (2001). Prefrontal regions supporting spontaneous and directed application of verbal learning strategies: Evidence from PET. *Brain, 124*, 219–231.

Savage-Rumbaugh, E. S., & Lewin, R. (1994). *Kanzi: At the brink of the human mind.* New York: Wiley.

Savage-Rumbaugh, S., McDonald, K., Sevcik, R. A., Hopkins, W. D., & Rupert, E. (1986). Spontaneous symbol acquisition and communicative use by pygmy chimpanzee (*Pan paniscus*). *Journal of Experimental Psychology: General, 115*, 211–235.

Savage-Rumbaugh, E. S., Pate, J. L., Lawson, J., Smith, S. T., & Rosenbaum, S. (1983). Can a chimpanzee make a statement? *Journal of Experimental Psychology: General, 112*, 457–492.

Savage-Rumbaugh, S., Shanker, S. G., & Taylor, T. J. (1998). *Apes, language, and the mind.* Oxford: Oxford University Press.

Saver, J. L., & Damasio, A. R. (1991). Preserved access and processing of social knowledge in a patient with acquired sociopathy due to ventromedial frontal damage. *Neuropsychologia, 29*, 1241–1249.

Savoy, R. L. (2002). Functional magnetic resonance imaging fMRI. In V. Ramachandran (ed.), *Encyclopedia of the brain.* San Diego: Academic Press.

Saxe, R., & Kanwisher, N. (2003). People thinking about thinking people: The role of the temporo-parietal junction in "theory of mind". *NeuroImage, 19*, 1835–1842.

Schacter, D. L. (1986). Amnesia and crime: How much do we really know? *American Psychologist, 41*, 286–295.

Schacter, D. L. (1987). Implicit memory: History and current status. *Journal of Experimental Psychology: Learning, Memory and Cognition, 113*, 501–518.

Schacter, D. L., & Badgaiyan, R. D. (2001). Neuroimaging of priming: New perspectives on implicit and explicit memory. *Current Directions in Psychological Science, 10*, 1–4.

Schacter, D. L., & Slotnick, S. D. (2004). The cognitive neuroscience of memory distortion. *Neuron, 44*, 149–160.

Schacter, D. L., Cooper, L., & Delaney, S. (1990). Implicit memory for unfamiliar objects depends on access to structural descriptions. *Journal of Experimental Psychology: General, 119*, 5–24.

Schacter, D. L., Norman, K. A., & Koutstaal, W. (1998). The cognitive neuroscience of constructive memory. *Annual Review of Psychology, 49*, 289–318.

Schacter, S., & Singer, J. E. (1962). Cognitive, social, and physiological determinants of emotional state. *Psychology Review, 69*, 379–399.

Scherer, K. R., Banse, R., & Wallbott, H. G. (2001). Emotion inferences from vocal expression correlate across languages and cultures. *Journal of Cross-Cultural Psychology, 32*, 76–92.

Schlagger, B. L., & O'Leary, D. D. M. (1991). Potential of visual cortex to develop an array of functional units unique to somatosensory cortex. *Science, 252*, 1556–1560.

Schmidt, R. A. (1975). A schema theory of discrete motor skill learning. *Psychological Review, 82*, 225–232.

Schneider, W., & Shiffrin, R. M. (1977). Controlled and automatic human information processing: I. Detection, search and attention. *Psychological Review, 84*, 1–66.

Schnider, A. (2003). Spontaneous confabulation and the adaptation of thought to ongoing reality. *Nature Reviews Neuroscience, 4*, 662–671.

Schnider, A., & Ptak, R. (1999). Spontaneous confabulators fail to suppress currently irrelevant memory traces. *Nature Neuroscience, 2*, 677–681.

Schnider, A., Treyer, V., & Buck, A. (2000). Selection of currently relevant memories by the human posterior medial orbitofrontal cortex. *The Journal of Neuroscience, 20*, 5880–5884.

Schwartz, M. F., Montgomery, M. W., Fitzpatrick-DeSalme, E. J., Ochipa, C., Coslett, H. B., & Mayer, N. H. (1995). Analysis of a disorder of everyday action. *Cognitive Neuropsychology, 12*, 863–892.

Schweinberger, S. R. (1996). How Gorbachev primed Yeltsin: Analyses of associative priming in person recognition by means of reaction times and event-related brain potentials. *Journal of Experimental Psychology: Learning, Memory and Cognition, 22*, 1383–1407.

Schweinberger, S. R., Pickering, E. C., Burton, A. M., & Kaufmann, J. M. (2002a). Human brain potential correlates of repetition priming in face and name recognition. *Neuropsychologia, 40*, 2057–2073.

Schweinberger, S. R., Pickering, E. C., Jentzsch, I., Burton, A. M., & Kaufmann, J. M. (2002b). Event-related brain potential evidence for a response of inferior temporal cortex to familiar face repetitions. *Cognitive Brain Research, 14*, 398–409.

Schwoebel, J., Buxbaum, L. J., & Coslett, H. B. (2004). Representations of the human body in the production and imitation of complex movements. *Cognitive Neuropsychology, 21*, 285–298.

Scott, S. K. (2008). Voice processing in human and monkey brain. *Trends in Cognitive Sciences, 12*, 323–325.

Scott, S. K., & Wise, R. J. S. (2004). The functional neuroanatomy of prelexical processing in speech perception. *Cognition, 92*, 13–45.

Scott, S. K., Blank, S. C., Rosen, S., & Wise, R. J. S. (2000). Identification of a pathway for intelligible speech in the left temporal lobe. *Brain, 123*, 2400–2406.

Scott, S. K., Young, A. W., Calder, A. J., Hellawell, D. J., Aggleton, J. P., & Johnson, M. (1997). Impaired auditory recognition of fear and anger following bilateral amygdala lesions. *Nature, 385*, 254–257.

Scoville, W. B., & Milner, B. (1957). Loss of recent memory after bilateral hippocampal lesions. *Journal of Neurology, Neurosurgery and Psychiatry, 20*, 11–21.

Scragg, D. G. (1974). *A history of English spelling.* Manchester: Manchester University Press.

Sebanz, N., Bekkering, H., & Knoblich, G. (2006). Joint action: Bodies and minds moving together. *Trends in Cognitive Sciences, 10*, 70–76.

Seidenberg, M. S., & McClelland, J. L. (1989). A distributed, developmental model of word recognition and naming. *Psychological Review, 96*, 523–568.

Seidenberg, M. S., & Petitto, L. A. (1987). Communication, symbolic communication, and language: Comment on Savage-Rumbaugh, McDonald, Sevcik, Hopkins and Rupert (1986). *Journal of Experimental Psychology: General, 116*, 279–287.

Seidenberg, M. S., Plaut, D. C., Petersen, A. S., McClelland, J. L., & McRae, K. (1994). Nonword pronunciation and models of word recognition. *Journal of Experimental Psychology: Human Perception and Performance, 20*, 1177–1196.

Seidenberg, M. S., Waters, G. S., Barnes, M. A., & Tanenhaus, M. K. (1984). When does irregular spelling or pronunciation influence word recognition? *Journal of Verbal Learning and Verbal Behaviour, 23*, 383–404.

Seligman, M. E. (1971). Phobias and preparedness. *Behavior Therapy, 2*, 307–320.

Semenza, C. (1988). Impairment in localization of body parts following brain damage. *Cortex, 24*, 443–449.

Semenza, C., & Goodglass, H. (1985). Localization of body parts in brain injured subjects. *Neuropsychologia, 23*, 161–175.

Semenza, C., & Zettin, M. (1988). Generating proper names: A case of selective inability. *Cognitive Neuropsychology, 5*, 711–721.

Semin, G. R., & Manstead, A. S. (1982). The social implications of embarrassment displays and restitution behaviour. *European Journal of Social Psychology, 12*, 367–377.

Sergent, J., & Signoret, J.-L. (1992). Varieties of functional deficits in prosopagnosia. *Cerebral Cortex, 2*, 375–388.

Seron, X., & Noel, M. P. (1995). Transcoding numbers from the Arabic code to the verbal one or vice versa: How many routes? *Mathematical Cognition, 1*, 215–243.

Shah, A., & Frith, U. (1983). Islet of ability in autistic-children: A research note. *Journal of Child Psychology and Psychiatry and Allied Disciplines, 24*, 613–620.

Shalev, L., & Humphreys, G. W. (2002). Implicit location encoding via stored representations of familiar objects: Neuropsychological evidence. *Cognitive Neuropsychology, 19*, 721–744.

Shallice, T. (1979). Case study approach in neuropsychological research. *Journal of Clinical Neuropsychology, 1*, 183–211.

Shallice, T. (1981). Phonological agraphia and the lexical route in writing. *Brain, 104*, 413–429.

Shallice, T. (1982). Specific impairment of planning. *Philosophical Transactions of the Royal Society of London B, 298*, 199–209.

Shallice, T. (1988). *From neuropsychology to mental structure.* Cambridge: Cambridge University Press.

Shallice, T., & Burgess, P. (1996). The domain of supervisory process and temporal organization of behaviour. *Philosophical Transactions of the Royal Society of London B, 351*, 1405–1412.

Shallice, T., & Burgess, P. W. (1991). Deficits in strategy application following frontal lobe damage in man. *Brain, 114*, 727–741.

Shallice, T., & Evans, M. E. (1978). The involvement of the frontal lobes in cognitive estimation. *Cortex, 14*, 294–303.

Shallice, T., & Saffran, E. (1986). Lexical processing in the absence of explicit word identification: Evidence from a letter-by-letter reader. *Cognitive Neuropsychology, 3*, 429–458.

Shallice, T., & Warrington, E. K. (1977). The possible role of selective attention in acquired dyslexia. *Neuropsychologia, 15*, 31–41.

Shallice, T., Burgess, P. W., Schon, F., & Baxter, D. M. (1989). The origins of utilization behaviour. *Brain, 112*, 1587–1598.

Shallice, T., Glasspool, D. W., & Houghton, G. (1995). Can neuropsychological evidence inform connectionist modelling? *Language and Cognitive Processes, 10*, 195–225.

Shallice, T., Warrington, E. K., & McCarthy, R. (1983). Reading without semantics. *Quarterly Journal of Experimental Psychology, 35A*, 111–138.

Shammi, P., & Stuss, D. T. (1999). Humour appreciation: A role of the right frontal lobe. *Brain, 122*, 657–666.

Shapiro, K., & Caramazza, A. (2003). The representation of grammatical categories in the brain. *Trends in Cognitive Sciences, 7*, 201–206.

Sharma, J., Angelucci, A., & Sur, M. (2000). Induction of visual orientation modules in auditory cortex. *Nature, 404*, 841–847.

Shellock, F. G. (2004). *Reference manual for magnetic resonance safety, implants and devices.* Los Angeles, CA: Biomedical Research Publishing Company.

Shelton, J. R., & Martin, R. C. (1992). How semantic is automatic semantic priming? *Journal of Experimental Psychology: Learning, Memory and Cognition, 18*, 1191–1209.

Shelton, J. R., Fouch, E., & Caramazza, A. (1998). The relative sparing of body part knowledge: A case study. *Neurocase, 4*, 339–351.

Shibahara, N., Zorzi, M., Hill, M. P., Wydell, T., & Butterworth, B. (2003). Semantic effects in word naming: Evidence from English and Japanese Kanji. *Quarterly Journal of Experimental Psychology, 56A*, 263–286.

Shuman, M., & Kanwisher, N. (2004). Numerical magnitude in the human parietal lobe: Tests of representational generality and domain specificity. *Neuron, 44*, 557–589.

Shuren, J. E., Maher, L. M., & Heilman, K. M. (1996). The role of visual imagery in spelling. *Brain and Language, 52*, 365–372.

Sigman, M., Mundy, P., Ungerer, J., & Sherman, T. (1986). Social Interactions of autistic, mentally retarded, and normal children and their caregivers. *Journal of Child Psychology and Psychiatry, 27*, 647–656.

Simons, D. J., & Chabris, C. F. (1999). Gorillas in our midst: Sustained inattentional blindness for dynamic events. *Perception, 28*, 1059–1074.

Simons, D. J., & Levin, D. T. (1998). Failure to detect changes to people during a real-world interaction. *Psychonomic Bulletin and Review, 5*, 644–649.

Singer, T., Seymour, B., O'Doherty, J., Kaube, H., Dolan, R. J., & Frith, C. D. (2004). Empathy for pain involves the affective but not the sensory components of pain. *Science, 303*, 1157–1162.

Singer, T., Seymour, B., O'Doherty, J. P., Stephan, K. E., Dolan, R. J., & Frith, C. D. (2006). Empathic neural responses are modulated by the perceived fairness of others. *Nature, 439*, 466–469.

Singh, K. D. (2006). Magnetoencephalography. In C. Senior, T. Russell, & M. S. Gazzaniga (eds.), *Methods in mind*. Cambridge, MA: MIT Press.

Sip, K., Roepstorff, A., McGregor, W., & Frith, C. D. (2007). Detecting deception: The scope and limits. *Trends in Cognitive Sciences, 12*, 48–53.

Sirigu, A., Zalla, T., Pillon, B., Grafman, J., Agid, Y., & Dubois, B. (1995). Selective impairments in managerial knowledge following pre-frontal cortex damage. *Cortex, 31*, 301–316.

Skipper, J. I., van Wassenhove, V., Nusbaum, H. C., & Small, S. L. (2007). Hearing lips and seeing voices: How cortical areas supporting speech production mediate audiovisual perception. *Cerebral Cortex, 17*, 2387–2399.

Slotnick, S. D., & Schacter, D. L. (2004). A sensory signature that distinguishes true from false memories. *Nature Neuroscience, 7*, 664–672.

Smith, E. E., & Jonides, J. (1999). Storage and executive processes in the frontal lobes. *Science, 283*, 1657–1661.

Smith, M. C., Smith, M. K., & Ellgring, H. (1996). Spontaneous and posed facial expression in Parkinson's disease. *Journal of the International Neuropsychological Society, 2*, 383–391.

Smith, S. B. (1983). *The great mental calculators*. New York: Columbia University Press.

Snodgrass, J. G., & Vanderwart, M. (1980). A standardised set of 260 pictures: Norms for name agreement, image agreement, familiarity and visual complexity. *Journal of Experimental Psychology: Human Perception and Performance, 6*, 174–215.

Snowden, J., Griffiths, H., & Neary, D. (1994). Semantic dementia: Autobiographical contribution to preservation of meaning. *Cognitive Neuropsychology, 11*, 265–288.

Sodian, B., & Frith, U. (1992). Deception and sabotage in autistic, retarded and normal children. *Journal of Child Psychology and Psychiatry, 33*, 591–605.

Sohn, M. H., Ursu, S., Anderson, J. R., Stenger, V. A., & Carter, C. S. (2000). The role of prefrontal cortex and posterior parietal cortex in task switching. *Proceedings of the National Academy of Science, USA, 97*, 13448–13453.

Southgate, V., & Hamilton, A. F. C. (2008). Unbroken mirrors: Challenging a theory of autism. *Trends in Cognitive Sciences, 12*, 225–229.

Sparks, D. L. (1999). Conceptual issues related to the role of the superior colliculus in the control of gaze. *Current Opinion in Neurobiology, 9*, 698–707.

Spelke, E. S. (1998). Nativism, empiricism, and the origins of knowledge. *Infant Behavior and Development, 21*, 181–200.

Spiers, H. J., Burgess, N., Maguire, E. A., Baxendale, S. A., Hartley, T., Thompson, P. J., & O'Keefe, J. (2001a). Unilateral temporal lobectomy patients show lateralised topographical and episodic memory deficits in a virtual town. *Brain, 124*, 2476–2489.

Spiers, H. J., Maguire, E. A., & Burgess, N. (2001b). Hippocampal amnesia. *Neurocase, 7*, 357–382.

Sprengelmeyer, R., Young, A. W., Calder, A. J., Karnat, A., Lange, H., Homberg, V., Perrett, D., & Rowland, D. (1996). Loss of disgust: Perception of faces and emotions in Huntington's disease. *Brain, 119*, 1647–1665.

Sprengelmeyer, R., Young, A. W., Sprengelmeyer, A., Calder, A. J., Rowland, D., Perrett, D., Homberg, V., & Lange, H. (1997). Recognition of facial expression: Selective impairment of specific emotions in Huntington's disease. *Cognitive Neuropsychology, 14*, 839–879.

Squire, L. R. (1992). Memory and the hippocampus: A synthesis from findings with rats, monkeys and humans. *Psychological Review, 99*, 195–231.

Squire, L. R., Knowlton, B., & Musen, G. (1993). The structure and organisation of memory. *Annual Review of Psychology, 44*, 453–495.

Squire, L. R., Stark, C. E. L., & Clark, R. E. (2004). The medial temporal lobe. *Annual Review of Neuroscience, 27*, 279–306.

Stanescu-Cosson, R., Pinel, P., Van de Moortele, P.-F., Le Bihan, D., Cohen, L., & Dehaene, S. (2000). Cerebral basis of calculation processes: Impact of number size on the cerebral circuits for exact and approximate calculation. *Brain, 123*, 2240–2255.

Stark, M., Coslett, H. B., & Saffran, E. M. (1996). Impairment of an egocentric map of locations: Implications for perception and action. *Cognitive Neuropsychology, 13*, 481–523.

Starr, M. S., & Rayner, K. (2001). Eye movements during reading: Some current controversies. *Trends in Cognitive Sciences, 5*, 156–163.

Sternberg, S. (1969). The discovery of processing stages: Extensions of Donders' method. *Acta Psychologica, 30*, 276–315.

Stevens, S. S. (1935). The relation of pitch to intensity. *Journal of the Acoustical Society of America, 6*, 150–154.

Stewart, L., Battelli, L., Walsh, V., & Cowey, A. (1999). Motion perception and perceptual learning studied by magnetic stimulation. *Electroencephalography and Clinical Neurophysiology, 3*, 334–350.

Stoerig, P., & Cowey, A. (1997). Blindsight in man and monkey. *Brain, 120*, 535–559.

Stone, V. E., & Gerrans, P. (2006). What's domain-specific about theory of mind? *Social Neuroscience, 1*, 309–319.

Strafella, A. P., & Paus, T. (2000). Modulation of cortical excitability during action observation: A transcranial magnetic stimulation study. *Experimental Brain Research, 11*, 2289–2292.

Strauss, M. S., & Curtis, L. E. (1981). Infant perception of numerosity. *Child Development, 52*, 97–127.

Stroop, J. R. (1935). Studies of interference in serial verbal reactions. *Journal of Experimental Psychology: General, 106*, 404–426.

Stuss, D. T., Alexander, M. P., Floden, D., Binns, M. A., Levine, B., McIntosh, A. R., Rajah, N., & Hevenor, S. J. (2002). Fractionation and localization of distinct frontal lobe processes: Evidence from focal lesions in humans. In D. T. Stuss, & R. T. Knight (eds.), *Principles of frontal lobe function.* Oxford: Oxford University Press.

Stuss, D. T., Alexander, M. P., Hamer, L., Palumbo, C., Dempster, R., Binns, M., Levine, B., & Izukawa, D. (1998). The effects of focal anterior and posterior brain lesions on verbal fluency. *Journal of the International Neuropsychological Society, 4*, 265–278.

Stuss, D. T., Floden, D., Alexander, M. P., Levine, B., & Katz, D. (2001a). Stroop performance in focal lesion patients: Dissociation of processes and frontal lobe lesion location. *Neuropsychologia, 39*, 771–786.

Stuss, D. T., Gallup, G. G., & Alexander, M. P. (2001b). The frontal lobes are necessary for "theory of mind". *Brain, 124*, 279–286.

Styles, E. A. (2006). *The psychology of attention*, 2nd edition. Hove: Psychology Press.

Sumby, W. H., & Pollack, I. (1954). Visual contribution to speech intelligibility in noise. *Journal of the Acoustical Society of America, 26*, 212–215.

Sun, J., & Perona, P. (1998). Where is the sun? *Nature Neuroscience, 1*, 183–184.

Sur, M., & Leamey, C. A. (2001). Development and plasticity of cortical areas and networks. *Nature Reviews Neuroscience, 2*, 251–262.

Sur, M., & Rubenstein, J. L. R. (2005). Patterning and plasticity of the cerebral cortex. *Science, 310*, 805–810.

Sur, M., Garraghty, P. E., & Roe, A. W. (1988). Experimentally induced visual projections into auditory thalamus and cortex. *Science, 242*, 1437–1441.

Sutton, S., Tueting, P., Zubin, J., & John, E. R. (1967). Information delivery and the sensory evoked potential. *Science, 155*, 1436–1439.

Swayze, V. W. (1995). Frontal leukotomy and related psychosurgical procedures in the era before antipsychotics (1935–1954): A historical overview. *American Journal of Psychiatry, 152*, 505–515.

Swick, D., & Turken, A. U. (1999). Dissociation between conflict detection and error monitoring in the human anterior cingulate cortex. *Proceedings of the National Academy of Science, USA, 99,* 16354–16359.

Tager-Flusberg, H. (1992). Autistic children's talk about psychological states: Deficits in the early acquisition of a theory of mind. *Child Development, 63,* 161–172.

Tager-Flusberg, H. (2003). Developmental disorders of genetic origin. In M. De Haan, & M. H. Johnson (eds.), *The cognitive neuroscience of development.* New York: Psychology Press.

Tainturier, M.-J., & Caramazza, A. (1996). The status of double letters in graphemic representations. *Journal of Memory and Language, 35,* 53–75.

Tainturier, M.-J., & Rapp, B. (2003). Is a single graphemic buffer used in reading and spelling? *Aphasiology, 17,* 537–562.

Takahashi, N., Kawamura, M., Shinotou, H., Hirayama, K., Kaga, K., & Shindo, M. (1992). Pure word deafness due to left-hemisphere damage. *Cortex, 28,* 295–303.

Talairach, J., & Tournoux, P. (1988). *A co-planar stereotactic atlas of the human brain.* Stuttgart: Thieme Verlag.

Tanji, J., Okano, K., & Sato, K. C. (1998). Neuronal activity in cortical motor areas related to ipsilateral, contralateral and bilateral digit movements in the monkey. *Journal of Neurophysiology, 60,* 325–343.

Tartter, V.C. (1986). *Language processes.* New York: Holt, Rinehart & Winston.

Taylor, A. E., Saint-Cyr, J. A., & Lang, A. E. (1986). Frontal lobe dysfunction in Parkinson's disease. *Brain, 109,* 845–883.

Tervaniemi, M., Maury, S., & Näätänen, R. (1994). Neural representations of abstract stimulus features in the human brain as reflected by the mismatch negativity. *NeuroReport, 9,* 4167–4170.

Theoret, H., Kobayashi, M., Valero-Cabre, A., & Pascual-Leone, A. (2003). Exploring paradoxical functional facilitation with TMS. *Supplements to Clinical Neurophysiology, 56,* 211–219.

Thomas, K. M., & Casey, B. J. (2003). Methods for imaging the developing brain. In M. De Haan, & M. H. Johnson (eds.), *The cognitive neuroscience of development.* New York: Psychology Press.

Thomas, K. M., & Nelson, C. A. (1996). Age-related changes in the electrophysiological response to visual stimulus novelty: A topographical approach. *Electroencephalography and Clinical Neurophysiology, 98,* 294–308.

Thomas, M., & Karmiloff-Smith, A. (2002). Are developmental disorders like cases of adult brain damage? Implications of connectionist modelling. *Behavioral and Brain Sciences, 25,* 727–788.

Thomas, M. S. C., & Johnson, M. H. (2008). New advances in understanding sensitive periods in brain development. *Current Directions in Psychological Science, 17,* 1–5.

Thompson, L. A., Detterman, D. K., & Plomin, R. (1991). Associations between cognitive abilities and scholastic achievement: Genetic overlap but environmental differences. *Psychological Science, 2,* 158–165.

Thompson, P. (1980). Margaret Thatcher: a new illusion. *Perception, 9,* 483–484.

Thompson, P. M., Schwartz, C., Lin, R. T., Khan, A. A., & Toga, A. W. (1996). Three-dimensional statistical analysis of sulcal variability in the human brain. *Journal of Neuroscience, 16,* 4261–4274.

Thompson-Schill, S. L., D'Esposito, M. D., & Kan, I. P. (1999). Effects of repetition and competition on activity in left prefrontal cortex during word generation. *Neuron, 23,* 513–522.

Thompson-Schill, S. L., D'Esposito, M. D., Aguirre, G. K., & Farah, M. J. (1997). Role of inferior prefrontal cortex in retrieval of semantic knowledge: A reevaluation. *Proceedings of the National Academy of Science, USA, 94,* 14792–14797.

Thompson-Schill, S. L., Swick, D., Farah, M. J., D'Esposito, M., Kan, I. P., & Knight, R. T. (1998). Verb generation in patients with focal frontal lesions: A neuropsychological test of neuroimaging findings. *Proceedings of the National Academy of Science, USA, 95,* 15855–15860.

Tinbergen, N. (1951). *The study of instinct.* Oxford: Oxford University Press.

Tipper, S. P. (1985). The negative priming effect: Inhibitory priming by ignored objects. *Quarterly Journal of Experimental Psychology, 37A,* 571–590.

Tipper, S. P., Driver, J., & Weaver, B. (1991). Object-centred inhibition of return of visual attention. *Quarterly Journal of Experimental Psychology, 43A,* 289–298.

Titone, D. A., & Salisbury, D. F. (2004). Contextual modulation of N400 amplitude to lexically ambiguous words. *Brain and Cognition, 55,* 470–478.

Tooth, G. C., & Newton, M. P. (1961). *Leukotomy in England and Wales 1942–1954.* London: Her Majesty's Stationery Office.

Torjussen, T. (1976). Visual processing in cortically blind hemifields. *Neuropsychologia, 16,* 15–21.

Tranel, D., & Damasio, H. (1995). Neuroanatomical correlates of electrodermal skin conductance responses. *Psychophysiology, 31,* 427–438.

Tranel, D., Damasio, A. R., & Damasio, H. (1988). Intact recognition of facial expression, gender and age in patients with impaired recognition of face identity. *Neurology, 38,* 690–696.

Tranel, D., Damasio, H., & Damasio, A. R. (1995). Double dissociation between overt and covert face recognition. *Journal of Cognitive Neuroscience, 7,* 425–432.

Tranel, D., Kemmerer, D., Adolphs, R., Damasio, H., & Damasio, A. R. (2003). Neural correlates of conceptual knowledge for actions. *Cognitive Neuropsychology, 20,* 409–432.

Treisman, A. (1988). Features and objects: The four-teenth Bartlett memorial lecture. *Quarterly Journal of Experimental Psychology, 40A*, 201–237.

Treisman, A., & Schmidt, H. (1982). Illusory conjunctions in the perception of objects. *Cognitive Psychology, 14*, 107–141.

Treisman, A. M., & Gelade, G. (1980). A feature-integration theory of attention. *Cognitive Psychology, 12*, 97–136.

Troncoso, X. G., Macknik, S. L., Otero-Millan, J., & Martinez-Conde, S. (2008). Microsaccades drive illusory motion in the Enigma illusion. *Proceedings of the National Academy of Sciences, USA, 41*, 16033–16038.

Tulving, E. (1972). Episodic and semantic memory. In E. Tulving, & W. Donaldson (eds.), *Organisation of memory* (pp. 381–403). New York: Academic Press.

Tulving, E. (1983). *Elements of episodic memory*. Oxford: Oxford University Press.

Tulving, E. (1985). Memory and consciousness. *Canadian Psychologist, 26*, 1–12.

Tulving, E., & Schacter, D. L. (1990). Priming and human memory systems. *Science, 247*, 301–306.

Tulving, E., Kapur, S., Craik, F. I. M., Moscovitch, M., & Houle, S. (1994). Hemispheric encoding/ retrieval asymmetry in episodic memory: Positron emission tomography findings. *Proceedings of the National Academy of Science, USA, 91*, 2016–2020.

Tulving, E., Schacter, D. L., McLachlan, D. R., & Moscovitch, M. (1988). Priming of semantic autobiographical knowledge: A case study of retrograde amnesia. *Brain and Cognition, 8*, 3–20.

Turconi, E., Jemel, B., Rossion, B., & Seron, X. (2004). Electrophysiological evidence for differential processing of numerical quantity and order in humans. *Cognitive Brain Research, 21*, 22–38.

Turnbull, O. H., & McGeorge, P. (1998). Lateral bumping: A normal-subject analog to the behaviour of patients with hemispatial neglect? *Brain and Cognition, 37*, 31–33.

Turnbull, O. H., Della Sala, S., & Beschin, N. (2002). Agnosia for object orientation: Naming and mental rotation evidence. *Neurocase, 8*, 296–305.

Tyler, L. K., & Moss, H. E. (2001). Towards a distributed account of conceptual knowledge. *Trends in Cognitive Sciences, 5*, 244–252.

Umiltà, M. A., Kohler, E., Gallese, V., Fogassi, L., Fadiga, L., Keysers, C., & Rizzolatti, G. (2001). I know what you are doing: A neurophysiological study. *Neuron, 25*, 287–295.

Underwood, B. J. (1965). False recognition produced by implicit verbal responses. *Journal of Experimental Psychology, 70*, 122–129.

Ungerleider, L. G., & Mishkin, M. (1982). Two cortical systems. In D. J. Ingle, M. A. Goodale, & R. J. W. Mansfield (eds.), *Analysis of visual behaviour*. Cambridge, MA: MIT Press.

Uttal, W. R. (2001). *The new phrenology: The limits of localising cognitive processes in the brain*. Cambridge, MA: MIT Press.

Vaina, L. M., Solomon, J., Chowdhury, S., Sinha, P., & Belliveau, J. W. (2001). Functional neuroanatomy of biological motion perception in humans. *Proceedings of the National Academy of Sciences USA, 98*, 11656–11661.

Valentine, T. (1991). A unified account of the effects of distinctiveness, inversion and race in face recognition. *Quarterly Journal of Experimental Psychology, 43A*, 161–204.

Vallar, G., & Baddeley, A. (1984). Phonological short-term store and phonological processing, and sentence comprehension. *Cognitive Neuropsychology, 1*, 121–141.

Van Harskamp, N. J., & Cipolotti, L. (2001). Selective impairments for addition, subtraction and multiplication: Implications for the organisation of arithmetical facts. *Cortex, 37*, 363–388.

Van Harskamp, N. J., Rudge, P., & Cipolotti, L. (2002). Are multiplication facts implemented by the left supramarginal and angular gyri? *Neuropsychologia, 40*, 1786–1793.

Van Lancker, D., & Klein, K. (1990). Preserved recognition of familiar personal names in global aphasia. *Brain and Language, 39*, 511–529.

Van Orden, G. C. (1987). A rows is a rose: Spelling, sound, and reading. *Memory and Cognition, 14*, 371–386.

Van Orden, G. C., Johnston, J. C., & Hele, B. L. (1988). Word identification in reading proceeds. from spelling to sound to meaning. *Journal of Experimental Psychology: Learning, Memory and Cognition, 14*, 371–386.

Vargha-Khadem, F., Carr, L. J., Isaacs, E., Brett, E., Adams, C., & Mishkin, M. (1997a). Onset of speech after left hemispherectomy in a nine-year-old boy. *Brain, 120*, 159–182.

Vargha-Khadem, F., Gadian, D. G., Copp, A., & Mishkin, M. (2005). FOXP2 and the neuroanatomy of speech and language. *Nature Reviews Neuroscience, 6*, 131–138.

Vargha-Khadem, F., Gadian, D. G., Watkins, K. E., Connelly, A., Van Paesschen, W., & Mishkin, M. (1997b). Differential effects of early hippocampal pathology on episodic and semantic memory. *Science, 277*, 376–380.

Vargha-Khadem, F., Isaacs, E., & Mishkin, M. (1994). Agnosia, alexia and a remarkable form of amnesia in an adolescent boy. *Brain, 117*, 683–703.

Vargha-Khadem, F., Watkins, K., Alcock, K., Fletcher, P., & Passingham, R. (1995). Cognitive and praxic deficits in a large family with a genetically transmitted speech and language disorder. *Proceedings of the National Academy of Science, USA, 92*, 930–933.

Veen, V. van, & Carter, C. S. (2002). The anterior cingulate as a conflict monitor: fMRI and ERP studies. *Physiology and Behavior, 77*, 477–482.

Velmans, M. (2000). *Understanding consciousness*. London: Routledge.

Verfaellie, M., Koseff, P., & Alexander, M. P. (2000). Acquisition of novel semantic information in amnesia: Effects of lesion location. *Neuropsychologia*, *38*, 484–492.

Verfaellie, M., Reiss, L., & Roth, H. L. (1995). Knowledge of new English vocabulary in amnesia: An examination of premorbidly acquired semantic memory. *Journal of International Neuropsychological Society*, *1*, 443–453.

Vesalius, A. (1543). *De humani corporis fabrica*. Basel: Oporinus.

Viessens, R. de (1685). *Neurographia universalis*. Lyons: Certe.

Vigliocco, G., Antonini, T., & Garrett, M. F. (1997). Grammatical gender is on the tip of Italian tongues. *Psychological Science*, *8*, 314–317.

Volkow, N. D., Wang, G.-J., Fowler, J. S., Logan, J., Gatley, S. J., Hitzemann, R., Chen, A. D., Dewey, S. L., & Pappas, N. (1997). Decreased striatal dopamine responsiveness in detoxified cocaine-dependent subjects. *Nature*, *386*, 830–835.

Vuilleumier, P., Henson, R. N., Driver, J., & Dolan, R. J. (2002a). Multiple levels of visual object constancy revealed by event-related fMRI of repetition priming. *Nature Neuroscience*, *5*, 491–499.

Vuilleumier, P., Schwartz, S., Clarke, K., Husain, M., & Driver, J. (2002b). Testing memory for unseen visual stimuli in patients with extinction and spatial neglect. *Journal of Cognitive Neuroscience*, *14*, 875–886.

Vuilleumier, P., Valenza, N., Mayer, E., Reverdin, A., & Landis, T. (1998). Near and far visual space in unilateral neglect. *Annals of Neurology*, *43*, 406–410.

Wagner, A. D., Koutstaal, W., & Schacter, D. L. (1999). When encoding yields remembering: Insights from event-related neuroimaging. *Philosophical Transactions of the Royal Society of London B*, *354*, 1307–1324.

Wagner, A. D., Poldrack, R. A., Eldridge, L. L., Desmond, J. E., Glover, G. H., & Gabrieli, G. D. E. (1998a). Material-specific lateralization of prefrontal activation during episodic encoding and retrieval. *Neuroreport*, *9*, 3711–3717.

Wagner, A. D., Schacter, D. L., Rotte, M., Koutstaal, W., Maril, A., Dale, A. M., Rosen, B. R., & Buckner, R. I. (1998b). Building memories: Remembering and forgetting of verbal experiences as predicted by brain activity. *Science*, *281*, 1188–1191.

Walsh, V. (2003). A theory of magnitude: Common cortical metrics of time, space and quantity. *Trends in Cognitive Sciences*, *7*, 483–488.

Walsh, V., & Cowey, A. (1998). Magnetic stimulation studies of visual cognition. *Trends in Cognitive Sciences*, *2*, 103–110.

Walsh, V., & Rushworth, M. (1999). A primer of magnetic stimulation as a tool for neuropsychology. *Neuropsychologia*, *37*, 125–135.

Walsh, V., Ashbridge, E., & Cowey, A. (1998a). Cortical plasticity in perceptual learning demonstrated by transcranial magnetic stimulation. *Neuropsychologia*, *36*, 363–367.

Walsh, V., Ellison, A., Battelli, L., & Cowey, A. (1998b). Task-induced impairments and enhancements induced by magnetic stimulation of human area V5. *Proceedings of the Royal Society of London B*, *265*, 537–543.

Ward, J. (2003). Understanding oral spelling: A review and synthesis. *Neurocase*, *9*, 1–14.

Ward, J., Stott, R., & Parkin, A. J. (2000). The role of semantics in reading and spelling: Evidence for the "Summation Hypothesis". *Neuropsychologia*, *38*, 1643–1653.

Warren, J. D., Scott, S. K., Price, C. J., & Griffiths, T. D. (2006). Human brain mechanisms for the early analysis of voices. *NeuroImage*, *31*, 1389–1397.

Warrington, E. K. (1982). The fractionation of arithmetical skills: A single case study. *Quarterly Journal of Experimental Psychology*, *34A*, 31–51.

Warrington, E. K., & James, M. (1986). Visual object recognition in patients with right hemisphere lesions: Axes or features? *Perception*, *15*, 355–356.

Warrington, E. K., & Langdon, D. (1994). Spelling dyslexia: A deficit of the visual word-form. *Journal of Neurology, Neurosurgery and Psychiatry*, *57*, 211–216.

Warrington, E. K., & McCarthy, R. (1983). Category specific access dysphasia. *Brain*, *106*, 859–878.

Warrington, E. K., & McCarthy, R. A. (1987). Categories of knowledge. *Brain*, *110*, 1273–1296.

Warrington, E. K., & McCarthy, R. A. (1988). The fractionation of retrograde amnesia. *Brain and Cognition*, *7*, 184–200.

Warrington, E. K., & Shallice, T. (1969). The selective impairment of auditory verbal short-term memory. *Brain*, *92*, 885–896.

Warrington, E. K., & Shallice, T. (1980). Word-form dyslexia. *Brain*, *103*, 99–112.

Warrington, E. K., & Shallice, T. (1984). Category specific semantic impairments. *Brain*, *107*, 829–854.

Warrington, E. K., & Taylor, A. M. (1973). The contribution of the right parietal lobe to object recognition. *Cortex*, *9*, 152–164.

Warrington, E. K., James, M., & Maciejewski, C. (1986). The WAIS as a lateralizing and localising diagnostic instrument: A study of 656 patients with unilateral cerebral lesions. *Neuropsychologia*, *24*, 223–239.

Washburn, D. A., & Rumbaugh, D. M. (1991). Ordinal judgments of numerical symbols by macaques (Macaca mulatta). *Psychological Science*, *2*, 190–193.

Wassermann, E. M. (1996). Risk and safety of transcranial magnetic stimulation: Report and suggested guidelines from the International Workshop on the safety of Repetitive Transcranial Magnetic Stimulation, June 5–7. *Electroencephalogy and Clinical Neurophysiology*, *108*, 1–16.

Wassermann, E. M., Cohen, L. G., Flitman, S. S., Chen, R., & Hallett, M. (1996). Seizures in healthy people with repeated "safe" trains of transcranial magnetic stimulation. *Lancet, 347*, 825–826.

Watkins, K., & Paus, T. (2004). Modulation of motor excitability during speech perception: The role of Broca's area. *Journal of Cognitive Neuroscience, 16*, 978–987.

Watkins, K. E., Vargha-Khadem, F., Ashburner, J., Passingham, R. E., Connelly, A., Friston, K. J., Frackowiak, R. S. J., Mishkin, M., & Gadian, D. G. (2002). MRI analysis of an inherited speech and language disorder: Structural brain abnormalities. *Brain, 125*, 465–478.

Weaver, I. C. G., Cervoni, N., Champagne, F. A., D'Alessio, A, C., Charma, S., Seckl, J., Dymov, S., Szyf, M., & Meaney, M. J. (2004). Epigenetic programming by maternal behavior. *Nature Neuroscience, 7*, 847–854.

Wechsler, D. (1981). *Wechsler Adult Intelligence Scale – Revised.* New York: Psychological Corporation.

Wechsler, D. (1984). *Wechsler Memory Scale – Revised.* New York: Psychological Corporation.

Weekes, B., & Chen, H. Q. (1999). Surface dyslexia in Chinese. *Neurocase, 5*, 161–172.

Weiskrantz, L. (1956). Behavioral changes associated with ablations of the amygdaloid complex in monkeys. *Journal of Comparative Physiological Psychology, 49*, 381–391.

Weiskrantz, L. (1986). *Blindsight: A case study and implications.* Oxford: Oxford University Press.

Weiskrantz, L., Warrington, E. K., Sanders, M. D., & Marshall, J. (1974). Visual capacity in the hemianopic field following a restricted occipital ablation. *Brain, 97*, 709–728.

Wenzel, E. M., Arruda, M., Kistler, D. J., & Wightman, F. L. (1993). Localization using non-individualized head-related transfer functions. *Journal of the Acoustical Society of America, 94*, 111–123.

Wernicke, C. (1874). *Der aphasiche symptomenkomplex.* Breslau: Cohen and Weigart.

Westermann, G., Mareschal, D., Johnson, M. H., Sirois, S., Spratling, M. W., & Thomas, M. S. C. (2007). Neuroconstructivism. *Developmental Science, 10*, 75–83.

Westmacott, R., & Moscovitch, M. (2002). Temporally graded semantic memory loss in amnesia and semantic dementia: Further evidence for opposite gradients. *Cognitive Neuropsychology, 19*, 135–163.

Wheeldon, L. R., & Monsell, S. (1992). The locus of repetition priming of spoken word production. *Quarterly Journal of Experimental Psychology, 44A*, 723–761.

Wheeler, M. A., Stuss, D. T., & Tulving, E. (1997). Toward a theory of episodic memory: The frontal lobes and autonoetic consciousness. *Psychological Bulletin, 121*, 331–354.

Whitfield, I. C., & Evans, E. F. (1965). Responses of auditory cortical neurons to stimuli of changing frequency. *Journal of Neurophysiology, 28*, 655–672.

Wichmann, T., & DeLong, M. R. (1996). Functional and pathophysiological models of the basal ganglia. *Current Opinion in Neurobiology, 6*, 751–758.

Wickens, C. D. (1980). The structure of attentional resources. In R. S. Nickerson (ed.), *Attention and performance VIII.* Hillsdale, NJ: Lawrence Erlbaum.

Wilkins, A. J. (1971). Conjoint frequency, category size, and categorization time. *Journal of Verbal Learning and Verbal Behaviour, 10*, 382–385.

Wilkins, A., Shallice, T., & McCarthy, R. (1987). Frontal lesions and sustained attention. *Neuropsychologia, 25*, 359–365.

Williams, L. M., Senior, C., David, A. S., Loughland, C. M., & Gordon, E. (2001). In search of the "Duchenne smile": Evidence from eye movements. *Journal of Psychophysiology, 15*, 122–127.

Wimmer, H., & Perner, J. (1983). Beliefs about beliefs: Representation and the constraining function of wrong beliefs in young children's understanding of deception. *Cognition, 13*, 103–128.

Wing, A. M., & Baddeley, A. D. (1980). Spelling errors in handwriting: A corpus and a distributional analysis. In U. Frith (ed.), *Cognitive processes in spelling.* London: Academic Press.

Winston, J. S., O'Doherty, J., & Dolan, R. J. (2003). Common and distinct neural responses during direct and incidental processing of multiple facial emotions. *NeuroImage, 20*, 84–97.

Wise, R. J. S., Greene, J., Buchel, C., & Scott, S. K. (1999). Brain regions involved in articulation. *Lancet, 353*, 1057–1061.

Wise, R. J. S., Scott, S. K., Blank, S. C., Mummery, C. J., & Warbuton, E. (2001). Identifying separate neural subsystems within Wernicke's area. *Brain, 124*, 83–95.

Witelson, S. F., Kigar, D. L., & Harvey, T. (1999). The exceptional brain of Albert Einstein. *Lancet, 353*, 2149–2153.

Witkin, H. A., Wapner, S., & Leventhal, T. (1952). Sound localization with conflicting visual and auditory cues. *Journal of Experimental Psychology, 43*, 58–67.

Wixted, J. T. (2004). The psychology and neuroscience of forgetting. *Annual Review of Psychology, 55*, 235–269.

Wixted, J. T., & Stretch, V. (2004). In defence of the signal detection interpretation of remember/know judgments. *Psychonomic Bulletin and Review, 11*, 616–641.

Wohlschlager, A., Gattis, M., & Bekkering, H. (2003). Action generation and action perception in imitation: An instance of the ideomotor principle. *Philosophical Transactions of the Royal Society of London B, 358*, 501–515.

Wojciulik, E., Husain, M., Clarke, K., & Driver, J. (2001). Spatial working memory deficit in unilateral neglect. *Neuropsychologia, 39*, 390–396.

Wolf, S. M., Lawrenz, F. P., Nelson, C. A., Kahn, J. P., Cho, M. K., Clayton, E. W., Fletcher, J. G., Georgieff, M. K., Hammerschmidt, D., Hudson, K., Illes, J., Kapur, V.,

Keane, M. A., Koenig, B. A., LeRoy, B. S., McFarland, E. G., Paradise, J., Parker, L. S., Terry, S. F., Van Ness, B., & Wilfond, B. S. (2008). Managing incidental findings in human subjects research: Analysis and recommendations. *Journal of Law, Medicine and Ethics, 36*, 219–248.

Wolpert, D. M., & Ghahramani, Z. (2000). Computational principles of movement neuroscience. *Nature Neuroscience, 3*, 1212–1217.

Wolpert, D. M., Ghahramani, Z., & Jordan, M. I. (1995). An internal model for sensorimotor integration. *Science, 269*, 1880–1882.

Worden, F. G. (1971). Hearing and the neural detection of acoustic patterns. *Behavioral Science, 16*, 20–30.

Wurtz, R. H., Goldberg, M. E., & Robinson, D. L. (1982). Brain mechanisms of visual attention. *Scientific American, 246*, 124–135.

Wynn, K. (1992). Addition and subtraction by human infants. *Nature, 358*, 749–750.

Xue, G., Aron, A. R., & Poldrack, R. A. (2008). Common neural substrates for inhibition of spoken and manual responses. *Cerebral Cortex, 18*, 1923–1932.

Yin, R. K. (1969). Looking at upside-down faces. *Journal of Experimental Psychology, 81*, 141–145.

Yin, W. G., & Weekes, B. S. (2003). Dyslexia in Chinese: Clues from cognitive neuropsychology. *Annals of Dyslexia, 53*, 255–279.

Yoneda, Y., Mori, E., Yamashita, H., & Yamadori, A. (1994). MRI volumetry of medial temporal lobe structures in amnesia following herpes simplex encephalitis. *European Neurology, 34*, 243–252.

Young, A. W., Hellawell, D., & De Haan, E. H. F. (1988). Cross-domain semantic priming in normal subjects and a prosopagnosic patient. *Quarterly Journal of Experimental Psychology, 40A*, 561–580.

Young, A. W., Hellawell, D. J., Van de Wal, C., & Johnson, M. (1996). Facial expression processing after amygdalectomy. *Neuropsychologia, 34*, 31–39.

Zahn, R., Moll, J., Krueger, F., Huey, E. D., Garrido, G., & Grafman, J. (2007). Social concepts are represented in the superior anterior temporal cortex. *Proceedings of the National Academy of Sciences, USA, 104*, 6430–6435.

Zanini, S., Rumiati, R. I., & Shallice, T. (2002). Action sequencing deficit following frontal lobe lesion. *Neurocase, 8*, 88–99.

Zatorre, R. J., Belin, P., & Penhune, V. B. (2002). Structure and function of auditory cortex: Music and speech. *Trends in Cognitive Sciences, 6*, 37–46.

Zeki, S. M. (1969). Representation of central visual fields in prestriate cortex of monkeys. *Brain Research, 14*, 733–747.

Zeki, S. M. (1974). Functional organisation of a visual area in the posterior bank of the superior temporal sulcus of the rhesus monkey. *Journal of Physiology, 236*, 549–573.

Zeki, S. M. (1983). Colour coding in the cerebral cortex: The reaction of cells in monkey visual cortex to wavelengths and colours. *Neuroscience, 9*, 741–756.

Zeki, S. M. (1990). A century of cerebral achromatopsia. *Brain, 113*, 1721–1777.

Zeki, S. M. (1991). Cerebral akinetopsia (visual motion blindness): A review. *Brain, 114*, 811–824.

Zeki, S. M. (1993). *A vision of the brain.* Oxford: Blackwell.

Zeki, S. M., & Marini, L. (1998). Three cortical stages of colour processing in the human brain. *Brain, 121*, 1669–1685.

Zeki, S. M., Watson, D. G., & Frackowiak, R. S. J. (1993). Going beyond the information given: The relation of illusory visual motion to brain activity. *Proceedings of the Royal Society of London B, 252*, 212–222.

Zeki, S. M., Watson, J. D. G., Lueck, C. J., Friston, K. J., Kennard, C., & Frackowiak, R. S. J. (1991). A direct demonstration of functional specialization in human visual cortex. *Journal of Neuroscience, 11*, 641–649.

Zettin, M., Cubelli, R., Perino, C., & Rago, R. (1995). Impairment of letter formation: The case of "ideomotor" apraxic agraphia. *Aphasiology, 9*, 283–294.

Zihl, J., von Cramon, D., & Mai, N. (1983). Selective disturbance of movement vision after bilateral brain damage. *Brain, 106*, 313–340.

Zorzi, M., Houghton, G., & Butterworth, B. (1998). Two routes or one in reading aloud? A connectionist dual-process model. *Journal of Experimental Psychology: Human Perception and Performance, 24*, 1131–1161.

Zorzi, M., Priftis, K., & Umiltà, C. (2002). Brain damage – neglect disrupts the mental number line. *Nature, 417*, 138–139.

Zurif, E., Gardner, H., & Brownell, H. H. (1989). The case against the case against group studies. *Brain and Cognition, 10*, 237–255.

Zwitserlood, P. (1989). The locus of the effects of sentential-semantic context in spoken word processing. *Cognition, 32*, 25–64.

Author index

Subject index

Page numbers in **bold** indicate key terms.